THEATRE COMPANIES
OF THE WORLD

THEATRE COMPANIES

OF THE
WORLD

United States of America, Western Europe
(excluding Scandinavia)

Edited by
COLBY H. KULLMAN
and
WILLIAM C. YOUNG

GREENWOOD PRESS
New York · Westport, Connecticut · London

Library of Congress Cataloging-in-Publication Data

Main entry under title:

Theatre companies of the world.

  Bibliography: p.
  Includes index.

  Contents: v. 1 Africa, Asia, Australia and New Zealand,
Canada, Eastern Europe, Latin America, The Middle East,
Scandinavia — v. 2 United States of America, Western Europe
(excluding Scandinavia)

  1. Theater—Handbooks, manuals, etc. I. Kullman,
Colby, H. II. Young, William C., 1928– .
PN2052.T48 1986   792'.09   84–539
ISBN 0-313-21456-5 (set)
ISBN 0-313-25667-5 (lib. bdg. : v. 1 : alk paper)
ISBN 0-313-25668-3 (lib. bdg. : v. 2 : alk paper)

Library of Congress Catalog Card Number: 84–539
ISBN 0-313-21456-5 (set)
ISBN 0-313-25667-5 (v. 1)
ISBN 0-313-25668-3 (v. 2)

First published in 1986

Greenwood Press, Inc.
88 Post Road West
Westport, Connecticut 06881

Printed in the United States of America

The paper used in this book complies with the
Permanent Paper Standard issued by the National
Information Standards Organization (Z39.48–1984).

10 9 8 7 6 5 4 3 2 1

TO

Joan McCabe Moore
in Appreciation for Her Encouragement
and Her Assistance

AND TO THE MEMORY OF
William C. Young
WITH LOVE

Contents

UNITED STATES
OF AMERICA

Jill N. Brantley, Area Editor

Introduction

Houston's Alley Theatre and the District of Columbia's Arena Stage are two of almost a dozen theatre companies that existed in the United States by 1950. These groups were the forerunners of a theatrical revolution that swept the nation during the 1950s, 1960s, and 1970s. By 1960 another dozen companies had joined their ranks, producing professional work in an atmosphere far removed from the influence of the Broadway stage. Among them were the Dallas Theater Center, Los Angeles' Center Theatre Group (formally the UCLA Theatre Group), the Milwaukee Repertory Theater Company, and the New York Shakespeare Festival, all drawing large and appreciative audiences for their outstanding productions. Foundation support encouraged their efforts. Early in the 1960s the Ford Foundation gave the money to establish a Theatre Communications Group designed to promote cooperation among the nation's professional, community, and university theatres. Since then hundreds of theatre companies have blossomed in many of the nation's cities. Minneapolis' Guthrie Theatre, New Haven's Long Wharf Theatre, New York City's Negro Ensemble Company, and the Seattle Repertory Theatre are among the most important of these regional troupes.

Sometimes the creative genius of a single individual inspired the founding of a company, as is the case with Nina Vance's Alley Theatre and Joseph Papp's New York Shakespeare Festival. More often, a group of founding "fathers" collaborated in establishing a professional theatre company for their region. During the winter of 1950 a group of some forty Washingtonians, spearheaded by Zelda Fichandler, planned the formation of the Arena Stage; in December 1953 Mary Widrig John gathered a few friends to organize a nonprofit stock corporation, Drama, Incorporated, an enterprise that was eventually to lead to the development of the Milwaukee Repertory Theater Company; and in March 1959 Oliver Rea, Peter Zeisler, and Tyrone Guthrie breakfasted at New York's Plaza Hotel, where they considered establishing a first-class repertory theatre in the American heartlands, a theatre destined to carry Guthrie's name.

The first years of many regional theatre companies were a fight for survival in theatre structures that challenged the most resourceful of artistic directors.

The Alley Theatre started business in an eighty-seven-seat dance studio that opened onto an alley; Minneapolis' Children's Theatre Company began in a borrowed back room of an Italian restaurant, moving the following year to an abandoned police station; and the Long Wharf performed in a meat and produce terminal that was designed primarily for cold storage.

From such inauspicious beginnings, quality companies quickly established themselves as leaders in the American theatrical scene by producing exciting new playscripts; giving talented directors unique opportunities; serving as a training ground for some of the nation's finest actors and actresses; providing theatre schools for elementary and secondary level students, actors workshops for various minority groups, and advanced training programs for adult students interested in every aspect of theatre production; and creating exchange programs with important companies in other countries. It is no surprise that the Tony Awards now recognize work done by the nation's regional theatre companies.

As resident theatres reach larger and larger audiences, meet new challenges, and discover new sources of income, regional companies in the United States will continue to complement and supplement the best the Broadway stage has to offer.

COLBY H. KULLMAN

ALLEY THEATRE
615 Texas Avenue
Houston, Texas 77002

Those people who have been intimately connected with the Alley Theatre from its beginnings like to state that the Alley literally began with 214 penny postcards. The number has no special significance; it was merely the amount of money that Nina Vance had in her purse at that time in 1947. The postcards invited interested people to a meeting to discuss the founding of a new theatre group for Houston. Over one hundred people attended this first meeting and decided to form the Alley Theatre, so-named since the facilities they planned to use (an eighty-seven-seat dance studio) opened onto an alley at 3617 Main Street. The group presented its first play, *A Sound of Hunting*, on November 18, 1947, a production that ran for ten nights.

During the second year of operation, the property was condemned for use as a theatre by the fire marshall, and it became imperative for the Alley Theatre to relocate. New facilities were found in an abandoned fan factory at 709 Berry Avenue, a relatively small building that was hastily converted to a 231-seat arena theatre. The new playhouse opened on February 8, 1949, with a strong production of Lillian Hellman's *The Children's Hour*. During the next nineteen years these premises were the home of the Alley Theatre, and it was during these years that the company acquired the excellence which gave it national prominence, and, later, an international reputation.

From the founding of the Alley, the group was totally amateur, but by 1951

Vance saw the need to begin to use some professional actors. This necessity arose because of a lack of rehearsal space and because the amateur actors from the community, most of whom worked during the day, had so little time to rehearse. Professional actors could be available to rehearse during the day and to act at night. Many of the amateur actors fought the hiring of professionals, but the issue was finally decided in the fall of 1952 when members voted the group professional status. At first just one or two professional actors supplemented the amateur group, but the Alley became an all-Equity house in 1954, with its production of Miller's *Death of a Salesman* starring Albert Dekker.

The repertoire of the Alley Theatre from 1947 to 1969 was a skillful blend of typical Broadway fare combined with standard classical plays and interspersed with some contemporary dramas by new playwrights. Among the more interesting productions were Eugene O'Neill's *The Iceman Cometh*, Samuel Beckett's *Waiting for Godot*, William Saroyan's *The Cave Dwellers* (starring and directed by Eugenie Leontovich), O'Neill's *A Moon for the Misbegotten*, Ben Jonson's *Volpone*, Chekhov's *The Three Sisters*, and Friedrich Dürrenmatt's *The Physicists*.

From 1960 the Ford Foundation took an active interest in the Alley as a major regional theatre. The first grant, awarded in 1960, was for $156,000 to pay the salaries of a ten-member Equity company for three years. Before that grant had expired, the Ford Foundation made a major commitment of $2.1 million, $1 million of which was to assist in the building and equipping of a new theatre, and the remainder to supply supplementary operating funds for the first ten years of life of the new playhouse at $110,000 per year. The Alley Theatre immediately began a major fund drive in the summer of 1961 to match the Ford Foundation grant. The people of Houston responded admirably, the schoolchildren contributing their dimes and the townspeople their dollars to the sum of an additional million dollars.

The architect chosen to design the new Alley Theatre was Ulrich Franzen, a New York-based designer. From his drawing board came a new $3.5 million Alley Theatre, a spectacular affair of poured concrete with four soaring towers and a basically linear design. The building is reminiscent of those designed by Frank Lloyd Wright. It contains two basic theatres: the main stage with 798 seats, and a smaller theatre with 296 seats. The main stage might be called a multispace theatre, since the audience is seated in a fan-shaped playing area. The smaller stage is similar to the old Alley Theatre in that it is an area surrounded by seats on four sides. The theatre was opened on November 26, 1968, when Vance directed a production of Brecht's *Galileo* in the new Alley.

Throughout its history, the basic philosophy of the Alley has remained to present a repertoire from all types of dramatic literature, classical to contemporary. There has been at least one premiere production each year. During the 1977–1978 season there was a production of the Soviet play, *Echelon*, the first production of its type in the United States.

During 1979–1982 the Alley's production schedule included Chekhov's *The Cherry Orchard*, Shakespeare's *Romeo and Juliet*, Herb Gardner's *The Goodbye*

People, Hugh Leonard's *Da*, Harold Pinter's *Betrayal*, Ernest Thompson's *On Golden Pond*, and the Southwest premiere of Mark Rozovsky's *Strider*. The company's musical productions of *Oh Coward!* (music and lyrics by Noel Coward, adaptation by Roderick Cook) and *The Threepenny Opera* (book and lyrics by Bertolt Brecht, music by Kurt Weill, and translation by Marc Blitzstein) were successful. Agatha Christie's *Black Coffee* and *The Mousetrap* added a popular murder mystery to the 1979–1980 and 1980–1981 seasons, respectively.

In addition to its regular active programs of plays, there is a theatre school, the Alley Merry-Go-Round, which is one of the nation's largest, for young people from the fourth grade through high school. The program is not intended to prepare professional actors, but to help young people "to develop greater imagination, keener observation, and stronger concentration," as well as to improve their "poise, diction, and posture." The school enrolls approximately three hundred students each semester.

In February 1980 founding director Nina Vance died and was succeeded by a team of four directors who took charge of the 1980–1981 season. On April 1, 1981, Pat Brown was chosen the Alley's new artistic director. More premiere productions, a directors' training program, and an exchange with Alan Ayckbourn's Stephen Joseph Theatre-in-the-Round in Scarborough, England, are a few of the many developing programs at Houston's Alley Theatre.

COLBY H. KULLMAN and
WILLIAM C. YOUNG

AMERICAN CONSERVATORY THEATRE
415 Geary Street
San Francisco, California 94102

The American Conservatory Theatre (ACT) is San Francisco's resident professional theatre and one of the few major companies that actually practices the repertory system of performance. It has presented more than 150 stage productions ranging from the classics of world drama to outstanding contemporary works and has attracted a total audience of over 5 million playgoers since its founding in 1965. To achieve all this, the ACT operates on an annual budget of roughly $4 million and employs more than 250 people, including actors, directors, teachers, designers, writers, craftsmen, administrators, and technicians. Currently, its season at the elegantly Victorian Geary Theatre offers some 280 performances of nine plays in repertory to audiences numbering more than three hundred thousand every year. ACT also sponsors engagements of nonrepertory productions at the smaller Marines' Memorial Theatre and at the Geary Theatre, when the company itself is not performing there. In addition to playing in true repertory, it is the largest and most active of the nation's forty-five major resident professional companies and also the only company whose performances are concurrent with, and inseparable from, a continuing program of theatre training to company members, as well as to those who go there to study in a variety of theatre programs.

William Ball, founder and general director, began ACT as a resident company at the Pittsburgh Playhouse with help from the Rockefeller Foundation, the Pittsburgh Playhouse, and Carnegie-Mellon University. In giving the name "American Conservatory Theatre" to the new company being formed in 1965, Ball and his colleagues sought to underscore not only its national character but also its basic premise of ongoing teaching and training. ACT did not achieve its current success, however, without a struggle. In fact, finding itself homeless in the summer of 1966 because of artistic and administrative conflicts between Ball and the playhouse management, ACT ended its cross-country search for a home in San Francisco, where the company has remained since 1967. Almost immediately, however, the company nearly went broke because it was leasing not only the Geary Theatre but also the smaller Marines' Memorial Theatre two blocks away and staging up to twenty-four plays in repertory in each of its first three seasons. By 1969 the company was nearly $500,000 in debt. These initial financial problems have since been overcome by steadily growing box office support, grants, and other engagements. The crisis has passed, the program has been reduced, and the future has become more secure. ACT now produces nine to fifteen plays a season, and attendance at the Geary is up to 92 percent of capacity as compared to 30 percent in the two-theatre years.

Founded as a contrast to producer-oriented commercial theatres where the all-powerful demands of the box office are often more important than the needs of the artist and where opportunities for creative growth are often severely limited, ACT operates on the principle that actors must continue to grow creatively throughout their professional lives and can be encouraged in this growth by performing almost simultaneously in different roles and in different acting styles. In addition, at the same time that ACT artists continue their growth through ongoing training, they also pass on their knowledge to younger members of their profession. Following this philosophy has enabled ACT to become the most active resident theatre in the country and one of the only true repertory theatres whose productions alternate nightly and whose permanent company is employed not for a single part in the single production but for several roles in several productions.

The ACT professional company is only one-half of the American Conservatory Theatre. The other one-half is the conservatory itself, and the heart of the conservatory is the Advanced Training Program, where approximately eighty-five acting students take part in two-year and three-year courses each season and more than five hundred others receive part-time or short-term training. The acting conservatory, a unique feature of ACT, is perhaps the most extensive actor training program in the United States. In the old linked buildings at 450 Geary Street, across from the Geary and Curran theatres a block from Union Square, conservatory classes involving several hundred people begin every morning. They cover such areas as voice production, dance, fencing, mime, stage movement, stage combat, music, yoga, make-up, improvisation, voice, history, literature, hairdressing, wigmaking, music design, and acting. Allen Fletcher, conservatory director, and his associates audition approximately one thousand young performers in San Francisco, Chicago, New Orleans, and New York between January and June each year. They choose approximately forty-five to join the conservatory as first-year students. After a year of training, one-half of the group is asked to return for a second year. A third year, again by invitation only, emphasizes performance in student projects and on the Geary Theatre stage and may include a Master of Fine Arts degree in acting. At ACT, where training and performing nourish each other, most of the teachers are ACT actors and directors, and students work closely with the professional company as it rehearses, performs, and creates. Actors are encouraged to apply what they learn to their work on stage and also to teach their fellow company members and students. Actors teach, teachers act, actors direct, and directors act while students learn techniques and discipline through close association with performing professionals. The company and the school are, therefore, interdependent, and the actors never stop being students and the students are never asked to stop being actors.

Daring, vigor, and vivid theatricality have been cited as hallmarks of ACT productions. Along with the works of Shakespeare, Ibsen, and Chekhov, the company has performed such popular shows as Brandon Thomas' *Charley's Aunt* and Joseph Kesselring's *Arsenic and Old Lace*; has made old, forgotten works like George M. Cohan's *The Tavern* and Arthur Wing Pinero's *Dandy Dick* into new successes; and has staged expensive productions like Edmond Rostand's *Cyrano de Bergerac* and Ibsen's *Peer Gynt*. It has also secured the rights to popular works from New York and London such as Peter Shaffer's *Equus*, Tom Stoppard's *Travesties* and *Night and Day*, and Sam Shepard's *Buried Child*. In addition, tours to Hawaii, Russia, and Japan have further expanded the influence of the ACT concept of the theatre as well as have the distinguished artists who have trained and performed with ACT: Marsha Mason, Peter Donat, Michael Learned, Cicely Tyson, René Auberjonois, Kitty Winn, Ed Flanders, Ken Ruta, and Sada Thompson. As a result of this vast expanse of showmanship, ACT has educated and entertained several million people over the years.

ACT began a program of community involvement in 1967, during its first repertory season in San Francisco, and has continued to expand and diversify community activities in successive seasons. Part of a movement in which resident professional theatres seek and find their identities in relation to the areas they serve, rather than from a single theatre capital, ACT has reached out into the community to learn its needs and to help fill them by providing student matinee performances, free theatre tickets to senior citizens and welfare groups, performances in student assemblies, and playreading programs. One vehicle for such interaction is the Summer Training Congress which provides 150 students with ten weeks of intensive professional training. The program emphasizes the performance-oriented subjects regularly provided for the professional ACT company. The Black Actor's Workshop, formed in cooperation with representatives of Bay Area Black theatres, meets three times a week, November through May, and uses black culture as a perspective to increase actors' technical skills. The Asian American Theatre Workshop is a year-round program to train performers and develop playwrights and to encourage the contribution of Asian-Americans to contemporary theatre. The Evening Extension Program offers ten weeks of classes in the spring for students and members of the community who want to broaden their theatrical talents and skills. It also provides training in such non-performance areas as children's theatre organization, theatre management, and public relations. The Young Conservatory introduces theatre to students nine through eighteen years of age with summer programs and after-school classes; some schools give academic credit for a student's work at ACT. The Master of Fine Arts program involves third-year students in the Advanced Training Program, and the Plays in Progress series of the new works finds second-year students and professional actors working side by side in presenting first productions of outstanding plays by new authors in a workshop environment. In providing advanced study in a variety of performance-oriented subjects to its own membership and to young people who come from campuses and cities all over the United States, ACT fulfills its dual objectives: a producing organization and a full-time professional conservatory.

In short, ACT has provided San Francisco with a large, ongoing, professional theatre that lives and works in the area where it performs. Moreover, in combining within its organization a conservatory for training young actors, taught by members of the company, it has provided the community with professional schooling unavailable before its move to the Bay area. In 1979 ACT won the prestigious Tony Award for imagination, professionalism, and bold theatrical style, as well as for contributions to the national and world theatre community through training programs. ACT's *A Christmas Carol* (1981) was one of the first productions to appear on the newly formed ABC ARTS cable channel. Many reviewers considered it "a class act." A thriving enterprise, financially as well as artistically, and the recipient of extensive grants from the Ford Foundation and the National Endowment for the Arts, ACT also enjoys strong local support and a subscription audience of over twenty-one thousand. This, together with the caliber of its work, makes it a candidate for the best repertory company in the United States.

BEVERLY ANN BENSON

AMERICAN REPERTORY THEATRE
Loeb Drama Center
64 Brattle Street
Cambridge, Massachusetts 02138

In 1979 Robert Brustein, founder of the Yale Repertory Theatre and for thirteen years the Dean of the Yale School of Drama, left New Haven for Boston, bringing with him a core of Yale Repertory company members. The resulting company, the American Repertory Theatre, opened its first production, *A Midsummer Night's Dream*, at the Loeb Drama Center in March 1980.

The American Repertory Theatre (ART) is a professional resident company affiliated with Harvard University, which provides about twelve percent of the ART yearly budget. As part of this relationship with Harvard, Company members currently present over twenty theatre-related courses at Harvard each year, including Extension School and Summer School courses.

Brustein, the founder of the ART, has been the artistic director of the company since its beginnings. Robert J. Orchard has served as managing director of the ART from its founding in 1980. Directors for various performances during the five seasons have included Alvin Epstein, Jonathan Miller, Lee Breuer, Andrei Serban, Peter Sellars and, of course, Brustein himself.

A typical ART performance season includes five productions at the Loeb Drama Center and several experimental plays at the Hasty Pudding Theatre. During its first five seasons, ART presentations have included world premieres of plays such as Mark Leib's *Terry by Terry* and Marsha Norman's *'Night, Mother* and *Traveler in the Dark*. Offerings have not, however, been limited to new plays: the company has also presented classics such as William Shakespeare's *As You Like It*, Henrik Ibsen's *Ghosts*, Anton Chekhov's *Three Sisters* and Richard Brinsley Sheridan's *The School for Scandal*, and a number of musical productions, including a presentation of Handel's opera *Orlando* staged by Peter Sellars.

The ART, currently playing at ninety-four percent of capacity, has been quite successful—particularly in a city where there had been no major equity theatre company since the late 1960s. There has, however, been some unevenness in the choice of plays and in production quality. The company's second season (1980–1981) illustrated some of the difficulties inherent in the ART's risk-taking approach to its productions. That season included among its offerings an unsuccessful American premiere of a British comedy, Charles Wood's *Has "Washington" Legs?* and the highly experimental and controversial *Lulu*, directed by Lee Breuer and adapted by Michael Feingold from Frank Wedekind's "Earth-Spirit" and "Pandora's Box." The more innovative and controversial aspects of the ART should not have come as a surprise to subscribers. Brustein, the ART's artistic director, declared in 1972 in an essay on English repertory theatre, "What I am still seeking is a theatre willing to risk its existence in order to advance its frontiers, continually questioning its direction even at the loss of its comfort and security." (Robert Brustein, *The Culture Watch: Essays on Theatre and Society, 1969–1974* [New York: Alfred A. Knopf, 1975], p. 71.) Like its predecessor, the Yale Repertory Theatre, the ART has displayed its willingness to take risks in its productions, particularly in its hiring of daringly experimental directors.

A highlight of the 1982–1983 season was the widely praised world premiere of Marsha Norman's *'Night, Mother*, which later won a Pulitzer Prize. *'Night, Mother* moved to Broadway, as have productions of Jules Feiffer's *Grown Ups*

(1980) and Eugene O'Neill's *A Moon for the Misbegotten* (1983–1984). Other particularly noteworthy presentations have included William Shakespeare's *A Midsummer Night's Dream* (1980), Molière's *Sganarelle* (1981–1982, 1984), and Samuel Beckett's *Waiting for Godot* (1983).

In addition to its usual season, in 1982 the ART mounted a successful eleven-week tour of seven countries. One of the productions on the tour, *Sganarelle*, directed by Andrei Serban, was recorded in London for British television. The ART was also one of five U.S. companies chosen to perform at the 1984 Olympics Art Festival, where company members presented productions of *The School for Scandal*, directed by Jonathan Miller, and Luigi Pirandello's *Six Characters in Search of an Author*, directed by Robert Brustein.

The ART seems likely to carry on its successful mix of modern plays and reinterpreted classics: recent productions have included Shakespeare's *Love's Labour's Lost*, and a new collaborative work by Sam Shepard and Joseph Chaikin, a controversial production of Samuel Beckett's *Endgame*, and the American premiere of *the CIVIL WarS*.

MARYKAY MAHONEY

ARENA STAGE
6th and Maine Avenue, S.W.
Washington, D.C. 20024

The Arena Stage prides itself in being three times a threefold theatre. First, it is three theatres in one: an eight hundred-seat, theatre-in-the-round—Arena Stage proper; a traditional but intimate, five hundred-seat, end-stage—the Kreeger Theater; and a cabaret-like, 180-seat—the Old Vat Room. Second, it serves three theatres through the new material Arena supplies for Broadway, and an international audience reached by Arena as an "ambassador" theatre company. Third, Arena is philosophically committed to three main purposes: to premiere new American and European plays and playwrights, to give established plays new and timely renderings, and to revive plays that have failed in commercial theatre.

Arena Stage is organized under the corporate name of the Washington Drama Society, Inc. It is headed by Zelda Fichandler, producing director, and Thomas Fichandler, executive director, and employs approximately 175 people. It maintains a permanent acting company nucleus of about fifteen actors, some of whom have been with Arena more than twenty years. This company is supplemented by actors from around the country, who may act with Arena on a semi-permanent basis. Directors may be permanent staff members or visitors. Arena uses a wide range of set designers; many develop their creative talents there and others are well-known designers, attracted by Arena's facilities and stimulating production choices. Costumes, sets, and properties are made in Arena's own workshops.

Arena owns outright its present buildings and one-half the land on which it stands. As a nonprofit theatre, its financing is secured through subscription and private foundation, government, and corporation support. Attendance for the three theatres averages 86 percent capacity. Arena has an active patrons organization.

Arena Stage seeks, according to founder Zelda Fichandler who was quoted in publicity materials provided by Arena Stage,

to bring life to life. And by doing this we are indissolubly connected to the world we live in and to the people we live for. We are a theater for audiences. We are not an idle or esoteric experiment. We live to illuminate life and make it more meaningful and more enjoyable.

The stage is repeatedly applauded locally and nationally for its commitment to "challenging audiences" rather than "pacifying them." Arena sees the theatre as a "laboratory where we examine our lives." The facilities and production choices reflect this philosophy.

Arena Stage, to a degree rare among American theatres, has had, in the persons of Zelda and Thomas Fichandler, a continuity of leadership in the evolution and implementation of its vision from its beginning. Arena Stage was organized in the winter of 1950 by a group of some forty Washingtonians—including an attorney, a policeman, a tennis professional, a jeweler, and a professor—spearheaded by Zelda Fichandler, a Cornell Phi Beta Kappa (Russian language and literature), who was about to receive her M.A. in theatre arts from the George Washington University. The organizers had no credentials as theatrical producers, but they were united by a common bond to bring professional theatre to Washington and perhaps were touched by the beginnings elsewhere of what was to become the "regional theatre movement." They put together a formidable drive to raise $15,000 in ten days to exercise an option on the Hippodrome, an old movie theatre in downtown Washington.

The converted Hippodrome had an arena form and seated 247 on all four sides of the stage. Between August 1950 and July 1955, Arena put on fifty-five productions in the Hippodrome, beginning with Oliver Goldsmith's *She Stoops to Conquer*. Audiences, actors, designers, and directors were challenged and delighted by the arena shape, which so involved audiences, achieving immediacy through simplicity. But the Hippodrome had limits. Some were amusing: actors having to run around the block to make entrances; others were serious: the small seating capacity meant Arena could not pay its production costs.

To overcome these limits, Zelda Fichandler, at the end of the successful American premiere of Agatha Christie's *The Mousetrap*, boldly closed the theatre for a year to look for better facilities. The new facilities were the former Heurich Brewery in Foggy Bottom and were christened "the Old Vat," a play on the "Old Vic" and the former use of the new environs. The Old Vat opened in November 1956 with a successful premiere of the full-length version of Arthur Miller's *A View from the Bridge*. The Old Vat seated five hundred in the area surrounding what had been the brewery's ice storage space. Some forty productions were presented in the Old Vat, including Ray Lawler's *Summer of the Seventeenth Doll*, Christopher Fry's *The Lady's Not for Burning*, Herman Wouk's *The Caine Mutiny Court Martial*, and the American premiere of Félicien Marceau's *The Egg*.

During the Old Vat period, Arena made a number of important organizational advances. It became a subscription-based company, providing actors with more stable employment and securing audiences who were not simply "shopping for a hit." The production schedule was established as a fall through spring season, with summer for planning. Arena began to receive foundation grants to develop new plays and encourage establishment of a permanent theatre company. But the Old Vat was scheduled to be demolished to make way for a new highway; Arena had once again to look for a new home.

Ground was broken to begin construction of Arena Stage's permanent home in October 1960. The first theatre of the three-theatre complex, the Arena, itself was a landmark in American theatre building because of the close collaboration between architect, actors, and producers. Architect Harry Weese worked with Zelda Fichandler, Thomas Fichandler, and the Arena Stage company to design the theatre around the ideals of the company. Realization of these designs cost over a million dollars and was made possible by the financial expertise of World Bank executive J. Burke Knapp and Thomas Fichandler. Foundation grants offered $300,000; other gifts, $75,000; bond sales, $225,000; and a mortgage, $250,000. Among the foundations responding to Arena's popular support were the Arts of the Theatre Foundation, the Eugene and Agnes E. Meyer Foundation, the Old Dominion Foundation, the Rockefeller Foundation, the Philip M. Stern Family Fund, and the Twentieth Century Fund. A later grant of $863,000 by the Ford Foundation paid for the mortgage, repaid bonds, bought the site, and allowed for building improvements.

The premiere production in the Arena was Bertolt Brecht's *The Caucasian Chalk Circle* (1961). Other significant productions included John Whiting's *The Devils*, Eugene O'Neill's *The Iceman Cometh*, Charles Gordone's *No Place to Be Somebody*, and the world premiere of Howard Sackler's *The Great White Hope*.

Audiences filled Arena to about 90 percent capacity. Projects such as the Living Stage, a first theatre-in-education program, grew to provide a full set of improvisational theatre experiences. Plays for children, training programs for the resident company, internships for high school and college students, and programs in local prisons were developed. Classes and rehearsals needed more space.

In August 1968 construction began on the Kreeger Theater (named for Washington philanthropist David Lloyd Kreeger, a major contributor to its building fund). The Kreeger is a marked contrast to the Arena, having a "flexible-end stage." The Kreeger opened in January 1971 with the American premiere of Peter Barnes' *The Ruling Class*.

Since 1971 Arena Stage has offered seasons presenting a total of eight plays in Arena and Kreeger and two or three special attractions. From September to July there is activity in either Arena Stage, the Kreeger Theater, or both.

In 1975 Arena added the Old Vat Room, formerly a large meeting space that was redesigned as a place of experimental theatre. The Old Vat is the home of Arena's "In the Process" series, an informal workshop for playwrights. "In the Process" lets new writers try their craft free of commercial pressures. In an "In the Process" production, the playwright works with directors and cast before and during a simply staged production. Audiences participate in an open discussion following the performance. Subscriptions just about sold out performances of the "In the Process" series. This program, supported by grants from the Andrew W. Mellon and Ford foundations, was temporarily suspended when support funds ran out. New funding is being sought.

In recent years, the cabaret space has hosted numerous Arena Stage special events, including Mary Kyte, Mel Marvin, and Gary Pearle's *Tintypes: A Ragtime Review*, *The Flying Karamazov Brothers*, and *Banjo Dancing*. Such events have been well attended, developing a new Arena audience and generating additional income.

Arena Stage has outstanding production facilities because architect Harry Weese (the designer of the stations of Washington's metro system) worked closely with the acting company, developing plans for both the Arena Stage (built in 1960) and the Kreeger Theater addition (built in 1968). When construction of Arena began, there were few Americans with experience in theatre architecture because no new theatre on a new site had been built in the United States for over fifty years.

Arena Stage is a 30-foot by 36-foot rectangle, surrounded on all four sides by tiers of seats, backed by an outer row of boxes. It seats 811. Rows are sharply banked to heighten the audience's sense of "leaning into the play." Zelda Fichandler has called the stage "a neutral cube of space, rather than a flat playing area." By use of lighting and platforms, the stage can be greatly contracted or expanded and can represent one place or a number of places. The stage can be entered through tunnels at each corner, from under the stage or by aisles through the house.

The Kreeger, in contrast, is an end-stage theatre with a fan-shaped house seating five hundred. Like the Arena, the Kreeger is designed for heavy use of lighting effects. The stage is fully trapped, allowing its various parts to be set at various levels. But, unlike the Arena, the action in the Kreeger is focused by the back wall of the stage. Panels on each side make it possible to expand and contract the width of the stage. Many features of traditional theatre may be created at the Kreeger but are not part of its permanent design—such as the proscenium, the house curtain, and a cyclorama.

Additional facilities include the Rehearsal Room, which duplicates the playing area of the Arena; the Old Vat Room, a 180-seat cabaret style room; shops; workrooms; and offices.

Arena Stage had become increasingly noted for world and American premieres of significant plays. Included in this distinguished list are Lorraine Hansberry's *A Raisin in the Sun*, Howard Sackler's *The Great White Hope*, Arthur Kopit's *Indians*, Michael Weller's *Loose Ends*, István Örkeńy's *Cat's Play*, and David Storey's *In Celebration*.

A number of actors, directors, and designers have had important career experiences at Arena, including Edward Herrmann; Jane Alexander; Jon Voight; Stacy Keach, Jr.; Ned Beatty; James Earl Jones; Esther Rolle; Alan Schneider; Edwin Sherin; Robin Wagner; Santo Loquasto; Ming Cho Lee; and Marjorie Slaiman. Visiting playwrights have included Arthur Miller, Arthur Kopit, Paddy Chayefsky, István Orkeńy, Preston Jones, Thornton Wilder, and Lillian Hellman.

The 1980–1981 season, marking the thirtieth anniversary of Arena Stage, included productions of Bertolt Brecht's *Galileo*, Vernel Bagneris' *One Mo' Time*, Moss Hart and George S. Kaufman's *The Man Who Came to Dinner*, Nikolai Erdman's *The Suicide*, and Jean-Paul Sartre's *Kean*.

Arena Stage has been widely rewarded for its pioneering work in American theatre, receiving the 1971 Margo Jones Award for "significant contributions to the dramatic art of new plays" at the National Theatre Conference and the 1976 Antoinette Perry ("Tony") Award for theatrical excellence (the first theatre outside New York City so honored). In addition, Arena Stage was the first American company to be given permission by the State Department and the Soviet Ministry of Culture to tour the USSR. In 1980, it was the first American theatre company to participate in the prestigious Hong Kong Arts Festival.

JILL N. BRANTLEY
(Adapted from materials provided by Arena Stage.
Quotes in the article are from the company's publicity materials.)

CENTER THEATRE GROUP/MARK TAPER FORUM
135 North Grand Avenue
Los Angeles, California 90012

The debut of the Center Theatre Group at the new Mark Taper Forum on April 9, 1967, aroused more than the usual fanfare and speculation. Having chosen John Whiting's *The Devils* for his inaugural production, artistic director Gordon Davidson had to withstand charges of obscenity from both the general public and many of the thirty thousand patrons who had subscribed for the premiere season. So great was the outcry that the Los Angeles County Board of Supervisors soon appointed a citizens' panel to determine whether any future play might exceed the limits of propriety. In this singularly appropriate manner, the Center Theatre Group launched its continuing campaign to offer new, provocative drama and reinstate the theatre as a vital and sometimes unsettling force in the Los Angeles community.

Prior to its association with the Taper and the adjoining Ahmanson Theatre, the company had operated for nine years as the UCLA Theatre Group, originally under the direction of John Houseman. In 1964, when Houseman felt pressed by other commitments, he invited thirty-one-year-old Gordon Davidson to sign on as assistant director for a production of *King Lear*. The two had met in 1958 when Davidson was stage manager for the American Shakespeare Festival Theatre; Davidson later held similar positions with the Phoenix Theatre, Martha Graham Dance Company, and Dallas Opera. When Houseman left UCLA in 1965, Davidson took over as managing director and produced eleven plays, including the highly successful *Candide* and *The Deputy*. With the opening of the Mark Taper Forum (named after a prominent Los Angeles financier and cultural patron) as part of the Music Center complex, the Theatre Group severed its UCLA connection and moved to its first permanent home—an experimental theatre equipped with a pentagonal thrust stage, cyclorama projection wall, and semicircular auditorium with a seating capacity of 742. On opening night the new company was officially installed by its founders, Center Theatre Group board president Lew R. Wasserman, adviser Robert Whitehead, and director Elliott Martin.

As the only major regional theatre in the United States that follows a year-round schedule, the Taper usually presents five or six plays each season, often with two or more plays running concurrently in a repertory festival. A subscription system that ensures 70 percent attendance frees Davidson somewhat from the usual concerns about critical reception and popular success, especially since box office receipts account for only one-half of the theatre's revenues. The remainder is supplied by the Music Center Fund, the National Endowment for the Arts, and private foundations. Davidson therefore believes that:

The least important factor in planning a season is figuring out what an audience wants to see. You have to get your own vision organized first, discover what it is you want to make in the theatre and then find a way to communicate that. If your ideas are valid, you find that generally the audience will go along with you.

The Taper also enjoys the advantage of having a large pool of television and film actors living in the Los Angeles area, which allows Davidson to cast each production separately instead of maintaining a repertory company. The wide availability of experienced actors, however, prevented his theatre from becoming a training ground for young performers until the formation of a twenty-member repertory company in 1981. Under the supervision of Ellis Rabb, the company will be regularly featured in repertory festivals of two or more plays. Its development represents, in Davidson's view, "*the* challenge for us in the eighties and certainly the next step for the Mark Taper Forum."

From 1967 through the 1981–1982 season, the Center Theatre Group has appeared in over two hundred productions, and in keeping with its commitment to new work, almost two-thirds of these have been world or American premieres. Among the most notable have been *In the Matter of J. Robert Oppenheimer* by Heinar Kipphardt; *The Trial of the Catonsville Nine* by Daniel Berrigan, S.J.; *Savages* by Christopher Hampton; *The Shadow Box* by Michael Cristofer; *Zoot Suit* by Luis Valdez; and *Children of a Lesser God* by Mark Medoff. Since these and other Center Theatre Group plays have gone on to be produced at other regional theatres and on Broadway, the company has gained a national reputation in a remarkably short time. Other Forum programs have been designed specifically to encourage promising writers, directors, actors, and technicians. The much-acclaimed New Theatre for Now series (originally directed by Edward Parone) has supported a wide range of innovative work under different formats— Monday night readings, festivals in various Los Angeles locales, and low-budget productions on the Taper main stage as part of the regular subscription series. *The Trial of the Catonsville Nine* and *Zoot Suit* originated in this program and, altogether, New Theatre for Now has sponsored over eighty new plays in ten seasons. Although occasionally suspended through lack of funding, the series was revived in the spring of 1982 with productions of four contemporary works.

More experimental in nature is the Forum Laboratory, located in the ninety-nine-seat John Anson Ford Cultural Center in Hollywood. Here plays can be developed in workshop sessions, rehearsed more thoroughly for production elsewhere, or presented to a select audience. Since 1972, more than sixty programs have been staged at the Lab. The Improvisational Theatre Project, meanwhile, uses story theatre and other theatre game techniques for improvised and scripted performances. Directed by John Dennis, the Improvisational Theatre Project has appeared at the Taper main stage and Lab, traveled to local schools and community centers, and toured both statewide and nationally. Most recently, an occasional series of dramatic sketches and readings has been presented in the informal setting of the Itchey Foot Ristorante, a three-minute walk from the Taper. "Sundays at the Itchey Foot" offers an hour-long entertainment that coincides with and expands upon the current main stage production; it can be seen after the matinee or before the evening performance.

As a complement to these diverse programs supporting original drama, the subscription series regularly features revivals of the classics. Shakespeare has been represented by *Othello*; *Henry IV, Part 1*; *Hamlet*; *The Tempest*; and *Twelfth Night*, while major works by Ben Jonson, John Webster, Molière, Chekhov, George Bernard Shaw, Oscar Wilde, and Sean O'Casey have also appeared. To the objection that the Taper should remain exclusively experimental, Davidson replies that worthy new plays are difficult to find and that the classic repertory challenges the director and actor to widen their perspective. He adds that "finally the mark of a theatre is to create, not only new material, but new ways of looking at material. . . . There's something about reviving a classic in its own time. If you do it well enough the audience should be able to make the connection with now."

Recognition of the Center Theatre Group's efforts for quality drama both new and old culminated in 1977 when *The Shadow Box* received the Pulitzer Prize and Tony Award for Best Play and Davidson won a Tony as Best Director. More significantly, the Taper became only the second theatre to receive a special Tony Award commending its excellence as a representative of the growing regional theatre movement in America. In addition to citing its dedication to new plays, the award saluted its cooperation with the Hartford Stage and Washington, D.C.'s Arena Stage in permitting Christopher Durang's *A History of the American Film* to appear at all three theatres during the same season. The Taper was also recognized for such innovations as offering related plays like *The Importance of Being Earnest* and Tom Stoppard's *Travesties* on alternate nights. In 1980 the theatre achieved another major "triple" when John Rubenstien and Phyllis Frelich won the Best Actor and Best Actress awards, respectively, for the production of *Children of a Lesser God*, which was also designated Best Play.

While Davidson's tenure as artistic director has provided the Center Theatre Group with unified goals and a consistent public image, a further reason for its cultural and financial success is its willingness to appeal to all segments of the population without condescension or compromise. Project DATE (Deaf Audience Theatre Encounter), for example, offers summaries and signed, preshow seminars as well as performances and postplay discussions for deaf audiences. An infrared sound listening system in the theatre provides maximum audibility for the hearing-impaired as audio signals are transmitted through headphone or the patron's own hearing aid. Discounts are also available for students and senior citizens, while Operation Discovery reserves one-dollar tickets for halfway houses, prisons, churches, and community groups. In addition, the recent purchase of the 1,199-seat Aquarius Theatre in Hollywood has greatly expanded the Taper's audience. An experimental space on its large stage is currently the home of the New Theatre for Now series. These and other initiatives are essential to the Taper's role in the community, according to Davidson, for "the connections that audiences make are very profound. We try to use the Forum as a forum, because people in Los Angeles tend to be hermetically sealed in their cars. We try to develop the capability for you to perceive, to decide, to change."

DANIEL BARRETT

CHILDREN'S THEATRE COMPANY
2400 Third Avenue South
Minneapolis, Minnesota 55404

Since its beginning, the Children's Theatre Company (CTC) has chosen young people as its primary audience. The company believes that this audience demands and deserves the same high standards expected in professional adult theatre.

Originally called the Moppet Players of Minneapolis, the company began in 1961, under the administration of Beth Linnerson, in a borrowed back room of an Italian restaurant, Mama Rosa's. A year later, the company moved to a 150-seat theatre fashioned out of an abandoned police station. John Clark Donahue, who joined the company when it was barely a year old, became artistic director in 1964 and has remained in that position until the present.

The all-volunteer Moppet Players set out to develop new plays in which children and adults shared in the production. In addition to the staging of these plays, classes were organized in creative dramatics, dance, and play production.

In 1965 John Clark Donahue approached the Minneapolis Institute of Arts, a museum, to ask for the use of its 646-seat lecture hall, which contained a narrow 26-foot proscenium stage, no fly-space, and only a narrow corridor as backstage area. Nevertheless, the company flourished, and the difficulties involved in presenting a large cast on a very small stage were used to telling dramatic advantage. The Institute of Arts, recognizing the potentialities of CTC, made it a permanent and significant part of the museum's program, renaming it the Children's Theatre Company of the Minneapolis Institute of Arts. The CTC returned to independent status in 1975.

For the first few years at the institute, CTC productions consisted of adaptations of classics, such as *The Emperor's New Clothes*, *Rumpelstiltskin*, and *Cinderella*, made by members of the staff of four, and original plays, such as John Donahue's *Good Morning, Mr. Tillie* and *Hang on to Your Head*. The number of performances increased from forty in 1965–1966 to 127 in 1969–1970. The company moved into national prominence with the showing of *Good Morning, Mr. Tillie* at the American Theater Association annual convention in Washington, D.C., in the summer of 1970 and of *Hang on to Your Head* at the Fourth World Congress of ASSITEJ (Association Internationale Théâtre Enfance Jeunesse) in Montreal and Albany in 1972. Also in 1972, a documentary film about the CTC, *A Children's Theatre* by D. A. Pennebaker, was commissioned by the National Endowment for the Arts/U.S. Office of Education.

The next major stage in the company's development came in 1970 when the Rockefeller Foundation made a substantial contribution to promote overall growth; old programs were expanded and new ones created. A large portion of the subsidy was used to encourage the writing of new plays, bring in guest writers, assemble scripts, and document their creation. Samples of these scripts can be found in *The Cookie Jar and Other Plays* by John Clark Donahue and *Five Plays from the Children's Theatre*, both published by the University of Minnesota Press in 1975. Additional funds from the Rockefeller Foundation provided support during the difficult year when the company was without a home or a stage while a new theatre was being constructed.

The new theatre was built in close collaboration between the Japanese master architect, Kenzo Tange, and the members of the CTC. With a 746-seat proscenium theatre, a studio theatre, a dance studio, and classroom space, it is the largest performing arts facility in the United States designed primarily for young children. The impact of the new theatre can be seen in the growth of the company from a season of forty performances to 28,548 people in 1965–1966 to a season of 123 performances to 114,875 people in 1974–1975, the year in which the theatre was opened.

The new theatre has allowed the company to develop especially lavish works, using sets and costumes that can be kept in repertoire, without losing the experimental energy that characterized its developing stages. Productions in the new theatre have included adaptations of *Treasure Island* and *The 500 Hats of Bartholomew Cubbins* by Timothy Mason, *The Snow Queen* by Michael Dennis Browne, *The Three Musketeers* by Frederick Gaines, and *The Marvelous Land of Oz* by Thomas Olson and Gary Briggle, as well as such original plays as *The Dream Fishers* by John Clark Donahue and *Falling Moons* by Kirk Ristau.

CTC productions usually start with only a title or an idea, and the play is developed in rehearsal. In publicity materials provided by the group, John Clark Donahue said, "All our work has been originated with us, either original plays developed completely in rehearsal or adaptations of classics also done in this way." Casting is done and rehearsal starts with only a scenario. In five to six weeks, the director, designer, composer, writer, and all the company contribute their unique skills as the play moves toward opening night. Sometimes the final scenes are not even sketched out until a few days before the play opens. Clearly, this process gives a special chaos to rehearsals and a special cohesiveness to the production. Through this method which Frederick Gaines, a writer with the company, calls "the first theatre democracy I've ever worked in," all the components—set, costumes, lights, music, acting, choreography, and plot—because they have been created together, are fused together in the final production.

The willingness to take such risks reflects the experimental quality of CTC. By spring 1981, the company had developed thirty original works. Its sixty-four adaptations of classic tales have been equally original in their approach, ranging from *Hansel and Gretel* entirely in German to *Sleeping Beauty* in the manner of a Japanese Kabuki company and *The Story of Babar* with "little" elephants over eight feet tall. Even the very young audiences (preschool), as well as those of elementary school age, respond to this spirit of innovation. In addition, the company performs some classic works by such authors as Chekhov, Richard Sheridan, Georges Feydeau, Molière, Leonid Andreyev, and Shakespeare for its teenage and adult audiences.

Along with producing plays, and as an essential arm of the theatre, since its beginning in the abandoned police station the CTC has always conducted a program of classes in the performing arts. According to the company's publicity, John Clark Donahue's view is that "the arts have a great role, potentially, in learning, in the future of education. The arts should be a catalyst for education because the art experience is a method of opening all the pores and learning possibilities of any situation." To carry out this educational purpose, the Children's Theatre School was officially founded in 1969, in cooperation with the Minneapolis Public Schools Urban Arts Program. It is now the largest fully professional theatre school for young people (ages eleven to eighteen) in the nation and maintains classes in both the performing arts and technical theatre. The school also has an intern program designed to provide working experience in theatre for high school graduates and college students.

The CTC received the Margo Jones Award in 1981 for theatrical excellence, with a special note from the awards committee, "It is terribly important that this not be confused with a special children's theatre award." As the note affirms, this award is given only to professional theatres of the highest quality without regard to the ages of their audiences. Such recognition confirms CTC's conviction that theatre for children need not be second best and that, in John Clark Donahue's words, "Theatre formulated around the literature, ideas, and fantasies of youth has an artistic viability which not only speaks to children but reaches to adults who . . . can touch those emotions and moments in themselves that were so real when they were children."

VICTORIA S. POULAKIS and
RICHARD SHAW

CIRCLE IN THE SQUARE THEATRE
1633 Broadway
New York, New York 10019

We believe that theatre is an art form and not a business for profit; . . . To move people, to help people is what we all want. The theatre is one of the greatest forces yet devised by man to accomplish this. . . . We are all here because we urgently believe in the re-affirmation of ourselves, our friends and our society. It seems to me that a fine way to express this faith is by developing and supporting a theatre which is open to all segments of the society. The only aristocracy that exists in the theatre belongs to those who can communicate with people, and those who help to make communication happen. ("Report of the Artistic Direction.")

Theodore Mann
August 15, 1972

This statement of philosophy by Theodore Mann, artistic director of the Circle in the Square Theatre since its founding thirty-three years ago, summarizes the aspirations and contributions of this company in New York.

Dedicated to both preserving and enriching American dramatic traditions, Circle in the Square has attempted to present powerful productions of classic plays with established actors, while at the same time to provide an arena for new dramatic work and new talented actors. It has sought to accomplish these objectives with an ever-expanding program that involves two theatres (one now used primarily for experimental productions, the other for the classics); a theatre school and workshop; and numerous civic activities. One measure of its success is that in 1975–1976, the twenty-fifth anniversary season, Circle in the Square received a special Tony Award and the Outer Critics Circle Award.

Circle in the Square was founded in 1951 on Bleecker Street in Greenwich Village, by converting an abandoned night club into a three-sided theatre. The building was scrubbed and stripped of its night club trappings, platforms that had been used for loading food produce were used for the stage, and the former night club's show girl and stripper costumes were remade to dress the cast.

The three-sided theatre concept was quickly adapted by other theatre companies because of its several advantages: all seats offer an unobstructed view of the stage; the stage is an open space, requiring minimal scenery; and the audience is close—no further than ten rows from stage in the original theatre—permitting them to participate in the play, providing the backdrop, and affecting the actors with emotional interaction. Because of all these advantages, when the new Circle in the Square Theatre was designed for the Uris office building on Broadway, the three-sided concept was a focal consideration.

Theodore Mann, artistic director, is one of the founders, along with Jose Quintero, Emilie Stevens, Jason Wingreen, Aileen Cramer, and Edward Mann. Paul Libin is managing director. The Board of Directors includes such well-known figures as Dustin Hoffman, Mike Nichols, Beverly Sills, and Joanne Woodward.

The genesis of the Off-Broadway theatre movement, which nurtured American actors, playwrights, and directors, can be said to have occurred with the Circle. It helped to build or establish the reputations of artists such as George C. Scott, Jason Robards, Geraldine Page, Colleen Dewhurst, Dustin Hoffman, Cicely Tyson, and James Earl Jones; directors Alan Arkin, William Ball, Michael Cacoyannis, Theodore Mann, and Jose Quintero; and playwrights Terrence McNally, Jules Feiffer, Adrienne Kennedy, and Murray Schisgal.

The Circle has successfully produced the works of many American playwrights: Tennessee Williams' *Summer and Smoke* and *Camino Real*; John Steinbeck's *Burning Bright*; Thornton Wilder's *Our Town* and *Plays for Bleecker Street* (written especially for the Circle); Eugene O'Neill's *The Iceman Cometh*, *Long Day's Journey into Night*, *A Moon for the Misbegotten*, *Desire Under the Elms*, *Ah, Wilderness!*, and *Hughie*; Jules Feiffer's *Little Murders* and *The White House Murder Case*; Saul Bellow's *Last Analysis*; and many others.

In addition, the Circle introduced American audiences to Jean Genet's *The Balcony*, Brendan Behan's *The Quare Fellow*, and Athol Fugard's *Boesman and Lena*, and revived such classics as Euripides' *The Trojan Women*, Gerhart Hauptmann's *Iphigenia in Aulis*, and Luigi Pirandello's *Six Characters in Search of an Author*.

Many of the same leading artists return, now to the newer Broadway Circle in the Square, from television and film work, attracted not only by the opportunity to keep in touch with live theatre but also by the four-month-only stint required for each play.

In 1972 the Broadway Circle opened, seating 650, more than double the size of the original Greenwich Village theatre. The Broadway Circle in the Square was envisioned as a way to infuse new life into the tired musical-comedy formula offered so long to Broadway audiences. It sought to provide classical theatre with important actors customarily absent from the Broadway scene. Some of its productions have included Irene Pappas in Euripides' *Medea*, George C. Scott, Nicol Williamson, Julie Christie, Cathleen Nesbit, Elizabeth Wilson, and Lillian Gish in Chekhov's *Uncle Vanya* (directed by Mike Nichols), Maureen Stapleton in Williams' *The Glass Menagerie*, Vanessa Redgrave in Ibsen's *The Lady from the Sea*, and Richard Chamberlain and Dorothy McGuire in Williams' *The Night of the Iguana*. Highly acclaimed performances were given in 1982 by George

C. Scott as Garry Essendine in Noel Coward's *Present Laughter* and Colleen Dewhurst as Argia in Ugo Betti's *Queen of the Rebels*.

Besides presenting four major productions per season at the Broadway theatre and several productions at the Greenwich Village theatre, the Circle operates a Theatre School. Begun in 1961 and administered by Mary Kerney Levenstein, it includes a two-year graduate professional program and an undergraduate program affiliated with the New York University School of the Arts. Approximately three hundred students train with working professionals in the New York theatre and are associated with a performing theatre company, the Circle.

The Circle also engages in community service programs, including a free ticket distribution program for senior citizens and the economically disadvantaged; half-priced tickets for students; free weekly readings of new plays to the public; and three student productions each semester. As a nonprofit, tax-exempt operation, the Circle has consistently attracted a large subscription audience.

Circle in the Square's expanding operations over the years have been infused with the same artistic aspirations and dedication: to present good theatre as a means of communication among people. Colleen Dewhurst has explained the admiration and love performers feel for Circle in the Square: "For me the Circle in the Square has always been a new beginning, a haven, a home." It is a place where the actor may feel "at ease, free to experiment, to be a natural part of the whole." (*Circle in the Square Newsletter*, September-October 1982, p. 1).

RUTH MIKKELSON
(Quotes in the article are
from the company's publicity materials.)

DALLAS THEATER CENTER
3636 Turtle Creek Boulevard
Dallas, Texas 75219

The Dallas Theater Center was founded in 1954 as a new kind of resident theatre designed to grow from the talents of its own people. Twenty-five years later, Paul Baker, founding director and now managing director of the Theater Center, described the goal of the company: "We wanted to find a new dimension for creative aliveness, to involve our audience in an active participation which required more of them than mere spectatorship." (Introduction, *Dallas Theater Center, 1959–1979: Twenty Dynamic Years*, p. 3.) To accomplish this goal, Baker and the other founding fathers felt that a vital theatre should have multiple personalities, for it "combines the performer, the teacher, the playwright, the director, the designer, the administrator, the student, and the technician"—all become "a part of the creative art which makes theatre" (p. 3). By working together, the actors and theatre artists create a new world vision which they share with the audience.

An imaginative, living, growing theatre characterized by an innovative spirit of adventure, the Dallas Theater Center was built and supported by the citizens of Dallas under the founding leadership of Robert D. Strecker, Paul M. Raigorodsky, and Beatrice Handel, who gave Baker the freedom to develop the artistic and scholastic dimensions of the theatre program.

At a 1954 summertime, backporch meeting of members of the Dallas Little Theatre, community theatre oldtimers shared their thoughts with newcomers. Together they decided to establish a living, vital theatre that would house a permanent resident company, produce quality theatre, and train talented individuals for professional careers. The group spent the next four years realizing its dream by erecting a theatre structure along the wooded shores of scenic Turtle Creek, just a few miles north of Dallas' central business district.

Opening on December 28, 1959, with a dramatic adaptation of Thomas Wolfe's *Of Time and the River* (adapted for the stage by Eugene McKinney and Paul Baker and directed by Paul Baker), the Dallas Theater Center formally unveiled its $1 million building and Kalita Humphreys Theater, named in honor of the Texas-born actress who made her stage debut in Dallas and died in 1954 in a plane crash. Designed by Frank Lloyd Wright, the Theatre Center immediately became a showplace for productions. Like so many of Wright's buildings, this, his last great design (his first theatre building), fits naturally into the wooded acreage on both sides of Turtle Creek, forming an organic bond with the surrounding landscape.

Freeing the actors and the audience from the confines of a proscenium stage, Baker sought a stage that would be adaptable, intriguing, and exciting. The result was an 85-foot stage that included three acting areas: (1) a central stage with a 32-foot circular revolving stage bordered on one side by a stage apron with steps and on the other side by upstage space ending in a cyclorama; (2) two side stages flowing from the central stage and bringing the action to the audience; and (3) two balconies above the side stages, duplicating their acting areas. Only twelve rows in depth, the auditorium seats seem to flow naturally into the stage area. With right angles excluded from the basic design, seats and stage seem to embrace each other as walls and ceiling gently angle and curve, passing from stage to auditorium and back to stage. With form following function, the theatre's space appears to be in constant movement, uniting the audience with the plays and players. In 1973 the Board of Directors of the Dallas Theater Center presented the building as a gift to the city of Dallas.

Since its founding, the Dallas Theater Center has produced over one hundred world premieres by such prominent playwrights as Robert Anderson, Paddy Chayefsky, Preston Jones, and Mark Medoff as well as by many less prominent playwrights. Among these premieres are productions of Glenn Allen Smith's *Sister* (1962–1963, directed by Ivan Rider), Robert Anderson's *The Days Between* (1964–1965, directed by Paul Baker), Paddy Chayefsky's *The Latent Heterosexual* (1967–1968, directed by Burgess Meredith), Sallie Laurie's *Stillsong* (1975–1976, directed by Paul Baker), Sally Netzel's *Sam* (1975–1976, directed by Bryant J. Reynolds), and Mark Medoff's *Firekeeper* (1977–1978, directed by Paul Baker).

During the 1973–1974 season, the company premiered *Jack Ruby, All-American Boy*, a play by John Logan in association with Paul Baker. As Baker and Logan explain, the play represents "an effort on the part of artists at the Dallas Theater Center to achieve, through the dramatic form, a certain perspective on the tragedies that occurred in Dallas in November 1963" (*Dallas Theater Center, 1959–1979: Twenty Dynamic Years*, p. 40). Pursuing the American Dream from the Chicago ghetto where he grew up, Ruby was unable to escape the neglect, persecution, and violence of his ghetto background and make his fortune in a new environment. Ruby's quest grows into a grotesque distortion of the American Dream that ends in his tragic death.

One of the Dallas Theater Center's most famous premieres involved Preston Jones' *A Texas Trilogy* presented during the 1974–1975 season—a production that marked a breakthrough for one of the Theater Center's own playwrights. *The Last Meeting of the Knights of the White Magnolia, Lu Ann Hampton Laverty Oberlander*, and *The Oldest Living Graduate* (the three plays in the trilogy) "celebrated" Bradleyville, a composite West Texas town of six thousand, bypassed by railroads and superhighways, permeated by dust and disappointment, and inhabited by people of dimension and substance. On New Year's Eve 1974, the Dallas Theater Center presented the entire trilogy in a marathon event lasting from 7:00 P.M. until 2:00 A.M., with supper served in the lobby around 10:00 P.M.

Among the many outstanding productions staged by the Dallas Theater Center are Dylan Thomas' *Under Milk Wood* (1959–1960, directed by Burgess Meredith); Thornton Wilder's *The Matchmaker* (1960–1961, directed by Paul Baker in association with Ken Latimer); William Shakespeare's *The Taming of the Shrew* (1960–1961 and 1968–1969, directed by Ivan Rider); Jean Giraudoux's *The Madwoman of Chaillot* (1961–1962, directed by Angna Enters); Rick Besoyan's *Little Mary Sunshine* (1961–1962, directed by Ivan Rider); Eugene O'Neill's *Long Day's Journey into Night* (1965, directed by Paul Baker); Eugene McKinney's *A Different Drummer* (1964–1965, directed by Ryland Merkey); William Shakespeare's *The Tempest* (1965–1966 and 1966–1967, directed by Paul Baker in association with Ken Latimer); Paddy Chayefsky's *The Latent Heterosexual* (1967–1968, directed by Burgess Meredith); William Shakespeare's *Twelfth Night* (1967–1968, directed by Norman Ayrton); Tennessee Williams' *A Streetcar Named Desire* (1967–1968, directed by Ryland Merkey); William Shakespeare's *Macbeth* (1968–1969, directed by Paul Baker); Archibald MacLeish's *J.B.* (1971–1972, directed by C. Bernard Jackson); James Goldman's *The Lion in Winter* (1971–1972, directed by Don Eitner); Aristophanes' *Lysistrata*, adapted by Patrick Dickinson (1971–1972, directed by Takis Muzenidis); Jerome Lawrence and Robert E. Lee's *Inherit the Wind* (1974–1975, directed by Jerome Lawrence); Peter Shaffer's *Equus* (1976–1977 and 1977–1978, directed by Ryland Merkey); Jack Heifner's *Vanities* (1977–1978, directed by Ryland Merkey); George S. Kaufman and Edna Ferber's *The Royal Family* (1977–1978, directed by Ryland Merkey); Robert Bolt's *A Man for All Seasons*

(1979–1980); Philip Barry's *Holiday* (1979–1980); Edmond Rostand's *Cyrano de Bergerac* (1980–1981); Ernest Thompson's *On Golden Pond* (1980–1981); Mark Medoff's *Children of a Lesser God* (1980–1981); and Eric Peterson and John Gray's *Billy Bishop Goes to War* (1983–1984).

Many of the Dallas Theater Center's American and world premieres have appeared in the Down Center Stage, a fifty-six-seat, small proscenium playhouse located in the basement adjacent to the workshop area. Formally opened on October 29, 1964, with a production of Arthur Kopit's *Oh Dad, Poor Dad, Mama's Hung You in the Closet and I'm Feeling So Sad*, this small experimental theatre has since staged over one hundred productions, more than fifty of them world premieres. Among them are Randy Ford's *R. U. Hungry* (1967–1968, directed by Paul Baker); Ronald Wilcox's *The Finger Tomb* (1967–1968, directed by Bob Baca); Glenn Allen Smith's *Curious in L.A.* (1973–1974, directed by Ken Latimer), Sue Ann Gunn's *Why Don't They Ever Talk about the First Mrs. Phipps?* (1974–1975, directed by Lynn Trammell); Iris Rosofsky's *Puppy Doesn't Live Here Anymore* (1974–1975, directed by Sallie Laurie); Sally Netzel's *Stand-off at Beaver and Pine* (1975–1976, directed by Mary Lou Hoyle); Lewis Cleckler's *Hermit's Homage* (1976–1977, directed by Matt Tracy); Paul R. Bassett's *War Zone* (1976–1977, directed by Randy Bonifay); Kevin O'Morrison's *Ladyhouse Blues* (1976–1977, directed by John Logan); Sallie Laurie's *Door Play* (1977–1978, directed by Mary Sue Jones); David Blomquist's *Cigarette Man* (1977–1978, directed by Ken Latimer); Sam Haven's *Cheese Garden* (1979–1980); and Fred Getchell's *Stagg and Stella* (1980–1981).

Since its founding, many major honors have been awarded the Dallas Theater Center. During the summer of 1964, the Theater Center represented the United States at the Théâtre des Nations Festival in Paris, France. It was the first American theatrical company outside of New York to perform at this annual event. Four years later, managing director Paul Baker was given the prestigious Margo Jones Award for "daring and continuous new play production."

Staging Jean Genet's *The Blacks* in 1970 (directed by Reginald Montgomery and Herman Wheatley), a group of black artists from the Dallas Theater Center began the Janus Players, a group that promoted minority theatre in the early 1970s. Mexican-American actors were quickly incorporated into the group which performed plays such as Douglas Turner Ward's *Day of Absence* (1971, directed by Judith Davis); Jean Anouilh's *Antigone* (1971, directed by Reginald Montgomery); Lonne Elder III's *Ceremonies in Dark Old Men* (1972, directed by Reginald Montgomery); and El Teatro Campesino's *La Conquista de Mexico* (1972, directed by Cecilia Flores).

Established during the 1969–1970 season, "The Magic Turtle" refers to the special series of plays performed on Saturday mornings for children of all ages. The series includes both classics such as A. A. Milne's *Winnie-the-Pooh* (1972–1973) and Joel Chandler Harris' *The Adventures of Br'er Rabbit* (1975–1976) as well as the premieres of new scripts such as Deanna Dunagan's *Pecos Bill*

(1969–1970) and Louise Mosley's *King Midas and the Golden Touch* (1974–1975).

The community-centered Dallas Theater Center offers special matinees for students, senior citizens, and disabled children. Through its Artist-in-the-School Program, members of the company conduct classes in such subjects as mime, techniques of play production, and the plays of Shakespeare. Productions of classics such as Shakespeare's *A Midsummer Night's Dream* are brought to the schools where they are performed for and discussed by appreciative audiences. Free performances of plays on human problems are given in schools, churches, and community centers; and MimeAct, the company's mime troupe, acts in neighborhood parks and in hospitals.

The Dallas Theater Center works with Trinity University to offer the talented theatre artist a unique opportunity to gain extensive professional experience at a major residential theatre while pursuing a Master of Fine Arts degree in drama. Adhering to the concept of "the individual as a dynamic, creative force," the two-year program stresses seven "focus" areas: acting, design, directing, movement and mime, playwriting, technical theatre, and teen and children's theatre.

The Dallas Theater Center has achieved its goal of becoming a creative source of energy for the Dallas community—an energy so vital it has influenced the national and international theatre scene.

COLBY H. KULLMAN

GUTHRIE THEATER
Vineland Place
Minneapolis, Minnesota 55403

In March 1959 Oliver Rea, Peter Zeisler, and Tyrone Guthrie breakfasted at New York's Plaza Hotel and began tinkering with what became over the months a more clearly defined goal: to break the stranglehold Broadway had on the American theatre scene. Four years later, on May 5, 1963, as a result of their efforts, *Hamlet* opened at the Tyrone Guthrie Theater in Minneapolis, Minnesota, and it was not long before they could boast that they had established a first-class repertory theatre in the American heartlands.

The three men brought impressive credentials to their task: Rea was a successful Broadway producer; Zeisler was a respected production manager; and Guthrie, an Irishman, had administered both the Old Vic and Sadler's Wells in London, as well as founded and directed the Stratford Festival Theatre in Canada. In his book, *A New Theatre* (New York: McGraw-Hill, 1964), Guthrie describes how they came together to challenge the pervasive influence of New York theatre. He goes on to outline the philosophy that guided their venture:

Our programme would be classical; only those plays would be chosen which had seemed, to discriminating people for several generations, to have serious merit. . . . One play in four should be an American play of potential classic status; this to be offered to any city which felt deprived of live theatre and would like to take us under its wing (pp. 41, 45).

The project tantalized seven cities—Boston, Chicago, Cleveland, Detroit, Milwaukee, Minneapolis, and San Francisco—but it was Minneapolis that finally won the plum. Not only was Minneapolis beyond the aura of New York, but it also offered the promise of a wide regional base; the new theatre would hope to claim as its audience the entire upper Midwest. Beyond that, financial backing for the $2,225,000 theatre was generous: the T. B. Walker Foundation donated $500,000 and land adjacent to the Walker Art Center, and the community threw itself into ticket-selling and fund-raising with heartwarming enthusiasm. Because they were trying to avoid the "make it or break it" syndrome which characterized Broadway productions, Guthrie and his associates had decided that their new theatre would follow the European example and operate as a nonprofit-distributing trust and as a public service. This meant that, while they had to bank on good ticket sales, they also had to be assured of financial support from private funds. The Twin Cities of Minneapolis and neighboring St. Paul encouraged them on both scores from the beginning. By 1962, 1,200 women from all over Minnesota had organized as the Stagehands and launched a season-ticket drive. Their coffee klatches and dinner parties, as well as more formal presentations by members of the Speaker's Bureau, were a success—by March 25, 1963, almost twenty-two thousand season tickets had been sold. Beyond that, donations poured in from over three hundred thousand individual sources. A hefty $337,000 Ford Foundation grant helped make the theatre project viable, but, more importantly, the success of the initial fund-raising and ticket-selling campaign suggested that genuine public interest could be maintained. Over the years, this has proven true. Roughly 70 percent of the theatre's budget has been earned, largely from ticket receipts, while 30 percent has continued to come from outside funds.

As money came in, architectural plans for the new theatre unfolded, and Guthrie proved that his sense of the dramatic extended beyond stage action. Along with Minneapolis architect Roger Rapson, technical consultant Jean Rosenthal, and costume designer Tanya Moiseiwitsch, Guthrie helped design an exciting eight-level theatre with an innovative main stage auditorium. Its thrust stage is the visible sign of the Guthrie Theater's commitment to the classics. Since it was planned that Greek and Renaissance drama would be the backbone of much of this new company's rotating repertoire, Guthrie was keen to forego the proscenium stage, which had its roots in the seventeenth-century Italian opera and which fostered what he felt was the inane idea that drama can give the "illusion" of reality. A thrust stage, on the other hand, would emphasize the ritualistic and participatory aspects of drama and help remind audiences that they were not simply guzzling more television. Deciding to boldly underline the pioneering spirit of their theatrical experiment, the designers went beyond a simple thrust stage and created a seven-sided, asymmetrical platform, approximately 32 feet by 35 feet, which comes forward at a slight angle into an audience of 1,441 seats. These seats, upholstered in a variety of colors, wrap around the stage in a 200 degree arc, and no seat is more than 52 feet from the center of the stage. Here again Guthrie's philosophy was at work. Intimacy, he was convinced, is crucial to the theatrical experience because it helps generate the necessary "heat and excitement" which the audience adds to the ritualistic environment.

Thrust stage productions require less elaborate sets. Instead, the audience's visual attention turns to costumes. At the Guthrie, where all the seats are so relatively near the stage, close audience scrutiny requires scrupulous attention to costume detail. The Guthrie's costume shop, which ingeniously and meticulously produces everything from armor to bodices to jewelry, has earned itself well-deserved fame for its imaginative and lavish wardrobes. One of the most notable included the larger-than-life masks designed by Tanya Moiseiwitsch for Tyrone Guthrie's production of *The House of Atreus*.

The Tyrone Guthrie Theater has remained in the forefront of the regional theatre movement. It had the advantages of not having to struggle from the ground up and of starting with strong financial support, skillful direction, and an eye-catching theatre. Over the years, its productions have been consistently expert, and its high standards and national reputation have been crucial in bolstering other regional theatres.

Nonetheless, it too has had its setbacks. Like other regional theatre companies, it has had difficulty establishing a permanent repertory company, though in 1985 plans for a resident ensemble company have been renewed. Actors and actresses have come and gone. Worse still, so have artistic directors. The theatre flourished under Guthrie's lead and scored successes with productions such as *The Three Sisters*, *The Cherry Orchard*, and *The Miser*. But Guthrie left in 1965, and, though particular plays like *Uncle Vanya*, *The Resistible Rise of Arturo Ui*, and *The Caucasian Chalk Circle* were favorably received, the theatre floundered and was $194,000 in debt when Michael Langham picked up the reins in 1971. His first two productions, *Cyrano de Bergerac* and *The Taming of the Shrew*, drew record audiences of 90 percent. Other highly praised favorites staged during his directorship included, *She Stoops to Conquer*, *Oedipus the King*, and *Love's Labour's Lost*. *A Christmas Carol* scored so well that it is now presented annually as a straight-run during the Christmas season. When Langham left in 1977, troubles cropped up again. Indeed, it would seem that whenever the Guthrie has departed from its original plan to concentrate on the classics, the audience reception has been measured. Certainly when Alvin Epstein took over in 1978, his penchant for new plays and premieres caused raised eyebrows. His resignation in 1979 left the theatre casting about for a new, permanent artistic director and determined to lure theatregoers with the tried and true.

The current artistic director at the Guthrie is Liviu Ciulei. A Romanian, he trained as an architect and then went to work in scene design. The Guthrie welcomed this innovative director, who is known for his keen sense of the visual, and applauded his plans to meld the realistic and the avant-garde.

Recent productions at the Guthrie have included Shakespeare's *The Tempest* and Hume Cronyn and Susan Cooper's *Foxfire* (1981); a day-long production of Ibsen's *Peer Gynt* (1982); Damon Runyon's *Guys and Dolls* and Chekhov's *The Seagull* (1983); a musical adaptation of Gorky's *Summerfolk* entitled *Hang On to Me* and Molière's *Tartuffe* (1984). In 1985-86 a return was planned to a rotating repertoire and productions were to include Barbara Field's adaptation of *Great Expectations*, Rostand's *Cyrano de Bergerac*, Tom Stoppard's *On the Razzle*, and Thornton Wilder's *The Rainmaker*.

From time to time, the Guthrie has sent some of its productions on national tours, *The House of Atreus* and Isaac Bashevis Singer and Eve Friedman's *Teibele and Her Demon*, for example. Various productions have also toured regional states. It has also sponsored two experimental theatres, the Other Place and the Guthrie 2. The very existence of these theatres suggests the confusion with identity which has sometimes plagued the Guthrie—should new theatre be presented on the main stage, or should it be relegated to the experimental stage? Guthrie 2 is now closed because the Scandinavian vaudeville hall that housed it was condemned, but there are hopes of raising funds and resurrecting the theatre elsewhere. In other areas of outreach, the Guthrie Theater remains active. Tens of thousands of people have taken advantage of backstage tours, discussion/demonstration programs, and pre- and post-performance activities. Students continue to benefit from classes and workshops as well as from internships and apprenticeships.

KATHLEEN COLLINS BEYER

LONG WHARF THEATRE
222 Sargent Drive
New Haven, Connecticut 06511

Before its inaugural season in 1965, the Long Wharf Theatre's chances for success, or even survival, seemed problematical. New Haven's academic community and rich theatrical heritage assured a healthy subscription list, but the new theatre could not rely on local industries for large-scale financial support. Equally unpropitious was the location of the playhouse on the outskirts of town in a meat and produce terminal, a concrete building designed primarily for cold storage. Furthermore, a tight operating budget permitted only a skeleton professional staff, many of whom received little or no pay for their services. Despite these unpromising conditions, the Long Wharf established a 99 percent attendance record during its first summer season, and over the years it has emerged as one of the most innovative and respected regional theatres in the country.

The underlying philosophy of the company has remained true to the aspirations of its founders, Jon Jory and Harlan P. Kleiman. As graduate students at the Yale School of Drama, they had grown dissatisfied with the conservative tendencies of many regional theatres and desired instead to perform lesser known works of established authors as well as new plays by contemporary writers. After soliciting funds for six months, they opened the theatre on July 4, 1965, and their varied repertoire and low ticket prices attracted capacity audiences. One year later, Jory and Kleiman felt confident enough to offer a summer season consisting of four world premieres. The results were nearly disastrous. Attendance was cut in half, and the theatre was still recovering when Jory and Kleiman departed in 1967.

Jory's successor as artistic director was twenty-six-year-old Arvin Brown, a Yale colleague who had directed three Long Wharf productions and supervised the resident children's company. Since his appointment, revivals of the classics have added balance to the seasonal programs, but the theatre's reputation still rests on its support of new or undervalued drama. This support has taken various forms: first U.S. productions of Maxim Gorky's *Country People* and *Yegor Bulichiov*; American premieres of David Storey's *The Contractor* and *The Changing Room*; performances of Michael Cristofer's *The Shadow Box* and D. L. Coburn's *The Gin Game* prior to their debut in New York, where each won the Pulitzer Prize for Drama; and ten world premieres, including that of David Rabe's *Streamers*. Brown has shown a special regard for twentieth-century American dramatists, particularly O'Neill, whose *Ah, Wilderness!* was memorably revived in 1974–1975. Like many Long Wharf productions, it later appeared on Broadway, although Brown dismisses the idea that his theatre operates as a tryout center for New York. Indeed, he believes that regional theatres consistently offer productions superior to Broadway's at a greatly reduced cost. For maintaining its own high standards and presenting diverse but uniformly excellent drama, Long Wharf in 1978 became the third theatre (following the Arena Stage and Mark Taper Forum) to receive a special Tony Award for its contribution to the regional theatre movement.

Part of Long Wharf's success stems from its ability to turn apparent liabilities into advantages. The size of the New Haven community, as well as the competition with the Yale Repertory Theatre, has forced the company to draw its patrons from a wider region. Now over 40 percent of the fourteen thousand subscribers come from outside New Haven County. The playhouse, too, has been a surprising asset. With a capacity audience of 484 seated on three sides of its thrust stage (the closest viewers being only 5 feet from the actors) the theatre fosters a feeling of intimacy that has influenced both the choice of plays and the painstaking preparation of scenery and costumes. Funding remains a primary concern, especially now that the budget is the fifth largest among the country's regional theatres. Yet the directors have recently expanded their eight-play season so that each main stage production runs approximately six weeks, a change made to accommodate increasing ticket demand.

Above all, Brown states that he regards Long Wharf as an actors' theatre, for "if you concentrate on plays that delve into the exploration of personality and personality interaction, you're creating the world of the actor." During its first ten years, the theatre maintained a repertory company hired at the beginning of each season. Since 1975, however, casts have been selected from what Brown calls a "floating rep," a corps of approximately twenty-five actors who perform at the Long Wharf periodically but are free to pursue more lucrative opportunities in the commerical theatre or in films. Consistent with this policy is his encouragement of guest artists, among them Geraldine Fitzgerald, Colleen Dewhurst, Eileen Atkins, Stacy Keach, Al Pacino, and Richard Dreyfuss. To critics who believe this system undercuts a sense of ensemble, Brown contends that working together at regular intervals instills the necessary familiarity and cohesion among actors. Meanwhile, their wider perspective and independence tend to dispel the hothouse atmosphere that can stifle the traditional repertory company.

Recently, Long Wharf has enlarged both its operation and audience. The opening in 1977 of Stage II, a two-hundred-seat "open space" adjacent to the main stage, has provided an ideal area for works in progress, play readings, and workshops. Since Stage II now presents only two plays each season (usually for six weeks apiece), a new program does not need to be booked far in advance. The further use of this space on behalf of emerging playwrights is one of Brown's hopes for the future.

Another long-range goal, the formation of a touring company, has already been realized. Beginning in September 1980, a group of twenty-two actors and technicians embarked on the most extensive tour ever attempted by a regional theatre, one comprising seventy engagements in thirty-two states. In addition to performing James Goldman's *A Lion in Winter* and Noel Coward's *Private Lives*, the cast and crew offered workshops and seminars during brief residencies at several of the colleges and universities they visited. Brown welcomed the tour as an opportunity for "valuable feedback from an enormous constituency," although he must have anticipated a favorable response—twenty-six of the twenty-eight weeks had been sold out in advance. Theatres like the Long Wharf, Executive Director M. Edgar Rosenblum says, "have an obligation to make our work as widely available as possible within our capabilities. We tour, not like a commercial operation to increase profits, but from a sense of public responsibility."

Long Wharf is also one of the few regional theatres to have gained an international reputation. Four productions have been transferred to London, and *The Gin Game* eventually traveled to Moscow. In addition, the company was the only one to perform at the 1980 Winter Olympics.

With attendance running at 96 percent, Brown anticipates no radical change of direction for his theatre. Rather, he wishes to expand the relationship between the stage, television, and film, an intention he has partially fulfilled. Five Long Wharf productions, including *Ah, Wilderness!* and Peter Nichol's *Forget-Me-Not Lane*, have been filmed by National Public Television. The increased exposure is advantageous, but Brown characteristically hopes that the primary benefit will be a strengthened company:

I find that film and stage, when they work at their best, can be enormously complementary. The actor who works on stage all the time finds a new discipline in having to scale down for the camera, and the actor who works on camera finds a new joy in being able to expand himself into the larger scale that the stage demands. I think there's a real health to that.

DANIEL BARRETT

MILWAUKEE REPERTORY THEATER COMPANY
929 North Water Street
Milwaukee, Wisconsin 53202

The Milwaukee Repertory Theater Company is the classic illustration of successful regional theatre: the bold dream of a few far-sighted individuals, the search for public support, the crisis of identity, the movement of personnel to and from other regional companies, the grants from major corporations, and finally the branching out into aspects of the theatrical experience unimaginable to the company's founders only a few decades earlier.

In Milwaukee's case, the story began on December 28, 1953, when Mary Widrig John gathered a few friends to organize a nonprofit stock corporation, Drama, Incorporated. The majority stockholder, Mrs. John became the new company's first manager at its initial meeting on April 15, 1954. The Oakland Theater, a movie-house at 2842 North Oakland, was leased in July as plans quickly raced ahead. Charles McCallum, one of the company's co-founders, oversaw the remodeling, which featured an arena stage and modern unistrut lighting. Fred Miller, a local brewer whose civic efforts also included bringing major league baseball to Milwaukee, served as fund-raising chairman until December 17, 1954, when he died in an airplane crash. Nearly completed, the "Milwaukee City Circle" was renamed in his honor. The Fred Miller Theater opened on January 25, 1955, with Jeffrey Lynn in Samuel Taylor's *Sabrina Fair*.

Mrs. John envisioned the Fred Miller as a professional theatre that would follow the star system. Under this system, imported celebrities—including Eva LeGallienne, Leo G. Carroll, and Edward Everett Horton—combined with the limited number of seats, 348, to insure demand. Financially, the Fred Miller Theater was a great success. The first season's twenty weeks became thirty weeks in the following year. The second season also saw the start of a professional drama school with McCallum as director of administration.

Internal strife, elaborately reported by the press, however, suggested that the Fred Miller had made a false, or at best ill-advised, start. The continuing controversy was such that Mrs. John's control of the company came under legal challenge. On October 3, 1958, a court-ordered reorganization took effect: the public, which had contributed over $115,000 to Fred Miller's newfound cause, was declared the owner of the theatre. Edward Mangum, co-founder with Zelda Fichandler of the Arena Stage in Washington, replaced Mrs. John as managing director. Mangum was himself soon replaced by a New Yorker, Ray Boyle, whom Mangum had brought in as guest director. Boyle resigned in July 1961, and the star system, which had spawned so much of the company's unhappiness, was abolished for the sake of the resident company. The theatre's twenty-year retrospective booklet lists the stars for the plays of the first seven years, but beginning with the 1961–1962 season directors alone are named. The directors and not the stars were now the major imports, and this fact reflects the growing interdependence of the regional theatres. The end of the star system meant chiefly an increasing emphasis on serious and innovative drama.

This new emphasis on the plays was given impetus when Ellis Rabb's recently formed traveling Association of Producing Artists (APA) arrived as if by miracle in 1961. The APA's Fall Drama Festival provided some breathing space for the Milwaukee company, which was still unsure of itself after its reorganization. Jack McQuiggan, a founding member of APA, remained in Milwaukee as manager and later as artistic director; the enduring McCallum became managing director in 1963. *The Tender Trap* and *Song of Norway* had been swept aside by more weighty plays, such as Chekhov's *The Seagull* and Pirandello's *Six Characters in Search of an Author*, but also missing were the 95 percent of capacity crowds the theatre had known only a few seasons earlier. After the 1963–1964 season, as if to signify the change of spirit that the company was determined to effect, the Fred Miller Theater became the Milwaukee Repertory Theater (MRT).

Since the mid-1960s Milwaukee's theatre has seen more than a change of name. When McQuiggan left in 1966 for the Trinity Square Repertory in Providence, McCallum hired as artistic director Tunc Yalman, his former fellow student at the Yale School of Drama. There followed a period in which attendance rose and fortune smiled on the MRT. The Rockefeller Foundation funded new plays in the MRT's Theater for Tomorrow Series. The Theatre Communications Group welcomed the MRT to its association of the thirteen American theatre companies most likely to survive. Alfred Lunt and Lynn Fontaine traveled to Milwaukee to enjoy the MRT's production of *Design for Living* by Noel Coward. Before leaving after the 1970–1971 season, Yalman had proved that a rotating repertory system could be a success. He also saw the company established in 1969 in its new home, the 504-seat, three-quarter arena, Todd Wehr Theater in central Milwaukee's Performing Arts Center. By this time, the ambiance and scope of the theatrical world were very different from what they had been when Mary John founded a theatre.

The decade of the 1970s was one of continued confidence at the MRT. The Court Street Theater, a ninety-nine-seat converted warehouse, became the quarters of the MRT's new plays and experimental work in 1973. The use of the 1,388-seat Pabst Theater for celebrations such as the annual event, *A Christmas Carol*, also reflects the MRT's growth. *An Easter Cycle of English Mystery Plays* was presented in churches throughout southern Wisconsin in 1972, and *A Christmas Carol* went on tour in 1974. In 1975 and 1977 the company toured the five states of the upper Midwest. Robert E. Ingham's *Custer* and a production matching O'Neill's *Long Day's Journey into Night* with his *Ah, Wilderness!* received high praise in the 1977–1978 season. The company had gained national prominence by 1978 when it toured nine states. A Midwest tour is now a regular annual event. The 1978–1979 season, the MRT's twenty-fifth, presented nineteen plays, including nine world premieres and two American premieres. Energy was also found to host the American debut of the Waseda Theater Company of Japan. The 1980–1981 season included new plays (Larry Shue's *The Nerd*, Amlin Gray's *Six Toes*, David Mamet's *Lakeboat*, and Daniel A. Stein's *Stark Mad in White Satin*), as well as popular classics (Edmond Rostand's *Cyrano de Bergerac*, Bertolt Brecht's *Mother Courage and Her Children*, Shakespeare's *Julius Caesar* and *The Taming of the Shrew*, and Tennessee Williams' *A Streetcar Named Desire*).

The 1982–1983 season was highlighted by premiere productions of Larry Shue's *The Foreigner*, Felipe Santander's *The Government Man*, and William Stancil's *The Pentecost*. The MRT performed in Japan in 1981 and 1983. In 1982 it traveled to England.

Nagle Jackson, who vigorously fostered new drama at the MRT, became artistic director in 1971. Since John Dillon assumed Jackson's role in 1977, he has brought playwrights into the company as full-time writers-in-residence. In 1974 Sara O'Connor replaced McCallum as current managing director. Her 1983-84 budget was approximately $2.2 million.

The MRT's stated philosophy embraces a commitment to providing new and classical theatre for Milwaukee and the Midwest. Among regional theatres, this may seem to be an ambitious but routine-sounding aim. Nevertheless, the MRT's productions in prisons, hospitals, and playgrounds; its commissioning of new plays; as well as the variety of theatre-related social and cultural events sponsored by the volunteer Laura Sherry League, give further proof of how lively and genuine such a commitment can be.

JAMES BEYER

NEGRO ENSEMBLE COMPANY
Theatre Four, Incorporated
424 West 55th Street
New York, New York 10036

The Negro Ensemble Company (NEC) is vigorously moving into what may be its permanent status as America's most prestigious and respected black theatre company. Born in the revolutionary heat of the 1960s, the NEC has attained critical and popular success nationally and internationally. Despite financial woes and funding crises, the tenacious, creative founders of the NEC continue to plan, expand, and adjust as the company seeks self-sufficiency.

On January 2, 1968, the NEC presented its first public performance, *Song of the Lusitanian Bogey*, written by Peter Weiss and directed by Michael Schultz, at the 145-seat St. Marks Playhouse in New York City's East Village. St. Marks Playhouse would be NEC's home for the next thirteen years. Although this first production had only a four-week run, it won critical acclaim. Now, as one of the oldest professional black theatres in America, the company faces the 1980s with a new home, the 299-seat Theatre Four on West 55th Street between Ninth and Tenth avenues. "This move is the first phase in implementing our new plans for the future," says Douglas Turner Ward, the fifty-year-old co-founder and artistic director of the company.

Who were the architects of this company and how did NEC happen? The idea and the plan for black-oriented theatre of some permanence was based on the practical and shared experience of three people, two blacks and one white.

The year was 1964. Robert Hooks, a professional actor, had just founded the Group Theatre Workshop and started training talented young people from his neighborhood of Manhattan's lower West Side. Douglas Turner Ward, actor-playwright, had just written two satirical one-act plays, *Happy Ending* and *A Day of Absence*. Hooks decided to produce Ward's plays Off-Broadway using the members of his workshop. Thus, a common theatrical interest brought these two men together. The third man, Gerald S. Krone, became a part of the collaboration when he was asked to manage the production. The plays became an instant success and had a run of fourteen months.

This venture brought the three founders of NEC together and gave them their first experience of working with the ingredients of black theatre that were soon to become the basic aims and goals of the Negro Ensemble Company. They had organized a training program; a black producer had produced a black writer's play; fourteen black actors had been involved; and a black audience had been gained.

The year was 1966. *Happy Ending* and *A Day of Absence* were still running when Douglas Turner Ward was asked to write an article for the *New York Times* expressing his ideas about theatre. On August 14, 1966, Ward's often quoted article appeared, wherein he called for the establishment of a permanent, autonomous theatre company where black artists could decide, promote, and oversee their own creative destiny. He wrote provocatively of:

A theatre evolving not out of negative need, but positive potential; better equipped to employ existing talents and spur the development of future ones. A theatre whose justification is not the gap it fills, but the achievement it aspires toward—no less high than any other comparable theatre company of present or past world fame.

A theatre concentrating primarily on themes of Negro life, but also resilient enough to incorporate and interpret the best of world drama—whatever the source. A theatre of permanence, continuity and consistency, providing the necessary home-base for the Negro artist to launch a campaign to win his ignored brothers and sisters as constant witnesses to his endeavors . . . so might the Negro, a most potential agent of vitality, infuse life into the moribund corpus of American theatre.

A Ford Foundation executive, impressed by Ward's ideas, asked him to submit a proposal. Ward, together with Hooks and Krone, presented a plan envisioning a company which combined an extensive training program for aspiring artists with a professional theatre for the continuous production of works relevant to black life. The foundation agreed to fund it for three years, with Ward as artistic director, Hooks as executive director, and Krone as administrative director. Thus the NEC came into existence.

With a financial commitment secured, the three pioneers made their personal commitment to the dream of organizing a black-oriented theatre. It was a dream that others before them had attempted to implement, but for various reasons (often financial) was never fully or permanently realized.

Determined to open only four months after receiving the grant, the founders conducted an intensive nationwide search for actors for the new resident professional company. And on schedule, rehearsals began in the fall of 1967 with a company of fifteen. At the same time, the tuition-free training programs for young blacks as actors, playwrights, designers, technical staff, and theatre personnel were launched.

The road traveled between an idea and the execution of that idea is often filled with ups and downs shaded with the myriad colors of a rainbow. After making such a far-reaching commitment, the NEC was hard-pressed to find quality plays by blacks that first season. It was not that none existed, but, rather, so few had been published that there was no body of black plays from which to draw.

In an effort to get that premiere 1967–1968 season on the boards, ironically, the first two productions were by white writers, *Song of the Lusitanian Bogey* by Peter Weiss and *Summer of the Seventeenth Doll* by Roy Lawler. A mixed and controversial reception followed.

Amid positive approval by white critics and thunderous criticism by some members of the black community, Ward pointed to the need for plays by blacks. At the same time, he defended his position by emphasizing the relevance of the then revolutionary statement in Weiss' play that gave open and pointed opposition to white oppression, that is, Angolan colonialism. The other two major productions of that premiere season were by an African writer and a well-established black American writer, *Kongi's Harvest* by Wole Soyinka and *Daddy Goodness* by Richard Wright.

The NEC began receiving black plays from all over the country as soon as the word got around that it was a place where a black playwright could get his work read and possibly produced. In addition, the young playwrights in the training program proved productive, and new works were often given a workshop presentation in what was called the Repertory Workshop. Since the first season, there has been no need to use works by white writers. Today, the NEC has developed and collected an unsurpassed body of black dramatic literature.

Included in NEC's second season bill were *God Is a (Guess What?)* by Roy McIver and *Ceremonies in Dark Old Men* by Lonne Elder III, which, together with *Daddy Goodness* by Richard Wright (mounted the first season), went out on NEC's first national tour. During 1969 and 1970 many people were given their first opportunity to witness black theatre as these three productions crisscrossed the nation. By 1969 the NEC had become an accepted member of America's professional theatre as it received a special Tony Award for Distinguished Achievement in Theatre.

That same year, the NEC went on its first international tour, where its productions of *Song of the Lusitanian Bogey* and *God Is a (Guess What?)* were featured in the World Theatre Season at the Aldwych Theatre, which is the London home of the Royal Shakespeare Company, and at the Premia Roma Festival in Italy. Members of the company also intrigued an international audience with a special "Black Jazz Night."

The NEC was named an official cultural representative at the 1972 Munich Summer Olympics where it presented two of its outstanding productions—Derek Wolcott's *The Dream on Monkey Mountain* (1970–1971 season and also presented in Bermuda) and Phillip Hayes Dean's *The Sty of the Blind Pig* (1971–1972 season). The NEC's international connection continued, and in 1977, under the auspices of the Virgin Islands Art Council, the company did a residency there which included conducting training programs and workshops, and presenting a production of Paul Carter Harrison's *The Great MacDaddy* (presented at St. Marks during the 1972–1973 and 1976–1977 seasons).

In 1973, in response to critical acclaim and demand for tickets, the NEC production of Joseph Walker's *The River Niger* moved on to Broadway to the 1,100-seat Brooks Atkinson Theatre where it ran for months, winning a Tony Award as the best play of the year. And then in 1975 Leslie Hill's *The First Breeze of Summer* became the NEC's second production on Broadway, when it opened at the Palace Theatre. It was later produced for national presentation on the Public Broadcasting System network, marking the NEC's second television production. The year before, *Ceremonies in Dark Old Men* had been made into a two-hour prime time special for the ABC network.

Then in 1980, the NEC returned to Broadway when *Home* by Samm-Art Williams moved to the Cort Theatre and became the third NEC play to be nominated for a Tony as best play.

All seasons have offered an exciting, electric variety of plays that have examined "the black experience" from diverse points of view. Ward, who is responsible for the selection of NEC plays, feels that these differing points of view are a natural phenomenon since people do not necessarily think alike. Early on, however, Ward's position had brought criticism from the more militant blacks who felt that the productions should focus more directly on the struggle of blacks in America. This criticism has long since subsided as many recognize the need for the various nuances of black life and the wisdom exercised by Ward in making that ideological decision for the NEC. In addition, the criticisms regarding the word "Negro" in the company name, as well as the NEC's location, no longer need any response.

It would be difficult to single out the most important award or achievement of this distinguished troupe. There have been many outstanding successes and accomplishments marking the company's steady development—even during some lean years.

Many of NEC's alumni have become outstanding in American theatre and television. They include Samm-Art Williams, Joseph A. Walker, Lonne Elder III, Phillip Hayes Dean, Rosalind Cash, Frances Foster, Sherman Hemsley, Denise Nicholas, Esther Rolle, and Richard Roundtree.

The NEC has provided tuition-free training for over 3,500 persons in all areas of theatre, but now, for economic reasons, the formal classes have been phased out. An on-the-job training program with focus on the backstage crafts is now in operation. Ward says that the institution is still committed to training and hopes to have a full program when it is financially suited.

To this end—the move to Theatre Four (which has twice the number of seats as St. Marks) is a step toward self-sufficiency. At St. Marks, NEC's productions were running at a permanent loss. Ward said, "Even at capacity, we could only gross about $7,000—and the production on a weekly running basis was up to $15,000."

In the theatre's publicity materials, Ward describes the move to Theatre Four as an interim step in the company's search for the ideal theatre, which it hopes to find within three years. He said,

We need to finally acquire a home theatre with 500 to 700 seats at most. This will give us the possibility of getting returns at the box-office that can be a major part of our budget, so that we won't be so dependent on outside subsidy. Finally, it is our goal to have a theatre which will allow us to provide the services of a Black cultural institution.

JANIE SYKES KENNEDY,
J. SCOTT KENNEDY,
and JAMES SCOTT KENNEDY, JR.

NEW YORK PUBLIC THEATER
425 Lafayette Street
New York, New York 10003

The original production of Gerome Ragni and James Rado's *Hair* opened at the New York Public Theater in 1967. Two years earlier, the New York Shakespeare Festival, led by producer Joseph Papp, had acquired the landmark Astor Library Building on Lafayette Street in lower Manhattan and converted it to a complex of theatres to be used primarily for the production of new American plays.

Since that opening in 1967, the New York Public Theatre has produced well over one hundred plays, including Charles Gordone's *No Place to Be Somebody* (the first play by a black to win a Pulitzer Prize), *The Two Gentlemen of Verona* (a rock adaptation of Shakespeare's comedy), David Rabe's *Sticks and Bones* and *The Basic Training of Pavlo Hummel*, Richard Wesley's *The Black Terror*, Jason Miller's *That Championship Season*, Miguel Pinero's *Short Eyes* (the first play by a Puerto Rican to win the Drama Critics' Circle Award), David Rabe's *Streamers*, *A Chorus Line* (book by James Kirkwood and Nicholas Dante, music by Marvin Hamlisch, and lyrics by Edward Kleban), Ntozake Shange's *For Colored Girls Who Have Considered Suicide/When The Rainbow Is Enuf*, Elizabeth Swados' *Runaways*, Thomas Babe's *Fathers and Sons*, and Des McAnuff's *The Death of von Richthofen as Witnessed From Earth*.

In 1976 the theatre began a major renewal of the building under architect Giorgio Cavaglieri, resulting in the present multitheatre complex, with theatres ranging in seating capacity from 55 to 299. This variety of spaces allows the theatre to house small workshops in photography, drama, and film, readings, seminars, and a cabaret, in addition to its regular productions.

The New York Public Theater, along with the New York Shakespeare Festival's Delacorte Theatre (a 2,300-seat, open-air amphitheatre in Central Park where Shakespeare is presented to the public free every summer), extends its audiences and subsidizes its regular programs by sending the most successful productions to Broadway and on tour. The popular success of *A Chorus Line* and *For Colored Girls . . .*, along with ticket sales (20 percent) and government and private contributions (20 percent), allowed LuEsther Mertz, chairman of the board, to hail 1977 as "the year the New York Shakespeare Festival got in the black."

The prestige of the New York Public Theater and its president, Joseph Papp, attracts the best American actors, directors, and designers. Among the actors in recent productions are Estelle Parsons, Irene Worth, Zohra Lampert, Christopher Plummer, Joel Gray, Geraldine Page, Rip Torn, Madeline Kahn, Tommy Lee Jones, and Peter Boyle.

The Public Theater presents a year-round season, extending from September through August and Tuesday through Sunday with weekend matinees.

M. NOEL SIPPLE

SEATTLE REPERTORY THEATRE
Seattle Center, P.O. Box B
Seattle, Washington 98109

In 1977, after Seattle's passage of a bond issue designating the construction of a $4.8 million theatre facility, Duncan Ross (artistic director at that time) and Peter Donnelly (producing director) noted: "With the new theatre plant the Repertory will be able to fully function as the major professional company it has become. The arts are now an integral part of the Northwest lifestyle—and the new theatre will surely help preserve that lifestyle for decades to come."

This major professional company, the Seattle Repertory Theatre (which moved into its new building in fall 1983), opened its first season on November 13, 1963, at the Seattle Center Playhouse with a production of *King Lear*. Incorporated as a nonprofit organization, the theatre was originally underwritten by

Century 21, Incorporated. It is now managed by a board of directors, of which Nancy Alvord is the president.

Using a core of twelve to fourteen actors and additional guest artists, the Repertory produces six plays per season (between October and May) in the Seattle Center Playhouse, owned by the city of Seattle. The Playhouse, designed by Paul Hayden Kirk, has a proscenium stage and seats 895. At present the supportive operations are located throughout the city. When the new building (containing a proscenium stage and seating 850) is completed, all activities will be under one roof. The Repertory operates with a budget of which 75 percent comes from season subscribers and single-ticket sales, 25 percent from contributions by individuals, foundations, and funding from PONCHO (Patrons of Northwest Civic, Cultural, and Charitable Organizations) and the Corporate Council on the Arts.

Among the many significant productions during the first seven years of the Repertory's existence were classical and contemporary plays, such as Shakespeare's *Twelfth Night*, Chekhov's *The Cherry Orchard*, Arthur Miller's *Death of a Salesman*, Christopher Fry's *The Lady's Not for Burning*, Bertolt Brecht's *The Threepenny Opera*, Friedrich Dürrenmatt's *The Visit*, and Arthur L. Kopit's *Indians*. In the Off Center Theatre were performed three premieres: Clarence Morley's *Christopher* (1967–1968), Jon Swan's *Three Cheers for What's-Its-Name* (1968–1969), and Nathan Teitel's *Initiation* (1969–1970).

In 1969 the Seattle Repertory Theatre traveled to the Bergen National Festival in Norway. The theatre's favorably reviewed production of Edward Albee's *Who's Afraid of Virginia Woolf?* and Jon Swan's *Short Sacred Rite of Search and Destruction* (a premiere) marked the first time a U.S. regional theatre company participated in the Festpillene. Two years later, in 1971, the Repertory staged a nationally acclaimed special production of *Richard II*, with Richard Chamberlain making his American Shakespearean debut in the title role.

In the summer of 1971 an innovation was introduced: "Rep 'n Rap." Sponsored by the King County Arts Commission, this program (replacing the earlier Theatre-in-the Park) consisted of post-show discussions with the audience. The first "Rep 'n Rap" presentation was George Bernard Shaw's *Village Wooing*, with Susan Ludlow and Clayton Corzatte. In subsequent seasons *Thurbermania* (selected works of James Thurber), *The Diary of Adam and Eve* (adaptation of Mark Twain), *Crazy Quilt* (a patchwork of American humor assembled from the work of Will Rogers, James Thurber, and Mark Twain), and Phil Shallat's *Discovering Tutankhamun* were presented.

During 1974–1975 the Seattle Repertory Theatre began operating a second house, the 2nd Stage, in downtown Seattle. For three seasons (1975–1977) it staged five plays each spring, including two special presentations. Among the plays were Max Frisch's *Biography*, Joe Orton's *Entertaining Mr. Sloane*, and two premieres: Alexey Arbuzov's *Once Upon a Time* and Marguerite Duras' *Suzanna Andler*. Other special presentations were two Leonard Melfi one-acts, featuring Valerie Harper and Anthony Zerbe, and Hume Cronyn and Jessica Tandy's *The Many Faces of Love* with Hume Cronyn and Jessica Tandy.

Another innovation, the "Hub Cities" touring concept, was instigated in 1975. While productions had toured since 1965, the Seattle Repertory Theatre now expanded its programs. Wilder's *The Matchmaker* toured Washington in 1975; George M. Cohan's *Seven Keys to Baldpate* and George Kelly's *The Show Off* went beyond Washington to Oregon, Idaho, Nevada, and Utah in 1976–1977.

The theatre's main stage productions during the 1970s included several world premieres: Lloyd Gold's *A Grave Undertaking* (1974–1975) and *Music Is* (based on *Twelfth Night*), adapted and directed by George Abbott, with music and lyrics by Richard Adler and Will Holt, and choreography by Patricia Birch (1976–1977). Highlights of the 1976–1977 season consisted of Peter Shaffer's *Equus* and a special thirteen-day Alaskan tour of *The Rhythm Song* (compiled and scripted by Megan Dean), sponsored by the National Endowment for the Arts.

The 1977–1978 season was devoted to six works on the theme "The Many Faces of Comedy": Barbara Wersba's *The Dream Watcher* (a premiere with Eva LeGallienne in the leading role), Edna Ferber and George S. Kaufman's *The Royal Family*, Peter Nichols' *The National Health*, Chekhov's *Uncle Vanya*, Shakespeare's *Much Ado About Nothing*, and Georges Feydeau's *13 Rue de l'Amour*. During "Albee on Albee," a special presentation of that season, dramatist Edward Albee read selected excerpts from his works and gave an informal lecture, "The Playwright vs. the Theatre."

An additional feature at the 2nd Stage has been a "plays-in-progress" program. Funded in 1978 by PONCHO, it was created to enable a writer to examine a new script in a workshop atmosphere. Under Jack Bender's direction, Percy Granger's *Eminent Domain* was presented as a development-rehearsal in April 1978.

During the 1979–1980 season the theatre offered several free programs: a postplay discussion series two nights a week and "Sunday at Sunday's," readings and poetry presentations by actors in Sunday's Restaurant on Sunday. Another free attraction was a staged reading of Arthur Miller's new play, *The American Clock*.

Among the 1980–1981 productions at the theatre were O'Neill's *Ah, Wilderness!*, Garson Kanin's *Born Yesterday*, and August Strindberg's *The Dance of Death*. In 1982 appeared Christopher Hampton's controversial *Savages*, which had been produced first at London's Royal Court Theatre in 1973 and later in Los Angeles and Berkeley.

Recent artistic directors of the Seattle Repertory Theatre have been Duncan Ross, John Hirsch, and now Daniel Sullivan. Robert Egan is associate director.

The philosophy of the Seattle Repertory Theatre has been to provide a variety of theatrical experiences, as exemplified by the "Rep 'n Rap" sessions and the "plays-in-progess" program. In collaboration with the Seattle Arts Commission, the theatre has also offered free matinees of main stage productions. To take theatre to even wider audiences, the Seattle Repertory Theatre has sponsored special touring attractions such as *Dear Love*, starring Myrna Loy, and Emlyn Williams as *Charles Dickens*. Furthermore, under the auspices of Washington State's Cultural Enrichment Act, schoolchildren have seen many performances, including *Hamlet*, *Indians*, *The Crucible*, *Our Town*, and *Richard II*.

The Repertory's producing director, Peter Donnelly, is optimistic about the future: "The theatre's growth has followed a steady course, both in . . . subscriber support and in the pursuit of quality." The artistic directorate, begun with John Hirsch as artistic director and Daniel Sullivan as resident director, proved successful in 1979–1981. Donnelly reports that

In hiring . . . [them], the board provided for internal succession of artistic directors. Now Bob Egan (the Rep's associate artistic director) is getting the kind of experience that will make him capable of running his own theatre in a short time. This system of internal succession is being watched closely by the national theatre community.

LAURA H. WEAVER
(Quotes in this article are
taken from the company's
publicity materials.)

WESTERN EUROPE
(excluding
Scandinavia)

Leon M. Aufdemberge, Area Editor

Austria

INTRODUCTION

In most significant ways, Austria's municipally funded theatres are like those in West Germany, with two exceptions: there are not as many of them, and Austria has a theatre center for the country, its capital, Vienna. The first is readily explained in that Austria is largely a rural country. The second cannot be explained; it has always been true and does not show much sign of changing, except, perhaps, in the summer.

Vienna has nearly all of Austria's theatres. The best theatre, opera, and ballet companies are all located there; if a singer, actor, or dancer is good, sooner or later Vienna will make a lasting claim. Vienna also trades people (especially *regisseurs* [stage managers]) with the rest of the German-speaking countries, including East Germany.

This picture changes in the summer when the festivals begin. Both the Vienna and the Salzburg festivals focus on opera, though a good deal of theatre is staged at both, which is not as well publicized. As part of these festivals, usually at least one great Austrian actor (Oskar Werner, for example) returns to the stage. Salzburg also has an excellent marionette theatre, which is described later in this section.

Theatre in the provinces of Austria is uneven in quality, although opera in the smaller cities of Graz and Linz is apt to be quite good. With certain exceptions, theatre companies throughout Austria produce the same bill of fare as those in West Germany. Austria has had a number of fine playwrights, most of whose works, because of their highly literary qualities or their use of argot, are seldom performed outside German-speaking theatres. Austria's most literary playwright is the nineteenth-century Franz Grillparzer, whose work is not performed much outside Austria and is given the same kind of reverence nationally that the French give Racine. Grillparzer is much admired for his use of language, though his stage machinery frequently creaks. More accessible in terms of charm are two nineteenth-century comic writers: Ferdinand Raimund, fantastical and light, and the Viennese Molière, Johann Nepomuk Nestroy, best known as the playwright whose *Einen Jux will er sich machen* (*He Wanted to Have a Good Time*) furnished Thornton Wilder with *The Matchmaker*. These three are played rather consistently in Austria, though Nestroy (whose language is the most Viennese) is now frequently done in all the German-speaking theatres.

Among the best twentieth-century playwrights are Hugo von Hofmannsthal, who also wrote opera librettos for Richard Strauss, and his contemporary, Arthur Schnitzler, who, while not as literary as von Hofmannsthal, proved more lasting. Austria's only well-known contemporary playwright is Fritz Hochwälder, who can scarcely be called a great playwright. With the inadequate financial remuneration given playwrights in Austria, the country has discouraged native drama. Hence, modern plays presented in Austria generally come from foreign countries.

Vienna has a thriving theatre, however. On a good evening in Vienna one may choose among eighteen theatres, including an English-speaking one. The theatre is well attended and well subsidized, and represents some of the greatest in the German-speaking world, with the Burg leading the way. It is apt to be rather conservative as Vienna tends to be so, but it is thoughtfully done and highly literary.

LEON M. AUFDEMBERGE

SALZBURG MARIONETTE THEATRE
(Das Salzburger Marionetten Theater)
Schwarz Strasse 24, Salzburg, Austria

Puppet shows have been a source of entertainment in Austria since the Middle Ages, but the country's great puppet mastery was not achieved until the eighteenth century. Prince Esterhazy had a marionette theatre built in 1766, for which Franz Joseph Haydn composed a series of short operas. During the whole of the romantic period, puppet theatres flourished, with Heinrich von Kleist waxing most eloquently over the puppet, which he thought to be superior to the living actor. A number of puppet theatres in Europe were founded in the nineteenth century, some of which still exist.

The queen of all Austrian puppet theatres is undoubtedly the Salzburg Marionette Theatre. The founder was a sculptor, Anton Aicher, who visited the famous Marionette Theatre of Papa Schmidt in 1902 and was immediately smitten by the puppets. Even though Schmidt did not like visitors backstage, he was touched by the young man and shared the secrets of his craft. Soon Aicher had opened his own theatre in the Pulvermühle, the "gunpowder mill" near the castle of Leopoldskron in Salzburg. The amateur performances there soon led to the opening of a real puppet stage in the Künstlerhaus, the first performance by the Salzburg Marionette Theatre being given on February 27, 1913, with Mozart's pastoral opera *Bastien und Bastienne*. This opera was repeated several times to enthusiastic audiences and by the end of June a series of regular performances began to take place in the little theatre. Plays were performed, some of which included the character of the Salzburger Kasperl, who gabbed extemporaneously with the audience. The following autumn, the company opened a theatre in the Dreifaltigkeitgasse, which was to be its home for the next fortynine years. In the early years opera and plays were part of the repertory of the Salzburg Marionettes, the live singers and actors taking their cues from a series of ingeniously placed mirrors.

From the very first, "Professor Aicher's Artistic Marionette Theatre" was a family affair with some outsiders assisting. The amateur poet, Hans Seebach, wrote plays for the marionettes, including the popular *The Wild Animals*. Rudolf Simmerle wrote songs especially for Kasperl. But the central part of the company was and is the Aicher family itself. World War I made the operation of the theatre very difficult. The eldest son, Burgel, who was business manager, died of an illness contracted in a prisoner-of-war camp. Herman, the youngest son, made the practical suggestion that the family open a branch of the theatre in Vienna. The project failed and Herman realized why: the puppets had become old-fashioned. He returned to Salzburg to refashion the theatre, to provide better lights, and to produce more ambitious works. The favorite character Kasperl was more or less retired, although he did make several sporadic return appearances. In the process of adding new artists to sing, a soprano, Elfride Eschenlahr, was hired, later to become Mrs. Herman Aicher. As a wedding gift the theatre was legally deeded to the couple.

Soon new and more exciting works entered the repertory with musical works by Gluck, Adam, and Offenbach. The marionettes became larger, better costumed, and more like "real" people. New plays were written to showcase the wonders of the marionettes. The theatre began to tour, but a series of disasters plagued the company. In 1930 Anton Aicher died. Later, the traveling restrictions imposed by the government in the 1930s made touring prohibitive. An invitation from the USSR in 1935, however, prompted two things: first, the building of a portable theatre and, second, the making of new and larger marionettes. The maximum height had been 42 centimeters; the new marionettes would top 1 meter. The theatre was very popular in the USSR with audiences sometimes numbering over three thousand. In 1937 the troupe played in Paris at the World Exhibition; again the theatre was a triumph.

In 1938, when Austria was annexed by Germany, the Aichers found themselves in Scandinavia. The return trip to Austria was a very difficult one, but they made it back to their homeland. During World War II the theatre played all over the war zone, often at the front lines. Mishaps were frequent, but the theatre troupe remained intact except for Herman, who was drafted. In 1945 the theatre, under the direction of Herman Aicher, reopened in Salzburg, even though their building had been damaged in the war. At first the performances were forbidden to Austrians, the shows being strictly for the occupying forces, who frequently paid for their admission in groceries. Fortunately, these restrictions were later removed. In 1947 the Salzburg Marionettes began to tour, and tour they still do.

A severe blow was dealt to the company in 1949 when its theatre building was condemned; the Aichers began to think about building another house, though this was slow to come.

The company continued to prosper, and in 1952 came a landmark production, Mozart's *The Magic Flute*, done not with live singers but as a radio performance that had been reproduced on tape. From this time all the manipulator would have to depend on was the puppet as there would be no more live voices. The scenery for this production (which is still in the repertory) was designed by Günther Schneider-Siemssen, one of Europe's top designers. Later, he designed a new stage for the company, which placed the manipulators above the marionettes and not in back of the sets. He also introduced the revolving stage and designed new and more intricate lighting effects. In the late 1950s tours began to become longer and more involved. In 1961 the theatre moved to a new theatre on Kapitelplatz, which, though a marvelous house, was superseded by another theatre in 1972 (architect, Professor Keidl), which was fashioned from part of the Hotel Mirabell. The new theatre, which seats 340, represents the utmost in comfort with the decor, not surprisingly, a faintly Salzburg baroque.

The company employs thirteen people, ten of whom actually operate the marionettes with one person to each marionette. Generally, a new production takes two years to open: one year is spent in planning and one in building and staging. As with stage productions, there is a *regisseur*, and some of Germany's and Austria's best known *regisseurs*, such as Otto Schenk, Johannes Schaaf, and Peter Stanchina, have been with the theatre to stage operas. There is almost always a new production every year with six or seven repeats and at least four Mozart operas in the yearly repertory. Ten years is usually the limit for a production, though Strauss' operetta *Die Fledermaus* has been in the repertory for twenty-five years and Mozart's *Die Entführung aus dem Serail* (*The Abduction from the Seraglio*) almost as long. Most productions are designed by Schneider-Siemssen. There is almost always at least one play, operetta, and ballet in the repertory plus the operas. The theatre pays a flat royalty to the recording companies for use of their work, and generally only the static parts of the operas are cut.

The season in Salzburg runs from Easter to the end of September plus a two-week season at Christmas. After that it tours, alternating countries. (It generally plays the United States every two years.) There are plans for an English-language production of Antoine de Saint-Exupéry's *The Little Prince*. The organization generally plays six days a week in Salzburg, and during the height of the tourist season gives two performances a day. Tickets range from $15 to around $20, but there is a huge overhead and the Austrian government provides no subsidy. Despite the high prices, July and August performances are frequently sold out before the season starts. The Salzburg Marionette Theatre is one of the top tourist attractions in Austria.

The company's philosophy, does it sell?, may seem crass but as a private enterprise the theatre must make its own way. Many years ago, for an anniver-

sary, the troupe mounted Ferdinand Raimund's fantastic *Die Diamants des Geis-
terkönigs* (*The Diamonds of the Ghost Kings*). Despite good critical reviews,
the lavish production lost money and was soon yanked from the repertory. In
the 1930s the company experimented; today experimentation is no longer possible. All productions must sell and be capable of touring. Even marionettes are
remade when a production has left the repertory. In addition, almost everyone
in the organization helps with the building or dressing of the marionettes when
a new production is bring prepared in the atelier of the theatre building itself.

The people who work for the company are devoted and enthusiastic and seem
more like a family than co-workers. One is apt to forget that imaginary beings,
not real people, are on stage, for the strings do disappear and the personality of
the marionette takes over, creating a magical experience for the theatregoer.

LEON M. AUFDEMBERGE
(With thanks to Frau Gretl Aicher,
artistic leader since 1977, and
Dr. Ackermann of the theatre staff)

THEATRE IN THE BURG
(Burgtheater)
Dr. Karl Lueger Ring 2
A1014 Vienna 1, Austria

According to legend, the Theatre in the Burg was born in Vienna when the
Empress Maria Theresa said, "Spektakle müssen halt sein" (We must have
shows). In 1741 Karl Joseph Sellier converted the derelict Ballhaus on the
Michaelplatz into a theatre. The opening performance in the new "Konigliches
Theater Nachst der Burg" was Carcano's opera *Amleto*. In 1776 the Emperor
Joseph II elevated the status of the theatre to the Imperial and National Theatre
which was to take precedence over the French- and Italian-language houses.
Thus was born the Theatre in the Burg. As might be suspected, in the early days
of the theatre both operas and plays were part of the repertory.

In 1814, the same year as the Congress of Vienna, Joseph Schreyvogel took
over the management of the Theatre in the Burg, and under his leadership the
theatre attained its first high recognition. During his regime Franz Grillparzer
became the resident playwright at the salary of 1,000 gülden per year. The first
performances of his *Sappho* (1818), *Des Meeres und der liebe Weller* (*Of the
Sea and the Dear Waves*, 1823), and *Ein treuer Diener seines Herrn* (*A True
Servant of His Lord*, 1828) were all done at the Theatre in the Burg. Even though
Chancellor Prince Metternich kept a tight rein on censorship, social criticisms
were found in all these plays, albeit hidden. Schreyvogel also established a firm
policy of ensemble in the theatre. He introduced the Viennese to quality productions of Shakespeare (*Romeo and Juliet, Hamlet, King Lear*) and to classic
repertory as well. The first play by Ferdinand Raimund was offered, *Der Verschwender* (*The Prodigal*). On October 12, 1887, the new theatre was finally

opened with Beethoven's overture, "The Consecration of the House," followed by Grillparzer's unfinished play, *Esther*, and Schiller's *Wallensteins Lager* (*Wallenstein's Camp*). The manager at this time was Adolf von Sonnenthal, who remained in this position for only one year, although he had been a member of the acting company for thirty years.

Probably the greatest reformer the Burg has ever had was Max Burckhardt (manager, 1890–1906), who was deemed an outsider by the members of the theatre staff when he first joined the company. He had been an official of the Ministry of Education and a lecturer in civil law at the university. Burckhardt soon assured the company that he was a man of the theatre. He introduced new playwrights to the repertory: Ibsen, Gerhart Hauptmann, and Arthur Schnitzler, whose *Liebelei* (*Light-o'-Love*) was first presented at the Burg in 1895. Burckhardt also engaged Josef Kainz to act in the company, Kainz's *Hamlet* being particularly famous. The great actor Friedrich Mitterwurzer finally became a permanent member of the company in 1894, playing Shylock, Richard III, Macbeth, and King Philip in Schiller's *Don Carlos*. Perhaps Burckhardt's greatest achievement was his introduction of low-priced Sunday matinees, at which the working class of Vienna could see quality productions at reduced prices.

The first important director to begin his tenure in the twentieth century was Hugo Thimig (1912–1917), the founder of a famous theatrical family, who introduced Burg audiences to the most recent plays of Arthur Schnitzler, Hugo von Hofmannsthal, Gerhart Hauptmann, and Ferenc Molnár. In the aftermath of World War I, the Imperial and Royal Burgtheater would simply become the Burgtheater. In 1922 the Akademie Theater, linked with the Burg, opened its doors with Goethe's *Iphigenia auf Tauris*. The theatre celebrated its 150th anniversary in 1926 with Gotthold Lessing's *Minna von Barnhelm*, with Else Wohlgemuth as the title character and Paul Hartmann as Tellheim.

Under National Socialism Lothar Müthel became the director but was by no means a Nazi tool. Müthel engaged *regisseurs* such as Adolf Rott and actors such as Kathe Dörsch, Horst Caspar, and Curt Jürgens. Many actors were forced to leave the country in order to survive. One, Ernst Arnst, died in a concentration camp despite the pleas of his fellow actors to free him.

In 1945 a bomb dropped on the Theatre in the Burg, destroying part of the house. Then in April 1945 the whole of the theatre went up in flames and only the two grand staircases and underground part of the building survived. In the same year, the company's first postwar performance was given, Grillparzer's *Sappho*, with Maria Eis as the title character. The temporary home of the company at this time was the Ronacher Theatre, which would house the Burg for the next ten years.

The first postwar director was Raoul Aslan, who, with the help of *regisseurs* such as Adolf Rott, Leopold Lindtberg, and Walter Relsenstein, created miracles in economically deprived Vienna. The new intendant's first job was to show the city the works of American, French, Russian, and British playwrights, works that had been forbidden during the war. His next tasks were to establish the

Burg as an international house by touring and to bring back some of the actors who had long been absent. Helene Thimig, for example, returned in 1945 to play Christine in *Mourning Becomes Electra* (1946). Joseph Gielen was director from 1948 to 1956 and staged a number of important works including Paul Claudel's *The Satin Slipper* (1949), Arthur Miller's *The Crucible* (1954), Shakespeare's *Julius Caesar*, and many other outstanding plays. He also engaged such well-known actors as Atilla Hörbiger and Josef Meinrad.

In 1950 the reconstruction of the old theatre was entrusted to the local architects, Michael Engerblaut and Otto Niedermoser, who restored what they could and modernized the rest, particularly the backstage area. The new house opened on October 16, 1955, with Grillparzer's *König Ottokars Glück und Ende* (*King Ottokar's Fortune and End*), with Ewald Balser as Ottokar and Hörbiger as Rudolf. The director at the time was Adolf Rott (1954–1959), who called the new theatre "a miraculous emanation of the heart."

Rott directed a series of brilliant productions: *Don Carlos* (1955), with Oskar Werner as Carlos and Werner Krauss as King Philip; Schiller's *Mary Stuart*; and Berthold Viertel's staging of *Othello* (1962), with Ewald Balser as the title character. Rott introduced a number of new Austrian authors to the Burg audience and invited a number of foreign troupes to perform at the Burg. These foreign groups include the Old Vic, the Comédie Française, the Hamburg Schauspielhaus, and other important companies. During these years the company of the Theatre in the Burg also went on a number of tours.

Ernst Haeussermann, director from 1959 to 1968, had formerly been an actor with the company. He began to present cycles of plays; for example, Shakespeare (to coincide with the four-hundredth anniversary of his birth) was the most favored with Leopold Lindtberg (*regisseur*) and Teo Otto (set designer), who were doing a series of the major history plays. *Richard II*, *Richard III*, *Henry IV, Parts 1 and 2*, and *Henry V* were given splendid productions. A series of plays by Ferdinand Raimund was directed by Rudolph Steinboeck with sets by Oskar Kokoschka. Haeussermann tried to include dramatists from the entire history of the Austrian theatre, from Johann Nestroy to Fritz Hochwälder. During the 1967–1968 season the Burg made a world tour of eleven countries, including the United States, giving ninety-three performances of eight plays on three continents.

Haeussermann was followed as managing director by Paul Hoffmann, who resigned after two years because of ill health. Gerhard Klingenberg was director from 1971 to 1976. He was a noted *regisseur* and did a number of works, including a modern dress, antifascist *Julius Caesar* in 1971. Barrault visited the company in 1973 and staged Molière's *Le bourgeois gentilhomme*. The great Italian director, Giorgio Strehler, directed the company in 1974 in a production of Carlo Goldoni's *The Countryside Trilogy*. Other guest directors at this time included Otto Schenk, Walter Felsenstein, Werner Düggelin, Peter Hall, Jean-Paul Roussillon, and Otto Tausig.

In 1972 Klingenberg inaugurated a "Junge Burg" series at the Akademietheater to interest young people. Audience dress was informal and prices were low. In honor of the Burg's bicentennial, Klingenberg offered nine new productions in the 1976 season. In 1977 Achim Benning replaced Klingenberg as managing director, generally continuing in his same tradition.

The great strength of the Burg has always been its acting company, though its directors have obviously played a very important role in its life, particularly since World War II. Like the Comédie Française, the Burg has a number of traditions and has frequently been branded a conservative house. This "conservative" label is perhaps true, but the Burg does excel in several areas, one of its principal virtues being the production of Austrian authors. Nowhere else in the world is it possible to see Raimund, Nestroy, and Grillparzer (all of whom are quite untranslatable) under one roof and done so well.

The Burg has two houses: the larger home theatre, seating 1,310 people, with standing room for 210 (always a necessity in Vienna); and the Akademietheater (located on Lisztstrasse), with 496 seats and 26 standing room places. The Akademie is used for small, more intimate, or experimental productions. One of the greatest successes the Burg has had in years was Adolf Dresen's production of Brecht and Weill's *Die Dreigroschenoper* (*The Threepenny Opera*) done in 1978. Actors, as might be suspected, work at both houses as do the directors. The Burg averages about 75 percent attendance over a season, with the Akademie averaging 85 percent. The main house presents about nine productions each year plus a number of revivals, while the Akademie does twelve productions. There are approximately 140 actors in the company, 90 men and 50 women. In any one season there are sixteen directors, mostly guests, and five dramaturges. The technical staff numbers in the hundreds. The public can choose among various subscription programs, and the Austrian government gives a healthy subsidy to the theatre. All in all, the Burg is a sound, well-organized, tidy operation.

The Burg is a popular institution; audiences return season after season to see their beloved stars. (Plays seem to take second place, with directors third.) Max Reinhardt once said that he learned all he knew about the theatre from the top of the Theatre in the Burg. While the Burg may have once seemed too conservative an institution, in the last few years such new *regisseurs* as Hans Neuenfels (who did Frank Wedekind's *Franziska* in 1979 and shocked many theatregoers) have given new blood to it. It seems a livelier institution for this infusion of new talent. Whatever the future holds for the Burg, the playhouse will always be unique in Vienna.

LEON M. AUFDEMBERGE

THEATRE IN THE JOSEFSTADT
(Theater in der Josefstadt)
Josefstädter Strasse 26
A-1080 Vienna, Austria

The Viennese have traditionally been an entertainment-loving people. At the end of the eighteenth century a number of theatres were built in the city, particularly for light entertainment. The most important of these plans was the Theatre in the Josefstadt, which opened on October 24, 1788, with *Lustspiel Liebe und Koketterie* (*Love and Coquetry*), by one Salomon Friedrich Schletter. Located in a garden on Kaisergasse, now Josefstädter Strasse, the theatre was first managed by Karl Meyer.

Its aim was to furnish popular entertainment, including *singspiels* (operetta). By 1791 its reputation was such that Kaiser Leopold II allowed the theatre to play during Lent and to display the imperial eagle.

A number of important actors came early to the Josefstadt, including the noted actor/playwright Ferdinand Raimund, who debuted as Karl Moor in Schiller's *Die Räuber* (*The Robbers*) in 1814. The next year Raimund had phenomenal success as Adam Kratzerl von Kratzerfeld in Johann Alois Gleich's *Die Musikanten am Hohenmarkt* (*The Musicians in the High Market*). Two playwrights also worked for the theatre in the first decades, Ferdinand Eberl (active in the theatre from the late 1780s through the 1790s) and Carl Friedrich Hensler (theatre poet and director from 1822 to 1825). The theatre was drastically renovated in 1822, taking over other buildings in the street. The remodeling was done by Joseph Kornhäusel, and the new Biedermeier facade was especially admired. For the opening of the theatre, Beethoven wrote his overture "Die Weihe des Hauses" ("The Consecration of the House"), which he conducted.

Among several important actors who came to the Josefstadt in the 1820s were Wenzel Scholz, an extremely popular comedian who came in 1826 and enjoyed a huge following, and the great actor/playwright Johann Nepomuk Nestroy, who made a guest appearance in 1829.

In the 1830s the theatre began to play many musical works. One important play that had its premiere at the Josefstadt in 1834 was Raimund's *Der Verschwender* (*The Prodigal*), with the playwright returning to the theatre to play Valentin.

From 1837 to 1850 the theatre was led by Franz Pokorny, who instituted royalty payments to playwrights. The greatest success of his era was Franz Todd and Anton Emil Titl's *Der Zauberschleier* (*The Magic Haze*), which was kept in the repertory until 1902, being played 402 times. The young Franz von Suppé came to the house as music director in 1840. Two important actresses arrived in the 1850s, Marie Geistinger and Josephine Gallmeyer. Joseph Hoffmann (1855–1865) was a singer before becoming director and opening a second theatre, the Thalia, in 1856 (it existed until 1870). It was designed for musical entertainments. The first Vienna production of Wagner's *Tannhäuser* was at the Thalia in 1857. Two years later the theatre presented one of the first European productions of Harriet Beecher Stowe's *Uncle Tom's Cabin* with Negro spirituals. In 1861 the theatre gave the premiere of Bruno Zappert's burlesque *Ein Böhm in Amerika*, which was played over six hundred times before being taken wearily out of the repertory.

Karl Costa (1882–1885) and Karl Blasel (1885–1889) pushed hard for good performances, with Blasel especially remembered for the number of Nestroy plays he included in the repertory. In 1888 the theatre celebrated its centenary with appropriate ceremonies and plays. Theodore Giesrau (1889–1894) had many long-running *bomben* (literally bombs, but in Vienna meaning hits), all comedies. Included in the repertory of the company during the leadership of Ignaz Wild (1894–1899) were light dramatic productions of everything from popular ballet to Gilbert and Sullivan.

With Josef Jarno (1899–1923) the theatre attained international standing. Jarno was an actor in his native Budapest before working in Berlin at the Deutsches Theater (with Otto Brahm), where he was especially good in modern playwrights, including Hauptmann and Strindberg. When Jarno took over the theatre, it was nearly bankrupt. He slowly built the repertory of the company so that it included not only *Schwank* (farces) and operettas, but also serious writers, such as Strindberg, Wedekind, Shaw, Molnár, and Wilde. He was aided by his wife ("Die Frau") Hansi Niese. Among the popular works done in his early seasons were Georges Feydeau's *The Girl from Maxim's* (1899), which was Jarno's first play with the company and starred Annie Dirkens as Crevette; Schnitzler's *Liebelei* (*Light-o'-Love*, 1902), with Niese as the protagonist; Strindberg's *Intoxication* (1902), with Lili Petri as Henriette; Wedekind's *Der Marquis von Keith*, with Jarno in the title role (1903); Gogol's *The Inspector General* (1904), with Jarno as Chlestakov; Wilde's *An Ideal Husband* (1906), with Jarno as Goring; Ibsen's *The Master Builder* (1907), with Jarno as Solness; Henri Bataille's *Poliche* (1908), with Jarno in the title role; Strindberg's *Creditors* (1910), with Jarno as Gustav; Strindberg's *The Dance of Death* (1912), with Jarno as Edgar; and Goethe's *Faust* (1912), with Jarno as Mephisto.

Then in 1913 came Jarno's greatest role, the title character in Ferenc Molnár's *Liliom*, which he not only played in Vienna, but also took on tour. Whenever the cashbox was running low after World War I (which was frequently), *Liliom* was revived. Jarno played it over 150 times until he left the Josefstadt in 1923. After the war, Jarno was forced to drop the kind of plays he had been doing and to play more light comedies to balance the budget. Hence, there were few post-*Liliom* hits. Among them were Imre Földes, *Lili Grün* (1916), with Gisela Werbezirk as the protagonist; Franz Herczeg's *Blaufuchs* (*Blue Fox*, 1917), with Leopold Konstantine in the lead role; Strindberg's *The Father* (1919), with Jarno as the Captain; Nestroy's *Lumpazivagabundus* (*The Vagabond*), with Niese as Knieriem (1923); and Strindberg's *Stormy Weather*. Jarno left the Josefstadt in 1923, continuing to work for several more years in Vienna. He died in 1932, heart-broken; his wife died two years later.

In June 1923 Max Reinhardt agreed to assume direction of the company, and, with him, the entire philosophy of the organization changed radically, with all changes personally instituted. The first major alteration was in the theatre itself, which was remodeled by Carl Witzmann. Particular attention was given to the foyers and refreshing rooms, which were given a red and gold baroque feeling. In terms of the acting company, Reinhardt brought many of the great names in German and Austrian theatre to work either in the permanent company or as guest artists. The following artists worked in the early years of Reinhardt's reform: Paul Hartmann, Eugen Klöpfer, Fritz Kortner, Werner Krauss, Else Lehmann, Alexander Moissi, Gerda Muller, Hermann Romberg, Die Thimig: Hugo and Hermann (brothers) and Helene (sister), who was Frau Reinhardt, and Gustav Waldau. Reinhardt also brought in a succession of prize *regisseurs*, most of whom were in the Reinhardt vein—very "directorial," very complete, with much interest in the relationship between production and the stage scenery. All of this cost money, so it was fortunate that Reinhardt had sound financial backing, mostly from Camillo Castiglioni, a banker.

The greatest change, however, was in repertory, with the theatre concentrating on two specialties: classic repertory with emphasis on Shakespeare; and modern German plays, including many important premieres. Reinhardt also invited many dancers to do *Tanzmatinees* (dance matinees) at the theatre. Reinhardt was also working in Berlin and Salzburg during his years at the Josefstadt!

The first of Reinhardt's productions was Goldoni's *The Servant of Two Masters*, April 1, 1924, with Die Thimig (Hermann and Helene) in the lead roles. This brilliant *commedia dell'arte* production, with its high style, set the tone for the Reinhardt period. It would include a mass of important productions (uncredited works were staged by Reinhardt): Schiller's *Kabale und Liebe* (*Intrigue and Love*, 1924); Hugo von Hofmannsthal's *Der Schwierige* (*The Difficult Man*, 1924); Shakespeare's *The Merchant of Venice* (1924), *King Lear* (1925), and *A Midsummer Night's Dream* (1925); Franz Werfel's *Juarez und Maximilian* (1925); John Galsworthy's *Loyalties* (1925); Hofmannsthal's *Christinas Heimreise* (*Christina's Homecoming*, 1926, regie Stephan Hock), with Gustav Gründgens as Florindo; the premiere of Hauptmann's *Dorothea Angermann* (1926), with Dagny Servaes as Dorothea; and Ivan Turgenev's *A Month in the Country* (1926, regie Ivan Schmith), with Helene Thimig as Natalie.

Beginning in 1927 Reinhardt staged plays at the theatre, though the company remained very much "Die Schauspieler im Theater in der Josefstadt unter der Führung von Max Reinhardt" (the actors in the Joseftheatre in Vienna under the direction of Max Reinhardt). Instead of Reinhardt's staging there were productions by people he had trained, especially Paul Kalbeck, Otto Preminger, and Emil Geyer. The repertory changed as well, with the theatre playing twentieth-century works almost exclusively and classics becoming rarer. The most significant works during these years were as follows (again uncredited productions are Reinhardt's): Frantisek Langer's *Peripherie* (1927); Stephan Kamare's *Leinen aus Ireland* (*Linen from Ireland*, 1928, regie Kalbeck), which proved an enormous success; Ferdinand Bruckner's *Die Verbrecher* (*The Criminal*, 1929, regie Geyer); Shaw's *The Apple Cart* (1930), with Ernst Deutsch as Magnus; Ben Hecht and Charles MacArthur's *The Front Page* (1931, regie Preminger); and Jacques Deval's *Mademoiselle* (1932).

In September 1933 Reinhardt gave up the leadership of the organization and was replaced by Preminger who ran the theatre for only two years. During his time the repertory of the company was almost exclusively popular comedies, with the only significant classic production being Reinhardt's staging of Goethe's *Faust* (1933) and Schiller's *Mary Stuart* (1934), with Helene Thimig as Elisabeth. The big successes were all very boulevard or Broadway, such as Koloman von Mikszáth's *The Love of Young Nosty* (1933, *regie* Preminger); Jacques Deval's *Tovarisch* (1933, *regie* Florian Kalbeck), with Lili Darvas as Tatiana; the premiere of Hans Jaray's *Christiano zwischen Himmel und Hölle* (*Christiano between Heaven and Hell*); and a huge success in Sidney Kingsley's *Men in White* (both 1934, *regie* Preminger).

It was during the era of Ernst Lothar (1935–1937) that Preminger and Reinhardt had their last European productions. Preminger's came in 1935 with Emmet Lavery's *Die erste Legion* (*The First Legion*) and Reinhardt's in 1937 with Werfel's *In einer Nacht* (*In a Night*). Lothar's repertory was extremely liberal, with many of his plays touching on toleration and pacificism. This is surprising considering what would happen in 1938. The most often played author in the period was Grillparzer. Lothar depended on two guest artists, Ernst Deutsch and Albert Bassermann. In retrospect, the most important productions were not necessarily the most popular works (uncredited productions are Lothar's): Grillparzer's *Ein treuer Diener seines Herrn* (*A True Servant of His Lord*, 1935) with Bassermann as Bancban; Gotthold Lessing's *Nathan der Weise* (*Nathan the Wise*, 1936), with Bassermann in the title role; Jean Giraudoux's *The War of Troy Will Not Take Place* (1936); Clare Booth Luce's *The Women* (1937, *regie* Kalbeck), which was revived after the war; and Shaw's *The Doctor's Dilemma* (1938, *regie* Kalbeck), with Deutsch as Ridgeon.

During the Nazi years Reinhardt, Preminger, and Lothar would all be in the United States: Reinhardt and Preminger in New York and Hollywood, and Lothar in Colorado. When Reinhardt died in October 1943, a memorial service was conducted for him at the Josefstadt behind *very closed* doors. Even so, the Nazi hierarchy heard about it and were most unhappy. Many of the great actors who had worked with the three expatriates were also in the United States, including Kortner, Bassermann, and Deutsch.

After the *Anschluss*, Robert Volberg took over the leadership for a while, producing one hit which he played over and over, Lessing's *Minna von Barnhelm* (*regie* Kalbeck), with Paula Wessely as Minna. Then, in the fall of 1938, Heinz Hilpert (a Reinhardt disciple) took over the joint directorship of both the Deutsches Theater in Berlin (something Reinhardt had done) and the Josefstadt, which meant more or less a common company. When he took over, Hilpert promised that he would not turn the theatre into a Germanic company, which was true; what was also true (but he did not say) was that he would not perform Nazi plays. Although he did a lot of comedies including Shaw, nearly all the big productions were classics, very much in the Reinhardt manner. Three important actresses rose to popularity in the period: Paula Wessely, Vilma Degischer (the first primarily Josefstadt actress to be a Kammerschauspieler [player in small, intimate theatres]), and Hilde Krahl. The works the company would like to remember from these bad years include the following (uncredited productions are Hilpert's): Shakespeare's *As You Like It* (1938); Raimund's *Der Bauer als Milliönar* (*The Peasant as Millionaire*, 1939), which celebrated the 150th anniversary of the theatre; Shakespeare's *The Taming of the Shrew* (1939), with Wessely and Attila Hörbiger as the battling couple; Chekhov's *The Three Sisters* (1940, *regie* Hans Thimig); Friedrich Hebbel's *Gyges und sein Ring* (*Gyges and His Ring*, 1941) and *Maria Magdalena* (1941), the latter with Krahl as Klara; Shakespeare's *Much Ado About Nothing* (1942); Shaw's *Pygmalion* (1942, *regie* Wolfgang Liebeneiner), with Wessely as Eliza; Hauptmann's *Michael Kramer* (1942); Ibsen's *A Doll's House* (1943), with Krahl as Nora; and Friedrich Hölderlin's *Empedokles* (1943), with Degischer as Panthea. In 1943 the company had two successes, Julian Kay's *Vagabunden* (*regie* Hilpert) and Franz Füssel's (real name Martin Costa, whose father had been *direktor* of the Josefstadt from 1882–1885) *Der Hofrat Geiger* (*regie* Bruno Hübner), with Alfred Neugebauer in the title role. Both were revived after the war with great success. Although all German theatres were supposedly closed in the fall of 1944, the Josefstadt continued to play through April 2, 1945, with the theatre surviving the war.

The first performance after declaration of peace was *Der Hofrat Geiger* (*Privy Councillor Geiger*) on May 1, 1945, with the official premiere following on June 8. This was a program of European one-acts (Chekhov, Courteline, and Nestroy), staged by the new *direktor*, Rudolf Steinboeck. Steinboeck had been a *regisseur* with the company during the war years, and, as with most German companies of the period, the Josefstadt performed many plays that would have been unthinkable during the Nazi years, mostly major works from Western Europe and America. Steinboeck added two houses to his main stage, the Kleines Haus in the former Weiner Winkel and the Kammerspiele in der Rotenturmstrasse. During the early Steinboeck era, the company began to tour, and at the end of the era, the organization began a vigorous subscription program. Steinboeck also liked touring guest productions. Most important in the era, in terms of productions, were works from the present century (uncredited productions are Steinboeck's): Priestley's *Time and the Conways* (1945); Hugo von Hofmannsthal's *Der Schwierige* (*The Difficult Man*, 1945), with Anton Edthofer in the title role; Wilder's *Our Town* (1946, *regie* Hans Thimig); Brecht's *Der gute Mensch von Sezuan* (*The Good Woman of Setzuan*, 1946), with Wessely as Shen Te/Shua Ta; Hermann Bahr's *Das Konzert* (1947, *regie* Franz Pfaudler); Kay's *Vagabunden* (1947); Wilder's *The Skin of Our Teeth* (1947), with Attila Hörbiger as Mr. Antrobus and Adrienne Gessner as Mrs. Antrobus; John van Druten's *The Voice of the Turtle* (1948); Carl Zuckmayer's *Barbara Blomberg* (1948), with Wessely in the title role; Ibsen's *The Lady from the Sea* (1949, *regie* Ernst Ginsberg), with Wessely as Ellida and Deutsch as the Stranger, which toured West Germany; Miller's *Death of a Salesman* (1950, *regie* Lothar), with Edthofer as Willy; and Wilde's *An Ideal Husband* (1952). By the end of the period a lot of famous actors and *regisseurs* had returned from exile to the Josefstadt.

Franz Stoss had been *direktor* of the Theatre in the Burg in the postwar era, and in 1951 he came to the Josefstadt as organizational leader, becoming *direktor* in 1953. In the following year Ernst Haeussermann, who had formerly been employed at the Burg as an actor and had worked with Reinhardt in Hollywood, became co-director with Stoss, continuing in this arrangement until 1958. In 1954 the company was completely reorganized under a limited corporation, which brought more financial stability to the organization. The city provided additional subsidy. Steinboeck invited many outside companies to become part of the season, while Haeussermann and Stoss continued the program. In terms of repertory in this period, the company staged many contemporary plays, with several guest artists in both the acting company and in the *regisseur*'s staff. The following productions were particularly good: Maxwell Anderson's *Joan of Lorraine* (1953, *regie* Walter Firner), with Krahl as Joan; Herman Wouk's *The Caine Mutiny Court Martial* (1954, *regie* Werner Kraut); John Patrick's *The Teahouse of the August Moon* (1954, *regie* Jaray), with Oskar Karlweis as Sakini; von Hofmannsthal's *Der Schwierige* (1954, *regie* Steinboeck); Sartre/Dumas' *Kean* (1955, *regie* Jaray), with Paul Hoffmann in the title role; Fritz Eckhardt's *Rendevouz in Wien* (1955, *regie* Werner Kraut), with Ernst Waldbruun as Windburger; Shakespeare's *Hamlet* (1956, *regie* Müthel), with Oskar Werner as Hamlet; Ibsen's *Ghosts* (1956, *regie* Müthel), with Helene Thimig-Reinhardt as Mrs. Alving, which toured; Turgenev's *A Month in the Country* (1957, *regie* Peter Scharoff), with Krahl as Natalie; and Werfel's *Jacobowsky and the Colonel* (1958, *regie* Franz Reichart). In 1956 the company went on an extended tour, first to Paris, and later to South America and New York; it was the first German-language company to play in New York after the war.

In 1959 Haeussermann left to become head of the Burg, a few streets away, and Stoss became the sole *direktor*. Once the joint directors had set the policies in terms of repertory (mostly modern with some classics), *regisseurs* (safe and solid), and acting company (fairly stable though with lots of guests), there were no huge changes in the company, except for the addition of absurdist plays to the repertory. The most important productions in the era and the leads were as follows: Shakespeare's *Much Ado About Nothing* (1959, *regie* Leonhard Steckel); O'Neill's *Ah, Wilderness!* (1960, *regie* Otto Schenk); William Saroyan's *Lily Davon* (1960, *regie* Steinboeck); Jean Anouilh's *Poor Bitos* (1961, *regie* Heinrich Schnitzler), with Leopold Rudolf in the title role; Luigi Pirandello's *Right You Are—If You Think You Are* (1962, *regie* Werner Kraut), with Helene Thimig-Reinhardt as Signora Frola; Beckett's *Waiting for Godot* (1962, *regie* Edwin Zbonek); Shakespeare's *Cymbeline* (1963, *regie* Dietrich Haugk); Hellman's *The Little Foxes* (1963, *regie* Heinrich Schnitzler); Odön von Horváth's *Kasimir und Karoline* (1964, *regie* Otto Schenk); the premiere of Ernst Waldbrunn and Lida Winiewicz's *Die Flucht* (*The Flight*, 1965, *regie* Hermann Kutchera); Molière's *The Misanthrope* (1965, *regie* Haugk), with Michael Heltau as Alceste; Carlo Goldoni's *The Venetian Twins* (1966, *regie* Haugk), with Maximilian Schell; Paddy Chayevsky's *The Tenth Man* (1966, *regie* Michael Kehlmann); Sławomir Mrożek's *Tango* (1967, *regie* Kutschera); Goldoni's *Trilogy of Country Dwellers* (1968, *regie* Peter Beauvais); Ibsen's *Hedda Gabler* (1968, *regie* Haugk), with

Eva Korbler in the title role; Peter Handke's *Kaspar* (1969, *regie* Hans Holl-mann), with Peter Matic in the title role; the premiere of Arthur Schnitzler's *Das Wort* (*The Word*, 1969 *regie* Haeussermann); Gotthold Lessing's *Emilia Galotti* (1970), which was Fritz Kortner's last production before his death and which toured extensively (Klaus-Maria Brandauer as the prince); and David Storey's *Home* (1972, *regie* Kutschera).

In 1968 Ernst Haeussermann left the Burg, returning shortly as *regisseur* to the Josefstadt, and in 1972 he became co-director (to 1977), again with Stoss. These were good seasons, with fine productions, but with scarcely any major policy change. There were many new *regisseurs*, however. Practically all of the plays performed during the era were from the modern period. While the major productions were primarily from the current century, there were some exceptions: Ibsen's *The Wild Duck* (1972, *regie* Heinrich Schnitzler); István Örkény's *Cat's Play* (1972, *regie* Leopold Lindtberg); Bahr's *Der arme Narr* (*The Poor Fool*, 1973, *regie* Haugk); Hofmannsthal's *Der Schwierige* (1974, *regie* Haeusser-mann); Nestroy's *Zu ebener Erde und Ersten Stock* (*On Level Ground and the First Floor*, 1975, *regie* Lindtberg); Jason Miller's *That Championship Season* (1975, *regie* Hermann Kutscher); Neil Simon's *The Good Doctor* (1976, *regie* Haugk); and Italo Svevo's *A Husband* (1977, *regie* Edwin Zbonek).

Since 1977 Haeussermann has run the company by himself, with Stoss still a part of the acting company. In the seasons since, there have been several major changes. The first is the decision not to use the Konzerthaus for plays, substituting works *aus der Reihe* (out of the subscription series) for "touchy" plays, which, if proven successful, can later be taken into the regular subscription series. Another change is the current author/*regisseur* program in which distinguished playwrights have been asked to stage their works. So far only Friedrich Dür-renmatt and Pavel Kohout have been involved, but a number of others have been invited to come to the Josefstadt. Haeussermann continues to bring a wide variety of plays to the theatre, especially from the current century, with some classics for contrast. In the last few years a number of productions have been well received by the Viennese critics: Giraudoux's *The Madwoman of Chaillot* (1977, *regie* Bernhard Wick), with Joanna Maria Gorvin in the title role; Pirandello's *Six Characters in Search of an Author* (1978, *regie* Ernst Haeussermann); Gotthold Lessing's *Nathan der Weise* (*Nathan the Wise*, 1979, *regie* Hoffmann); Peter Ustinov's *Photo Finish* (1979, *regie* Walter Davy); Henry Denker's *A Far Coun-try* (1979, *regie* Ernst Haeussermann), with Curt Jürgens as Freud; Botho Strauss' *Trilogie des Wiedersehens* (*Trilogy of Reunions*, 1980, *regie* Gorvin); Arthur Schnitzler's *Der einsame Weg* (*The Lonely Way*, 1980, *regie* Brandauer); Oscar Wilde's *Lady Windemere's Fan* (1980, *regie* Jaray); and Arthur Schnitzler's *Zug der Schatten* (*Shadow Train*, 1981, *regie* Michael Kehlmann).

Currently, the theatre operates two houses, the Josefstadt itself, which seats 785, and the Kammerspiele which seats 528. Generally, the company does nine new productions in the first house and five in the second, plus two more *aus der Reihe*. The permanent acting company numbers thirty-one actors and thirty-two actresses, with a number of guests who work part of a season or for only one play. Generally, around sixteen *regisseurs* are hired over the season, with Haeussermann generally the only permanent one, though some acting guests also work as *regisseurs*. There are also three dramaturges as well as a full technical staff with each *regisseur* allowed to select his or her own designer. On the whole, it is a very well-run company, with the atmosphere very friendly.

The general philosophy of the company is to find a good play and then to do it well. Choice of plays and *regisseurs* tends toward the conservative as the theatre is a private organization and has to make its own way. However, it does receive about one-half of its current 104 million schilling budget from a subsidy. The theatre is very popular and runs at about 80 percent capacity. Most of the plays it does are modern, with the company generally doing two or three classics a year. There are a couple of Austrian plays every year and generally a Nestroy or a Raimund. Its season is usually set with the other theatres in the city, so there is no overlap of plays. The plays are chosen by the *direktor* and his dramaturges.

The Josefstadt is a theatre rich in traditions, not only from the people who have acted in or staged plays there, but in the feeling of the house as well. Each performance begins with the tradition of the Lampe Luste, where the raising of the chandeliers signals the beginning of a performance. While richness of tradition sometimes produces a stereotyped performance, with the Josefstadt it only makes everyone work harder.

LEON M. AUFDEMBERGE
(With thanks to Klemens Paul Schindler)

Belgium

INTRODUCTION

Belgium is a country very much separated by two languages. This separation is very apparent in the two different theatres in the country, which have very little contact. One thing is clear, however: while the two major playwrights in Belgium in the twentieth century have been French-speaking (Maurice Maeterlinck and Michel de Ghelderode), the bases for their plays have been the more spiritual and mystical area north of Flanders.

The French-speaking theatre in Belgium is centered in Brussels; in addition, there is now a very highly regarded company in the Louvain-la-Neuve. The main French-speaking theatre is the Théâtre National de Belgique, Bruxelles. Founded in 1945, it serves not only its home city but the Walloon area as well, and it also appears in the important festival at Spa. There are a number of so-called Les Théâtres agrées (or officially recognized theatres), which maintain a permanent company of at least eight actors and are subsidized by both city and national governments. In addition, a number of experimental companies receive help. The theatres in French-speaking Belgium have a tendency to be independent of one another.

The Flemish theatres are very much in contact. They even publish a yearbook, *Teater Jaarboek voor Vlaanderen*, which is a record of all the theatre activities in Flanders and is published under the auspices of the *Minister van Nederlandse Kultuur*. The principal Flemish companies are in Antwerp, Ghent, and Brussels.

In addition, the government in Flanders subsidizes *Grote Repertoiregezelschappen* (established repertory companies), which must do at least eight plays each season. The government also issues grants for touring companies (Antwerp has a very good one), small studio companies, and experimental and educational theatres.

The Flemish companies have much more varied programs than the French and one added advantage. Flemish companies seem more welcome in the Netherlands than are the French ones in France. Dutch companies also play in Flanders with some frequency.

The government has rather valiantly tried to encourage all the companies in both languages to tour to smaller towns in the country. Most Belgian towns have some sort of theatre, but few have facilities for large productions. Hence, some theatres may mount smaller productions to tour. Belgium also has a rather good railroad system, which means people from outlying areas can come into a city for an evening of theatre and return in short order.

LEON M. AUFDEMBERGE

ATELIER THEATRE OF THE LOUVAIN
(Atelier Théâtral de Louvain-la-Neuve)
Ferme de Blocry, Place de l'Hocaille
1348 Louvain-la-Neuve, Belgium

Until recently, French-speaking theatre in Belgium was to be found in the capital city, Bruxelles, with touring companies sent to outlying areas. In 1961, however, Professor Raymonde Pouillart, with the assistance of Armand Delcampe, founded the Théâtre Universitaire à Louvain (TUL) primarily to present plays in the area. TUL is part of a decentralization movement that began developing in Belgium after World War II. Louvain (or in Flemish, Leuven) is located in Brabant Walloon, which is on the dividing line between the French- and Flemish-speaking areas of Belgium. The university itself was the scene of some clashes in language which eventually brought a split.

In its early seasons, the TUL concentrated on the modern playwrights (most with a social philosophy), such as Samuel Beckett, Nikolai Gogol, Michel de Ghelderode, and Friedrich Dürrenmatt. It also invited a number of troupes, mostly from France, to present plays at the university, such as the Théâtre Antique de la Sorbonne, the Théâtre National de Strasbourg, and Belgian troupes, such as the Rideau de Bruxelles. Also popular were concerts of avant-garde music with composers such as Léo Ferré and Xenakis.

In 1968, under the auspices of the Centre d'Etudes Théâtrales, the Atelier Theatre of the Louvain was born, its purpose largely that of the TUL. However, it began to present more troupes from outside French-speaking Europe, troupes such as the Living Theatre and the Bread and Puppet Theatre from the United States. The new company, which was much more professional in outlook, philosophy, and actual make-up, became more ambitious in the 1970s with its first important single production coming in 1970: Jean-Pierre Willemaer's *C'est un dur métier que l'exil* (*Exile Is a Bad Trade*), (*mise-en-scène* [directed by] Pierre Laroche assisted by Anne Malengreu and Anne Wibo), which dealt with the problems of Turkish exiles. The university was soon split, with the French part moving to Louvain-la-Neuve. In 1975 the theatre followed.

The first permanent home for the company was the small (180 to 200 seats) Théâtre Blocry (architect Hernandez), which was inaugurated in November 1976. The company was invited in 1977 to become part of the Festival d'Avignon, presenting (with the Théâtre de l'Est Parisien in a co-production) Shakespeare's

La tragique histoire d'Hamlet, prince de Danemark, staged by the noted Swiss *metteur-en-scène* (the director) Benno Besson (who has worked a great deal in East Berlin at the Volksbühne), with sets by Ezio Toffolutti and the title role played by Philippe Avron. This production played in Avignon, Paris, and Louvain-la-Neuve, also touring France and Belgium. The same year the company had a splendid success with Alexey Arbuzov's two-character piece, *Old-Fashioned Comedy* (*mise-en-scène* Yuta-Ka Wada).

The troupe returned to the Avignon Festival in July of 1978 with a Besson-staged production of Brecht's *The Caucasian Chalk Circle*, with Avron as Azdak. This production was done with the Théâtre National de Chaillot de Paris and played an extensive tour in Belgium, France, and Italy. At the same festival the company also played Beckett's *Waiting for Godot*, in a production by Otomar Krejca, who was born in Poland but has worked with companies in West Germany and France. In the cast were Rufus as Estragon and Georges Wilson as Vladimir. This production inaugurated a new theatre in Louvain-la-Neuve, the Théâtre Jean Vilar (named in honor of the noted French *metteur-en-scène*). It was one of the first theatres in Belgium with an open stage and places for 640 to 700 spectators. (Architect Jean Potvin worked in conjunction with Arsene Joukovsky, who also assisted in the planning of the Blocry.) In 1978 Krejca became a permanent *metteur-en-scène* for the company.

The company returned to Avignon in July 1979 with a much admired production (again by Krejca) of Alfred de Musset's *Lorenzaccio*, with sets by Jan Koblasa and with the role of Lorenzo de Medici played by Philipe Caubère. This production toured Belgium, France, and Switzerland. During the same year, a co-production with the Théâtre du Soleil of Paris involved a dramatization of Klaus Mann's novel *Mephisto* (*mise-en-scène* Ariane Mnouchkine), which played not only in Belgium and France, but also in West Germany (where the novel was forbidden because of libel).

In 1980 the company took its production of Chekhov's *The Three Sisters* (*mise-en-scène* Krejca) to Canada and toured Belgium, France, Switzerland, and Italy. This production was an ideal presentation of the Chekhov play, as it was intensely moving, especially in the last act, though by no means lugubrious or maudlin. Since then the company has staged notable works, including Beckett's *Endgame* (1981, *mise-en-scène* Delcampe) with André Lenaerts as Hamm, and Schnitzler's *The Greek Cockatoo* (1981, *mise-en-scène* Krejca).

The company consists of fifteen actors and six technical people who are permanent, with the total organization numbering thirty. The company also runs a theatre school in conjunction with the organization, with third- and fourth-year students acting in productions. The company mounts two new productions a year, each production remaining in the repertory for at least two and sometimes three years. The theatre also invites eight outside productions a year, with each production playing twelve performances. With all its activities, the company plays about 250 performances a year. Because its prices are popular (250 to 300 Belgian francs), the company has a sizable deficit, which is met by an adequate though not extensive subsidy. In 1980 the budget ran to 65 million BF, of which 44 percent came from a state subsidy, 15 percent from the University of Louvain, and 41 percent from the box office. Plays are chosen by the *directeur* to fit the company and thus avoid hiring outside actors. The company produces its own journal, *Cahiers théâtre Louvain* (edited by Armand Delcampe), which features articles on *metteurs-en-scène*, productions, and various other aspects of theatre. A second journal, *Arts du Spectacle* (managed by Andre Veinstein and Pierre-Aimé Touchard), is already in preparation.

The theatre has a very popular philosophy (in the best sense of the word). In a letter from M. Delcampe which has been translated by Kay Rossiter, Delcampe explains:

We think that it is necessary to attempt every day to make concrete this Utopia: to make day after day an artistic theatre of high intelligence and sensitivity and to present it to the greatest number possible. This is a thing which seems simple, even simplistic, but it is in fact a complex thing of which one will never see the end. . . . (ellipses are Delcampe's).

Consequently, low prices and high standards are enforced. The positive results of the company derive, in part, from the fine work of Krejca who owes much to Stanislavsky, though he is by no means heavily realistic. Most of the company's achievements can be credited to Delcampe's determination. In its first season in Louvain-la-Neuve (1975–1976), the company had three hundred people on subscription and thirty thousand spectators for the season; currently the company has seven thousand people as subscribers, and in the 1980–1981 season there were one hundred eighty thousand spectators.

The company would like to intensify the work of both the company and its school. It will continue its policy of touring and guest productions, which are necessary because of economic conditions but do not, as Delcampe says "*défigurer son visage artistique propre*" ("disfigure our own artistic image" [letter from Delcampe]). As long as Delcampe is there to lead the company, nothing short of the dissolution of the theatre could disfigure it.

LEON M. AUFDEMBERGE
(With thanks to Armande Delcampe)

NATIONAL THEATRE OF BELGIUM
(Théâtre National de Langue Française)
Centre Rogier, Brussels, Belgium

During the closing days of World War II, the Belgians experienced a resurgence of pride and gave some thought to founding a national theatre. There had already been subsidized theatres in Belgium, most notably in Antwerp. Four people are generally given credit for the founding of the two national theatres: Herman Tierlinck (Flemish), Jules Pelacre (French), and Jacques and Maurice Huismann (Flemish, but French-speaking). The two theatres would be subsidized:

a French-speaking one in Brussels and a Flemish-speaking one in Antwerp. These two theatres would be equally important in subsidy and resources.

Before World War II, a traveling company called the Comédiens Routiers took plays throughout French-speaking Belgium. During the war, the group continued to tour, although with extreme difficulty. After the war, they entertained the Belgian, French, English, and American troops, especially with evenings of pantomime (Jacques Copeau was a big influence). At the end of the war the directors of the Comédiens Routiers were the Huismann brothers, who were entrusted in 1945 with the founding of a French-language national theatre in Brussels. The first play chosen was a dramatization of an old Belgian legend, *Les Quatre Fils de Aymon* by Herman Closson, done in 1946. This was followed by Shakespeare's *Romeo and Juliet*, with both staged by Jacques Huismann. Both productions received excellent reviews, and the theatre was off to a good start. In the first several seasons, the choice of plays gave Brussels theatregoers a first opportunity to view the works of many writers: García Lorca's *Blood Wedding*; Wilder's *Our Town*; and, in 1952, the first international success, Miller's *Death of a Salesman* (*Morte d'un Commis-Voyageur*), which later played Paris as a premiere for Parisians. Most of the plays in the early years of the company were staged by Jacques Huismann, who in 1949 was made sole director of the theatre.

The repertory of the 1950s was very solid and included the first French-language production of T.S. Eliot's *The Cocktail Party* and Miller's *The Crucible* (*La Chasse aux Sorcières*, 1953), with productions by Huismann. Two especially remembered productions from this era were Brecht's *The Good Woman of Setzuan* (1954) and Fernand Crommeynck's *Une Femme Qu'a le Cour Trop Petit* (*A Woman with a Small Heart*, 1956). Later in the decade came Michel de Ghelderode's *Barabbas* (1955) and a huge success with the Krasna *Rashomon* (1959), in a production by Raymond Roleau.

Early in the history of the company, it began touring, especially in the lower (French-speaking) part of the country. In 1952 the troupe played London (as it has several times since), and in 1955 it toured South America (Brazil, Uruguay, and Argentina) for three months with a repertory of eight plays, including Shakespeare's *Twelfth Night*; Sheridan's *The School for Scandal*; Ghelderode's *Barabbas*; and, of course, *Les Quatre Fils de Aymon*.

The repertory of the 1960s remained international in flavor with productions of Chekhov; Schéhadé's *Emigre de Brisbane*, which played the Festival of Baalbeck; Hugo's *Ruy Blas*, which toured to Montreal; and others. On October 21, 1961, the company moved into a new home in the Centre Rogier, with two theatres: La Grande Salle, which seats 756, and La Petite Salle, which holds 321. The opening was preceded by a long parade with each performer wearing his or her favorite costume. It was, as they say, "a bash." In the late 1960s the company traveled to Paris (1965, 1967, and 1969), Baalbeck (1966), Canada (1967), and East Berlin (1967).

In the 1970s the theatre sought international status, in terms of both repertory and *metteurs-en-scène*. Frank Dunlap of Britain's national theatre staged *Antony and Cleopatra* (1970) in Gide's translation; Ghelderode's *Pantagleige* (1971); and Shakespeare's *Pericles* (1973), plus others.

In the present decade, there have been outstanding productions of Dario Fo's *The Seventh Commandment* (1970), staged by Arturo Corso; Peter Nichols' *Public Health* (1972), staged by Huismann; Peter Shaffer's *Equus*, in a production by Jo Dua; Robert Bolt's *The Testimony of Lenin* (1979), staged by Huismann; and Shakespeare's *Romeo and Juliet* (1979), with Otmar Krejca doing the staging.

The National Theatre of Belgium has an ambitious program. There are generally nine productions each season, split between the theatres. Each play has a set run, although popular productions have been returned. There are two permanent stagers with the company; the rest are guests. The acting company has approximately sixty members (it varies from season to season), split about thirty-seven men to twenty-three women. There is a large technical staff, and it is a pleasant place in which to work.

The theatre maintains a fairly conservative international policy. It tries to present a balanced season, split between classics and moderns. It would like to perform more Belgian works but finds few of quality. Several smaller theatres in Brussels do regular seasons of Belgian playwrights, reducing pressure, but the National Theatre of Belgium continues to read new Belgian scripts. It has a large number of pleased subscribers. Students are admitted at reduced prices but attend in small numbers. Brussels is basically conservative, and its theatre seems to reflect this attitude. Jacques Huismann has been with the theatre from the beginning and shows little sign of wanting to retire. Under his leadership, the National Théâtre seems to have a healthy outlook.

LEON M. AUFDEMBERGE

NETHERLANDS "TONEEL GENT"
(Nederlands Toneel Gent)
Sint-Baafsplein 7
9000 Ghent, Belgium

In 1965 a permanent theatre company, the Netherlands "Toneel Gent," moved into Ghent's old civic theatre, beginning a healthy period of theatre history in this great artistic city. The first play staged opened on October 9, 1965. It was Schiller's *Mary Stuart* (*regie* Georges Vitaly), with Joanna Geldof as Mary and Suzanne Juchtmans as Elisabeth, and was partly funded by Coca-Cola. In the first season came Constantijn Huygens' *Trintje Cornelis* (*regie* Frans Roggen); Tennessee Williams' *Summer and Smoke* (*regie* Dré Poppe), with Maria Verheyden as Alma; Shakespeare's *As You Like It* (*regie* Dom de Gruyter), with Juchtmans as Rosalinde; and the Schmidt/Jones musical *110 in the Shade* (*regie* Eddy Verbruggen).

The first director for the company was Dré Poppe, who had been active in

Belgian television. Many of the policies set in the first season continue today: a repertory of both classic and modern works, a program that would include touring, an exchange of plays with other Flemish-speaking companies, and frequent talks with the audience about the work of the company (*"Gesprekken in de Foyer"*).

The second season opened with Sophocles' *Oedipus Tyrannos* (*regie* Roggen), with Jef Demedts in the lead role and choreography by Lea Daan. This season was marked by several large-scale works, which could have proven too ambitious for the young company but fortunately were not: Jean Anouilh's *Becket, or the Honor of God* (*regie* Kris Betz), with Demedts as the King and Werner Kopers as Thomas; Brecht's *Mr. Puntila and His Hired Man, Matti* (*regie* Paul Anrieu); and Miller's *The Crucible* (*regie* Walter Eysselinck). There were also a couple of popular comedies, plus Harold Pinter's *The Homecoming* (*regie* Demedts).

Albert Hanssens, who had been the company's *administratief-directeur* from 1965 to 1967, became the *directeur* in 1967, staying until 1973. While he continued the policy of balanced repertory, he had a special liking for Flemish writers and produced a number of their plays. He did not have quite the luck with his classics, however, which had marked the first two seasons. Most of the interesting things done in this era were modern: Chekhov's *The Three Sisters* (1968, *regie* Walter Eysselinck); José Triana's *The Night of the Assassins* (1968, *regie* Jef Demedts); Peter Nichols' *A Day in the Death of Joe Egg* (1969, *regie* Marcel de Stoop); Anouilh's *The Rehearsal* (1969, *regie* Roggen); Molière's *Les femmes savantes* (1969, *regie* de Stoop); Mart Crowley's *The Boys in the Band* (1969, *regie* Demedts); Alain Decaux's *The Rosenbergs Can Not Die* (1970, *regie* Demedts); Schiller's *Don Carlos* (1970, *regie* de Stoop); Anouilh's *Cher Antoine* (1971, *regie* Kopers); John Hopkins' *This Story of Yours* (1971, *regie* de Stoop); Peter Nichols' *Forget-Me-Not Lane* (1971, *regie* Kees van Iersel); Ibsen's *A Doll's House* (1972, *regie* Eysselinck), with Juchtmans as Nora; Pinter's *Old Times* (1972, *regie* Demedts); Cyril Buysse's *Driekkoning-enavond Epiphany* (1972, *regie* van der Berghe), with Blanka Heirman as Vrouw Cloet; Gaston-Marie Martens' *Paradijsvogels* (*Paradise Birds*, 1972, *regie* Demedts); Hugo Claus' *Interieur* (1973, *regie* Jean-Pierre de Decker); and Simon Gray's *Butley* (1973, *regie* Harry Kümel), with Kopers in the title role.

In 1973 the new director for the company became Walter Eysselinck, who had already had a number of striking successes as a *regisseur* with the company. Eysselinck's repertory was much the same as the repertories of his predecessors, although he used more modern British writers. He also pulled in *regisseurs* from outside the company, including some non-Belgian ones. This was a fairly good period for classics, as well as modern works, and the company was adaptable to a variety of styles from Shakespeare to American musicals. The best works done in the era were from a wide area: Jason Miller's *That Championship Season* (1973, *regie* Demedts); Molière's *Le misanthrope* (1973, *regie* Jo Dua), with Werner Kopers as Alceste; David Storey's *The Contractor* (1974, *regie* de Decker), with decor from the Royal Court Theatre production; Buysse's *Hetrecht van de sterkste* (*The Right of the Strongest*, 1974, *regie* van den Berghe); Shakespeare's *Richard II* (1974, *regie* Paul Anrieu), with Kopers in the title role; Nikolai Gogol's *The Inspector General* (1975, *regie* Radu Penciulescu); and Peter Shaffer's *Equus* (1975, *regie* Eysselinck), with Demedts as Dysart.

In 1976 Eysselinck left for a post at the University of Pittsburgh and was replaced by another university man, Jacques van Schoor. The choice of the repertory was esoteric and not balanced. Complaints appeared in the press stating that van Schoor did not have enough practical knowledge to run a theatre. The most popular works done in this era were decidedly modern: Gerhart Hauptmann's *The Beaver Coat* (1976, *regie* van den Berghe), Per Olov Enquist's *The Night of the Tribaden* (1977, *regie* de Decker), and Buysse's *Het gezin van Paemel* (*The Paemel Family*, 1977, *regie* van den Berghe).

Jef Demedts, who had been an actor and *regisseur* for the company, became its *directeur* on the first day of 1978. So far this had been a very good period. Greater effort has been made to push productions toward the ensemble spirit. The repertory still remains part classic, part modern, though modern plays are much more in the ascendancy.

Important physical changes have been made in the theatre itself, which has recently been blessed with a new lighting system. A renovation of the auditorium has cut the seating from a tight one thousand to a more comfortable seven hundred fifty. Among the recent successes for the company, one could number the Peter Weiss adaptation of Kafka's *The Trial* (1978, *regie* Walter Tillemans), with Demedts as Joseph K.; Brecht's *The Good Woman of Setzuan* (1978, *regie* Walter Tillemans); Mino Roli and Lucian Vincenzoni's *Sacco and Vanzetti*; Carlo Goldoni's *The Chioggian Brawls* (1978, *regie* Walter Moeremans); Molière's *Le bourgeois gentilhomme* (1979, *regie* Rafael Rodriguez); Ibsen's *Ghosts* (1979, *regie* Ulrich Grieff), with Chris Boni as Mrs. Alving; Chekhov's *The Seagull* (1980, *regie* de Decker), with Boni as Arkadina; and Martin Sherman's *Bent* (1981, *regie* de Decker).

The Netherlands "Toneel Gent" season consists of thirteen works, of which ten are mounted by the local company, with one each from the Flemish civic companies in Brussels and Antwerp and one other from another company, possibly from Holland. The company numbers sixteen actors and eight actresses, with guests as necessary. There are generally seven *regisseurs* in a season, four of whom are permanent (and also act) and three guests. Plays are selected by a committee, which includes the *directeur*, the dramaturge, and members of the company who also have some voice in selecting the *regisseur*. No *regisseur* is ever forced to do a play he does not like. The company has its own technical staff, headed by André Fonteyne with Andrei Ivaneanu (who is from Romania and very good) as its chief designer. Its annual subsidy runs to 38 million BF which comes from the city of Ghent and the province of Oost-Vlaanderen. Most plays run about two weeks, with those playing engagements in other theatres (Brussels and Antwerp) running longer. The company also plays every production in several other towns close to Ghent. In addition, there are a number of special performances from many companies (both from Belgium and Holland), which play single performances during the season. All these activities are covered in its newspaper, the *NTG Nieuws*.

The company believes that the theatre should be for everybody. International as well as Flemish in scope, the company therefore tries to please a wide range of spectators and always includes a couple of popular comedies in the repertory. Even so these are not always the best-sellers of the season. The repertory of the company encompasses a variety of plays, with the committee that chooses plays reading many scripts each season. The company generally does at least one Flemish work a year, with the plays of Hugo Claus (who has done some translations for the company) most often repeated. Plays with a social background are most common.

One of the company's best characteristics is the ensemble spirit that exists both backstage and on. Many members of the acting company and its administrators have been with the troupe for years. Its main function is to serve Ghent, a city famous for its visual arts. With the Netherlands "Toneel Gent," Ghent becomes a city famous for its theatrical art as well.

LEON M. AUFDEMBERGE
(Thanks to Rudi Lekens,
Zaekelijk Leider for the company)

ROYAL DUTCH THEATRE
(Koninklijke Nederlandsce Schouwberg)
Komedienplaats, Antwerp, Belgium

The Royal Dutch Theatre was founded in 1853 when two amateur groups, De Dageraad and De Scheldegalm, came together to form the National Toneel (the National Theatre). The person responsible for this amalgamation was Victor Driessens, who played the "hoofdrol" (leading role) in the company's first play, *De Dronkaard* (*The Drunkard*) by P. F. Van Kerckhoven. The first director of the group was August Leytens, and the first performance was held in the Théâtre des Varietés on the Mechelsplein.

The first several seasons featured the usual nineteenth-century popular fare and considerable touring, including a summer season in Rotterdam beginning in 1862. By the 1870s the group was strong enough to begin to play a more classical repertory, opening its season in 1870 with Victor Hugo's *Hernani*. A new theatre was built especially for the company on the Kipdarpburg (the center of the town), opening in 1874. At the same time the company took a new name, the Nederlandsce Schouwberg. By the 1880s, under the direction of Frans van Daeselaer, a real surge took place in the production of the classics, especially Shakespearean plays. The company mounted strong productions of *Julius Caesar*, *The Winter's Tale*, *The Merchant of Venice*, *Romeo and Juliet*, and *Hamlet*, with Jan Dilis as the Dane. In 1887 came the first play by the Dutch writer Joost van der Vondel, *De Leewendalers* (*The Lion Sellers*). Several actresses in the company attained some prominence, including Catherina Beersman and Julie Verstraet—the Flemish Sarah Bernhardt.

By the late 1890s the theatre came under the influence of the Théâtre Libre in Paris and Die Freie Bühne in Berlin. More Ibsen plays began to be performed, as well as works of the new crop of German playwrights. In 1903 a signal honor was given the company, when the King's Cabinet allowed the company to prefix its name with the title Koninklijke (royal). Louis Bertrijn became director in 1912 and remained until 1920. He had a very difficult time, as many of the male members of the company left Holland at the outbreak of World War I (Holland was a neutral country). All the same, there were several notable productions in this era, especially that of *The Merchant of Venice* (1918) with Pier Janssens. By the 1920s, under the regime of Jan Oscar de Gruyter (1920–1929), the theatre came under the influence of Max Reinhardt and more emphasis was given to the staging of plays. In addition, more Flemish plays began to be produced, such as works by Herman Tierlinck, Willen Putnam, Gaston Martens, and others. De Gruyter pushed the number of plays from six to nine per season. In the 1930s there was a string of directors, the most prominent of whom was Joris Diels, who had been a *regisseur* with the company. In 1934 the group moved to a different theatre, an older house that for years had been the home of the French company in town and that had been designed by Bruno Bourla in 1834. This is still the home of the company.

In the 1930s the group adopted a policy of a repertory of partly classical and partly modern works. The modern include some Flemish works, a policy it still follows today.

The theatre continued to perform during the German occupation of the 1940s, and in 1942 the city of Antwerp voted to subsidize the group for the first time in its history. During the war, the playhouse was badly damaged but still usable. After the war, in 1946, the theatre was officially made a "National Toneel van Belgie" (National Theatre of Belgium), under the directorship of Firmin Matier, who was its director until 1963. In the following year a studio was opened in conjunction with the main theatre to play more experimental works, under the leadership of Herman Tierlinck. In 1955 the theatre toured to Paris with two plays written in Dutch. The repertory of the 1950s included many writers who had been forbidden by the Nazis, with Brecht especially becoming a house regular. Two of the greatest successes of the 1950s were Ben Rayaard's productions of *A Midsummer Night's Dream* (1954) and *Peer Gynt* (1956). In 1967 the name "National Theatre" had spread to other theatres and the company decided to return to its old name.

During the last few years, the group has staged a number of excellent productions, including Shaw's *Caesar and Cleopatra* (1960), Jos Gever's *Slissne Bompa* (1964), Brecht's *The Good Woman of Setzuan* (1962), Herman Heyerman's *Schakels* (*Chains*, 1964), Molière's *Tartuffe* (1964), Miller's *After the Fall* (1965), Shakespeare's *King Lear* (1966), Hugo Claus' *Vrijdag* (*Friday*, 1970), Sartre/Euripides' *The Trojan Women*, Georg Büchner's *Danton's Death*

(1977), and Shakespeare's *The Merchant of Venice* (1979), with Don de Gruyter, the current director of the company, as Shylock.

By 1968 it was clear that the old theatre was inadequate for the company, and plans were formulated to open a new one; these plans were canceled because of lack of funds. A new theatre, however, was built in the early 1980s. The new house, designed by architects Verbruggen-Appel-Hahn, is one of the best equipped playhouses in Europe with an excellent large theatre and two smaller ones.

The company has twenty-two actors and eleven actresses. This smallness guarantees an actor or actress will play at least one good part each season. The director generally chooses the season and the *regisseurs*, assisted by the members of his staff, but, in honor of the 125th anniversary of the theatre, the 1978–1979 season was chosen by the entire company. The company usually does nine plays a season, each play being performed for three weeks, with popular works occasionally returning the following season. In addition, the company tours to Flemish-speaking Belgium (Ghent, Louvain, Courtrai, and so on) and occasionally into Holland (Rotterdam and Amsterdam). Sometimes the company plays in Brussels for the large Flemish-speaking population. This theatre company is very popular within the city in which it makes its home. It has a large budget (80 million Belgian francs), with the state contributing 30 million, the city 5 million, and the remainder coming from the box office and the cities in which the company plays.

The theatre likes to think of itself as providing the best for everyone, with the season balanced to provide for a wide picture of drama. Shakespeare and Brecht are probably the most popular writers with the group. The theatre holds a great attraction for young people; it provides special low rates to make attendance easier for them. Subscriptions are also available in a variety of plans for those who like to attend the theatre on a regular basis.

The theatre maintains close contact with the people of the city of Antwerp, as well as with various organizations of the city, in order to understand what the people are thinking. For all of these reasons the Royal Dutch Theatre has attuned itself to the life of its present city.

LEON M. AUFDEMBERGE

East Germany

INTRODUCTION

All theatre in East Germany is controlled by the state. Commercial theatre in any style was abolished with the founding of the Democratic Republic of Germany in 1949. While state control has meant a number of significant differences from theatre in Western Europe, especially in terms of repertory, there are many resemblances to other German-speaking theatres.

The East German theatre is very much a *regisseur*'s (stage manager's or stage director's) theatre, but it is not as experimental as the West German theatre. East Germany has stage work from theatre to theatre, but the concept of a freelance *regisseur* does not exist, with most apt to be identified with one house and to have less mobility than in West Germany. Some East German *regisseurs* work in other German-speaking theatres; some go "out" to other European countries and even the United States. There are uncomfortable signs that the East German government may be in the process of ending this cultural emigration. Stage directors from capitalist countries rarely work in East German houses, though it has happened. Most often *regisseurs* from other Socialist countries are invited as guests.

There are not nearly as many theatres in East Germany as there are in West Germany simply because only one-quarter of the East German populace lives in large cities. East Germany has about 80 theatres, whereas West Germany has 225.

East Germany also tends to spend less on its theatre than West Germany does. Approximately 80 percent of the West German theatre budget comes from subsidy, whereas in East Germany the average runs to about a fifty-fifty split between box office and subsidies (though figures are exceedingly difficult to obtain). This means that most East German theatres tend to stage fewer productions per year and to keep them in the repertory longer, many remaining for years. In contrast, the average life of a production in West Germany, Austria, and German-speaking Switzerland is one to two years.

Most East German houses are comfortable, especially those outside Berlin.

The East German government has worked overtime to make life in the provinces (and this means theatres as well) as pleasant as possible. Most theatre houses have bars, and during the intermissions, couples circle the foyers in a traditional ritual. Tickets are cheap (rather cheaper than a film) and, except for hot tickets, need not be bought ahead. Frequently, tickets are purchased for East German workers and given gratis. However, as the work day in East Germany is long and workers must rise early, many workers skip the theatre. Thus, a house may be *ausverkauft* (sold out) and still have banks of empty seats. The East German theatre management has learned to live with this situation.

In East German houses, too, despite being *regisseur*-centered theatres, the intendant (general manager) seems to have more clout and to set the style for the theatre. Houses in East Germany do tend to have less diversity than those in the West, particularly in the matter of style of production. Productions in many East German houses have a quality of sameness to them, though some (as at Rostock or the Volksbühne in Berlin) present a variety of approaches.

The greatest difference in the East German houses, however, is found in the business of repertory. After 1945 many houses in the Russian sector of occupation tried a variety of approaches to the problem of repertory. After 1949 a good deal of drama became lost to the East German playgoer. No theatre has a written policy forbidding certain types of plays, though some (absurdist drama being the most conspicuous example) are strictly *verboten*. There are occasional productions of playwrights from capitalist countries (Edward Albee, Arthur Miller, Tennessee Williams, and Lillian Hellman are the most often done of American playwrights), but only if they are sufficiently critical of American life. Surprisingly, American musicals are popular, and practically every East German house has done the Alan Jay Lerner/Frederick Lowe *My Fair Lady*. Only the theatre at Rostock has a consistent policy of doing American plays.

The average East German is apt to see plays from three areas: the classics (Shakespeare, Schiller, and Goethe being the big three); Marxist drama from contemporary East German playwrights (with Brecht leading the group); and plays from other Socialist countries. Contemporary Russian playwrights are *de rigueur* in most East German houses, but they are probably the least popular playwrights in East Germany. Most East German playgoers prefer the dramatists of the older generation, especially Gorky and Chekhov.

How good is East German theatre? This is a difficult question to answer because, as in West Germany, there is a wide variety of houses. On the whole, East German houses tend to be rather conservative in staging plays, and many are not yet out of the post-Stanislavsky style (Leipzig, for example). In the more liberal houses, there is little difference between what is staged from one Germany to the other. Both theatres complain about the lack of great *regisseurs*, and the East Germans have an acute shortage of stage technicians.

Life is very secure for the East German actor. Once an actor is hired by a company, unless he or she is abysmally bad, the actor is there to stay. Of course, many actors who work in the provinces want to go to Berlin because that is where the television and movie industries are creating a lucrative pull for the actor. Most intendants in the provinces work overtime to make life as pleasant as possible for the company, though this is often a losing battle.

East German theatre does exist—Marxist oriented, rather conservative in style, somewhat limited in repertory, but perhaps (because tickets are cheaper) more accessible to the average playgoer than on the other side of the wall.

LEON M. AUFDEMBERGE

BERLIN ENSEMBLE
(Berliner Ensemble)
Bertolt-Brecht-Platz
104 Berlin, East Germany

When Bertolt Brecht left Germany in 1933 (it was the day after The Reichstag fire), along with his wife, Helene Weigel, and his son, Stefan, he probably knew he would one day return. The years of exile were spent in various places including Santa Monica, California (1941–1947), where he hated the Nazis, Hollywood's commercialism (which he never cracked), and Thomas Mann, in that order. In July 1947 came the Josef Losey/Charles Laughton version of *Galileo*, and in October of the same year came Brecht's funny/unfunny testimony before the Committee on Un-American Activities. Brecht left the United States for Europe the next month, going first to Paris and then to Zurich, looking for a place in which to light. The first postwar production he staged was his own adaptation of the Sophocles/Hölderlin *Antigone* (assisted by Caspar Neher), done in Chur, Switzerland, in 1948, with Helene Weigel in the title role. On October 27, 1948, Brecht and Weigel arrived in Berlin (the Soviet sector), and Brecht set to work at the Deutsches Theater (where he had lazily worked from 1922 to 1924). There he thought up projects, and attempted to get actors, some exiled in America (including Peter Lorre), to return to Germany to play for him.

The first production Brecht staged for the Deutsches Theater, which was the beginning of the Berliner Ensemble, was his own *Mutter Courage und ihre Kinder* (*Mother Courage and Her Children*), which opened on January 11, 1949, with Weigel as Anna Fierling and Angelika Hurwicz as Kattrin, and with Erich Engel assisting Brecht. If one were to select the most important production in any German-speaking country since World War II, it probably would be this one. Even critics who did not appreciate Brecht agreed that everything was in line, with Weigel especially well cast.

The first actual production for the Berliner was an Engel/Brecht production of *Herr Puntila und sein Knecht Matti* (*Mr. Puntila and His Hired Man, Matti*, November 8, 1949), with Leonard Steckel as Puntila. During the first seasons, Brecht brought in a series of actors whom he had admired before the war to be part of his company, ensuring them adequate rehearsal time (and time to experiment), plus the chance to take productions around East Germany. Among the productions done in the opening seasons (played at the Deutsches Theater) were Gorky's *Wassa Schlesnowa* (*Vassa Zheleznova, regie* Berthold Viertel), with Therese Giehse in the title role; the Brecht/Gorky *Die Mutter* (*The Mother,* 1951, *regie* Brecht), with Weigel as Pelagea; a second production of *Mutter Courage* (1951, *regie* Brecht/Engel); Brecht's adaptations of Gerhart Hauptmann's *Biberpelz* (*Beaver Coat,* 1951) and *Der rote Hahn* (*The Red Hen*), with the production by Egon Monk and Giehse as Frau Wolff (later Frau Fieltz); Heinrich von Kleist's *Der zerbrochene Krug* (*The Broken Jug,* 1952, *regie* Giehse), with Erwin Geschonneck as Adam; Goethe's *Urfaust* (1952, *regie* Monk); Brecht's *Die Gewehr der Frau Carrar* (*Mrs. Carrar's Rifles,* 1952, *regie* Monk assisted by Brecht), with Weigel as Carrar; the Seghers/Brecht/Besson *Der Prozess der Jean d'Arc zu Rouen 1431* (*The Trial of Joan of Arc at Rouen in 1431, regie* Benno Besson), with Käthe Reichel as Joan; and the premiere of Erwin Strittmatter's *Katzgraben* (*Cat's Ditch,* 1953, *regie* Brecht).

On March 19, 1954, Brecht moved his company into its own theatre, the Theater am Schiffbauerdamm, where he had seen the premiere of his and Kurt Weill's *Die Dreigroschenoper* (*The Threepenny Opera*) in 1928; it was in this theatre, full of plaster cherubs, that Brecht was to revolutionize much of twentieth-century theatre.

About this time, Brecht formulated nine principles in his "Some Characteristics of the Berliner Ensemble" which would govern the Berliner:

1. To show society is changeable.

2. To show human nature is changeable.

3. To show how human nature is dependent on social structure.

4. To show conflicts as social conflicts.

5. To show characters with a pure contradiction.

6. To show the development of characters' circumstances as discontinuous (erratic).

7. To make the looking at the dialectic pleasurable.

8. To lift up the achievement of the classic in a dialectical sense.

9. To produce a unity of realism and poetry.

A great deal has been written about Brecht's methodology in both rehearsals (lengthy with much discussion) and devices he used to achieve what he called *Verfremdung* (estrangement, but usually translated alienation), which was to be the final result for the spectator at this "epic theatre." Among the devices used to achieve *Verfremdung* were lantern slides, which told the plot to come (to get rid of suspense); the absence of colored light, which Brecht had despised as contributing to falsity; and his famous half curtain which let the audience "see but not too much." The great revolution, however, was not in staging, but in the acting style which threw off the excessive emoting that had marked (marred might be a better word) much of earlier German playing. Performances were arrived at analytically with great choice of details, with Brecht rather anti-Stanislavsky (though grudgingly admiring him). The result was an acting of great selectivity and coolness played by an astonishing company that included Helene

Weigel, Ernst Busch, Ekkehard Schell, and Norbert Christian. Brecht also paid close attention to the music he used (which was extensive); the most often used composers were Paul Dessau, Hans Eisler, and Hans-Dieter Hosalla.

During the next few years, Brecht worked with his company in honing style and in training other *regisseurs* to continue his work. He emphasized touring policies and going outside the German-speaking world, with the first international recognition coming to the Berliner in 1960 in Paris. Brecht also encouraged a number of young playwrights to become part of the company.

In the opening years at the Schiffbauerdamm, the company produced the following: Molière's *Don Juan* (1954), in Brecht's adaptation (*regie* Benno Besson), which was the first production in the new theatre; a Chinese folk play by Lon Ding, Tschu Dschin-Now, and Tschang Fan, called *Miller for the Eight* (1954, *regie* Manfred Wekwerth, adaptation by Elisabeth Hauptmann and Wekwerth); Brecht's production of his own *Der Kaukasische Kreide Kreis* (*The Caucasian Chalk Circle*, 1954), with Hurwicz as Grusche and Busch as Azdak; Johannes Becher's *Winterschlacht* (*Winter Battle*, 1955, *regie* Brecht/Wekwerth); Brecht's adaptation of George Farquhar's *The Recruiting Officer*, called *Pauken und Trompeten* (*Drums and Trumpets*, 1955, *regie* Besson); another Chinese play adapted by Yuan Miau-tse (further adapted by Peter Palitzsch and Carl Weber), called *The Day of the Great Learned Wu* (1955, *regie* Palitzsch/ Weber); and John Millington Synge's *The Playboy of the Western World* (*regie* Palitzsch/Wekwerth), with Heinz Schubert as Christy.

Brecht died on August 14, 1956, and Weigel (who had been the intendant from the beginning) took over the running of the company alone. Brecht died on the eve of the company's first engagement in London, where he admonished the troupe in a practical move to play lightly. The mid-1950s and the 1960s were a time of upheaval not only at the Berliner, but also in East Germany, and the company lost many of its mainstays. It kept two of its major designers, whom Brecht had used repeatedly, Karl von Appen and Caspar Neher, though Teo Otto stopped designing for the Berliner after Brecht's death. Certain of the trusted *regisseurs*, notably Egon Monk and Peter Palitzsch, moved westward, with Besson deserting in the late 1950s and Wekwerth going to the Deutsches Theater at the end of the 1960s.

The beginning of the 1950s, however, was quite fruitful, with a series of productions which Brecht had helped to plan: Brecht's *Das Leben des Galilei* (*The Life of Galileo*, 1957, *regie* Engel), with Ernst Busch in the title role; *Furcht und Elend des Dritten Reich* (*Fear and Misery in the Third Reich*, 1957, *regie* Lothar Bellog, Peter Palitzsch, Käthe Rülicke, Konrad Swinarski, and Carl M. Weber); *Der gute Mensch von Sezuan* (*The Good Woman of Setzuan*, 1957, *regie* Besson), with Käthe Reichel in the dual role of Shen Tel/Shui Ta; Vsevolod Vishnevsky's *The Optimistic Tragedy* (1958, *regie* Wekwerth/Palitzsch); *Der aufhaltsame Aufstieg des Arturo Ui* (*The Resistible Rise of Arturo Ui*, 1959, *regie* Wekwerth/Palitzsch), with Schalla as a Chaplinesque Ui; and Brecht's *Die*

Dreigroschenoper (*The Threepenny Opera*, 1960, *regie* Engel), with Wolf Kaiser as Mackie Messer.

In the early 1960s the company began to move toward new script and stagings of some of Brecht's lesser known works, frequently done by some of East Germany's new, university-trained *regisseurs*. In addition, there were evenings made up of some of Brecht's learning pieces, short pieces on Marxist themes. Typical of the new scripts was Helmut Baierl's *Frau Flinz*, staged by the Wekwerth/Palitzsch team in 1961 and then taken up by practically every East German house outside Berlin. The piece was an answer to *Mutter Courage*, who learned nothing from her condition, while Frau Flinz learned to become a good Marxist, with Weigel incidentally playing both characters. Other productions in the 1960s and into the 1970s include Brecht's *Die Tage der Commune* (*The Day of the Commune*, 1962, *regie* Wekwerth/Joachim Tenschert) and *Schweyk im Zweiten Weltkrieg* (*Schweyk in the Second World War*, 1962, *regie* Erich Engel/Wolfgang Pintzka); the Brecht/Shakespeare *Coriolan* (1964, *regie* Wekwerth/Tenschert), with Schall as Coriolan and Weigel as Volumnia; Heinar Kipphardt's *In der Sache des J. Robert Oppenheimer* (*In the Case of J. Robert Oppenheimer*, 1965, *regie* Wekwerth/Tenschert); Sean O'Casey's *Purple Dust* (1965, *regie* Hans-Georg Simmgen); Brecht's *Mann ist Mann* (*A Man's a Man*, 1967, *regie* Uta Birnbaum) and *Die Heilige's Johanna der Schlachthöfe* (*Saint Joan of the Stockyards*, 1968, *regie* Wekwerth/Tenschert), with Hanne Hiob (Brecht's daughter) in the title role; Peter Weiss' *Vietnam Diskurs* (*Vietnam Discourse*, 1968, *regie* Ruth Berghaus); Aeschylus' *Seven Against Thebes* (1969, *regie* Manfred Karge/Matthias Langhoff); Büchner's *Woyzeck* (1970, *regie* Hans-Dieter Hosalla); and O'Casey's *Cock-a-Doodle Dandy* (1971, *regie* Werner Hecht).

In April 1971 came the Berliner production of Brecht's early *Im Dickicht der Städte* (*In the Jungle of the Cities*), staged by Ruth Berghaus. Berghaus, Weigel's assistant, was appointed intendant when Weigel died on May 6, 1971. When Berghaus came, there were problems in the company; when she left, they were worse but not necessarily of her making. Weigel had problems at the end of her era in noncommunication—she chose to lock herself in her office, and the company seemed frozen out. Berghaus intensified this situation, which caused factions, with the Brecht family generally on one side, various parties on the other, and the company split into two divisions. As one actor said, "It was hard to know during the [Berghaus] era on any given day who was speaking to whom."

Perhaps Berghaus' main mistake was in trying to remake the company, specifically in trying to find various styles to fit the works the company did. Then too, Berghaus' choice of plays seemed arbitrary. Both of these were contrary to what the Berliner had done previously and added to the problems Berghaus inherited. It was small wonder that the years from 1971 to 1977 were bad for the Berliner, though not all of it was Berghaus' fault.

Nonetheless, there were a series of rather good productions during that period.

Some of the more controversial ones (the Wedekind and Strindberg works in particular) lasted only a short while in the repertory, although they drew fairly well. Among the important works staged during the Berghaus era were the usual Brecht: a second *Das Leben des Galilei* (*The Life of Galileo*, 1971, *regie* Fritz Bennewitz, with Wolfgang Heinz in the title role; *Turandot, oder Der Kongress des Weisswascher* (*Turandot, or the Congress of Whitewashers*, 1972, *regie* Peter Kupke/Wolfgang Pintzka); a new *Die Mutter* (*The Mother*, 1974, *regie* Berghaus), with Felicitas Ritsch in Weigel's old role; *Leben des Eduard II von England* (*Life of Edward II of England*, 1974, *regie* Schall); a new *Puntila* (1975, *regie* Kupke), with Schall as Puntila; and a return visit to *Der Kaukasische Kreide Kreis* (*The Caucasian Chalk Circle*, 1976, *regie* Kupke), with Schall as Azdak. There was also a series of productions of non-Brechtian plays and, while these were very well done for the most part, some of the choices of plays seemed curious for the Berliner: the premiere of Peter Hacks' *Omphale* (1972, *regie* Berghaus); Shaw's *Mrs. Warren's Profession* (1973, *regie* Pintzka), with Gisela May as Kitty; Frank Wedekind's *Frühlings Erwachen* (*Spring's Awakening*, 1974, *regie* B. K. Tragelehn); and a highly erotic Strindberg's *Miss Julie* (1975, *regie* B. K. Tragelehn), with Jutta Hoffmann in the title role. In April 1977 Berghaus left the Berliner to pursue her career as an opera *regisseur* (she was married to Paul Dessau), mainly in West Germany.

Berghaus was succeeded by Manfred Wekwerth and with him came Joachim Tenschert, who had worked closely with him as chief dramaturge at the Berliner from 1958 to 1970. Since 1977 they have done a number of co-productions of Brecht productions which are reevaluations, entirely new and not repeats of earlier productions. Several of the earlier productions at the Berliner had been immortalized with rather complete pictorial records in *Modell Buchs*. While these are fascinating visual records of these productions, Wekwerth and Tenschert have not bowed to them. In the Wekwerth era there have been repeats of Brecht plays done in earlier seasons: *Das Leben des Galilei* (1978, *regie* Wekwerth/Tenschert), with Schall as Galileo; *Mutter Courage und ihre Kinder* (1978, *regie* Peter Kupke; *Mann ist Mann* (1981, *regie* Konrad Zschiedrich); and *Turandot* (1981, *regie* Wekwerth/Tenschert); plus the first production of a play that was one of Brecht's favorites, *Die Ausnahme und die Regel* (*The Exception and the Rule*, 1980, *regie* Carlos Medina of the Institut für Schauspielregie).

There has also been a series of non-Brecht works. Wekwerth has done rather better than Berghaus in that the plays all have a Berliner stamp on them, with something of a unified style. In the last few seasons, these have included Dario Fo's *Don't Pay, Don't Pay!* (*regie* Zschiedrich); the premiere of Volker Braun's *Grosser Frieden* (*Greater Peace*, 1980, *regie* Wekwerth/Tenschert); and Claus Hammel's *Blaue Pferd auf rotem Gras* (*Blue Horse on Red Grass*, 1980, *regie* Christoph Schroth), plus others.

Each season the Berliner presents four to five new plays and revivals of perhaps fifteen works from previous seasons. Plays are carried over from season to season until literally the public no longer comes. Brecht's plays form over one-half the repertory. The choice of non-Brecht works in the Wekwerth era has been fairly liberal, with some surprises such as Shakespeare's *The Taming of the Shrew* which is currently part of the Berliner repertory. The choice of new plays and the continued presentation of Brecht's early works are sources of discussion among the administrators of the Berliner. The acting company numbers around forty-four men and twenty-four women, with guests (mostly from the nearby Deutsches Theater). In addition, the theatre has three dramaturges including Tenschert and Baierl, and a full technical staff with about 280 people. The theatre publishes a leaflet called "Mitteilungen und Notizen," which publicizes events in the theatre and the nearby Brecht Haus. There is also a canteen for all the workers. Laurence Olivier once observed that the Berliner was not so much a theatre as it was a "way of life."

The company's theatre began life in 1892 as the Neues Theater (architect Heinrich Seeling), but is currently known as the Theater am Schiffbauerdamm. The theatre holds around seven hundred people. The company also plays in a foyer and has a Probebühne (rehearsal stage) for experimental works, something Brecht wanted at the Berliner but never had. The company has done some work on television and has made records, but, more importantly, several of its important productions have been filmed. Thus, later ages can see what the playing of the Berliner was like in its truly great days of the 1950s and 1960s.

In the bar on the first floor (American second floor) is an extensive map, indicating where the Berliner has played. In its first seasons, it played engagements in East and West Germany, Austria (1950), and Poland (1952). Later, the company went to Paris (1954, 1955, 1957, 1960, and 1971), London (1965), and the Soviet Union (1957 and 1968), as well as Sweden, Finland, Italy, and the Eastern Bloc nations. Its most recent trip to the West was to the Theatre in the Burg in Vienna in 1978 in an exchange of productions. Recently, it turned down invitations to tour both Venezuela and the United States simply because it did not have enough money.

The company bases its decisions on the question "What would Brecht have done?" which is a long way from what Berghaus stressed. The company still spends a good deal of rehearsal time (ten to twelve weeks) discussing how a role should be played. Curiously, however, the company rarely discusses *Verfremdung* any more, for it is more or less taken for granted. At the end, Brecht himself saw the *Verfremdung Effekt* more in the plays than in the staging.

"How good is the Berliner?" is the most frequently asked question of theatre visitors to Berlin. Since Wekwerth's return to the company, the answer is "Excellent," but it is obviously not the company theatre of giants it once was. Still, enough remains on a good evening, and when a play like *Mutter Courage und ihre Kinder* is playing, to make a trip "over the wall" is not only desirable but also mandatory.

LEON M. AUFDEMBERGE
(With thanks to Joachim
Tenschert and his staff)

CITY THEATRE OF KARL-MARX-STADT
(Städtische Theatre Karl-Marx-Stadt)
Theater Platz 2
Karl-Marx-Stadt, East Germany

Theatre came to Chemnitz (the original name of Karl-Marx-Stadt) at the end of the fifteenth century with religious plays. In the sixteenth and seventeenth centuries there were traveling opera companies as well. By the end of the eighteenth century, a local rector by the name of Hager pushed to have new German dramatists, notably Gotthold Lessing, played in the city. The first important actor to work in the city was Johann David Beil in the 1770s. Shakespeare began to be played with some regularity in the city around 1800.

The first permanent theatre was built in 1805, followed by another, the Atkientheatre, in 1838 (architect John Traugott Heining). The work chosen to open the second theatre was a piece called *Des Fluches Losung* (*The Loosening of the Curse*), with the first head of the theatre being G. Kramer, later a friend of Richard Wagner. The same season the theatre company performed Goethe's *Faust* (*regie* Philip Bruer).

During most of the nineteenth century, the Atkientheatre was a convenient stopping place for a series of companies or guests, such as Wilhelmina Schroder-Devrient (1839) and Emil Devrient (1840). In 1862 the Aktientheater became the Stadtheater and three years later was completely renovated by the noted Berlin architect Eduard Titz. Through the 1860s to the 1880s, there were many guest appearances by prominent artists, such as Adalbert Matkowsky, Friedrich Haase, Pauline Ulrich, Franziska Ellmenreich, and Clara Ziegler. There were also local favorites who were building a reputation, such as Helene Odilon, Wilhelm Hasemann, and Paula Wolf, all of whom went on to larger theatres after Chemnitz. The first Ibsen play in Chemnitz came in 1878 with *The Pillars of Society*.

The first important intendant for the city was Louis Schindler (1883–1889), who made the theatre's reputation by the number of guest artists he imported. Schindler was succeeded by Richard Jesse, who was much loved and much respected, with the town generally referring to him as "Vater" ("Father"). Jesse stayed a long while (1889–1912) and saw great changes in his era. His early seasons were heavy with classics, and by the end of his era there were frequent productions of writers such as Ibsen, Hauptmann, and Hermann Sudermann. He also brought a number of guest artists to the city, many from the Burg in Vienna. The productions Jesse remembered at the end of his era included the following (all staged by Jesse): Shakespeare's *A Midsummer Night's Dream* (1889, Jesse's first production); Schiller's *Don Carlos* (1894) and *Die Jungfrau von Orleans* (*The Maid from Orleans*, 1894), with Marie Pospischel (from the Burg) in the title role; Ibsen's *A Doll's House* (1896), with Marie Reinhofer as Nora; Schiller's *Mary Stuart* (1897); Hauptmann's *Biberpelz* (*Beaver Coat*, 1899); O. E. Hartleben's *Rosenmontag* (*Rosy Monday*, 1901); Shakespeare's *Othello* (1906), with Adalbert Matkowsky in the title role; and Lessing's *Emilia Galotti* (1908). On September 1, 1909, a new opera house opened (architect Richard Möbius) in the presence of King Friedrich August of Sachsen, with Schiller's *Wallensteins Lager* (*Wallenstein's Camp*) and Act Three of Wagner's *Die Meistersinger*. In 1912 Jesse retired with the firm conviction he had done as much for the theatre in Chemnitz as he could.

Jesse was followed by Richard Tauber, father of the famous tenor (who was born in the city); like Jesse he would have a long tenure (1912–1930). Under his leadership the Chemnitz became an important theatre city for both plays and opera. Tauber continued the guest actor policy, but he had frequent and very important guest *regisseurs* as well. He also had a first-rate designer in Felix Loch, who was one of the first Germans to make extensive use of projected scenery. In 1925 the old Atkientheatre was renovated (architect Adolf Linnebach), opening with Heinrich von Kleist's *Der zerbrochene Krug* (*The Broken Jug*, *regie* Ludwig Seipp), with Karl Weining as Adam. In the early part of Tauber's period the company was noted for its playing of classics, with such works as Shakespeare's *Hamlet* (1915), with Weining in the title role; Goethe's *Faust* (1916), and Schiller's *Don Carlos* (1918, *regie* Alfred Fischer). At the end, however, it was the modern plays that were most admired and written about, many staged by some of the most famous *regisseurs* in Germany: Georg Kaiser's *Nebeneinander* (*Side by Side*, 1925, *regie* George Braatz); Walter Hasanclever's *Ein besserer Herr* (*A Better Man*, 1927, *regie* Heinz Pabst); Hauptmann's *Die Weber* (*The Weavers*, 1928, *regie* Leopold Jessner); Alfred Neumann's *Der Patriot* (1928, *regie* Pabst); Brecht's *Die Dreigroschenoper* (*The Threepenny Opera*, 1929, *regie* Pabst); the two Oedipus plays of Sophocles (1929, *regie* Jessner), with Karl Heinz Stein as Oedipus; and Carl Zuckmayer's *Katharina Knie* (1930, *regie* Seipp).

Heinz Hartmann took over from 1930 to 1933. He saw the changing times in Germany, and his era saw more classics, including his own production of Goethe's *Iphigenia auf Tauris* (1931), which was nicely reviewed in the Berlin papers. Chemnitz was one of the first cities in Germany to see Joseph Goebbels' ill-written play, *Der Wanderer* (*The Wanderer*, 1932, *regie* Robert Rohde). During the next era, the theatre company at Chemnitz was noted for its devotion to the Nazi cause.

During the era of National Socialism there was an antifascist underground in the city. The Chemnitz, however, was a dutiful company with a series of heads during this period: Karl Heinz Stein (1933–1935), Walter Pittschau (1935–1938), Hermann Schaffner (1938–1943), and Richard Rückert (1943–1944), all of whom kept fairly close to the policies laid down in Berlin. The major plus during the era was the acting company, which included Johannes Arpe, Oskar Kaesler, Karl Heinz Stein, and Gustav Wehrle. The repertory of the company was almost totally limited to German classics or "acceptable" modern ones. Those receiving most publicity were: Friedrich Hebbel's *Agnes Bernauer* (1934, *regie* Stein) and *Die Niebelungen* (1935, *regie* Pittschau); Raimund's *Die Verschwender* (*The Prodigal*, 1936, *regie* Otto Kastner); Schiller's *Die Räuber* (*The Robbers*, 1937, *regie* Karl Weining); Goethe's *Egmont* (1938, *regie* George Kiesau), which celebrated the one hundredth anniversary of the founding of the theatre, with Paul Hartmann in the title role; Shaw's *The Doctor's Dilemma* (1939, *regie* Benna Hattesen); G. Barmeister's *Kaiser Konstantines Taufer* (*Kaiser Konstantine's Baptism*, 1941, *regie* Schaffner); Goethe's *Stella* (1942); Hauptmann's *Rose Bernd* (1942); and Hebbel's *Agnes Bernauer* (1943, all the last *regie* Stein). In the last year of the war, the opera house was severely damaged, and the old theatre (which dated from 1838) was destroyed.

The next production of a play in Chemnitz came on July 21, 1945, with Klabund's (Alfred Henschke) *Kreidekreis* (*Circle of Chalk*, *regie* Johannes Arpe), in the local gymnasium. The first head of the company was Karl Görs, with Oskar Kaesler as head of the theatre. The company's repertory in these years was not far different from today's: classics interspersed with Socialist drama, with Görs one of the first intendants after World War II to include Soviet drama as part of a season, as well as Bertolt Brecht and Friedrich Wolf. After both prewar theatres were destroyed, the company played in a variety of theatres, including the Adventshaus and the Festsaal in the real gymnasium. Some of the works performed during the reconstruction era include Goethe's *Faust* (1946, *regie* Görs); von Hofmannsthal's *Jedermann* (1947, *regie* Kaesler); the premiere of Annamarie Bostrom's *Die Kette fallt* (*The Chain Drops*, 1948, *regie* Görs); Schiller's *Mary Stuart* (1948, *regie* Kaesler); Brecht's *Der Gute Mensch von Sezuan* (*The Good Woman of Setzuan*, 1949, *regie* Heinz W. Litten); Clifford Odets' *Golden Boy* (1950, *regie* Kaesler); and Günther Weisenborn's *Das Spiel von Thomaskantor* (*The Play of Thomaskantor*, 1951, *regie* Görs). In 1949 Görs opened a Schauspielhaus (the Theater on Karl-Marx Platz); and on May 26, 1951, the opera house reopened (architects for the rebuilding were Ochs and Hemmerling) with Beethoven's *Fidelio*, followed a few days later by Friedrich Wolf's *Der arme Konrad* (*regie* Kaesler). In December of the same year Görs was called to Dresden.

Kaesler took over for Görs, with Gottfried Kolditz becoming director of the spoken theatre. It was in this period that Chemnitz became the Karl-Marx-Stadt. This change is mirrored in the repertory of the company, which developed into one of the most rigidly Marxist in East Germany. It was in this period, too, that Kaesler initiated a popular theatre festival, to which troupes from all over the Socialist world were invited. The most significant works in the era were Socialist plays or classics treated in a Marxist fashion: Alexander Kornetjschuk's *The Elder Grove* (1951, *regie* Kaesler); Moroslav Stehlik's *The Glen* (1952, *regie*

Kolditz); Schiller's *Wilhelm Tell* (1952, *regie* Kaesler); Shaw's *Saint Joan* (1952, *regie* Kaesler), with Sigrid Hausmann in the title role; Shakespeare's *Hamlet* (1953, *regie* Kolditz), with Hans Richter in the title role, and *Romeo and Juliet* (1954, *regie* Kolditz); Lessing's *Emilia Galotti* (1955, *regie* Kaesler); and Schiller's *Wallenstein* cycle (1955, *regie* Kolditz), with Hans Kiessler in the title role.

Paul Herbert Freyer came to the company in 1956 and stayed until 1961. Although he did a number of good things for the opera and ballet companies, the spoken theatre declined under his leadership. One rather good *regisseur* who did work there during the period, Gerhard Keil, was best in staging German classic drama. Freyer had worked as a dramaturge in Crimmitschau and at the Maxim Gorky Theatre in East Berlin, and had also been intendant at Plauen. The Schauspielhaus probably slipped because of his choice of *regisseurs* and a rather esoteric choice of plays. One notable premiere in the era was Brecht's *Der Tage der Commune* (*The Day of the Commune*, 1956), with the production of Manfred Wekwerth and Benno Besson a sort of dry run before the Berliner Ensemble Production. Some of the better productions in the Freyer period include: Goethe's *Torquato Tasso* (1957, *regie* Keil); the Burian/Hasek *Good Soldier Schweyk* (1958, *regie* Freyer); Schiller's *Die Räuber* (*The Robbers*, 1959, *regie* Keil); and Lajos Mesterhaizy's *Men of Budapest* (1960, *regie* Keil).

Hans Dieter Mäde had worked in Rostock, Weimer, Erfuth, and the Gorky in East Berlin before coming to Karl-Marx-Stadt in 1961, and more than anything he made the *regisseur* an important person in the company. Making a conscious effort to reach the public, he chose his plays well. His best work was done in the classics, most of which he himself staged, and many of which were big cast plays in which Mäde pushed very hard for a tight ensemble; Brecht's *Das Leben des Galilei* (*The Life of Galileo*, 1962, *regie* Mäde); Alexey Arbuzov's *The Irkutsk Story* (1963, *regie* Mäde); Alexander Schtein's *Ocean* (1963, *regie* Mäde); Goethe's *Egmont* (1963, *regie* Siegfried Menzel); Shakespeare's *Hamlet* (1964, *regie* Erwin Alt); Goldoni's *The Chioggian Brawls* (1965, *regie* Mäde); and Schiller's *Don Carlos* (1965, *regie* Mäde). In 1966 Mäde moved on to Dresden.

Gerhard Meyer took over the leadership from Mäde. Meyer had the large task of bringing the theatre, opera, and ballet companies to their full potential: the opera and ballet were in fair condition but were not very well organized. He was successful largely through discipline in all these areas, with his most notable success in the spoken drama. His first Schauspiel director was Wolfram Krempl, who served from 1967 to 1970. Krempl began his era by reorganizing the theatre and making an excellent choice of plays. He also brought in a number of young *regisseurs*. The main problem in this period was that Krempl lost some of his major actors to Berlin, most notably Christian Grashof. His major productions were from the classics or modern Socialist drama: Rainer Kerndl's *Die seltsame Reise des Alois Fingerlin* (*The Strange Journey of Alois Fingerlin*, 1967, *regie* Krempl); Odön von Horváth's *Kasimir und Karoline* (1968); Schiller's *Kabale und Liebe* (*Intrigue and Love*, 1969, *regie* Krempl), with Grashof as Ferdinand;

the premiere of Alfred Matusche's *Das Lied meines Weg* (*The Song of My Way*, 1969, *regie* Jochen Ziller); and Brecht's *Der Gute Mensch von Sezuan* (*The Good Woman of Setzuan*, 1970, *regie* Hartwig Albiro).

Hartwig Albiro took over the running of the theatre in 1971. The combination of Albiro, Meyer, and Dieter Görne (chief dramaturge) has turned this company into one of the most important in East Germany. Albiro had worked at Grolitz and the Berliner Ensemble before coming to Karl-Marx-Stadt. In interviews most East German intendants speak about the great cooperation among the various elements in the company, though with varied results on the stage. Karl-Marx-Stadt is noted for this excellence, careful planning of repertory and staging, and just plain running the theatre day after day. Despite one bad problem (a fire in the Schauspielhaus in 1976), the company has set an enviable record in achievement. Albiro has brought a number of young *regisseurs* to the company and has focused on ensemble, lightness, and versatility, and on playing, with a vigorous training program for the actor. A number of fine *regisseurs* work in Karl-Marx-Stadt.

Under Albiro some of the major productions have included the premiere of Alfred Matusche's *Prognose* (1971, *regie* Piet Drescher); Schiller's *Die Räuber* (1971, *regie* Albiro); Shakespeare's *Twelfth Night* (1972, *regie* Drescher); Pirandello's *Liolà* (1972, *regie* Drescher); Carlo Goldoni's *The Liar* (1973, *regie* Albiro); Michail Schatrow's *Valentin and Valentina* (1973, *regie* Meyer); Volker Braun's *Hinze and Kinze* (1973, *regie* Drescher); Sean O'Casey's *Red Roses for Me* (1974, *regie* Drescher); Pablo Neruda's *Brightness and Death of Joaquin Murieta* (1975, *regie* Drescher); Shakespeare's *Timon of Athens* (1975, *regie* Albiro); Goethe's *Faust I* (1976, *regie* Drescher); the premiere of Volker Braun's *Tinka* (1976, *regie* Albiro), with Dagmar Jaeger in the title role; Goldoni's *The Bell Tower* (1977, *regie* Albiro); Brecht's *Der Kaukasische Kreide Kreis* (*The Caucasian Chalk Circle*, 1978, *regie* Albiro); Shakespeare's *Macbeth* (1978, *regie* Drescher); the premiere of Peter Hacks' *Arter Ritter* (*Poor Knight*, 1979, *regie* Irmgard Lang); and Eugène Labiche's *Pots of Money* (1980, *regie* Albiro), with Gerd Preusche as Champboury.

On October 5, 1980, a reconditioned Schauspielhaus opened with a very Marxist production of Georg Büchner's *Dantons Tod* (*Danton's Death*; *regie* Albiro), with Bernhard Baier in the title role. Since then the company has gone on to do the same sort of repertory it has done previously: the Thomas Wolfe/Kelti Frings *Look Homeward, Angel* (1980, *regie* Axel Richter); Brecht's *Mutter Courage und ihre Kinder* (*Mother Courage and Her Children*, 1981, *regie* Siegfried Höchst), with Anny Stoger as Courage; Heiner Müller's *Der Auftrug* (*The Commission*, 1981, *regie* Axel Richter); the Sastre/de Rojas *Celestina* (1981, *regie* Irmgard Lange); and Grischa Ostrovsky's *The Storm* (*regie* Grigori Shesmer).

The strength of the acting company lies in the combination of *Generalintendant/Schauspielhausdirektor*/chief dramaturge. Gerhard Meyer is a strong head for the operation, but all the members of the organization hold extensive discussions before making any decision as to repertory, *regisseurs*, acting company, and the like. As a result, it is a highly democratic company. In addition, Carl Riha, a strong *regisseur* in his department, is an excellent opera head.

Each season the theatre company mounts six to eight new productions as well as revivals. Modern plays dominate, but it obviously does a number of classics. Meyer devotes a good deal of his energy to talking to the public, which is why the theatre is popular (at 90 percent capacity on an average). The theatre is particularly popular with the young; the company tries to mount several plays a season which will appeal to them, either children's plays or plays for young adults. The company generally numbers around thirteen women and twenty men, and it does have some guests. Three dramaturges and a technical staff serve the theatre and opera companies, as well as the ballet. The company plays in the opera house, its main theatre, the Schauspielhaus (419 seats), and in the local cultural center, which has two theatres. It has also played in various theatres around town. The company has done some touring, especially in East Germany.

The City Theatre of Karl-Marx-Stadt is concerned, first, for the playgoer and for what he wants. Second, it cares about the actor, especially the actor's working conditions and craft (the theatre maintains a vigorous training program). Third, it has a concern for people, as exemplified in the company's repertory, which includes some plays from the West. These concerns have made the company exemplary.

LEON M. AUFDEMBERGE
(With thanks to Hartwig Albiro)

CITY THEATRE OF LEIPZIG
(Städtische Theater Leipzig)
Karl-Marx-Platz 12
7010 Leipzig, East Germany

The first important theatre in Leipzig was the Komödienhaus, which opened on October 10, 1766, with Johann Elisas Schlegal's *Hermann*, financed by a local merchant, Gottlob Benedikt. The company then occupied the theatre headed by Heinrich Gottfried Koch, one of Germany's earliest theatre greats. The Koch company played the usual classics, but also some of the earliest performances of Gotthold Lessing. The Komödienhaus was frequently attended by the young Goethe in his student days. In 1777, through orders from the local duke, it became part of the series of theatres occupied by the company from Dresden, an arrangement that was to carry on into the next century. The premiere of Schiller's *Die Jungfrau von Orleans* (*The Maid of Orleans*) took place in the theatre in September 1801, with Schiller attending the third performance. The work was also performed by the Secondasche Gesellschaft, one of the many companies that played guest performances during the early part of the eighteenth century. A rebuilt theatre (architect Friedrich Weinbrenner) opened on August 26, 1817, with Schiller's *Die Braut von Messina* (*The Bride from Messina*), this time with a permanent company ensconced in the theatre. The organization was called the Theater der Stadt Liepzig, under the directorship of Hofrat Dr. Küstner. This new troupe began to attract a number of important guest actors, including Eduard Genast, Emil and Ludwig Devrient, Pius Alexander Wolff, and F.A.A. Wurm.

The early years of the Leipzig theatre were noted for their liberality (despite some troublesome strictures of an omnipresent censor), especially under the directorship of Dr. Carl Christian Schmidt (1845–1848). The company played not only classics, but also works of such authors as Carl Gutzkow, Heinrich Laube, Gustav Freytag, and, above all, Friedrich Hebbel.

One of Germany's greatest actresses, Clara Ziegler, was a member of the troupe from 1867 to 1868, making her debut as Brunhilde in Hebbel's *Die Niebelungen*. She opened a new opera house, known as the Neue Theater (architect Ferdinand Langhans), on January 28, 1868, playing the title role in Goethe's *Iphigenie auf Tauris* to "hysterical applause." Heinrich Laube, frequently referred to as *"der alte Puritaner des Schauspielkunst"* ("the old Puritan of the art of the theatre"), became director in 1869 for one season. In that season he brought Friedrich Mitterwurzer to the company, as well as a favorable number of Shakespeare and Schiller plays. Friedrich Haase (1870–1876) was an actor/ *regisseur* combination, and his era was noted for Shakespearean productions. Both Haase and his successor, August Förster (1876–1882), had a stormy time with the Leipzig public. A number of important actors played the theatre during their tenure, however, including Marie Geistinger, Joseph Kainz, Anna Haverland, Franziska Ellmenrich, Josephine Wessely, and Otto Sommerstoff.

In 1882 the opera and theatre companies were combined under the single directorship of Max Stägemann. His most important single product was Otto Devrient's staging of *Faust*, which was part of a Goethe cycle (1883), with a classic cycle following in 1885 and a Shakespeare cycle in 1904. Modern playwrights represented during Stägemann's leadership include Ibsen, Hermann Sudermann, and Frank Wedekind. The premiere of Wedekind's *Erdgeist* (*Earth Spirit*) took place in 1898 in Leipzig, under the instigation of the Literarische Gesellschaft headed by Carl Heine.

Stägemann died in 1905 and was succeeded by Arthur Nikisch and Robert Volkner, with Volkner eventually taking over until 1912. In this period there were masses of guest artists and important single productions of a mixture of modern and classic works: Tolstoy's *The Power of Darkness* (1906, *regie* Lothar Mehnert); the two parts of *Faust* (1907, *regie* George Witkowsky); Goethe's *Götz von Berlichingen* (1908, *regie* Carl Dalmonico); Friedrich Hebbel's *Maria Magdalena* (1910, *regie* Dalmonico), with Lina Monnard as Clara; and Ibsen's *The Pillars of Society* (1911, *regie* Adolf Winds).

With the name of Max Martersteig (1912–1918), Leipzig had a truly important *Generalintendant* (theatrical manager), one who was a combination actor, *regisseur*, theatre leader, and historian. In terms of playwrights, his specialties in staging were Christian Dietrich Grabbe, Ibsen, Shakespeare, and Lessing. Martersteig's own personal style was marked by neo-romanticism and emphasis on atmosphere.

Some of Martersteig's major productions during the period include plays from a variety of periods: Shakespeare's *Coriolanus* (1912); Schiller's *Wallenstein* cycle (1913); Ibsen's *When We Dead Awaken* (1913); Ernst Hardt's *Gudrun* (1914); Ibsen's *Ghosts* (1915); Goethe's *Torquato Tasso* (1916); Strindberg's *The Father* (1916); Shakespeare's *As You Like It* (1916); and the premiere of Wilhelm Schmidtbonn's *Die Stadt der Besessenen* (*The City of Besessenen*, 1917).

Martersteig was followed by Wolfgang Alexander Meher Waldeck (1918–1920) and a quiet period. The tenure of the next *Generalintendant*, Guido Barthol, was anything but quiet, however, the whole marked by experimentation in the staging of both classics and modern works. One of the first things Barthold did was to remodel the Altes Theater (dating from 1766), opening it in 1922 with Schiller's *Die Verschwörung des Fiesco zu Genua* (*The Conspiracy of Fiesco Against Genoa*, *regie* Alwin Kronacher). The repertory has the usual classics, with the company becoming known for its playing of modern playwrights: Bertolt Brecht, Frank Wedekind, Walter Hasanclever, Ernst Toller, Fritz von Unruh, and Carl Zuckmayer. This led to occasional stinkbombs in the theatre, especially in the latter period, when the Nazis hated a good deal of the repertory in both the Schauspielhaus and the opera. The acting company included several important actors, notably Lothar Körner, Herbert Hubner, Joachim Gottschalk, Grete Scheer, Robert Meyn, and Leipzig's great classic actress, Lina Carstens. Added to these were a number of important *regisseurs*, including Detlef Sierck (later Hollywood's Douglas Sirk) and Erich Schönlank.

Among the important productions in this remarkable period (heavy with premieres) were Shakespeare's *As You Like It* (1921, *regie* Hans Rothe); the premiere of Hans Henny Jahn's *Die Krönung Richard III* (1922, *regie* Rothe); the premiere of Brecht's *Baal* (1923, *regie* Kronacher), with Körner in the title role; Ernst Toller's *Hinkemann* (1924, *regie* Paul Wieke); Fritz von Unruh's *Heinrich aus Andernach* (1925, *regie* Kronacher); Shakespeare's *Troilus and Cressida* (1925, *regie* Kronacher) and *King John* (1926, *regie* Kronacher); Shaw's *Saint Joan* (1926, *regie* Kronacher), with Scheer in the title role; the premiere of Hans Rothe's *Der brennende Stall* (*The Burning Stable*, 1928, *regie* Kronacher); Brecht's *Die Dreigroschenoper* (*The Threepenny Opera*, 1929, *regie* Erich Schönlank), with Meyn as Mackie; Toller's *Das Maschinenstürmer* (*The Machine Warder*, 1930, *regie* Schönlank); Ferdinand Bruckner's *Elisabeth von England* (1930, *regie* Sierck), with Carstens in the title role; Goethe's *Clavigo* (1932, *regie* Sierck); and Ibsen's *An Enemy of the People* (1932, *regie* Otto Kasten), with Otto Bassermann as Stockmann in a guest appearance and one of his last appearances in Germany before emigrating.

Sierck took over the Schauspiel from 1932 to 1935, and with him the company passed from experimentation to the playing of classics, with part of the company emigrating. Kronacher's departure was the saddest loss. Most of the significant

productions during the transitional period were staged by Sierck: Gerhart Hauptmann's *Florian Geyer* (1932, *regie* Sierck), with Körner in the title role; the
Walter Hasanclever/Panter *Christopher Columbus* (1932, *regie* Otto Werther);
Schiller's *Die Räuber* (*The Robbers*, 1932, *regie* Sierck); Hebbel's *Agnes Bernauer* (1933, *regie* Sierck); Schiller's *Die Jungfrau von Orleans* (*The Maid of
Orleans*, 1934, *regie* Sierck), with Carstens as Isabeau; and Shakespeare's *Macbeth* (1934, *regie* Sierck), with Walter Reymer in the title role.

Paul Smolny became head of the Schauspiel from 1935 to 1944, and Hans
Schüler was *Generalintendant* from 1937 to 1947. As with most German companies, Leipzig staged many classics during the era of National Socialism. There
was a mass of plays during Schüler's stewardship; as a result, the Schauspielhaus
(which dated from 1902) was taken over as a second theatre for plays. The
company became known as the Bühnen der Reichsmessestadt, Leipzig. Fortunately for Schüler, the company did comparatively few Nazi plays; most of its
modern works were comedies that were neither particularly good nor political.
The major productions during the period were mostly from the past: Heinrich
von Kleist's *Prinz Friedrich von Homburg* (1936, *regie* Schüler); Hebbel's *Die
Niebelungen* (1938, *regie* Smolny); Shakespeare's *Hamlet* (1938, *regie* Smolny),
with Peter Lühr as the title (one of his best roles); Schiller's *Wallenstein* cycle
(1940, *regie* Smolny), with Hans Jungbauer in the title role; Schiller's *Die Braut
von Messina* (*The Bride of Messina*, 1940, *regie* Smolny), with Carstens as
Isabella (one of her important roles); the Sophocles/Hölderlin *Oedipus Tyrannos*
(1942, *regie* Smolny); Kleist's *Penthislea* (1942, *regie* Smolny); and Schiller's
Die Räuber (*The Robbers*, 1943, *regie* Smolny). In 1943 and 1944 all three
theatres in Leipzig would be destroyed.

Schüler was one of the few German *Generalintendants* who kept his job in
1945. The first production after the war took place on September 27, 1945, with
Georg Büchner's *Woyzeck*, staged by Schüler in the Weisses Saal of the Zoo.
The company used a variety of theatres in the postwar era. In 1946 Schüler
helped found the Theater der Jungen Welt to present plays for children and young
people. The reformed company did many Socialist plays (especially Russian)
and classics. Some of the most significant works done during the post-war period
included Paul Raynal's antiwar *The Tomb Beneath the Arch of Triumph* (1945,
regie Schüler); Gotthold Lessing's *Nathan der Weise* (*Nathan the Wise*, 1946,
regie Schüler); A. M. Afinogenow's *Maschenka* (1946, *regie* Schüler); and Grischa Ostrovsky's *Wolves and Sheep* (1947, *regie* Lühr).

In 1947 Schüler left abruptly, and Max Kruger eventually took his place.
During this period the German Democratic Republic was born, as reflected in
the repertory which begins rather broadly in 1947 but at the end of Kruger's era
in 1950 includes very few plays from the West. During this time there was a
feeling of upheaval, with certain important people dropping out (Peter Lühr for
one) and others beginning to emerge who would remake the company, such as
Karl Kayer, Johannes Arpe, and Heinrich Voigt. Among the company's significant works during Kruger's leadership were Schiller's *Don Carlos* (1947, *regie*

Albert Fischel); O'Neill's *Mourning Becomes Electra* (1948, *regie* Fischel); the premiere of Friedrich Wolf's *Wie Tiere des Waldes* (*How Brutish the Woods*, 1948, *regie* Hans-Joachim Büttner); Goethe's *Faust* (1949, *regie* Arpe); Brecht's *Herr Puntila und sein Knecht Matti* (*Mr. Puntila and His Hired Man, Matti*, 1950, *regie* Hans Michael Richter); and the Leon Feuchtwanger anticolonialist *Kalkutta, 4 Mai* (*Calcutta, 4 May*, 1950, *regie* Voigt).

Max Burghardt became *Generalintendant* in 1950, leading the company through 1954. Although there were many small-cast shows during these years, the most important were large-scale works, staged by a rather wide variety of *regisseurs*. The most important premiere in Leipzig after the war may have been Romain Rolland's *Robespierre* (1952, *regie* Arthur Jopp and Burghardt), with Martin Flörchinger as Robespierre, with sets by Paul Pilowski. Burghardt concentrated on the classics; modern plays almost always came from East German writers. Among the long-playing works in the Burghardt years could be named Shaw's *Saint Joan* (1950, *regie* Fritz Wendel); Shakespeare's *Measure for Measure* (1951, *regie* Wendel); Schiller's *Mary Stuart* (1951, *regie* Arpe); Gorky's *Yegor Bulychyov and Others* (1953, *regie* Wendel); Shakespeare's *Hamlet* (1953, *regie* Wendel); and the premiere of Johannes Becher's *Winterschlacht* (*Winter Battle*, 1954, *regie* Burghardt with Frithjof Ruede).

Johannes Arpe was head from 1954 to 1958, and the most important event during his tenure was the opening of the Schauspiel on September 28, 1955. The play was Schiller's *Wilhelm Tell* (*regie* Arpe), with Carl Bruno in the title role. This theatre was the old Zentral Theater, dating from 1901, which had been remodeled by K. Souradny, R. Brumer, and F. Herbst. As was true of the previous period, most significant productions were heavy on the classics side: Shakespeare's *Twelfth Night* (1956, *regie* Jopp); Schiller's *Wallenstein* (1957, *regie* Arpe), with Hans-Joachim Rechnitz in the title role; the premiere of Heiner Müller's *Der Lohndrücker* (*Press for Wages, regie* Günter Schwarz); and Shakespeare's *Romeo and Juliet* (1958, *regie* Arpe).

Karl Kayser had been an actor in Leipzig in the postwar era, left, and returned in 1958 to take over the company, where he remains. Kayser's work as a *regisseur* has been a mixture of Marxist and Stanislavsky elements, with lots of thought on acting and special emphasis on classics. Kayser's acting company is one of East Germany's best, with Günther Grabbert, Christa Gottschalk, Manfred Zetsche, and Hans-Joachim Hegewald. One of Kayser's first official duties as *Generalintendant* was to supervise the final construction of a new Operahaus am Karl-Marx-Platz (architects Kunz Nierade and Kurt Hemmerling), which seats 1,682. It opened on October 9, 1960, with Wagner's *Die Meistersinger von Nurnberg* (*regie* Joachim Herz).

Kayser's long reign can be divided into two parts. In the first, Kayser set a policy of repertory which the theatre would favor and has rather rigorously stuck to it. Following are the works Leipzig considered most important in the late 1950s and 1960s (when no *regisseur* is mentioned, credit the production to Kayser): Schiller's *Don Carlos* (1959); Gorky's *False Money* (1960, *regie* Smiszek); Miller's *Death of a Salesman* (1961, *regie* Richter), with Heinz Suhr as Willy; Shakespeare's *Richard III* (1961, *regie* Voigt), with Grabbert as the crafty king; Schiller's *Die Räuber* (*The Robbers*, 1962); Brecht's *Das Leben des Galilei* (*The Life of Galileo*, 1962, *regie* Voigt); Shakespeare's *Timon of Athens* (1963, *regie* Voight), with Hegewald as Timon; Ibsen's *Peer Gynt* (1964), with Grabbert as Peer; Schiller's *Kabale und Liebe* (*Intrigue and Love*, 1964); both parts of *Faust* (1965), with Zetsche as Mephisto and Grabbert as Faust; Schiller's *Mary Stuart* (1966), with Gottschalk in the title role; Shakespeare's *Macbeth* (1967), with Grabbert and Gottschalk as the royal couple; Armand Gatti's *V as in Vietnam* (1968, *regie* Müller); James Baldwin's *Blues for Mr. Charlie* (1969; and Helmut Sakowski's *Wege über Land* (*Passage over Land*, 1969).

In many ways, the second part of Kayser's tenure as *Generalintendant* looks much like the first: the same kind of plays, but with much more variety in *regisseurs* in the last few years. The following have received a good deal of favorable comment in both the East and West German press: Shakespeare's *Hamlet* (1971), with Friedhelm Eberle in the title role; Miller's *The Crucible* (1972), with Grabbert as John Proctor; the premiere of Volker Braun's *Die Kipper* (1972, *regie* Müller); Shaw's *Caesar and Cleopatra* (1973, *regie* Müller) with Grabbert as Caesar; Schiller's *Wallenstein* plays (1974), with Zetsche as Wallenstein; Williams' *A Streetcar Named Desire* (1975, *regie* Richter), with Gottschalk as Blanche; Brecht's *Das Leben des Galilei* (*The Life of Galileo*, 1976, *regie* Joachim Tenschert), with Grabbert as Galileo; Schiller's *Don Carlos* (1976); the premiere of Franz Xavier Kroetz's *Agnes Bernauer* (1977); Brecht's *Die Dreigroschenoper* (*The Threepenny Opera*, 1978, *regie* Fritz Bennewitz); Shakespeare's *King Lear* (1979), with Grabbert as Lear; Schiller's *Wilhelm Tell* (1980), with Hegewald in the title role; Goethe's *Faust I* (1981), with Eberle as Faust; and Lessing's *Nathan der Weise* (*Nathan the Wise*, 1981, *regie* Peter Röll), with Grabbert as Nathan.

There are five main theatres in Leipzig: the Operahaus, which is used for both opera and ballet; the Schauspielhaus, which seats 1,079; the Kellertheater (located in the Operahaus), which is used for small productions; the Musikalische Komödie; and the Theater der Jungen Welt (the children's-young people's theatre), which is located in Weissen Saal of the Zoo. Every day there are five thousand theatre tickets for sale in the city, and Karl Kayser is pretty much in charge of all theatres.

The company generally does nine new productions a year, plus revivals of around thirty works from previous seasons. Productions are carried over from season to season until the public loses interest. The repertory of the theatre is the usual East German split of classics and modern Socialist works. In addition, there are usually three or four works from outside the Eastern Bloc, provided the plays have something to say about the problems of society. (Tennessee Williams, Clifford Odets, and Arthur Miller are the most popular American writers.) Plays and *regisseurs* are selected by the administration of the company in a lengthy process.

The current acting company totals twenty-four women and forty-three men, plus three dramaturges. There is a huge technical staff which serves all branches of the theatre with a central atelier. Leipzig is very much an ensemble company, but if one element could be said to be most prominent it would be acting, which Leipzig has traditionally prized. Because of its good production record, Leipzig is frequently asked to tour in East Germany and in Eastern Bloc countries. It has also played frequently in West Germany, with some places sending productions back. All in all, Leipzig is well served with theatre.

One of the chief criticisms of the Kayser era—that it has been very much a one-man theatre—is in many ways true. Kayser has been very interested in all branches of the theatre and is conversant not only in spoken drama, but also the opera and ballet. In the last few years, however, he has been delegating more authority to others in the company. Kayser has been much decorated by the East German government and has been the East German president of the International Theatre Institute.

On the whole Leipzig is safe, dependable theatre, with a high standard. It tends to be conservative in its choices of plays and rather old-fashioned in its staging styles, but it is by no means stuffy or dull. There are some signs that these standards are loosening: some non-Western, non-Marxist works are being discussed and even Samuel Beckett has been mentioned as a possibility for staging. Whatever the future holds for the theatre in Leipzig, Karl Kayser will be a large part of it.

LEON M. AUFDEMBERGE
(With thanks to the dramaturge
staff of the theatre)

GERMAN NATIONAL THEATRE OF WEIMAR
(Deutsche National Theater Weimar)
Theaterplatz, Weimar, East Germany

In 1756 Herzog Ernst August Konstantin of Weimar wanted a resident theatre company in the city and invited the company of Karl Theophilus Döbbelin (who had been part of the Neuber troupe) to come to Weimar. Unfortunately, Ernst August died in 1758, and his widow, Anna Amalia (later a friend of Goethe), could not afford a resident company. Things were dormant until 1768 when Anna Amalia invited the troupe of Heinrich Gottfried Koch (also from the Neuber troupe) to Weimar, and the Koch company presented a variety of plays and *singspiels* (operettas). The Koch troupe had one good actor, Johannes Brückner, known for his naturalistic style.

The resident company in 1771 became that of Abel Seyler, who presented contemporary authors, including Gotthold Lessing. The business manager for this company and its lead actor was Konrad Ekhof, who is generally called the father of German acting. Ekhof was not a young man but persisted in playing juvenile roles and generally got away with it. The Seyler troupe was very popular in Weimar, but in 1774 was forced to move on when the theatre burned.

In 1774 the young Johann Wolfgang Goethe arrived to be an adornment for the court. (He remained in the city until his death in 1832.) In the next year a new theatre was built in the city, the Liebhabertheater, and it was this theatre to which Goethe was attracted, though the company was amateur. One of Goethe's fellow players was Charlotte von Stein, his muse for a while. Corona Schröter ("ein Engel," says Goethe) was invited in 1776 as a professional to become part of the court performances, with Goethe acting in these as well. Some of the plays done in the Liebhabertheater included Goethe's Erwin und Elmire and Die Geschwister (Brother and Sister, both 1776).

Ekhof returned as a guest artist in 1778, and his visit served as an impetus to the young Goethe to improve standards in the court theatre. For the next several seasons, Goethe contributed plays and his acting to several productions. His greatest acting triumph came in his own Iphigenie auf Tauris (1779), in which he played Orestes and Schröter took the title role. A new Hoftheater, built by Anton Hauptmann, opened in 1780 with Sigmund von Seckendorff's musical tragedy, Robert und Kalliste. Goethe and Schröter took the lead roles. For the new theatre Goethe contributed his own Jery und Bätely (Jery and Bately, 1780) and his adaptation of Aristophanes' The Birds (also 1780). After that, the local troupe went downhill when Goethe's attentions turned elsewhere.

On January 1, 1784, the troupe of Joseph Bellomo became the resident professional company in Weimar. It presented many contemporary writers, including Goethe (Clavigo was especially admired), August Iffland, August von Kotzebue, Schiller (Die Räuber, The Robbers), and Shakespeare with the first Weimar Hamlet (Schröder translation) appearing in 1778. Schiller traveled to Weimar in 1787, though Goethe was out of town (he was in Italy). The two poets met the following year. By 1789 the Bellomo troupe performances were so poor that, when invited to Graz in 1790, both the local court and Goethe were pleased to see them go. A number of people were invited to come as head of the Weimar theatre, but no one wanted the rather small rewards the local duke promised. On January 17, 1791, Goethe was selected as temporary intendant, a job he would hold until 1817.

The period of 1791 to 1805 (the death of Schiller) is generally referred to as the Golden Age of Theatre in Weimar, and indeed it was. To help shape his troupe, Goethe invited Franz Joseph Fischer (then appearing in Prague) to become principal regisseur with most of his acting company from the Bellomo troupe.

The first production for the new company took place on May 7, 1791, with Iffland's Die Jäger (The Hunter). Goethe added a second summer theatre at Luchstadt in 1791, and it was here that a prose version by Schiller was presented (1791). Goethe, who was then in his classic period, rejected it, though the performance may have been at fault (the actors had learned their roles in four days).

As Goethe became more secure in his job (in his early seasons, he too frequently left it to his assistant Franz Kirms), theatre performances became increasingly better, especially those in which Heinrich Vohs had learned his part and was feeling well. In the spring of 1796, August Wilhelm Iffland, actor and playwright, made a guest appearance at the Weimar theatre, bringing both his lead roles and plays. Goethe's observation of Iffland as an actor made Goethe realize that he would have to add more and better actors to the company. By this time he had several good actors, namely, Vohs, Anton Genast, Heinrich Becker, and Johann Graff, and one fair actress, Frau Vohs. To the troupe Goethe added Christiane Becker-Neumann, Pius Alexander Wolff, Friedrich Haide, and Amalia Malcolmi (later Frau Wolff). From these he forged his "Weimarer stils," which was a highly idealistic (not naturalistic) style of playing. Goethe, however, made a big mistake in hiring Karoline Jagermann as an actress and lead soprano. Although she was a handsome woman (she later was the local duke's mistress) and adept in both opera and spoken drama, she made frequent demands on Goethe that were difficult to fulfill. Yet at the beginning she was another "Engel."

On October 12, 1797, a new theatre, built from Hartmann's old house, opened with the first part of Schiller's Wallenstein trilogy, *Wallensteins Lager* (*Wallenstein's Camp*), plus August von Kotzebue's *Die Korsen* (*The Corsicans*). It was to this theatre that Schiller contributed his last great plays: the last two parts of the Wallenstein plays, *Die Piccolomini* (*The Piccolomini*) and *Wallensteins Tod* (*Wallenstein's Death*, both 1799), with Graff as Wallenstein and Jagermann as Thekla; his translation of Shakespeare's *Macbeth* (1800), with Vohs in the title role; *Mary Stuart* (1800), with Jagermann as Elisabeth and Frau Vohs as Maria (both had triumphs); *Die Braut von Messina oder Die Feindliche Brüder* (*The Bride of Messina, or The Enmity Between Brothers*, 1803), with Haide as Tell; and his translation of Racine's *Phèdre* (1805). In addition, in 1803 there was a triumphant production of *Die Jungfrau von Orleans* (*The Maid of Orleans*), with Malcolmi as Johanna. Schiller also did working adaptations or translations of works by Lessing, Euripides, Goethe, and Louis-Benoît Picard. Goethe's contributions in this period were his translations of Voltaire's *Mahomet* (1800) and *Tancrede* (1801), as well as the premieres of the second version of *Iphigenie auf Tauris* (1802) and *Die naturlich Tochter* (*The Natural Daughter*, 1803). Goethe also opened a new theatre in Lauchstädt in 1802 (architect Johann Götze, a friend of Goethe's). The following year Madame de Stäel came to visit Goethe (who pretended illness to put off their meeting), Schiller, and the theatre at Weimar. She was only moderately impressed, partly because she spoke no German.

Schiller's death on April 29, 1805, was a serious blow to Goethe. Schiller's plays, however, have formed a large percentage of the theatre's repertory to the present day. The period from 1805 to Goethe's retirement in 1817 was a bad one, as Goethe suffered from ill-health, and the recurrent wars in Germany (with Weimar occupied by the French) caused additional hardships. Goethe continued the same sort of repertory, adding productions of the Spanish Calderón, as well as those of two contemporary Germans, Zacharias Warner and Heinrich von

Kleist. Warner is remembered today as the source for one minor Verdi opera (*Attila*), but Kleist is a major writer in German theatre. Nonetheless, Kleist's one comedy (and perhaps the best of all German comedies), *Der zerbrochene Krug* (*The Broken Jug*, 1808), was a horrible failure at Weimar in 1808 mostly because of Heinrich Becker's slow performance as Adam. Goethe himself was responsible for two productions of his own plays: *Egmont* (1812), which used the Beethoven for the first time, and the premiere of *Torquato Tasso* (1807).

Conflict over a guest production and his more or less continuous battles with Jagermann caused Goethe to retire in 1817. After that the company was run by a consortium, with Goethe paying scarce attention to what was going on in his former theatre. On May 25, 1825, the theatre burned. A new house (architect Clemens Coudray) opened on September 3, 1825, with Rossini's *Semiramide*, with Jagermann in the title role. Under the directorship of Hofmarschall von Spiel Spiegel (1828–1847), Weimar saw the first production of *Faust* (part one in 1829, part two in 1831), with Karl La Roche as Mephisto. Goethe was out of town for both performances. In March 1832 Goethe died and was buried next to Schiller in Weimar.

The directorships of Freiherr von Ziegefar (1847–1855) and Freiherr von Beaulieu Marconnay (1854–1857) included many plays by Goethe, Schiller, and Shakespeare. In this period Franz Liszt was head of the music (1841–1859), with the premiere of Wagner's *Lohengrin* (1850) taking place in Weimar. Many important guest actors made appearances in the theatre during the middle of the century, the most important being Bogumil Dawison in the 1850s.

The tenure of Franz Dingelstedt (1857–1867) was a model period for the theatre in Weimar. There were many productions of classics, especially Shakespeare, and among contemporary writers Dingelstedt liked Franz Grillparzer and Friedrich Hebbel. Major productions which he himself staged included Shakespeare's *The Winter's Tale* (1859); Molière's *L'avare* (*The Miser*, 1860); Hebbel's *Niebelungen* trilogy (premiere, 1861); a cycle of Shakespeare's histories (1863–1864); Hebbel's *Judith* (1864); and Shakespeare's *As You Like It* (1865).

Dingelstedt moved on to Vienna and was followed by Baron von Loën as director (1867–1887). While this was an important time for opera, one major person worked in the acting company, Otto Devrient. His production of both parts of *Faust* (1876), with himself as Mephisto, is still studied by scholars. Bronsart von Schellendorf (1887–1895) was also very good for opera; Richard Strauss headed up musical activities during part of this period.

It was during the directorship of Herr von Vignau (1895–1908) that the old house closed with Goethe's *Iphigenie auf Tauris* (February 16, 1907) in a production by Karl Weiser with Paul Wiecke as Orestes. A new house opened on January 11, 1908, with Goethe's *Vorspiel auf der Theater* (*Prelude on the Stage*) and Schiller's *Wallensteins Lager* (*Wallenstein's Camp*). Carl von Schirach (1908–1919) was head when the theatre passed from a grand-ducal, court theater to a country theatre (1918). Schirach presented many premieres as well as the works of some non-German writers new to Weimar, such as August Strindberg.

Ernst Hardt became director in 1919. On January 11 the theatre became the Deutsches Nationaltheater, presenting Schiller's *Wilhelm Tell* (*regie* Eugen Wilhelmini). Hardt staged the usual classics, including Goethe's *Faust* (1920) and the First Quarto of *Hamlet* (1922) which were much admired. There were also productions of Herbert Eulenberg, Georg Kaiser, Gerhart Hauptmann, and Carl Sternheim.

The tenure of Franz Ulbrich (1924–1933) is best remembered as the period when the Bauhaus was located in Weimar, which meant principally that Oscar Schlemmer did some sets for both the theatre and ballet companies. This was a very good period, with many splendid classic productions and some modern works (this time with few shocks), especially Eulenberg and Shaw. Ulbrich's biggest accomplishment was his staging of a series of Faust plays in 1925, including both parts of Goethe's play the *Urfaust*, and works by Christopher Marlowe, Christian Grabbe, and Gotthold Lessing. Among the major productions during these years were Shakespeare's *Macbeth* (1924, *regie* Friedrich Sebrecht); the premiere of Herbert Eulenberg's *Der Rote Mond* (*The Red Moon*, 1924, *regie* Ulbrich); Grabbe's *Don Juan und Faust* (1925, *regie* Ulbrich), with sets by Schlemmer; Shakespeare's *Henry IV* (1927/1928, *regie* Sebrecht), with Wilhelm Holz as Falstaff; Schiller's *Die Räuber* (*The Robbers*, 1928, *regie* Sebrecht); Edmond Rostand's *Cyrano de Bergerac* (1929, *regie* Helmuth Ebbs); Georg Büchner's *Dantons Tod* (*Danton's Death*, 1930, *regie* Ebbs); Ferdinand Raimund's *Der Verschwender* (*The Prodigal*, 1931, *regie* Ebbs); Schiller's Wallenstein cycle (1931, *regie* Ulbrich); and Shakespeare's *King John* (1932, *regie* Ulbrich). In 1933 Ulbrich was called to Berlin to begin a rather spotty career as head of the State Theatre, a job he got partly by being one of the first to stage Mussolini's Napoleon play, *The 100 Days*, which Weimar did not admire in 1931.

During National Socialism Weimar had only a middling record. Many of the artists who had worked in the Ulbrich era went elsewhere, and the two directors, Ernst Nobbe (1933–1936) and Hans Severus Ziegler (1936–1944), did not have sufficient personal drive to make Weimar the theatre city it had once been. As with most other German companies, there were a string of classics, but Weimar seemed to have even more. The best known actor during the period was Falk Harnack (later a *regisseur*). The productions praised in the theatre magazines during the period included Shakespeare's *Richard II* (1934, *regie* George Kruse), *Hamlet* (1934, *regie* Hans König), and *Richard III* (1936, *regie* Otto Roland); Goethe's *Götz von Berlichingen* (1937, *regie* Max Brock), with Heinrich George in the title role; Heinrich von Kleist's *Penthislea* (1938, *regie* Walter Grünssig); Carlo Goldoni's *Mistress of the Inn* (1938, *regie* Harnack); Shakespeare's *Twelfth Night* (1939, *regie* Roland) and *Measure for Measure* (*regie* Lutz Heinle); Kleist's *Prinz Friedrich von Homburg* (1940, *regie* Grünssig); and Ibsen's *Ghosts* (1941, *regie* Heinle). In 1945 the theatre was partially destroyed, just before the town was occupied by the Russians.

By early 1946, all forms of theatrical activity in Weimar were in full swing.

Hans Weiseg was the first *Generalintendant* (1945–1947), and two actor-*regisseurs* in prominent view were Hans-Robert Bortfeldt (who came in 1945, later *Generalintendant* from 1947 to 1950) and Lothar Müthel (chief *regisseur* in Weimar from 1947 to 1950). Christa Lehmann came in 1947 as a major addition to the acting company. The biggest year for Weimar during the postwar era was the Goethe year of 1948, when the theatre presented a long cycle of Goethe plays. Both Wieseg and Bortfeldt wanted a wide variety of plays. The first theatres the company used after the war were the Weimarhalle and the Kammerspiele. The opening seasons featured works such as Friedrich Wolf's *Die Matrosen von Cattaro* (*The Sailors of Cattaro*, 1946, *regie* Kurt Bertschée); Clifford Odets' *Awake and Sing* (1947, *regie* Hans Streline); Friedrich Hebbel's *Herodes und Mariamne* (1947, *regie* Müthel), with Lehman as Mariamne and Müthel as Herodes; and Brecht's *Furcht und Elend des dritten Reich* (*Fear and Misery in the Third Reich*, 1947, *regie* Bortfeldt). On August 28, 1948, the Nationaltheater reopened with Goethe's *Faust* (*regie* Bortfeldt); Müthel was Mephisto. The second part followed the next year. Other productions during this era include Goethe's *Torquato Tasso* (1949, *regie* Bortfeldt); Molière's *Le misanthrope* (*The Misanthrope*, 1949), with Müthel staging and playing Alceste; and Lessing's *Nathan der Weise* (*Nathan the Wise*, 1950, *regie* Bortfeldt).

Karl Kayser, also a very Stanislavsky-oriented actor-*regisseur* combination, came in 1950 as *Generalintendant*, and with him the whole complexion of the theatre became very Marxist. Kayser permitted only two types of plays during the period: classics and modern Socialist drama. This was very much Kayser's era, in which he staged and acted in the following: Vsevolod Vishnevsky's *The Optimistic Tragedy* (1951); Goethe's *Egmont* (1951); Schiller's *Wilhelm Tell* (1951); Jaroslav Klima's *Fortune Falls Not from Heaven* (1952); Schiller's Wallenstein cycle (1953), with Horst Koch in the title role, and *Die Jungfrau von Orleans* (*The Maid of Orleans*, 1954); Alois Jirasek's *Jan Hus* (1955), with Kayser playing the title role; Hedda Zinner's *Teufelskreis* (*Devil's Circle*, 1955); Johannes Becher's *Winterschlacht* (*Winter Battle*, 1955); and Shakespeare's *Hamlet* (1958). Kayser established a Kammerspiele in May 1957, in the Schloss Belvedere, and the next year he left to be *Generalintendant* in Leipzig.

Kayser's successor, Otto Lang, was also very Marxist in orientation, but his years at Weimar (1958–1973) were different: he had a variety of *regisseurs*, and even differences in staging styles were in evidence. Lang had worked in various German theatres and in the USSR. One of the first people he brought to Weimar was Fritz Bennewitz as *Schauspieldirektor*, who retained the post until 1976. In 1963 Bennewitz in turn brought Ekkehard Kiesewetter as a *regisseur*, who became *Stellvertretender Schauspieldirektor* (deputy director of the theatre) from 1963 to 1972. This period was characterized by a number of stylish *regisseurs*. Lang had studied with Heinz Hilpert and Fritz Odemar. Bennewitz may be the most analytic *regisseur* in East Germany, combining Brechtian staging ideas with more psychological techniques. He is therefore very good for Brecht and Shakespeare. Kiesewetter's forte was Socialist-realist drama, and his work was as emotionally hot as Bennewitz's was analytically cool. Occasionally, Bennewitz and Kiesewetter worked together with good results.

Lang stressed acting during his long directorship, and there were certainly a number of fine actors at Weimar: Lehmann, Herbert Sievers, Fred Diesko, Wolfgang Dehler, Dietrich Mechow, and Manfred Zetsche. The opening seasons of the Lang period featured excellent classic productions, including Schiller's *Die Verschwörung des Fiesco zu Genua* (*The Conspiracy of Fiesco Against Genoa*, 1958, *regie* Lang); Shakespeare's *A Midsummer Night's Dream* (1959, *regie* Jean Peter Dierichs); Schiller's *Don Carlos* (1959, *regie* Lang); Shakespeare's *Hamlet* (1961, *regie* Bennewitz), with Zetsche as Hamlet; Goethe's *Faust I* (1961, *regie* Lang), with Zetsche as Mephisto; and one modern Socialist play, Wsewold Iwanow's *Panzerzug* (1960, *regie* Lang).

Beginning in 1962, however, Bennewitz, with his staging of Brecht's *Die Dreigroschenoper* (*The Threepenny Opera*), offered more highly disciplined productions in which all facets of a work would mesh. In the remaining years of Lang's tenure there would be a string of much admired productions, with classics in the majority: Shakespeare's *Twelfth Night* (1962, *regie* Bennewitz), with Lang as Malvolio, and *Richard III* (1964, *regie* Bennewitz), with Dehler in the title role; Maxim Gorky's *Wassa Schlesnowa* (*The Mother*, 1964, *regie* Kiesewetter); a string of Bennewitz-staged works, including both parts of Goethe's *Faust* (part one in 1965, two in 1967), with Dehler as Faust and Diesko as Mephisto; Brecht's *Das Leben des Galilei* (*The Life of Galileo*, 1966), with Herbert Sievers and Mechow both playing Galileo, and *Der Tage der Commune* (*The Day of the Commune*, 1966, *regie* Bennewitz); yet another Brecht in *Leben des König Eduard II von England* (*Life of King Edward II of England*, 1968, *regie* Bennewitz); Volker Braun's *Hans Faust* (1968, *regie* Bennewitz); Shakespeare's *A Midsummer Night's Dream* (1969, *regie* Bennewitz); Ibsen's *Peer Gynt* (1970, *regie* Bennewitz), with Heine in the title role; Ben Jonson's *Bartholomew Fair* (1970, *regie* Bennewitz), with Lehmann as Ursula; Fernando de Rojas' *Celestina* (1971, *regie* Bennewitz), with Lehmann in the title role; Shakespeare's *Hamlet* (1972, *regie* Bennewitz); Brecht's *Der Kaukasische Kreide Kreis* (*The Caucasian Chalk Circle*, 1972), with Mechow as Azdak; and Molière's *George Dandin* (1973), with Mechow in the title role.

Since 1973 the *Generalintendant* for Weimar has been Gerd Beinemann, with two *Schauspieldirektors*: Bennewitz (to 1976) and Christa Lehmann (1976–). The year 1973 also marks the beginning of the remodeling of the theatre; it reopened on March 1, 1975, with Goethe's *Faust* (*regie* Bennewitz), starring Manfred Heine. Bennewitz has continued to stage his fine classic productions, including Shakespeare's *Othello* (1974), with Heine in the title role, *The Merchant of Venice* (1976), with Victor Dräger as Shylock, and *King John* (1980); and yet another treatment of Goethe's *Faust* (1980/1981). But Beinemann has recognized that one cannot run a theatre on one *regisseur* alone (and Bennewitz works other houses); these years have therefore been heavy with productions by new *regisseurs* who have staged mostly modern works: Brecht's *Mutter Courage und ihre Kinder* (*Mother Courage and Her Children*, 1977, *regie* Heinz-Uwe Haus), with Lehmann as Anna Fierling; Gorky's *Children of the Sun* (1978, *regie* Sandu Manu); Friedrich Dürrenmatt's *Besuch der Alten Dame* (*Visit from the Old Lady*, 1979, *regie* Harry Buckwitz); Schiller's *Mary Stuart* (1980, *regie* Walter Niklaus); Carlo Gozzi's *The Raven* (1980, *regie* Horst Hawemann); Michail Welitschkow's *Die Flucht* (*The Flight*, 1981, *regie* Dieter Roth); Chekhov's *The Cherry Orchard* (*regie* Galina Woltschek), with Sylvia Kuzicnezski as Madame Ranevskaya; and Goethe's *Torquato Tasso* (1981, *regie* Klaus Tews).

The Nationaltheater at Weimar is one of the most attractive and, since 1975, one of the most comfortable in East Germany. It has a pleasant but plain neoclassical facade (Goethe would have approved) and the Goethe-Schiller Denkmal (1857, sculptor Rit Reitsche) outside. The company uses its main theatre (which seats around one thousand) and two experimental stages, its Probebühne and Foyer III (with flexible seating in both). It stages around six new productions a year as well as revivals from the previous season. The repertory is the usual East German balance of Marxist works and classics, but Weimar rather prides itself on having plays from outside the Eastern Bloc. The acting company runs to eleven men and twenty-six women and is considered very good. It plays both Weimar and Jena and has done some touring. It also has strong ties to its local school of performing arts, the Franz Liszt Hoch Schule.

Weimar's reputation is out of proportion to its size as a city and owes much to Goethe and his work with the theatre. Since 1865, Weimar has been the home of the Shakespeare Gesellschaft. Weimar has its annual Shakespeare Tage, which attracts scholars from around the world. This devotion to the past does not preclude experimentation. Especially in the last seasons, there has been some deviation from the normal fare in East German houses, such as the 1979 production by the Polish film director Andrej Wajda of Stanislaw Wyspánski's *November Night*. And all this started because Goethe came to town in 1774.

LEON M. AUFDEMBERGE
(With thanks to the dramaturge
staff of the theatre)

GERMAN THEATRE AND INTIMATE THEATRE
(Deutsches Theater und Kammerspiele)
Schumanstrasse 13a, 104 East Berlin
East Berlin, East Germany

The Deutsches Theater is frequently referred to as the East Berlin home of the classics. Its true name is the Max Reinhardt Deutsches Theater, though no one ever calls it by that name. It sits on a pleasant street in East Berlin, adorned by a bust of Max Reinhardt, which stands in front of the playhouse. Its history goes back to 1850 when the Friedrich Wilhelm Städtische Theater opened. The playhouse presented mostly operettas, light fare to Berliners. Then, in 1883, the playhouse was rented to a young theatre leader, Adolf L'Arronge, to present stronger and more literary dramas. The new organization was called the Deutsches Theater, and its opening production was Schiller's *Kabale und Liebe* (*Intrigue and Love*). Most of L'Arronge's company was young and rather transient, since members tended to leave the group as they gained a reputation. L'Arronge did Shakespeare, German classics, and a few Ibsen plays during his regime.

In 1889 a development occurred which largely shaped the future of the Deutsches Theater. Largely under the leadership of Paul Schlenter, Otto Brahm, one of Berlin's leading critics, organized a new theatre company to present contemporary works. It was called Die Freie Bühne and patterned itself after André Antoine's Théâtre Libre in Paris. Its opening production was Ibsen's *Ghosts*, presented on September 29, 1889. In 1894 Otto Brahm became head of the Deutsches Theater, and under his directorship the theatre became a much more modern organization, while continuing to do its share of the classics. In the 1890s the theatre became more than anything a home for the work of Gerhart Hauptmann. Many of his early works were done here, some for the first time; they include *Kollege Krampton* (*Colleague Krampton*, 1892), the German-language premiere of *Die Weber* (*The Weavers*, 1894), *Der Biberpelz* (*The Beaver Coat*, 1893), *Florian Geyer* (1896), *Der Versunkene Glocke* (*The Sunken Bell*, 1896), *Fuhrman Henschel* (1898), *Schluck und Jau* (1900), *Michael Kramer* (1900), *Der rote Hahn* (*The Red Hen*, 1901), and *Rose Berndt* (1903). As might be suspected, Brahm also produced many Ibsen plays. A number of prominent actors flocked to the company at this time, people like Louise Dumont (who would become Germany's most famous Ibsen actress), Rosa Bertens, Else Lehmann, Emanuel Reicher, Albert Bassermann, and the Viennese Max Reinhardt.

Reinhardt was to be the leader of the Deutsches Theater from 1904 until he left Germany in 1932. Reinhardt left his mark on German staging, both good and bad. The present adjective "Reinhardtish," for example, is hardly a compliment, suggesting a play overproduced and overdirected. On the positive side, he did set a style for staging that was a revelation in the German theatre. His acting company had the best talent in Germany: Albert Bassermann, Alexander Moissi, Joseph Schildkraut, Paul Wegener, Paul Hartmann, Fritz Kortner (also a *regisseur*), Oskar Homolka, Elisabeth Bergner, Gustaf Gründgens, Helena Thimig, Elisabeth Flickenschildt, and many others. New and exciting *regisseurs*, including Bernhard Reich, Heinz Hilpert, Hans Schweikart, and Karl-Heinz Martin, worked for Reinhardt.

The greatest worker, however, was Reinhardt himself. He did cycles of Shakespeare, Wedekind (when he was by no means popular), Hauptmann, and Ibsen. The great productions rolled out of the Deutsches Theater: *The Merchant of Venice* (1905), *The Winter's Tale* (1907), *Romeo and Juliet* (1907), Schiller's *Die Räuber* (*The Robbers*, 1908), *King Lear* (1908), *Faust I* (1909) and II (1911), *Hamlet* (1909), Schiller's *Don Carlos* (1909), *Macbeth* (1916), *As You Like It* (1919), and the premiere of Shaw's *The Apple Cart* (1929). His last production was Calderón's *The Great World Theatre* in 1932.

Reinhardt used the revolving stage to good effect. He relied heavily on a *regiebuch*, that is, a complete record of what the director would do with blocking the play, which was prepared before the play went into rehearsal. He made use of psychological lighting, but, most of all, he loved the idea of a concept. In 1906 Reinhardt opened the Kammerspiel, a 420-seat theatre in connection with the Deutsches Theater. It was here that he did more intimate works. The first production was Ibsen's *Ghosts*, more or less in honor of Otto Brahm.

Reinhardt brought his company to the United States in 1927. In addition to his other work, Reinhardt helped to develop the talents of a number of new German playwrights. One of these was Odön von Horváth, whose work, *Geschichte aus Wiener Wald (Tales of the Vienna Woods)*, was given a production in 1931, with Peter Lorre as Alfred. Brecht worked at this theatre from 1924 to 1926, but he did not care for the theatre or Reinhardt, whose style of staging he found repulsive. Brecht retaliated by being notoriously lazy. He wanted to rename the theatre "The Epic Smoking Theatre." It was during these years that Brecht wrote *Mann ist Mann (A Man's a Man*, 1926), and his play *Baal* was presented there in 1926, with Oskar Homolka as the title character. Also during Reinhardt's regime, Adolf Zuckmayer's play *De Hauptmann von Kopenick (The Captain from Kopenick)* was presented in 1931.

Then, in 1932 Reinhardt left the Deutsches Theater, eventually going to the United States. Heinz Hilpert became the new intendant of the company in 1934 and remained in the position until 1945. Since Hilpert's forte had always been Shakespearean productions, he staged a series of the Bard's plays: *Romeo and Juliet* (1935), *Twelfth Night* (1939), *Richard II* (1939), *King Lear* (1940), and *Antony and Cleopatra* (1942). In addition, he did many of the plays by George Bernard Shaw and Somerset Maugham, but dropped them from the repertory during World War II. Caspar Neher was the head designer for the company, beginning in 1934, and is especially remembered for his sets for *King Lear* and *Antony and Cleopatra*. Later he would become one of Brecht's designers for the Berliner Ensemble. Many of the best people of the Reinhardt era fled Germany with the coming of the Nazi regime. The theatre itself was damaged during the war (especially the Kammerspiele), and the entire operation closed in 1944, when nearly all German theatres closed their doors.

By 1945 a large number of Berlin theatres were reopened, playing for 50 pfennig or sometimes groceries. The first intendant after the war was Gustav von Wangenheim, and the opening production was Gotthold Lessing's *Nathan der Weise (Nathan the Wise)*, on September 7, 1945, with Fritz Wisten as *regisseur* and Paul Wegener in the title role. It was a play that praised Jewish kindness and wisdom and obviously had not been played in the German theatre for many years. It was a good choice for the reopening. The new intendant stayed for only one season. During that time he staged *Hamlet* and Schiller's *Kabale und Liebe (Intrigue and Love)*. He was replaced by Wolfgang Langhoff, who remained until 1963.

The Langhoff regime represented one of the great eras of the Deutsches

Theater. It was marked by a time of fervent experimentation. Langhoff had lived in Zurich during the war and had kept abreast of the new playwrights emerging in all parts of the world. Under his directorship, the theatre went from a "hit-or-miss" organization, begging for funds, to a solid organization. Gustaf Gründgens came early in Langhoff's tenure to stage Shaw's *Captain Brassbound's Conversion* (1946) and Frank Wedekind's *Der Marquis von Keith* (1947). Gründgens acted as well in a production of *Oedipus Tyrannos* (1947). But it was Langhoff who did the best known productions, both as director and actor: Georg Büchner's *Woyzeck* (1947), Brecht's *Furcht und Elend des dritten Reiches* (*Fear and Misery in the Third Reich*, 1947), Vsevolod Vishnevsky's *The Optimistic Tragedy* (1948), *Measure for Measure* (1948), Clifford Odets' *Golden Boy* (1950), Shaw's *Mrs. Warren's Profession* (1950), Goethe's *Egmont* (1952), and many others. In 1954 Peter Hacks began a long relationship with the theatre, when Langhoff staged his *Die Schlacht bei Lobositz* (*The Battle at Lobositz*), and eventually Hacks worked as dramaturge at the theatre (1960–1963). There have been a number of premieres of Hacks' works at the playhouse.

Langhoff's style was strongly influenced by Reinhardt (careful preparation before starting a production), Brahm (theatre as a social entity), Brecht (a friend), and Stanislavsky (he talked a lot with his actors). Perhaps his greatest production was the Brecht/Eric Engel staging of Brecht's *Mutter Courage und ihre Kinder* (*Mother Courage and Her Children*), first done in 1949 and eventually carried into the repertory of the Berliner Ensemble (with some of the actors from the Deutsches Theater). Benno Besson, Adolf Dresen, and Hans-Diether Meves all worked for Langhoff and eventually became some of East Germany's strongest *regisseurs*.

In 1963 Langhoff resigned to be replaced by Wolfgang Heinz, who had been an actor at the Deutsches Theater from 1920 to 1924 and had been a *regisseur* under Langhoff. The cold war had a great influence on the repertory, and the choice of plays began to narrow under his leadership. There were some excellent productions, particularly those by Besson, who staged *Tartuffe* (1963), the Hacks/Aristophanes' *Peace* (1962), *Oedipus Tyrannos* (1967), and other plays. Heinz staged *Hamlet* (1964) and *Faust I*. Fritz Bornemann staged Max Frisch's *Andorra* (1966) and the *Marat/Sade* play of Peter Weiss (1967) plus Schiller's *Mary Stuart* (1968). The emphasis during the Heinz era was clearly on productions and not on repertory, though some adventurous work was done. The absurdists, however, were clearly ignored during this period.

Heinz was succeeded by Hans Anselm Perten. Perten's real love was the theatre in Rostock, and he remained only two seasons in Berlin, returning to the city he loved. In 1972 Gerhard Wolfram became intendant, having worked in Halle, Dresden, and Leipzig before coming to Berlin. He is still intendant of the Deutsches Theater.

Many of Germany's finest *regisseurs* work at the Deutsches Theater, including Friedo Solter, who staged Goethe's *Torquato Tasso* (1976), *King Lear* (1976), and other plays. Adolf Dresen works here, as does Horst Schönemann, whose best production was Ulrich Pleenzdorf's *Die Neuen Leiden des Jungen W.* (*The New Sorrows of the Young W.*, 1973).

The earmark of the Deutsches Theater from the Brahm era to the present time has been its impeccable choice of plays. Even during the Nazi years, the Deutsches Theater was the place to see plays of high literary merit. The theatre stages twenty works each season. Twelve plays will be new works to be seen in three houses. A large theatre seats 856, the Kammerspiele seats 480, and a small house, with flexible seating, is used for experimental productions. The acting company numbers eighty (fifty men and thirty women), with ten *regisseurs* and nine dramaturges. The theatre stresses ensemble over stars and solid staging over novelty. Its choice of plays is obviously governed by what the government decrees, though the theatre has been criticized on several occasions for its choice of plays ("not correct enough").

Since Berlin is not only East Germany's capital but also its center of theatre activity, most good talent eventually gravitates there. Since World War II a number of first-rate actors and *regisseurs* have worked at the Deutsches Theater, and the playhouse continues to attract some of Germany's first-rate talent. In addition, the theatre has been instrumental in developing one of East Germany's best writers, Peter Hacks. The theatre feels its strength lies in the fact that it is a theatre of equality.

LEON M. AUFDEMBERGE

MAXIM GORKY THEATRE
108 East Berlin
Am Fesungsgraben 2
East Berlin, East Germany

Of all the theatres described in this section, the Maxim Gorky Theatre in East Berlin is perhaps the loveliest. Located just off the most famous of all Berlin streets, Unter den Linden, the theatre was built in 1827 by Theodore Ottmer to designs by Karl K. Schinkel, Berlin's great neoclassic architect. It was originally a concert hall, the Singakadamie, in which both Felix Mendelssohn-Bartholdy and Franz Liszt conducted. In 1947 the building was redesigned as a theatre and named the Theater des Hauses der Kultur der Sowjetunion, under the directorship of Robert Trösch. The first production staged by the new company was Soviet writer Boris Lawrenjow's *The Breach*. The troupe did many other Soviet writers, including a much-discussed production of Vsevolod Vishnevsky's *The Optimistic Tragedy* (1948, *regie* William Langhoff).

In 1952 the theatre was renamed the Maxim Gorky Theatre, with a new company under the leadership of Maxim Vallentin, one of East Germany's leading Marxist *regisseurs*. Vallentin also staged the first production, Lawrenjow's *For Those at Sea* (October 30, 1952), with Hans-Peter Minetti as Borowski. In the early years of the theatre, Vallentin concentrated on Russian works and on writers from other Socialist countries. There were also productions of plays by Shakespeare, Molière, Shaw, and modern German writers, such as Julian Hay, Friedrich Wolf, and Johannes Becher, and some German classics.

The style of the company was, from the beginning, Socialist-realistic, very Stanislavsky, and very ensemble. In the company in the early years were actors such as Hans-Peter Minetti, Sabine Krug, Hilmar Thate, Walter Jupe, and Friedel Nowack. Rather than look for lead actors, however, the company strove for uniformity. This meant that some of the most highly regarded actors in the company did leads in one play and walk-ons in another.

Fortunately, a number of East Germany's leading *regisseurs* became attracted to the company quite early, and it enjoyed an admirable list of tightly realized productions from the very beginning: Miloslaw Stehlik's *The Way to Life* (1952, *regie* Werner Schulz-Wittan/Achim Hübner); Anatoli Surow's *The Green Signal* (1953, *regie* Vallentin); the premiere of Friedrich Wolf's *Das Schiff auf der Donau* (*The Ship on the Donau*, 1955, *regie* Vallentin); Schiller's *Die Räuber* (*The Robbers*, 1955, *regie* Vallentin), with Albert Hetterle as Karl; Ibsen's *Ghosts* (1956, *regie* Werner Schulz-Wittan), with Nowack as Mrs. Alving and Thate as Oswald; and Stehlik's *Peasant's Life* (1957, *regie* Schulz-Wittan).

Gorky's masterpiece, *Night Hotel* (usually translated in English as *The Lower Depths*), was produced in 1957, a production that established the Maxim Gorky as a major East German company. The work was approached as a complete recreation of the period, and the company worked marvelously together, with actors who normally played large roles with the company talking smaller parts. The work was restudied in 1961 and was kept in the repertory until 1973, playing 267 performances.

In the late 1950s, with new *regisseurs* joining, often for one production, the style of the company became more expansive. Among the new *regisseurs* who came for a longer period were Horst Schönemann and Hans Dieter Mäde, both of whom had made major names for themselves elsewhere. The company also began to play works that were not necessarily in the Socialist-realist column. Among the works done about this time were Ewan MacColl's comedy (based on Aristophanes' *Lysistrata) Unternehmen Olzweig* (*Undertaking Olive Branch*, 1957, *regie* Joan Littlewood); a double bill of Heiner Müller's *Der Lohndrucker* (*The Undercutter*) and *Die Korrektur* (*The Correction*, 1958, *regie* Mäde), with the latter a premiere; Grischa Ostrovsky's *Thievery and Love* (1959, *regie* Schulz-Wittan); Gorky's *Enemies* (1959, *regie* Mäde); Vratislav Blazek's *And on Christmas Evening* (1960, *regie* Mäde), with Hetterle as the father; and Heinrich von Kleist's *Der zerbrochene Krug* (*The Broken Jug*, 1961, *regie* Vallentin), with Kurt Steingraf as Adam.

In the early 1960s and through the rest of the decade, there was a movement to perform more works from other Eastern Bloc countries, more premieres, and even some plays from the capitalist world, provided they fit the philosophy of the company. Lorraine Hansberry's *A Raisin in the Sun* was presented in 1963 (*regie* Mäde) but had only scant success. Of course, the company did not neglect works by earlier playwrights. Productions of the 1960s included many plays from all over, with the following especially noted: the premiere of Ewan MacColl's *Rummelplatz* (1961, *regie* Mäde); Lajos Mesterhazy's *The Eleventh Commandment* (1962, *regie* Helfried Schöbel/Schönemann); the Jules Verne/Pavel Kohout *Around the World in 80 Days* (1962, *regie* Schönemann); the premiere of Claus Hammel's *Um Neun an der Achterbahn* (*Around Nine on the Roller Coaster*, 1964, *regie* Schönemann); Max Frisch's *Don Juan oder Die Liebe zu Geometrei* (*Don Juan, or the Love of Geometry*, 1966, *regie* Wolfram Krempel), with Alexander Lang as Don Juan; the premiere of Manfred Freitag and Jochen Nestler's *Seemannsliebe* (*Sea Man's Life*, 1967, *regie* Kurt Veth); and Pirandello's *Liola* (1968, *regie* Hans-George Simmgen).

Albert Hetterle became intendant in 1968, an appointment that marked a change in management but not in philosophy. One of the first things Hetterle did was to form a Foyertheater to play smaller cast works. He kept to the kind of plays done earlier, but there were several new *regisseurs* including Fritz Bornemann, Karl Gassauer, and Wolfram Krempel. Among the major productions in the first years of Hetterle's era were Gogol's *The Inspector General* (1969, *regie* Simmgen); Franz Freitag's *Der Egoist* (1969, *regie* Frank Beyer); Michail Schatrow's *Bolschevik* (1969, *regie* Bornemann), with Hetterle as Swerdlow; Rudi Strahl's *In Sachen Adam und Eva* (*In the Concerns of Adam and Eve*, 1970, *regie* Gerhard Konig); Gorky's *Wassa Schelesnowa* (1970, *regie* Hetterle), with Manja Behrens in the title role; Goldoni's *La donna di garbo* (*The Clever Woman*, 1971, *regie* Karl Gassauer); Lessing's *Minna von Barnhelm* (1972, *regie* Hetterle), with Jutta Hoffmann as Minna; Armin Stolper's *Himmelfahrt zu Erde* (*Ascension to Earth*, 1972, *regie* Wolfram Krempel); Gorky's *Barbarians* (1972, *regie* Mäde); Michail Schatrow's *Campanella and the Commander* (1973, *regie* Mäde), with Hilmar Baumann as the Commander; Strindberg's *Erik XIV* (1974, *regie* Mäde), with Hetterle in the title role; Gorky's *The Last Ones* (1975, *regie* Wolfgang Heinz); and the premiere of Hacks' *Rosie Träumt* (*Rosie Dreamed*, 1975, *regie* Krempel).

In the last half of the 1970s and to the present, the Gorky has enjoyed a very good period. Hetterle has continued to expand the *regisseurs'* staff as some of his regulars left to become heads of theatres in the provinces. Since 1978 he has had as resident playwright Jürgen Gross, whose works are frequently done in East Germany. Many of the productions are not in the slavishly realistic style of the earlier age, particularly those of Thomas Langhoff. The important productions include: Peter Hacks' *Ein Gesprach im Hause Stein über den abwesenden Herr von Goethe* (*A Conversation in the Stein House over the Absent Herr von Goethe*, 1976, *regie* Krempel), with Karin Gregorek as Charlotte Stein; a new production of *The Lower Depths* (1977, *regie* Langhoff); the premiere of Jürgen Gross' *Match* (1978, *regie* Krempel); Hauptmann's *Einsame Menschen* (*Lonely People*, 1978, *regie* Langhoff); Valentin Rasputin's *Money for Maria* (1979, *regie* Hetterle), with Monika Hetterle as Maria; Chekhov's *The Three Sisters* (1979, *regie* Langhoff); Gross' *Geburtstagsgaste* (*Birthday Guest*, 1980, *regie* Krempel); Shakespeare's *A Midsummer Night's Dream* (1981, *regie* Lang-hoff); Gogol's *The Inspector General* (1981, *regie* Boris Luzendo of the Maxim Gorky Theatre in Minsk in the USSR); and Jordan Raditschokow's *Attempt to Fly* (1981, *regie* Grischa Ostrovsky).

The model for the organization of the company was more or less based on the Moscow Art Theatre, with choice of repertory similar in the two theatres. Socialist Realism is very much the style of the company. So, despite the fact that *regisseurs* are an important component in the theatre, one suspects acting may be more significant.

The company's repertory consists largely of naturalistic plays of either the late nineteenth century or Socialist works of the twentieth century. The company does four to six new works every year, and there is generally a premiere, as well as revivals of popular plays from previous seasons. Plays are kept in the repertory until they no longer draw.

The acting company numbers fifteen women and twenty-nine men and, because of the ensemble feeling in the theatre, this total tends to remain rather stable. There are four dramaturges, and the theatre has its own *atelier* (studio) for building the scenery.

The company has toured East Germany and various Socialist countries and plays host to other theatres from other parts of the Socialist world. The Gorky has its own paper which bears the name of the theatre. The whole organization has a cheerfulness about it which extends to the women who are in the ticket booth. The theatre is frequently sold out, not only because its main house is small (460 seats), but also because its productions are very good. The Studio Bühne (with flexible seating) is almost always sold out. It currently has an ongoing relationship with the Maxim Gorky Theatre in Minsk and is exchanging *regisseurs* with them.

So, despite the limitations (the company finds this a virtue) of the rather uniform style of the acting company, the Gorky is still a good place to go. One of the company's many strengths, and there are many, is that plays in the repertory for a long while tend to remain fresh. This is no small accomplishment and something upon which the theatre prides itself.

LEON M. AUFDEMBERGE

PEOPLE'S THEATRE
(Volksbühne)
Luxemburg Platz
X102 East Berlin, East Germany

The name Volksbühne (People's Theatre) is one of the oldest in German theatrical history and has reference to two things: an organization, founded in the 1890s and still existing across West Germany, which buys theatre tickets for members; and several theatres which are (or were) Volksbühnes. In Berlin there are two Volksbühnes; one in East Berlin and another in West Berlin, founded in 1949 with Rudolf Hammacher as intendant.

The Volksbühne movement was founded by the Freie Bühne in the 1890s. Cecil W. Davis, in his history of the Volksbühne organization, *Theatre for the People* (Austin, Texas: University of Texas Press, 1977), states that the Freie Bühne was "born of a marriage between political and artistic movements, socialism and naturalism" (p. 1). It brought theatre to people who were too poor to attend commercial or state theatres in Berlin.

The original organization was founded by Otto Brahm, an early champion of Ibsen in Germany and at one time one of Berlin's most important critics. The opening performance was Ibsen's *Ghosts*, given in 1889, uncut and greeted alternately with boos, hisses, and cheers. From this original group came others, and at various times there have been the Freie Bühne; the Volksbühne; the Freie Volksbühne; and the Neue Freie Volksbühne—each competing with the others, though all having the same aims. The last two had begun to merge in 1913 when a new theatre, the Volksbühne, the product of the Neue Freie Volksbühne, was dedicated. The opening performance came on December 30, 1914, with Bjørnstjerne Bjørnson's *When the Vineyards Are in Blossom*. The director of the new theatre, located on Bülowplatz, was Emil Lessing, and its architect was Walter Kaufmann. From the very first it was clear that, although this was Berlin's first modern theatre, it was inadequate in both sight lines and acoustics, though many critics praised the decoration. Over the top of the theatre appeared the caption: *Der Kunst dem Volke* (Art of the People).

The period from the end of World War I until Hitler's rise was a fervent time for the merged organizations and for the new theatre. From 1915 to 1918 Max Reinhardt staged many classics, particularly Schiller and Shakespeare. In 1918 Friedrich Kayssler took over, remaining until 1923; he made the theatre one of the most experimental in Germany, with premieres such as Ernst Toller's *Masse Mensch* (*Mass Man*, 1921). Jurgen Fehling was his chief *regisseur*. Kayssler was followed by Fritz Hall, who invited Piscator to be part of the producing organization. Piscator was apt to be quarrelsome but presented many well-received productions. It was here the term "Epic Theatre" was first used in the staging of Alfons Paquet's play, *Flags*, which dealt with German immigrants in Chicago. Hall was succeeded by a number of directors (including Heinz Hilpert and Karl Heinz Martin), until the Nazis took over the building as state property in 1934. In 1939 the Volksbühne organization was dissolved. Plays continued to be staged at the theatre under the management of Eugen Klopfer, who was a great *regisseur* and also a great follower of National Socialism. In 1945 the theatre was damaged by bombs, and the next year the company disbanded.

The Volksbühne organization was refounded in 1945 by many of the same members who had been pushed out by the Nazis. For a while there were two competing Volksbühne organizations, one in the Russian sector and one in the other three. Eventually, the one in the Russian sector was disbanded. In 1947 the Russians decided to reopen the old theatre, now located on the renamed Karl

Liebknecht Platz (still later it was to become the [Rose] Luxemburg Platz) but it was to be 1954 before the theatre finally opened. The theatre was partly renovated by the architect H. Richter. The first intendant for the new theatre was Fritz Wisten. He had opened that theatre with Alexander N. Alfingeoz's *Maschenka*. The repertory of the theatre included German, American, and British works, but Russian, particularly Soviet, plays would be most prominent. Eventually, this theatre was given to Brecht to be the home of the Berliner Ensemble, and Wisten brought his old company to the newly opened theatre. The opening performance was Schiller's *Wilhelm Tell*, with Wisten as *regisseur* and Franz Kutschera in the lead role.

Wisten invited a number of prominent *regisseurs* to be part of the theatre, including Fritz Borhemann, Ernst Kahle, and Benno Besson. Wisten staged a number of works himself, including plays by Tolstoy and Goethe. In 1956 he founded the ''Theaters in 3 Stock'' (Theatre on the Third Floor) to stage more intimate works. Heiner Müller began a long association with the theatre as a playwright in 1957, with a dramatization of John Reed's *Ten Days That Shook the World*. Wisten was followed by Wolfgang Heinz (1962–1963), who remained for only one season but long enough to stage a memorable *Florian Geyer* by Hauptmann and the Piscator version of Tolstoy's *War and Peace* with Hannes Fischer helping stage the Tolstoy work. Heinz was followed by Maxim Vallentin, from 1963 to 1966, a period when the theatre began to solidly mirror the current politics of the East German government. Vallentin had spent World War II in the Soviet Union. His forte was staging Gorky and contemporary Russians. Strangely, the most remembered productions came from elsewhere: Besson's production of Molière's *Tartuffe*, with Fred Duren in the title role (1963); Dürrenmatt's *Der Besuch der Alten Dame* (*The Visit from the Old Lady*, 1965, *regie* Bornemann), with Manja Behrens as Klara; and Peter Hacks' *Moritz Tassow* (1965, *regie* Besson).

Vallentin was replaced by Karl Holán, who remained from 1966 to 1974. Under his guidance, the Volksbühne would expand its repertory (to more international plays) and its acting company. Bornemann staged Peter Weiss' *Marat/Sade* play in 1967, followed by a meticulously staged Schiller's *Mary Stuart* and a *Don Carlos* by the same author, both in 1968. Other important productions were Shaw's *Caesar and Cleopatra* (1969, *regie* Otto Fritz), with Wolf Kaiser as Caesar and Angelica Domröse as Cleopatra; Ostrovsky's *The Forest* (1970, with production by the Manfred Karge/Matthias Langhoff team); the Müller/Aristophanes' *Weiberkomedie* (*Women's Comedy*, 1971, *regie* Marquardt); Ernst Kohler's *Der Geist von Cranitz* (*The Spirit of Cranitz*, 1971, *regie* Marquardt); and others.

In 1968 the theatre began to stage Dario Fo, the delightful Italian Marxist writer. Perhaps the best known production of the era was Besson's staging of Brecht's *Der Gute Mensch von Sezuan* (*The Good Woman of Setzuan*) in 1970, with Ursula Karusseit as Shen Te/Shui Ta. Besson had first staged the play at the Berliner Ensemble without success. This production proved a great success and is still in the repertory with fresh sets and costumes added as needed. Besson followed this with Molière's *The Doctor in Spite of Himself* (1971); Carlo Gozzi's *King Stag* (1972), which was one of the most enchanting productions ever seen in East Berlin; and Peter Hacks' *Margarete in Aix* (1973). Pieter Hahn joined the Volksbühne in the late 1960s to become its top designer, especially for the Langhoff/Karge team. He worked on *Othello* (1970), Ibsen's *The Wild Duck* (1973), and other productions.

Besson became intendant in 1974 and remained until 1978. He made the house known for its stage productions, including some of his best work: *As You Like It* (1975, with sets by Eric Toffolutti) and *Hamlet* (1977). Heiner Müller contributed two of his best plays: *Die Schlacht* (*The Battle*, 1975) and *Die Bauern* (*The Peasants*, 1976). Brigette Soubeyran staged Racine's *Britannicus* (1975), which is especially remembered for the fluidity of staging style; and there was a notable production of Gorky's *The Beautiful Green Bird*, with staging by Helmut Strassburger. In 1977 Besson left to freelance and was replaced by Dr. Fritz Rodel.

The Volksbühne, one of the best acting companies in East Germany, is composed of sixty actors, forty men and twenty women. The theatre does four to six new major productions on the main stage and several in its other houses. In addition, it presents a number of revivals of popular works from previous years and carries over productions from year to year. The theatre employs five *regisseurs* and five dramaturges to assist them. Its best ongoing relationship has been with the well-known East German dramatist, Heiner Müller, whose work is frequently done in West Germany as well. Müller has had six plays and two translations done at the theatre.

The Volksbühne considers itself very much a people's theatre as its choice of playwrights reflects—Gozzi, Goldoni, Shakespeare, Schiller, Goethe, Ibsen, and Molière. (Surprisingly, the production of Racine's *Brittanicus* was popular). Audiences like good productions and will return to see the same piece if it is well staged. The plays are chosen by the intendant with the help of his staff, especially Hans-Dieter, who is one of Germany's best *regisseurs* and now heads the artistic end of the theatre, and Dr. Werner Heinitz, the chief dramaturge. Plays are selected with an eye to the box office but not heavily so. There are some subscriptions to the house, but the theatre relies on single box office sales.

The Volksbühne has four houses—the Grosses Haus, which seats eight hundred and plays daily, and three smaller houses, all of which seat about one hundred. The actors work among the houses. Since 1977 the theatre has started a heavy touring policy, going to Paris, Lyon, Zurich, Turin, Sophia, Prague, and Helsinki. In 1978 *The Good Woman of Setzuan* went to Amsterdam. The company would like to do more touring in the future, but East German houses are of late feeling an economic pinch. Since only part of the income of the theatre comes from subsidy, the Volksbühne must be responsive to what its customers want. Its policy is to hire young *regisseurs* with lively ideas, lest the theatre fall into dull practices. One of these new *regisseurs* is Jürgen Gosch, whose production of Georg Büchner's *Leonce und Lena* was a success for the theatre in 1979. Among its older group of *regisseurs* is the Karge/Langhoff team, which occasionally works in the West.

The Volksbühne differs from the other East German houses in that it probably does more international works and it has made a specialty of more modern works from East Germany and elsewhere. It very much reflects the Marxist government of East Germany (as do all East German houses), but political position is not the only reason for doing a play. To be produced at the Volksbühne means one thing for a play—it must be a good one. Its *regisseurs* are some of East Germany's best, although Besson works elsewhere these days. All these factors make the Volksbühne one of the most popular and best theatres in East Germany.

LEON M. AUFDEMBERGE

PEOPLE'S THEATRE OF ROSTOCK
(Volkstheater Rostock)
33 Patriotischer Weg
Rostock, East Germany 25

On October 5, 1896, a theatre was built in Rostock by the noted Berlin architect, Heinrich Seeling, in heavily baroque style. The opening performance was Schiller's *Wilhelm Tell* (*regie* Carl Habermayer), with the young Paul Wegener as Stauffacher, followed by the second act of Wagner's *Lohengrin*. The first director for the company was Carl Hagen, whose main passion was Wagner. Fortunately, Habermayer set the style for the acting company doing cycles of plays, including a Schiller cycle (1896–1897) and a Shakespeare history cycle (1900). Habermayer's single productions included Rostand's *Cyrano de Bergerac* (1899), with himself in the title role; Shakespeare's *Richard III* (1900); Bjørnstjerne Bjørnson's *Beyond Our Power*; Goethe's *Faust*(1901); and Maurice Maeterlinck's *Monna Vanna* (1902). A number of guest artists appeared at the theatre during this period, including Maria Reisenhofer, Franziska Elmenreich, Rossa Poppe, Irene Treisch, and an artist who frequently returned, Adalbert Matkowsky.

After Hagen's death in 1905, the theatre was managed for one season (1905–1906) by Adolf Wallhöfer, another Wagner enthusiast. Rudolf Schaper (1906–1916) continued the guest artist policy and tried to balance the repertory between operas and plays. Schaper liked Ibsen especially. A goodly number of plays by Gerhart Hauptmann, August Strindberg, and Hermann Sudermann were also done during his tenure. The theatre was closed for part of World War I but reopened in the 1916–1917 season, under the leadership of Otto Ockert. Ockert so greatly strengthened the Wagnerian and Strauss parts of the operatic repertory that the theatre was sometimes called the Second Bayreuth.

Under Ludwig Neubeck (1919–1925) there was a better balance between operas and plays. He had a very good *regisseur*, Hanns Donadt, who specialized in big-cast spectacles, such as Goethe's *Faust I* (1924) and Ibsen's *Peer Gynt*

(1925). Two guest artists much admired during the period were Hermine Körner and Paul Wegener.

Ernst Immish was *Generalintendant* from 1925 to 1935 and was instrumental in making the theatre more modern in both repertory and staging style. Critics outside Rostock began reviewing plays; there are reviews and pictures in German publications of works such as Hans J. Rehfish's *Nickel und die 32 Gerechten* (*Nickel and the 32 Just Men*, 1925, *regie* Ernst Schwitzkein), Leo Lenz's *Leonie* (1927, *regie* Alfred Nicolai), the premiere of Rolf Lauckner's *Die Entkleidung des Antonio Canosa* (*The Disrobing of Antonio Canosa*, 1927, *regie* Ludwig Seipp), Robert Walther's *Die grosse Hebammenkunst* (*The Great Art of Midwifery*, 1928, *regie* Erich Hell), Graham Rawson's *Soldatenschicksal* (*Soldier's Destiny*, 1928, *regie* Harald Röbbeling), Hebbel's *Gyges und sein Ring* (*Gyges and His Ring*, 1928, *regie* Röbbeling), the Brecht/Weill *Die Dreigroschenoper* (*The Threepenny Opera*, 1928, *regie* Röbbeling), Shakespeare's *Hamlet* (1930, *regie* Johannes Lehmann), and Goethe's *Egmont* (1932, *regie* Carl Haberlein).

During the Nazi era, the theatre was led by Friedrich Wacker (1935–1945), who emphasized German classics and guest artists. He kept a small company that became smaller during the war. He changed the theatre's name to the Theater der Seestadt Rostock. (After World War II, the company would be called Volkstheater Rostock.) Among the works performed during this period were Shakespeare's *King Lear* (1935, *regie* Wacker), with Werner Krauss as a guest artist in the title role; Felix Dhünen's *Uta von Naumburg* (1936, *regie* Eugen Brabander); Schiller's *Mary Stuart* (1937, *regie* Wacker), with two guest artists, Maria Koppenhöfer as Elisabeth and Käthe Dorsch in the title role; Heinrich von Kleist's *Prinz Friedrich von Homburg* (1937, *regie* Wolfgang Kaehler); Hauptmann's *Florian Geyer* (1937, *regie* Wacker); Goethe's *Egmont* (1939, *regie* Edward Hermann); Hauptmann's *Michael Kramer* (1940, *regie* Hermann); and Schiller's *Kabale und Liebe* (*Intrigue and Love*, 1941, *regie* Hermann). In 1942 the Stadttheater was destroyed in a bombing raid, and the next year a new theatre was opened, rebuilt from the old Philharmonie, which had been an old labor meeting hall. The theatre survived the war.

The first performance after the war was a concert, including orchestral and operatic works done on May 5, 1945; works by Chekhov and Curt Goetz followed later the same month. The first head after the war was Johannes Semper, who contributed a great deal to the opera and spoken theatre. He tried to introduce a highly popular repertory to Rostock, including Broadway and West End successes. The most publicized plays of his period include the premiere of Hedda Zinner's *Caféhaus Payer* (*The Coffeehouse Payer*, 1945, *regie* P. Ayer) and Tolstoy's *The Power of Darkness* (1948, *regie* Otto Ulrich).

The regime of Heinrich Allmeroth (1949–1952) was more significant for several reasons. First, he had two notable resident *regisseurs*, Adolf Peter Hoffmann and Victor Dräger, and several good guest stagers. He also had an exceedingly fine actor in Norbert Christian, who doubled as a *regisseur*. While the classics were stressed, there were several good Brecht productions. Among the most significant works of this period were Goethe's *Götz von Berlichingen* (1949, *regie* Dräger); Brecht's *Herr Puntila und sein Knecht Matti* (*Mr. Puntila and His Hired Man, Matti*, 1950, *regie* Egon Monk, who later worked for the Berliner Ensemble); Schiller's *Die Räuber* (*The Robbers*, 1950, *regie* Dräger); Goethe's *Faust I* (1950, *regie* Hoffmann, who also played Mephisto); Shakespeare's *Hamlet* (1951, *regie* Hoffmann), with Christian in the title role; and Goethe's *Faust II* (1952, *regie* Hoffmann who again played Mephisto). In 1952 Benno Besson began an extensive relationship with the theatre, staging Brecht's adaptation of Molière's *Don Juan*; Joseph Noerden was in the title role and Christian played Sganarelle. Christian left the company shortly thereafter for Brecht's Berliner Ensemble, where he repeated his role.

In 1952 Hans Anselm Perten came from Wismar to be *Generalintendant*, and, with him, Rostock became one of the leading theatres in East Germany. Perten began his career rather cautiously in Rostock with a series of classic productions: Shakespeare's *Measure for Measure* (1953); Schiller's *Mary Stuart* (1955), with Christine van Santen (Rostock's best known actress) in the title role; Shakespeare's *Antony and Cleopatra* (1955); Ibsen's *Ghosts* (1955); and *A Doll's House* (1956), with van Santen as Nora. During this same period, Besson continued his Brecht stagings: *Der gute Mensch von Sezuan* (*The Good Woman of Setzuan*, 1956), with Käthe Reichel as Shen Te/Shui Ta; *Die Dreigroschenoper* (*The Threepenny Opera*, 1959), with Erwin Geschonneck as Mackie Messer; and *Die Heilige Johanna der Schlacthöfe* (*Saint Joan of the Stockyards*, 1961), with Reichel as Johanna.

In 1956 Kurt Barthel, who wrote under the name Kuba, became a playwright and the chief dramaturge for the theatre. His influence was seen in the more ambitious staging style of Perten in the late 1950s and a much more Marxist approach to both repertory and staging. Kuba also contributed several works as premieres for the company, all staged by Perten: *Die Legende von Klaus Störtebeker* (1959) with music by Günter Kochan, and van Santen as Margaretha von Dänemark; and his adaptation of Büchner's *Dantons Tod* (*Danton's Death*, 1962). His death in 1967 was a severe shock to the company, and he was much missed.

In the late 1950s and 1960s the repertory of the company was expanded as was the number of actors. The company began to tour, not only in East, but also in West, Germany. Perten's productions began to be reviewed in all the leading East German theatre magazines, with the repertory of the theatre coming from both classic and modern eras. Some major productions of this period include Shakespeare's *Richard III* (1957), with Hermann Wagemann in the title role; Lessing's *Minna von Barnhelm* (1957); Schiller's *Wallenstein* cycle (1959); Chekhov's *The Seagull* (1960), with van Santen as Nina; Shakespeare's *Henry IV* (1960); Dreiser/Piscator's *An American Tragedy* (1961); Jerome Kilty's *Dear Liar* (1962), with van Santen as Mrs. Campbell and Gerd Micheel (Rostock's most noted actor) as Shaw; Hauptmann's *Hamlet in Wittenberg* (1962), with Micheel in the title role; Rafaele Solana's *There Ought to Be Women Bishops*

(1963), with Erika Donkelmann as Matea; Shakespeare's *Hamlet* (1964), with Micheel in the title role; Tennessee Williams' *Orpheus Descending*, with Micheel as Val; Claus Hammel's *Morgen kommt der Schornsteinfeger* (*Tomorrow the Chimney Sweeper Comes*, 1969); and James Baldwin's *Blues for Mr. Charlie* (1969).

In 1965 Perten staged the German Democratic Republic premiere of Peter Weiss' remarkable play, whose abbreviated title is the *Marat/Sade*play. It was a major success for the company and toured in East and West Germany as well. In the lead roles were Micheel as Marat, Ralph Borgwardt as de Sade, and van Santen as Charlotte Corday, with marvelously atmospheric sets by Falk von Wangelin. This began a long relationship between Weiss and Perten which continues today. The other Weiss plays staged in the 1960s were *Die Ermittelung* (*The Investigation*, 1965), *Nacht mit Gästen* (*Night with Company*, 1966), *Gesang von Lusitanischen Popanz* (*Song of the Lusitanian Bogey*, 1967), and *Vietnam Diskurs* (*Vietnam Discourse*, 1968).

From 1970 to 1972 Perten was intendant of the Deutsches Theater in East Berlin, taking part of Rostock's company with him. Gerd Puls took over for these years. Part of the slack of Perten's move was taken up by Horst Smiszek, one of East Germany's leading *regisseurs*, who worked for the theatre from 1971 to 1972. In 1972 Perten returned to Rostock.

Since his return, Perten has broadened his repertory, both in the number of plays presented and the types of plays he does. Certain playwrights have been repeats with the company: O'Neill, Hammel (who has contributed several premieres), and Weiss. Perten has also broadened the scope of the company to include *regisseurs* with different styles; thus, the major productions now done at Rostock are not always done by Perten himself. Since 1972 the major productions at Rostock have included Weiss' second version of *Hölderlin*(1973) with Micheel in the title role; O'Neill's *Long Day's Journey into Night* (1973); Antonio Buero Vallejo's *The Sleep of Reason* (1973) with Micheel as Goya; Manfred Steubel's *Ratcliff rechnet ab* (*Ratcliff Deducts*, 1974); Ernst Schumacher's *Die Versuchung des Forschers* (*The Temptation of the Investigators*) with Hans Peter Minetti as Einstein; Rolf Hochhuth's *Lysistrata und die NATO* (1975); Sławomir Mrożek's *Tango* (1975, *regie* Jozef Gruda); the premiere of Hammel's *Rom, oder die zweite Erschaffung der Welt* (*Rome, or the Second Creation of the World*, 1975); Edward Albee's *Who's Afraid of Virginia Woolf?* (1976); Hammel's *Das gelbe Fenster, das gelbe Stein* (*The Yellow Window, the Yellow Stone*, 1977); Buero Vallejo's *The Charitable Institution* (1977); Hochhuth's *Tod eines Jägers* (*Death of a Hunter*, 1977); O'Neill's *A Touch of the Poet* (1978), with Thomas Weisberger as "Con" and van Santen as Nora; the Weiss/Kafka *The Trial* (1978); Thornton Wilder's *Our Town* (1978, *regie* Wolfgang Kretchmer); Friedrich Dürrenmatt's *Die Frist* (*The Appointed Time*, 1979); the premiere of Hammel's *Humboldt und Bolivar oder der neue Continent* (*Humboldt and Bolivar or the New Continent*, 1979); Strindberg's *The Father*, in a new translation by Weiss (1980); Michail Schatrow's *Blue Horse on Red Grass*

(1980, *regie* Böttger); Hochhuth's *Die Juristen* (*The Jurists*, 1980); O'Neill's *Mourning Becomes Electra* (1980), with van Santen as Christine; Hochhuth's *Arztinhen* (*Lady Doctors*, 1981); Dürrenmatt's *Die Panne* (*The Breakdown*, 1981, *regie* Wilfred Kretschmer and Uwe-Detlev Jessen); the premiere of Monika Latzsch's *Häuschen mit Butler* (*House with Butler*, 1981, *regie* Jessen); the premiere of Hammel's *Die Prussen kommt* (*The Prussians Are Coming*, 1981); and Shakespeare's *Love's Labour's Lost* (1981, *regie* Jörg Kahler). Practically all the modern plays have been German Democratic Republic premieres.

The People's Theatre of Rostock is one of East Germany's most active, if not the most active, theatre. Generally, it stages about seven new productions a year. In addition, it carries over so many revivals that there are about thirty-five plays in the current repertory. One of the most important things Perten has accomplished in his years as *Generalintendant* is the number of theatres he has added to the company, so there are now seven houses: its recently renovated Grosses Haus, which seats over six hundred, and a series of smaller theatres (the Kleines Haus, the Intimes Theater, the Opera in Barocksaal, the Atelier Theater, the Kleine Komödie Warnemünde, and Studio 74). In addition, the company plays the Klubhus Neptune and the Theater Güstrow outside the city. Perten stages at least two works a year and also works in the opera as a *regisseur*. The acting company numbers twenty-two women and forty-eight men.

Perhaps the most interesting thing about the Rostock company outside Perten's own productions is the choice of repertory. No other company inside or outside Berlin has such a wide-ranging choice of plays available in any *Spielzeit*. Perten balances his repertory between classic and modern. Of course, a number of Marxist playwrights are exhibited every season; alongside these are writers, such as Eduardo de Filippo and Buero Vallejo, and frankly commercial writers, such as Barillet and Grédy, and Perten's own program in staging O'Neill. There is also a very active children's company. In addition to the theatre and opera, Perten is interested in the training of youth for the theatre and in the running of the drama school in Rostock which he helped found. Because of all these wide-ranging qualities, the Volkstheater and its *Generalintendant* Hans Anselm Perten have won the admiration of all German-speaking countries. All uncredited theatre productions in this article are by Hans Anselm Perten.

LEON M. AUFDEMBERGE

France

INTRODUCTION

The two major changes in French theatrical landscape after World War II were the decentralization of the theatre and the rise of the *metteur-en-scène* (stage director). Before World War II, there was no single theatre outside Paris that would have been termed significant; now there are dozens, all of which, except the Théâtre National Populaire, were founded after 1945. Most major cities now have some sort of theatre, many with permanent companies. Most of these developments can be credited to two ministers of culture, Jeanne Laurent and André Malraux who encouraged prominent theatrical figures in Paris to go to the provinces. Standards for these companies are generally very high, frequently higher than those of boulevard theatres, especially the quality of the repertory.

Decentralization has affected not only the provinces, but Paris as well; several good companies are located both in Paris (away from the boulevards) and in the suburbs. Most of these companies perform high-quality productions at low prices. Even the Comédie Française has the Odéon, which hosts theatre productions from the provinces.

The French government classifies all theatrical-producing organizations as follows:

1. The Maisons de la Culture, which import plays from both Paris and the provinces at high cost. These are frequently handsome buildings, the one at Firminy being designed by Le Corbusier.

2. The Centres Dramatiques Nationaux, which are funded by both state and local governments. Many of these have permanent companies.

3. The Théâtres Municipals, which are local theatres and import touring productions without any particular program in mind.

4. The Théâtres et Compagnies Dramatiques, which are funded by only local bodies.

5. The Théâtres Nationaux, which are few in number and are funded by the state.

6. The private theatres, most of which operate as do Broadway or West End theatres, though a few have companies that operate on a permanent basis, such as the Renaud-

Barrault company and the Théâtre du Soleil, and many also receive some form of subsidy.

Before World War II France had a small number of important *metteurs-en-scènes*, including Louis Jouvet, Jacques Copeau, and Gaston Baty, to which the name of Antonin Artaud has recently been added. Since the end of the war, a number of great ones have emerged, including those who make Paris their permanent home (Jean-Louis Barrault and Ariane Mnouchine) and those who choose to work in the provinces (Roger Planchon and Chéreau). Most of the new stagers have been pushing new playwrights as well, especially in the last ten years. The playwrights seem generally happy to work for the 13 percent commission. The great hope is that eventually a Jean Giraudoux or even a Paul Claudel will emerge.

LEON M. AUFDEMBERGE

ATTIC OF TOULOUSE
(Grenier de Toulouse)
3, rue de la Digue
31300 Toulouse, France

While the Attic of Toulouse was not officially founded until 1945, as early as 1943 several members of the troupe met informally for drama classes with Mires Vincent. Among them were Maurice Sarrazin (who was eventually to become the director of the Attic), Simone Turck, Jacque Duby, Renée Salabert (the future Mrs. Duby), Pierre Negre, and Pierre Chovy, with Daniel Sorano becoming a member soon after. Eventually, all of them would join the company. Some members of the informal group were in classes at the local Conservatory and found the instruction rather stifling. In 1944 part of the group left for Paris to play in Claude André Puget's *Les jours heureux* (*The Happy Days*), *mise-en-scène* Vincent. The trip did not prove altogether profitable, and they returned soon to reform in the *grenier* (attic) of the Sarrazin household and to plan a theatre company with Sarrazin as head.

The first performance was Racine's *Brittanicus*, a play that proved to be beyond the troupe's abilities. The production was changed to a bill of one acts, and the Racine work was reserved for a later date. The one acts were Georges Courteline's *La peur des coups* (*The Fear of Hitting*), Chekhov's *The Wedding Proposal*, and excerpts from Puget's *Les jours heureux*. Sarrazin and Jacques Duby shared staging responsibilities. The first public performance came on May 15, 1945, in the village of Septfonds. The bill, to which Paul Géraldy's *Les grande garçons* (*The Big Boys*) was added, was played in various towns in the region before it finally played to good reviews in Toulouse.

From 1945 to 1960 the group was itinerant, rehearsing in Toulouse to go on the road. While Toulouse was only part of the itinerary, the Attic was considered an important troupe almost from the beginning. The opening selection of the second season was Jean Anouilh's *Eurydice*, with Sarrazin staging. It was followed by an adaptation of Plautus' play *Poenulus*, called *Le Carthaginois* (*The Carthaginian*) in which Daniel Sorano scored a personal triumph as Milfion. This play, staged by Sarrazin, was revived several times over various seasons and played over 250 times throughout France. It eventually had a successful engagement in Paris, where it won the young company the Premier Prix du Concours des Jeunes Compagnies. In 1949 the company was made a Centre Dramatique (Center for Drama) and was awarded a subsidy by the government, but it was not a permanent theatre.

Throughout the 1940s and 1950s the repertory of the company relied heavily on the classics, particularly French classics. Many of the lead roles were played by Sorano, and the sets were by Pierre Lafitte or Maurice Melat. The great successes were as follows (unless otherwise stated they were staged by Sarrazin): Shakespeare's *Romeo and Juliet*; Nikolai Gogol's *The Marriage* (1949, *mise-en-scène* Duby); Molière's *Les fourberies de Scapin* (*The Cheats of Scapin*), with Sorano a winning title character; Aristophanes' *An Assembly of Women* (1950); Jean Cocteau's *La machine infernale* (1950); Shakespeare's *The Taming of the Shrew* (1951), with Sorano and Sarrazin in true repertory fashion playing small roles; Molière's *L'avare* (*The Miser*, 1953), which was revived several times; Shakespeare's *Much Ado About Nothing* (1955); Pierre Carlet de Marivaux's *Le jeu de l'amour et du hasard* (*The Game of Love and Chance*, 1956, *mise-en-scène* Simone Turck); Beaumarchais' *Le barbier de Séville* (1956); Jean Giraudoux's *Electre* (1957); Beaumarchais' *Le mariage de Figaro* (1957, *mise-en-scène* Turck); Luigi Pirandello's *Right You Are—If You Think You Are* (1958, *mise-en-scène* Turck), which played in Barcelona and won the Festival Prize there; Molière's *L'école des femmes* (*The School for Wives*, 1959); and Bertolt Brecht's *Mother Courage and Her Children* (1959, *mise-en-scène* Jacque Mauclair). During this time the company was very stable. The only major defection was Sorano, who left in 1952 to be part of the Renaud-Barrault company.

In the 1960s the Attic began to tackle more ambitious plays, to play fewer classic plays, and to stage more modern works. In 1964 the city of Toulouse remodeled a movie-house and gave it to the troupe, calling it the Théâtre Daniel Sorano in memory of the actor who had died in 1962. The troupe was to call this its home until 1969, when the local mayor decided he ought to choose the plays for the company. Sarrazin rejected the mayor's decision, and once again the troupe was back in the Sarrazin home. The Attic was to remain there for six months until friends of the company talked the French government into buying a movie-house and converting it into a home for the troupe, with the company paying rent to the government. The productions of the 1960s included such works as Molière's *Tartuffe* (1960, *mise-en-scène* Jean Bousquet); Tolstoy's *Tania* (1961); Shakespeare's *Twelfth Night* (1961); Jules Romains' *Knock* (1963); Beckett's *Waiting for Godot* (1964, *mise-en-scène* Roger Blin); the Romains/ Zweig/Ben Jonson *Volpone* (1965); Shakespeare's *King Lear*, with Sarrazin staging and playing the title role (1966); Armand Gatti's *V comme Vietnam* (*V as in Vietnam*, 1967), with the author staging the work; and Shakespeare's *Hamlet* (1969).

In the last fifteen years Sarrazin has enlarged the company's repertory considerably to include classics as well as more modern experimental works. Successes have included not only French works, but also many scripts from outside France, such as productions of Carlo Goldoni's *Le Marquis de Montefosco* (1970, *mise-en-scène* Jean-Pierre Vincent); Sarrazin's own *La Pièce*, with himself as stager (1971); Molière's *Don Juan* (1972); Shakespeare's *Julius Caesar* (1973); Brecht's *The Life of Galileo* (1973), with Sarrazin as both *metteur-en-scène* and playing Galileo; Molière's *L'avare* (1975), with Sarrazin again staging and playing the title character; Georges Feydeau's *La dame de Chez Maxim* (1976), with Betty Bek as La Mome Crevette; the Brecht-Kurt Weill *The Threepenny Opera* (1978), with staging by Sarrazin and Jean Favarel; Paval Kohout's *Poor Assassin* (1978); Gogol's *The Inspector General* (1979); Pirandello's *Right You Are—If You Think You Are* (1980, *mise-en-scène* Jean Favarel); and two Dumas works: *La dame aux camélias* by Dumas *fils* (1981, *mise-en-scène* Jean-Louis Martin Barbaz), with Sylvie Genty as Marguerite, and *Kean* by Dumas *père* (*mise-en-scène* Mario Franceschi), with Jean-Paul Zehnacker in the title role.

As a theatre company the Attic has earned enormous respect for itself throughout France, largely through Sarrazin's devotion to Toulouse. He has been chief administrator, head *metteur-en-scène*, and the lead actor for many productions. The theatre mounts three or four works a year; the rest of the season is made up of works from other theatres. As a rule plays open in Toulouse and then tour. Popular works are revived the following seasons when they do more touring. In the first years of the company, the troupe played many small towns in the area. Now the performances are more concentrated in large cities where patrons can afford the theatre's large productions. The Grenier has played throughout France, including several trips to Paris, and has performed in Algeria and Germany as well.

The company relies on a policy that enables the spectator to buy seats at reduced prices. The Attic has its own newspaper, *Theatre à Toulouse*, which announces plays coming up in the theatre. In Toulouse the company plays in four houses: its main house, which seats three hundred (le Grenier); the Théâtre Daniel Sorano, which has places for six hundred (the current mayor has no desire to pick plays and is a friend to the company); a small room in the permanent theatre, with no permanent seating; and occasionally the Théâtre du Capitole, which has seats for fifteen hundred. The theatre frequently plays host to other theatre companies from France and elsewhere, including the Pip Simmons group from England and Mummenschanz from Switzerland. It also sponsors music concerts and likes to have actors or *metteurs-en-scène* talk about a new play before it opens, either at the theatre or before organizations around town which regularly buy tickets. The theatre is very popular in the city and is frequently sold out. Only occasionally does the public stay away from a good production, as it did in 1979 when the theatre presented Arnold Wesker's *I'm Talking About Jerusalem* (production by Jean-Claude Bastos). Despite excellent reviews, it did not attract an audience.

The company has a nucleus of actors hired for the season, generally five or six; the rest of the productions are staffed by local actors. Only occasionally does Sarrazin hire an actor from Paris. As it is a Centre Dramatique National, it receives a subsidy from both the state (3.5 million francs) and the city of Toulouse (1.1 million francs), which is about 80 percent of its budget. Sarrazin is very serious in his duties as administrator and stager (to say nothing of his acting). This is probably why the Attic of Toulouse is admired not only in Toulouse, but throughout France as well.

LEON M. AUFDEMBERGE
(With the assistance of Josette Borja
of the theatre staff.)

CENTRE THEATRE OF LIMOUSIN
(Centre Théâtral du Limousin)
59, rue Montmailler
87000 Limoges, France

The Centre Theatre of Limousin was founded in 1964 by Jean-Pierre Laruy and Georges-Henri Régnier, both of whom had been active in theatre since childhood. Régnier began as a dancer at age five in Lille, later training as an actor (very Stanislavsky) in Paris, where he earned a precarious living as a super at the Comédie Française. Later, he worked with Jean-Louis Barrault as an assistant.

At the age of ten Laruy began his training as an actor, later studying at the Conservatory at Oran (his home city). He began staging plays at thirteen, and at sixteen he mounted a production of Paul Claudel's *L'échange* (*The Exchange*) at the Festival de Merz-el-Kebir. Eventually, he came to Paris where he studied at the Sorbonne. At the Lycée Henri IV, he came under the influence of Charles Dullin and of his teacher, Lucien Arnaud. Later, he, too, worked with Barrault as an actor, and still later, with the Troupe du Lycée Louis le Grand, where he played with Patrice Chéreau and Jean-Pierre Vincent. In 1961 with Régnier, Laruy founded Le Jeune Théâtre at the Cité Universitaire, where the two produced works by Claudel, Fernando Arrabal, Samuel Beckett, and Racine.

In 1964 George Lerminier, French inspecteur du théâtre, decided in a spirit of decentralization to transfer the young company to Limousin. In 1966 it therefore became the Centre Théâtral du Limousin. The company was designed to serve not only the city of Limousin, but also other small towns in the region. The first production staged in the 1964–1965 season was a double bill of Jules Renard's *Poil de Carotte* (*Red Head*) and Jean Cocteau's *La voix humaine* (*The Human Voice*), both staged by Laruy. (Unless otherwise stated in the following, Laruy did all the staging.)

During the years of the joint directorship, both staged productions, with Régnier doing most of the stage design. The repertory included largely French classics and a few modern surprises. A number of guest artists complemented the small company. The largest productions of the first years were the Corneille/Molière *Psyché* (1965, *mise-en-scène* Laruy and Régnier); Albert Camus' *Caligula* (1965, *mise-en-scène* Laruy and Régnier); Bertolt Brecht's *Antigone* (1965); Beckett's *Fin de partie* (*Endgame*, 1967), with Pierre Dux as Hamm; Claudel's *L'échange* (1968, *mise-en-scène* Régnier); Pierre Carlet de Marivaux's *La fausse suivante* (*The False Follower*, 1969); a collective script, *Premenons-nous en Limousin* (*Let's Walk Around Limousin*, 1970); Tennessee Williams' *The Milk Train Doesn't Stop Here Anymore* (1971); Eugene Ionesco's *Rhinocéros* (1972), with Laruy as Berender; and Alfred de Musset's *On ne badine pas avec l'amour* (*No Trifling with Love*, 1972). Actors who worked with the company during these years included Monica Boucheix, Frédéric Cerdal, Lucien Barjon, Frégoli, Christian Duc, and Héléna Bossis.

Régnier departed the company in 1972 to become head of the Théâtre de Bourges. Laruy stayed on, and in that same year the company became a Centre Dramatique National. Laruy has retained many of the same writers used in the earlier repertory. Some of them have become specialties of the company, especially Jean Giraudoux. Laruy has added a number of localities in France which the company regularly visits and has lengthened the visits to each city. In addition, the company has begun to play internationally on a regular basis. In recent years the company has done tours in Libya, Jordan, Tunisia, Algeria, Switzerland, Belgium, and Germany. In 1976 Laruy mounted a production of Racine's *Phèdre* in conjunction with the National Theatre of Egypt, with Samiha Ayoub in the title role. More recently (1980), the company has toured its production of Molière's *L'école des femmes* (*The School for Wives*) to West Germany, with Laruy both playing Arnolphe and staging the work.

The theatre continues the high standard of production it established during the double directorship. In the last years there have been Roger Vitrac's *Victor ou Les enfants au pouvoir* (*The Children to Power*, 1972), with Laruy playing the title role; Brecht's *Mother Courage and Her Children* (1973), with Mary Marquet as Ann Fierling (her last role); Rene de Obaldiea's *Du vent dans les branches de sassafras* (*The Wind in the Branches of the Sassafras*,1973); the Dostoyevsky/Camus *Les possédés* (*The Possessed*, 1974); Giraudoux's *Intermezzo* (1975); Giraudoux's *La Duchesse de Langeais* (1976); Dario Fo's *Mistero Buffo* (1976, *mise-en-scène* Hassan Geretly); Giraudoux's *Judith* (1977), with Anna Delueze in the title role; August Strindberg's *The Dance of Death* (1977); Alfred Jarry's *Ubu Roi* (1979, *mise-en-scène* Cerdal), with Frédéric Cerdal staging the work and playing the monstrous title role; *XVIIe et des Poussières-Les Farceurs avant Molière (1590–1640)* (*The XVIIth Century and the Pollen-Farceurs Before Molière [1590–1640]*), with the adaptation and *mise-en-scène* by Cerdal (1980); and Daniel Depland's *La mouche verte* (*The Green Mouth*, 1981).

The Centre Theatre generally does four new productions a year; the rest of its season is made up of productions from other theatres, including a variety of attractions such as plays and musical events for both adults and children. The company works eleven months a year, with the permanent company numbering four and the rest of the company hired as needed. The theatre has twenty-three permanent employees, and Laruy serves as *directeur-animateur, administrateur general*. The large technical and administrative staff tries to be as self-sustaining as possible. Its subsidy, which is currently somewhat over 2 million francs, comes from the city of Limoges, the department of Haute-Vienne, and the Ministry of Culture. Its main theatre is Le Petit Théâtre de la Visitation, which is a former chapel dating from the sixteenth century.

In recent years more modern works have been staged with special emphasis on a local playwright, Daniel Depland. The repertory also retains classical pieces. This balance of the classic and modern is characteristic of France's provincial theatres.

LEON M. AUFDEMBERGE

COMÉDIE FRANÇAISE
(La Comédie Française)
Salle Richelieu, Place Colette
Paris, France

L'Odéon and Le Petit Odéon
18, rue Vaugiraud
Paris, France

The Comédie Française is frequently called "la maison de Molière," because its founding owes a great deal to Molière and his troupe. Molière first appeared before Louis XIV in October 1658, thereby beginning a long relationship between the Sun King and the great French playwright. Louis both protected Molière (he finally persuaded the Church to bury him) and paid for numerous performances by Molière's company. At the time of the playwright's death in 1673 there were two rival companies: one at the Hôtel de Guénégaud headed by Molière and another at the Hôtel de Bourgogne, headed by the actor La Thorillière. On August 18, 1680, three weeks after the death of La Thorillière, Louis instructed the two acting companies to merge: the Comèdie Française had been formed. The first performances were on August 25, 1680, when the two united companies presented Racine's *Phèdre* and a minor play, *Les Carrosses d'Orléans* (*The Carriages of Orleans*). The letter solidifying the agreement was dated October 21, 1680.

According to Louis' decree, the new company would employ fifteen actors and twelve actresses, and the royal subsidy would total 12,000 livres. The theatre in which it would play was located in the Hôtel Guénégaud on the rue Seine. The players would be accorded certain rights: full civil and religious privileges; the sole right to play its own repertoire (Molière, Corneille, and Racine) forbidden to other French companies; and protection (which also meant freedom from interference) by the government. All of these rights would be lost during the Revolution a century later. In 1689 the company moved to a new theatre, the Jeu de Paume de l'Etoile on the rue Fossés-Saint Germain-des-Prés.

During the eighteenth century the company was blessed with new plays and great acting. A few actor-playwrights submitted pieces to the company, but the great writers for the group came from the outside. Alain-René Lesage saw his great comedy *Turcaret* presented by the Comédie in 1707, Voltaire began a long association with the company with his *Oedipe roi* in 1718, and Pierre Carlet de Marivaux, after a long string of successes with the rival Comédiens Italiens, joined the ranks of playwrights for the Comédie with his *La seconde surprise de l'amour* (*The Second Surprise of Love*) also in 1718. Diderot created his *Père de famille* (*Father of the Family*) in 1758, which was a success for the company, and in 1775 Beaumarchais gave his play *Le barbier de Séville* to the repertory of the Comédie Française. Beaumarchais wrote *La folle journée* (*A Day's Madness*) in 1778, but because of its revolutionary sentiments it was forbidden performance until 1781, when it was received with hysterical success and acclamation. The play is better known by its second title, *The Marriage of Figaro*. Voltaire, returning from a long exile, wrote his tragedy *Irène* (1778) for the theatre, where it was received with what would be known in French history as the *Triomphe de Voltaire*, the evening ending with the crowning of a bust of Voltaire on the stage. During the century the Comédie continued to revive the three great dramatists who still form the nucleus of the repertory: Molière, Racine, and Corneille.

The greatness of the plays produced by the Comédie Française during the century was equaled by its acting company: actresses such as "Duclos" and "Clarion" were famous for their Racine heroines; the gracious Louise Contat; "Dangeville," who was a favorite subject for Watteau; and, above all, Adrienne Lecouvreur, who was adept at both tragedy and comedy. Famous actors included Le Kain, who was Voltaire's favorite actor; La Rive, who did many Racine roles; and, in the latter part of the century, the "great glory of French acting," Talma, who was with the company from 1787 to 1826.

In 1765 the first of the Comédie's many scandals took place when "Dubois," an actress of scant talent and less manners, was forbidden to play her usual roles. She appealed to the Duc de Richelieu, and the actors who refused to play with her were thrown into a comfortable, but nevertheless real, jail. The actors were eventually set free. In 1770 the company was installed in a new theatre on the terraces of the Hôtel de Conde. The stage left (toward the center) was designated *cour*, and the stage right (toward the garden) was designated *jardin*, designations that still exist in the French theatre. In 1782 the company moved again to another theatre which is now l'Odéon, but the joy of playing in the new theatre was short-lived. Two forces split the company: Talma and the Revolution.

In 1787, when Talma joined the company, the actors and the public began to split into two factions: Talma, seconded by his intelligent wife Julia Carreau, were in the spirit of the Revolution, and they would eventually splinter their group from the Comédie and form the Théâtre de la République; a rival group would form behind the traditionalists and become the Théâtre de la Nation. The Comédie Française ceased to exist. In 1793 the second group was denounced by the Jacobeans and twenty-six actors were imprisoned; six were eventually guillotined, and the rest deported. These were perhaps the darkest days for the Comédie. Not only did the company no longer exist, but also the traditional rights of its actors had been abolished.

On May 14, 1799 (25 Floriel, Year VII), the group reconstituted itself under the auspices of the minister of the interior (François de Neufchâteau), who appointed the first real adminstrative head, Mahérault. The company would appear at a fairly new theatre (the old one had been damaged by fire), built by the architect Louis, on the rue de la Loi in 1785. It remains the company's home. Talma would be the leading actor with the company until his death in 1826. The leading actress was Mlle. Mars, who would remain with the company until her retirement in 1839.

Napoleon greatly admired Talma, and perhaps for this reason he took time from his duties as emperor to sign the Decree of Moscow (October 1812), which would reestablish the relationship between the company and the French state: that of a self-governing theatre which would be under the supervision of the superintendent of public entertainment. Despite a number of changes, this decree is more or less the ruling force of the Comédie today.

At the beginning of the nineteenth century, a new vigor began to show in the company's acting style, a style that would be associated largely with that of Talma, who combined the discipline of French classic acting with the romantic spirit. Many playwrights began to be inspired by his style, which hit its apogée in 1830 on the famous opening night of Victor Hugo's *Hernani*, generally called *La bataille d'Hernani*, with Firmin as the title character and the aging Mlle. Mars as the young heroine, Doña Sol. It was the signal for a battle royal between the classicists and the romantics. Only the first line of the play could be heard clearly; the rest of the drama was obscured by the catcalls of the traditionalists and the frequent applause of the new order.

During the Second Empire the theatre was troubled by outbreaks of cholera, which closed the theatre from time to time; recurrent problems with the government over subsidy; and Rachel. The last-named, whose full name was Elisa Rachel Félix (1820–1858), was born with two strikes against her as far as an acting career was concerned: she was Jewish and she was far from attractive. Nevertheless, she became one of the most splendid actresses the Comédie has ever known. Playing both classic roles (Phèdre, Andromaque, and Pauline in *Polyeucte*) and modern (Eugène Scribe wrote *Adrienne Lecouvreur* for her, based on the life of the famous actress), she conquered all before her untimely death in Venice after a disastrous tour of America in 1858. She alternately captivated and drove to despair the administrative head of the Comédie, Arsène Houssaye, who had come to the theatre in 1850. It was Houssaye who turned the Comédie into what one critic called "A Temple of the Bourgeois," reflecting the taste of Louis Napoleon, his close friend.

Rachel was followed by the actress most people probably associate with the Comédie Française, Sarah Bernhardt, who was also Jewish and also not a great beauty. She joined the company in 1862 as a *pensionnaire* who was given room, board, and pocket money. She made her debut in Racine's *Iphigenie*; she had only a small role, and she was at best mediocre. In the following January she slapped Mme. Nathale, a *sociétaire* (a member of the society of the company) and was dismissed by the head of the company, Edouard Thierry. She made her reputation for greatness at the rival l'Odéon, but she returned to the Comédie in 1872 and departed again in 1880. Her attitude toward the Comédie was a mixture of reverence and disgust: while an actress with the company, she once told a visiting member of royalty to remove his hat while inside the theatre. After she left the Comédie, she once spied a group of people waiting at the stage door. After discovering that the people were there to await the actors, she inquired, "Are they going to hiss them?"

Her leading man on many occasions (and probably lover) was Jean Mounet-Sully, who was as handsome as he was talented. He was especially famous for his Hamlet. The Divine Sarah's greatest triumph at the Comédie came when, by a fluke in casting, she played the title role in *Phèdre* in 1874. She would always consider this her greatest role; she said it took her two hours to get herself ready for the role and one hour to unwind after she had performed it. Eventually, she would play it all over the Western world, but this was after she had left the company. (Mounet-Sally also had a triumph as her Hippolyte.)

The administrative head of the company during the latter part of Bernhardt's career with the Comédie was Emile Perrin, who frequently cast her in unflattering or minor roles. Sarah retaliated by making the part a major role by the strength of her acting. In 1877 she played Doña Sol in *Hernani*, and she was frequently called by the name of this character by her adoring public and the aging Victor Hugo. In 1879 she became a *sociétaire* by threatening to quit the Comédie on the eve of its first trip to London. In the following year, Perrin cast her in a part she refused to play, and she really did leave the company.

Other great players with the Comédie during this era included: Paul Monet, who was the first actor to play with bare legs in classic tragedy (causing a furor) and who was with the company from 1889 to his death in 1922; Julia Bartet, who did both classic and modern parts and is famous for probably being the first actress to use a telephone as a property on the stage; the two Coquelins, younger and older; Gustave-Hippolyte Worms; and the amiable Edmond Got, who would play at the Comédie from 1845 to 1895.

Tragedy struck in the disastrous fire of 1900 which was caused by a careless electrician. The house was preparing for a matinee of Racine's *Bajazet* and, despite the heroic efforts of firemen and actors, a young *pensionnaire*, Jane Henriot, suffocated. It made the French revise the safety code for theatres. Fortunately, the Divine Sarah was off on one of her frequent tours, and the company played at her house until repairs were made on the theatre. The Comédie also quietly dropped a lawsuit against its former *sociétaire* (Bernhardt), which had been pending since she left the company. Actors who joined the group at this time included Madeleine Roch, Marie-Thérèse Pierat, Cecile Sorel (who would leave in 1933 for the Casino de Paris), and Pierre Fresnay.

In honor of the three-hundredth anniversary of Molière's birth, all of his plays were presented in 1922. In the same decade Madeleine Renaud, Marie Bell, and Fernand Ledoux all entered the doors of the Comédie. In 1929 Berthe Bovy created Jean Cocteau's *La voix humaine*. One of the strangest things to occur at the Comédie happened in 1933 when a production of Shakespeare's *Coriolan* (*sic*), with *mise-en-scène* by Emile Fabre, caused a riot. Both the right and left in Paris objected to the politics of the play.

By the mid-1930s the company began to expand its activities, making a couple of mediocre movies and broadcasting over the radio. The greatest expansion in the theatre came with its new *metteurs-en-scène*. The first one, Jacques Copeau, had already staged Molière's *L'école des femmes* (*The School for Wives*) in 1929. This was followed by his production of Racine's *Bajazet* (1937), the premiere of François Mauriac's *Asmodée* (1937), and Corneille's *Le Cid* (1940). Louis Jouvet, who, unfortunately, was never to act at the Comédie, staged *L'illusion comique* by Corneille (sets and costumes by Christian Berard) in 1937, but the play ran for only thirty-two performances. He also did the *mise-en-scène* for the premiere of Jean Giraudoux's *Cantique des cantiques* (*Song of Songs*), which ran for sixty-eight performances in 1938. This was followed by Pierre Lestrin-guez's *Tricolore* (also in 1938, music by Darius Milhaud), which ran for seventeen performances. In 1937 Gaston Baty staged Eugene Labiche's *Un chapeau de paille d'Italie* (*The Italian Straw Hat*) and would continue to work for the Comédie until after the Liberation. In the same period, Charles Dullin would stage a well-remembered production of Luigi Pirandello's *Right You Are—If You Think You Are*, with Berthe Bovy and Fernand Ledoux.

At the outbreak of the war, Edouard Bourdet was the director of the theatre and an officer in the reserves. He was killed in an accident in 1940, and Jacques Copeau was named interim director. Copeau was replaced in 1941 by Jean-Louis Vaudoyer. The occupation was a dark period for the French, but the Comédie continued to play throughout the period. Its brightest actor, Jean-Louis Barrault, joined the company in 1940 and staged a number of great productions during this bleak period. Barrault's wife was the famous actress Madeleine Renaud, whom he had married in 1939. He made his debut with the company in *Le Cid* (staged by Copeau), but Barrault considered himself "too light" and the performance a disaster. His greatest work with the company came with his own productions, particularly those of Paul Claudel's difficult works. His production of Claudel's *Le soulier de satin* (*The Satin Slipper*) in 1943 ran five hours (the cast included Renaud, Bell, Pierre Dux, and Barrault himself), and this when the curfew during wartime was 10:30 P.M. It was a triumph for both Claudel and Barrault. The actor also performed Hamlet, the year of his debut, and the following year he staged *Phèdre* for Marie Bell. In 1942 came the premiere of Henri de Montherlant's *La reine morte* (*The Dead Queen*), which established Montherlant's reputation as one of France's most significant modern playwrights. Two years later, "Raimu" joined the ranks of the Comédie for a brief stay, making his debut in Molière's *Le bourgeois gentilhomme*.

André Obey was made director of the theatre in 1946. One of his first decisions was to add a second house, the Salle Luxembourg, to be used mainly to stage new productions. Barrault left the same year, but Jacques Charon took up the loss left by this important member of the company. In 1947 Robert Hirsch joined the company, becoming a *sociétaire* in 1951. Both new members would make their fame as comedians of the rarest sort. Montherlant's *Port-Royal* had its premiere at the Salle Luxembourg in 1954, directed by Jean Meyer. In 1954 the company traveled to the USSR with *Le bourgeois gentilhomme*, with Louis Seigner as the comic Monsieur Jourdain. This production was also filmed with great success. The following year it toured the United States and Canada, and since that time the Comédie has made many tours to North Africa, Belgium, England, Portugal, Austria, Germany, and South America. In addition, during the 1950s the Comédie began to enlarge its repertoire, staging the works of a number of playwrights from the not too remote French past, particularly those of Georges Feydeau. These productions sparked a revival of interest in the works of this master of French farce which continues today.

Maurice Escande became the administrative head of the Comédie in 1960, staying until 1970. His greatest addition to the company was a series of productions which took a new look at the French classics. Examples are Antoine Bourseillier's direction of Molière's *Don Juan* with Jacques Charon (1967) and *L'avare* with Michel Aumont as the miser, which was staged by Jean-Paul Roussillon. Bourseiller also staged Molière's *Georges Dandin* in 1970, with Robert Hirsch; the production was especially notable for its sympathetic treatment of the title character. One of the most outstanding premieres during this decade was Jean Mercure's direction of Montherlant's *Le Cardinal d'Espagne* (*The Cardinal of Spain*) done in 1960. Ionesco made his first appearance at the Comédie with the premiere of *Le soif et le faim* (*Thirst and Hunger*) done in 1965, directed by J. M. Serreau and with Robert Hirsch playing the lead.

In 1970 Escande was replaced by Pierre Dux, who had been an actor with the company. Dux ceased using the Salle Luxembourg as the second stage and added l'Odéon and Le Petit Odéon to stage works by young French authors. Undoubtedly, he has done a great deal to revitalize the Comédie's staid repertory. Samuel Beckett's *Waiting for Godot*, in an excellent production by Roger Blin, was presented in 1977. Brecht's *Mr. Puntila and His Hired Man, Matti* made an appearance in 1975. Under Dux's administration, the Comédie's main theatre, the Salle Richelieu, has been completely renovated. Because of this improvement, the theatre had to be closed for a period of time during the 1970s, and the company played in a number of theatres in Paris, particularly the Théâtre Marigny. The house was finally reopened in 1976 with new and improved backstage facilities, a new foyer, completely redecorated halls, new and improved seating (with many of the old, bothersome partitions removed), and, most importantly, air conditioning. At the time of the reopening, it was decided to do away with the cumbersome habit of tipping the ushers. The Comédie is clearly one of the most comfortable and modern theatres in Paris.

Generally, the Comédie does five new productions and a repetition of seven or eight productions from previous years at the Salle Richelieu. Four productions are mounted at the Odéon, generally non-French plays, and half of these are guest productions from other French-speaking theatres. The Petit Odéon does three or four new works. All of these are available to the Parisian public on a wide series of subscriptions. The Comédie has its own scene shops, upholsterers, and property shop. Actors and technicians dine in their own cafeteria, which is subsidized by the theatre. The Comédie has a relatively stable company, as far as actors and technicians are concerned. The annual budget for the Comédie is a comfortable 58.9 million francs.

There are basically three categories of actors in the company: the *sociétaires honoraires*, the *sociétaires*, and the *pensionnaires*. The *sociétaires honoraires* are members who have been elected to *sociétaires* but who are retired (for example, Berthe Bovy and Louis Seigner), or not acting with the company at present (Pierre Dux still takes time off from his administrative duties with the company to act, but he is not a permanent member of the company), or have left the company but still return occasionally to act with the group (Marie Bell and Jean Piat). The *sociétaires* are elected by other *sociétaires* to be permanent members of the company. These would include Jacques Eyser (the senior member of the company), Jean-Paul Roussillon, Michel Etcheverry, Annie Ducaux, and Jean-Paul Noëlle. There are at present twenty-two men and fourteen women who are *sociétaires*. *Pensionnaires* are actors or actresses who are hired by the season or longer according to their acting ability. A *pensionnaire* can become a *sociétaire* by election, which means advantages in hiring (it is very difficult to get rid of a *sociétaire*) and in retirement. There are at present eighteen actors and twelve actresses who are *pensionnaires*. Jeanne Moreau was a *pensionnaire* at the Comédie for three seasons in the 1950s. Jean-Paul Belmondo also acted with the Comédie in the same decade, but he never achieved the status of *pensionnaire*.

The Comédie's repertory is both one of its great glories and great drawbacks. It has been called a great repository of the best of French drama. It has also been called a stuffy museum. The Comédie prides itself on its productions of great French plays, and it is with French plays that most playgoers associate the house. Since the theatre was founded, the Comédie has staged nearly thirty thousand performances of Molière, with *Tartuffe* the most performed play in the Comédie's repertory. Racine's plays come second, followed by Corneille and Jean-François Regnard. For a time in the 1960s the Comédie's repertory seemed to have grown stagnant. Yet with the opening of both the Odéon and the Petit

Odéon and the introduction of foreign authors into the repertory, the Comédie is beginning to rejuvenate itself. New productions of Molière by such *metteurs-en-scène* as Jacques le Marquet would seem to be turning the theatre back into "la maison de Molière." If sold-out houses are a sign of a healthy theatre, the Comédie has become one of the healthiest theatres in Europe, and seats, particularly on weekends, have become a scarce item at the Comédie's box office. Under the leadership of Pierre Dux, the Comédie has resumed its rightful place as the national theatre of France.

LEON M. AUFDEMBERGE

COMPANY OF RENAUD-BARRAULT
(Compagnie Renaud-Barrault)
Théâtre d'Orsay, 7, Quai Anatole
75007 Paris, France

In 1921 Madeleine Renaud joined the Comédie Française, and in 1940 her husband, Jean-Louis Barrault, followed. They became *sociétaires* in their years with the company but grew dissatisfied. Thanks to new legislation, which relaxed the company's rules, the two left the ranks of the Comédie and on October 17, 1946, a new company was born in Paris: the Company of Renaud-Barrault. The opening production was *Hamlet*, staged by and starring Barrault, using an adaptation by André Gide.

The first home of the new company was the Théâtre Marigny, which the company would use until 1957. In the first season, Barrault would stage Pierre Carlet de Marivaux's *Les fausses confidences* (*False Confessions*), *Baptiste* (a pantomime), and Armand Salacrou's *Les nuits de la colère* (*Nights of Anger*). Most of the season was financed by Barrault's film work.

For the next eleven years Barrault staged one production after another, with only minor failures, at least as far as the public was concerned. In 1947 came *The Trial* (adapted by André Gide from Kafka's novel) and Molière's *Amphitryon*. The next year Parisians delighted to Georges Feydeau's *Occupe-toi d'Amélie* (*Keep an Eye on Amélie*), followed by Paul Claudel's *Partage de midi* (*Break of Noon*). In most of the company's productions, Barrault staged the work and also acted with his wife. The company's list of productions is lengthy, but special mention should be made of Louis Jouvet's production of Molière's *Les fourberies de Scapin* (*The Cheats of Scapin*, 1948); Jean Vilar's production of André Gide's *Oedipe* (1951), Claudel's *Christophe Colombo* (1953), and Chekhov's *The Cherry Orchard* (1954), with Renaud as a touching and very French Madame Ranyevskaya.

Then in 1955 came perhaps the greatest achievement in Barrault's career, his production of Aeschylus' *Oresteia*, a work of total theatre with masks, light, music, mime, and all elements of ritualized theatre.

In the second season the company began to tour, a process Barrault has continued with the three companies he has formed. In 1953 he began to publish his *Cahiers de la Compagnie Renaud-Barrault*, a highly reputable and extremely scholarly literary journal.

In 1957 the company left the Marigny, played several Paris theatres, and did extensive touring. The troupe had an unexpected smash in 1958 when it produced Jacques Levy Offenbach's *La vie parisienne*. It became the hottest ticket in Paris for a long while. The same year Barrault revived Claudel's *Le soulier de satin* (*The Satin Slipper*), a work he had originally staged at the Comédie in 1943. It was a triumph.

At the invitation of André Malraux, the French minister of culture, Barrault became head of a national theatre at the Odéon in 1959 and taking most of his old company founded the Théâtre de France, which would be subsidized by the French government. Its opening production was Claudel's *Tête d'Or* (*Golden Head*) on October 21, 1959, again a triumph for Barrault. In the same year Barrault staged the French premiere of Eugene Ionesco's *Rhinocéros*, a work he has since revived. Until Barrault was removed in 1968 (in the middle of the Paris riots), he did a series of plays that were clearly well received by both critics and the public. He also invited a series of outstanding *metteurs-en-scène* to share staging responsibilities with him. Among his greatest productions were Georges Schéhadé's *Le voyage* (*The Voyage*, a premiere in 1961); Shakespeare's *The Merchant of Venice* (1961, with production by Marguerite Jamois); Brendan Behan's *The Hostage* (1962); Ionesco's *Le piéton de l'air* (*The Stroller in the Air*, 1963); Beckett's *Oh les beaux jours* (*Happy Days*, 1964), with Robert Blin staging and Renaud a heartbreaking Winnie; Shakespeare's *As You Like It* (1963); and Beaumarchais' *Le mariage de Figaro* (*The Marriage of Figaro*, 1964), with Barrault staging and eventually filming the work. The company's most expensive production came in 1965 with Jean Genet's *Les paravents* (*The Screens*), staged by Blin, with sets by André Acquart and with Amidou as Said and Maria Casarès as the mother. The play was highly critical of French colonial policy. There were frequent catcalls by elements of the far right. In 1965 came Marguerite Duras' *Des journées entières dans les arbres* (*Days in the Trees*), with Renaud as the oppressive mother and Jean Desailly as the gigolo son, with sets by Joe Browning and Renaud's costumes by Yves Saint-Laurent. Barrault opened the Petit Odéon in 1966 to stage more intimate works. The next year he organized an international theatre festival, the Théâtre des Nations, at the Odéon for troupes from outside Paris to present their best productions.

Barrault's ninth season started well with Edward Albee's *A Delicate Balance*, adapted by Matthew Galey, with Marie Bell and Renaud as the sisters. Other works followed until the evening of May 15, 1968, when student groups occupied the theatre partly because the theatre was state-subsidized and partly because it was on the Left Bank. When Barrault was ordered to eject the students, he refused even though the students were making a turmoil in the theatre. Barrault talked with the students and seemed genuinely interested in what they were doing. At the same time he was heartsick over the students' destruction of costumes which had been accumulated over a twenty-year period. Malraux eventually ejected both the students and Barrault.

Taking eighteen of his actors from the Théâtre de France, Barrault organized a new company with an old name, the Compagnie Renaud-Barrault. His first production was *Rabelais* done in the grossly misnamed Elysée Montmartre (it was actually an old boxing ring). Working with a "stage" that was more improvised than actual and with ropes, lights, and sound, he created yet another work of total theatre. It was a financial success for the troupe and enabled the group to continue, even without subsidies. In 1969 the company went on an extensive tour which took it to Germany, Belgium, the United States, and England. The next year more touring was followed by a production of *Jarry sur le batte*, an adaptation of Alfred Jarry's works, which was staged in the Elysée Montmartre. This production did not repeat the success of *Rabelais*.

The company returned to the Théâtre Recamier in 1971, and in 1972 it moved again to the old Gare d'Orsay, playing in a circus tent. In the same year, Barrault staged a revival of Paul Claudel's *Le soulier de satin*, including the fourth part, which he had never included. Since moving into the Gare d'Orsay, two theatres have been built in its interior.

In the last few seasons the company has presented several important productions including *Harold and Maude* (1973), adapted by Jean-Claude Carriere and staged by Barrault, with Renaud as Maude and Daniel Riviere as Harold; Peter Shaffer's *Equus* (1976, *metteur-en-scène* John Dexter), with François Perrier as the analyst, Dr. Dysart (a huge success); and *Also Sprach Zarathustra* (*Zarathustra Speaks*, 1979), adapted by Barrault from Nietzsche. In addition, Barrault has revived a number of his earlier successes.

Barrault and Renaud, having dedicated their whole lives to the theatre, expect professional conduct from their company at all times. Many actors have worked for Barrault since the Odéon days, and he has a devoted company as well as a loyal audience. He and Renaud seem to live in the d'Orsay. He has a restaurant in the theatre so that he can eat and meet the public there as well.

As mentioned earlier, there are two theatres in the Gare d'Orsay: a large theatre with a thrust stage, seating 900, and a smaller one with 170 seats. The company does three or four new works each year, as well as revivals. While there are some subscriptions, the theatre does not favor them. Actors are engaged by the season, but many return year after year. In addition, the theatre sponsors concerts, for Barrault is passionately fond of music. The theatre receives a small subsidy (2 million francs a year), which is minuscule compared to that of the Comédie.

The theatre at the Gare d'Orsay is probably doomed, and the company will probably have to move, perhaps to the Palais de Glace on the Grande Palais. Barrault would like to tour more, but many of his productions do not travel well.

LEON M. AUFDEMBERGE
(With thanks to Denise Duhamel
of the Renaud-Barrault staff.)

LARGE MAGIC CIRCUS
(Le Grand Magic Circus)
c/o Gay-Bellile, 4, rue de Candolle
75005 Paris, France

If one were to name the troupes in France which at once provide a good time, teach something political (subtly), assault audiences visually, and above all entertain, Le Grand Magic Circus would probably be number one on the list. Despite the company's sometimes rough financial past, particularly in its early years, perhaps no other troupe in Europe has been as zestful in its playing as this inventive, joyful band of happy actors.

From its founding, Jérôme Savary has been the mainstay of the troupe, writing original scripts, acting, and staging. He began his theatrical career in 1965, when he staged his own work, *Les boîtes* (*The Boxes*), *tragédie musicale*, which played not too successful engagements in Paris and Bourges. The following year, Savary founded Le Grand Théâtre Panique. Its first production was an adaptation of Fernando Arrabal's *Le labyrinthe*, succeeded in the following year by an original script, *Radeau de la Méduse* (*Raft of the Medusa*), written by Savary, who staged both works. *Le labyrinthe* played Vincennes, Frankfurt, Brussels, and London, with its outrageousness pleasing and startling audiences and critics. Savary decided to change the name of the company to Le Grand Cirque Panique in 1968, the same year the company began street plays in London. In the summer of the same year, the company came to New York, playing at Brandeis University and the Theatre Extension. At this time the company again changed its name, to Le Grand Panic Circus.

With its last name change in the fall of 1968 to Le Grand Magic Circus, the company dropped the concept of panic from its title and philosophy. Savary's model in the founding of the company was Jean Vilar. Its first work was appropriately a circus called *Le grand magic circus et ses animaux tristes* (*The Grand Magic Circus and Its Sad Animals*), which was played forty-two times and was the subject of a book. Two years later the troupe created more than two hundred *actions punctuelles*, (punctual actions) which were games the actors played with the public. The same year the company created *Noël*, which was a living creche.

In the summer of 1970 the Circus was invited to a festival of guerrilla theatre in Toronto. The work it created (in English) was *Zartan, le frere mal-aimé de Tarzan* (*Zartan, the Badly Loved Brother of Tarzan*), which was the company's first large-scale political statement. (Its subject was neocolonialism.) It utilized the full resources of the company, including mime, music, dancing, cabaret, spectacle, and, of course, clowning. The piece was eventually played at the Café La Mama in New York, followed by an engagement in Paris, and then toured to Yugoslavia, Iran, Belgium, Switzerland, and Holland.

In both 1971 and 1972 the troupe played extensively in the streets with some performances at the Olympics in Munich in 1972. *Les derniers jours de solitude de Robinson Crusoë* (*The Last Days of Solitude of Robinson Crusoe*) also came in 1972, which was not so much about Defoe's hero as it was about the solitude and desolation of modern man. This work played all over Western Europe.

The year 1973 was particularly active, beginning with the end of the tour of *Crusoë*. In April the troupe created *Cendrillon et la lutte des classes* (*Cinderella and the Class Struggle*) at the Rencontres d'Art Contemporain de La Rochelle, with the help of 150 people in the city of La Rochelle. In September, the troupe participated in its first film, *Le boucher, le star et l'orpheline* (*The Butcher, the Star, and the Orphan*), directed by Savary, starring Christopher Lee and Delphine Seyrig, and with the script by Savary-Topor. It was released in May 1974 to limited success.

In November 1973 the company journeyed to Strasbourg, where it opened with probably the archetypal production of the organization, *De Moïse a Mao, 5000 ans de l'aventures et l'amours* (*From Moses to Mao, 5,000 years of Adventures and Loves*). The work was done in conjunction with the Théâtre National de Strasbourg and covered a very wide canvas indeed. It was a selective look at the history of man from Adam and Eve to the present, with its cast of characters including Romulus, Napoléon, Valentino, Josephine Baker, and the Marquis de Sade. The text was a pastiche of Hugo, Molière, Shakespeare, Abraham Lincoln, and Jérôme Savary. This work eventually played thirty-four cities in France, as well as ten foreign countries.

There followed two highly successful attacks on modern civilization: *Goodbye Mister Freud* (1974) and *Grands Sentiments* (1975), the latter also playing an extensive tour. *Courage* came in 1977 at the Schauspielhaus in Bochum, West Germany, and has an interesting history. Savary originally was to stage Bertolt Brecht's *Mother Courage and Her Children*, but he wanted to take some liberties with it. When the Brecht family objected, Savary took the original Hans-Jakob Grimmelhausen novel and adapted it with Karsten Schalicke and his company. The following year, the troupe played in German, Dutch, and French *1001 Nights*, which dealt with Sinbad, Aladdin, and Ali Baba. It started out in Freiburg, West Germany, and eventually versions played in Rotterdam and France. This was probably the most colorful spectacle the company has ever done.

Melodies du malheur (*Melodies of Unhappiness*, 1979) was done in a co-production with the Théâtre de l'Olivier at Istres as a tribute to the theatre of the nineteenth century; the plot concerned the trials of *"le veuf et l'orpheline"* (the widower and the orphan). Since then the company has done two more works, both in 1981. The first of these was a surprise, a production of Molière's *Le bourgeois gentilhomme* (done in conjunction with a number of theatres), with Savary playing Jourdain. The second was a bilingual production (with the Deutsches Schauspielhaus in Hamburg) of life in the trenches called *Weinachten auf der Front/Noël au front* (*Christmas at the Front*), with the script by Savary, Roland Topor, and Helmut Ruge. It went on tour and came to the United States in April 1982.

A number of critics have attempted to describe the work of the company but to no avail, for the troupe is extremely eclectic, utilizing the full resources of the theatre, from intimate cabaret to grand spectacle. The company is obviously dedicated politically, though it neither harangues nor takes a lofty view. Rather, the company tells the audience where its sympathies lie and lets it go at that. The company has tackled every subject imaginable. Its closest equivalent in America would be a blend of *Saturday Night Live* with a circus, plus night club techniques, but not strictly revue, with all acts centering around one theme.

The company does no set number of works a year; rather it does whatever runs longest. It has toured all over France (ninety-nine places), as well as eighty-nine cities in twenty foreign countries on four continents. The company is composed of twelve actors (including Savary), five musicians (again including Savary), and a technical staff. Until 1975 the troupe was not subsidized and despite its successes had some bad financial times. In that year it was taken over by an organization under the supervision of Christian Gay-Bellile. Savary was given freedom to follow his theatrical activities and not worry about finances. The troupe currently receives a subsidy from the French government of 350,000 francs, as well as a number of other subsidies from various sources.

Savary does not work solely with this one troupe; he has also staged a number of fine works with both opera and spoken drama companies in Germany. The future of the company is tied up with Savary who in both writing and staging has guided this most madly childlike but highly sophisticated company.

LEON M. AUFDEMBERGE

NATIONAL THEATRE OF EAST PARIS
(Théâtre National de L'Est Parisien)
17, rue Malte-Brun
75020 Paris, France

By one of those tremendous errors of judgment, Guy Rétoré was twice turned down by the Conservatoire, the acting school connected with the Comédie Française. Instead, he went to work for the Société Nationale des Chemins de Fer, the French national railway system. While an employee of the SNCF, he began to direct plays for an amateur group of railway employees. This gave him a taste for the theatre, and in 1950 he left the railway for a life in the theatre and to begin staging plays in Ménilmontant in the northern part of Paris. In 1951 he created his own theatrical group called La Guilde, using a hall in the 20th Arrondisement of Paris. The first play to be presented was Molière's *Le médecin malgré lui* (*The Doctor in Spite of Himself*), which was a moderate success. In 1952 the company presented Ruíz de Alarcón's *La vérité suspecte* (*The Suspected Truth*) and the following year Jean Chatenet's *La nuit des fous* (*The Night of the Madmen*). In 1954 the play was *La fille du roi* (*The Daughter of the King*) by Jean Cosmos, who was deeply involved with the company.

In 1955 came the first great success for La Guilde, Shakespeare's *King John*, which established the company's reputation and suggested Rétoré as a rising director. Another moderate success came in 1957 when Cosmos adapted George Farquhar's *The Recruiting Officer* as *Les grenadiers de la reine*. In the same year, the company received the Grand Prix au Concours de Jeunes Compagnies.

The next year Rétoré opened a new theatre, the Théâtre de Ménilmontant, in a converted hall. Le Guilde also revived its former successes, and with the Théâtre National Populaire, it presented Molière's *L'étourdi* (*The Absent-Minded*) and began to present evenings of poetry readings, concerts, and films, a policy the company still follows.

The 1959–1960 season, however, is generally considered to be the founding season of the National Theatre of East Paris. By that time the company had what it considered to be a permanent home, a first-rate director who would stage all its works, and a large devoted public. In that season, Rétoré staged *Macbeth*, with Victor Garrivier as the title character, and Molière's *L'avare* (*The Miser*). In addition, La Guilde sponsored a number of musical offerings.

In 1961 the company decided to move into a better theatre, as the old one had become inadequate. It found an old cinema (Le Zénith) and in 1962 the Ministre d'Etat Chargé des Affaires Culturelles acquired the theatre for the company and renamed the group the National Theatre of East Paris, with Guy Rétoré as its director. The following year the cinema was completely renovated, a fly gallery and backstage equipment were added, and the foyer was remodeled. The new house opened the same year with Jean Cosmos' adaptation of Nikolai Gogol's *The Overcoat*, with Jean Turpin as the proud possessor of "le manteau." That season (1963–1964) the company presented four major works and also began its policy of inviting other theatre companies from the provinces or elsewhere to share its stage. Merce Cunningham came from the United States to perform with his dance company. The first film series was begun, the first art exhibits were held, the theatre magazine was founded, and a great number of poetry readings and musical concerts were sponsored by the theatre.

The 1960s were a fervent time for the National Theatre of East Paris, both as a producing organization and as a host to other companies. The Piccolo of Milan performed, as did the Teatro Stabile of Turin, the Théâtre de Caen, and the Orchestre de Paris. One of its greatest successes came in 1964 with a very Elizabethan production of *Arden of Feversham*. This was followed by Alain-René Lesage's *Turcaret*, which toured the United States; Eugène Labiche's *Le voyage de Monsieur Perrichon* (*The Trip of Monsieur Perrichon*); and John Arden's *Live Like Pigs* (1969), a controversial work. All of these productions were staged by Rétoré, as was Peter Hacks' *The Battle of Lobositz* (1968), which represented the Parisian public's introduction to this East German writer. In 1969–1970 came three solid successes: Alfred de Musset's *Lorenzaccio* (praised especially for its careful analysis of the script); the Bertolt Brecht-Kurt Weill *The Threepenny Opera*; and George Bernard Shaw's *Major Barbara*. These were again staged by Rétoré. By the middle of this decade, a number of permanent policies had been established. It would be a theatre that would take artistic chances, and it would choose plays that Parisian commercial theatres normally ignored, especially the works of Brecht and Hacks. It would support the life of the community in which it lived by doing plays the public would like to see (but not boulevard successes) and by presenting concerts, poetry readings, and films for people who did not usually go to the theatre. It would not be a static company, and it has not remained so; it is a popular theatre in every sense of the word.

In the present decade, the theatre has continued to grow. At the beginning of the 1970s Rétoré had to divert more of his creative energy toward administration; he directs only two productions in any season, with guest directors doing the rest. In 1971 the theatre became a national theatre, joining the Comédie Française, l'Odéon, and the Théâtre National Populaire as theatres subsidized by the French government.

The theatre continues to present a wide and varied choice of plays. Brecht is a staple, two of the theatre's greatest successes being productions of *Saint Joan of the Stockyards* (staged by Rétoré in 1971) and *Mr. Puntila and His Hired Man, Matti* (1979, also staged by Rétoré). Shakespeare continues to be popular with the group, with notable productions of *The Tempest* (*mise-en-scène* by Bernard Sobel, 1973), *Macbeth* (staged by Rétoré, 1972), and *As You Like It* (*mise-en-scène* by the East German Benno Besson). A very Marxist version of *Hamlet* (*mise-en-scène* by Besson) was presented in 1977 and repeated at the Avignon Festival, while *Julius Caesar*, staged by Rétoré, was produced in 1979. Shaw, never a great favorite in France, has been well represented, especially by a production that is fondly remembered by the public, *Androcles and the Lion* (Rétoré, 1975).

The continual progress of the National Theatre of East Paris is reflected in the varied choice of its repertory. Hacks has already been mentioned, and the Parisian public got one of its first looks at the work of Odön von Horváth when the company brought *Don Juan Returns from the War* to its stage in 1976. African playwrights have also been represented with Aimé Césaire's *A Season in the Congo*, which was a solid success in 1967. Sean O'Casey's works, always difficult to translate, have been presented several times. Paul Claudel has long been considered too intellectual for a "popular" theatre, but in 1977 *L'otage* (*The Hostage*) was roundly applauded (*mise-en-scène* by Rétoré).

In the 1970s the company began to produce its own scripts, one of its most controversial works being *dans les eaux glacées du calcul egoiste* (*on the icy waters of self-interest*) with texts by Brecht, François Rabelais, Federico García Lorca, Vladimir Mayakovsky, Jacques Prévert, Karl Marx, and other writers. In the 1973–1974 season, the group opened a small theatre next to its main stage, the Petit TEP, to present experimental works. The Petit TEP has been the home for political experimental works, musical events, and poetry readings.

The National Theatre of East Paris generally produces four or five major works a year in the main theatre and a varied number in the small house. Rétoré and his staff choose the plays. The larger house seats one thousand spectators, while the smaller house seats only one hundred. The company is subsidized by the

French government; in 1979 the amount of subsidy was nearly 9 million francs, which represents approximately 75 percent of the group's budget. Most actors are engaged by the company for one show only, and perhaps six or seven are engaged by the season. A large number of actors return season after season, which makes the company appear to have more continuity than it actually does. The technical staff of fifteen is engaged for the season and builds all the sets for the company in the theatre's own workshops.

One of the troupe's chief distinctions has been that it has tried to reflect the life of the Parisian quarter in which the theatre is located, but in the last few years this effort has been difficult. When the theatre opened in the 20th Arrondisement, the population was very stable, most of the people working in what in America would be called blue collar jobs. In the middle 1970s a large part of the population moved to the suburbs. Old buildings were replaced by new luxury apartments. Rétoré has tried to retain his old audience by keeping a low admissions policy, popular subscription prices, and a wide variety of activities in the theatre. He has attracted new audiences moving into the district by adding fresh attractions, such as musical offerings, and by keeping the quality of attractions as good as those offered on the boulevards. By maintaining these policies and by keeping in touch with political organizations, this theatre has managed to reflect the varied strata that live in the area.

LEON M. AUFDEMBERGE

NATIONAL THEATRE OF STRASBOURG
(Théâtre National de Strasbourg)
1, rue Général-Gourard
67000 Strasbourg, France

The National Theatre of Strasbourg (originally the Centre Dramatique de l'Est or CDE) began in October 1946 when representatives of the cities of Colmar, Julhouse, and Strasbourg met at the Hotel de Ville in the city of Colmar to form a theatre company to serve Alsace-Lorraine. Later, Metz joined the group of cities; and in 1947 Jeanne Laurent, the French minister of culture, announced the formation of the new Centre Dramatique de l'Est, with its home theatre the Théâtre Municipal in Colmar.

The first director was Roland Piétri, then director of the Comédie des Champs-Elysées. It was he who finally formed the company, opening with a work by a Lorraine author, Jean-François Noël, *Le survivant* (*The Survivor*). The work, never a success in the French theatre, was received coldly in Colmar and with some hostility on its subsequent tour. The troupe's second work was Molière's *Le misanthrope*. Here the company was on surer ground and played to larger and more appreciative audiences. During the first season, the troupe mounted seven productions, which proved too many.

Piétri had a difficult time with the founders of the company and at the end of his first season was replaced by André Clavé. Clavé was successful with the first work he staged for the troupe, François Mauriac's *Asmodée*, with Bernard Ledoux, a *sociétaire* of the Comédie Française, as guest artist. Clavé brought with him a number of fine actors from Paris, upgrading the company and thereby attracting larger audiences. His choice of plays included many French works. In this first season Clavé staged, in addition to the Mauriac work, Molière's *Le bourgeois gentilhomme* (*The Bourgeois Gentleman*), and Ledoux did the *mise-en-scène* for Molière's *Tartuffe* and also played the lead, a role he had often played at the Comédie Française. Clavé staged works as varied as Shakespeare's *Hamlet* (1948–1949), Shaw's *Saint Joan* (the same season), Shakespeare's *Macbeth* (1950–1951), and Max Campserveux's *Les Centaures* (also 1950–1951). Clavé continued the touring policies set in the first season, adding several more cities to the itinerary, including Paris. By the end of his directorship the company was mounting ten or eleven productions a year.

In 1952 Jeanne Laurent decided to reorganize the company, and Clavé was reluctantly replaced by one of the great names in the French theatre, Michel Saint-Denis. Saint-Denis organized a theatre school for the company on the lines of the Old Vic School, which he had headed in London. The first director of the new school was Suria Magito. Saint-Denis also did the *mise-en-scènes* for a number of well-remembered productions, including Shakespeare's *Romeo and Juliet*, *Twelfth Night*, and *A Midsummer Night's Dream*; Pedro Calderón's *The Mayor of Zalamea*; George Bernard Shaw's *The Devil's Disciple*; and Corneille's *Le menteur* (*The Liar*). In October 1954 the CDE was transferred to Strasbourg, and in 1956 Saint-Denis organized the Tréteaux, a small troupe formed to take short or small-cast plays to towns in the vicinity of Strasbourg. This new organization was not, however, to take the place of the regular touring company.

In June 1957 Saint-Denis resigned for reasons of health and was replaced by Hubert Gignoux, with Pierre Lefèvre replacing Magito as head of the school. Gignoux had been both an actor and a *metteur-en-scène* and had first worked in Lyon, later touring with the Comédiens Routiers before becoming its managing director. During World War II, he had been a prisoner of war and had worked with marionettes in a prison camp. After the war he opened a marionette stage in Paris with George Goubert, and in 1949 (with Goubert as an actor in the troupe) he became the first head of the Centre Dramatique de l'Ouest in Rennes. In his first season, Gignoux opened a new theatre for the company (designed by Pierre Sonrel), the first large theatre to be opened in France since the Liberation. The first play in the new house was *Hamlet*, with Gignoux playing the lead. Gignoux's leadership was similar to that of Saint-Denis. Although he put more emphasis on the company's going to Paris, he disliked playing Paris as he was a firm believer in decentralization. Gignoux staged many works for the company, the best known success being Friedrich Dürrenmatt's *The Visit from the Old Lady* (1960). Valentine Tessier as Klara won for the company the Prix du Syndicat de la Critique. Other works which Gignoux staged for the company included Eugene O'Neill's *The Hairy Ape* (1961); Dürrenmatt's *The Physicists*

(1964); and, perhaps his most solid achievement as a *metteur-en-scène*, Claudel's *Le soulier de satin* (*The Satin Slipper*, 1966).

The repertory, while varied, emphasized the French classics. Clearly, the repertory was well balanced, and the company's acting and staging were of a high caliber. Gignoux also liked to tour productions to small towns in the area. One of the most popular works was Thornton Wilder's *Our Town* (*Notre petite ville*). Under Gignoux, the troupe also played in Belgium, Germany, and French-speaking Switzerland. He was an extremely likable director and enhanced the company's standing.

In 1974 Gignoux resigned, to be replaced for one season by André-Louis Pérenetti. Pérenetti became director of the Théâtre National de Chaillot in 1975, and Jean-Pierre Vincent was made the head of the Théâtre National de l'Est. Vincent had been part of the Théâtre de l'Espérance (Compagnie Vincent-Jourdheil) and had assisted Peter Brook in his Paris production of Shakespeare's *Timon of Athens*. Since his politics were distinctly to the left, he seemed a curious choice for Strasbourg which tends to be rather conservative.

Vincent made sweeping changes in both the personnel and repertory. His first production was a collective dramatization by most of the acting company and the administrative staff of Emile Zola's *Germinal*, with over thirty authors listed on the title page of the published version. The work was extremely controversial, and some features of the staging, particularly the nudity, were shocking to the audience. Nevertheless, the work was well attended, especially by the young, who found the new director much to their liking. In the same season the troupe played *Ah Krou* (text by Bernard Chartreux and Joan Jourdheil); *Dimanche* (*Sunday*) by Michel Deutsch and Dominique Müller; and Brecht's *Baal*, staged by André Engel in a local stable.

The company was successful with collective scripts, including Michèl Foucher's *La table* and the *Théâtre complet de Kafka*, with scenario by Engel and Bernard Pautrat. The first script has been played frequently throughout the area around Strasbourg and consists of fragments of interviews which Foucher made in factories, homes, and offices. Starting from a simple question: "What is a woman's relationship to a simple object like a table?," the script discusses woman's role in the world today from the viewpoints of mother, wife, prostitute, and *soubrette* (an elegant female servant). The work was a monodrama, played by Foucher and assisted by Denise Peron and Yolande Marzolff, *metteur-en-scène* and choreographer, respectively. Because the work is simple to perform, it does not have to be played in a theatre and has been staged in many places where plays are seldom performed.

During Vincent's tenure the company has probably become one of the most discussed theatres in France. What are his beliefs? First, he wants to bring theatre closer to people's lives; this he has done by performing in places outside the theatre (stable, warehouse, private homes), which are both unexpected and closer to people's everyday lives. Second, Vincent seeks the roots of popular ideas (workers' lives, woman's role in the world today, liberation movements, popular literature, and so on), and explores those themes for plays. He spends an enormous amount of his time talking to people in the community about what they want, what they are interested in. He has tried to do plays that provoke discussion, and most of his works have been fairly nonpolitical despite his personal feelings. For example, he admires the poetic and individualistic early Brecht much more than the more political and doctrinaire later Brecht. Most of all, he approaches theatre as a collective art, where everyone, audience included, must be part of the work. He particularly favors collective scripts and at the same time frequently stages more conventional writers (O'Casey, de Musset, and Molière).

Thirteen actors are employed in the permanent company, and more are hired for individual pieces; they come from either Strasbourg or Paris. In addition to the technical staff, there are five dramaturges for the theatre who largely work on the theatre's collective exercises. Generally, the theatre mounts three works per theatrical year; the rest of the season is imported from other French companies. The company does some touring, particularly of its small pieces, but the large collective pieces, which have brought the theatre the most notoriety, have been impossible to tour.

The annual subsidy for the theatre is 9 million francs. The city of Strasbourg also gives the company a small subsidy, and the Council General du Bas-Rhin awards another small amount yearly. In addition, the school connected with the company receives a government subsidy, and staff members teach in the school. Vincent has publicly stated that his subsidy is not adequate, especially as compared with that of the Comédie Française.

Of course, Vincent's radical ideas have upset many people in Strasbourg. Some of the older patrons have turned in comfort to the more staid Opera, which is nearby. Vincent has tried to win these playgoers back by doing "safe" productions, and there are signs he may be succeeding. Vincent wants a theatre that appeals to everybody, not just the young.

LEON M. AUFDEMBERGE
(With thanks to Jacques Blanc of the theatre staff
and Byron Lippert, who helped with translating.)

PLAYHOUSE OF SAINT-ETIENNE
(Comédie de Saint-Etienne)
Centre Dramatique National
Maison de la Culture
42001 Saint-Etienne, France

Saint-Etienne has one of the best theatre companies in France, which is surprising for a city its size (about two hundred thousand). The fame of the company can be traced largely to its founder, Jean Dasté, who began the company in 1947 as one of the first manifestations of theatrical decentralization in France.

Dasté has been called an apostle of theatre in the provinces. Unlike many figures in French theatre who came from the provinces to work in Paris, Dasté reversed the process. Dasté was born in Paris in a depot for *fiacres* (small wagons for two people). Early in his life he became a student of Jacques Copeau at the School of the Lieux—Colombier (Place of Colombier). He eventually worked for Michel Saint-Denis and Compagnie des Quinze and for Maurice Jacquemont at La Compagnie des Quatre Saisons (which played two seasons in New York in the 1930s).

During the 1940s Dasté worked in many theatres in the provinces. In 1946 he decided to found a company outside Paris where he could both manage and stage plays. He chose Grenoble for his first company, founding the Comédie de Grenoble in 1946. The following year he was offered the chance to head a new Centre Dramatique National in Saint-Etienne. He came to Saint-Etienne because he thought the city needed a company and the valley of the area (about four hundred thousand inhabitants) would give the company a chance for growth. The first production was Molière's *Le médecin malgré lui* (*The Doctor in Spite of Himself*), with Dasté as *metteur-en-scène* and Lucien Brahem as set designer. It was a success. In the first season, the company presented ninety performances of five works.

In the first season about 80 percent of the repertory consisted of French classics. The troupe also toured in the area around Saint-Etienne, as well as in French-speaking areas in Europe (Belgium and Switzerland). Most of the works were staged either by Dasté or Alain-René Lesage. Lesage staged the company's first big success, Molière's *Le bourgeois gentilhomme*, in the 1950–1951 season. Early in the company's history, the Société des Amis de la Comédie was formed to foster the work of the theatre.

Dasté was lead actor, stager, and administrator for the company. He is best known outside France for his roles in two films, Jean Renoir's *La grande illusion* and Jean Vigo's *Zero de conduite*. His wife, Hélène (a daughter of Jacques Copeau), was a designer for the company, and his daughter, Jean, staged a number of works for the troupe and also wrote some children's plays. Dasté's staging style was brilliantly eclectic. Whether he was staging Molière, Claudel, Shakespeare, Brecht, or Japanese Nō dramas, he always found the style for the play, rather than trying to impose only one style on the plays. His best productions would probably include Eugène Labiche's *Le voyage de M. Perrichon* (*The Voyage of Mr. Perrichon*, 1947–1948); Molière's *L'école des maris* (*The School for Husbands*, 1948–1949); Shakespeare's *Measure for Measure* (1949–1950); Seami Motokiyo's *Kagekiyo* (1950–1951); Molière's *Les femmes savantes* (*The Learned Ladies*, 1953–1954); Shakespeare's *Macbeth* (1954–1955); Claudel's *L'annonce faite á Marie* (*The Tidings Brought to Mary*, 1954–1955); Brecht's *The Caucasian Chalk Circle* (1956–1957), co-directed with John Blatchley (who has singly done several Brecht productions for the company), with sets by Abd El Kadar Farah; Copeau's *L'illusion* (*The Illusion*, 1959–1960); O'Casey's *The Plough and the Stars* (1961–1962); Heinrich von Kleist's *The Broken Jug* (1961–1962); John M. Synge's *The Playboy of the Western World* (1963–1964); and

Molière's *Le médecin malgré lui* (*The Doctor in Spite of Himself*, 1969–1970). Dasté tried to keep his productions uncluttered, and his actors liked him because he always had time to talk to them. He also tried to find a variety of *metteurs-en-scènes* for his company, and he never kept one author as his sole property. He staged Molière for the company, but so did Alain-René Lesage; Dasté did several Shakespeare productions, but so did John Blatchley.

The first theatre for the company was the Grenier (attic) of the local Ecole des Mimes. In 1962, as part of the cultural movement that was sweeping France, a new cultural center was announced for Saint-Etienne, and Dasté seemed assured of a prominent place in the plans. The company moved in 1963 to a second theatre in the Mutilés du Travail, opening the theatre with Molière's *Monsieur de Pourceaugnac* (*Mr. de Pourceaugnac*, staged by Phillippe Dauchez), which was to be the first subscription season. In anticipation of the opening of the new Maison de la Culture, Dasté began organizing concerts, poetry readings, and a film series, but when the center opened in 1969 Dasté was given the right to wait for a place in the center. (Eventually, the offices for the theatre did find a place in the Maison de la Culture.) Dasté decided instead to open a second, small, experimental theatre, the Théâtre Copeau.

During the 1960s Dasté began to devote more of his time to administration and less to staging. In the same decade, the company's repertory became less devoted to classics, particularly French classics, and more to new French authors. Finally in 1971, Dasté decided to resign as head, but he continues to take an active part in the life of the company. He was replaced by Pierre Vial, who was initially hired for three years. Vial reorganized the Trétaux, which was an organization Dasté had founded to take plays to small villages in the area. Vial also began summer tours for the company, but they were soon discontinued because of cost. Under Vial the repertory became more avant-garde, and the touring for the regular company expanded. In December 1974 the French Ministry of Culture announced that Vial's contract would not be renewed, a decision that angered many subscribers to the theatre. The ministry proved intractable, and in 1975, with a production of Brecht's *The Life of Galileo*, Vial said farewell to a brilliant three years.

Vial was succeeded by a co-directorship of Daniel Benoin and Guy Lauzin from 1975 to 1978, when Lauzin left and Benoin continued alone. Both men were proven *metteurs-en-scènes* before they came to Saint-Etienne, and both were far more interested in developing new scripts or projects than were their predecessors. The major physical change for the company was a complete renovation of the old theatre in the Salle des Mutilés, with the old balcony demolished and the whole theatre renovated (architect Gürler Akdora), with improved sight lines and acoustics.

A number of excellent productions have been staged in the last few years in Saint-Etienne, including Georg Büchner's *Woyzeck* (1975, production by Benoin); Shakespeare's *As You Like It* (1976, production by Lauzin), which toured extensively; Shakespeare's *King Lear* (1976, production by Benoin); Roger Vaillard's musical play, *Héloise et Abélard* (1977, production by Benoin); Pierre Bourgeade's *Deutsches Requiem* (1979), which Benoin staged in its Paris premiere in 1974 and revised for Saint-Etienne; and Serge Goubert's *Proust, ou la Passion d'être* (1979), with Benoin getting excellent reviews for his *mise-en-scène*. *Proust*, a world premiere, was written by a professor from Lyon and was a dramatization of Proust's life, interspersed with scenes from the novels. Two actors played Proust: Gilles Segal played the aging Proust surrounded by his medicine bottles, and Alain Bonneville played the young Proust surrounded by his dilettante friends. The work was revived in the 1979–1980 season when it toured in the United States.

The Playhouse of Saint-Etienne generally does four major works a year, chosen by its managing director, who is also responsible for most decisions in running the troupe. He also stages two works for the company. The theatre season is supplemented by plays from other French companies. The company's repertory tends to be very modern, and there is almost always a work with a woman's philosophy. The Maison de la Culture also has a season of plays, generally boulevard successes from Paris. It also sponsors concerts and art shows. In addition, there is a local opera company.

The permanent company numbers about five, with the rest hired for one play in either Lyon or Paris. Some members of the permanent company have been with the theatre for over ten years. Since it has an excellent reputation with actors, getting actors to play in Saint-Etienne is generally quite easy. There are also ten people on the technical staff, and an additional fifteen are involved in the administration of the company. The theatre is well run and stable, and is popular with the people in the area. (There are currently 5,400 subscribers.) The theatre publishes its own newspaper, *Public*, which tells subscribers what is coming up.

The theatre plays four houses in the city: the main stage, called the Théâtre de la Comédie (located on Avenue Emile Loubet); two small houses nearby, the Théâtre Copeau and the Atelier; and since the 1970s, the huge theatre in the Maison de la Culture, where it stages an occasional production. In addition to plays, the company also sponsors *Variété* (variety shows), which are evenings of popular music or whatever seems to interest the general public.

The only obstacles in the theatre's progress have apparently been created largely by the government. Its present director, Daniel Benoin, holds a doctorate in business and is largely self-trained in the theatre. He believes in a theatre of the here and now without becoming faddish or playing pieces that will interest only a few people. (Molière productions are still presented.) It is one of those rare theatre companies which has managed to maintain its original high standards. As proof of its quality, one need only point to the number of times it has been invited to present a play at another theatre. It also plays Paris with some regularity and has toured in several countries.

LEON M. AUFDEMBERGE
(With thanks to Christine Räia of the
theatre staff and Daniel Benoin.)

POPULAR NATIONAL THEATRE
(Théâtre National Populaire)
Place de la Liberation
69100 Villeurbanne, France

The history of the Théâtre National Populaire (TNP) begins not with the conventional date, 1951, and with Jean Vilar, but in 1912 when Joseph Paul-Boncour, a well-known journalist, began to complain of a lack of popular theatre in Paris. In 1920 Paul-Boncour was voted 110,000 francs by the Chamber of Deputies to found a popular theatre at the Trocadéro. Firmin Gémier was named its first director, and, on November 11 (Armistice Day), he opened the doors of the Popular National Theatre in a ghastly auditorium with 4,500 seats. Gémier had earlier worked with the Théâtre Antoine and had traveled with several touring organizations. Although he was to live most of his life in Paris, he was an early champion of decentralization in the French theatre.

Most of the company's early repertory was very light (operettas, former boulevard successes, or frank imitations of the Comédie Française). Gémier was by no means popular with the government, and, when the first financial crisis hit the theatre (March 1922), it would take the government eight months to figure out whether it wanted to keep Gémier on (it did).

In many ways Gémier was ahead of his time. As mentioned above, he favored decentralization of the theatre, which largely came to pass after World War II. He created a number of productions that were full of life and color (critics frequently called him vulgar) and that appealed to popular taste. He also wanted an international repertory (which set him in opposition to the Comédie Française) and staged not only Shakespeare, but also modern authors from abroad. Before his death in 1933, he was a champion of Eugene O'Neill. Unfortunately, Gémier combined his directorship of the Popular National Theatre with his directorship of other theatres and never could give the group his full attention. Alfred Fourtier became director in 1933, to stay only two years as it was decided in 1935 to demolish the old Trocadéro. Sporadic attempts were made in the 1930s and 1940s to revive the company at the new Palais de Chaillot, under several directors (notably Pierre Aldebert), but little was accomplished.

In 1947 Jean Vilar created the first Festival of Avignon because the town seemed popular with tourists and the Palais des Popes (Palace of the Popes) a good place for plays in the open air. In his first seasons with the festival, he did such popular works as Alphonse Daudet's *L'Arlésienne* and Edmond Rostand's *Cyrano de Bergerac* to attract audiences. Then in the 1950s the works began to be more difficult, and in 1951 he staged Heinrich von Kleist's *The Prince of Homburg* and Corneille's *Le Cid*, both with Gerard Philipe. Because of the success at Avignon, at the time of Aldebert's death in 1951, Vilar was offered the directorship of the TNP. He hesitated two days and then accepted. The theatre at the Palais de Chaillot was enormous (2,800 seats), the public was far from sure, and the subsidy ridiculously low. Still the challenge was there and

Vilar opened his first season in 1952 with Molière's *L'avare* (*The Miser*) and Henri Pichette's *Nuclea*. Neither was a success, and the French press called for his resignation.

Vilar almost acquiesced. In the fall of 1952 he had his first popular success, a revival of *The Prince of Homburg* with Philipe. From then until his resignation in 1963, he was the pride of the same French press, which suddenly claimed it had "discovered" him. In the same year came Vilar's staging of T. S. Eliot's *Murder in the Cathedral* (he had staged the French premiere in 1945), with himself as Thomas. From that year on there came an almost unbroken string of triumphs, not only for Vilar the *metteur-en-scène*, but also for Vilar the actor.

He invited a number of French actors to work for the troupe for small wages and the compensation of great roles. In 1952 came Brecht's *Mother Courage and Her Children*, with Germain Montero as the title character; in 1953 he staged Molière's *Don Juan* (with Vilar), Georg Büchner's *Danton's Death*, and Shakespeare's *Richard II* (with Philipe). In 1954 Victor Hugo's *Ruy Blas* (with Philipe) was presented, and the next year *Le triomphe de l'amour* (*The Triumph of Love*), with Maria Casarès, which played havoc with the notion that only the Comédie Française could do Pierre Marivaux. In 1956 the theatre mounted Molière's *Les femmes savantes* (*The Learned Ladies*) and Racine's *Phèdre* (*Phaedra*, with Casarès triumphant in the title role), and made a tour in the Soviet Union with *Don Juan*, *Le triomphe de l'amour*, and Hugo's *Maria Tudor*. Daniel Sorano staged Molière's *Le malade imaginaire* (*The Imaginary Invalid*) for the company in 1957, and the next year Vilar staged Luigi Pirandello's *Henry IV*, with himself as the title character. George Wilson came in 1958 to stage his first production for the company, Molière's *L'école des femmes* (*The School for Wives*); the same year Vilar staged a marvelously funny production of Alfred Jarry's *Ubu Roi*. In 1959 Rene Clair was invited to stage Alfred de Musset's *On ne badine pas avec l'amour* (*No Trifling with Love*), with Suzanne Flon and Philipe. In 1959 Vilar staged Shakespeare's *A Midsummer Night's Dream* (himself as Oberon) and Armand Gatti's *Le Crapaud-Buffle* (*The Toad Buffalo*).

The 1960s witnessed several triumphs for the company with Vilar's staging. The first year of the decade, Vilar did Alain-René Lesage's *Turcaret*, Sophocles' *Antigone*, and Brecht's *The Resistible Rise of Arturo Ui* (with Wilson as Ui), and Roger Blin did the French premiere of Beckett's *Krapp's Last Tape*. In the following year Vilar directed Aristophanes' *The Peace* and O'Casey's *Red Roses for Me* (with G. Requier). Other productions of the early 1960s staged by Vilar included Jean Giraudoux's *La guerre de Troie n'aura pas lieu* (*The War of Troy Will Not Take Place*, 1962) and Robert Bolt's *A Man for All Seasons* (1963), his farewell production. In 1963 Wilson staged Brecht's *The Life of Galileo*, with himself in the title role; in the same year he was announced as new director of the TNP.

What were Vilar's major accomplishments for the TNP other than the obvious ones of staging and acting?

1. A thoroughly popular repertory. Vilar took frequent polls at his theatre to determine what the public wanted. More than anything, his public liked modern foreign works, even if they were avant-garde, providing they were well done. If French classics were played, they would be done by well-known actors, such as Philipe or Casarès or even Vilar. Evidently, Vilar did his work well, for in the 1960–1961 season about 90 percent of all seats were sold.

2. A low admission price. When Vilar first became director the price for admission ranged from 2 to 6 francs; when he left the tariff was 5 to 8 francs.

3. A fair treatment of actors. One of the provisions made by the French government when Vilar became director was that he have a permanent company. Vilar tended to keep the number low but with good salaries and to pay the rest of the actors (engaged on a one-play basis) well in order to keep them away from the blandishments of film, television or other theatres. Generally, Vilar kept a permanent company of about twenty-five actors each season.

4. An insistence that the play should be well staged and never "staged down" to the public. He always claimed that he was a servant of the play and that his staging style was apt to be a little dry. He was influenced by Brecht (who admired him as well) and his love of music (he organized concerts as well as producing plays).

5. A desire to tour. Vilar did many of his productions at Paris and Avignon, as well as in tours to thirty-two foreign countries before his retirement.

6. An encouragement of new French talent. In order to support promising young playwrights, in the 1960s Vilar took a lease on the Théâtre Recamier (six hundred seats) and presented the works of unknown French authors (Gatti, Boris Vian, and so on).

7. A theatre that would serve its people. Vilar took as his model not the commercial theatres of Paris, but the theatres in the provinces—in Saint-Etienne, Rennes, and elsewhere. To keep his public, he organized concerts as well as ballet performances, modern dance productions, poetry readings, and the like.

All in all, Vilar's era with the TNP was a great one in French theatre. He stepped down largely for personal reasons. (He died in 1971 much mourned by his public.)

George Wilson had acted and staged a number of productions with the company, but was not nearly as dynamic as Vilar. Despite several very well-staged productions, either by him or other *metteurs-en-scène*, the public never responded as it should have and in 1971 Wilson was replaced. He began his directorship with a good production of Maxim Gorky's *The Children of the Sun* (1964); other noteworthy works included Friedrich Dürrenmatt's *Romulus the Great* (1964); Brecht's *Mr. Puntila and his Hired Man, Matti* (1965); John Osborne's *Luther* (1965), with Pierre Vaneck as the German reformer; Giraudoux's *La folle de Chaillot* (*The Madwoman of Chaillot*, 1966), with Edwige Fullière in the title role; and Brecht's *The Resistible Rise of Arturo Ui* (1969). Michael Cacoyannis' staging of Shakespeare's *Romeo and Juliet* (1968) in Copeau's translation and Claude Rey's staging of Marguerite Duras' *L'amante Anglais* (*The English Lover*), with Madeleine Renaud as Claire and Claude Dauphin as Pierre (1968), were also praiseworthy. But by 1970 it was clear the public was not coming, and in that year the French Ministry of Culture announced that Wilson's contract would not be renewed.

Soon afterwards, Jacques Duhamel, then French minister of culture, announced that the TNP would transfer its place of operation from Paris to Villeurbanne (a suburb of Lyon), with Roger Planchon, Patrice Chéreau, and Robert Gilbert as a triumvirate of directors. Planchon had been working at the Théâtre de la Cité of Villeurbanne since 1957, and in 1971 Chéreau was nominated its artistic director. When Planchon took over the directorship of the Théâtre de la Cité, the theatre had been bankrupted by "popular" seasons of operetta. His opening production was Shakespeare's *Henry IV*, which ran five hours and yet was massively attended. Planchon took to the streets and asked his prospective audience what it would like to see; the answer was Alexander Dumas *pere*'s *The Three Musketeers*. So Planchon dramatized *Les trois mousequetaires*, which played ninety-eight times in Villeurbanne alone and toured to Paris, most of Europe, and eventually the United States. Other works Planchon staged at Villeurbanne included Brecht's *The Good Woman of Setzuan* (1958), with Isabelle Sadoyan; Marivaux's *La second surprise de l'amour* (*The Second Surprise of Love*, 1959); Christopher Marlow's *Edward II* (1960); Molière's *Tartuffe* (1962); Shakespeare's *Troilus and Cressida* (1964); O'Casey's *Purple Dust* (1966); Racine's *Bérènice* (1966); and Molière's *Georges Dandin* (1967). Planchon himself wrote several works for the company, including *La remise* (*Refund*, 1962), *Les libertins* (*The Libertines*, 1967), *Dans le vent* (*In the Wind*, 1968), and *La mise en pièces du Cid* (*The Taking Apart of the Cid*, 1969), the last-named about culture and politics in Villeurbanne. In 1970 Planchon was invited to become director of the new Maison de la Culture in Lyon. Instead, he renewed his contract with Villeurbanne, provided the theatre was refurbished. While the theatre was being redone, Planchon took the troupe to Paris (one of many visits) and on tour. The troupe went everywhere in Europe, to the Scandinavian countries, and to Africa, and it came to the United States in 1968 with *Georges Dandin* and *The Three Musketeers*.

Chéreau had originally run the theatre at Sartrouville, a suburb of Paris, where he had staged a fantastic number of works, frequently filled with striking visual images, much violence, and shocking scenes. His best known production there was probably *Richard II*, with the king, a second-rate poet, finally digging himself into a sand pit. Chéreau quit the theatre in the riots of 1968 to stage plays in Italy. Robert Gilbert, the least known member of the triumvirate, had been an actor in Planchon's troupe at Villeurbanne.

What the TNP got in Villeurbanne was largely an old name for an old company, with all the Parisians staying where they were and the company at Villeurbanne getting a distinguished name and its accompanying trademark. Some actors have appeared from the old Parisian-based theatre as guests, but this was about all to come down from Paris. The opening production at Villeurbanne in May 1972 was an adaptation by Jean Vauthier of Marlowe's *The Massacre at Paris*, staged by Chéreau. Actors, dressed in Chicago gangland style, strode about a set that was part swimming pool. Alida Valli played Catherine de Medici in a broad style, and the whole production was marked by wild extravagance, full of killing, mayhem, and darkness ("lighting" by Andre Diot). The Duc de Guise (Planchon) dressed like Brecht of the 1920s (costumes by Jacques Schmidt). One critic called his review "Les Egarts de l'histoire" ("the Sewers of History"). It was a great sendoff for the new company, with Parisians clamoring to see the production. It proved too costly to tour, however, so only those who came down to Villeurbanne saw it (it only played eighteen times).

In 1972 Planchon staged an original work of his own, *La langue au chat* (*The Tongue of the Cat*). In the following year Chéreau staged Tankred Dorst's revolutionary work, *Toller*, and Planchon presented Molière's *Tartuffe*. In 1974 Chéreau did the *mise-en-scène* for *La dispute* (*The Dispute*), and Planchon did his own production of his own work, *Le cochon noir* (*The Black Pig*). *Tartuffe* was typical of many works done by the TNP and deserves some discussion. Planchon had done the work once with the previous company at Villeurbanne. This production, while based on the previous one, was not a carbon copy by any means. The work was startlingly original (which is characteristic of much of the company's work), with the family monstrous (they ate all the time), and the relationship between Tartuffe and Organ based on deep religious conviction. The house was full of religious images of the suffering Christ. Tartuffe was treated much more sympathetically than normal, and his final arrest seemed more monstrous than comic. It might be added that there were perhaps three laughs the whole evening, and the production was probably the longest *Tartuffe* on record. The work was much discussed in the French press, particularly when it played in Paris. When a lady from Buenos Aires objected to the production, Planchon answered her complaints in the program. It was all very gentlemanly.

In 1975 the company had a huge success, staged by Planchon, with *Folies bourgeoises*, which was a pastiche of boulevard comedies done in Paris in 1913. Planchon staged his own play, *Gilles de Rais* (known as *Bluebeard*) in 1976. Planchon presented Shakespeare's *Antony and Cleopatra* and *Pericles, Prince of Tyre* in 1978 and Harold Pinter's *No Man's Land* in 1979.

The TNP does five productions a year; the rest of the season (about twelve others) is made up of works from other French houses, generally Marseilles, Tourcoing, Grenoble, Ivry, and the Jeune Théâtre National. In exchange, the company has guest appearances in other houses and tours extensively, most frequently to Paris. In 1978 it went to East Germany, the Soviet Union, and Japan. Its home theatre is in the city complex, which was built in the 1930s and renovated in 1972. The theatre seats nine hundred and is frequently sold out. The chief criticism lodged against the troupe is that it is difficult to get tickets. The company has a record number of subscribers, and the "complet" sign is normal at the box office.

This very active company has only a small permanent company: generally only six actors are signed for the season. The theatre hires its extra actors from Paris or occasionally Lyon. Certain actors tend to return season after season for one play, making the company seem larger. It receives a hefty subsidy of 10 million francs from the French government.

No real attempt is made to balance the season. The TNP simply likes to offer its subscribers what is best. Most decisions are made by its triumvirate, with Planchon of late making more and more decisions, as Chéreau absents himself for either staging operas or directing films. (Chéreau did no productions in 1978–1979 or 1979–1980.) Wilson generally makes most of the financial decisions.

It is hard to imagine two men more unalike in the French theatre than Vilar and Planchon, to say nothing of Chéreau. Vilar thought he was the servant of the script; Planchon frequently twists the words of a script; and Chéreau is almost infuriatingly clever. Yet all have had a popular following and have spent a considerable amount of time talking to their public about what they want. The classics are included at Villeurbanne; in the 1979–1980 season Planchon staged Racine's *Athalie* and Molière's *Don Juan*. In the same season there were productions by Robert Wilson and Andrey Wajda. The price of tickets is quite low, a subscription costing about 65 francs for five productions. The company plays within the region, notably in Saint-Etienne, Grenoble, Valence, and Chalons-sur-Saône. In addition, it sponsors some concerts and has invited foreign troupes to Villeurbanne. In June 1978 it sponsored twenty-five productions from twenty companies in one week in various theatres in the town. It would like to do more of this in the future.

What makes the TNP a popular theatre? Every director of the company would probably give a different answer, but all share the notion that the public should be asked what it wants to see. Consequently, the troupe presents not boulevard successes, but works which the theatre staff selects (not all by itself) and which it thinks the public will like. Giuseppi Verdi, as did Lope de Vega, once said that the only real judge of success is the box office, to which the TNP adds: fill the theatre but don't insult the audience's intelligence. The audience may at first be baffled by quality or differences in staging, but gradually it will appreciate what is being done. Then put a price on it which the public can afford to pay.

LEON M. AUFDEMBERGE

POPULAR THEATRE OF FLANDERS
(Théâtre Populaire des Flandres)
68 Avenue du Peuple Belge
59000 Lille, France

Since 1953 Lille has housed one of France's most important theatre companies, the Théâtre Populaire des Flandres (TPF). Its founder was Cyril Robichez. The company's first work was Jean Davrincourt's *Les bourgeois de Calais*. It was presented for two performances and was staged by Robichez, who would be the only director for the company until 1961. In its first seasons the company generally presented very short runs of performances (anywhere from two to eight) of such works as Lope de Vega's *The Star of Seville* (1954), T. S. Eliot's *Murder in the Cathedral* (1955), Brecht's *The Rifles of Mother Carrara* and *Fear and Misery in the Third Reich* (1956), Günther Weisenborn's *Tyl Eulenspiegel* (1958), and Molière's *Les fourberies de Scapin* (*The Cheats of Scapin*, 1959).

In 1954 Robichez founded a school in conjunction with the company which would teach music as well as theatre arts. Two years later the company began a series of exchanges with companies in nearby Westphalia, and in 1960 the troupe began an extensive touring program in France with a portable stage and a repertory selected with an eye for both adults and children. The same year the French Ministry of Culture gave the company permanent national troupe status, which insured government subsidy. But what the company needed most was a permanent home.

In the 1960s a series of events drastically altered the life of the company. The most important occurred in 1962 when the city gave the troupe an old building, the Hôtel des Archives, to refashion as a theatre. It was called the Petit Théâtre du Pont Neuf, with seats for 100 to 140 people. This meant longer runs for plays and increased the number of plays done each year. The company's great successes of the 1960s included the Zweig/Jules Romains/Ben Jonson *Volpone*(1960), Victor Hugo's *Marie Tudor* (1961, *mise-en-scène* Robichez), John Steinbeck's *Of Mice and Men* (1962, *mise-en-scène* Robichez), Jean Anouilh's *Antigone* (1962, *mise-en-scène* J. Boyer), Molière's *Le malade imaginaire* (*The Imaginary Invalid*, 1963, *mise-en-scène* Robichez), Corneille's *Le Cid* (1965, *mise-en-scène* Robichez), Brecht's *The Exception and the Rule* (1965, *mise-en-scène* Robichez), Eugene O'Neill's *Long Day's Journey into Night* (1965, *mise-en-scène* J. Boyer), Ferenc Molnár's *Liliom* (1965, *mise-en-scène* Robichez, who also played the title role), P. A. Breal's *Les Hussards* (1967, *mise-en-scène* Robichez), Molière's *L'avare* (*The Miser*, 1968, *mise-en-scène* Robichez), the anonymous *La farce de Maître Pathelin* (1968, *mise-en-scène* Jacques Mussier), and Fernando Arrabal's *Guernica* (1969, *mise-en-scène* Robichez).

In the 1970s the theatre experienced a number of ups and downs. On its plus side, the company continued its touring policy, going to theatres throughout France, Belgium, Holland, and Northern and Central Africa. In 1970 the TPF created a *passeport culturel* which entitles holders to substantial discounts on tickets. In 1977 Robichez founded the Carrefour International du Théâtre which presents visiting troupes from all over the world, with performances in November and December. Among the troupes presented were the Bread and Puppet Theatre, the Living Theatre, the Théâtre National Daniel Sorano of Sénégal, and Yoshi and Company from Japan. The theatre has also established close ties with other companies in the area to share expenses in the mounting of a production.

On the negative side, the theatre has had two bad problems, perhaps the worst a company can have. The first was its theatre. In 1973 the company was forced to leave its home when its theatre was torn down. The city of Lille then gave the troupe a space to use, which it fashioned into a theatre, the Théâtre Daniel Salengro. The second problem was money. Fortunately, L'Association des Amis du TPF was formed to help bail out the company and to provide money for a new theatre.

Beginning in the 1970s the repertory became more modern. Robichez continues to stage about half the works done for the company, but with his devoted audience he can do more contemporary plays and not have to depend so much on the mixture of classics and moderns which is so favored in other regional houses. Among the successes in the last decade have been Jules Romains' *Knock, ou Le triomphe de la médecine* (1970, *mise-en-scène* Robichez), Molière's *Le médecin malgré lui* (*The Doctor in Spite of Himself*, 1972, *mise-en-scène* Robichez), Luigi Pirandello's *Tonight We Improvise* (1972, *mise-en-scène* Jean Marie Schmitt), Sean O'Casey's *The Shadow of a Gunman* (1973, *mise-en-scène* Bernard Maigrot), J. F. Regnard's *Le légataire universel* (*The Residuary Legatee*, 1974, *mise-en-scène* J. Mussier), Edward Albee's *Who's Afraid of Virginia Woolf?* (1974, *mise-en-scène* Robichez), Ibsen's *An Enemy of the People* (1977) with Robichez both playing Stockmann and staging the work that became perhaps the greatest hit in the TPF's history, Sławomir Mrożek's *Tango* (1978, *mise-en-scène* Robichez), the Gorky/Brecht *The Mother* (1979, *mise-en-scène* Pierre Etienne Heymann), and Eugene Ionesco's *Le roi se meurt* (*Exit the King*, 1980) with Robichez again staging and playing the lead role.

The company produces three to four new works a season and also plays host to several more productions from other theatres. The company employs about six actors for the season, and the rest are hired as demanded. Robichez is its only permanent *metteur-en-scène*, with the rest guests. The theatre does not employ dramaturges on a permanent basis; however, either a dramaturge is hired for each production or Robichez acts as one. The annual budget for the company in 1980 was 5 million francs, of which the state provided 29 percent, the regional council 39 percent, the council general of the north 6 percent, the council regional of Pas-de-Calais 2 percent, the city of Lille 8 percent, and the box office 15 percent. In addition, some money is received from the various towns where the company plays.

Since its beginning, Popular Theatre of Flanders has been more of a regional theatre than a theatre for the city of Lille. Robichez has said that his company is not an *"esthétique chapelle"* but rather a theatre made to conquer the region with *"moyens nobles"* (lofty means). The rocky times of the early 1970s, when the loss of the physical theatre and financial problems threatened to close the company, are definitely over. The company is looking forward to a new theatre which Robichez has dubbed a Théâtre Comédie Quotidien. The company began as Robichez's personal vision and remains so today.

LEON M. AUFDEMBERGE

SUNSHINE THEATRE
(Théâtre du Soleil)
Bois de Vinennes, Parc Floral
Paris 12e, France

To go from obscurity to one of the leading theatres in France in fifteen short years, as the Théâtre du Soleil has done, is surely a sign of artistry. Founded in 1964 by Ariane Mnouchine and ten others (both actors and technicians) opposed to France's ordinary commercial theatres, the company began in obscurity as a collective. It remains one of the few collective theatre organizations in the country. Its first production, staged by Mnouchine, was a production of Maxim Gorky's *The Petty Bourgeois* and received good reviews. The next production was Philippe Lestard's *Capitaine Fracasse*. Both works were moderate successes, but in 1966 came the production of Arnold Wesker's *The Kitchen*, making the group one of the most talked about in Paris.

The Kitchen was staged by Mnouchine in the Cirque de Montmartre. The choice, dealing with work, was an obvious one for the collective. The actors worked with props (trays, utensils) but not actual food, which caused a great deal of discussion about the aesthetics of the production. The concept of actors being closely identified with their roles and the immediacy of the production made the whole evening very alive.

The Wesker play was followed in 1968 by Shakespeare's *A Midsummer Night's Dream*, also staged by Mnouchine in the Cirque Montmartre. The play was done in modern dress and stressed the savage in nature. There was grandeur in the playing, and the verse was spoken well, but the production was marked by its eroticism and perversity. In 1969 the group (at the Elysée Montmartre) gave its first production of a collective script, *Les Clowns*, which first played Aubervilliers, Milan, and Avignon before settling down to a comfortable run in Paris. Since then nearly all the theatre's productions have been collective exercises in which the director, doubling as *metteur-en-scène*, and the actors start work from a premise.

Les Clowns was followed by *1789*, which premiered in 1970. The work was first done in Milan and then transferred to Paris at the renovated Cartoucherie de Vincennes, where it became the hottest ticket in Paris for a long while. The play consisted of a series of episodes dealing with the French Revolution and Les Etats Généraux. As Mnouchine explained, it had a "positive spirit." The sets were well engineered by Roberto Morosco and Guy-Claude François. A second piece on the French Revolution, *1793*, also appeared in 1970. The second work was much more serious and less positive than the first. In both works, the audience stood or wandered about, from scene to scene, among the various playing areas scattered around the large hall. Music, dancing, singing, puppets, and masks played a large part in both productions. Mnouchine and the actors performed an enormous amount of research (with many actual speeches from the period) for both plays. Improvisation was employed to arrive at the final script; some actors found their characters early (sometimes four or five characters) and then helped others. This cooperative exercise paid off in both critical acclaim and at the box office. After the run of *1793*, both works played in tandem for a time so that the audience could contrast the works. The works also toured in Warsaw and England.

Following the pieces on the French Revolution, there was a long pause before the group presented a new work. As the last pieces dealt with the past, it seemed obvious that the new work should deal with the present. This new presentation, ironically entitled *L'âge d'or* (1973), was again staged in the Cartoucherie de Vincennes, where the audience could roam from one acting area to another. This time a variety of techniques were used, including *commedia dell'arte*, clown shows, cabaret performances, Chinese theatre, Brechtian alienation exercises, masks, and broad gestures. The story focused on the daily life of an Algerian immigrant, Abdallah, well played by Philippe Caubère. While it was a political play, it was not politically dogmatic, as the company was more anxious to spark discussion than to be doctrinaire.

After *L'âge d'or*, there was again a long break in production, this time prompted by the company's move in another direction. In 1976 Mnouchine was invited to direct her first film, produced by Claude Lelouch, the critically acclaimed *Molière*, with Philippe Caubère in the title role. The film employed the company, as well as a number of celebrated French actors and *metteurs-en-scène*, including Roger Plancon, Hubert Gignoux, and Jean Dasté. It played at the New York Film Festival in the fall of 1979. Most critics have said it is probably the best film on theatre life since *Les enfants du Paradis*.

Following *Molière*, part of the troupe played Molière's *Don Juan*, with Caubère as the lead and *metteur-en-scène*. This revival was an attempt to recapture the play's original treatment, as most modern productions look at the play from either a Freudian or Marxist viewpoint, sometimes both. This was followed in May 1979 by *Mephisto*, a collective script based largely on the writings of Klaus Mann, but also on works by Thomas and Erika Mann, Chekhov, Karl Valentin, and many others. The work was a look at the rise of Nazi Germany from 1923 to 1939. Again music, dancing, cabaret techniques, and many speeches from the era were combined in the text. After playing in Paris, the work toured in Avignon and Louvain, Belgium (in cooperation with the Atelier Théâtral of that city) and played Paris again in the 1979–1980 season.

Apparently, the company has been greatly influenced by Vladimir Mayakovsky and Jacques Copeau. Mnouchine, however, insists that her work has been much more influenced by the English Joan Littlewood (and the theatre workshops) and work in such exercises as *Oh! What a Lovely War*. The actors are called upon to be both authors and players. Mnouchine sees her company as fulfilling large social needs—hence the choice of repertory and subjects. In an attempt to make the audience part of the production, the company interviews the people to find out what they want in terms of a theatre and what their lives are like. The company has also played in prisons.

The company began as a collective with eleven people, most of whom are still with the company. Not all the actors play in every piece. Some drop in and out of the company and play in commercial productions or other theatres before returning. In order to belong to the collective, the potential member must petition, be elected, and buy into the organization. Eventually, members of the corporation (now numbering fifteen, including both actors and technical people) should share in the company profits, though most money from play profits must fund the next production. The whole company (including the cooperative members) works for straight salary; salaries increase as revenues from plays increase. The company has about twenty-two actors on salary, and an additional eighteen people in the technical end or in administration. The company receives a subsidy from the French government of over 1.3 million francs. In 1973 Mnouchine, with other French directors, took to the streets to protest the amount of money allocated to state theatres and the small amount for nonstate or city-operated theatres. This inequity is a perennial problem in France and is not likely to be solved in the near future.

While the collective makes all company decisions, most ideas for pieces begin with Mnouchine. The company plays in Paris in the ancient Cartoucherie of Vincennes, near the old Chateau, and in the spacious Bois de Vincennes. A number of buildings are located in the compound; the administrative offices are in one building and the theatre in another. The building next to the administrative offices is the Théâtre de l'Aquarium, another collective with which the Théâtre du Soleil has a friendly relationship. All buildings in the compound are nicely weathered. In 1979, while the company played in Louvain, the theatre was occupied by the young Théâtre de l'écure, which played an adaptation from Chekhov called *Amours de poisson*. The Théâtre du Soleil hopes that this visit will be a prologue to visits from other companies.

LEON M. AUFDEMBERGE
(With the help of Lilian Andreone and
Jean-Pierre Henin of the Théâtre du Soleil.)

THEATRE AT THE TOP OF THE WORLD
(Théâtre du Bout du Monde)
(Centre Dramatique National de l'Ouest)
9 bis Avenue Jean Janvier
35100 Rennes, France

This company began in 1940 when a group of students in Rennes formed an amateur theatrical company, Les Jeunes Comédiens de Rennes, under the directorship of a lawyer, Jean-Louis Bertrand. Two of the students, George Goubert and Guy Parigot, grew so enamored of the theatre that they dropped their original professional plans and decided to devote themselves to the theatre. Les Jeunes Comédiens was an ambitious troupe, tackling such traditional pieces as Alexandre Dumas *fils' La dame aux camélias* and such works as Beaumarchais' *Le barbier de Seville* and Molière's *Les fourberies de Scapin* (*The Cheats of Scapin*). From 1940 to 1945 the troupe played more and more ambitious works, with productions steadily improving in quality. In 1946 the troupe began to tour, even playing Paris. One of its major successes was Jean-Louis Bertrand's *Merlin et Viviene*, based on an old Breton legend. In 1948 Goubert and Parigot became directors of the Centre Regional d'Arte Dramatique de Bretagne, the same year French Minister of Culture Jeanne Laurent decided to found at Rennes the Centre Dramatique de l'Ouest with part of that company formed from the Jeunes Comédiens (Hélène Batteaux, Roger Guillo, and, of course, Goubert and Parigot).

Hubert Gignoux was selected to be the new head of the company. He had considerable experience in the professional theatre before coming to Rennes. Fortunately for him, much good-will had already been generated by the Jeunes Comédiens and by a more than serviceable theatre in the town, le Théâtre Municipal, one of France's most beautiful. The company's first play was presented in the 1949–1950 season, Eugène Labiche's farce *Un chapeau de paille d'Italie* (*An Italian Straw Hat*), which was staged by the noted *metteur-en-scène* Maurice Jacquemont (who was also a good friend of Gignoux), with sets by a Breton painter, Jean le Moal. It was a difficult play to do—perhaps too ambitious for the young company—and was only a middling hit with the public. (A later revival did much better.) The second production was John Millington Synge's *The Playboy of the Western World* (staged by Gignoux), which was not a success. The third, a French classic, Molière's *L'avare* (*The Miser*), was enormously popular. It was staged by Gignoux, and it played an extensive tour. That season the company also mounted Paul Claudel's *L'echange* (*The Exchange*, *mise-en-scène* Gignoux) and a huge success, Molière's *Georges Dandin*, paired with *L'impromptu du grand siecle* (*The Impromptu of the Grand Century*), with the production by Jacquemont.

Gignoux led the company from 1949 to 1957, establishing the company not only in Rennes and the surrounding area, but also in Paris. Gignoux helped create a solid feeling of ensemble in terms of acting, with himself staging two or three works a year. He also liked to use guest actors, although most of the lead roles were played by members of the company. Gignoux favored a largely classical repertory, with a few modern works for variety. The major productions of the era reflect this preference: Molière's *L'école des femmes* and *La critique de l'ecole des femmes* (1950, *The School for Wives* and *The Critique of the School for Wives*, *mise-en-scène* Gignoux) with Philippe Noiret, the Zweig/Jules Romains/Ben Jonson *Volpone* (1951, *mise-en-scène* Gignoux) with George Wilson, Molière's *Le malade imaginaire* (*The Imaginary Invalid*, 1952, *mise-en-scène* Henry Grangé), Jean Giraudoux's *Intermezzo* (1952, *mise-en-scène* Jacquemont) with Noiret, Chekhov's *The Three Sisters* (1952, *mise-en-scène* Gignoux), Beaumarchais' *Le barbier de Seville* (1953, *mise-en-scène* Andre Maheux), Jules Romains' *Knock* (1953, *mise-en-scène* Gignoux), Molière's *Le misanthrope* (1954, *mise-en-scène* Gignoux), Shakespeare's *The Merchant of Venice* (1954, *mise-en-scène* Gignoux), Racine's *Les plaideurs* (*The Litigants*, 1955, *mise-en-scène* Goubert), Molière's *Le médecin malgré lui* (*The Doctor in Spite of Himself*, 1955, *mise-en-scène* Parigot), P. A. Breal's *Les Hussards* (1956, *mise-en-scène* Goubert), Claudel's *L'otage* (*The Hostage*, 1956, *mise-en-scène* Gignoux), and Gignoux's last classic production, *Hamlet* (1956), which he adapted. During a good deal of this period Gignoux's main designer was René Allio, one of France's most distinguished set designers.

Gignoux left for the company in Strasbourg in 1957 and was replaced by

Goubert and Parigot who had been with the company since the beginning. Both men had acted in each other's plays and were (and remain) close friends. Both had great rapport with the company and were proven *metteurs-en-scène*. During this period of the joint directorship (1957 to 1975), the company's touring activities were enlarged, not only in the area, but throughout France and internationally as well; and the company's policy of inviting other productions to the theatre, established in the 1951–1952 season, became more prevalent. The greatest change came in the repertory. Gignoux had favored the classics. Under the co-directorship, there was a movement toward twentieth-century plays, including some premieres, with a special emphasis on French authors. In 1958 the name of the company was changed to the Comédie de l'Ouest, although the name of the organization has remained the Centre Dramatique de l'Ouest. In 1968 a new Maison de la Culture was opened in Rennes which included two theatres. The company left its old home with mixed emotions; Parigot and Goubert became directors of the Maison.

For Parigot the list of good productions would include Friedrich von Schiller's *Mary Stuart* (1957), Molière's *Tartuffe* (1959), Shakespeare's *Othello* (1961), Chekhov's *The Cherry Orchard* (1961), Molière's *Les femmes savantes* (*The Learned Ladies*, 1962), Carlo Goldoni's *The Coffee House* (1952), Heinrich von Kleist's *The Prince of Homburg* (1963), Alfred de Musset's *On ne badine pas avec l'amour* (*No Trifling with Love*, 1963), Pierre Marivaux's *Les fausses confidences* (*The False Confidences*, 1964), Shakespeare's *Twelfth Night* (1966), Molière's *L'avare* (*The Miser*, 1967), Shakespeare's *The Taming of the Shrew* (1968), Max Frisch's *Biography* (1969), Louis Gaulis' *Capitane Karaghuez* (1970), de Musset's *Les caprices de Marianne* (1971), and Fernando Arrabal's *L'architect et l'Empereur d'Assyrie* (1974). As might be ascertained, Parigot favored the classics.

Goubert favored a much more modern repertory, and his list would include Marcel Pagnol's *Marius* (1957), Pedro Calderón de la Barca's *La vida es sueño* (1959), O'Casey's *Juno and the Paycock* (1960), Molière's *Monsieur de Pourgeaugnac* (1963), Boris Vian's *Les bâtisseurs d'empire* (*The Empire Builders*, 1966), and Friedrich Dürrenmatt's *The Marriage of Mr. Mississippi*(1967), Dario Fo's *The Archangels Don't Play Electric Billiards* (1967), Alfred Jarry's *Ubu Roi* (1970, with production by Goubert and a collective), George Bernard Shaw's *Androcles and the Lion* (1972), and Robert Bolt's *A Man for All Seasons* (1975) with Pierre Spadoni assisting in the production. Goubert's biggest role with the company was his crafty king in Shakespeare's *Richard III*, done in the Shakespeare year of 1964 with the production by Pierre Barrat.

In addition to these two men's productions, there was an enviable list of productions by other stage directors, including the premiere of Per Jakes Hélias' *Le grand valet* (1961, *mise-en-scène* Roger Guillo), Sophocles' *Antigone* paired with *La ville aux sept portes* (*The City with Seven Gates*) adapted by Jeannette Granval from texts of Sophocles and Aeschylus (1962, *mise-en-scène* Barrat),

Brecht's *Man Is Man* (1965, *mise-en-scène* André Steiger), Federico García Lorca's *Blood Wedding* (1966, *mise-en-scène* René Lafforgue), Prosper Mérimée's *Les Espagnols en Danemarck* (*The Spaniards in Denmark*, 1966, *mise-en-scène* Pierre Vial), and Molière's *Don Juan* (1969, *mise-en-scène* Barrat).

In 1974 the Ministry of Culture in Paris decided to take the directorship of the Maison de la Culture from the co-directors, and the next year the company was placed under a one-man rule. Goubert left to become director of the Théâtre National at the Palais de Chaillot. Since 1975 there have been no sweeping changes in policy, but there has been a name change to the Théâtre du Bout du Monde. Rather than changes, there has been a reaffirmation of what the two men did together.

One of the theatre's accomplishments in the last few years has been to present scripts either set in the area or written by local authors, or both. One local author, Guillame Kergourlay, works as a literary advisor for the company and has contributed two scripts, *La chasse presidentielle* (*The Presidential Hunt*, 1973, *mise-en-scène* Goubert) and *Tard dans la Nuit* (*Late in the Night*, 1977, *mise-en-scène* by the author). Another local writer is Per Jakes Hélias, whose *Le grand valet* has already been mentioned. This script, originally done in 1961, was revived by the company in 1976 (*mise-en-scène* Guillo). The company has also presented a collective dramatization and production of Paul Feval's celebrated work *Le bossu* (*The Hunchback*, 1977), with this work filmed as well.

Some of the major works since 1975 have included Molière's *L'avare* (1975, *mise-en-scène* le Bonniac), a children's play by Jeannette Granval and Robert Angebaud, with the help of Hélias, called *Jobik et les sept chemins de l'Ankou* (*Jobik and the Seven Ways of Ankou*, 1977, *mise-en-scène* Angebaud), James Saunders' *The Next Time I'll Sing to You* (1976, *mise-en-scène* Angebaud), Samuel Beckett's *Oh les beaux jours* (*Happy Days*, 1977, *mise-en-scène* Parigot and Granval) with Annie Legrand as Winnie, Brecht's *Dialogues of the Exiles* (1978, *mise-en-scène* Angebaud), Ionesco's *Le roi se meurt* (*Exit the King*, 1980, *mise-en-scène* Bernard Lotti), and *Molière-Bulgakov* adapted from Mikhail Bulgakov's work with the adaptation and production by Angebaud (1980).

As is true of the many good provincial companies which dot France, this company serves not only its home city, Rennes, but also the surrounding area. The season is a series of major productions by the company (perhaps eight with some revivals) and various productions from other companies. The company plays in two houses in the Maison de la Culture, both of which are named after distinguished *metteurs-en-scène*: the Salle Jean Vilar, which seats 1,100, and the Salle Jean-Marie Serreau, which seats 420. In October 1979 the company opened a small, two-hundred-seat house, the Théâtre de la Parcheminerie, named after the street on which it is located. The opening production was Brecht's *The Resistible Rise of Arturo Ui*, staged by Pierre Debauche with Parigot in the title role. This theatre will house more experimental works by the company as well as a series of small productions from other companies. In addition to France, the company has played often in England (mostly universities), Italy, and Algeria, and, in 1964, it circled the globe with *Les femmes savantes*. The company also plays Paris in order to reach the critics there.

The permanent company numbers about twelve; many of the actors have been with the company for years. In addition, some actors are hired for one play, generally from Paris, although Parigot likes to hire local actors whenever possible. The theatre has its own atelier located in the theatre building. (Parigot and Goubert had their hands in designing the building, and it shows most happily.) The theatre publishes its own journal, *Le Courrier Dramatique de l'Ouest*, as does the Maison de la Culture with its *Confluent*. The company maintains an excellent relationship with the Maison and with its head, Cheriff Khazadak. Khazadak's job is to see that the two theatres are filled with plays not only by the resident company, but also by all kinds of touring productions including ballet, musical programs, films, and generally what the public wants.

In recent years the company has played mostly modern works, but the classics are by no means ignored. In its first years audiences, particularly in small towns, disliked modern plays; now modern works, even Beckett, are taken in stride. The company was one of the first in France to play Dario Fo. Although the company has no subscription plan in Rennes, other cities where the company plays have such plans. Instead, the company relies on heavy (and rather well-done) publicity and on discounts for large groups of students. The company is subsidized by the French government in the amount of 3.5 million francs, to which other authorities add another 1.1 million francs.

The theatre, while one of the handsomest in France and very comfortable, has problems with attendance. On a good soccer night, attendance is quite poor. Nevertheless, the attendance record for the company is very high in Rennes and commendable in the smaller places. With its modern repertory and its high standard of performance, the company is one of the leading provincial companies in France.

LEON M. AUFDEMBERGE

Great Britain

INTRODUCTION

Great Britain has a broad range of theatre companies: (1) university theatre companies such as those at Birmingham and Wolverhampton; (2) touring troupes, which are privately financed and in need of a minimum audience guarantee in order to book a particular theatre; (3) professional acting companies at London's fringe theatres; (4) national companies such as the Abbey Theatre Company, the English Stage Company at the Royal Court Theatre, the National Theatre Company, and the Royal Shakespeare Company; (5) and regional companies of varying merit. The Bristol Old Vic, senior member of the four premiere provincial theatre companies of Great Britain, pioneered the revival of regional theatres. Along with the Birmingham Repertory Theatre Company, Glasgow's Citizens' Theatre, and Manchester's Royal Exchange Theatre Company, it provides an exceptionally high caliber of theatrical production.

During the 1970s rapid inflation, decreasing opportunities for theatre personnel, and a lack of new and innovative materials with which to work brought major changes in Great Britain's theatre. The importance of London's West End as a theatre center has decreased as the quality of productions has increased at London's fringe and the nation's provincial theatres. Relatively new companies with outstanding casts have premiered award-winning plays. The national companies have developed relationships with theatres outside London: the National Theatre Company with the Theatre Royal in Edinburgh and the Royal Shakespeare Company with Newcastle. Tight money has forced the repertory companies to consider more one-set and small-cast plays, smaller orchestras, and fewer touring productions. Large-scale touring musicals have become rare. As expensive renovation of theatres designed to accompany touring companies decreased, touring productions themselves increased and presented more regional dramas. Precariously poised between boom and bankruptcy, London's fringe theatres have expanded the possibilities for producing imaginative and original playscripts.

The National Theatre Company's impressive theatre complex on the South

Bank of the Thames and the Royal Shakespeare Company's new home in London's Barbican Centre have helped to generate renewed enthusiasm for Great Britain's theatre companies. British theatre is alive and thriving in London *and* in the provinces.

COLBY H. KULLMAN

ABBEY THEATRE COMPANY
Lower Abbey Street
Dublin 1, Ireland

In *Our Irish National Theatre* (1913), reprinted by Hugh Hunt in *The Abbey: Ireland's National Theatre 1904–1978* (1979), p. 18, Lady Augusta Gregory wrote:

We propose to have performed in Dublin . . . certain Celtic and Irish plays, which whatever their degree of excellence, will be written with a high ambition, and so to build up a Celtic and Irish school of dramatic literature. We hope to find in Ireland an uncorrupted and imaginative audience trained to listen by its passion for oratory, and believe that our desire to bring upon the stage the deeper thoughts and emotions of Ireland will ensure for us a tolerant welcome, and that freedom of experiment which is not found in theatres of England. . . . We will show that Ireland is not the home of buffoonery and easy sentiment . . . but the home of an ancient idealism.

That manifesto, issued by William Butler Yeats, Lady Gregory, and Edward Martyn in 1898, eventually led to the formation of the Abbey Theatre, which in December 1979 celebrated its seventy-fifth anniversary. The purpose delineated by the founders has continued.

Referring to the Abbey Theatre as "a writers' theatre," current Artistic Director Joe Dowling emphasizes the need "to encourage and promote new Irish dramatic material for our stage." However, despite the need for continuity with the past, tradition must also be "redefined and revivified for each succeeding generation of theatregoers," acknowledges Micheál Ó hAodha, chairman of the Board of Directors.

After the 1898 meeting of Yeats, Lady Gregory, and Martyn at Duras House, on the shores of Galway Bay, George Moore also became interested in their project. As a result, in May 1899 the Irish Literary Theatre began in Dublin; the first plays presented were Yeats' *The Countess Cathleen* and Martyn's *The Heather Field*. Two years later appeared a play that would become significant for the future of Irish theatre. On October 21, 1901, the Irish Literary Theatre produced Douglas Hyde's *Casadh an tSúgáin* (*The Twisting of the Rope*), the first play in Irish to be staged at a recognized theatre. Furthermore, two years later W. F. Fay, the director of that play, and his brother, Frank Fay (bringing with them the Irish National Dramatic Company, which had produced Yeats' *Cathleen Ni Houlihan* in 1902), joined the Irish Literary Theatre to form the Irish National Theatre Society. The arrival of the Fay brothers, with their expertise in stagecraft, added a new dimension to the group.

At the first meeting of the Irish National Theatre Society on February 1, 1903, Yeats, George W. Russell (AE), Douglas Hyde, and Maud Gonne were elected officers, and among the other members were the two Fay brothers.

In the "Rules of the Irish National Theatre Society," which according to Hugh Hunt (p. 39) may be found in the National Library of Ireland (ms. 13068), the society wished

to create an Irish National Theatre, to act and produce plays in Irish or English, written by Irish writers, or on Irish subjects; and such dramatic works by foreign authors as would tend to educate and interest the public of this country in the higher aspects of dramatic art.

In 1904 the society found a patron. Annie Fredericka Horniman, an English-woman, bought and gave to the society a small music hall theatre (in the former Mechanics Institute on Abbey Street, Dublin) with an annual subsidy. That building, with a patent granted to Lady Gregory, became the Abbey Theatre. The patent stipulated that performances in the Abbey be confined to plays by Irish authors, plays of Irish life, plays translated from Continental languages, and plays more than a hundred years old. (A later escape clause gave the theatre twenty-four nights a year free of restrictions). On December 27, 1904, the Abbey opened with Yeats' *On Baile's Strand* and Lady Gregory's *Spreading the News*.

During the early years of the Abbey its actors and actresses included, among others, Sara Allgood, the Fay brothers, J. M. Kerrigan, Fred O'Donovan, Máire (Molly) O'Neill, and Máire Nic Shiubhlaigh. Some of the early productions were Yeats' *Shadowy Waters* (1906); Lady Gregory's *The Rising of the Moon* (1907); and William Boyle's comedies (popular plays in the Abbey's repertoire): *The Building Fund* (1905) and *The Eloquent Dempsey* (1906).

The Abbey soon welcomed the emergence of John Millington Synge, an influential new playwright. Synge, who had visited the Aran Islands several times between 1898 and 1902 and who had seen Douglas Hyde's *Casadh an tSúgáin*, wanted to use peasant life as the material for drama. He combined that interest, however, with an interest in a poetic ideal. Even before the society obtained the Abbey Theatre, Synge's *In the Shadow of the Glen* (1903) and *Riders to the Sea* (1904) were performed in Molesworth Hall. After the Abbey opened, it presented Synge's *The Well of the Saints* (1905) and *The Playboy of the Western World* (1907), which provoked celebrated disturbances. After Synge's death (1909), the Abbey staged his *Deirdre of the Sorrows* in 1910. Synge's work established what became known as the Abbey play, with its country char-acters and setting, naturalistic framework, and poetic realistic dialogue. (Later, the Abbey play also included tenement and prison settings.)

In 1908 and 1910 occurred two events that significantly affected the artistic and financial future of the Abbey Theatre. In 1908 the Fay brothers left, forming their own company to present Abbey plays in New York, Chicago, and elsewhere. By this time, however, they had given the theatre a distinctive style of acting, emphasizing naturalness, restraint, the spoken word, and teamwork (rather than the star system). The chief influences on this theatre have been not only the Celtic revival, J. T. Grein's Independent Theatre in London, Aurélien-Marie Lugné-Poe's Théâtre de l'Oeuvre (dedicated to the Symbolist cause), and Ibsen and the Norwegian theatre, but also the French actor Constant-Benoit Coquelin and André Antoine's Théâtre Libre.

In 1910 the Abbey Theatre, having failed to close on May 6 for King Edward VII's death, lost the support of Miss Horniman. Its financial survival was assured, however, by appeals for funds by Lady Gregory and Yeats, and by tours. In 1910 a new patent was granted and a limited liability company formed.

During 1911–1912 the Abbey toured British cities and the United States. In Philadelphia, a performance of *The Playboy of the Western World* again caused controversy; the company was arrested for presenting a play corrupting morals.

After Synge's death some of his contemporaries were still writing plays for the Abbey, for example, Yeats (*The Land of Heart's Desire*, 1911) and Lady Gregory (*The Full Moon*, 1910). Although William Boyle, protesting the staging of *Playboy*, withdrew his plays from the Abbey's repertoire, other new playwrights appeared. Two of these were Padraic Colum, who wrote realistic plays about country life (for example, *The Land*, 1905) and George Fitzmaurice (*The Country Dressmaker*, 1907). Another movement away from romantic, poetical theatre consisted of plays by the Cork Realists, including Lennox Robinson and T. C. Murray. Lennox Robinson's early plays were *The Clancy Name* (1908) and *The Cross Roads* (1909). Murray contributed *Birthright* (1910) and *Maurice Harte* (1912).

In 1919 Lennox Robinson, who had been the Abbey's manager from 1909 to 1914 and who served as playwright and director at various times until 1918, again became manager. Under Robinson's direction worked such actors and actresses as May Craig, Barry Fitzgerald, Arthur Shields, and especially the versatile F. J. McCormick. Among the roles McCormick played between 1918 and 1947 were Lear, Oedipus, Seamus Shields in *The Shadow of a Gunman*, and Joxer Daly in *Juno and the Paycock*.

As a result of political upheaval, including a curfew, the Abbey suffered financially during 1914–1923. Through the efforts of Ernest Blythe, minister of finance and later managing director of the Abbey, the theatre was saved from bankruptcy by an annual grant from the Irish Free State. In 1924 the Abbey Theatre became the first state-subsidized theatre in the English-speaking world.

Plays by Yeats, Gregory, Robinson, and Murray continued to be performed during this period: Yeats' *The Player Queen* (1919); Lady Gregory's "Wonder Plays," for example, *The Golden Apples* (1920); Robinson's *The Whiteheaded Boy* (1916); and Murray's *Autumn Fire* (1924). Important new playwrights included two who provided the Abbey's repertoire with plays for a number of years: George Shiels (*Bedmates*, 1921) and Brinsley Macnamara (*The Rebellion in Ballycullen*, 1919).

The most significant new playwright, however, was Sean O'Casey, famous for his trilogy on Dublin tenement settings and for his portrayal of turmoil from the General Strike of 1913 to the end of the Civil War. In 1923 appeared *The Shadow of a Gunman* (about the Black and Tan War); in 1924, *Juno and the Paycock* (about the Civil War of 1922) and *Nannie's Night Out*; and in 1926, *The Plough and the Stars* (which caused outbursts because of O'Casey's treatment of the 1916 Easter Rebellion). A later play, *The Silver Tassie* (about World War I), was rejected by Yeats in 1928 but was belatedly performed in 1935 and acclaimed in its 1972 production by Hugh Hunt.

In 1927 the Abbey gained a supplementary theatre. The Peacock Theatre, in another portion of the former Mechanics Institute, opened on November 13 with the New Players' presentation of Georg Kaiser's expressionistic play, *From Morn to Midnight*. Seating one hundred people, this small theatre housed the Dublin Gate Theatre, the Abbey School of Acting, and the Abbey School of Ballet.

In the late 1920s and the 1930s Yeats, disappointed with the failure of verse drama, turned to small private audiences for his presentation of poetic dramas influenced by Nō plays. Although his version of *Oedipus the King* (1926) did succeed, many of his last plays were in prose: *The Only Jealousy of Emer*, rewritten in prose as *Fighting the Waves* (1929), and *The Words upon the Window Pane* (1930). *Purgatory* (1938), in verse, was the last Yeats play performed by the Abbey before his death in 1939.

In the 1930s Abbey actors who performed while the contract players toured the United States included Frank Carney, Cyril Cusack, Eric Gorman, Ria Mooney, Nora O'Mahony, and Shelah Richards. Among the new dramatists during this period were Denis Johnston, Paul Vincent Carroll, Louis D'Alton, and Teresa Deevy. Plays by Johnston included *The Moon in the Yellow River* (1931) and *Blind Man's Buff* (1936); by Carroll, *Shadow and Substance* (1937), winning the New York Critics Award for the Best Foreign Play of 1936–1937; by D'Alton, *The Man in the Cloak* (1937); and by Deevy, *The King of Spain's Daughter* (1935).

In 1938 one of the dreams of the founders of the Irish National Literary Theatre was fulfilled. Although Lady Gregory had tried as early as 1912 to have plays performed in the Irish language, it was only in 1938, with the advocacy of Ernest Blythe, that plays in Irish began to be produced at the Abbey. In 1938 Hugh Hunt, who had become producer in 1935 (accompanied by designer Tanya Moiseiwitsch), directed a revival of *Casadh an tSúgáin*. On December 26, 1945, the Abbey performed the pantomime *Muireann agus an Prionnsa*, Micheál Ó hAodha's adaptation of Lady Gregory's *The Golden Apples*.

In the 1940s the Abbey's repertoire included additional plays by George Shiels (for example, *The Rugged Path*, 1940, the first long-running play at the Abbey), Lennox Robinson, and Brinsley Macnamara. The theatre also produced plays by Walter Macken (*Mungo's Mansion*, 1946) and M. J. Molloy (*Old Road*, 1943). Among important actors and actresses in the 1940s were Harry Brogan, Máire Ni Dhomhnaill, Bill Foley, Geoffrey Golden, Siobhan McKenna, Angela Newman, Philip O'Flynn, and Micheál Ó hAonghusa.

In the early morning of July 18, 1951, a few hours after a performance of

The Plough and the Stars, a fire broke out in the back stage of the Abbey, destroying the premises. After the fire the Abbey first performed at the Rupert Guinness Hall and in August leased the Queen's Theatre, where it remained from 1951 to 1966. The move to larger quarters meant a less intimate atmosphere, fewer revivals, and longer runs of popular plays, for example, Walter Macken's *Home Is the Hero* (1952) and Louis D'Alton's *This Other Eden* (1953). Another change at the Queen's consisted of the Abbey's beginning to present a one-act play in Irish after a main performance.

During its exile the Abbey continued to perform plays by M. J. Molloy, such as *The Wood of the Whispering* (1953). It also presented Brendan Behan's play of prison life, *The Quare Fella* (1956), Joseph Tomelty's *Is the Priest at Home?* (1954), John Murphy's *The Country Boy* (1959), and John McCann's *Twenty Years A-Wooing* (1954). Works by the significant new dramatists John B. Keane, Hugh Leonard, and Brian Friel began to appear: Keane's *Hut 42* (1962) and *The Man from Clare* (1963), Leonard's *The Big Birthday* (1956), and Friel's *The Enemy Within* (1962).

In 1959 plans for the new Abbey, prepared by Michael Scott with consultant Pierre Sonrel (a French architect), had been approved by the Dublin Corporation and contributions were authorized by the government. Not until 1966, however, was the new building ready for occupancy.

On July 18, 1966, the new Abbey opened in a building seating 628 (one hundred more than the original one), with *Recall the Years*, a theatrical presentation of the Abbey Theatre's history up to 1951. Following this presentation, scripted by Walter Macken and directed by Tomás Mac Anna, the Abbey on August 15, 1966, again staged *The Plough and the Stars*, the last play performed before the fire that destroyed the old Abbey. The most popular play at the new Abbey in 1966 was *Tarry Flynn*, adapted by P. J. O'Connor from a novel by Patrick Kavanagh.

Incorporated into the new Abbey is the Peacock, which seats 157 and can stage plays in a semi-arena arrangement, as well as in the proscenium. Completed in 1967 and opened with Myles Na gCopaleen's *An Beál Bocht* (*The Poor Mouth*) on July 25, this small stage (located under the main auditorium) is used for experimental drama, Irish-language plays, verse plays, and one-man shows.

In its first several years in the new Abbey, the theatre produced successful adaptations, *The Shaughraun* and *Borstal Boy*. The new production of Dion Boucicault's 1875 melodrama, directed by Hugh Hunt with Cyril Cusack playing the part of Conn, also appeared at the Aldwych Theatre, London, during the World Theatre Season in 1968. The other 1967 success, *Borstal Boy*, was adapted by Frank McMahon from Brendan Behan's autobiography and directed by Tomás Mac Anna. After a performance at the Dublin Theatre Festival, *Borstal Boy* went on to Broadway and in 1970 received a Tony Award.

During 1967–1969 Irish-language plays appeared at both the Abbey and the Peacock. In a departure from traditional pantomime, the Abbey in 1969 presented *Séadna* by An tAthair Peadar Ó Laoghaire and adapted by Tomás Mac Anna;

among the plays staged at the Peacock were *Faill ar an bhFeart* by Séamus O'Neill (1967) and *An Giall* (1968), Brendan Behan's first draft of *The Hostage*.

While the Abbey continued to emphasize the performance of plays by Irish writers (and in 1969 for the first time produced Samuel Beckett's *Waiting for Godot*), it also engaged in international projects. Returning to the policies of the 1920s and 1930s, it produced foreign classics, such as Eugene O'Neill's *Long Day's Journey into Night* (1967). A 1968 highlight consisted of the Abbey's Dublin Theatre Festival offering, Chekhov's *The Cherry Orchard*, directed by Marie Knebel from the Red Army Theatre of the Soviet Union. For the latter production Siobhan McKenna and Cyril Cusack joined the regular Abbey players. Finally, an international seminar on national theatres was held during September 30–October 8, 1968.

During the 1970s the Abbey staged a number of revivals, including *Macbeth* (the first Shakespearean play to be presented at the Abbey in forty years), directed by Hugh Hunt (1971), and Yeats' version of *King Oedipus*, this time (1973) by a Greek director, Michael Cacoyannis. In 1978 the Abbey performed *Stephen D*, Hugh Leonard's adaptation of James Joyce's *A Portrait of the Artist as a Young Man* and *Stephen Hero*, originally produced at the Gate in 1962.

Important revivals of Synge and O'Casey also appeared. For the 1971 centenary of Synge's birth the Abbey performed *Riders to the Sea*, *The Playboy of the Western World*, and (for the first time) *The Tinker's Wedding*; and the Peacock staged *Deirdre of the Sorrows*. O'Casey's plays produced again at the Abbey consisted of *The Shadow of a Gunman* (1971), *The Silver Tassie* (1972), and in 1976 (for the fiftieth anniversary of its first performance) *The Plough and the Stars*, which has never been out of the Abbey's repertoire. Directed by Tomás Mac Anna, this Golden Jubilee production, with Siobhan McKenna and Cyril Cusack, toured the United States as part of the bicentennial celebrations. O'Casey's later plays were also presented during the 1970s: at the Abbey—*Purple Dust* (1975), *Cock-a-Doodle Dandy* (1977), *The Star Turns Red* (1978); and at the Peacock—*Figuro in the Night* (1975) and *The Moon Shines on Kylenamoe* (1975).

There were new ventures at the Abbey and the Peacock in the 1970s. For example, the first play by Americans entered the Abbey's repertoire. Tomás Mac Anna directed Richard F. Stockton and Richard Herd's *Prisoner of the Crown* (1972), a play about the arrest and trial of Roger Casement. In 1975 the Abbey presented *Innish*, a successful musical based on Lennox Robinson's play of the 1930s. The most successful new play at the Peacock in 1972 was Brendan Behan's posthumous *Richard's Cork Leg*, of which the first act was written by Behan and the second was composed by Alan Simpson from notes left by Behan.

Political plays about various periods appeared on the Abbey's stage during the 1970s. One of the most famous was Brendan Behan's play about the Irish Republican Army (originally performed at Joan Littlewood's Theatre in London in 1958), *The Hostage* (1970). Directed by Hugh Hunt, this production later toured Europe. At the Peacock, G. P. Gallivan's documentary *The Dáil Debate* (1971) presented in theatrical form the debates in Dáil Eireann on acceptance of the Anglo-Irish Treaty of 1922. Equally significant productions included (at the Peacock) *A State of Chassis* (1970) by John D. Stewart, Tomás Mac Anna, and Eugene Watters, a revue on the Irish political situation in the North and the South, and (at the Abbey) Brian Friel's *The Freedom of the City* (1973), based on the events of Bloody Sunday in Derry.

Other important new plays were Thomas Murphy's *The Morning After Optimism* (1971), performed for the Dublin Theatre Festival; Edna O'Brien's first play for the Abbey, *The Gathering* (1974); and more plays by accomplished new playwright Brian Friel, including *Philadelphia Here I Come* (1972), an earlier success on Broadway.

On December 27, 1979, the Abbey celebrated its seventy-fifth anniversary. During 1979–1980 Abbey players performed for large audiences in Dublin, and in London presented a widely acclaimed production of Hugh Leonard's *A Life*, a sequel to *Da*. Celebrations continued in 1980 to mark the centenary of Sean O'Casey: his *Juno and the Paycock*, *Red Roses for Me*, and *The Shadow of a Gunman* were performed. Other scheduled events included a festival of films recalling great performances of the Abbey players and exhibitions of paintings, drawings, and sketches associated with the Abbey. Finally, Hugh Hunt's new history, *The Abbey: Ireland's National Theatre 1904–1979*, was published by Gill and Macmillan, Dublin.

In the 1980s, the Abbey has become more international, as evidenced by its touring Europe and the United States, hosting overseas companies, guest directors, and producing plays by writers from other countries. It has not, however, abandoned its original purpose, reaffirmed in 1976 by Tomás Mac Anna, a former artistic director: "to present the best Irish plays by Irish writers." In addition to earlier plays by Yeats, Synge, O'Casey, Paul Vincent Carroll, M. J. Molloy, and Walter Macken, it has performed new Irish plays in both theatres, including plays in the Irish language.

The financial future is optimistic thanks to the Irish government's subsidizing the Abbey with an equivalent of $1 million a year. Its artistic future is also secure. In publicity materials provided by the Abbey, Joe Dowling, who became artistic director of the Abbey in 1978, has called attention to the Abbey's standards for writing and acting:

Along with the development of a strong naturalistic writing tradition, the Abbey has always had a great reputation for the quality of its acting and[,] like the Moscow Arts Theatre and the Comédie Française, has a specific and unique style of acting.

The Abbey's long-range plans, according to Dowling, are

to maintain and adapt its traditions of writing and acting to meet the changing trends in both the cultural and social life of the country while at the same time be aware of its position as a show place of what is best in Irish classical literature and drama.

One of Dowling's specific suggestions for the future is to wean Irish audiences of romantic notions of Ireland and to deal with current issues facing a young, industrialized population and with the violence of the country. He also proposes that writers come to the theatre for advice before they write plays. The future of the Irish theatre, suggests Micheál Ó hAodha in 1974 in *Theatre in Ireland*, may lie in the experimental work of the Peacock (of which Pat Laffan became director in 1976) in its role as a theatre workshop. That future began with the Peacock's 1981–1982 productions of Sean McCarthy's *Childish Things*, Antoin O Flaharta's *Gaeligeoirí*, Neil Donnelly's *The Silver Dollar Boys*, and Eilís Dillon's *The Cats' Opera*.

LAURA H. WEAVER
(Quotations without direct attribution
were supplied by publicity materials
of the Abbey Theatre Company.)

BIRMINGHAM REPERTORY THEATRE
Broad Street
Birmingham B1 2EP, England

The modern repertory movement was founded when Barry Jackson built the first theatre designed for repertory playing in England in 1913. His Birmingham Repertory Company developed from the Pilgrim Players, a group of amateur actors who met to read and act at Jackson's country house in Moseley. For the opening of the new theatre on Station Street in Birmingham, they turned professional to produce *Twelfth Night*, thus setting a course that eventually took the new company through productions of thirty-four of Shakespeare's plays. In its first season, the Birmingham Repertory Theatre presented plays by Euripides, Shakespeare, Richard Sheridan, George Bernard Shaw, Oscar Wilde, Edmond Rostand, Arthur Schnitzler, Maurice Maeterlinck, Lady Augusta Gregory, and William Butler Yeats, as well as a new play by O. B. Chatwin.

In most seasons since 1913, the company has produced plays new to the world or to England, by such playwrights as Leonid Andreyev, Luigi Pirandello, Elmer Rice, and Jean Anouilh, along with English favorites. Barry Jackson (1879–1961) was knighted for his contribution to the theatre in 1925. His aims were to expand public taste, to present a cross-section of drama, and to give living authors the chance to see their works performed. He insisted on fresh creative work, whether putting *Cymbeline* into modern dress in 1923 or producing a proletarian play by Thomas Muschamp in 1960, his last full season. Talented artistic directors have carried on his aims, working since 1971 in a new theatre on Broad Street.

The poet, actor, and playwright John Drinkwater was a member of the original company. His play, *Abraham Lincoln*, premiered in 1918 and, like many of the company's productions, moved from Birmingham to London the following year for more than four hundred performances and a subsequent tour of the United States. In 1923 *Cymbeline*, with Cedric Hardwicke as Iachimo in white-tie, was the first modern-dress Shakespeare. Having brought *Cymbeline* into the present, the company courageously moved Shaw's *Back to Methuselah* out of the library and onto the stage, a feat London theatres had refused. The philosophic play, in five parts, occupies four evenings and one matinee performance, moving its audience from Eden to a future "As Far As Thought Can Reach." Edith Evans and Cedric Hardwicke acted in a production that delighted Shaw, and it moved to London in 1924.

Enthusiastic about Shaw, Sir Barry Jackson founded the Malvern Festival in 1929, with a first season devoted entirely to Shaw. In 1930 Rudolf Besier's *The Barretts of Wimpole Street* opened at Malvern and then moved to the Station Street theatre in Birmingham. Besier was popular but not all of Jackson's experiments were successful.

Although Birmingham was proud of the theatre where Jackson developed such players as Peggy Ashcroft, John Gielgud, and Laurence Olivier, the citizens gave their box office support to films and football. Discouraged in 1934, Jackson, who had spent 100,000 pounds of his private fortune in its support, was ready to close the theatre. However, he stayed on as director when a local nonprofit trust was formed. In 1937 an experimental play by Christopher Isherwood and Birmingham native son W. H. Auden, *The Ascent of F6*, filled the house. The theatre was closed briefly early in World War II, reopening in 1942 to houses packed with war workers for productions of Shakespeare and West End comedies.

After the war, a new director, only twenty years of age in 1945, came to Birmingham to direct Paul Scofield in *Man and Superman*. Peter Brook divided Tanner's long speeches into lucid segments for Scofield and later in the same season directed him in Shakespeare's *King John* and Ibsen's *The Lady from the Sea*. The 1945 season concluded with a revival of the perennially popular *1066 and All That*, first produced at Birmingham in 1934. Sir Barry Jackson took Peter Brook, Paul Scofield, and John Harrison with him to the Memorial Theatre in Stratford in 1946 to bring new life to a dull administration.

In his last year, Sir Barry Jackson staged the three parts of *Henry VI*, which had not been performed consecutively since 1906. In the year he died, the company produced *Antony and Cleopatra*, one of the few Shakespearean plays they had not yet attempted. Sir Barry Jackson saw Elizabeth Spriggs play Cleopatra two weeks before his death on April 3, 1961. John Harrison succeeded him as artistic director.

The Station Street theatre is a handsome building and ideally located, but its backstage and restaurant facilities are inadequate. A new theatre, proposed before Sir Barry's death, was completed in 1971. The Old Rep looks like a theatre; that is, playbills catch the eye on a busy street, a marquee offers shelter, and the facade invites ground-level entry. Inside, each of 464 seats offers an unobstructed view of the stage. The New Rep, despite the glittering beauty of an inverted arch design by Graham Winteringham, suggests a beached, three-deck excursion steamer. Set well back from the street, it has also been seen as a cathedral, a crematory, and a civic monument. For several directors, cast forth like Jonah in recent years, it must seem "very like a whale." The main auditorium has nine hundred seats in a single steep rake from an enormous proscenium stage. An attached Studio Theatre provides variable staging for audiences of 120. The advantages offered by attractive restaurants and bars, some inexpensive, are countered by the location on Broad Street, fifteen minutes from the center of the city.

With *First Impressions*, a very popular musical adaptation of *Pride and Prejudice*, Peter Dews carried the company through the difficult transition from the old auditorium of 464 seats to the new one with 900. Other spectacular shows attracted audiences who, it was thought, would later support the classical repertory. However, when Michael Simpson filled the 1972–1973 season with a program dominated by classics, attendance fell drastically. With his Studio Theatre programs and appointment of David Edgar as the first resident dramatist, Simpson was more successful. A reasonably good season in 1973–1974 encouraged Simpson to plan seven premieres for 1974–1975, but he was limited by severe budgetary restrictions before his resignation.

The Birmingham Repertory Theatre receives its principal support from the Arts Council of Great Britain and the City of Birmingham. The Arts Council favors adventurous programs and balanced budgets; these objectives are difficult to reconcile in a large theatre with very high running costs. Programs to make the formal spaces of the theatre familiar to more people include a late-night Folk Club in the Studio on Fridays, occasional rock concerts, Playdays for young people, Youth Theatre' productions, a Young Rep society, and restaurant bars open to the public every day for lunch and supper.

Clive Perry, who became artistic director in 1976, has been remarkably successful in attracting audiences for his own programs and for such visiting companies as Ballet Rambert and the National Theatre. The Birmingham Repertory Company, in turn, sent its productions of *Measure for Measure* and *The Devil Is an Ass* to the National Theatre, the Edinburgh Festival, and to other European cities in 1977–1978. Peter Farago's *Iniquity*, a Studio Theatre adaptation of Leo Tolstoy's *The Kreutzer Sonata*, had a subsequent season at the Royal Court Theatre in London. The near-capacity audiences Perry attracted not only balanced the budget but also produced a surplus for 1977–1978.

The 1978–1979 season brought a contemporary production of *The Merchant of Venice* and the British premiere of Arnold Wesker's *The Merchant*, based on the three Venetian stories used by Shakespeare. In another innovative production, Peter Farago set Molière's *The Misanthrope* in de Gaulle's France. In the Studio, resident playwright David Edgar offered *Mary Barnes*, a play about alternative treatments for madness. This production also had a subsequent success at the London Royal Court.

Recently, the Birmingham Repertory Theatre has produced Sheridan's *The School for Scandal* and John Vanbrugh's *The Provoked Wife*, as well as the world premiere of Stephen Bill's *Piggy Back Riders*, a play with a Birmingham setting. For the tenth anniversary of the new theatre in 1981, the company revived

Shaw's *Major Barbara* and brought its Edinburgh Festival productions of Leonard Bernstein's *Candide* and Shakespeare's *As You Like It* to Birmingham. The Studio Theatre premiered Vince Foxall's *Strictly Entre Nous*, a tour-de-force for two actors on the life of W. H. Auden. The 1982 season included productions of Foxall's *Strictly Entre Nous*, Frederick Mohr's *Bozzy*, Arthur Schnitzler's *La Ronde*, and David Gale's *Slips*.

Clive Perry maintains the artistic policy of presenting at least one major new production each season, in the tradition promoted by Sir Barry Jackson. His programs are aligned to the popular and artistic demands of a large-scale auditorium and the largest regional playhouse stage in England.

MARY R. DAVIDSON

BRISTOL OLD VIC THEATRE COMPANY
King Street
Bristol, England

The Bristol Old Vic is the senior member of the four premier provincial theatre companies in Great Britain. Along with the Birmingham Repertory Company, the Glasgow Citizens Theatre, and Manchester's Royal Exchange Theatre, it provides theatre of an exceptionally high caliber to the citizens of Bristol and has pioneered the revival of provincial theatre in Great Britain.

The Bristol Old Vic is the lineal descendant of Bristol's Theatre Royal. Its theatre building is the oldest in the country and is on the roll of historical monuments (which makes renovation or structural changes to the fabric a matter of parliamentary concern). The theatre, built on King Street in the heart of Bristol, was the culmination of the wishes of a group of Bristol's leading citizens and merchants. Their efforts to build the theatre ran into great opposition from the city's Puritan clergy. Various stratagems were utilized to overcome this resistance, including disguising the performances as "Musicales" or "Rhetoricks." The theatre, an almost exact replica of the London Drury Lane Theatre of that day, eventually opened its doors in 1766. The first director was William Powell, a colleague of David Garrick, and the first play to be presented was Richard Steele's *The Conscious Lover*. Powell asked Garrick to contribute a special prologue and epilogue to the play, which were read by one of the actors. The theatre flourished, and many famous actors such as the Kembles, Sarah Siddons, Edmund and Charles Kean, William Charles Macready, Samuel Phelps, Henry Irving, Frank Forbes-Robertson, Ellen Terry, Max Beerbohm-Tree, and Sybil Thorndike appeared on its stage.

In 1777 the theatre received the royal patent and changed its name to the Theatre Royal. With the exception of two interludes, it has been in continual use since its origin. In 1819 the father of the actor William Macready took over its management and ran the theatre for ten years. For two of those years, his son shared the management and appeared often on its stage. By the early twentieth century, the shape of the city of Bristol had changed. The commercial heart of the city shifted from King Street, west across the river, leaving the theatre stranded in a dock area that soon became a slum. Business diminished, and the theatre soon fell upon bad times. By 1920 the theatre was rundown and suffered periods of disuse. The competition of newer, better located theatres, and the cinema, as well as the deterioration of the neighborhood, conspired to bring about a closing of the theatre. It eluded closure by presentations of third-rate variety shows and pantomimes, but its existence was marginal.

The Theatre Royal was rescued from almost certain demolition by an urban renewal scheme developed by the city of Bristol, which restored King Street to its old prominence. However, the new prosperity did not extend to the theatre. By this time, the auditorium had deteriorated to such an extent that it could not attract patrons, and even vaudeville and pantomime could not succeed in keeping the theatre open. It stood empty until the early days of World War II. Several schemes were developed either to change the theatre into a warehouse or to pull it down and build a commercial structure in its place.

In the early 1940s the crisis concerning the Theatre Royal's existence mobilized several civic-minded Bristol citizens to develop a plan to save their historic theatre. They were able to persuade the government, through one of its wartime committees (the council for the Encouragement of Music and the Arts), to buy the structure and provide funds to refurbish it. This was an exceptional occurrence since the country was at war, and the council's funds were primarily earmarked for the entertainment of troops and citizens. A management reorganization occurred, and the government became part-owner of the theatre, along with a group of Bristol citizens. The new Board of Trustees' philosophy was to invite the best English touring companies to perform at the theatre. The London Old Vic Company was contacted and asked to provide the greatest number of performances at the Theatre Royal. The London company agreed, and thus the long association between the two theatre companies came into existence. The newly renovated theatre opened in 1943 with Oliver Goldsmith's *She Stoops to Conquer*. In the same year it premiered J. B. Priestley's *Desert Highway*. The theatre also saw the 1946 opening of his *Jenny Villiers*, a play about the Theatre Royal.

This scheme seemed to work fairly well for a while. Prominent touring companies came to Bristol, and its citizens experienced an inordinately high level of theatrical excellence. However, the theatre was only a depot for touring companies. It had no theatrical company of its own. By 1945 the lack of a resident company became obvious. By relying on touring companies exclusively, the theatre soon ran out of companies of acceptable caliber and fell to inviting second-rate touring groups. This immediately affected its box office receipts. The trustees decided to abandon their previous policy of being a stop on the touring circuit and to develop their own resident company. This was to be accomplished by strengthening their relationships with the London Old Vic Company. It was proposed that the London Old Vic take over the management of the Theatre Royal, supplying productions, actors, directors, designers, and so on. The Theatre Royal would utilize these personnel as well as develop local talent who, if they proved successful, would transfer to the London theatre. In effect, the Theatre Royal was to be the western branch of London's Old Vic. The plan was acceptable to the London management and to the government. The government also agreed to financially underwrite the scheme. The Theatre Royal became an outpost of the London Old Vic and was thus renamed the Bristol Old Vic in keeping with its new status.

The new company was organized and directed by Val May, and presented its first performance in 1946, opening with George Farquhar's *The Beaux' Strat-agem*. The company mounted a series of excellent productions. Two of its most famous productions came into existence in the early 1950s. In 1952 it presented a memorable version of *The Two Gentlemen of Verona*, and in 1954, it premiered Julian Slade and Dorothy Reynold's long-running *Salad Days*. During this period, the company was also developing its own talent; such players as Moira Shearer, Eric Porter, John Neville, Peter O'Toole, Dorothy Tutin, Richard Pasco, and Barbara Leigh-Hunt either got their start with the company or became resident members of the theatre early in their careers.

By the end of the 1950s the reciprocal agreement between the Bristol and London Old Vics was abandoned, and the Bristol company took over sole direction of its operation and artistic future. The government also withdrew from participation on the Board of Trustees. Today the board is composed of such various groups as the University of Bristol, the National Trust, the Arts Council of Great Britain, the Bristol and Gloucestershire Archaeological Society, the Council for the Preservation of Ancient Bristol, the Society for the Protection of Ancient Buildings, the Council for the City of Bristol, and the Bristol Municipal Charities.

The severing of the connection between the two companies provided an impetus to greater artistic activity in the Bristol group. Arthur Miller's *The Crucible* had its British opening in 1954 in Bristol. In 1960 Hale's *The Tinker* (by Laurence Dobie and Robert Sloman) transferred to London's West End with its original Bristol cast. This was the first Bristol Old Vic drama to do this. Full Bristol Old Vic Company transfers to London are now very common, and they supply the London theatre with much of its drama offerings. The Board of Trustees has also expanded the activities of the theatre company. In 1961 they took over the management of the Little Theatre on Colston Street. The Little Theatre now provides a second auditorium for the Bristol Old Vic Company. The company has also developed a drama school (the Bristol Old Vic Theatre School) in cooperation with the University of Bristol's Drama Department. The drama school provides training to aspiring actors and serves as a talent funnel for the parent company.

The company has also acquired property in and around King Street, and in 1972 it embarked on a $1.8 million renovation and expansion plan. The trustees bought the Coopers Hall on King Street, an abandoned eighteenth-century Palladian guild hall, and turned it into an impressive entrance to the auditorium. Previous to this move, the theatre's entrance was to be reached by going down a side alley on King Street. Extensive renovation to the main theatre was carried out, and an experimental theatre (the Young Vic) was built alongside the Coopers

Hall entrance. Long-needed backstage modernization was also carried out. These changes have made the Bristol Old Vic one of the most comfortable, attractive, and modern theatres in Great Britain. Because the theatre is on the list of National Monuments, its eighteenth-century structure and charm have been preserved.

The Bristol Old Vic now manages three auditoriums. The Theatre Royal has 660 seats. The Little Theatre and the Young Vic have 360 and 150 seats, respectively. The Bristol Old Vic continues to present plays of extremely high caliber, and its actors are of the first order. The list of resident players for the 1976 season illustrates the high acting standards of the company. For that year it engaged Michael Hordern, Felicity Kendal, Mike Gwilym, Daniel Massey, Jane Lapotaine, and Constance Cummings, among others. Such famous plays as *War and Peace*, *A Severed Head*, *Portrait of a Queen*, *The Killing of Sister George*, *The Italian Girl*, and *Conduct Unbecoming* premiered in Bristol and later transferred with their original casts to London. The 1981–1982 season included productions of William Wycherly's *The Country Wife*, Brecht's *The Resistible Rise of Arturo Ui*, Shakespeare's *Henry V*, Arthur Wing Pinero's *The Magistrate*, and P. G. Wodehouse's *Good Morning, Bill*. According to tradition the Bristol Old Vic ends each season with a musical. In 1982 the company presented two musicals: a small-scale production of Victoria Wood's *Good Fun* and a large-scale production of *A Funny Thing Happened on the Way to the Forum* (book by Burt Shevelove and Larry Gelbart; music and lyrics by Stephen Sondheim). The 1982–1983 season began with Jean Anouilh's *Ring Round the Moon*. Two highly successful productions followed: Simon Gray's *Quartermaine's Terms*, an elegy for a foreign language teacher that drew an excellent performance from Ian Price; and John O'Keefe's *Wild Oats*, a revival of the eighteenth-century play in which the Shakespeare-spouting Rover was played by Ian Price and the patient Quaker wife by Tessa Peake-Jones. The first months of 1983 saw productions of Clifford Odets' *Awake and Sing* and John Webster's *The White Devil*.

In 1980 artistic director Richard Cottrell left the Bristol Old Vic and was succeeded by John David.

The Bristol Old Vic has an international reputation and has been asked to tour all over the world. The citizens of Bristol have the unique opportunity to be exposed to some of the finest theatrical experiences in the world. The company's standard of excellence is extremely high, and it is hoped that the financial retrenchments occurring in Great Britain at the present time will not force the management either to curtail their activities or to lower their standards.

CHARLES NEURINGER

CITIZENS' THEATRE
Gorbals, Glasgow G5 9DS, Scotland

The Citizens' Theatre opened on October 11, 1943, with a production by James Bridie, entitled *Holy Isle*, in the old Athenaeum Theatre. This site, the first home of the Citizens' Theatre, was far from ideal, both in regard to facilities and to its longtime association with "amateur" productions. It remained the only practical solution, however, because wartime building restrictions limited available choices.

It was with the third production—Paul Vincent Carroll's *Shadow and Substance*—that the theatre began to establish itself. During its first year, a guarantee against loss was secured from the Council for Encouragement of Music and the Arts. This guarantee was possible because the directors of the Citizens' group had raised £1,500 in donations. At the end of the first season, the company found it had broken even.

During the two years spent in the old Athenaeum Theatre, Scottish writing and acting flourished. At the end of the season, two tours were presented: one on the continent with *The Forrigan Reel*, and one on the west of Scotland with *Mr. Bolfry*, both by James Bridie.

The most important name associated with the early years of the Citizens' Theatre was James Bridie, a dramatist of international stature. It was his goal to see the establishment of a fully professional Scottish National Theatre which would present both Scottish playwrights and the pick of world drama. This philosophy predominated until the late 1950s. Bridie produced a minimum of one play per year during that period, including such productions as *Gog and McGog*, 1949; *The Golden Legend of Shults*, 1952; *Meeting at Night*, 1953; and *Marriage Is No Joke*, 1954. Other well-known Scottish playwrights of these times included Robert David McLellan: *Toom Byres*, 1945, *Jamie the Saxt*, 1947, *Flouers o' Edinburgh*, 1952, *The Laird of Torwatletie*, 1953; Robert Kemp: *Victory Square*, 1945, *The Scientific Singers*, 1950, and *What the Stars Foretell*, 1953; and Robins Millar: *The Sell Out*, 1955, and *Royal Scotch*, 1957.

Two years after its debut, a move to the Royal Princess Theatre across the river marked the second stage in the theatre's history. The first production in its new home, *Johnson Over Jordan* by J. B. Priestley, was on September 11, 1945. Owned by Harry McKelvie, the Royal Princess was offered to the Citizens' Theatre for a ten-year lease on generous terms. This, plus a gift of £10,000 from Sir Frederick Stewart, allowed the Citizens' Theatre to make this significant move. Celebrating its one hundredth birthday in 1978, the Royal Princess was renowned for a long thread of pantomimes, running annually from autumn to summer. This series of pantomimes was considered an annual treat for families from all around and left its mark on the Citizens' Theatre in that much of the material produced is big, broadly based, and colorful.

Since the war, the Citizens' Theatre has experienced varying fortunes. Although audience figures had dropped because of the influx of television, by the 1960s the theatre once again attracted significant audiences. This trend was reversed toward the end of that decade when attendance fell to 30 percent of capacity. Many reasons were presented for this decline. Not only is the Royal Princess in an unattractive part of the city, but also the building has been condemned and progress toward building a replacement has been slow. Another important reason can probably be attributed to a change in philosophy. When the Citizens' Theatre began, links with Glasgow were strong. Moreover, local actresses and actors, such as Molly Urquhart and Duncan Macrae, were favorites of the audience; the theatre was a generally Scottish company of actors who could play in both Scots comedy and other drama. Since the late 1950s directors have been predominately Englishmen; and, with this change to English directors, the predominately Scottish company has disappeared.

The theatre is currently directed by a triumvirate—Giles Havergal, Philip Prowse, and Robert David MacDonald—who, since 1970, have concentrated on an international repertoire based on the classics. The style of productions has gained a high reputation in Britain and international recognition in the form of invitations to appear as British representatives at prestigious European drama festivals. Scottish plays no longer figure in the repertoire, except those by Robert David MacDonald, one of the three resident directors and the resident dramatist of the company. He has written seven new plays and has translated works by Chekhov, Beaumarchais, Genet, Gogol, Goldoni, Lermontov, Brecht, and Büchner.

One of the more interesting developments in the history of the Citizens' Theatre was the establishment of the Close Theatre Club in 1965. This was a small "experimental" theatre originated by Michael Goldberg, chairman of the Citizens' Board. Under the same auspices and roof as the Citizens' Theatre, the Close Theatre Club was small and compact, seating 150 persons around three sides of the acting area. The closeness achieved total involvement between actors and audience. Because the Citizens' Theatre and the Close Theatre Club interchanged both actors and directors and because the play alternated on the big proscenium and the little open stage, the combination became a powerful magnet for directors and actors. Although an ideal complement to the Citizens' Theatre, the Close Theatre Club was destroyed in 1973 by fire, bringing this extremely interesting and electric stage in the life of the Citizens' Theatre to an end.

The Citizens' Theatre generally presents six to ten plays between September and April. Some of the more recent successful productions include *Summit-Conference* (1978) by Robert David MacDonald, a play concerning the meeting of Hitler's mistress, Eva Braun, and Mussolini's mistress, Clara Petacci; Noel Coward's comedy *Semi-Monde*, which was given its world premiere on September 12, 1977, although written in 1927; and *Painter's Palace of Pleasure*, designed and directed by Philip Prowse (1978). More recently, the company presented the British premiere of Goldoni's *La Villegiatura (The House Party)*; and *A Waste of Time*, based on *A la recherche du temps perdu (A Remembrance of Things Past)* by Marcel Proust, and *Chinchilla*, both by Robert David MacDonald. Successful 1985 productions included Friedrich Schiller's *Mary Stewart*, Noel Coward's *Blithe Spirit*, and Sean O'Casey's *The Plough and the Stars*. The company represented Great Britain at the Holland Festival (1981), the Cologne Theater der Welt (1981), and the Venice Festival (1981). They also appeared at the Edinburgh Festival in 1980.

The original theatre built in 1878 has been saved by substantial grants from the Glasgow District Council, which enabled comprehensive upgrading of all backstage areas and the auditorium.

Another unique aspect of the company's work is that the theatre charges an overall seat price and has pioneered a scheme for admitting unemployed persons free of charge.

JOAN SARGENT SHERWOOD

ENGLISH STAGE COMPANY at THE ROYAL COURT THEATRE
Sloane Square, London SW1, England

The English Stage Company (ESC) was founded by Edward Blacksell, Ronald Duncan, the Earl of Harewood, and Oscar Lewenstein in 1954, a time when new writers had few opportunities to stage their work. Conceived as a writer's theatre, that has remained its basic policy through six artistic managements: George Devine (1956–1965); William Gaskill (1965–1972); Oscar Lewenstein (1972–1975); Nicholas Wright and Robert Kidd (co-directors, 1975–1976); Stuart Burge (1977–1979); and Max Stafford-Clark, who succeeded Burge in 1979.

The ESC had the good fortune at its beginning to persuade Neville Blond, a wealthy Manchester businessman, to become chairman of the ESC Council. Although he claimed to know little about the art of the theatre, he knew a great deal about business and management. Astute in financial matters, he served the ESC well for fourteen years. He died in 1970.

The ESC also used good judgment when it asked George Devine to fill the crucial position of artistic director. Devine accepted on condition that Tony Richardson join him as his associate. Richardson became assistant artistic director in January 1956. George Devine (1910–1966) had been active in theatre as a student at Oxford, where in 1932 he had invited John Gielgud to produce and star in *Romeo and Juliet*, in which Peggy Ashcroft played Juliet, Edith Evans the Nurse, and Devine Mercutio. In the same year, Devine made his professional debut in London, later spent a season at the Old Vic, and in 1936 joined the London Theatre Studio as producer and teacher. Founded by Michel Saint-Denis in 1936, the studio adopted the Jacques Copeau system of actor training. The war closed the studio, but Saint-Denis later took this philosophy to the Old Vic Theatre Centre. Devine again joined Saint-Denis at the Old Vic after the war. The association affected Devine deeply. He carried with him the ideas of Copeau and Saint-Denis as he shaped the philosophy of the English Stage Company at the Royal Court Theatre.

In 1956 the ESC Council formed an Artistic and a Management Committee to assist in operation of the theatre. The Artistic Committee, consisting of Duncan, Lewenstein, and Lord Harewood as chairman, was to read and evaluate plays, with power of veto before an option could be taken by the artistic director. The Management Committee was to set budgets, offer business counsel, and tend to general operation of the theatre plant. In actual practice, the Artistic Committee did not function effectively; at least this was the belief of the artistic directors, who usually found group decisions on artistic matters unacceptable. What a good theatre requires, Nicholas Wright once said, is a benevolent despot whose vision is unhampered by the diverse opinions of a committee. Eventually, the ESC abandoned the Artistic Committee; none has been active at the Court for many years. Because financial decisions influence artistic decisions, however, the artistic directors have often clashed with the Management Committee in the budgeting of productions.

George Devine guided the ESC at the Royal Court to international prominence in the 1950s and 1960s. New voices began to be heard on the London stage. The works of John Osborne, Edward Bond, Ann Jellicoe, N. F. Simpson, Arnold Wesker, John Arden, and others deliberately eschewed traditional West End dramatic values and explored postwar shifts in social and political conduct. They helped shape the character of the Royal Court as a house for new social realism. Devine also saw the need to provide a theatrical platform for established foreign writers, whose serious art held little attraction for commercial producers. Consequently, the plays of Bertolt Brecht, Eugene Ionesco, Samuel Beckett, Jean-Paul Sartre, Max Frisch, and Jean Genet, for example, were brought to the English stage, some for the first time. Their ideas and innovative dramatic techniques influenced British theatre practices for the next decade. In addition, Devine advocated the revival of classic dramatists. (Wycherly, Ibsen, Thomas Middleton, Shakespeare, and Shaw were among those produced.) He was not interested in preserving museum pieces; the old plays must be staged with a fresh and imaginative awareness of their truths.

When George Devine turned artistic leadership of the Court to William Gaskill (1930–) in January 1965, the character and policies of the ESC had been firmly established; and Gaskill, who had begun his association with the Court as early as 1957, wished to carry on these aims. John Osborne's *A Patriot for Me*, Edward Bond's *Saved*, and John Arden's *Serjeant Musgrave's Dance*, all produced in 1956, furnished examples of Gaskill's seriousness of purpose. Without Gaskill's determination to produce the plays of Edward Bond, they probably would not have been done. He championed Bond's work at a time when the ESC Council preferred to avoid the public controversy the plays inevitably aroused; in addition, the council feared Bond's pieces would not fare well at the box office. Gaskill also encouraged Nicholas Wright to establish the Theatre Upstairs, a space on the Court's second floor that could accommodate the staging of new plays on minimal budgets. Gaskill's presentation of controversial works stimulated a new barrage of attacks upon the long outmoded censorship policies of the Lord Chamberlain's Office. Although attacks upon British stage censorship had long been made, it was largely a result of the ESC's willingness to fight in court for its right to present serious drama without interference that censorship in Great Britain came to an end, with the passage of the Theatre Acts of 1968.

Bond's *Early Morning* (1968), the last play banned by the Lord Chamberlain, and his earlier play, *Saved*, were revived by Gaskill early in the 1969 season to celebrate the theatre's newly gained freedom.

Under Gaskill the Royal Court's prestige continued to grow, but there were (and still are) enormous financial strains that made operation difficult and uncertain. Like other noncommercial theatre operations, the Royal Court Theatre has struggled constantly, not merely to gain solvency but to stay in existence. Hardly a season has passed, since the Court's opening, in which threats of closure have not reverberated through its council meetings, rehearsals, and staff offices. Although the Arts Council grants have been raised continuously over the years (from £7,000 in 1956–1957 to £350,000 in 1979–1980), they have not kept abreast of inflationary costs of operation.

The first four productions staged by the ESC in 1956 cost a little over £1,000 each, but in 1980–1981 *Hamlet*, with Jonathan Pryce in the title role, cost £29,426. The ESC depends upon production costs from a box office income, which frequently does not exceed 50 percent capacity. In 1979 Nicholas Wright's *The Gorky Brigade* had production costs of £18,395, but in its run of twenty-seven performances, the presentation had a box office average of only 15 percent. However, the ESC usually has sufficient box office successes to balance failures.

In 1969 Gaskill, weary from the theatre's financial stresses and his four years of hard work, told the ESC Council that he wanted a leave of absence. Instead, the council recommended the appointment of Lindsay Anderson and Anthony Page as associate artistic directors. This afforded Gaskill relief from the sole burden of the Court's operation. Gaskill, Page, and Anderson together planned the season and then more or less took turns as artistic director. Despite production of much good work, the arrangement proved unsatisfactory, and in 1972 William Gaskill resigned. Oscar Lewenstein, co-founder of the ESC and longtime member of the ESC Council and its committees, was immediately elected new artistic director.

Oscar Lewenstein (1917–), unlike his predecessors, had no acting or directing experience, but had spent some twenty-five years working in noncommercial theatre operations as a manager and independent producer. In 1946 he became the general manager of the Glasgow Unity Theatre, a post he retained until 1950. In that year he became associated with Anthony Hawtrey at the Embassy Theatre, and in 1952 he was named general manager of the Royal Court Theatre (prior to its occupation by the ESC in 1956). Between 1955 and 1971 Lewenstein produced over fifty plays, some in the West End and some in association with the ESC at the Royal Court. In the 1960s, Lewenstein became associated with John Osborne, Tony Richardson, and others in the production of films under the Woodfall Films banner. Many of the films relied upon Royal Court writers, actors, and directors, who carried the Royal Court style of social realism to the screen. Some of the most notable of these were *Tom Jones* (1963), *The Girl with the Green Eyes* (1964), and *The Sailor from Gibraltar* (1967), all directed by Tony Richardson, and *The Knack* (1965) and *The Bed Sitting Room* (1969), directed by Richard Lester.

When Lewenstein accepted the post of artistic director of the ESC in 1972, Lindsay Anderson and Anthony Page remained as associate directors, and Albert Finney joined the staff at Lewenstein's invitation as a third associate director. Under Lewenstein, the Court emphasized plays dealing with political, social, and ethical issues. Brian Friel's *Freedom of the City*, Athol Fugard's *Sizwe Banze is Dead*, Edward Bond's *Bingo*, John Osborne's *A Sense of Detachment*, David Storey's *Life Class*, Sam Shepard's *Tooth of Crime*, Matura's *Play Mas*, and Joe Orton's *Loot*, *What the Butler Saw*, and *Entertaining Mr. Sloane* were among the dramas he produced. Lewenstein maintained the high standards set by his predecessors at the Court, through his astute selection of plays and his effective use of exceptional directors, actors, and designers.

The appointment of Nicholas Wright and Robert Kidd to succeed Oscar Lewenstein as artistic director of the ESC was principally an attempt to break with traditions of the past and to turn the reins over to experienced young people with fresh ideas. Both Nicholas Wright (1941–) and Robert Kidd (1943–1980) had grown up professionally at the Court, chiefly as directors. But their co-directorship of the ESC became something of a disaster, for which neither should be blamed. Two obstacles could not be overcome: first, the Royal Court Theatre, long undersubsidized, had financial problems that now reached crisis proportions; second, the theatre could not be run by two individuals who often disagreed. Wright and Kidd produced some fine pieces (notably David Hare's *Teeth 'N Smiles*, Edward Bond's *The Fool*, and Peter Gill's *Small Change*), and a few mistakes (Richard O'Brien's *T Zee* and David Storey's *Mother's Day*). They resigned their posts in December 1976. Wright remained for several weeks to help the new artistic director, Stuart Burge (1918–), with the transition.

Although Burge began his career as an actor, in 1952 he was appointed director of the Queen's Theatre, Hornchurch, where he directed over sixty productions. He later directed at the Bristol Old Vic, the Old Vic, Stratford, Ontario, and the Nottingham Playhouse.

After assuming leadership of the ESC at the Royal Court, Burge reviewed the aims of the company. "Our work here," he said, "is to produce new scripts, and the writing should be radical . . . it should be controversial—socially or politically dangerous" (Conference on the English Stage Company at the Royal Court Theatre, Louisiana State University, October 10, 1981). Productions of Martin Sherman's *Bent*, Alan Brown's *Wheelchair Willie*, David Edgar's *Mary Barnes*, and Caryl Churchill's *Cloud Nine* fulfilled these aims. In addition, John Osborne directed a successful revival of his own play, *Inadmissible Evidence*, and Burge staged a Restoration farce, Edward Ravenscroft's *The London Cuckold*.

Max Stafford-Clark (1941–), who replaced Burge as artistic director in late 1979, had been director of the Traverse Workshop and the Joint Stock Company. At the Court he had staged David Hare's *Slag* (1971) and Howard Brenton's

Magnificence (1973). Under Stafford-Clark, the ESC presented an innovative production of *Hamlet* (with Jonathan Pryce in the title role) and new plays by Nicholas Wright (*The Gorky Brigade*), David Lan (*Sergeant Ola and His Followers*), Andrea Dunbar (*The Arbor*), and Caryl Churchill (*Top Girls*), among others. In an interview with the author in April 1980, Max Stafford-Clark stated, "As we begin the 1980s . . . the Royal Court will continue to present and champion contemporary writing to the limits that our abilities and our subsidy allow."

BILLY J. HARBIN

NATIONAL THEATRE
South Bank, London SE1 9PX, England

Three foundation stones and a 128-year span from suggestion to completion of its own theatre indicate the long and complex history of the National Theatre of Great Britain. Indeed, for 115 years its record was one of efforts, not productions, of dramas not enacted upon a stage.

In 1843, at the urging of the novelist Sir Edward Bulwer-Lytton, the Theatres Act had broken the monopoly on the production of straight drama of the three London "patent" theatres: Drury Lane, Covent Garden, and the Haymarket. In 1848, inspired by the purchase of Shakespeare's possible birthplace for the nation, the publisher and passionate supporter of popular education, Effingham Wilson, first proposed a national theatre. It would be "A House for Shakespeare" to be purchased by "national subscription" and held "in trust for the nation" to preserve a heritage that might otherwise be threatened by populism and commercial interests. Although Wilson soon abandoned his campaign, Bulwer-Lytton responded to his pamphlet with enthusiasm and singlehandedly kept the idea alive until his death in 1873.

In 1879, spurred by the London visit of the Comédie Française, the cause of the National Theatre was revived. A year earlier Henry Irving, the great actor-manager, had written a well-publicized paper on the subject for the Social Science Congress in which he proposed a "large, elastic, and independent" single institution subject to no state interference. In contrast, Matthew Arnold, in one of his most famous and influential essays, *The French Play in London* (August 1879), called for a coherent organization, subject to some state control, with a number of "Nationals." Arnold declared that a national theatre was needed for moral instruction in the "good life," a thought G. B. Shaw echoed in his 1910 "interlude," *The Dark Lady of the Sonnets*, in which Shakespeare pleads with Queen Elizabeth I to "endow a great play house . . . for the better instruction and gracing of your Majesty's subjects."

Irving's brilliant career ended in financial ruin, dramatically illustrating the economic dangers, to even a great actor, of private management. In 1904, the year of Irving's death, the actor and director Harley Granville-Barker and the theatre critic William Archer wrote *A National Theatre: Scheme and Estimates*, which was privately circulated and eventually published in 1907. The turn of the century had seen a great flowering of British theatre, and their deliberately modest proposal made a dream seem practical and reasonable, a blueprint for action. They described a large-scale repertory theatre which would require a new building, were neutral in principle about state subsidy, suggested a board of trustees to appoint a director and a general staff, and discussed such detailed matters as a repertoire of plays, actors' salaries, the director's powers, and the size of the company. A national theatre should be "visibly and unmistakably a popular institution, making a large appeal to the whole community." The book gained the support of such eminent men of the theatre as James Barrie, Arthur Wing Pinero, John Galsworthy, and a fervent George Bernard Shaw; it became the "bible" of the National Theatre movement.

In the same year the book was written, a rich, retired brewer, Richard Badger, in memory of his years as a schoolboy at Stratford-on-Avon, pledged £2,500 to start a fund for a statue of Shakespeare. A Shakespeare Memorial Committee was formed to raise sufficient funds. However, National Theatre supporters eventually persuaded the committee that a theatre would make a finer memorial to the Bard, and in July 1908 the Shakespeare Memorial National Theatre Committee (SMNT) was formed with objectives closely based on the Archer and Granville-Barker scheme. A handbook was issued in 1909 listing the aims of a "Shakespeare National Theatre." Naturally, Shakespeare would be in the repertory, along with other English classical dramas. The theatre company would produce translations of representative works of foreign drama, old and new, further the development of English modern drama, and "stimulate the art of acting." An appeal for funds was launched, and the banker Carl Meyer donated £70,000. The cause of the National Theatre became fashionable, and enthusiasm increased as the three-hundredth anniversary of Shakespeare's death approached. However, £500,000 was required, and other donors were not readily forthcoming.

In 1916, on April 23, St. George's Day and the traditional date of Shakespeare's birth, H. J. MacKinder, a sympathetic Member of Parliament, introduced a Private Member's Bill on the subject. The bill generated a wide-ranging discussion about state patronage of the arts in which MacKinder quoted Matthew Arnold. Although the bill passed by a sixty-four vote margin, it failed to gain the more than two-thirds majority a Private Bill required. However, the SMNT committee was encouraged and in the autumn of 1913 purchased its first site, a freehold acre for £50,000, in Bloomsbury. A year later, when war was declared, the committee was temporarily dissolved, and in 1916 a hut was put up on the site for the entertainment of wounded soldiers.

During the war, the London theatre deteriorated in range and in quality. The Entertainments Tax was introduced in 1916 to raise money for the war effort (it was not repealed until 1958); it made the theatrical profession an even riskier financial undertaking, and donations to the SMNT decreased. Only the Old Vic under Lilian Baylis, in its role as a "people's theatre," continued its Shakespearean productions.

The regional repertory companies were growing, however, and impressed by this movement, a young publisher named Geoffrey Whitworth formed the British Drama League in 1919 with Granville-Barker as its first chairman. Among the many aims of the league was support for a national theatre. The SMNT executive committee met again in July 1918, after a hiatus of four years, and decided to "temporarily" shelve any plans. Consequently, the committee lost many of its best supporters to the league. The Bloomsbury site became a liability and was sold in 1922. Various sites were suggested in the twenties and thirties but all were rejected as unsuitable. Even though it pressed the government for subsidies, to be taken from the Entertainments Tax, for a national theatre, the SMNT was visibly waning in enthusiasm. However, in January 1930 the Drama League held a meeting in Kingsway Hall which formally united it with the SMNT Committee in its goal of a national theatre. (Also in 1930, Granville-Barker revised the *Scheme*, advocating two theatres, a large and a small, under one roof; thus, the company would be fully occupied during a season.) Fund-raising improved because of such dedicated supporters as Whitworth, Mrs. Alfred Lyttelton continuing her husband's work, and Sir Israel Gollancz, but the sums still fell far short of the goal.

In 1937 a small site was purchased for £75,000 in Cromwell Gardens opposite the entrance to the Victoria and Albert Museum. The famous architect Edwin Lutyens was engaged, and detailed plans were produced. But once again war broke out, and a water tank for fire engines was erected on the site. The effort between the wars was not futile, however. The basis of fund-raising and sponsorship had broadened as a result of the league's support, and the principle of government aid was becoming more acceptable. In addition, the Kensington site would later prove a useful bargaining tool.

In 1940 the Council for the Encouragement of Music and the Arts (CEMA), which later became the Arts Council, was established. In June 1942 the London County Council (LCC) (reconstituted in 1965 as the Greater London Council [GLC]) offered to exchange the Kensington site for a larger one on the South Bank as part of its ten-year-old plans to create a cultural complex there. The LCC asked the SMNT committee to submit plans for a theatre on the south side of Waterloo Bridge, very close to where the National Theatre now stands. However, another major theatre across the Thames might draw audiences away from the Old Vic where a new, superb company had been formed under the leadership of Olivier, Richardson, and John Burrell. But the Old Vic had been badly damaged by bombs in 1941, and no one knew what would happen when the war ended. In late 1944 a union between the Old Vic and the SMNT was proposed; this led to a formal agreement, announced in January 1946, that a new joint committee was now formed to spearhead "one body under the name of the National Theatre." Thus, the National Theatre cause emerged from World War II, in contrast to World War I, greatly strengthened and united.

On August 9, 1946, the Arts Council of Great Britain was established by Royal Charter; however, it had funds of only £235,000 when the National Theatre needed £1 million. By now the National Theatre had ceased to be just a worthy cause and had become a project supported by the LCC, all three political parties, the embryonic Arts Council, and the newly formed Labour government. Publicity in favor of a national theatre was increasing, and in November 1948 the National Theatre Bill was introduced into the House of Commons. By February 1949 it had passed both Houses without a division. The sum of £1 million, which provided neither for the equipment of the theatre nor its annual running expenses, would be given "subject to such conditions as the Treasury may think fit"—cautious words that would mean a delay of fifteen years.

The pound was devalued in 1949, and it became obvious that the National could not be built in time for the 1951 Festival of Britain. In a symbolic gesture a foundation stone was laid beside the Royal Festival Hall on July 31, 1951, by the now Queen Mother. (A year later it was quietly moved to a new site beside the County Hall.)

Despite these economic difficulties, money from the Arts Council, with some funds from the SMNT, became available in 1949 to the Old Vic, which was remodeled and reopened in 1950. But theatres were closing around the country; there was a dearth of new plays; television posed a new threat; and since 1948, when the Olivier/Richardson/Burrell troika ended, the Old Vic had entered a period of decline. Its fortunes did not revive until 1953, and by that time its survival, not as a nucleus for a new National Theatre, but as a company, was in question.

In 1953 a new South Bank scheme was unveiled which proposed shifting the National Theatre to a site nearer the County Hall. However, the Arts Council issued a gloomy report in 1956, and the prospect for a national theatre looked more remote than ever. Other priorities loomed large, and many proposed that the regional theatres, now suffering great economic hardships, be saved first. The National had a few zealous supporters in Parliament (notably Olivier, Lyttelton, and Jennie Lee, later the minister for the arts) and in the Arts Council (chiefly, Lord Cottesloe, then its chairman, and Lord Goodman who succeeded him). In 1960 the priority of the National Theatre was reviewed by the Arts Council, and the report envisaged the establishment of the National by 1964 with a subsidy of £2.3 million. But in March 1961 the government announced that money would not be released for the National; Arts Council funds would be increased to help regional theatres, the Old Vic, and the Royal Shakespeare Company, which that month had received its Royal Charter. The LCC, under Isaac Haywood's leadership, offered a site between the County Hall and Hungerford Bridge rent free and £1.3 million toward the building if the Treasury would release £1 million for the National. The Labour councillor Hugh Jenkins, later arts minister, moved that the theatre should be built without delay; the resolution unanimously passed.

Also in 1961 a merger of the Old Vic and the Royal Shakespeare Company was proposed, but the latter withdrew. This withdrawal did not delay the establishment of the National, however. An agreement was reached between the government and the LCC in mid-July. Two new boards were established to replace the old joint council; the National Theatre Board (under the chairmanship of Lord Chandos) would supervise the National Theatre company, and the South Bank Theatre Board (under the chairmanship of Lord Cottesloe) would control the building. It was also decided to establish the National Theatre company without waiting for the theatre to be built. Olivier joined the various boards when his appointment as the National's first director was officially announced on August 9, 1962. (Olivier was then director of the Chichester Festival Theatre, the first large-scale, modern "open-stage" theatre whose design would influence the National.) On February 8, 1963, the National Theatre was formally incorporated under the Companies Act.

It was also agreed with the governors of the Old Vic that the National would occupy their theatre from August 5, 1963, until its own building was ready. In his first major press conference on August 6, 1963, Olivier stated that "We aim to give a spectrum of world drama and to develop in time a company which will be the finest in the world." This "spectrum" was reflected in the first season which opened on October 22, 1963, with Peter O'Toole in *Hamlet* and included Ibsen's *The Master Builder*, Sophocles' *Philoctetes*, Beckett's *Play*, Farquhar's *The Recruiting Officer*, and *Othello*. Of the first season's fifteen productions, twelve were well received, Farquhar's comedy being the first major success of the National's career. Olivier as Othello firmly established the National's reputation in the public's mind. The production played to standing room only, and his astonishing performance quickly became legendary. Throughout the first season attendance figures topped 86 percent of capacity. From the start, however, the National was undercapitalized, and after the first year, there was a £22,500 deficit. Nevertheless, it was an impressive beginning.

A month after the National opened at the Old Vic, Denys Lasdun was chosen to design a theatre on a scale never before attempted in Britain. Inspired by the Greek amphitheatre at Epidauras, Lasdun started at the "heart" of the building, the main auditorium, with his first consideration being a sense of direct, unobstructed communication between actors and audience. For two years he consulted with leading directors, designers, and actors, and numerous designs were considered. In the spring of 1964 it was agreed that two major theatres, an open stage and a proscenium, as well as a studio theatre, were needed; a year later, the overall plan for the National seemed complete.

In February 1967 the GLC proposed a new site, downstream next to Waterloo Bridge, and by September 1967 formal planning permission was given for the 4.7-acre Prince's Meadow site on King's Reach. Work began on the substructure the following spring. In March 1969, because of inflation, an amendment to the National Theatre Act of 1949 was passed which increased the government's financial contribution to £3.75 million. By 1972 yet more money was needed, and in February 1973 the National Theatre and Museums of London Bill became law; this legislation raised the total sum to £9.8 million. In May of that year a "topping out" ceremony was held, presided over by Olivier and Lord Cottesloe, but the interior of the building remained to be finished.

In November 1974 another National Theatre Bill, made necessary by a 20 percent inflation rate, was passed by Parliament after a rather acrimonious debate over the National's position and priorities, its policies, power, and privileges. The bill removed the statutory ceiling on the government's contribution to the project so that the building could be completed as quickly as possible.

The next four years continued the complex history of architectural, economic, and political problems as costs escalated, stirring political debate and causing government support to fluctuate, and contractual and construction troubles mounted as contractors encountered grave financial difficulties and unmeetable deadlines. In addition, sophisticated technical innovations such as computerized stage lighting and complex revolving stage drums, more ambitious and experimental than any attempted before by British theatre contractors, needed to be installed and tested.

While its new home slowly arose on the South Bank, the National company continued to present its "spectrum" of world drama at the Old Vic. The first new British play produced at the National was John Dexter's brilliant 1964 production of Peter Shaffer's *The Royal Hunt of the Sun*. This production established the National's reputation for theatrical athleticism, for mime and visual effects. Another new play that was an outstanding success was Tom Stoppard's *Rosencrantz and Guildenstern Are Dead* (1967). This, along with such plays as Noel Coward's *Hay Fever*, William Congreve's *Love For Love*, and Arthur Wing Pinero's *Trelawny of the 'Wells,'* helped establish the National's reputation as a most marvelous company for comedies. The classics were also well represented with, among others, Olivier's triumphant productions of Chekhov's *Uncle Vanya* and *The Three Sisters*. These early days also made the names of many previously "unknown" young professionals, such as Ronald Pickup, Derek Jacobi, Colin Blakely, Maggie Smith, and Frank Finlay, to name only a few. In September 1965 the National was the first foreign company invited to play at Moscow's new Kremlin Theatre, a two-and-a-half-week visit that was hugely successful. The Russian visit demonstrated the value of having a company that could, in some way, represent Britain; the National was demonstrably justifying its existence.

Of course, not all productions were successful, and despite such "hits" as Gaskill's brilliant production in 1969 of George Farquhar's *The Beaux' Stratagem* and the huge 1971 success of Peter Nichol's *The National Health*, directed by Michael Blakemore, the deficits continued to mount because of inflation, undercapitalization, falling attendance, and increasingly critical reviews. The summer of 1971 saw the worst crisis of the National's life thus far. A disastrous excursion was made to the new theatre in St. Martin's Lane. Attendance was low, and the season closed after thirty-nine weeks; the year ended with an £80,000 deficit. However, the "tide was turned" when Olivier, directed by Blakemore, appeared in his last major role at the National as James Tyrone in Eugene O'Neill's *Long Day's Journey into Night*. The 1972-1973 season was very successful with outstanding productions: Blakemore's of Ben Hecht and Charles MacArthur's *The Front Page*, Dexter's of Molière's *The Misanthrope*, and Stoppard's *Jumpers* directed by Peter Wood, with Michael Hordern brilliant as the rambling philosopher. The season, however, saw the "end of an era" when, on March 13, 1973, Olivier, after two grave illnesses and ten successful years as director, announced his retirement. Peter Hall, the founder of the Royal Shakespeare Company, succeeded him as director.

The 1973-1974 season was a flowering time with productions of Peter Shaffer's *Equus*, Sheridan's *The School for Scandal*, Shakespeare's *Macbeth* and *Measure for Measure*, Chekhov's *The Cherry Orchard*, Euripides' *The Bacchae*, and Hall's first National production, *The Tempest*, with Gielgud as Prospero. If the National had entered its new building that year, as had been planned, it would have done so with the best company and the best overall range of productions yet in its brief history. Construction delays prevented the move, and the 1974-1975 season, which included forty-one weeks of touring, had its only undoubted successes in the early spring with productions of Shaw's *Heartbreak House* with a superb cast and the triumph of Pinter's *No Man's Land* with outstanding performances by Gielgud as Spooner and Richardson as Hirst.

Two months later, in June 1975, the Building Services manager was the first employee to move into the new building, and on February 28, 1976, the National gave its last performance, the documentary *Tribute to the Lady* with Peggy Ashcroft playing Lilian Baylis, at the Old Vic. On March 16, 1976, the Lyttelton, although not completely finished, opened with Ashcroft's superb, almost solo, performance in Beckett's *Happy Days* followed by eight other productions, including Hall's productions of *Hamlet*, Pinter's *No Man's Land*, and Ibsen's *John Gabriel Borkman*, in the next five months. On October 4, the Olivier opened with Albert Finney in an uncut Christopher Marlowe's *Tamberlaine*, and on October 25 the Olivier was officially inaugurated when Lord Cottesloe welcomed the Queen and the Duke of Edinburgh and handed over the building on behalf of the South Bank Theatre Board to the National Theatre Board. In March 1977 the Cottesloe staged its first public performances.

A description of Lasdun's unique and innovative 5.5 acre, £16 million concrete building with its cantilevered terraces properly belongs in a history of theatre architecture. Integrated under one roof, its three theatres have a total of 2,450 seats. The Olivier has an open stage with 1,160 seats in a fan-shaped auditorium, the Lyttelton, with an adjustable proscenium, has 890 seats in two tiers, and the Cottesloe contains two tiers of galleries on three sides, has infinitely flexible floor space, and can hold up to 400 spectators. The National Theatre is serving, as Peter Hall, its current director, envisioned in 1974, as a showcase for British talents, without laying down any restrictive definitions as to what kind of talents. It continues to present a "spectrum" of world drama, of which only a brief sampling can be given. Continental drama has been represented with productions of Henrik Ibsen's *The Wild Duck*, Arthur Schnitzler's *An Undiscovered Country*, Georg Büchner's *Danton's Death*, Anton Chekhov's *Uncle Vanya*, Ivan Turgenev's *A Month in the Country*, Molière's *The Hypochondriac* and *Don Juan*, Bertolt Brecht's *The Life of Galileo* and *Schweyk in the Second World War*, and, in their first major London productions, Heinrich von Kleist's *The Prince of Homburg* and Calderón's *The Mayor of Zalamea*. Shakespearean productions have included *A Midsummer Night's Dream*, *Much Ado About Nothing*, *Richard III*, *As You Like It*, and *Othello*, and in its declared "museum function," the National has produced Dekker's *The Shoemaker's Holiday* and Thomas Kyd's *The Spanish Tragedy*. Britain's theatrical heritage has also been represented by, among others, Oscar Wilde's *The Importance of Being Earnest*, George Bernard Shaw's *Major Barbara*, J. B. Priestley's *When We Were Married* and *Eden's End*, Arthur Wing Pinero's *The Second Mrs. Tangueray*, and Terence Rattigan's *The Browning Version* and *Harlequinade*. In November 1981, in its first venture into Greek drama in seventeen years, Hall's production of Aeschylus' *The Oresteia* opened at the Olivier, an ideal venue for Greek tragedy. It was a daring, admirable production, with an all-male cast wearing full masks.

In March 1982 the National presented its first musical, Loesser's *Guys and Dolls*, which became an "overnight success," breaking all records. This was followed in July by Richard Eyre's production at the Cottesloe of John Gay's masterpiece *The Beggar's Opera*. American playwrights have been represented by revivals of Arthur Miller's *The Crucible*, Edward Albee's *Who's Afraid of Virginia Woolf?*, and Sam Shepard's new play, *True West*. Among new British dramas have been three short plays by Pinter, which included the brilliant *A Kind of Alaska* featuring a superb performance by Judi Dench, Edward Bond's *Summer*, Arnold Wesker's *Caritas*, Ayckbourn's *Way Upstream*, David Storey's *Early Days* with a triumphal performance by Ralph Richardson, Tom Stoppard's *On the Razzle*, and the "smash hit" of the 1979-1980 season, Peter Shaffer's *Amadeus* with Simon Callow as Mozart and Paul Scofield as Salieri.

In its brief history the National Theatre has followed Henry Irving's hope that a state theatre would "attempt and achieve success in every worthy branch of historic art." Successive governments, through periods of great economic hardship, have shared Shaw's belief that "a National Theatre is worth having for the sake of the National Soul."

CAROLYN ELY NEURINGER

NOTTINGHAM PLAYHOUSE
Wellington Circus
Nottingham NG1 5AF, England

The Nottingham Playhouse has long enjoyed a reputation as one of the leading repertory companies in Britain. It is run by the Nottingham Theater Trust Limited, a nonprofit distributing body consisting of twenty-two community figures. Formed as a private company in 1948, the trust took over the running of the Old Playhouse, a converted cinema in Goldsmith Street. The first director of productions was Andre Van Gyseghem. In 1952 John Harrison became director, succeeded in 1957 by Val May. Under May, the playhouse group was recognized for having the highest standards of production of any repertory company in the country.

Performances were consistent and reliable, characterized by precision teamwork and polished professionalism. The company favored naturalistic drama and well-crafted comedies that could, and did, transfer easily to London's West End. Some experimental work was produced in the attached studio theatre.

In 1961 Frank Dunlop became artistic director, and in 1962 John Neville joined the company as associate director. At this time plans were made to build a new theatre; and in 1963, in anticipation of the move, a triumvirate was formed with Dunlop, Neville, and Peter Ustinov. The new playhouse opened officially on December 11, 1963. It was then one of the most modern theatres in Northern England. Designed by Peter Moro, it has a cylindrical auditorium, a variable-speed revolve 26 feet in diameter, a fly tower, and two mechanically operated forestages that can be raised to add a 13-foot apron to the stage area or lowered to provide an orchestra pit. Its cost, £370,000, was raised from private contributions and the Nottingham City Council.

The move into the new theatre marked a new era for the playhouse company. By 1965 John Neville had become sole artistic director, and the theatre was enormously popular. Neville, who had established a reputation at the Old Vic as one of the leading classical actors of the day, brought glamor and grand style to the playhouse. Charismatic and dynamic, he was able to draw a widely diverse audience and an impressive array of well-known performers to the theatre. At a time when most theatres were struggling to survive, the playhouse averaged 85 percent capacity for productions ranging from Greek tragedy to contemporary comedy. Leading performers included Robert Ryan in Shakespeare's *Othello* and O'Neill's *Long Day's Journey into Night*; and Cleo Laine (as Ellen Terry) and John Neville (as George Bernard Shaw) in the premiere production of *Boots with Strawberry Jam*. Neville gave many notable performances, including Hamlet and Richard II. The company was at its best in virtuoso rather than team acting and with classic rather than new plays. The quality of new scripts did not equal the acting talent made available to the company. By the late 1960s, the playhouse was one of seven theatres in Britain designated by the Arts Council as a major regional theatre. But the end of the 1960s brought a troubled time for the playhouse. In a dramatic move, partly intended as a bid to get more money from the Arts Council, John Neville resigned. The governing board and community groups expressed hope he would reconsider. Weeks later, believing his objectives had been accomplished, Neville withdrew his resignation, but the board declined to reinstate him. Neville's devoted theatregoers were outraged. The resulting public furor brought to attention several important questions: How much autonomy should a private, albeit non-profit, company be allowed in the control of public funds? (That year, the Nottingham Theater Trust Limited had received £50,000 from the Arts Council, £22,000 from the city council, and £8,000 from the county council, plus box of-fice revenues.) How much can and should public opinion influence decisions? Who should have final authority in determining artitic and/or financial policies—the artistic director or the governing board? What is the proper role of the Arts Council in such matters? Are council members authorized to offer management advice as well as financial assistance for the operation of the theatres? These questions point to the very difficult balancing act still required of the director, who must come to terms with the demands of an audience, a governing board, and subsidizing agencies, as well as his own artistic integrity.

Stuart Burge was appointed to succeed Neville in 1968 and admirably set about achieving harmonious working relationships and consistently high production standards. The playhouse saw first-rate revivals of such plays as Chekhov's *The Sea Gull* and Shakespeare's *King Lear* and premieres of Peter Barnes' *The Ruling Class* and Barnes' adaptation of Frank Wedekind's *Lulu*. Both productions transferred successfully to London.

In 1973 Richard Eyre became a joint director, and he succeeded Burge the following year. Eyre had worked as an assistant director to John Neville at the playhouse before joining Clive Perry as associate director at the Edinburgh Festival. He came to Nottingham with an abiding interest in contemporary drama and an unfailing ability for recognizing promising new talent. Under his direction, the playhouse became known for its support of fine new performers and playwrights. Nearly one-half of the productions during Eyre's first year represented new work. He premiered *Brassneck* by David Hare and Howard Brenton. A spectacularly staged show about municipal corruption in a small Midlands town, it played to full houses. Also successful was *Bendigo* by Ben Campbell, Andy Andrews, and Dave Hill, a zany music hall account of a legendary Nottingham prizefighter. Eyre commissioned Howard Brenton's *The Churchill Play*, as well as a new version of Adrian Mitchell's *The Government Inspector*. In 1975 Ken Campbell's *Walking Like Geoffrey* and Trevor Griffiths' *Comedians* premiered. *Comedians*, a play that takes a look at politics through a school for stand-up comics, went on to receive notice as one of the best plays of the year, and to run at the National Theater, Wyndham's, and on Broadway.

The playhouse maintained a permanent company of about thirty performers, including James Warrior, Roger Sloman, Jonathan Pryce, Mary Sheen, and Tom Wilkinson. The playhouse also supported its own Theatre in Education Company—the Roundabout Company—directed by Sue Birtwistle. The Roundabout toured programs to local schools, ran drama workshops for young people and teachers, and performed plays for children in the playhouse. By the end of Eyre's five-year directorship, the Nottingham company was widely recognized for its achievements in the vanguard. In 1978 Geoffrey Reeves became artistic director; he was succeeded in September 1980 by Richard Digby Day.

Richard Digby Day brought a commitment to first-rate entertainment and an enlightened sense of the role of the theatre to Nottingham Playhouse, as he prepared to expand the importance of the theatre in the community during the 1980s. Faced with competition from active touring companies, other newly built or refurbished community theatres, and the television and film industry, Day believed the regional theatres must be responsive to local audiences and offer theatrical experiences not to be found elsewhere. For his initial season, he offered sure audience-pleasers like Sandy Wilson's *The Boy Friend*, as well as Shaw's *Mrs.*

Warren's Profession and Dylan Thomas' *Under Milk Wood*. The autumn schedule also included Arthur Miller's *A View from the Bridge*, directed by Crispin Thomas, who became associate director in January 1981, and Hugh Witemore's experimental *Stevie*, the story of the eccentric woman poet Stevie Smith. Appealing to a wide range of ages as well as interests, Day staged Ken Campbell's comedy for children *Old King Cole* and a new family play by children's writer David Wood. The spring of 1981 saw productions of Francis Gray's *Fantasy in "C"* and *Comedy of Errors* by the New Shakespeare Company of Regents Park. During the 1981–1982 season, Shakespeare's *A Midsummer Night's Dream*, Friedrich von Schiller's *Mary Stuart*, Somerset Maugham's *Our Betters*, Shakespeare's *The Taming of the Shrew*, Ibsen's *Peer Gynt*, and *No, No, Nanette* (score by Vincent Youmans and book and lyrics by Frank Mandel, Otto Harbach, and Irving Caesar), were featured attractions. The 1982–1983 season was highlighted by productions of Miller's *The Crucible*, Shakespeare's *Much Ado about Nothing* and *Antony and Cleopatra*, Gilbert and Sullivan's *H.M.S. Pinafore*, and Alan Ayckbourn's *How the Other Half Loves*. Day's favorite contemporary playwrights are John Arden and Edward Albee, but he prefers producing Shaw.

Day concentrated on building a large core company of performers and guest artists who will maintain a permanent close relationship with the playhouse. This group already included Jill Bennet, Miriam Carling, Basil Hoskins, Evelyn Laye, Imelda Staunton, and Judy Campbell, among others. Day was also committed to expanding the company's role in the community. A series of noontime sessions at Nottingham's Central Library, devised and performed by playhouse company members, focused in turn on Byron, Tennyson, Wilfred Owen, W. H. Auden, Virginia Woolf, and Lytton Strachey. Designated productions featured post-performance discussion sessions. For example, after certain performances of *Mrs. Warren's Profession*, company members discussed Shaw as a music critic, drama critic, and social and political commentator. The Nottingham Playhouse Touring Company, Roundabout, directed by Danny Hiller, has devised new shows for senior citizen groups, as well as schoolchildren. They tour youth clubs, community homes, and prisons. The Nottingham Playhouse is partially subsidized by the Arts Council and the Nottingham City Council. Assistance from the Arts Council has risen considerably, from £177,303 in 1975–1976, to £269,835 in 1979, but more than 75 percent of the company revenues comes directly from the supporting community. The Playhouse Company seems prepared to take on new and important roles; it is working with imaginative ways to bring the community into the theatre and to take the theatre into the community.

JO BRANTLEY BERRYMAN

ROYAL EXCHANGE THEATRE COMPANY
Saint Anne's Square
Manchester M2 7DH, England

It seems unlikely that a theatre company could find a congenial home in a stock exchange, but the Royal Exchange Theatre of Manchester has done just that. In an imaginative and bold venture beginning in 1972, the theatre company acquired the name and the Great Hall of Manchester's former stock exchange. Now, a steel and glass modern marvel of a theatre-in-the-round has been built inside the Great Hall, and audiences have been given season after season of first-rate, highly professional theatre. The theatre company has managed to combine the best of old and new—not only in its futuristic new theatre constructed inside a Victorian landmark, but also in its staging of both experimental new plays as well as quality revivals and established classics. This admirable state of affairs has been reached only after an extended period of evolution for both the theatre company and the Exchange building.

The theatre company traces its beginnings to 1959, when a group of actors, directors, and designers formed the '59 Theatre Company. Many of this group, including Finnish director Casper Wrede, Italian designer Richard Negri, and Anglicized American actor James Maxwell, had trained at the Old Vic Theater School, at that time run by Michel Saint-Denis, Glen Byam Shaw, and George Devine. Michael Elliott began working with Wrede in 1954, directing a number of plays for the British Broadcasting Corporation (BBC). Five years later, Wrede became the director, and Elliott his associate, for the '59 Company. The '59 Company's first season at the Lyric Theater, Hammersmith, was ambitious; it included the first English production of Georg Büchner's *Danton's Death* and Ibsen's difficult *Brand*. The productions of the unsubsidized company were critically acclaimed but financially unsuccessful. For the next decade, the group worked together informally and occasionally, doing productions for film and television, the Royal Shakespeare Company, the National Theater, and the Old Vic. Michael Elliott brought together many of the '59 group for the 1962–1963 season at the Old Vic, its last season before becoming the home of the National Theater.

Drawn together by their professional values and their desire to create their own theatre, the group reformed in 1968. Calling themselves the '69 Theatre Company to maintain continuity with the earlier group, they began working at the University Theater of Manchester. Their first production, *Hamlet*, with Tom Courtenay, opened at the Edinburgh Festival. Its success began the momentum for the group's rapidly growing national reputation. During the next five years, the company staged twenty-one productions in Manchester and took seven of these to London, including R. C. Sherriff's *Journey's End* and Oliver Goldsmith's *She Stoops to Conquer*. Performers included Paul Scofield, Edward Fox, Dame Edith Evans, and Dame Wendy Hiller. Yet the '69 Company was working only twenty weeks a year in Manchester. Only three full-time members of the company lived in the area. Rehearsals often had to be held in London. The theatre, on one of Manchester's back streets, was tiny. Artistic directors were not paid. With money and space critical problems, the time had come for the group either to break up or to find a more permanent home.

At the very time that the '69 Company was rehearsing its first production, *Hamlet*, the Royal Exchange Company Limited in Manchester, on December

31, 1968, closed its doors. Neither group was then particularly aware of the other. But soon after its arrival in Manchester, the theatre company had the good fortune to become associated with one of Manchester's distinguished citizens, stockbroker Peter Henriques. Heading an unofficial support group for the company, Peter Henriques worked tirelessly to raise money and community interest for the theatre. Just at the critical time, he came up with the proposal of using the empty Great Hall in the Exchange building as a temporary, stop-gap theatre. It proved to be a felicitous suggestion. The Exchange building, in the center of the city, was easily accessible, and the Great Hall, covering over three-quarters of an acre, was certainly spacious. The history of the Exchange building itself was colorful enough to sound like living theatre.

The first Exchange building had been erected in 1729 and at that time was used on occasion as a theatre for dramatic and musical performances. Instead of devising a new use for the Exchange building, the '69 Company was actually restoring an old one. The first recorded theatrical production in Manchester took place in the Exchange in 1743: George Farquhar's *The Recruiting Officer. Macbeth* was also performed there. But by 1772, the area had deteriorated and the Exchange building was demolished. A place for the derelict and disreputable, the site became known as "Penniless Hill." Not until 1809 was a new Exchange built. In 1812 the building was the scene of a riot, a Reformist demonstration against the authorities. Windows, furnishings, and paintings were smashed until the militia arrived and the mob was dispersed. But the incident marked the beginning of more than three decades of political, economic, and social reform with both industrial and reformist leaders belonging to the Manchester Exchange.

The Exchange was also witness to more decorous occasions. In the autumn of 1851, Queen Victoria and Prince Albert visited Manchester. It was the first time a reigning sovereign had visited the city; and for the formal presentation of the Lord Mayor's Loyal Address to the Queen, the Exchange Building had been selected and refurbished. The Queen was so pleased by her reception in Manchester that she not only knighted the mayor, but also decided that thereafter the Exchange should be known as the Manchester Royal Exchange.

After an act of Parliament in 1866, a new Royal Exchange was constructed. Completed in 1874, the new Exchange's Great Hall was built 9 feet above street level, with shops and offices below. The Hall covered an area of 1.7 acres. It was the largest room in the world used for commercial purposes. At its peak, nearly ten thousand members met at the Exchange, with trading connected mainly to the cotton industry. On December 22, 1940, one-half of the building was destroyed by enemy bombing. Reconstruction was finally completed in 1953, but the Hall was reduced to half its original size. As Manchester became less important as a center for cotton trading, the business of the Exchange declined, and by 1968, the Exchange was closed. The Great Hall remained unused until it reopened for the Royal Exchange Theatre Company. In 1972 the company arranged a twenty-five-year lease of the Great Hall. Peter Henriques created an Appeals Committee to raise funds, a group of trustees was formed, and the Arts

Council of Britain and the City Council promised support. The company began to formulate plans for a new theatre.

In 1973 the City Council donated £8,000 for the building of a temporary tent theatre inside the Exchange building for the Manchester Festival. Constructed of timber and scaffolding, discarded seats and canvas, and donated fabric, the theatre was erected within a month, supposedly for a three-week period. It remained for ten months. The Royal Exchange Theatre Company performed plays by George Bernard Shaw, J. B. Priestley, Samuel Beckett, and T. S. Eliot. The 450-seat theatre was filled to capacity. When the local authorities and the insurance companies finally insisted that it be dismantled, over £140,000 had been raised for the new theatre's building fund. Plans for the new theatre were well underway. Richard Negri, one of the company's artistic directors, had conceived the model of the theatre and now worked in collaboration with architects Levitt Bernstein Associates. Proceedings, however, were not without problems. The theatre had been designed to be free standing, but it was discovered that with the weight of a full house, the structure would have sunk ignominiously through the floor and into the shops below. The imaginative solution of suspending the theatre from the four main columns in the Hall considerably increased the time and cost involved. From an original estimate of £400,000, costs soared to over £1 million. The completion of the theatre was delayed eighteen months. Another setback was the death of Peter Henriques, who had been a constant source of support. In his honor, the company created a special memorial fund to be used to commission new works. This fund insures the performance of new plays each season.

The Royal Exchange Theatre was officially opened on September 15, 1976, by Sir Laurence Olivier. Braham Murray directed the initial production, Richard Sheridan's *The Rivals*, with Patricia Routledge, Tom Courtenay, Christopher Gable, James Maxwell, and Trevor Peacock. During the 1976–1977 season, the company mounted ten productions, including Chekhov's *Uncle Vanya*, directed by Michael Elliott; Thornton Wilder's *The Skin of Our Teeth*, directed by Richard Negri and James Maxwell; and *Leaping Ginger*, a new musical by Trevor Peacock and directed by Braham Murray. There were eight productions during 1977–1978, including a stage adaptation of *Crime and Punishment* by Paul Bailey, directed by Michael Elliott; and *A Family*, a new play by Ronald Harwood, directed by Casper Wrede, with Paul Scofield. Several productions were dramatized novels, including *Crime and Punishment*; *The Adventures of Huckleberry Finn*, adapted by David Terence; and Evelyn Waugh's *The Ordeal of Gilbert Pinfold*, adapted by Ronald Harwood. One of the most highly acclaimed productions in 1978 was Michael Elliott's direction of Ibsen's *The Lady from the Sea*, with Vanessa Redgrave as Ellida. After an initial run in Manchester, the Royal Exchange Theatre Company took the play to the Round House in London, where it continued to receive high praise. Other excellent productions in 1979 were Elliott's revival of T. S. Eliot's *The Family Reunion*, Arthur Wing Pinero's *The School Mistress*, and the British premieres of Neil Simon's *The Last of the*

Red Hot Lovers and Hugo von Hofmannsthal's *The Deep Man*. In 1981 productions of Christopher Marlowe's *Doctor Faustus* (with Ben Kingsley and James Maxwell) and Shaw's *Heartbreak House* (with Alfred Burke, Nigel Stock, and Eleanor Bron) were highly successful. The year 1982 saw the Royal Exchange's first Greek drama when Sophocles' *Philoctetes* was directed by Michael Elliott, who used a new translation by Dr. Christopher Grace.

There is no permanent company of actors; each play is cast individually by the directors. Michael Elliott has said that, while permanent companies often do the very best work, it is unfair to the actors to keep them tied up for long periods, preventing them from taking good parts elsewhere. As a result, the company attracts major performers and new talent; and actors return again and again to appear in appropriate roles. The theatre company has also tried to establish consistently high standards not only on, but behind, the stage. The designers and technicians are first rate.

As a regional, repertory company, the Royal Exchange is subsidized by the Arts Council of Britain and also receives financial assistance from the Manchester City Council and the Greater Manchester Council. The Arts Council contributed £138,000 in 1976, £160,000 in 1977–1978, and £216,500 in 1978–1979 for general operating costs. The Greater Manchester Council contributes approximately £130,000 a year, and the Manchester City Council guarantees the rent and rates of the building. The building costs for the new Royal Exchange Theater have been met by grants and public appeal. Of the £1.2 million needed, £275,000 was raised from the Greater Manchester Council, £100,000 from the Manchester City Council, and £300,000 from the Arts Council; £340,000 has been raised so far from public appeal. The company plans to continue offering a wide range of plays; it has demonstrated a preference for high-brow drama. Its consistently high-quality work has made this company one of the most ambitious and admirable in the business, and has established the Royal Exchange as a major regional theatre.

JO BRANTLEY BERRYMAN

ROYAL SHAKESPEARE COMPANY
Stratford-upon-Avon and London
Royal Shakespeare Theatre
Stratford-upon-Avon
Warwickshire CV37 6BB, England

The Royal Shakespeare Company is generally recognized as the preeminent theatre company in England; it is among the best in the world, not only for Shakespeare, but also for classics and new plays. In its artistic achievement, its rich history, and its impact on world theatre, it stands today as the most influential single theatre enterprise in the English-speaking world. Besides frequent tours of England, the Continent, North America, and the Commonwealth, the RSC (as it is commonly called) mounts a diverse repertory in four theatres: the Royal Shakespeare Theatre (seating 1,400) and the Other Place (150 to 200) in Stratford-upon-Avon, the company's home, and the Barbican Theatre (1,150) and the Pit Theatre (150 to 200) in the newly completed Barbican Centre in London.

In 1979, the last year for which records are complete, on a budget of £4.6 million ($11 million) the RSC mounted thirty-five productions: eleven in Stratford, nineteen in London, two in the West End, two for a small-scale tour in England, and one for a European tour. Tours and tourists ensure that its audiences, like its repertoire, are cosmopolitan. Its theatre-in-education programs and the planned Guildhall school for theatre at the Barbican make it a vital part of England's educational scene. And its long history of theatrical experiment has made the RSC a major theatre influence throughout the world.

It was not always so. The history of the theatre company from its beginnings in the nineteenth century records a fascinating chapter in theatre history, amply documented in the promptbooks and theatre records of the Shakespeare Centre Library in Stratford-upon-Avon. (These records are available on microfilm by application to Dr. Levi Fox, Director of the Shakespeare Birthplace Trust, and may also be studied on microfilm at the University of Illinois Library.)

The inspiration for a Shakespeare theatre in Stratford goes back to David Garrick's celebrations in 1769, a gala festival with masquerades, commemoratory orations, and fireworks. Yet it sprang into being only in 1879, with the opening of the Shakespeare Memorial Theatre, sponsored in large part by the local brewer Charles Edward Flower, who raised the money (much of it his own) and built the theatre on the banks of the Avon. In the decades following, brief two- or three-week spring festivals, featuring six or seven Shakespeare plays, made up the repertory. Frank Benson (1858–1939), whose company otherwise toured the provinces and occasionally played in London, was festival director from 1886 to 1919. Under his hand, the festival company grew into seasoned professionals, who in later years proudly called themselves Old Bensonians. With the end of World War I came W. Bridges-Adams (1889–1965). "Unabridges" Adams, as he was called, paid more attention to the text than had Benson, restoring some of the convenient and conventional cuts made in earlier days, and adding a summer season to the festival.

When the theatre burned in 1926, Adams helped carry the company through. Actually an unexpected blessing, the fire provided the opportunity to build a newer and better theatre, and the international appeals and tours that came with this effort made the Shakespeare Memorial Theatre (which finally reopened in 1932) a truly national and international institution.

With several internal modifications, the 1932 theatre is the one that remains the RSC's main Stratford stage today. Ben Iden Payne (1881–1976), an Old Bensonian himself, took over in 1932. Payne introduced the new idea of "Elizabethan" staging—a thrust stage, an upper acting area, and continuous action—and, more importantly, brought in guest directors like Theodore Komisarjevsky from Moscow to use the new theatre to experiment with new approaches—expressionism, for one—and to help free the Stratford theatre from its provincialism.

After World War II, Sir Barry Jackson (1879–1961), founder of the Birmingham Repertory Theatre and famous for his innovative modern-dress Shakespeare during the 1930s, transformed the seasonal festival into a year-round operation, with a permanent administration, an extended season running from spring to fall, and scene and costume shops in Stratford. Jackson, who came in 1946 and left in 1948, was succeeded by Anthony Quayle (1913-), who was joined in 1953 by Glen Byam Shaw (1904–). They worked together as co-directors until 1956, Shaw continuing until 1959. In the 1950s the company drew the best talent from London's West End, an occasional occurrence before.

Quayle and Shaw both came from the crowd of talent who made the Old Vic famous during the 1930s. Now, after the war, they brought to Stratford a dazzling array of stars—Peggy Ashcroft, Laurence Harvey, Charles Laughton, Vivien Leigh, Laurence Olivier, Michael Redgrave, Clive Revill, Godfrey Tearle, Margaret Webster, and Emlyn Williams, to name only a few. They also nurtured new talent, including directors Peter Brook and Peter Hall and actors Richard Burton, Ian Holm, Emrys James, and Keith Michell. And they raised the level of artistic accomplishment so that theatre at Stratford ranked with the best in London. Tourists came from all over the world to see the performances, and the company—now really two companies, one in Stratford and one on the road—embarked on ambitious world tours to Australia (1949, 1952–1953), Germany (1950), Canada and the United States (1953–1954), and Russia (1958–1959).

With Peter Hall (1930-), in 1959 came a yet more fundamental change. From the Shakespeare Memorial Theatre Company, with its now outdated suggestions of reverence for the local shrine, Hall changed the name and the character of the company, rechristening it in 1961 the Royal Shakespeare Company. Although the enterprise has boasted a royal charter since 1925, Hall's twofold aim was to make it truly "royal" in the sense of representing the best the nation could produce and creating a "company" that would foster new talent and secure the best established talent through long-term contracts for associate artists. To these ends, the RSC established its London base at the Aldwych Theatre (in 1960); it sought out the best young actors; and it began a policy, still in force, whereby it would take its productions on tour—either small-scale tours in Great Britain or full company tours abroad. Transfers of successful productions to the West End or to Broadway followed. The World Theatre Season each spring brought leading theatre companies from abroad to perform in the RSC's London theatre. By forming a company grouped around a core of the best actors, the associate artists, and by offering sustenance to the best young actors, in the years following the RSC has succeeded as a theatre company whose life is self-renewing.

An important part of this self-renewal rests in the RSC's commitment to new plays and experimental work. Both were fostered by Trevor Nunn (1940-), who became artistic director in 1968, with Terry Hands (1941-) sharing joint artistic directorship from 1979. To foster new work, the Stratford and London branches of the RSC opened small studio theatres in which both experienced associate artists and younger members of the company act in new plays and new stagings of classic plays.

Productions transfer from one theatre to another, usually from the main house in Stratford to the main house in London and from the studios interchangeably, with Shakespeare and classic drama usually originating in Stratford and new plays or non-Shakespearean plays in London. While Shakespeare has remained the center of the RSC's interest, bringing together the best actors and directors in the theatre has inevitably meant the company would seek the best in dramatic literature and theatrical innovation. Its repertoire is wide ranging and eclectic.

With the expansion of the repertoire and the number of theatres over the past two decades has come another kind of growth. Beginning in the 1960s, the RSC has mounted tours with small companies of actors to bring theatre to smaller cities and towns in Britain, many of which had not seen live professional theatre since the days of Frank Benson. On a larger scale, the Newcastle-on-Tyne season (seven weeks) has established another, provincial venue for the RSC's work. In its main theatres and on tour, the company has pioneered in bringing audiences, especially of students and teachers, into workshops with its artists. In 1979, for instance, the audiences participating in such workshops, in Stratford and London alone, numbered eight thousand. The Royal Shakespeare Theatre in Stratford participates in similar programs affiliated with the University of Warwick and the University of Birmingham's Shakespeare Institute, allowing students from Britain and abroad to meet with RSC artists and discuss their work.

To distill a company philosophy from such a diverse and eclectic group seems nearly impossible. True, the RSC's *esprit de corps*, very real and deeply felt, springs from a dedication to the best and highest standards of theatre art. Anyone in the RSC could make a better salary acting in television or films alone. What this means in human terms, however, is a bond of company loyalty that is life-long, not for all members surely, but for most. Because so many of the best actors and directors now performing or producing in England have come from the RSC, and because they share the company's dedication to excellence, there is a spirit in it that cannot be named.

Inflation has inhibited, for instance, a hoped-for third Stratford theatre of medium size (six hundred seats) for classic plays. Yet the camaraderie of excellence in adversity has knit together what must be recognized as the best permanent theatre company in England today—fostering new talent and presenting established actors in productions garnering the critics' highest praise season after season.

To practice the art of theatre at this high level requires not only gifted artists, an experienced technical staff, and an astute management all dedicated to their art, as well as an established reputation for excellence ensuring good box office, but it also requires substantial subsidies. RSC expenditures for 1979 totaled more than £4.5 million. How are these monies spent? About £1.2 million went for artists' salaries (27 percent of the total expenditure). (Overall, wages accounted for 62 percent of the RSC's expenses.) Income from the box office came to £2.4 million. The balance was in grants by the Arts Council of Great Britain (£1.9 million) and by corporate funders (£67,000). Were the box office alone to support the RSC, ticket prices would have to be increased to nearly two times their current level. Of course, the greatest cost is in operating the theatres and mounting productions (about 59 percent, including publicity but excluding tour costs). Management accounted for less than 5 percent of the RSC's 1979 expenditures.

Despite its subsidy, for 1979 the RSC operated at a deficit of £100,000. Hard pressed by inflation and retrenchment in the arts, the Royal Shakespeare Company has nonetheless continued to maintain a standard of artistic achievement and to expand into new areas of endeavor, most notably regional and educational. From past strengths, present blessings flow.

What the future holds for the RSC seems promising but uncertain. The establishment of the National Theatre in London, "the Opposition" as it is known in Stratford, poses a great challenge, competing for first-rate actors and funding needed to sustain the RSC's current level of operation. The National Theatre also offers a challenge due and just to the RSC's hegemony. From such challenges, which the RSC met from the Old Vic, much good theatre may result. After some tentative ventures into film (Peter Hall's film of *A Midsummer Night's Dream*, for instance, and Trevor Nunn's *Hedda Gabler*), the RSC has made videotapes of the 1976 *Macbeth* and the 1983 *Nicholas Nickleby*, with more such theatre-for-television productions in the offing. From this, the potential for the metamorphosis of the best theatre productions into equally satisfying television productions seems promising as a way not merely of recording what the company has done (of interest primarily to theatre historians) but of creating new productions of lasting value. If there is a new theatre for the RSC in the 1980s (such as the RSC found in the 1960s and 1970s), television offers exciting promise.

MICHAEL MULLIN

Greece

INTRODUCTION

Generous subsidies, first-rate acting, and quality direction characterize the three state theatres in Greece: the National Opera in Athens, the National Theatre of Greece (also in Athens), and the State Theatre of Northern Greece in Salonica.

The idea for a Greek national theatre became a reality in 1900 when the Vascilon Theatron (Royal Theatre) was built. Due to severe financial troubles, it folded in 1908, reopening in 1930 as the National Theatre of Greece. This time it survived. Designed primarily as a theatre to play the classic Greek plays, the company still emphasizes the works of the fifth century B.C., which it performs regularly in the ancient theatres of Epidaurus, Dodoni, Herode Atticus, and Philippi. These are the productions most often seen by outsiders during the summer season when the company plays out-of-doors.

In 1969, the State Theatre of Northern Greece was founded by an act of the Ministry of Culture and Science. As a part of the decentralization movement in the Greek theatre, it was designed to serve the local community. Like the National Theatre of Greece, it has a two-season year: a fall-winter season (with Easter at the end) and an outdoor-summer season. In its attempt to get as close as possible to the life of the people in the city of Thessaloniki and the surrounding area, the company sends out actors, directors, and other theatre personnel to talk to local groups about upcoming productions which are usually selected from the best of classical and contemporary plays, from Greece and abroad.

Well attended and lavishly subsidized by the government, the Greek Art Theatre in Athens is one of the best of the many private theatre companies thriving in the provinces as well as in Athens. Praised for its vigor, the company has a winter season devoted to modern repertory and a summer season with one work presented on the outdoor circuit.

The most promising development in Greek theatre today involves the creative productions of a new generation of playwrights, including Loula Anagnostaki, Iakovos Kambanellis, Dimitris Kedaidis, Yeorgos Maniotis, and Yeorgos Skourtis. Thanks to government awards, many of these playwrights are able to devote much of their time to writing for one of the country's many outstanding theatre companies, most of whom are attempting to produce original, new Greek plays each season.

LEON M. AUFDEMBERGE
and COLBY H. KULLMAN

GREEK ART THEATRE
(Teatro Technis)
44, Stadium Street
Athens, Greece

On the whole, 1942 would seem to be a dreadful year for the founding of a theatre in Athens. Greece had been devastated in the Occupation, yet in that year Karolos Koun founded the Teatro Technis (Greek Art Theatre). The first production was Ibsen's *The Wild Duck* done at the Teatro Alikis, opening on October 17. Koun had studied in both Athens and Istanbul, and had staged a number of plays (both classic and modern) before founding his own theatre. In 1941 he had founded a drama school, which still functions alongside the theatre. The Art Theatre's repertory in its first seasons was made up of naturalistic writers (including some Greek writers), with Henrik Ibsen, Luigi Pirandello, and George Bernard Shaw being the most often played.

After the Liberation, the repertory moved toward more international writers, such as Arthur Miller, Thornton Wilder, Federico García Lorca, Eugene O'Neill, and Tennessee Williams, as well as works by the playwrights done during the Occupation. Some of the most significant works performed in the early years of the company included the following (unless otherwise stated in the body of this article, Koun was responsible for the production): Gregorios Xenopoulos' *Stella Volandi* (1944), Williams' *The Glass Menagerie* (1946), García Lorca's *Blood Wedding* (1948), Williams' *A Streetcar Named Desire* (1949) with Melina Mercouri as Blanche, and Miller's *Death of a Salesman* (1949). The philosophy of the company in its early years in both repertory and playing was poetic realism. Despite its popularity, financial hardships forced the company to close in 1949.

In 1954 a new company was formed with largely a young group of actors. The new theatre was an arena house, formed from a basement cinema. The new theatre was to be a place where Athenians could see the classic writers (Shakespeare above all), as well as the best new playwrights of Europe. The most publicized plays done were Wilder's *Our Town* (1954) and *The Skin of Our Teeth* (1954), Sean O'Casey's *The Plough and the Stars* (1955), Shakespeare's *Twelfth Night* (1956), and Bertolt Brecht's *The Caucasian Chalk Circle* (1957) and *The Good Woman of Setzuan* (1958).

In 1957 the theatre staged its first production of a classic Greek work, a fantastic look at Aristophanes' *Plutus*. Some years later Aristophanes' *The Birds* was a big hit; it was done at the Herod Atticus Theatre as part of the Athens Festival. *The Birds* also played in Paris (1962), London (1964, 1965, and 1967), the USSR (1965), Poland (1965), and in other cities in Western Europe. Aeschylus' *The Persians* came in 1965, touring extensively, as did Aristophanes' *The Frogs*. Other popular works in this era were Williams' *Sweet Bird of Youth* (1959) with Mercouri as the Princess, Chekhov's *Uncle Vanya* (1960), Brecht's *The Resistible Rise of Arturo Ui* (1961), Max Frisch's *Andorra* (1962), O'Neill's *The Iceman Cometh* (1963), Dimitriou Vezantiou's *The Babylonians* (1964), Georgy Sebastikoglu's *Aggela* (1965), Iakovou Kampaneles' *The Homecoming of Ulysses* (1966), and Peter Weiss' *Marat/Sade* (1966). In addition, there were productions of a number of absurdist writers, such as Edward Albee, Eugene Ionesco, and Samuel Beckett.

During the time of the Colonels' regime, the Arts Theatre suffered the loss of one of its favorite playwrights, Brecht. Strangely enough, however, absurdist playwrights continued to be done. The biggest successes of the period were two classics (both presented in 1969): Aristophanes' *Lysistrata* and Sophocles' *Oedipus Tyrannos* with Georgy Lazanis in the title role. These productions toured in London in the same year to generally good reviews. The other major productions in this troubled time were from both the classics and moderns: Shakespeare's *Measure for Measure* (1968), Beckett's *Waiting for Godot* (1969), Büchner's *Woyzeck* (1970), Beckett's *Endgame* (1970), and Shakespeare's *A Midsummer Night's Dream* (1971). On the whole, the repertory might be interpreted as safe without necessarily being subservient.

Since the return of freedom to Greece (1974) and the thirtieth anniversary of the founding of the theatre in 1972, there has been a major shift in the repertory of the company. The works of new young playwrights have been presented in a series of premieres. Among the writers of the older generation are Demetrios Koromilas and Gregorios Xenopoulos. Among the new writers are Iakovos Kambanellis, Loula Anagnostaki, Dimitris Kehaidis, and Yeorgos Skourtis. Since 1975 the Arts Theatre has appeared every summer at the outdoor festivals of Athens and Epidaurus with Aeschylus' *Seven Against Thebes* (1975), Aristophanes' *The Acharnians* (1976) and *Peace* (1977), Euripides' *The Bacchae* (1977), Sophocles' *Oedipus Tyrannos* (1978) with Lazanis in the title role, Aristophanes' *The Knights* (1979, production by Lazanis), Euripides' *The Trojan Women* (1979), and Aeschylus' *The Oresteia* (1980). Many of these productions have toured other cities in Europe and have brought deserved success to the company.

In addition to its Greek repertory, the company continues to present international works in order to achieve balance. Some of its major productions from outside Greece in recent seasons include Witold Gombrowicz's *The Operetta* (1972), Brecht's *Fear and Misery in the Third Reich* (1974), Dario Fo's *Isabella and the Three Ships* (1974), Carlo Goldoni's *The Servant of Two Masters* (1976), and Il Ruzzante's *La Mosketa* (1978, production by Lazanis). But the mainstay of the repertory remains its Greek works, and several, such as Iakovos Kambanellis' *The Four Feet of the Table* (1979), have received rave reviews in both the Greek and foreign press.

As with most Greek theatres, the Greek Art Theatre has two seasons: the winter season, which is devoted to a generally modern repertory, in which it presents six works; and its summer season, in which it does one work on the outdoor circuit. At present it controls three houses: its arena stage on Stadium Street (Aghiou Stadiou), which seats 230; the Veaki Theatre on Stounara Street, with places for 456; and a summer theatre on Ioulianou Street, with 420 places. Its acting company is composed of forty performers, and some use is made of guests. Its annual budget runs to 24 million drachmas, of which 20 percent is subsidy.

Plays are chosen by Koun with his staff, who read a mass of modern Greek plays to choose a season. Since 1968 the theatre has been governed by the Greek Theatre Society, composed of twenty-five members, which include theatre employees, playwrights, people interested in the arts in general, and prominent Athenians. The Board of Directors is composed of seven members who serve for three years and are elected by the society. Koun is managing director for the society and also plays a major role in running the dramatic school connected with the theatre. The fame of the theatre company is perhaps reflected best in its many recent tours. This fame can largely be credited to its founder and mainstay, Karolos Koun.

Every major Greek theatre is esteemed for a particular reason. The National Theatre commands respect because of its long history and its pioneering in the production of Greek classic drama. The State Theatre of Northern Greece is admired because it serves an area of Greece that might normally not be served by a theatre company. But for the Art, there is affection because of its vigor and its sense of vitality.

LEON M. AUFDEMBERGE
(With thanks to Olga Pavlatou of the theatre staff.
Translation help by Peter Georgaras and James Moutzouros.)

NATIONAL THEATRE OF GREECE
(Ethnicón Théatron)
65, Menandrou Street
Athens, Greece

The idea for a Greek national theatre began in 1891 when King George I began to lay plans with Dimitrios Coromlas, a respected Greek poet, for a theatre. The theatre did not become reality until 1900 when the Vascilon Théatron (Royal Theatre) was built. The opening performance was on November 24, 1901, with Angelos Vlachos as managing director and Thomas Economu as what might be called artistic director. The theatre did 144 works before it folded in 1908 because of severe financial problems. The house continued to be used as a commercial theatre, and in 1922, it changed its name to the Ethnicón Théatron (National Theatre).

The theatre was reopened as a state facility on May 5, 1930, when Fotos Politis, the artistic director, staged two works, Aeschylus' *Agamemnon* and Gregorios Xenopoulos' *The Divine Dream*, with the well-known poet Ioannis

Gryparis as managing director. Much respected as a director, Politis staged a string of productions, including Shakespeare's *Julius Caesar* (1932), with the young Alexis Minotis as Marc Antony; *Anna Christie* (1932), with the translation by Katina Paxinou, who also played the lead; George Bernard Shaw's *The Devil's Disciple* (1933), with Minotis as Dick Dudgeon; Euripides' *Cyclops* (1934); and Friedrich von Schiller's *Don Carlos*, which Politis staged in 1934, the year of his death. Minotis and Paxinou acted in Ibsen's *Ghosts* the same year.

The 1930s were years of growth for the theatre. Early in its history touring was begun, especially of Greek classic plays, which have always been the nucleus of the repertory. Early in its career the company played classic works in its theatre on Aghiou Constantiou Street. But in 1936 Dimitri Rondiris took classic drama outdoors, when he staged Sophocles' *Electra* in the Odeon of Herod Atticus and Euripides' *Hippolytus* the following year. Rondiris, who eventually became managing director, was a disciple of Max Reinhardt and had worked at the Burgtheater in Vienna. He was an advocate of playing classic tragedy out-of-doors, and eventually he would take the company to many of the classic theatres throughout Greece, including Epidaurus in which he staged Sophocles' *Electra* in 1938.

In 1939 the company toured the same *Electra* (Paxinou played Electra) and Shakespeare's *Hamlet* (Minotis as Hamlet) in Germany and eventually in London. Before the war, Rondiris staged well-received productions of Beaumarchais' *The Marriage of Figaro* (1936); Shakespeare's *King Lear* (1938) and *Romeo and Juliet* (1939); Eugene O'Neill's *Beyond the Horizon* (1939); and many others.

Despite the privations of the Occupation, the theatre continued to play, particularly many French works staged by Rondiris, including a return of *The Marriage of Figaro* (1941) and Molière's *The Miser* (1942), but there were also good productions of Gregorios Xenopoulos' *The Student* (1941) and Schiller's *Intrigue and Love* (1942). The postwar era was a difficult time for the theatre, as Greece was rocked by civil wars; it was not really until the early 1950s and the return of Paxinou and Minotis that the company's fortunes began to improve. One of the young actresses who worked for the National Theatre in the 1940s was Melina Mercouri, playing O'Neill, Anouilh, and Tennessee Williams before going on to other theatres and politics.

In the 1950s the company's work split into three parts: the fall-winter season in Athens, the summer work in outdoor theatres, and the international tours. In the late 1940s and into the 1950s, the repertory began to expand rapidly, with many works added from the international scene, both classic and modern, including its productions of Edmond Rostand's *Cyrano de Bergerac* (1948) and John Patrick's *The Hasty Heart* (1950), both by Rondiris; and Minotis' staging of both Federico García Lorca's *The House of Bernarda Alba* (1954), with Paxinou as Bernarda, and *Blood Wedding* (1959), with Paxinou as the mother. In 1952 the company began to tour outside Greece, and since then it has regularly played Paris, London, and the United States.

But the National Theatre of Greece was founded largely as a theatre to play classic Greek works, and with these the best work of the theatre has been found. Since 1954 the company has played regularly in both the Theatre of Herod Atticus and Epidaurus, as well as Dodoni and Philippi. A variety of directors have used these theatres, and all four of the major directors who work regularly on the outdoor stage have had a wide difference in staging styles. Rondiris is the oldest, and his great work was probably in the handling of the chorus. His best classic Greek productions would include Aeschylus' *The Persians* (1939), Euripides' *Hippolytus* (1954), Aeschylus' *Oresteia* (1949, 1959), and Euripides' *Medea* (1960), with Aspasia Papathanassiou as the title character. It might be added that for a long while Rondiris was head of both the National Theatre and the Festival at Epidaurus; the jobs are now being handled by two people. Alexis Minotis is another respected director; his best work has been characterized by a staging of great scenes. His best productions would include Sophocles' *Antigone* (1956), *Oedipus Tyrannos* (1955), and the productions of *Oedipus at Colonus* (1958 and 1975), both of which featured Minotis as Oedipus and both of which toured extensively; Euripides' *Hecuba* (1955), with Paxinou as the title character; Aeschylus' *Prometheus Bound* (1957); and Euripides' *Bacchae* (1962). He continues to direct for the outdoor festivals; he produced Euripides' *The Phoenician Women* in the summer of 1979. Takis Mouzenidis is the most eclectic and intellectual of the four. He has staged such works as Menander's *Dyskolos* (1960); and Euripides' *Helena* (1962), *Andromache* (1963), *The Suppliants* (1966), *Rhesus* (1968) and *Electra* (1969). Alexis Solomos is the most modern of the four and is adept at both tragedy and comedy. He has staged Aristophanes' *Thesmophoriazousai* (1957); Aeschylus' *The Suppliants* (1964); and Aristophanes' *Lysistrata* (1969), *The Knights* (1976), and *The Brides* (1979). Other directors who have staged classic works for the National Theatre with some success include Stavros Doufexis, Spyros Evangelatos, and Giorgios Theodossias.

The National Theatre of Greece believes its staging of the works of the fifth century B.C. to be the most important part of its work. Certainly these productions are among those most often seen by outsiders. The actors in the company seem to like playing in the Greek choruses because it gives them a chance to speak and move at the same time. It is often said of the National Theatre that, even if the acting of a Greek tragedy is ordinary, the work of the chorus is always good. This is in large part thanks to the choreographers of the company, Maria M. Horss and Dora Tsatsou-Symeonidi.

The Greek National Theatre also plays an international repertory in its fall-winter season. In the last few years the most notable productions have included O'Neill's *Mourning Becomes Electra* (1971, staged by Mouzenidis), with Mary Arani as Christine and Vasa Monenidou as Lavinia; Paul Zindel's *The Effect of Gamma Rays on Man-in-the-Moon Marigolds* (1974), in a translation by Stella Kranai and staged by Lambros Kostoupolos; Georg Büchner's *Danton's Death* (1975, staged by Minotis); Schiller's *Don Carlos* (1976, staged by Salomos); George Skourt's *Knot* (1976, staged by Kostas Bakas); Shakespeare's *Twelfth Night* (1976, staged by Evangelatos); Ken Kesey's *One Flew over the Cuckoo's Nest* (1976, staged by George Massalas); Brecht's *The Visions of Simone Ma-*

chard (1976, staged by Stavros Doufexis); Margarete Lymberaki's *The Other Alexander* (1977, staged by George Massalas); Beckett's *Endgame* (1977), with Minotis as Hamm; Albert Camus' *Caligula* (1977, staged by Timarchos Moudatsakis), with Kosta Kastemas as the title character; Gregorios Xenopoulos' *The Student* (1978, staged by Stayas Papadakis); Williams' *The Glass Menagerie* (1978, staged by Michael Cacoyannis), with Vasso Mano Lidou as Amanda; Shakespeare's *King Lear* (1978, staged by Minotis, who also played the king); and August Strindberg's *The Ghost Sonata* (1979, staged by Solomos).

The Greek National Theatre is the country's oldest theatre company, and because of its tours it is the best known outside Greece. Its current director is Alexis Minotis, who works as an actor, director, and manager of the company. As is true of other large Greek companies, it has two seasons, previously described. The company is a large one (about one hundred) and employs guest artists, such as Dinos Eleopoulos, who enacted *The Amphytrion* of Plautus in 1978. The National Theatre has employed many great Greek actors, including Minotis, Paxinou, Aspasia Papathanassiou, Anna Synodinou, and Mary Arani. The theatre is also connected with an acting school.

The company generally does eight works in its fall-winter season, split between classics and modern, Greek and international. It only plays fifth century B.C. works in its outdoor summer season (generally doing four), but it does perform them indoors on tour outside Greece where stages are larger. The home theatre has two stages: a large theatre that seats about seven hundred, and a smaller theatre that has flexible seating and holds about two hundred.

The company has played rather regularly at the Theatre Festival in Paris and throughout Germany, Russia, and Japan. Its most recent tour to the United States was in honor of the bicentennial, performing Sophocles' *Oedipus at Colonus* and Aristophanes' *The Knights*. It also tours in Greece and always plays a short season in the spring in Thessaloniki. To fund all its activities, the government gives it a subsidy of around 100 million drachmas.

The Greek National Theatre has surmounted a number of obstacles to become Greece's most revered theatre. It survived economic difficulties in the 1930s, the Occupation and civil war of the 1940s, the Colonels of the 1960s and 1970s when many people (including Minotis and Paxinou) left, and the many strikes by its actors. Its strong point is undoubtedly its staging of classic Greek drama, though its work with other forms is quite good, if a trifle conservative.

LEON M. AUFDEMBERGE
(Translation help by Ionna Butzos)

STATE THEATRE OF NORTHERN GREECE
(Kratikon Theatre Voreiou Ellados)
Queen Sophia Street 2
Thessaloniki, Greece

The first permanent theatre company established in Thessaloniki (often called Salonika) since Roman times came in 1940 when the Bulgarians, then occupying the city, decided to form a theatre troupe to play in their native Bulgarian. The Greek government countered with a decision to open a theatre for the native Greeks instead, using local actors and headed by Leon Koukulas. The company generally staged two or three works a year, including Friedrich von Schiller's *Intrigue and Love*, Gregorio Martínez Sierra's *The Cradle Song*, works by Carlo Goldoni, and, of course, Greek plays, both classic and modern. At the end of the Occupation, their work done, the company disbanded, and until 1969 the city had to be satisfied with what Athens decided to tour.

In 1969, as part of the decentralization movement in the Greek theatre, the Ministry of Culture and Science opted to form a new company in Thessaloniki. Named the State Theatre of Northern Greece, it was designed to serve the local community. The first managing director was Socrates Karandinos, with the president of the artistic board (unpaid) a prominent local writer, George Theotakas. The first production was Sophocles' *Oedipus Tyrannos*, staged in the ancient theatre in Philippi and greeted by large critical and popular acclaim. This production was followed by a fall season in what was formerly the Royal Theatre. In 1962 the young company moved into a new theatre designed by architect Vassilos Kassandras and built by the Society of Macedonian Studies, which still owns the theatre but puts no pressure on the running of the company.

During the company's first years, policies were set which still govern the theatre, both in repertory style and type of plays to be performed. Before it could begin to experiment, the company wanted to serve the local community by giving it types of plays it wanted to see. Many of the plays done in the opening season were modern Greek works which the company would first play in Thessaloniki and then take on tour. Karandinos (who is still honorary manager of the company) also founded the drama festival at Philippi, where he staged several classic Greek works, including the opening *Oedipus Tyrannos* and Aristophanes' *Lysistrata* (1965). His taste in drama was wide and varied, and by the late 1960s the repertory of the company began to be very international, with Tennessee Williams and Samuel Beckett being especially popular. Although his staging was considered academic, Karandinos did encourage other young directors to be freer. His best production was undoubtedly Molière's *Don Juan* (1966), which played both the home theatre and the Athens Festival. Other noteworthy productions in his era were done by Minos Volonakis in 1965, when he staged Samuel Beckett's *Waiting for Godot* and Bertolt Brecht's *The Good Woman of Setzuan*. In the same year, the theatre began to play at the Athens Festival and continues to do so. In 1967 Karandinos was ousted by the *junta*.

The "Time of the Colonels" was a difficult time for all Greeks; those in the theatre particularly suffered because many actors were outspoken in their criticisms. George Kitsoupoulos, who was chosen to be managing director of the company, had been a theatre critic in the city; and, though he was not a stage director, he knew the theatre well. He founded the *Nea Skini* (new stage) in the nearby YMCA to present works of a more experimental or intimate nature. Although Brecht was forbidden, many other modern European writers were introduced into Thessaloniki during the period. Friedrich Dürrenmatt's *Romulus the Great* was an enormous success in 1973, when staged by Mary Vostangi, as was Max Frisch's *Count Öderland* (1974) with the production by Alexis Salomos, but perhaps the best staging of the era was done by Thomas Kotsoupolos with his production of Eugene Ionesco's *Exit the King* in 1970. Other good productions in this era were *Oedipus Tyrannos* (1968), with the production by Kotsoupolos, who also played the title role; Edmond Rostand's *Cyrano de Bergerac* (1968), with the staging by Kostis Michelidis and with Andreas Zissimatos as the long-nosed hero; Aristophanes' *Plutus* (1969), with the staging by Kyryaos Jaratsaris; Shakespeare's *King Lear* (1970), with Kotsoupolos both staging and playing the title role; Goethe's *Faust I* (1970), with the production by Spyros Evangelatos; and Aeschylus' *Prometheus Bound* (1970), with Kotsoupolos doing the staging honors. One good byproduct of the era was that Kotsoupolos chose a lot of different directors to stage Greek tragedies, and the approach was much more modern than Karandinos' textbook stagings.

Another shakeup in the government came in 1974, when both the Colonels and Kotsoupolos were ousted from their jobs. The new managing director was Minos Volanakis, who had been both an actor and a director for the company. He had been exceedingly anti-*junta* and had spent part of the years of the Colonels in exile. He quarreled with his artistic board, but he improved the company by expanding the repertory and the number of actors. He brought back Brecht with his own production of *Mr. Puntila and His Hired Man, Matti* (1976), which was probably the biggest success the company has ever had. Two other works with political overtones were staged during his short tenure: Lope de Vega's *Fuente ovejuna* (1977), with staging by George Michaeclidis; and Euripides' *Medea* (1977), with Melina Mercouri as the title character and Volonakis as the director.

In 1977 Volonakis resigned and was replaced by Spyros Evangelatos, who had already directed a number of works for this company and the National Theatre of Greece before becoming the manager for the State Theatre of Northern Greece. (Evangelatos is also managing director of Amphi-Theatre in Athens, a company founded in 1975 to do both classic and modern plays. The spirit of the company is very experimental. It has played not only in Greece, but also in Austria and Russia.) His tenure has already been marked by a number of significant changes and additions. He has encouraged the performance of many new works (both Greek and international) and has staged a series of premieres by new Greek authors. He recently founded an opera company that does two works a year from the standard repertory. His own approach to classic Greek works has been very modern (much use of masks and music) without being necessarily radical. In the last few years, the most outstanding works done by the company have been Brecht's *The Caucasian Chalk Circle* (1977, direction by Nick Pezelis); Ibsen's *Hedda Gabler* (1978, direction by Evis Gabzieidis), with Antigone Valakou as Hedda; Shakespeare's *Julius Caesar* (1978, direction by Evangelatos); and, above all, Evangelatos' production of Aeschylus' *The Persians*, which toured Romania

(1978) and the Soviet Union (1979) to triumphant crowds before playing the summer theatre circuit in Greece in 1979. In the 1979–1980 season there were two outstanding productions: Goldoni's *The Chioggian Brawls* (production by Evangelatos) and Manolis Sckouloudis' adaptation of Dostoyevsky's *The Idiot*. The summer production of 1980 was Sophocles' *Antigone*; it was staged by Evangelatos and toured Epidaurus, Philippi, and Thassos.

The State Theatre of Northern Greece has two seasons a year (interspersed with vacations): a fall-winter season (with Easter at the end), and the outdoor summer season. The company itself is large, consisting of one hundred actors (more men than women) and a large technical staff, with about three hundred people working for the theatre. Its subsidy is over 100 million drachmas, which is paid by the Greek government. The theatre mounts about twenty works a year, of which half are Greek plays, both classic and modern. The classic works, however, are mounted only for the outdoor stage. There are generally two or three ancient Greek dramas, two or three from the nineteenth or twentieth centuries, and four or five modern Greek plays with some premieres. The rest are from the international repertory with Shakespeare, Brecht, and Beckett being the most often repeated.

There are several small producing organizations within the framework of the company, including a children's theatre, the Theatre of Thrace (which plays in that area and has about fifteen actors in the company), and the *Nea Skini* (now located in the home theatre) for experimental works or small-cast plays. A recent addition to the company was a small troupe (ten to twelve actors) to play in Pontos, which is a dialect from Asia Minor that is spoken in the area by a small number of people but that, surprisingly, several actors in the company speak. In 1978 Evangelatos decided to produce a play especially written for them. In 1973 a theatre school was founded, with the company and a number of other people working for both the theatre and the school. It was the first company in Greece to play true repertory fashion.

About twenty to thirty performances are given of each major work, and a work is never yanked because it is not attracting a large audience. If a play proves very popular, it may be revived the next year, as was the successful production of *The Persians*. Most new Greek works are played in the *Nea Skini*. The company uses two theatres in the fall-winter season: the main stage, *Kenitri Skini*, which seats just over 1,000, and the *Nea Skini*, with places for 250. Since 1977 a summer season in Thessaloniki has been played in the outdoor Park Theatre. It is a popular theatre with good attendance; yet the management would like more subscriptions as most seats sold are singles and are bought at the last minute.

The theatre encourages young talent in acting, directing, and playwriting. Each year it sponsors a competition for the best new script. The winning playwright receives a financial prize, and his or her play is staged by the company. The State Theatre of Northern Greece has not produced a major play as yet, but many of the plays have been interesting.

The repertory of the company is chosen by the managing director and its dramaturge, Nikolas Bakolas, who is best known in Greece as the translator of William Faulkner's *The Sound and the Fury* and F. Scott Fitzgerald's *The Great Gatsby*. Both Evangelatos and Bakolas read many plays each year (both Greek and international) and suggest works to the artistic board (all unpaid), who then set the season. The theatre likes to keep its company stable. In the past few seasons, it has hired a number of guest artists, including Dimitris Papamihael, Aleka Katseli, Eleni Hatziargiri, Thomas Kotsoupolos, Lykourgos Kalergis, Elsa Vergi, Anna Synodinoux, Antigone Valakou, and, of course, Melina Mercouri. Most of the directors for the company are guests, with Evangelatos staging two or three works a year. The summer directors generally think Greek tragedy is easier to stage than Aristophanes' comedies, and the latter have even had some minor rewriting to bring the jokes up to date.

The State Theatre of Northern Greece does more work within a wider area than perhaps any other theatre in Europe. From its earliest seasons it has consistently tried to get as close as possible to the life of the people in the city of Thessaloniki and surrounding area. One of the activities it encourages is to send out an actor, a director, or an author (especially with a premiere) to talk to local groups about an upcoming production. It tries as much as possible to use local actors and technicians. Its main work is to present plays to Northern Greece (which is a wide area), but it also pays an annual visit to Athens at Easter, when the National Theatre visits Thessaloniki. As its director observed when asked for a statement of the philosophy of the company, ''The State Theatre of Northern Greece is a dynamic, lively theatre, for it is a theatre for everyone, for people of all walks of life, offering quality work with the best plays of the classical and contemporary stage, from Greece and abroad.''

LEON M. AUFDEMBERGE
(With thanks to Nicholas Bakolas and,
of course, Spyros Evangelatos.)

Italy

INTRODUCTION

Italy has benefited mightily from decentralization in theatre since World War II. Before the war, all theatrical roads led to or came from Rome, which is still true in cinema. There were exceptions such as Turin and Milan, which supported *stabili* (or city-sponsored companies) independent of Rome. Before the war most commercial companies were more or less based on the talents of one actor, what in English is called the actor/manager company.

After World War II, many great Italian performers left theatre for the more lucrative film industry. Since the 1950s, many have returned for part of a season, and some still build companies around themselves. Since the war, companies have been formed around Anna Magnani, Rosella Falk, Alida Valli, Vittorio Gassman, Raf Vallone, and others, who have taken a play (or two) around Italy for a season and then generally disbanded. Only one actor/manager could be said to be a permanent fixture in Italy, the playwright/actor/manager/*registra* (stage director) Eduardo de Filippo, whose Teatro di Eduardo was founded in 1945 and is still in existence. Many Italian cinema actors make a guest appearance at a *stabile*, though rather infrequently.

Italy's many touring companies play commercial hits, often from outside the country; most are based or begin rehearsals in Rome. These companies go everywhere, frequently playing in opera houses left over from the nineteenth century. Commercial theatres receive some form of government subsidy if they produce works of sufficient literary worth.

The *teatri stabili* which dot the map from Catania to Milan have done the most significant work in recent Italian theatre. Foremost among these companies is the Piccolo Teatro di Milano, founded in 1947 by the late Paolo Grassi with Giorgio Strehler. This organization has largely been the model for the rest of the companies, although it was not by any means the first *stabile* in Italy. There were permanent companies in Italy before the turn of the century, including one in Milan, the Teatro Manzoni de Milano, which was organized in 1912 by Marco Prago. Rome had one as early as 1905, the Compagnia Stabile Romana. Most of the *sta-*

bili died young but were clearly significant. Mussolini pushed for companies in cities outside Rome, but for the most part these were half-hearted. During the fascist era, Rome was practically the only place where important theatre was played.

What is a *teatro stabile*? The name translates as a company with its base in one city. However, there is an Italian saying which translates, "There is nothing so mobile as a *stabile*." Companies are funded by the Italian government, their local city, and generally the government of their local area. Therefore, all *stabili* tour in response to an obligation and to make money too. All *stabili* offer a season made up of plays from the home theatre, as well as what other *stabili* (or commercial companies) have to offer. There are *stabili* in most major cities, though in cities such as Bologna they have disappeared for political and economic reasons. Some are in smaller cities like the Stabile dell'Acquila, founded in 1965 by Luciano Fabioni.

The most important person in all these organizations is the general manager who sets the tone for the company and is usually a stage director. Most of these people are shrewd politicians (necessary in Italy to survive) and many heads of theatres in Italy are politically very leftist. As bureaucrats in Italy tend to be quite conservative, it is often difficult to get the government to cooperate with a theatre. Stage directors are almost universally leftist in Italy. A number, such as Strehler or Luca Ronconi, work internationally. Most of these produce a form of highly experimental theatre. The most experimental companies are also in Rome (generally in Trastevore); many tend to be rather short-lived, but they are very good.

The actor probably has the most difficult time in Italian theatres. Because of the *stabili*'s economic problems they usually keep small permanent companies and add actors as necessary. Some actors have protected themselves by banding into cooperatives, the best known of which is the Gruppo della Rocca, based in Florence. The cooperatives also receive government subsidy.

Italy has a good deal of theatre, and much of it is very good indeed. However, it is plagued by some distressing problems. For one thing it has too many actors who do not work often enough. This is a common problem in many countries, but in Italy it seems highly acute. Second, subsidies in the *stabili* have not kept pace with inflation. Third, currently, there is the pull of television; and on a big soccer night in Italy there are apt to be few people in any theatre. The *stabili* have countered by presenting better produced plays, but most companies tend to do fewer each season. All in all, the theatre in Italy seems secure, but it could be healthier.

LEON M. AUFDEMBERGE

COLLECTIVE COMPANY OF PARMA
(Compagnia del Collettivo)
Teatro Due, Viale Bassetti 12
43100 Parma, Italy

Unlike many professional Italian theatre companies, the Collective Company of Parma operates as a cooperative with ten members of equal standing. Although it enjoys state funds and the support of the municipality (the use of the theatre and utilities in exchange for an alternative theatre outside the circuit of national companies), it is autonomous and absorbs profits, losses, and architectural improvement costs. Founded in 1971, it evolved from a politically engaged splinter group of the University Theatre, which developed during the aftermath of the protest movement of 1968. Academic in nature, the University Theatre had been founded in 1953–1954 and was linked with international theatre festivals. The festivals have continued to provide stimulation and space to experiment for locally based companies throughout Europe and beyond.

The Collective Company of the City of Parma provides the city with about two hundred performances a year by national and international companies. Its productions number about two a year, and it has had the long-standing collaboration of Bogdan Jercoviĉ, a distinguished Yugoslav director. Major works produced in the years 1971–1981 included the following: *Blame the Devil* by Dario Fo; *Pulcinella's Son* by Eduardo de Filippo; *Criminal Novel* and *Fifth Estate* (adaptations of J. V. Philes' "L'emprecateur" and F. Camon's "Il Quinto Sato"); *Gargantua* (adapted from Rabelais' work); *God* by W. Allen; and *Project Shakespeare* (a synthesis of Shakespearean plays).

All company productions are presented in Parma, other Italian cities, and abroad at various theatre festivals.

GIANNA SOMMI PANOFSKY

GENOA'S THEATRE
(Teatro di Genova)
Via Nicolò Bacgalupo, 6
Genoa, Italy

As early as 1944, Gian Maria Guglielmino, Giannino Galloni, and Ivo Chiesa had founded a permanent company in Genoa, calling it the Teatro Sperimantle Luigi Pirandello. While the group specialized in Pirandello, it also played William Butler Yeats, Eugene O'Neill, and Ugo Betti. In 1947 Galloni and Giulio Cesare Castello became its directors. (Both were distinguished stage directors.) Under their co-directorship, the group began to play a wide repertory, including the Italian premiere of George Bernard Shaw's lengthy *Back to Methuselah* (1947, *regia* Galloni), though they did not do it all. From this company came another (whose principal director was Galloni) which was a true *stabile*, named the Teatro d'Arte della Città di Genova. Among its more important productions were Konstantin Simonov's *The Russian Question* (1947), Armand Salacrou's *The Night of Anger* (1947), and Machiavelli's *Mandragola* (1948), all staged by Galloni.

While the Teatro d'Arte was developing its brief history, another company was formed (again in 1947), the Piccolo Teatro Eleonora Duse, whose first director was Aldo Trabucco. In its first seasons it produced many stage hits from abroad, particularly England. In 1949 the Duse and the Teatro d'Arte merged, becoming the Piccolo Teatro della Città di Genova; the first directors were Roberto Rebora and Nino Furia who were heads from 1950 to 1952. The company was eventually directed by Camillo Pilotto and Nino Furia (1952–1953), Galloni and Furia (1953–1954), and Furia alone (1954–1955). Despite the frequent changes of leadership, the company established itself as one of the most important in Italy's *stabili*. It did a wide range of plays (both Italian and foreign, classic and modern), with some of Italy's most distinguished directors (particularly Alessandor Fersen and Mario Ferrero), and designers (Emmanuele Luzzati and Pier Luigi Pizzi), and a number of Italy's most distinguished actors. It was the first company to experiment with arena staging (in its first seasons) in an improvised house in the Palazzo Cattaneo Adorno. Its chief distinction, however, was in its list of works: Carlo Goldoni's *La vedova scaltra* (*The Artful Widow, regia* Galloni); Molière's *The Miser* (1950, *regia* Galloni); Goldoni's *Arlecchino, servitore di due padroni* (*The Servant of Two Masters*, 1951, *regia* Galloni); Beaumarchais' *The Barber of Seville* (1952, *regia* Fersen); Maxim Gorky's *The Petty Bourgeois* (1952, *regia* Fersen); Goldoni's *La famiglia dell'antiquario* (*The Antiquated Family*, 1953, *regia* Galloni); Jean Anouilh's *Colombe* (1954, *regia* Fersen), with Lina Volonghi (Genoa's great joy in an actress) as Madame Alexandra; and Ben Jonson's *Volpone* (1955, *regia* Fersen), with Camillo Pilotto in the title role. In 1953 *Celestina* toured in Spain, the first international tour for the company.

All of this was a plus, but the company was blighted by financial problems. Fortunately, in 1955 the company was taken over by Ivo Chiesa, one of Italy's leading men of the theatre. In 1946 Chiesa had founded the distinguished Italian theatre periodical *Sipario*. He worked as a critic and served as an administrator at the Piccolo Teatro di Milano (1952–1953). He is generally acknowledged to be one of the chief renovators of the Italian theatre since World War II. His regard for repertory has been especially praised. When Chiesa inherited the company he had a permanent theatre (on the Piazza Tommaseo), but he also had a monstrous debt and an erratic public. Chiesa pushed for excellence in production by using the Fersen-Ferrero combination in his early seasons and later Luigi Squarzina, and he had a vigorous subscription program. He also added a number of important actors to the company, especially Alberto Lionello, who joined in 1960. In addition, he kept many of the actors from earlier seasons. Among his most distinguished early productions were Achille Torelli's *I mariti* (*The Husbands*, 1955, *regia* Ferrero); Jean Giraudoux's *Ondine* (1956, *regia* Ferrero), with Valeria Valeri in the title role; Shakespeare's *Measure for Measure* (1957, *regia* Squarzina), with Renzo Ricci as the Duke; the Fabbri/Dostoyevsky *I demoni* (*The Demons*, 1957, *regia* Squarzina); Valentino Bompiani's *La Conchiglia all'orecchio* (1958, *regia* by the author); Anouilh's *L'hurluberlu* (1959, *regia* Squarzina); Eugene O'Neill's *A Moon for the Misbegotten* (1959, *regia* Virginio Puecher); Nikolai Gogol's *The Inspector General* (1959, *regia* Puecher), with Franco Parenti in the title role; the premiere of Carlo Rietmann's *La grande speranza* (*The Great Hope*, 1960, *regia* Squarzina); Ibsen's *The Pillars of Society*

(1960, *regia* Paolo Giuranna), with Lionello as Tanner and sets by Pizzi; Pirandello's *Ciascuno a suo modo* (*Each in His Own Way*, 1961, *regia* Squarzina), with Lionello as Diego; and Beaumarchais' *The Marriage of Figaro* (1962, *regia* Puecher), with Lionello as Figaro. In 1958 the company went to South America with a repertory of seven plays.

The 1962–1963 season saw a number of major changes in the company, one of which was in its theatre. Until then, the company had been playing in one house and had been doing runs of one play. In 1962 the company began playing in two major houses, the Duse and the Politeama Genovese (they are actually next to each other). The company was enlarged so that one part could play in Genoa and another could tour. In the same year, Squarzina became co-director of the company. Squarzina pushed hardest for more experimental work, particularly with the classics, and for more premieres, including his own works.

In his first season as co-director, Squarzina staged a memorable Jean-Paul Sartre's *The Devil and the Good Lord* (1962), with Lionello as Goetz. He followed this play with the greatest success the company has ever had, Goldoni's *I due gemelli Veneziani* (*The Two Venetian Twins*, 1963), with "Lionello" as the twins Zanetto/Tonio. This production toured Italy and throughout Europe (including Russia), later playing engagements in Canada (Expo '67 in Montreal) and the United States. It continued in the repertory in revivals through the late 1970s. Other notable successes in the 1960s included both classic and modern works: August Strindberg's *The Dance of Death* (1963, *regia* Squarzina); Shakespeare's *Troilus and Cressida* (1964, *regia* Squarzina), with Glauco Mauri as Thersites; Vico Faggi's *Il processo di Savona* (*The Savona Trial*, 1964, *regia* Paolo Giuranna); Arthur Miller's *After the Fall* (1964, *regia* Franco Zeffirelli), with Giorgio Albertazzi as Quentin and Monica Vitti as Maggie; O'Neill's *The Iceman Cometh* (1965, *regia* Squarzina), with Tino Buazzelli as Hickey; Shaw's *The Doctor's Dilemma* (1966, *regia* Paolo Giuranna); the premiere of Squarzina's *Emmeti* (*M.T.*, 1966, *regia* Squarzina himself); Georges Feydeau's *A Flea in Her Ear* (1966, *regia* Squarzina), with Lionello as Chandebise/Poche; Sławomir Mrożek's *Tango* (1967, *regia* Squarzina); Goldoni's *Una delle ultima sere di carnevale* (*One of the Last Evenings of Carnival*, 1968, *regia* Squarzina); Euripides' *Bacchae* (1968, *regia* Squarzina); Goldoni's *I rusteghi* (*The Rustics*, 1969, *regia* Squarzina); the Faggi/Squarzina *Cinque giorni al porto* (*Five Days at the Harbor*, 1969, *regia* Squarzina); and the Kezich/Squarzina/Flaubert *Bouvard e Pechuchet* (1969, *regia* Squarzina). Some of the productions named above, particularly Squarzina's own *Emmeti*, upset some playgoers, but at the same time attracted many new patrons. In this period the company began inviting other companies to share the facilities of the theatres, a practice the company has retained.

In the first half of the 1970s, the company continued its policies of presenting both classic and modern plays, conducting a wide range of touring (though mostly in Italy), and presenting as many premieres as possible, particularly the documentary-style productions of Squarzina.

Among the most important productions of this period were Brecht's *Mother*

Courage and Her Children (1970, *regia* Squarzina), with Lina Volonghi as Anna Fierling; a work based on the works of Molière and Mikhail Bulgakov called *Il Tartuffo ovvero Vita amori autocensura e morte in scene del signor di Molière nostro contemporaneo* (*Tartuffe or Life, Loves, Self-assessment, and Death in the Scenes of Molière, Our Contemporary*), which was adapted and staged by Squarzina (1971), with Eros Pagni in the protagonist's role; Enzo De Benart, Squarzina, and Ruggero Zangrandi's *8 Settembre* (1971, *regia* Squarzina), which was a premiere; Shakespeare's *Julius Caesar* (1971, *regia* Squarzina); Brecht's *The Caucasian Chalk Circle* (1974, *regia* Squarzina), with Pagni as Azdak; O'Neill's *Long Day's Journey into Night* (1974, *regia* Squarzina), with Lilla Brignone as Mary Tyrone; Peter Shaffer's *Equus* (1975, *regia* by the young Marco Sciaccaluga), with Pagni as the analyst and Giovanni Crippa as the boy; the premiere of the Faggi/Squarzina *Rosa Luxemburg* (1976, *regia* Squarzina), with Adriana Asti in the title role; and Squarzina's farewell production with the company, Aleksandr Ostrovsky's *The Forest* (1976).

In 1976 Squarzina left the company to become head of the Teatro di Roma; Chiesa has led the company alone since that time. In many ways the company's policies remain the same, particularly in terms of the repertory and the actors it uses. In recent years there has been a more experimental approach to the classics, as well as fewer premieres. The company's most recent outstanding productions include Edward Bond's *The Sea* (1976, *regia* Armando Pugliese); Ibsen's *The Wild Duck* (1977, *regia* Luca Ronconi); Friedrich Dürrenmatt's *The Accomplice* (1977, *regia* Marco Sciccaluga); Arthur Schnitzler's *The Green Cockatoo* and *Countess Mizzi* (1978, *regia* Ronconi); Molière's *The Learned Ladies* (1978, *regia* Sciaccaluga); Goldoni's *La donna serpente* (*The Snake Woman*, 1979, *regia* Egisto Marucci); Alain-René Lesage's *Turcaret* (1979, *regia* Marucci), with Pagni in the title role; Remigo Zena's *La bocca del Lupo* (*The Wolf's Mouth*, 1980, *regia* Sciaccaluga), done in the local dialect; Arthur Miller's *The American Clock* (1981, *regia* Elio Petri); Frank Wedekind's *King Nicolo* (1981, *regia* Egisto Marucci); and Thomas Middleton's *Women Beware Women* (1981, *regia* Terry Hands).

Genoa's Theatre has two houses in its home city: the Politeama Genovese (which seats eleven hundred) and the Teatro Eleonora Duse (which seats six hundred). The Genovese is actually an old theatre, dating from 1871 (architect N. Bruno). It was damaged in the war but reopened in 1955 (architects Dante Datta and Marco Lavarello). The Duse was built in 1953 by the same architects. The company generally does three or four major works a season, and several revivals. The season is made up of the plays from the home company, as well as a wide number from other theatres. (In the 1981–1982 season there were sixteen in all.)

The company has played in approximately 130 Italian cities and towns, with all major productions playing Milan and Rome. In addition, it has done several international tours, notably with *I due gemelli Veneziani*, and Goldoni's *La donna serpente* was recently taken to Russia. The acting company numbers from forty to sixty, depending on the season and the number of revivals. Generally there are three or four stage directors (*registras*) each season.

The company tends toward the left, but not in any doctrinaire fashion. Plays are selected for their reflection of contemporary life, whereas *registras* are selected for their experimental approach to staging. One of the company's best features is the publication of its play scripts. Before a play opens, its text is available, with articles about the play and the social conditions that produced the work. The company also has a theatre school of approximately thirty students who work with the troupe. As with most *stabili*, much of the company's budget derives from its subsidy. In its 1978–1979 season the total budget for the company came to over 2 billion lira, of which the stage contributed 650 million, the city of Genoa 386 million, the province of Genoa 45 million, the Ligura Regione 72.5 million, the Cassa di Risparmio of Genoa 6 million, the Consorzio del Porto 1 million, and the Camera di Commercil 10 million. The rest came from box office receipts. In addition to its productions, the company has close ties with the local theatre museum, currently the Civico Museo Biblioteca dell'attore, which has just moved to new quarters in the Villetta Serra. Its current director is Sandro D'Amico. The museum is noted for its excellent library, its collection of costumes of Adelaide Ristori, and the archives of Tomasso Salvini. Recently, the museum has begun a new journal, *Teatro Archivo*.

From its early beginnings, with its small theatre, to the present two houses, the company has had a rather steady history of excellence, mostly because of the persistence of its much-admired head, Ivo Chiesa. In summing up the excellence of the company, one would note the high literary quality of the theatre's productions, coupled with a distinguished acting company and a series of varied *registras*. In the 1980–1981 season the city of Genoa honored Chiesa for his twenty-five years of service to the city. Many people have since remarked that the honor was small in proportion to what Chiesa had done for the city.

LEON M. AUFDEMBERGE
(With thanks to Salvatore Arico and
Carlo Repetti of the company.)

GIACOMO CUTICCHIO'S PUPPET THEATRE
(Teatro dei Pupi Giacomo Cuticchio)
Vicolo Ragusi, 6
Palermo, Sicily

The great days of Sicilian puppetry date back to the nineteenth century. The plots of most plays deal with the Paladins, of the days of the wars between the Saracens (Evil) and the Christians (Good). The characters are easily recognized: Christians are always stage right, the Saracens on the left; Saracens wear baggy trousers, Christians wear various distinguishing emblems—Orlando wears an eagle on his helmet and a cross on his shield, while Rinaldo has a lion with a bar on his shield; green means evil, red equals valor. In the past, the plays performed were like old movie serials, to be continued the next night. Now, the theatres present one long play.

The Cuticchio family owns two theatres in Palermo: Giacomo Cuticchio has the theatre in the Vicolo Ragusi, and Giralomo Cuticchio has a theatre in the Via Bara. All puppets come from the family's workshop near the Duomo. The theatres are owned and operated by family members. The one on the Vicolo Ragusi is owned by Giacomo, the father, who is in retirement. His wife sells the tickets (1,500 lira) from a window and takes care of the souvenir business (pieces of scenery, booklets, postcards, and the puppets themselves). One of the granddaughters operates the player piano. Two of the sons do most of the manipulation of the puppets, aided by a grandson. Two sons also do the male voices, while a daughter does the voices for all the female roles. In the workshop, Mimmo (from the other Cuticchio branch) makes the metal parts of the puppets; Guido makes the rest, while their mother makes costumes. A grandson, Giacomo, helps with the manipulation; he likes the work but thinks it has no future. It is on Mimmo and Guido that both theatres seem to depend.

The theatre sits on an alley, and performances begin around nine. First, there is a long overture, played by the granddaughter on the player piano. This is followed by a somewhat corny prologue by a puppet who smokes a pipe, which the family says is strictly for the tourists. Then comes the play. There are sometimes long waits between scenes, though no one seems to mind. The puppets are manipulated like marionettes, with rods as they are far too heavy for strings. They can do almost anything an actor can do (draw swords, move their heads, and so on). All entrances are announced by another puppet, and battles are fought with much stomping and shouting by the manipulators. The sets are colorful, if garish. It is all quite enjoyable and done as if among friends.

The great days of the Sicilian puppet theatre are clearly over; what one sees now is the tail end of a dying art. Although the puppets look as good as ever, the manipulation is clumsy and the voices are mediocre at best. Still it is an art form meriting preservation. The Italian government is making some effort, through a small subsidy, to keep it alive, though clearly it is not enough. Most of the family members work other jobs, and the grandchildren seem to favor other professions. In the last few years, the theatre has gone to Rome, Spoleto, Turin, and Berlin to help pay bills. Part of the charm of the performances comes with the theatres themselves. Sicilians seem to prefer television and, thus, may be losing one of their authentic art forms at a time when critical and scholarly interest in puppetry is at its height.

LEON M. AUFDEMBERGE

LITTLE THEATRE OF MILAN
(Piccolo Teatro di Milano)
Via Rovello, 2
Milan, Italy

After World War II, Milan was the first city to found a still-existent *stabile*, the Little Theatre of Milan (the Piccolo). The company was founded in 1947 by

Paolo Grassi, its first director, and Giorgio Strechler, its principal *registra* and current head. At that time Milan was an impoverished city. Consequently, when the company was given an old movie theatre (the Excelsior), it seemed likely that it would follow the pattern of other companies by surviving only a few years. But the theatre still exists largely through the efforts of Grassi and Strehler.

Grassi was best known as a critic (mostly for *Avanti*), though he had also been a *registra* for several companies before founding the Piccolo. Strehler had also been both a critic and *registra*, as well as an actor, who had worked with Grassi in an avant-garde company, the Palcoscenico, in the early 1940s. Strehler had escaped to Switzerland during the war and had worked with several companies there before returning to Italy in 1945. At the time of the founding of the Piccolo, it was evident that the two men knew about the theatre from various angles.

The first performance for the Piccolo came on May 14, with Maxim Gorky's play, *The Lower Depths*, staged by Strehler. In many ways the choice of play was an odd one. Gorky's play has a rather depressing philosophy and seems rather downbeat for the Milanese public of that time. On the other hand, it does have a message of hope and is not a play of despair. The play was well attended. From the very beginning, the Piccolo was considered one of Italy's most important theatre companies. In the same season it was invited to play *The Lower Depths* at the International Theatre Festival in Venice. Among the young company of twenty-five were a number of actors who have since become known internationally, largely through their work with the company: Lilla Brignone, Marcello Moretti, Giorgio de Lullo, and Gianni Santuccio. Acting occasionally, Strehler played Alyosha in the opener, which also had an excellent designer in Gianni Ratto.

In the first season, the company played Salacrou and Calderón; then followed the work that made the company internationally famous, Strehler's staging of Carlo Goldoni's *Arlecchino, Servitori di due padroni* (*The Servant of Two Masters*, 1947), with Moretti in the title role. If one were to select the most famous single production in Italy since 1945, it would certainly be this one. This work started the Goldoni revival, which continues to the present not only in Italy but also outside. Strehler focused on the theatrical quality of the *commedia dell'arte* elements in the script, and the work was played quite lightly (but truthfully). Since then the work has been revived constantly and has played on every habitable continent, except Australia, in thirty foreign countries (including cities in the United States and the Soviet Union in the 1959–1960 season), 159 Italian towns, and 160 foreign locales. Moretti was Arlecchino until his death in 1961; in recent years the role has been played by Ferruccio Soleri. Since this work, Strehler has gone on to stage eight more Goldoni works for the company.

In its first seasons, the Piccolo toured Italy, and then in the 1949–1950 season, it took its prize Goldoni work to Switzerland. During this time it produced a gigantic number of successes characterized by the poetic realistic style of the company, a style that is still in evidence. A partial list of the significant works in the first years would include the following (unless otherwise specified Strehler was the *registra*): Luigi Pirandello's *I giganti della montagne* (*The Giants of the Mountain*, 1947); Molière's *Don Juan* (1948, *regia* Orazio Costa), with Santuccio in the title role; Shakespeare's *Richard II*, with Santuccio in the title role, and *The Tempest* (1948); T. S. Eliot's *Murder in the Cathedral* (1948), with Santuccio as Thomas; Carlo Gozzi's *Il Corvo* (*The Crow*, 1948); Chekhov's *The Seagull* (1948), with Brignone as Arkadina; Thornton Wilder's *The Skin of Our Teeth* (1948), with Brignone as Sabina; Shakespeare's *The Taming of the Shrew* (1949); Pirandello's *Questa sera si recitta a soggetto* (*Tonight We Improvise*, 1949); Henry Becque's *La Parisienne* (1950), with Brignone as Clotilde; Shakespeare's *Richard III* (1950), with Renzo Ricci in the title role; Goldoni's *La putta onorata* (*The Honored Maiden*, 1950) and *Gl' innamorati* (*The Lovers*, 1950); Tennessee Williams' *Summer and Smoke* (1950), with Brignone as Alma; Molière's *The Misanthrope* (1950); Georg Büchner's *Danton's Death* (1950); Ibsen's *A Doll's House* (1951), with Brignone as Nora; Alfred de Musset's *You Can't Think of Everything* (1951); Shakespeare's *Henry IV* (1951), with de Lullo as Hal; Shakespeare's *Twelfth Night* (1951); Sophocles' *Electra* (1951), with Brignone in the title role; Goldoni's *L'amante militaire* (*The Military Lover*, 1951); Ernst Toller's *Hoppla! We're Alive* (1951); and Shakespeare's *Macbeth* (1952), with Santuccio in the title role.

In 1952 the theatre was completely renovated by Marco Zanuso and Ernesto N. Rogers, opening with Ferdinand Bruckner's *Elizabeth of England*, staged by Strehler, with Brignone in the title role. By this time the company had more than established itself as preeminent among the *stabili* in Italy. The company toured in Italy and outside in the early 1950s, adding new triumphs. The repertory for the Piccolo in the early 1950s began to change to a concentration on two areas: classic plays (especially Shakespeare and Goldoni) and plays from contemporary Italy (including some premieres). New actors began to work with the company at this time, including Laura Adani, Tino Carraro, Tino Buazzelli, and Sara Ferrati. What emerged in these years was the same sort of productions produced earlier: Nikolai Gogol's *The Inspector General* (1952), with Moretti as Chelestakov; Luigi Pirandello's *Sei personaggi in cerca d'autore* (*Six Characters in Search of an Author*, 1953); Carlo Bertolazzi's *Lulù* (1953), with Brignone in the title role; a premiere of Dino Buazzatti's *Un caso clinico* (*A Clinical Case*, 1953); Goldoni's *La vedova scaltra* (*The Crafty Widow*, 1953), with Adani as Rosaura; Shakespeare's *Julius Caesar* (1953), with Carraro as Brutus; the premiere of Enzo d'Errico's *La sei giorni* (*The Six Days*, 1953); Jean Giraudoux's *The Madwoman of Chaillot* (1954), with Ferrati in the title role; Goldoni's *La trilogia della villeggiature* (*The Trilogy of Country Dwellers*, 1954), with Carraro as Leonardo; Chekhov's *The Cherry Orchard* (1955), with Ferrati as Madame Ranevskaya; Federico García Lorca's *The House of Bernarda Alba* (1955); and Luigi Squarzina's *Tre quarti di luna* (*Three Quarters of the Moon*, 1955).

The mid-1950s marked a number of changes for the company. In 1955 Strehler was made a co-director with Grassi, which meant both participated equally in the company's decision-making. In terms of repertory, the company continued to play Shakespeare and Goldoni, as well as the usual Italians, and began to play documentary-style works (in the Milanese dialect) and a writer who became a specialty with the company, Bertolt Brecht. In 1952 Lucian Damiani joined the company to become its resident designer, with most of his major work coming after 1955. Needless to say, the company continued its policy of touring both in Italy and throughout Europe, with regular trips to Paris.

The first production Strehler staged in his co-directorship was an adaptation of Carlo Bertolazzi's *La povera gent* (*The Poor People*), played in the Milanese dialect and entitled *El nost Milan* (*Our Milan*, 1955), which was staged in a Brechtian/documentary style with sets by Damiani. Strehler followed this with a production of the Brecht/Kurt Weill *The Threepenny Opera* (1956), with sets by Teo Otto and with Mackie Messer played by Carraro. Both were huge successes and were revived both for Milanese audiences and on tour. Other productions staged in the late 1950s included Giovanni Verga's *Dal tuo al mio* (*From Yours to Mine*, 1956); Federico Zardi's *I giacobini* (*The Jacobites*, 1956), with Carraro as Robespierre; Shakespeare's *Coriolanus* (1957), with Carraro in the title role; Paolo Ferrari's *Goldoni e le sue sedici commede nuove* (*Goldoni and His Sixteen New Plays*, 1957), with Carraro as Goldoni; Brecht's fable, *The Good Woman of Setzuan* (1958), with Valentina Fortunato as Shen Te/Shui Ta; Pasquale Altavilla's *Pulcinella in cerca della sua Fortune* (*Pulcinella in Search of Fortune*, 1958, *regia* Eduardo de Filippo), with Achille Millo as Pulcinella; and Chekhov's *Platonov, or A Country Scandal* (1959), with Carraro in the title role.

From 1960 to 1968 (when Strehler left for a while), there were few large changes in the company. The repertory still concentrated on the big three: Shakespeare, Brecht, and Goldoni. Perhaps the major change was that Strehler began to share more staging duties with outside *registras*. Thus, the big productions of the 1960s were staged not only by Strehler, but also by some of Italy's best *registras*. The important productions of this era included Carlo Bertolazzi's *L'egoista* (*The Egoist*, 1960); Friedrich Dürrenmatt's *The Visit from the Old Lady* (1960), with Ferrati as Claire; Brecht's *Schweyk in the Second World War* (1961), with Tino Buazzelli in the title role; Pirandello's *Henry IV* (1962, *regia* Orazio Costa), with Carraro as the king; Brecht's *The Life of Galileo* (1963), with Buazzelli as Galileo; Eliot's *Murder in the Cathedral* (1964), *regia* Mario Missiroli; Goldoni's *La baruffe Chiozzette* (*The Chioggian Brawls*, 1964); Molière's *Monsieur de Pourceaugnac* (1965, *regia* Filippo); an adaptation in two parts by Strehler of Shakespeare's *Henry VI* trilogy, entitled *Il gioco die potenti* (*The Game of the Powerful*, 1965), with Renato de Carmine as Henry VI and Corrado Pani as Richard III; the Jean-Paul Sartre/Euripides *Trojan Women* (1965, *regia* Fulvio Tolusso), with Lina Volonghi as Hecuba; Arnold Wesker's *Chips with Everything* (1966, *regia* Rafaele Maiello); and the Peter Weiss *Marat/Sade* play, with sets by René Allio (1967, *regia* Maiello).

From 1968 to 1972 Grassi ran the theatre alone, with Strehler working principally with the Gruppo Teatro e Azione. During these seasons Grassi emphasized modern plays and obviously included some classics. Most of the *registras* used by the company were young and highly experimental, and not all of them were Italian. The company did fairly well in these seasons, but it sadly needed Strehler. Much of what was done during Grassi's solo era was well received, however, with the following works standing out: Arthur Adamov's *Off Limits* (1969, *regia* Grüber); Shakespeare's *Timon of Athens* (1969, *regia* Marcello Bellochi), with Salvo Randone in the title role; Brecht's *Saint Joan of the Stockyards* (1970), with Cortese as Johanna Dark and with Strehler doing the staging in a return visit; Pablo Neruda's *Splendor and Death of Joaquin Muriet* (1970, *regia* Patrice Chéreau); Tankred Dorst's *Toller* (1970, *regia* Chéreau); and Frank Wedekind's *Lulu* (1972, *regia* Chéreau again), with Cortese in the title role. In 1972 Grassi left the Piccolo to become head of La Scala, a post he held until 1976, when he quit over funding difficulties because the government refused him a subsidy to send the opera company to New York. (It came anyway, but Grassi decided to quit.) On March 14, 1981, Grassi died in Milan, missed by all who love the theatre.

Strehler returned to the Piccolo in 1972 to run the company alone, and these have been good years. He continues to stage plays with the same precision and logic that marked his early work with the company, though admittedly not as often. He continues to bring new people to the company, most recently a designer, Ezio Frigerio, who works alongside Damiani. To sum up what the company has done in the last few years would include Shakespeare's *King Lear* (1972), with Tino Carraro in the title role; the Brecht/Weill *The Threepenny Opera* (1973), with Domenico Modugno as Mackie; Massimo Dursi's *La vita scellerata del Nobile Signor Barbalú e la vita illuminata del suo re* (*The Wicked Life of the Noble Lord Bluebeard and the Illuminated Life of His King*, 1973, *regia* Lamberto Puggelli), with Francesco Graziosi as Bluebeard; Chekhov's *The Cherry Orchard* (1974), with Cortese as Madame Ranevskaya; Goldoni's *Il Campiello* (*The Little Plaza*, 1975); George Bernard Shaw's *Widower's Houses* (1976, *regia* Carlo Battistoni); Jean Genet's *The Balcony* (1976); the premiere of the Alfonso Sastre/Brecht/Strehler *La storia della bambola abbandonata* (*The Story of the Abandoned Doll*, 1977); Shakespeare's *The Tempest* (1978), with Carraro as Prospero; Molière's *The School for Wives* (1978, *regia* Enrico D'Amato), with Graziosi as Arnolf; Samuel Beckett's *Waiting for Godot* (1978, *regia* Walter Pagliaro); Pedro Calderón's *Life Is a Dream* (1980); August Strindberg's *Stormy Weather* (1980), with Carraro as the Gentlemen; Massimo Bontempelli's *Minn'e e la candida* (1980, *regia* Battistoni); and Brecht's *The Good Woman of Setzuan* (1981), with Andrea Jonasson as Shen Te/Shui Ta.

The Piccolo generally mounts three or four productions a year, as well as an indeterminate number of revivals to send on tour. Strehler generally stages one of the new productions. The main theatre is its own house, which seats a comfortable 650 (Brecht called it "a great little theatre"), and had been a palace, movie-house, and night club before the Piccolo took it over. It also uses the larger Teatro Lirico, one of Milan's most pleasant theatres, and plays other theatres in the city as well. The company generally numbers about forty during the season, with most actors hired for one play. The troupe gives about 350 performances a year over a ten-month period, with July and August being the dark months. Most of Italy's most famous actors, whose main reputation is stage work, have worked for the Piccolo at one time or another.

One of the most evident characteristics of the Piccolo is the high literary quality of the plays, which is a product of both Grassi's and Strehler's approaches to theatre. Both had been critics and knew the dangers of doing works for the sheer joy. More than anything else, the Piccolo has been noted for coupling the quality of its plays with its productions. Not only has Strehler staged plays eloquently, but he has also written about them with a good deal of insight. Fortunately, he has expressed his thoughts on theatre in *Per un teatro umano* (Milan: Feltrinelli,1974). He has also published production notes for several of his plays. Unfortunately, none of these is as yet available in English.

The company is interested in what the people want to see and in how well the company can do it. Accordingly, Strehler spends a great deal of his time talking to both his theatre staff and theatregoers. In this concern, the Piccolo has served as a model for the rest of the *stabili* in Italy, and the company has set the mark for similar companies throughout the world. It has always been a theatre for the people, and the public has reciprocated by filling the theatre season after season. (The sold-out record for the company in the last few seasons is almost total.) It is truly a humanist's theatre.

LEON M. AUFDEMBERGE
(With thanks to the publicity
department of the theatre.)

PERMANENT THEATRE OF AQUILA
(Teatro Stabile dell, Aquila)
Via Roma, 54
Aquila, Italy

In 1963 Luciano Fabiani, a local resident of Aquila, decided that what the city needed most was a *stabile*. His first problem in getting the city a company was an economic one. The Italian Ministry of Culture had decreed that no city under a certain population could have a *stabile*. (The city currently has sixty thousand inhabitants and was not much smaller at the time.) Fabiani persevered, however, and in the 1964–1965 season the Permanent Theatre of Aquila was born, with Fabiani as its first head. The first play produced was Luigi Pirandello's *L'uomo la bestia e la virtù* (*Man, Beast, and Virtue, regia* Paolo Giuranna), with Achille Millo (Aquila's first mainstay as an actor) as Paolino. The second was Carlo Gozzi's fable *L'amore della tre melarance* (*The Love of Three Oranges, regia* Silvano Agosti), which featured puppets by Maria Signorelli. This production also played at the Festival of Marionettes in Bucharest in the same season.

In the first seasons the company began to tour, particularly in the Abruzzi. Fabiani pushed for subscriptions, promising audiences highly polished productions staged by some of Italy's best *registras* and involving notable actors. In these early seasons (generally the company was doing two productions a year), there were Ignazio Silone's *Ed egli si nascose* (*And He Himself Is Hidden*, 1965, *regia* Giacomo Colli); the premiere of Italo Svevo's *L'aventura di Maria* (1966, *regia* Mario Maranzana), with Franca Nuti in the title role; Vittorio Alfieri's classic *Il divorzio* (*The Divorce*, 1967, *regia* Paolo Giuranna): Molière's *Tartuffe* (1967, *regia* Giuranna); Ferdinando Galiani's *Socrate immaginario* (*Imaginary Socrates*, 1968, *regia* Giovanni Poli); the John Osborne/Lope de Vega *A Bond Honored* (1968, *regia* Luigi Durissi), which played at the Rassegna in Venice Vicenza; and August Strindberg's *The Pelican* (1968, *regia* Giampiero Calasso).

In the 1968–1969 season Antonio Calenda staged his first work with the company, the premiere of Alberto Moravia's *Il Dio Kurt* (*The God Kurt*), with Luigi Proietti in the title role. This was an enormous success for the company and marked the beginning of a long association with Calenda, which continues today. The same season featured another strong premiere, Ignazio Silone's *L'aventura d'un povero Cristiano* (*The Adventure of a Poor Christian*), which later played at the Theatre Festival of San Miniato. In 1969 Calenda staged Shakespeare's *Coriolanus* with the company.

In the next season (1969–1970) Calenda had two astonishing successes which established the company internationally. The first was the premiere of Witold Gombrowicz's fantastic *The Operetta*, with sets by Franco Nonnis and music by Fiorenzo Carpi and Luigi Proietti. This work has recently been revived by the company. The second was a highly mythic production of Aeschylus' *Oresteia*.

By the early 1970s, the company began to mount more plays each season (with Calenda generally doing two) and to send revivals of its successes on the road. In addition, the company began to rely on bigger name artists and became famous for its playing of classic works, most notably Shakespeare and large-scale Italian works from the past. During this era, the critics and the public responded favorably to a number of productions, such as Pietro Aretino's *La Cortigiana* (*The Courtiers*, 1970, *regia* Calenda); the anonymous Elizabethan *Arden of Feversham* (1971, *regia* Aldo Trionfo); Jean Giraudoux's *The Madwoman of Chaillot* (1972, *regia* Giancarlo Cobelli), with Piera Degli Esposti in the title role; Gabriele D'Annunzio's *La figlia di Iorio* (*The Daughter of Iorio*, 1973, *regia* Cobelli), with Degli Esposti in the protagonist's role; Sem Bellini's *La cena della beffe* (*The Mocker's Supper*, 1974, with the *regia*, costumes, and sets by Carmelo Bene); Tasso's *Aminta* (1974, *regia* Cobelli); and Shakespeare's *Antony and Cleopatra* (1974, *regia* Cobelli), with Degli Esposti and Tino Schirinzi as the lovers.

Since the mid-1970s even more attention has been paid to the classics and to touring in Italy. In addition, Fabiani expanded his seasons to include more performances of plays produced in the home theatre, plus productions from outside. Recent successes for the company have included Sophocles' *Antigone* (1976, *regia* Calenda); the Italian premiere of Bond's *Lear* (1976, *regia* Calenda), with Giampiero Fortebraccio in the title role; Alberto Gozzi's *Casa Mozart* (*Mozart's House*, 1976, *regia* by the author); Shakespeare's *As You Like It* (1977, *regia* Calenda), with Lorenza Guerrieri as Rosalind; an anonymous religious play by a writer of the Abruzzi region (from the sixteenth century) entitled *Rappresentazione della Passione* (*Representation of the Passion*, 1978, adapted and staged by Calenda), which had its premiere in the Chiesa di Pietro a Coppito and later played in Aquila at the church of Santa Maria di Collemaggio; the Brecht/Gorky *The Mother* (1978, *regia* Calenda), with Pupella Maggio in the title role; a much-toured success with Shakespeare's *Richard III* (1979, *regia* Calenda), with Glauco Mauri in the title role; and a double bill of Samuel Beckett's *Krapp's Last Tape*, with Mauri in the title role; and Edward Albee's *The Zoo Story* (1980, *regia* Mauri).

In the 1980–1981 season Errico Centofani (who had been a vice director with Fabiani) took over as head. In his first two seasons, he continued to do the same kind of plays with the same *registras* as were done in the Fabiani era. (Fabiani continues as an advisor.) So far, there have been major successes in a new production of Gombrowicz's *The Operetta* (1980); Fabio Doplicher's *La parola e i Fuochi* (*The Word and the Fire*, 1980, *regia* Calenda, choreography by Amedeo Amodio), which was done on Italian television for Christmas 1980; and Rainer Maria Fassbinder's *Bremen Freedom* (1981, *regia* Maurizio Di Mattia).

The Permanent Theatre of Aquila does three or four productions a year, with six more added to make a season. The company plays around two hundred performances a year in either Aquila or on tour. The company frequently plays in the Abruzzi in such cities as Rieti, Todi, Perugia, and Spoleto. Large-scale works play in Rome, Florence, Milan, and so on; the company has played in Sicily and in cities of the far north. There have been performances at the festivals in Spoleto, Florence, and Venice. In May 1981 the company flew to Canada to play its passion play at the Toronto Theatre Festival (the city has a large Italian population), as well as in Ottawa and Thorald. The company wants to visit the United States in the near future.

The company is varied in terms of number of actors and actresses. Four make their home in the city, and about twenty-five to thirty others are hired in an average season. The company usually plays in the Communale (with seven hundred seats), but it has also played in the outdoor theatre in the city, in churches, in other theatres in the city, and in schools. The current budget for the company is 1.7 billion lira, of which 800 million is subsidy (paid by Rome, Aquila, and the Abruzzi Province).

The company selects plays that reflect contemporary social realities. Both directors of the company believe that theatre can change people; hence, they stress plays with some sort of social criticism. (There are obvious exceptions, of course.) In terms of playing style, the company is noted for its frequent experimentation (often in classics) with a variety of approaches, and the company is notably antinaturalistic. If one could choose one word to characterize the group, it would be vitality. Since Aquila is located away from any large city, the company has been free to develop in its own way. When it was founded, there were few subscribers; now it has the largest number of subscribers in percentage to population of any *stabile* in Italy (currently around two thousand). Casual visitors to the city are amazed by how many people know about the company, and it is an object of civic pride.

LEON M. AUFDEMBERGE
(With thanks to both Luciano Fabiani
and Errico Centofanti)

PERMANENT THEATRE OF BOLZANO
(Teatro Stabile di Bolzano)
13 Gall, Telser Telserdurchgang
Bolzano, Italy

Fantassio Piccoli had worked in various capacities in the Italian theatre since the 1920s, but during World War II he worked as a journalist. In 1947 he had founded, with a group of young actors, the Carrozone, which toured the north of Italy with a variety of plays, mostly classic Italian. In the young company were Valentino Fortunato, Adrian Asti, and Romolo Valli, as well as the *registra*, Aldo Trionfo. Among the works Piccoli staged for this company were Carlo Goldoni's *Un curioso accidente* (*A Curious Accident*, 1947); the anonymous eighteenth-century religious play (adapted by Jocopone da Todi) *Istoria de Jesù Nazareno* (*History of Jesus of Nazareth*, 1948); Goldoni's *Il Talismano* (*The Talisman*, 1949); and Plautus' *Miles Gloriosus* (1949). The Carrozone had such a fine reputation that in 1950 it was invited to become the Permanent Theatre of Bolzano with its most illustrious actors becoming part of the company.

Bolzano is a city in the extreme north of Italy, close to Austria, and German is frequently heard in the streets. During World War II, it was heavily bombed, and much of the city is new. In 1950 it needed something to boost civic pride, and a *stabile* seemed an important adjunct to the life of the city, though this did not mean the new company had an easy time. From the first, there were financial and physical problems. In terms of style, Piccoli stressed certain aspects: stylized scenery with heavy use of lighting (his main designer was Gianfranco Padovani) and a light, agile manner of playing, in contrast to the neorealism sweeping through Italian art of the time. The first theatre for the company, which was not altogether satisfactory, was the hall in the Conservatorio Monteverdi (with around six hundred seats).

In the first seasons the company toured, starting first in the North of Italy and moving gradually to more and more cities in the South. The repertory was international in scope, and in the first season the theatre gained an admirable reputation with a variety of vehicles (until 1966 all uncredited productions are

by Piccoli): a new production of Plautus' *Miles Gloriosus* (1951); Ferenc Molnár's *Liliom* (1951), with Valli as Liliom; Shakespeare's *Twelfth Night* (1951);
Euripides' *Medea* (1951); Chekhov's *Uncle Vanya* (1952), with Valli as Vanya;
and Cesare Meano's *Melisenda per me* (*Melisenda for Me*, 1953).

By 1953 the news was good and bad. The good news was that the theatre
company had become one of the most prestigious in Italy. The bad was that the
acting company was so good it was soon depleted, with its four most famous
artists going to other *stabili* (particularly in Milan) and later to films. Fortunately,
one actor who had been with Piccoli from the first became Piccoli's mainstay,
Ugo Bologna. (He would leave in 1957.) During the 1950s the company widened
its touring activities, playing Rome in the 1954–1955 season. The same season
it began inviting other companies to come to Bolzano, and soon after it went
outside Italy, to nearby Innsbruck. It had two serious problems in the 1950s:
changing theatres and financial difficulties. The company had lost its first theatre
early on, and, during the 1950s, it played in three cinemas in the city and a
hotel, all of which were difficult to set and light. In 1956 Memo Benassi, one
of Italy's grand old actors, was set to do the title role in Shakespeare's *King
Lear* when he grew sick and eventually died, which made the company lose
money from a prospective tour. During the 1950s, however, Piccoli would stage
many excellent plays: Silvio Giovanninetti's *Sangue verde* (*Green Blood*, 1953);
Ibsen's *The Lady from the Sea* (1955), with Germana Monteverdi as Ellida;
Alexandre Dumas *fils*' *The Lady of the Camellias*, with Monteverdi as Mar-
guerite; Shakespeare's *King Lear* (1957), with Annibale Ninchi as Lear, and
The Merchant of Venice (1958), with Ninchi as Shylock; García Lorca's *Dona
Rosita Remains Single* (1959); and Paul Claudel's *The Tidings as Brought to
Mary*, with Bruna Tellah as Violaine.

One of the last things Piccoli had done was to combine the company with the
city of Trento (Trent), becoming the Teatro Stabile Trento e Bolzano (the order
of names bothered Bolzano a lot). In 1966 Piccoli finally gave up, partly because
of finances and partly because too many productions were staged. The distinguished actor/*registra* Renzo Ricci took over for one good season (1966–1967),
including two fine productions, both of which he staged: Pirandello's *Henry IV*,
with himself in the title role, and Eugene O'Neill's *Long Day's Journey into
Night*, with Ricci and Eva Magni playing the elder Tyrones. Renzo Giovampietro
took over for one season (1967–1968), and he was responsible for three good
productions: Francesco Della Corte's *Processo per magia* (*Trial by Magic*);
Plautus' *The Twin Menaechmi*; and Cicerone's *Il governo di verre* (*The Governor
of Boars*), all staged by Giovampietro.

In 1968–1969 there was no artistic head, but Mario Antonelli and Pietro
Privitera made the decisions for the company. In this season the company re-
claimed its former name and began a subscription program. That season saw
two good works: Carlo Marcello Reitmann's *Il vento sotto la porta* (*The Wind
Under the Door*) and the early part of George Bernard Shaw's *Back to Methuselah*
(both directed by Privitera) in an Italian premiere. During this season the company

solved one of its recurrent problems, a permanent theatre, not with one but two theatres. The first to open was the Haus de Kulter, which was a big cultural center for the city; and the second, which opened soon after, was the Teatro Communale in Gries (in the western part of the city), which was specially renovated for the company.

The six seasons Maurizio Scaparro took over the company (1969–1975) were very good, in terms of both plays and acting, which meant more people on subscription. Scaparro brought a number of new works to Italy, some of them controversial, and most of them prompting discussion. In addition, a number of actors worked with the company for the first time, including Mario Scaccia, Laura Adani, Giustino Durano, and Pino Micol. Scaparro attracted a regular audience through the vigor of his productions, which were frequently experimental and challenging. Among the plays of these years were a number of works that brought both critical and audience pleasure (uncredited productions are Scaparro's): Ettore Petrolin's *Chiccignola* (1969), with Scaccia as the protagonist; Georges Feydeau's *What Shall We Tell People?* (1970, *regia* Scaccia); Michel de Ghelderode's *Red Magic* (1970); Strindberg's *The Father* (1970), with Scaccia in the title role; Saul Bellow's *The Last Analysis* (1971), with Scaccia as Bummy; Ariosto's *La Lena* (*The Breath*), with Adani in the protagonist's role; Nikolai Erdman's *The Suicide* (1972, *regia* Ruggero Miti), with Giustino Durano in the title role; Jan Kott's production of Shakespeare's *Hamlet* (1972), with Pino Micol in the title role, which was revived over three seasons and toured extensively; Massimo Dursi's *Stefano Pelloni detto Il Passatore* (*Stefano Pelloni Called The Passer*, 1973), which was also a big hit and toured extensively; Tonino Conti and Emmanuele Luzzati's *Tre Pulcinella—due carabinieried uno spazzino* (*Three Pulcinellas, Two Carabinieri, and One Scavenger*, 1974, *regia* Gian Roberto Cavalli); and John Ford's *'Tis Pity She's a Whore* (1974, *regia* Roberto Guicciardini). Many of these plays were set by Roberto Francia, who tended toward the abstract in design.

Alessandro Fersen was also highly regarded as a *registra* when he took over the company. This, too, was a good era with lots of excellent plays, many of them with large casts and outstanding sets, usually by Emmanuele Luzzati. Fersen was more solid in his productions, though unlike Scaparro he favored a mixture of classic with twentieth-century plays, from a variety of periods (uncredited productions are Fersen's): Fersen's own play *Leviathan* (1975), which he also staged; Lope de Vega's *Fuenteovejuna* (1975); Giovan Battista della Porta's *La fantesca* (*The Maidservant*, 1976); Georg Büchner's *Leonce and Lena* (1977); Hugo von Hofmannsthal's *Elektra* (1978, *regia* Antonio Taglioni); and Peter Müller's *Shameless Truth* (1979).

Fersen himself left in 1979. Although he had accomplished a good deal with the company, many problems remained, particularly in matters of organization and finance. In the 1979–1980 season the company had no artistic director. This season produced two excellent works, August Zucchi's *Il teatro comico di Carlo Goldoni* (*regia* the author), with Arnoldo Foà as Goldoni, and Heinrich von

Kleist's *The Prince of Homburg* (1979, *regie* Antonio Taglioni). The problems continued during the season, and there was some talk of disbanding the company. Fortunately, Marco Bernardi was appointed artistic director in 1979, and in his first two seasons the work of the company was uniformly good, particularly Bernardi's own productions, Shakespeare's *Romeo and Juliet* (1980) and John Cassavetes' *Knives* (1981), and a much-discussed look at Arthur Schnitzler's *Round Dance* (1981), staged by the Yugoslav stage director Bogdan Jercoviĉ.

The Teatro di Bolzano's main house is the Teatro Communale in Gries (425 places). The company also plays in the Haus der Kultur (650 seats), a theatre that is also used for a variety of other activities. The company does two major productions per season, plus a children's play; the rest of the season is made up of plays from other theatres, generally *stabili*. The season generally runs to about 100 percent capacity, partly because the Teatro Communale is small (too small, says the company). There are currently 1,350 people on subscription, which is very healthy for a city its size. During the 1980–1981 season the company gave 160 performances, which is about average. The subsidy for the organization comes not only from the state and the city, but also from the Provincia Autonoma Bolzano. The acting company totals around thirty, of which fifteen to twenty are hired for the entire season.

The main touring area for the theatre consists of the cities and towns around Bolzano, especially Merano and Trento; the company has also played all over Italy as well as in Germany, Malta, and Innsbruck. In addition to plays, the organization presents other programs such as film showings and talks, in order to meet the public's needs. The company has a friendliness and freedom which have pulled it through acute financial problems. The Teatro di Bolzano is managed by a *comisario* and a board of directors, and would like to achieve greater autonomy.

LEON M. AUFDEMBERGE
(With thanks to the publicity
department of the theatre.)

PERMANENT THEATRE OF PARMA
(Compagnia Stabile Città di Parma)
Teatro La Pedana Via Gian Battista
Fornovo, 43100 Parma, Italy

Traditional and purist in its approach to theatre productions, the Permanent Theatre of Parma presents the continuity of the old Teatro Universitario founded in 1953–1954. Under strains of ideological and generational rifts, the Teatro Universitario split in 1968. The "old" people, outvoted and stripped of funds, regrouped first under the name of Gruppo Eventi Teatrali (GET) in 1970 and recently, in 1977, as the Compagnia Stabile Città di Parma. Formed by seasoned actors and directors, the company does not enjoy professional status because it cannot provide the two-hundred-odd performances a year required by Italian law for state support. It does, however, have the illustrious tradition of producing a great number of modern plays as premieres in Italy. It has preserved an academically acquired taste for theatre of the grotesque and the absurd. Private donations, television filming of its productions, and unpaid actors make it possible for this group to survive financially and to produce some thirty performances each year.

Major productions during 1970–1980 included *R.U.R.* by Karel Capek; poetical collages on the Resistance: *L'incendio, Salvate l'uomo,* and *Non è finita; On the High Sea* by the Polish playwright Słowomir Mrożek, with music of Falavigna; *Karol,* also by Mrożek; *Escurial* by Michel de Ghelderode; *Love Is the Best Doctor* by Molière; and *The Contenders* by Jean Racine.

GIANNA SOMMI PANOFSKY

PERMANENT THEATRE OF TURIN
(Teatro Stabile Torino)
Piazza Castello, 215
Turin, Italy

In 1877 Cesare Rossi founded the Compagnia Città di Torino at the Teatro Carignano, which existed through the 1880s. Its great actress was Eleonora Duse, whose most famed role with the company was Santuzza in Giovanni Verga's *Cavalleria rusticana.* The company's main repertory, for which it was justly famous, was mostly Italian and French writers of the period.

In 1898 Domenico Lanza founded the Teatro d'Arte at the Teatro Gerbino, with its first manager A. de Sanctis. This company is generally considered the first modern *stabile* in Italy. The repertory of the company included a wide range of classics (especially Molière and Carlo Goldoni) and moderns (Ibsen and Paolo Ferrari). Its acting company included a number of great names in the theatre of Turin. Despite these accomplishments, the theatre folded in 1903.

Other attempts were made to form *stabili* in the city in the early part of this century, but they met with failure. It was not until after World War II that permanent companies based in the city became a reality. The first attempt came in 1946 with the Teatro Sperimentale di Torino, under the leadership of Eugenio Battisti and including Vallone and Gaultiero Rizzi in its company. In conjunction with the local university, it presented a wide variety of authors including Shakespeare, Thornton Wilder, Friedrich Hebbel, and August Strindberg. Its greatest successes came in 1946 with Georg Büchner's *Woyzeck* and Federico García Lorca's *Blood Wedding,* both staged by Vincenzo Ciaffi. In 1948 came the Teatro dei Cento (which did many of the classics) and, in 1952, the Centro del Teatro Popolare. In 1955, however, the local council decided, after a lengthy debate, to form a *stabile* in the city, with its first name the Piccolo Teatro della Città di Torino, and Nico Pepe as its first head.

Pepe was a good choice to lead the company as he knew the theatre from his long career as an actor. The opening performance for the company was on

November 3, 1955, at the Teatro Gobetti, with a double bill of Goldoni's *Gl'* *innamorati* (*The Lovers*) and Alfred de Musset's *You Can't Think of Everything* (both staged by Anna Maria Rimoaldi). Pepe led the company for only two seasons, but he and his productions were definite successes. Some of the productions staged during that time included García Lorca's *Mariana Pineda* (1955, *regia* Luigi Chiaverelli); Molière's *The Learned Ladies* (1955, *regia* Chiaverelli); E. d'Errico's *Best Seller* (1956, *regia* by the author); and Luigi Pirandello's *Liolà* (Gianfranco de Bosio), with Leonardo Cortese. The company's emphasis during these two seasons was decidedly on modern works.

Gianfranco de Bosio became the head in 1957 and would remain a long while. His background was as both a film and theatre *registra*, and he had worked in a number of theatres before coming to Turin. During his directorship, he was assisted first by M. Ferrari and then (1958) by Fulvio Fo, who directed the organization and administrative work of the company. As one of the first actions of 1957, the city took more control of the company (hence more subsidy). De Bosio invited important *registras*, as well as a number of important actors, to come to the city. In terms of repertory, de Bosio liked everything from Plautus to Vittorio Alfieri to Brecht; in short, he always strove for balanced seasons. In his first season with the company, there were short tours. Later, more elaborate tours were arranged, with some outside Italy. By 1960 the company was so established that it was invited to tour South America, with its production of Shakespeare's *The Tempest* (*regia* Giacomo Colli). In his first seasons with the company, de Bosio had a significant number of fine works, with his troupe including Massimo Dursi's *Bertoldo a Corte* (*Blockhead at Court*, 1957, *regia* de Bosio); Alfieri's *La congiura de'Pazzi* (*The Pazzi Conspiracy*, 1958, *regia* de Bosio), with Giulio Bosetti as Raimondo; Dario Fo's *Comica Finale* (*Comic Finale*, 1958, *regia* by the author with de Bosio); Giuseppe Dessi's *La giustizia* (*Justice*, 1959, *regia* Colli); Cesare Meano's *Nascita di Salomé* (*The Birth of Salomé*, 1959, *regia* Giacomo Colli); Giuseppe Dessi's *Qui non c'e guerra* (*But It's Not War*, 1960, *regia* de Bosio), with Lilla Brignone in a lead role; Brecht's *The Resistible Rise of Arturo Ui* (1961, *regia* de Bosio) with Franco Parenti in the title role; Vitalino Brancati's *Don Giovanni Involontario* (1961, *regia* de Bosio), with Renzo Giovampietro; Archibald MacLeish's *J. B.* (1962, *regia* Parenti), the premiere of Luigi Canodi's *Edipo a Hiroshima* (1963, *regia* Roberto Guicciardini); Eugene Ionesco's *Exit the King* (1963, *regia* José Quaglio), with Giulio Bosetti as Berenger; T. S. Eliot's *The Elder Statesmen* (1964, *regia* Quaglio); and Luigi Pirandello's *Henry IV* (1964, *regia* Quaglio), with Salvo Randone in the title role.

In 1964 Nuccio Messina took over the administrative part of the company, with de Bosio staying on as artistic director. Under Messina's directorship the company featured famous actors in great plays staged by some of Italy's most noted stage directors, with special emphasis on Franco Enriquez. The troupe went on many more tours—even to Eastern Europe including Russia—and played at festivals. After 1965, the company began to mount more plays each season and to hire more actors. Among the most important productions of this period were George Bernard Shaw's *Caesar and Cleopatra* (1964, *regia* de Bosio), with Giovanni Santucci and Adriana Asti in the title roles; Samuel Beckett's *Happy Days* (1965, *regia* Roger Blin), with Laura Adani as Winny; "Ruzante's" *L'Anconitana* (*The Girl from Ancona*); Goldoni's *La locandiera* (*The Mistress of the Inn*, 1965, *regia* Franco Enriquez), with Valeria Moriconi in the title role; Friedrich Dürrenmatt's *The Physicists* (1965, *regia* Enriquez); Shakespeare's *As You Like It* (1966, *regia* Enriquez), with Moriconi as Rosalind; Shakespeare's *Richard II* (1966, *regia* de Bosio), with Glauco Mauri in the title role and sets by Emmanuele Luzzati; Shakespeare's *The Taming of the Shrew* (1966, *regia* Enriquez); Natalia Ginzburg's *Ti ho sposato per allegria* (*I Have Married You for Merriment*, 1966, *regia* Luciano Salce); Chekhov's *The Seagull* (1967, *regia* Enriquez), with Brignone as Arkadina; Shakespeare's *The Merchant of Venice* (1967, *regia* Enriquez), with Glauco Mauri as Shylock; Pedro Calderón's *Devotion to the Cross* (1967, *regia* de Bosio); Shakespeare's *Richard III* (1967, *regia* Luca Ronconi), with Vittorio Gassman in the title role which was much revived and toured; and Molière's *The Misanthrope* (1968, *regia* Roger Mollien), with Mauri as Alceste. It was a brilliant era.

De Bosio left in 1968. Some seasons with changeable management followed: Giuseppe Bartolucci, Federico Doglio, Gian Renzo Morteo, Messina (1969–1970), and Bartolucci and Messina (1970–1972). During this era the company moved away from the classics and concentrated on modern repertory. It continued its policy of touring, with considerably less emphasis on guest artists and more on ensemble. To compensate there were more premieres. In 1968 the company began to work with the Teatro Piemontese, which took plays to the outlying areas. In 1969 the Permanent Theatre of Torino was founded as a separate organization, which worked within the company and produced plays for theatres within the city. This was a good era for design with Emmanuele Luzzati, Pier Luigi Pizzi, and Josef Svoboda all working for the company. Most of the strongest productions were modern works, including Pirandello's *L'amica delle mogli* (*The Friend of the Wife*, 1968, *regia* Giorgio de Lullo), with Rosella Falk as Marta; Ibsen's *Hedda Gabler* (1969, *regia* de Lullo), with Falk in the title role and with sets by Pizzi; the premiere of Mario Prosperi's *Persecuzione e morte di Gerolamo Savonarola* (*Persecution and Death of Gerolamo Savonarola*, 1969, *regia* Giovampietro); Vittorio Bersezio's *Le Miserie d' Monssu Travet* (*The Distress of Monssu Travet*, 1979, *regia* Giacomo Colli); August Strindberg's *A Dream Play* (1970, *regia* Michael Meschke), with Ingrid Thulin; Francesco Della Corte's *Atene Anno Zero* (*Athens, Year Zero*, 1970, *regia* Giovampietro); Brecht's *Mr. Puntila and His Hired Man, Matti* (1970, *regia* Aldo Trionfo), with Tino Buazzelli as Puntila and Corrado Pani as Matti, with sets by Luzzati; Georg Büchner's *Woyzeck* (1971, *regia* Virginio Puecher), with sets by Svoboda and performed in conjunction with La Scala in Milan; the premiere of Angelo Dallagiacoma's *Vita di William Shakespeare* (*Life of William Shakespeare*, 1971, *regia* Gazzolo); Vito Pandolfi and Franco Enriquez's *Isabella Comica Gelosa*

(*Isabella's Comic Jealousy*, 1971, *regia* by Enriquez); and Pirandello's *Sei personaggi in cerca d'autore* (*Six Characters in Search of an Author*, 1971, *regia* Enriquez), with Moriconi and Mauri as the embattled couple. In 1971 the company began to sponsor summer performances.

Aldo Trionfo became head in 1972, with Messina staying on one more season (1972–1973). Trionfo began to cut the annual number of productions, but the company probably toured as much. During his tenure there was a greater mixture of classics and modern dramas, done in more sensible productions with considerably less use of avant-garde techniques. Among the most honored presentations were Brecht's *The Life of Galileo* (1972, *regia* by the East German Fritz Bennewitz), with Buazzelli in the title role; Ibsen's *Peer Gynt* (1972, *regia* Al Trionfo), with Pani in the title role; the premiere of Tonio Conte and Trionfo's (adapted from Massimo D'Azeglio's work) *Ettore Fieramosca* (1973, *regia* Trionfo), with sets by Luzzati; Shakespeare's *King John* (1973, *regia* Trionfo), with Bosetti in the title role; Carlo Gozzi's *Turandot* (1973, *regia* Puecher); Sophocles' *Electra* (1974, *regia* Trionfo), with Marissa Fabbri in the title role; Luciano Codignola's *Bel-Ami e il suo doppio* (*Bel-Ami and His Double*, 1975, *regia* Trionfo); Vladimir Mayakovsky's *The Bathhouse* (1976, *regia* Mario Missiroli); and Gotthold Lessing's *Nathan the Wise* (1976, *regia* Missiroli).

Mario Missiroli took over the directorship of the company in 1976, with Giorgio Guazzotti joining him the following year. The focus shifted to tight ensemble shows and moved away from the guest star policy. As a result, the company has become very *registra*-centered, with considerable experimentation in production, especially Missiroli's. The repertory is balanced between the classics and modern drama. In the last few seasons the company has presented the following: Carl Sternheim's *Middle Class Hero's Life* (frequently called *The Maske Plays*, 1976, *regia* Missiroli); Molière's *Don Juan* (1977), with Giulio Broggi in the title role; Chekhov's *Uncle Vanya* (1977, *regia* Missiroli); Strindberg's *To Damascus* (1978, *regia* Missiroli); John Webster's *The Duchess of Malfi* (1978, *regia* Missiroli), with Anna Maria Guarnieri in the title role; Pirandello's *Come tu mi vuoi* (*As You Desire Me*, 1979, *regia* Susan Sontag), with Adriana Asti as L'Ignota and sets by Pizzi; Pirandello's *I giganti della Montagna* (*The Giants of the Mountain*, 1979, *regia* Missiroli); Jean Genet's *The Maids* (1980, *regia* Missiroli); Sergio Tofano's *Una losca congiura di Barbariccia contra Bonaventura* (1980, *regia* Franco Passtore); Frank Wedekind's *Music* (1981, *regia* Missiroli); and Goldoni's *La Villeggiatura* (*Country Dwellers*, 1981, *regia* Missiroli).

The Permanent Theatre of Turin presents three new productions a year, sometimes four, two of which are staged by Missiroli. In addition, the company does an indeterminate number of revivals. The acting company numbers around fifty and presents many visiting productions each season. In the 1981–1982 season there were twenty-four visiting productions, including some puppet performances. The company is subsidized by Turin, the province of Turin, and the

Piedmont area, with the total subsidy coming to approximately 1.3 billion lira. The company gives about 250 performances a year in about thirty theatres.

The company produces plays for a broad general public, plays from outside companies, and plays for children. The company also has an intense series of activities in both Turin and the Piedmont region, which vary widely each year. For example, in collaboration with the Assessor of Culture for the Common People of Turin, it does a number of special programs, especially during the summer, with the Punti Verdi, which is a large festival that brings together plays, dance companies, and music programs. The company also presents various programs during the regular season and organizes international conferences on theatre. In May 1981, for example, the company helped sponsor a conference on dramaturgy in Europe in the eighties.

The company has no permanent theatre; hence, a number of houses are used by both the home company and invited groups. The most handsome theatre used by the company is the Teatro Carignano, which was built in 1751 by Benedetto Alfieri but burned in 1786 and was restored by Giovanni Battista Feroggio. It seats eight hundred. Other theatres which the company uses are the Gobetti (built in 1828 by Leoni, with seating for 330) and the Teatro Adua (architect and date unknown, with places for five hundred). In addition, the company has used the handsome Teatro Alfieri, built in 1857 by Panizza.

Turin's theatre tries to meet the needs of the people, not only in this highly industrial city but in the outside areas as well. It has done so from the beginning.

LEON M. AUFDEMBERGE
(With thanks to Giorgio Guazzatti.)

ROCCA GROUP
(Il Gruppo della Rocca)
Borgo degli Albizi 15
Florence, Italy

The Rocca Group was founded in reaction to two forces which it found distasteful: politics and economics. Its political trend was evident from the beginning (influenced by Bertolt Brecht, Dario Fo, Patrice Chéreau, and the Piccolo Teatro di Milano), and it countered the commercialism of the Italian theatre by becoming a cooperative. The group was founded by eight people in 1969 as The Group, soon after changing its name to The Rocca Group as another organization carried the first name. The young founding members were led by Roberto Giucciardini.

The first production was Machiavelli's *Clizia*, staged by Guicciardini at the Teatro San Casciano in Florence. It was a moderate success as was the second production, a bill of farces by Brecht: *Lux in Tenebris, The Wedding*, and *How Much Does the Steel Cost?* In the 1970–1971 season there were two works: a collective work based on Aldo Palazzeschi's *Perelà uomo di fumo* (*Perelà, Man of Smoke, regia* Guicciardini) and Giralamo Strozzi and Stefano Merlini's didactic *La repubblica si fara'* (*The Republic Forms Itself, regia* Guicciardini). In 1971–1972 the play was again a collective, aided by Guicciardini, *Viaggio Controverso di Candido e gli altri negli Arcipelaghi della Ragione* (*Dubious Journey of Candide and the Others in the Archipelagos of Reason, regia* Guicciardini). This work was based on Voltaire and a number of other writers and became the company's first solid success.

In 1972–1973 the company had two successful performances: the first, a highly inventive production by Egisto Marucci of Shakespeare's *A Midsummer Night's Dream*, which stressed many of the erotic features of the play; and the second, the Brecht/Sophocles *Antigone* (*regia* Guicciardini), with Paila Pavese in the title role. Both works had their first nights in Prato and then toured throughout Italy. In the 1973–1974 season there were again two works: Massimo Duri's *Il tumulto dei Ciompi* (*The Revolt of the Carders, regia* Guicciardini), which dealt with a revolt of Florentine carders in 1378, and a rousing performance of Brecht's *Schweyk in the Second World War* (*regia* Egisto Marucci), with Marcello Bartoli in the title role. The 1974–1975 season was Guicciardini's last and proved controversial. The first production of the season was the Italian premiere of Odön von Horváth's *Italian Night*, which suffered from translation problems, despite the production by Guicciardini. The other was a collective exercise, entitled *Processo per aborto* (*Trial for Abortion*), which tackled one of Italy's most hotly debated subjects.

After Guicciardini's exit, much of what he had done was taken over by Marucci. In the next seasons, the company mounted Nikolai Erdman's *The Mandate* (1976, *regia* Marucci); an original production done by the group with Italo Dall'Orto from the novel by Luigi Compagnone, *Ballata e morte di Pulcinella Capitano del popolo* (*Ballad and Death of Pulcinella, Captain of the People*, 1977, *regia* Marucci), with sets by Luciano Damiani; and Samuel Beckett's *Waiting for Godot* (1977, *regia* Robert Vezzosi).

In 1978 came two substantial successes for the company: the first (which toured over several seasons) was Renzo Rosso's *Esercizi spirituali, Il Concerto* (*Spiritual Exercise, The Concert*), with the production by Alvaro Piccardi and the music by Nicola Piovani; and the second was Erdman's *The Suicide* (1978, *regia* Marucci), with Marcello Bartoli as Semyon Semyonovic Podsekalnikov. Since then the company has mounted *L'XI giornata del Decamerone* (*The XI Day of the Decameron*), based on Boccaccio's work adapted by Fabio Doplicher (1979, *regia* Guicciardini); Alexander Blok's *L'azzurro non si misura con la mento* (*Blue Is Not Measured by the Chin*, 1980, *regia* Bartoli); a highly successful production of the anonymous Elizabethan *Arden of Feversham* (1980, *regia* Antonello Mendolia, who also did the translation with Fiorenza Brogi); and Harold Pinter's *The Caretaker* (1981, *regia* Vezzosi).

The Rocca Group does two productions a year, sometimes four. It rehearses in Florence and then opens in a nearby city such as Prato, Pistoia, or Fiesole. It has no home theatre and tours extensively. The company has one resident *registra* and fifteen actors (twelve men and three women); others are hired as needed. When the company is in full production, it has sixty people on the payroll. The company plays eight months a year, presenting approximately three hundred performances in 136 places. The company is subsidized by the state Ministry of Tourism and Performances, which awarded it 410 million lira in the 1979–1980 season. While it is a cooperative with no manager, the company does listen to expert advice before making a decision. The company is seeking a better place to rehearse.

From its narrow and precarious beginnings, the Rocca Group has developed into the major experimental touring company in Italy. It regularly plays all the major *stabile* houses in Italy, as well as many small towns. Its reputation is such that its productions have been reviewed in periodicals outside Italy.

LEON M. AUFDEMBERGE
(With thanks to Donna Miles and
the theatre's publicity department.)

THEATRE OF EDUARDO
(Il Teatro di Eduardo)
Teatro San Ferdinando
Piazza Teatro San Ferdinando
Naples, Italy

If ever a playwright could be said to sum up the daily life of a city, that writer would be Eduardo de Filippo. Eduardo came from a long line of actors and was born in Naples in 1900. As a young man he acted with his brother Pippino and his sister Titina in the company of Eduardo Scarpetta, who was both an actor and a playwright. Since the company frequently worked under adverse conditions, Eduardo learned to perform a variety of functions in the theatre. Most of Scarpetta's plays were in the Italian realistic manner, some of which Eduardo later adapted. In 1931 Eduardo began to write plays, with his first important work coming in that year, *Natale in casa Cupiello* (*Christmas in the Cupiello House*). It included some satire on the fascist government, but most of it was hidden, lest the play be forbidden by the censor.

Eduardo began rather early to stage his own works, so it was no surprise that in 1932 he and his brother and sister founded their own troupe, the Teatro Umoristo I De Filipo. This company existed until 1945 when the two brothers split and Eduardo founded his own company, Il Teatro di Eduardo, with his sister as lead actress. The company was born during the Occupation in Naples, when conditions could not have been worse.

The new company's first play was the premiere of Eduardo's *Napoli milionaria!* (*Millionaire Naples*), written, staged, and with the lead role (Gennaro Iovine) played by Eduardo. The premiere took place on March 31, 1945, at the Teatro San Carlo in Naples and later toured in Rome and Milan. The play has been revived by the company and has been done on television, as have all of

Eduardo's major plays. In the first season the company also presented *Il berretto a sonagli (The Cap with Bells)* by Luigi Pirandello and *La scorzetta di limone (The Lemon Peel)* by Gino Rocca.

In December 1946 came another success, *Questi fantasmi! (These Ghosts!)*, which the company has also frequently revived. In these opening seasons, the pattern would be set: two or three plays would be taken on the road, one of which would be a new play by Eduardo and the other two revivals of Eduardo's old works, plus a work of another author. In the 1946–1947 season came Eduardo's greatest success and the work with which he is most closely identified, *Filumena Marturano*, with Titina playing the title role and Eduardo as Domenico Soriano. Eduardo was to stage this work (as he would all the plays listed in this article). It has been the most often revived of all of his plays and has been filmed twice. The play is both realistic and allegorical (the three sons, Eduardo says, are the three classes of Italian society), and the theme centers on how Italy could have a fresh start after the war. In 1947 came *Pericolosamente (Dangerously)* which was not a success.

All of Eduardo's early works share certain characteristics. They are realistic works, which criticize all strata of Italian society without becoming didactic or sentimental. Characters are neither virtuous nor villainous. He wrote all the early works in Neapolitan dialect (as he would all of his works), and they have been played that way throughout Italy.

In 1948 Eduardo took a big step forward by purchasing the old Teatro San Fernandino (original architect Camillo Lionti), which was built in 1797 and was severely damaged during the war. It took all the money he had as well as all the cash he was earning on his tours to finance the remodeling. The theatre was not to open until 1954, however.

With the stability of the company assured, Eduardo began to turn out a steady stream of plays and productions for the company, with himself in the lead role and as the only *registra*. In the late 1940s and early 1950s, he wrote for his company such classics as *Le bugie con le gambe lunghe (The Truth That Was Never Revealed*, 1948), *Le voci di dentro (Inner Voices*, 1948), *La grande magia (The Big Magic*, 1949), *La paura numero uno (Fear Number One*, 1950), and *Misera e nobilita (Misery Is Nobility*, 1953). Eduardo adapted the last-named play from a Scarpetta work.

On January 21, 1954, Eduardo inaugurated the Teatro San Fernandino (architect for the rebuilding, Cotugno) with a production of Antonio Petito's *Palummella zompa e vola (Palummella Jumps and Flies)*, which Eduardo staged with the help of Vittorio Viviani. (The company which opened the theatre was not the Teatro di Eduardo, but La Compagnia "La Scarpettiana," which Eduardo had founded and led for five years, though he did not act with it.) It was at this time that Titina retired from the company, with Dolores Palumbo becoming the leading lady for the troupe. In the 1950s Eduardo began to produce more plays by other authors rather than his own plays, with works by Pirandello, Dino Romano, Francesco Gabriello Starace, Athos Setti, and especially Scarpetta.

Eduardo's plays, however, were the most important works for the company: *Mia famiglia* (*My Family*, 1955), *Bene mio e core mio* (*My Darling and My Love*, 1955), *Il medico dei pazzi* (*The Doctor for the Crazy*, 1956), and *La fortuna in cerca di tasche* (*The Fortune in Search of a Pocket*, 1958), with the last two works adapted from Scarpetta. In 1955 the Teatro di Eduardo participated in the international theatre festival in Paris with *Questi fantasmi!*, returning in 1961 with Pasquale Altavilla's *Pulcinella in cerca della sua fortuna per Napoli* (*Pulcinella in Search of a Fortune in Naples*).

In 1959 came another of Eduardo's triumphs, *Sabato, domenica e lunedi* (*Saturday, Sunday, and Monday*), followed in 1960 by *Il sindaco del rione Sanità* (*The Director of the Sanità District*). In 1962 the company went on a long tour to Russia, Poland, Hungary, Austria, and Belgium with a repertory of *Filumena Marturano, Il sindaco del rione Sanità, Napoli milionaria!*, *Questi fantasmi!*, and Pirandello's *Il berretto a sonagli*. At about this time, the troupe began to appear regularly on television with at least one play done on this medium each season. Eduardo first put on the mask of Pulcinella in 1962 with his own *Il figlio di Pulcinella* (*The Son of Pulcinella*), which was a great tour-de-force for him. The work was a superb piece of buffoonery based on *commedia dell'arte*.

Because of rising costs, Eduardo did not take out a troupe in 1963–1964 but concentrated on presenting several of his plays on television. The next year the troupe had only a short tour, with only one play, Eduardo's philosophy of art, properly named *L'arte della commedia* (*The Art of Comedy*). From the mid-1960s to the early 1970s the company presented several of Eduardo's premieres: *Dolore sotto chiave* (*Grief under Lock and Key*, 1964), *Il cilindro* (*The Cylinder*, 1966), *Il contratto* (*The Contract*, 1967), the Scarpetta/Eduardo *Cani e gatti* (*Cat and Dog*, 1969), *Il monumento* (*The Monument*, 1970), and *Na santarella* (*The Saintly Woman*, 1972). In 1972 the company presented *Napoli milionaria!* at the World Theatre Season in London at the Aldwych to great critical acclaim. In the same year Eduardo was awarded the Premio Internazionale ''Antonio Feltrinelli'' by the Academia Nazionale dei Lincei.

In the 1970s and into the present decade, the company has done more and more revivals of previous seasons. There have been several new works by Eduardo in *Gli esami non finiscono mai* (*The Exams Never Finish*, 1973), one of Eduardo's best plays, and an adaptation of Scarpetta's *Lu curaggio de nu pumpiere napulitano* (*The Courage of the Neopolitan Firemen*, 1974), which had *commedia dell'arte* elements. Since 1975 all of Eduardo's new works have been done on television, but there have been the usual tours. In recent seasons there have been productions of Pirandello's *Il berretto a sonagli* (1979), and in the 1980–1981 season the company took on tour Rocca's *La scorzetta di limone* and two of Eduardo's early works, *Dolore sotto chiave* and *Sik-Sik, l'artefice magico* (*Sik-Sik, the Magic Craftsman*), which had been one of Eduardo's early successes (in 1932) but had not been done by the company since 1955. Eduardo was honored in June 1978 at the second International Festival of Popular Theatre in Rome, in which Eduardo enacted scenes from his plays, aided by many of his colleagues, including Vittorio Gassman, Monica Vitti, Valentina Cortese, Marcello Mastroianni, Nino Rota, and Mario Scaccia. Carla Fracci, lead ballerina from La Scala, danced a new ballet called *Filumena*, with music by Eduardo, played by Severino Gazzelloni.

The theatrical company Teatro di Eduardo obviously revolves around its main actor/playwright/*registra*, but the company has done extensive work on television as well. As a theatre person, Eduardo has been admired by people in the theatre as different as Sir Laurence Olivier and Bertolt Brecht. The company has done many plays by Scarpetta and Pirandello, the two playwrights who have influenced Eduardo the most, particularly Scarpetta in the idiom of the popular Neapolitan comedy. Some critics have also seen the influences of Chekhov, and Eduardo acknowledges his large debt to the *commedia* and to the tradition of Italian burlesque. While all of Eduardo's scripts are written in Neapolitan, the early plays are much more heavily written in the dialect; the later plays are closer to spoken Italian. Eduardo has insisted that his plays are not merely realistic and that all of his plays have associations that go beneath mere pictures of Neapolitan life to something more universal. Hence his popularity in countries other than Italy.

The company's permanent home is the seven-hundred-seat Teatro San Fernandino, in which rehearsals take place before tours. In the first decade of the tours, the company went all over Italy; now tours generally center in the three biggest cities, Naples, Milan, and Rome. Since the 1970s tours have been shorter, and the company has concentrated on recording Eduardo's plays on television for posterity. Eduardo has also staged his own plays, as well as the plays of other authors, at theatres throughout Italy. Because he is passionate about music, he has also staged operas. In the United States he has staged Gaetano Donizetti's *Don Pasquale* for the Lyric Opera of Chicago in 1974 and 1978.

The company generally consists of twenty to twenty-four actors; four or five of them are always young actors as Eduardo likes to train the novice players in the style of his own works. In the company's early years, actors generally were hired for an eleven-month tour; now the tours run to about eight months. The most frequently revived play in the repertory is *Filumena Marturano*, but Eduardo's favorite play is *Questi fantasmi*! His favorite role is Guglielmo Speranza in *Gli esami non finiscono mai* because it treats the relationship between the individual and society, a theme close to Eduardo's heart.

Eduardo has carried on a long love affair with the people of Naples, but not necessarily the city government (or the Italian government). As a result, he has not had the help of a large subsidy. Practically the whole income comes from the box office in single sales as Eduardo dislikes subscriptions ("If a play is bad, why should an audience sit through it?"). The company plays about 170 performances a year and has little trouble filling a theatre.

For the future, the company will probably concentrate more on television than on the live stage because Eduardo wants a record of his major plays for posterity. The major theme of his plays is that life goes on despite adversity. Although he refuses to align himself with any political party, his plays can be interpreted politically. As a person and playwright (the two are inseparable), he is both a man of Naples and a man of the world.

LEON M. AUFDEMBERGE

THEATRE OF EMILIA-ROMAGNA
(Emilia-Romagna Teatro)
Via Fonteraso, 1
Modena, Italy

Until 1964 the area of Reggio Emilia-Romagna was sporadically served by commercial touring companies from Rome and occasional visits from international companies. The area had no theatre of its own (except opera), and no attempt was made to coordinate the activities of the theatres dotting the region. In 1964 an association was formed to correct these inadequacies, and the directors of the theatres in Modena, Reggio Emilia, Ferrara, and the smaller Budrio, Fidenza, and Carpi met to discuss common problems about booking activities into each respective house. The organization was called ATER (Associazone Teatri Emilia-Romagna), with the cities of Parma and Ravenna joining soon after. The secretary of the organization was Mario Cadalora, whose home theatre was in Modena.

ATER's main function was to coordinate company bookings in order to insure an adequate number of activities in the theatres. One of the organization's chief accomplishments was to book avant-garde companies into this area, including the Living Theatre, which came with K. H. Brown's *The Brig* (1966) and *Frankenstein* (1967) and Charles Marowitz's Open Space productions of *Hamlet* (1966) and *Macbeth* (1969). It also provided backing for some Roman companies to escape censorship troubles there.

In April 1977 the twenty-three theatres that constituted ATER met to consider whether there should be a company for prose drama to play in the area (and eventually all of Italy). From this meeting emerged the theatre of Emilia-Romagna; it was not exactly a *stabile*, since it would not be based solely in one city, but would serve an area. Since ATER had already built up an audience, finding enough people was no problem. Companies booked by ATER had presented a rather steady stream of avant-garde theatre, so repertory was no problem either.

The head of the new organization was to be Mario Cadalora, and the company he selected as a nucleus was partly formed from an earlier cooperative troupe, Gli Associati, which consisted of several well-known actors, including Fulvia Fo, Giancarlo Sbragia, Sergio Fantoni, Paolo Giuranna, Sergio Fantoni, and Valentina Fortunato. The first production was the Italian premiere of Hugo von Hofmannsthal's *The Difficult Man* (*regia* Sergio Fantoni), with Sergio Fantoni as Hans Karl Bühl, presented in Corregio at the Teatro Asioli on October 30, 1977. In the same season the company also presented the Italian premiere of

Tolstoy's *The Power of Darkness* (*regia* Giuranna), with Fortunato as Marfisa, and the premiere of Diego Fabbri's *Il commedione* (*The Comedian*), with Sbragia staging the work and playing the protagonist, Belli, as well. In the first season the company visited eighty-seven places giving 321 performances and playing before 176,441 people. *Il commedione* was the biggest success—so much so it was revived the next season.

The 1978–1979 season opened with the revival mentioned above, followed by an Italian premiere of Heinrich Böll's *A Sip of Earth* (*regia* de Bosio), which was moderately successful. The last two works of the season were a study in contrasts: the first was an adaptation by Sbragia (who also staged the work and played Stepan) of Dostoyevsky's *The Demons* and the second was Francis Beaumont and John Fletcher's *The Maid's Tragedy* (*regia* Aldo Trionfo), with Paolo Mannoni as Evadne. During the same season, the company inaugurated a laboratory theatre to present new works: Bruno Sacchini's *Divus Dionisio* (*regia* Giovannia Pampiglione), adapted from Euripides' *The Bacchae*; Pietro Formentini's *Officina Rigoletto* (*regia* by the author); and Gregorio Scalise's *I custodi* (*regia* Pampiglione).

The next season (1979–1980) might well be called the year of the big production, with a series of established *registras*. It opened with Chekhov's *The Seagull* (*regia* Gabriella Gabriele Lavia), with Fortunato as Arkadina and with sets by Pier Luigi Pizzi. This production was well received, as was the next production, Giuseppe Giacosa's *Come le foglie* (*Like Falling Leaves*, *regia* Giancarlo Sepe). Maurice Maeterlinck's *The Blue Bird* followed this work, staged by Italy's Luca Ronconi, with sets by Saro Luturco. The season closed with an aesthetically satisfying Sophocles' *Oedipus Tyrannos* (translation by Edoardo Sanguineti), staged by Benno Besson, with Vittorio Franceschi in the protagonist's role. The work used masks and called for a vigorous program of acting training, especially for the chorus. The sets and costumes were by Ezio Toffolutti and have already achieved the status of a classic.

The Sophocles/Sanguineti work was revived to open the following season (1980–1981) with a moderately experimental production of Ibsen's *Hedda Gabler* (*regia* Massimo Castri) following, with Moriconi as Hedda. Moriconi also played the lead protagonist in *Turandot* by Carlo Gozzi, which came next (*regia* by Giancarlo Cobelli). This production was followed by Martin Speer's *Hunting Scenes from Lower Bavaria* (*regia* Walter Pagliaro), which many playgoers found hard going. The last work of the season was a visual delight, a co-production (with the Piccolo Teatro di Milano) of Brecht's *The Good Woman of Setzuan*. The 1981–1982 season consisted of revivals of all the above four plus one new production, Beckett's *Waiting for Godot* (*regia* Pagliaro).

The Emilia-Romagna has two functions: as a producer of plays (its *stabile* part) and as a kind of gigantic booking office (its ATER part). The plays are selected by the director with the help of three newspaper critics in the area. As is reflected by the plays produced, the company has a strong social commitment. Consequently, the works done in any one season usually revolve around problems in contemporary Italy, such as terrorism (*The Demons*) or social unrest (the Hofmannsthal work which opened the company's activities). The acting company numbers anywhere from forty-five to fifty, with more men than women. Actors come from all over Italy, especially Rome. As a separate company it plays in the area before touring, sometimes throughout Italy. Many actors have returned season after season, and some are on two-season contracts. Plays may be rehearsed in one place and frequently open in another.

As a booking organization, ATER handles sixty to seventy groups a season, ranging from one-person acts to large opera companies. The theatres choose from a variety of offerings. ATER has its own ballet company, ATER Balletto, which is run along American lines and was founded in 1977. One of ATER's recent activities (summer 1980) was the sponsorship of a floating theatre with the Festival at Dubrovnik and the Biennale di Venezia. (It went from Venice to Dubrovnik.) The festival presented musical programs (singers and orchestras) and *commedia dell'arte* performances. The voyage of Il Teatro del Mondo was the subject of a handsome book published by the three organizations.

Although the company has done some plays that have been indifferently received, for the most part the work has been of high quality. Since 1964 the area has become accustomed to all types of theatre, and even small towns have a constituency that responds to Beckett. Some people in Fidenza even find him rather dated.

LEON M. AUFDEMBERGE
(Thanks to Mario Cadalora)

THEATRE OF ROME
(Teatro di Roma)
Via Barbieri 21
Rome, Italy

Before World War II, Rome was the center of theatrical activity in Italy. After the war, with decentralization, Rome lost its power to make or break a theatrical reputation. Many of its *teatri stabili* have had rocky times and then died. Even today Rome supports experimental groups which, though good, have precarious existences because of the fickleness of Romans. This has been the case since the turn of the century. To understand the history of the Teatro di Roma, it is necessary to look at the histories of other *stabili* in the city.

Rome has had companies of actors since the High Renaissance; some of the Popes enjoyed their own private forms of theatre. In the baroque era, the city had several playhouses, though most major playwrights lived elsewhere. The first important Roman *stabile*, La Compagnia Stabile Romana, was founded in 1905 and was placed under the direction of Eduard Boutet and F. Garavagli. The company performed at the Teatro Argentina, where the Theatre of Rome now plays. Its opening production was Shakespeare's *Julius Caesar*, first performed on December 29, 1905.

The company was noted especially for its productions of Carlo Goldoni, Gerhart Hauptmann, Gabriele D'Annunzio, and Luigi Pirandello, but above all for Molière and Shakespeare. With a solid core of the finest Italian actors, it tackled such ambitious works as Aeschylus' *Oresteia*. It also had a great designer, Duilio Cambellotti. After World War I, the company changed managers and experienced financial problems, finally folding in the mid-1920s. In the 1920s and 1930s many theatre companies opened and folded.

An attempt was made in 1948 to form a *stabile* when Orazio Costa, one of Italy's most progressive *registras*, organized the Piccolo Teatro della Città di Roma. Costa was noted in Italy for his productions of Ibsen and Greek tragedies. For the company, he staged a variety of works, often with well-known guest artists, such as Rosella Falk, Tino Buazelli, and Vittorio Gassman. The company toured as far as South America. In 1951–1952 it was directed by Turi Vasile. It had many splendid hits, including the following (productions without *registras* named are Costa's): Pirandello's *Sei personaggi in cerca di autore* (*Six Characters in Search of an Author*, 1948), Vittorio Alfieri's *Oreste* (1949) with Gassman in the title role, Shakespeare's *Twelfth Night* (1950), Ferenc Molnár's *Liliom* (1950) with Nion Manfredi as Liliom, Georges Bernanos' *Dialogues of the Carmelites* (1952), Ugo Betti's *L'aiuola bruciata* (*The Burnt Flower Bed*, 1953), and Gennaro Pistilli's *La donna dell'uomo* (*The Women of Man*, 1954). In 1954, despite the best of intentions, it folded.

Then followed a number of other companies with many ups and downs. Vito Pandolfi tried again in 1965 with the Teatro Stabile della Città di Roma. This time it survived, even though it has had a very difficult time. Pandolfi, violently antifascist during the Mussolini regime, had worked after the war as a critic for several periodicals and later as a *registra*. His idea was to bring big actors and noted *registras* together, in a repertory of important plays. Critics applauded his efforts, but many thought he was not building a company. Pandolfi's major theatre was the Teatro Valle, although the company toured as much as it played in Rome. The theatre's best productions included both modern and classic works, directed by a succession of Italy's leading *registras*: Chekhov's *The Cherry Orchard* (October 25, 1965, *regia* Visconti) which opened the company with Rina Morelli as Madame Ranevskaya and Tino Carraro as Lopakhin, Giovanni Verga's *Dal tuo al mir* (*From Yours to Mine*, 1966, *regia* Paolo Giuranni), Sean O'Casey's *Red Roses for Me* (1966, *regia* Alessandro Fersen), Pirandello's *Vestire gli ignudi* (*Clothe the Naked*, 1966, *regia* Pandolfi) with Adriana Asti as Ersila, Shakespeare's *The Merchant of Venice* (1966, *regia* Ettore Giannini) with Paolo Stoppa as Shylock, Raffaele Viviani's *Napoli notte e giorno* (*Naples Night and Day*, 1967, *regia* Giuseppe Griffi), John Osborne's *Inadmissible Evidence* (1967, *regia* Alberto Arbasina), with Tino Carraro as Bill Maitland, Carlo Goldoni's *La bottega del caffè* (*The Coffee Shop*, 1967, *regia* Griffi Patroni), Brecht's *In the Jungle of the Cities* (1968, *regia* Antonio Calenda), Seneca's *Fedra* (1968, *regia* Ronconi), and T. S. Eliot's *The Cocktail Party* (1968, *regia* Mario Ferreri).

In 1969 Pandolfi departed, and for one season there was no head. It was hoped that Giorgio Strehler would take over the company, but he finally said no. Nevertheless, the 1969–1970 season was a very good one with productions of Richard Sheridan's *The School for Scandal* (1970, *regia* Sergio Tofano), and George Bernard Shaw's *Mrs. Warren's Profession* (1970, *regia* Leonardo Bragali) with Paola Borboni as Mrs. Warren. For the following two seasons the theatre produced nothing.

When the company reformed in 1972, it was with Franco Enriquez as artistic director. Enriquez had been an assistant to Visconti and Strehler and had worked with the Campagnia del Quattro. Like Pandolfi he hired guest artists and the best of *registras*. Under his guidance the repertory was mostly twentieth-century drama and included many premieres. His production style was experimental and arresting, which caused some scandals. Enriquez made much of touring and tried to get the people of Rome to come to the theatre, particularly the young, whom he tried to woo with special performances. Enriquez wanted people to talk about his company. The company also changed its name during this period to the Teatro di Roma. It was rewarded by more city support each season. During the Enriquez era, large-cast productions from many periods were staged: Goldoni's *Gli innamorati* (*The Lovers*, 1972, *regia* Enriquez), a bill of Beckett one-acts called *Beckett '73* (1973, *regia* Enriquez), Brecht's *The Good Woman of Setzuan* (1973, *regia* Benno Besson) with Valeria Moriconi as Shen Te/Shui Ta, Harold Pinter's *Old Times* (1973, *regia* Visconti) which Pinter objected to, Euripides' *Medea* (1973, *regia* Enriquez) with Moriconi in the title role, the premiere of Enzo Siciliano's *Vita e morte di Cola di Rienzo* (*Life and Death of Cola di Rienzo*, 1973, *regia* Alessandro Giupponi) with Glauco Mauri in the title role, Odön von Horváth's *Kasimir and Karoline* (1974, *regia* Enriquez), the premiere of Glauco Mauri's *I quaderni di conversazione di Ludwig van Beethoven* (*The Copy Books of Conversations of Ludwig van Beethoven*, 1974) with Mauri as both *registra* and protagonist, Shakespeare's *The Taming of the Shrew* (1974, *regia* Enriquez), a rather controversial production of Molière's *Tartuffe* (1975, *regia* Mario Missiroli), and Sophocles' *Philoktetes* (1976) with Mauri again in charge of the production and playing the protagonist, and the Cerami/Ortensi/Volponi *Il sipario ducale* (*The Ducal Curtain*, 1976, *regia* Enriquez). In the 1975–1976 season the company was co-directed by Mauro Carbonoli.

Since 1976 the company has been led by Luigi Squarzina, who from 1962 to 1976 had been one of the co-directors of the Teatro Stabile di Genova, where he had done wondrous things with both repertory and staging. As is true of Enriquez and Pandolfi, Squarzina specializes in large-scale productions, but he may be the most literary of the three. He is very baroque and makes much use of lighting and interesting stage groupings. He, too, has staged many premieres, but he has cut down on the number of productions. The company tours as much as it did in the past. It now makes its home in the Teatro Argentina (eight hundred seats), with its offices around the corner.

The following productions were highly praised by the Roman theatre critics (uncredited productions are by Squarzina): Pier Paolo Pasolini's *Il vantone* (*The Boaster*) based on Plautus' *Miles Gloriosus* (1976) with Mario Scaccia in the title part, Shakespeare's *Measure for Measure* (1977) with Luigi Vanucchi as the Duke, the premiere of Giorgio Albertazzi's *Uomo e sottosuolo* (*Man and Subsoil*, 1977, *regia* the author) which was based on Dostoyevsky, Ben Jonson's *Volpone* (1977) with Scaccia in the title role, Brecht's *Fear and Misery in the Third Reich* (1978) with sets by Uberto Bertacca, the Fernando de Rojas/Alfonso Sastre *Celestina* (1979) with Anna Maestri in the title role, Goldoni's *Il ventaglio* (*The Fan*, 1979), another production of Shakespeare's *Measure for Measure* (1980) with Massimo Foschi as the Duke, Shaw's *Heartbreak House* (1980) with Gianrico Tedeschi as Captain Shotover, and Ibsen's *John Gabriel Borkman* (1981, *regia* Memè Perlini) with Foschi in the title role. The 1981–1982 season marked the 250th anniversary of the Teatro Argentina; two plays presented that season dealt with eighteenth-century life: Alfredo Testoni's *Il Cardinale Lambertini* and Peter Shaffer's *Amadeus* (*regia* and translation Giorgio Pressburger) with Paolo Bonacelli as Salierei.

In addition to plays the Theatre of Rome sponsors theatrical exhibits; holds seminars and discussions on themes such as Elizabethan drama today (1978, sponsored with the University of Rome) and twentieth-century drama (1979); and gives workshops (ongoing since 1979). Its conferences have included Theatre in the Weimar Republic (1978), Shakespeare's Problem Comedies (1979), and Goldoni (1980). It has also sponsored performances and cultural activities throughout Rome, on street corners and in parks, as part of the "Estate Romana." The company appears at the summer festival of classic works at the Teatro Romano di Ostia Antica. Particularly interesting is its season for young people in the Teatro Flaiano. Generally, six plays are staged. It also appeals to young people with special performances of its plays in the regular season.

During the regular season the company does at least two works at the Teatro Argentina, both of which generally tour. The rest of the season offered to subscribers is made up of six productions from other theatres, some from outside Italy. Squarzina usually stages one work a season himself, and most often it is a classic. About thirty-six actors are hired each year—some for the whole season and others for only one play. Many actors return season after season, but contracts run for only one season. The company receives an annual subsidy of 500 million lira, which comes not only from the city and province of Rome, but also from the Regione Lazio and the Ministry of Tourism and Culture. The company generally plays about three hundred performances a year throughout Italy. It does not have a theatre school of its own, but it has warm ties with the National Academy of Dramatic Art.

The company is popular in Rome and throughout Italy, and is especially noted for the polish and ease of its productions. Politics have sometimes gotten in the way of the company's productions. Many of the people in the theatre outside Rome think the company should be mounting more than two plays a season since the company receives a healthy subsidy. What Squarzina does, he does well, and theatre should not always be measured by quantity.

LEON M. AUFDEMBERGE
(With thanks to the Publicity
Department of the theatre.)

The Netherlands

INTRODUCTION

The Dutch are enjoying a healthy theatre boom, despite the country's general economic slump. The government, at both state and local levels, is assisting the theatre as much as possible, awarding subsidies to many different kinds of companies, including experimental companies.

The Netherlands theatre companies are divided into three categories: (1) The municipally supported, which keep a permanent company and are subsidized not only by the city of the home theatre, but also by the national government, and frequently by the province. They are run with a managing director, permanent stage directors, a permanent acting company, dramaturges, and a technical staff, generally operating two theatres and touring extensively to other cities. (2) The experimental companies, which are surprisingly good because most are subsidized by the government. Practically every major city in Holland has one (Amsterdam has a couple), and, while there is practically no interchange between the municipally supported and the experimental companies, there is no open hostility. (3) The commercial theatre companies, which play current Broadway, West End, or boulevard hits and which tour. These occasionally receive government help.

The repertory of the first and third types derives largely from abroad. Their productions reflect what has been popular at theatres all over Europe, at least capitalist Europe. Plays are well presented, with every theatre company, both commercial and municipal, trying to get as much mileage from a success as possible by touring. Since the Netherlands is a small country, this is not a hardship on the actors; many either drive or take the train back home after a performance. Some companies play Northern Belgium as well as the Netherlands.

The Dutch theatre has two major plusses: its experimentation and the sheer number of companies. Not only do the small companies experiment, but within the municipally controlled houses there is also considerable probing of new ways to present plays, especially in the smaller subsidiary houses, which most companies have. On any given night in the Netherlands one is seldom more than a few kilometers from a play, and a good one at that.

Holland has not been able to nurture new playwrights. Of the municipally-funded companies described on the following pages, Toneelgroep Centrum does the most to foster new writing talent. The rest of the companies read many plays to find new talent, but most dramaturges have misgivings even about the plays selected for production. Holland seems very aware of its lack of new playwrights, and this is probably at least the beginning of a solution for the problem.

LEON M. AUFDEMBERGE

CENTRAL THEATRE GROUP
(Toneelgroep Centrum)
Leideskade 90
Amsterdam, Netherlands

The Central Theatre Group, though relatively young (founded in 1950), has established itself as one of Holland's most experimental companies. In its short history it has progressed from a company known only to a small portion of Amsterdam's theatregoing public to one reaching for international reputation. Yet it had a difficult time becoming established.

Dissatisfied with the existing Amsterdam companies, four Amsterdam actors founded the group: Egbert van Paridon, who is still with the company; Cas Baas; Jaap Maarleveld; and Wim Vasseur. Parts were distributed indiscriminately, and most productions were tired and perfunctory. The first production was *Als Ik König Was* (*If I Were King*) by Jaap Hoogstra, presented on September 2, 1950. It was staged by Cruys Voorbergh and ran for fifty-seven performances. The first major success came in the first season with *Gevecht Met de Zoon* (*Fight with the Son*) by Cas Baas and staged by Egbert van Paridon.

The first season the company did a number of Dutch and foreign classics. (*Romeo and Juliet* was produced in the third season, while *A Midsummer Night's Dream* followed in 1957.) During these early seasons a number of Dutch plays, written by new and unknown playwrights, were given, primarily because royalties to established playwrights were difficult for the company to pay. A number of children's plays were also presented to help train actors and to pay the bills. All this time the company did not have a permanent house and played in various Amsterdam theatres or factory halls.

By the early 1960s the company was sufficiently well established to begin paying royalties, and modern foreign writers began to be part of the company's repertoire. Tennessee Williams' *Suddenly Last Summer* was a success for the group, as was J. B. Priestley's *Pelican Island*. In 1962 the first Dutch performance of a Harold Pinter work was given, when *The Birthday Party*, staged by Walter Kous, was presented. Until 1974 the Central Theatre Group staged almost all the first performances of Pinter's works in Holland. In 1968 the company had a long run with Witold Gombrowicz's *Yvonne, Princess of Burgundy*. Other noteworthy productions of this period included Christopher Hampton's *When Did You Last See Your Mother?* (translated by Walter Kous and staged by Peter Oosthoek), Peter Nichols' *A Day in the Life of Joe Egg*, and Edward Bond's *Saved* (translated by Kous and directed by Peter Oosthoek).

The play most remembered by the theatre public of the 1960s was *Ajax Reyendord* by Gerber Hellinga, a play about a subject dear to most Hollanders: soccer. In 1970 Hellinga adapted Teho Thijssen's extremely popular novel, which had been read by practically everyone in Holland, *Kees de Jongen* (*The Boy Kees*). The play had a long run of 184 performances, was done throughout Holland, and later played a guest performance in Yugoslavia. The director was Peter Oosthoek, who had two actors playing Kees—an outer and an inner personality.

By the early 1970s many Dutch actors had begun to revolt against the conservative policies of most Amsterdam theatres, and the company became known as very avant-garde and a rallying point for the new actor and director. At this time, the company also made a decision to present mainly contemporary Dutch plays written by new writers. Strangely enough, however, two of the greatest hits of the 1970s were foreign: George Tabori's *The Cannibals*, staged in 1972 by Oosthoek, and David Rudkin's *Ashes* in a production by Eddy Habbema (1976).

In 1974 Herman Lurgerink (who had written other plays for the company) had a success with his work, *Babyfoon* (*Intercom for Baby*), staged by Oosthoek. It ran for 152 performances. The center acquired a resident dramatist in 1976, when it presented Tom Vorstenbosch's dramatization of Frederick van Eeden's novel, *Van de Koele Meren des Doods* (*From the Cool Lakes of Death*), in a production by Oosthoek. This was both a popular and critical success. In 1978 Vorstenbosch had a second success with his play *Mata Hari*. In 1979 Rob Scholten, also a resident playwright and literary manager, translated and adapted into a Dutch milieu Barrie Keefee's double bill of *Gotcha* and *Killing Time* (*regie* Habbema).

In 1975 the company moved into the Bellevue Theatre, after playing a number of theatres in Amsterdam. It is a relatively small house (250 seats) and has a smaller theatre (80 seats) for one-person shows. The company itself is comprised of eight actresses and fourteeen actors who are generally engaged by the season. It is subsidized by five authorities: the Dutch government, the city of Amsterdam, the provinces of Utrecht and North Holland, and the cities of Utrecht and Haarlem. In addition, the company receives income from the cities it plays.

Since the company has a Dutch philosophy (other companies in Amsterdam do present many foreign plays), the company likes to work in its home theatre, but it is also a touring organization. It plays in both theatres and open halls, and generally eschews large auditoriums. It frequently takes short plays to factories or places where workers congregate. Plays are chosen by Carel Aphenaar, with the help of the theatre staff. Most of the plays chosen are by modern Dutch authors. Holland's major playwright at present, Lodewijk de Boer, wrote *De*

Pornograaf for the company in 1978. The group likes to think of itself as an Amsterdam equivalent of the Royal Court in London. In addition, while on tour, the company stages productions from other Dutch companies in its home theatre. In 1979 the Bread and Butter Company of New York made a guest appearance at the Centrum after receiving the Erasmus Prize.

Although Holland has had a theatre since the Middle Ages and has had theatres since the eighteenth century, it still considers itself a young theatre country. Young playwrights need encouragement, and one of the producing organizations in Holland that provides a great deal of help is the Centrum. The play must have social relevance to be produced by the group. If the Toneelgroep Centrum has anything to say about it, Holland may one day be noted for its playwrights.

LEON M. AUFDEMBERGE

COOPERATIVE ORGANIZATION—THE WORK THEATRE
(Kooperative Vereinging het Werkteater)
Kattengrat 10
Amsterdam 10, Netherlands

Het Werkteater (the Work Theatre), founded in 1970 in Amsterdam, is highly experimental and appears likely to become a permanent feature of Dutch theatre life. The group was founded by twelve young people, who liked the theatre but were also interested in social causes. From its first season the group has been funded by the Amsterdam City Council and the Ministry of Culture. There was no need to perform, but the company did have a work space. It decided that no one would be head and that all decisions would be made cooperatively. This approach proved chaotic but rewarding. The group began with a series of small projects, the first of which was based on Maurice Maeterlinck's *Pelleas and Melisande* called *Dromenprojekt* (*Dream Project*) and played from November 1970 to January 1971. At the end of the first year the troupe was given permission to continue. Twelve pieces were performed in the first season. Two selections proved outstanding. *Allez-Hop*, commissioned by the Residentieorkest with music by Luciano Berio and performed by Cathy Berberian in the Congresgebow in Den Haag (conducted by M. Tabacnik), was an elaborate clown show played by the whole company. *De Avonduren van Beethoven* (*The Adventures of Beethoven*) was based on an idea by John Murat with the production by Rense Royaards. The group began to tour the first season.

The company began the second season (1971–1972) with a series of small pieces and several projects (including one based on William Faulkner's *Sanctuary*). It was in this season that it had its first substantial success (though long-running success was probably the last thing the company sought) in *Toestanden* (*In a Mess*). This work played from 1972 to 1975 and was eventually filmed. The *stimulator* (not a *regisseur* or stage director) was Marja Kok. This work also stressed improvisation, with the form of the play changing from audience to audience (as does all work of the company).

The company believes that all productions are equally important; hence, a description of some of the company's work is one way of summarizing what the company has done. An early project, *'T is maar een Meisje (It's Only a Girl)*, was inspired by Germaine Greer's *The Female Eunuch*. This production consisted of a series of cabaret scenes (*stimulators* Cas Enklaar and Marja Kok) dealing with female emancipation. In the same year KLM commissioned *Ondernemingsraadprojekt (Venture-Advice-Project)* in which the improvisations were based on the sort of problems the company would face now that part of the labor force would be present in its management.

Misdaad (Mishap, which played from 1973 to 1974) dealt with the problem of the individual in prison and was frequently performed in prisons where prisoners, guards, and officials sat together. The prisoners themselves frequently took parts in the play, either as themselves or as employees in the prison who they felt were oppressing their rights. *Ovondrood (Evening Redness,* which played from 1974 to 1977), centered on the problems of aging and dying, subjects to which the group has since returned. *Het feest voor Nico (The Party for Nico,* 1974–1975) was played in the tent with its *stimulator* Rense Royaards. Nico (skinny) is in conflict with his (fat) family because, after receiving his degree in engineering, he wants to use his knowledge in underdeveloped countries. This work was also done at the Festival Mondiale du Théâtre in Nancy in 1975.

Obesity also played a large role in *Dikke vrieden (Thick Friends,* 1976) which focused on a group of fat people who meet and discuss discrimination against their obesity. Eventually, they all join a therapy group. *Niet thuis (Not at Home,* 1975–1977) had as its subject children in homes not their own. *Hallo Medemens! (Hello Fellow Human!),* which played from the summer of 1976 through the summer of 1977, was a penetrating study of people's relationships as three women try to reach people in an outside circle. This was eventually done on television in 1979. A popular children's play was *Doodgewoon (Very East,* 1976–1977), based on Astrid Lindgren's *De Gebroeders Leeuwenhart (The Leeuwenhart Brothers),* with Peter Faber its *stimulator.*

Als de dood (Scared to Death, stimulator Shireen Strooker) was about the problems of dying and was played at the BITEF Festival in Yugoslavia in 1979. *Je moet er mee leven (You Must Live with It,* 1975–1979) was also about death and was played in Yugoslavia in 1979. Eventually, these two works were combined and entitled *Opname (In for Treatment),* filmed in 1979 (*regie* Marja Kok and Erike van Zuylen). Other recent plays have been *Gewoon Weg (Exceptional Way,* 1980, *stimulator* Dair Mohr) which discussed the problem of handicapped children, and *Zus of zo (Such and Such,* 1980), which was a collective exercise about homosexuality and played London in 1981.

The Work Theatre has a permanent theatre in Amsterdam where it performs once a week (on Fridays), always to a full house. It plays on tour in the Netherlands, using a tent seating 750. It also plays in theatres, hospitals, and jails, and has done a number of street performances. The company has played in France and England with several actors in the company fluent in the languages of the countries. There is no set number of plays per season. The troupe plays six to eleven performances a week, generally giving two performances an evening.

Each project begins with an actor or actress bringing in a subject for troupe discussion. Then all or part of the company researches the most likely subjects. From there the group begins to improvise, sometimes separating into two groups. From this improvisation emerges a basic framework. All performances are different from evening to evening as all pieces involve the audience. The troupe has made several films and has recently published a collection of three scripts, the scripts are an amalgamation of several performances of the same work. Entitled *Het Werkteater Drie Stukken* (Amsterdam: Van Gennep, 1979), this collection was edited by Daria Mohr.

The current troupe numbers twelve performers. Each actor or actress must be elected to the company. In addition, a number of guests have worked with the troupe. Approximately 70 percent of the operating budget comes from the generous government subsidy. The group is moving toward more performances with music, but whatever it does in the future must involve the audience. All performances of the Work Theatre end in an audience discussion of what they have seen.

Two factors keep the company from overcomplacency: its feelings for social causes and its fluidity. All of its projects are statements of social problems and the products of the company's collective thinking. No two performances are the same, as no audience is the same. The Work Theatre is a very committed theatre both in the terms of its projects and its acting company.

LEON M. AUFDEMBERGE

HAAGSE'S PLAYHOUSE
(Haagse Comedie) (at the Koninklijke Schouwburg)
Schouwburgstraat 8
The Hague, Netherlands

Although Haagse's Playhouse was founded in 1947, the theatre in which it plays is very old and the tradition of a city theatre is older still. There have been plays in The Hague since the Middle Ages and playhouses since the late Renaissance. It was not until 1908, with the Hagheselers founded by Edward Verkade, that a company identified with the city became an actuality. Verkade is one of the great names in Dutch theatre, not only in The Hague but also throughout Holland. This company did not last long, being replaced in 1917 by the Hofstadtoneel, under the leadership of Cor van der Lugt Melsert, which lasted until World War II. These two men are credited with founding a style, the "Haagse style," which was characterized by a coolness, underacting, and a civilized and refined approach to production. Most of the plays done by either troupe were naturalistic in style, which the public clearly liked.

During the Nazi Occupation, the Royal Playhouse (the Koninklijke Shouwburg) was an opera house for German troupes. A local troupe, the Residentie

Toneel, under the direction of Dirk Veerbeck, Bets Ranucci Beckmann, and Johan de Meester, did play at various houses until it folded in 1947. In that year, the city fathers decided to replace this company, and Veerbeck was given permission to found the new company. Two people were considered for director: Cees Leseur and Johan de Meester. Since both were out of the country—Leseur in the United States and de Meester in Belgium—the choice fell to Paul Steenberger, an actor. A large percentage of the old Residentie Toneel was to form the nucleus of the new company, which Leseur (now returned to Holland and made director) called De Haagsche Comedie. The first play chosen for the repertory was in honor of the American liberators. Howard Lindsay and Russel Crouse's *State of the Union* was presented in the fall of 1947; it was staged by Leseur and acted by Paul Steenberger. During its first season the company revolved around these two people. The repertory of the new company in its first year included many American works, such as the Moss Hart/George Kaufman *You Can't Take It with You*, Sidney Howard's *They Knew What They Wanted*, and Maxwell Anderson's *Anne of a Thousand Days*. There was also a place for the new French repertory, with Jean Anouilh's *Eurydice* appearing in the first season. Leseur staged about half of the first season. By the end of the season, it was clear that the company was among the leading ones in Holland.

Most of the plays in the first seasons were Broadway successes, current English hits, or boulevard works from France. These choices were made in order to bring people into the theatre and to help balance the budget. The company was grossly overworked in its first years, frequently doing two performances a day. In 1948 Loes Wieringa joined the company, later becoming business manager, a job she still holds.

In 1950 the pressure of being both manager and head *regisseur* of the company proved too much for one man, so Steenberger was made co-director with Leseur. Both men argued frequently, but when the evening performance rolled around, tranquility ruled on the stage. This relationship lasted until Leseur died in 1960.

By the middle of the 1950s the company's repertory became less and less popularly oriented, and classics assumed a larger part. The first Dutch production of a Christopher Fry play came in 1950 when Leseur staged *Venus Observed*. Shakespeare became more prominent in the same decade, as did Chekhov, Brecht, and Anouilh. In 1951 Karl Gutterman became the first house dramaturge.

In the same decade the two directors began to look outside Holland for *regisseurs*. Erwin Piscator came in 1952 to stage George Bernard Shaw's *Androcles and the Lion*, and the next year he repeated the success of the first with the same author's *Caesar and Cleopatra*. Since then outside *regisseurs* have included Michael Langham, Michael Croft, and Wilfred Minks.

In 1956 the company was sufficiently well known to be invited to the International Theatre Festival in Paris, presenting three one-act plays (by Michel de Ghelderode, Jean Anouilh, and Terence Rattigan), under the collective title of

Harlekinade. The company also assisted in establishing the Holland Festival in 1957. Then, in 1958, with Ledley Stoyn's *Little Toontje Drew a Horse*, Fie Carelsen, who had been with the company since its inception and was considered the *grande dame* of the Netherlands theatre, said farewell. But a sadder farewell was in store for the company. On January 1, 1960, after Peter Wood's production of Shakespeare's *The Winter's Tale*, Leseur, after making a name for the company, fell dead. It looked for a while as if the company would fold, but Steenberger and Loes Wieringa pulled it through.

The 1960s began sadly, but the company continued to prosper throughout the decade. New and avant-garde playwrights appeared in the repertory, such as Harold Pinter, Fernando Arrabal, Sławomir Mrożek, and a new small theatre was opened in the top of the house, "Het Pardijs" ("Paradise" or more prosaically "Attic"), to accommodate them. Peter Scharoff came in 1959 as a guest *regisseur*, but in the 1960s he became a permanent part of the company, best remembered for his Chekhov's *The Cherry Orchard* (1961), with Ida Wassermann as Madame Ranyevskaya. Steenberger continued as a stager, as did Dutch *regisseurs*, such as Johan de Meester, Frans van der Lingen, and Joris Diels. Diels staged *King Lear* in 1965 for Albert van Dalsum's farewell to the theatre after fifty-five years of acting.

The most outstanding production of this decade was Peter Zadek's production of Frank Wedekind's *Spring Awakening* (1964). By the early 1960s it was clear that the company needed a new introduction to staging. It had good *regisseurs* and was keeping abreast of new playwrights, but the new staging methods of Germany were foreign. Zadek reworked the company, and the results were sensational. Even an actor of the old school, such as Steenberger, said the treatment was refreshing. The public took to both the production and the renewed actors.

This renewed vigor was also seen in the work of the designer, Aart Verhoeven, who decided to change the name of the company to the Haagse Comedie. In 1964 an old church in the city, the Ooster Kerk (The Easter Church), was remodeled for rehearsal purposes, with a bar, library, and a foyer where the actors and the public could mingle. A new custom began in the 1967–1968 season of allowing high school students to observe rehearsals.

At the end of the 1960s Steenberger thought it was time to step down, although retirement was unthinkable. In 1968 Carl van der Ples was invited to become artistic director, with an eye (although he did not know it) to replacing Steenberger. At this time there were tremendous upheavals in the Dutch theatre, with two companies folding, one in Rotterdam and one in Amsterdam. But the company in The Hague prospered, and, to meet the needs of an expanded repertory, a new theatre was added to the permanent one. It was nicknamed "HOT." This theatre would be used to stage experimental works and to provide a showcase for new talents in acting, staging, and writing.

In August 1971 van der Ples became managing director of the main company, with Richard Nastasi becoming director of HOT. Two new *regisseurs* joined the company at this time, van Rooj and Guido de Moor. By 1972 and the twenty-fifth anniversary of the company, the days of upheavals in other companies which might have spread to this one were clearly past, and the company was on solid ground.

In the 1970s again the Haagse Comedie added new playwrights. Edward Albee first appeared in 1971 with *All Over*. Beckett was frequently done as was Odön von Horváth. The company also participated in the Feydeau revival throughout Europe. Perhaps the company's greatest accomplishment has been its encouragement of new Dutch writers. The opening of HOT provided an opportunity to see new works by untried authors without the threat of box office failure. HOT has clearly established itself. Perhaps the best work to come out of HOT has been *De Andere Weld* (*The Other World*) by Tom Vorstenbosuh. With two playhouses, the public can choose to see what it wishes. Of course, the young patronize HOT, and the older generation the main stage. Classics are best attended, often at capacity.

A typical season at the Haagse Comedie strives for balance between classics and modern, while HOT is consistently used for new plays. The company tries to do at least a couple of Dutch authors every year, with usually one-quarter of the repertory coming from the Netherlands.

The theatre is municipally owned, and the income from the box office must be shared with the city. The Koninklijke Schouwburg was built by Pieter de Swart in 1765 and was originally to be the wing of a palace that was never completed. The classic facade is older than the rest of the theatre. It was first used as a court theatre usually for French works, both operas and plays, but the history of the theatre as a house for Dutch works does not begin until Verkade's company. The house is fairly comfortable and seats 750, with HOT seating 360. HOT also has an art gallery collection.

The company's chief strengths are probably its large and varied repertory and its *regisseurs*. One of its most outstanding *regisseurs* has been Guido de Moore, who has done such works as Maxim Gorky's *Summer Folk* (1975) and Alfred de Musset's *Lorenzaccio* (1977). The company also is expected to tour and has played all over the Netherlands, as well as Northern Belgium. When on tour, other companies use its stage.

The company numbers about fifty, with thirty men and twenty women; other actors are hired as needed. The theatre employs four permanent *regisseurs* and invites four guests each season. It also has two dramaturges who read a great number of scripts each season; several resident translators; a large technical staff; and a resident musical advisor. The company publishes a summary of its season every year, which is very frank in its appraisal of how the year fared. Its budget runs to about 12 million guilders, of which one-half is subsidy and one-half is box office receipts.

Building on the past, Carl van der Ples continues to make the Haagse Comedie one of the outstanding theatres in Holland. Its philosophy may be stated succinctly: the best productions of the best plays for a wide audience. Now with two separate theatres (but actors and *regisseurs* working at both) it looks to a bright and ideal future, with a reverence for the past.

LEON M. AUFDEMBERGE
(Translation help by Frida Somers-Hatley)

PUBLIC THEATRE
(Publicksteater)
Stadtschouwburg, Marnixstraat 427
Amsterdam, Netherlands

Amsterdam's theatre companies date back to the seventeenth century, although plays have been done there since the late Middle Ages. The first municipally subsidized theatre came in 1810 when the city took over management of the Nieuw Amsterdamsche Stadtschouwburg, giving the theatre 10,000 florins to provide "entertainment for the public." A number of other theatres have been built in the city. The municipally controlled Stadtschouwburg opened in 1894 (architects J. and J. B. Springer and A. L. Van Gendt), with Victorien Sardou's *Madame Sans-Gêne*. The theatre, built in the prevailing style of Flemish Renaissance Revival, is all gables and decoration, and has been home for a series of municipally financed theatre companies.

One of the companies was the De Nederlandsce Comedie, founded in 1953 by Johann de Keester, who was famous as a *regisseur* for his Shakespeare, Joost van den Vondel (Holland's best loved playwright), and Greek productions. He and Hans Pentz van den Berg were the principal stagers for this company, which introduced a number of modern playwrights (Anton Chekhov, Tennessee Williams, and T. S. Eliot) to Amsterdam. De Nederlandsce Comedie was considered the country's leading theatre company until the middle 1960s, when productions began to become perfunctory and the acting stagnant. The public stayed home in droves, and in March 1969, a group of students staged a famous happening known as *action tomaat*, throwing vegetables at the actors in the company during a production of Tankred Dorst's *Toller*. In the accompanying furor the city council closed the theatre, and a new company, the Amsterdam Toneel, was formed. The new one lasted two years and was made up of many actors from the previous company.

In 1973 the city government approached Hans Croiset, head of the "Theatre" in Arnheim, about founding a new company that would be given the name of the Publicksteater. A new acting company was formed, which would have a few actors from the previous companies, but for the most part would be composed of fresh young talent. The opening production was Shakespeare's *A Midsummer Night's Dream* (*regie* Croiset), opening on September 23, 1973. It ran for fifty-six performances, which is considered a long run in Amsterdam, and was clearly a winner with the public. By the opening production, it was clear that public faith had been restored in the old Schouwburg. It was not the traditional heavy approach to a play, but a wildly extravagant playful production in mod clothing, a reflection of swinging Amsterdam. The actors, particularly Lou Landré as Puck, revealed that the old tired ways of dreadful acting in the theatre were over.

A second Shakespeare followed, *King Lear*, with the production again by Hans Croiset and with Max Croiset as the title character. Again successes were achieved with Nikolai Gogol's *The Inspector General* (*regie* Jan Grossman) and with an adaptation by George Farquhar's *The Recruiting Officer*, called *Le Hollandse Ronselaar* (*The Dutch Recruiting Officer*). By the end of the first season, the company had played 185 performances of which 69 were in Amsterdam, to nearly seventy-four thousand spectators.

In this first season, the theatre set the artistic policies that still govern it. First, the company would play the best of an international repertory, with special emphasis on the classics. Second, it would not only play Amsterdam, but would also tour, playing in twenty-five cities in Holland in its first season. Third, it would employ a number of young actors and *regisseurs*. Fourth, it would do only a small number of productions each season and concentrate all its energies on doing these well.

During the second season, the company played Carlo Goldoni, Chekhov, Brecht, and Joost van den Vondel's *Gysbreght van Aemstel*. Three of these productions were staged by Hans Croiset, the exception being the Dutch play. In the 1975–1976 season a rather new *regisseur* and co-director was added to the staff to take pressure off Croiset. He is Ton Lutz, who has become one of Holland's best known and experimental *regisseurs*. He did the production of the opener, Sophocles' *Electra*, as well as a pairing of Jean-Paul Sartre's *No Exit* and Jean Genet's *The Maids*. The fourth season saw a dip in the number of performances, largely because the local opera company with which the theatre company shares the house began to schedule more performances. The greatest success of the season was Euripides' *Medea* (*regie* Lutz), with Annet Nieuwenhuyzen as the title character and sets by Nicholas Wijnberg. Chekhov's *The Cherry Orchard* (*regie* Lutz), Shakespeare's *Hamlet* (*regie* Hans Croiset), and Brecht's *The Caucasian Chalk Circle* (*regie* Lutz) made up the well-balanced season.

The 1977–1978 season saw an excellent production of Sartre's *Dirty Hands*. The season had a big success in Hans Croiset's staging of Chekhov's rarely done work *Platonov*. In 1978–1979 the most ambitious work done was a double bill of Sophocles' two Oedipus plays, *Oedipus Tyrannos* and *Oedipus at Colonus*, both cut a third, and both played in one evening (*regie* Croiset).

The policy with regard to play selection was set in the first season and remains the same. The company does five works a year with plays generally balancing each other. It has now completed a cycle of the four major Chekhov plays, plus *Ivanov* and *Platonov*. The theatre company has a subsidy from both the state and city government, and some financial assistance from other cities it plays. It employs twelve actors and eight actresses in its permanent company, adding more if needed. In general, local actors are in plentiful supply in Amsterdam.

The theatre holds about nine hundred people. Because the theatre company shares the house with two other companies (opera and ballet), it plays only on Friday, Saturday, and Sunday. The theatre staff is separate from the other two staffs but cooperates with them. During the nights it does not play in Amsterdam, the company plays other Dutch theatres. The theatre publishes its own bulletin, *The Publicksteater Krant*, every three months, telling the public what is happening in the theatre. The journal is sent to all on subscription.

The company chooses plays from the standpoint of the theatre's philosophy. Holland has had a difficult time in recent years, suffering from the Occupation during the war and some bad years economically after the war. Although Hollanders are traditionally hard working, many people are frequently discouraged. The theatre seeks to demonstrate that problems can be worked out and that things can be changed. Chekhov and Brecht lead the way in this effort, despite the wide disparity in their philosophies.

The Publicksteater is a young company, both in its years of existence and in the ages of its members. It appeals to many young people in Amsterdam and in other cities in which it plays. Appealing more to the young, the theatre is planning more contemporary works now that a public has been attracted. The company has built a steady clientele of subscribers and has a loyal public. Clearly, the *action tomaat* is very much a thing of the past.

LEON M. AUFDEMBERGE

RO THEATRE
(RO Theater)
van Oldenbarneveltstraat 105
Rotterdam, Netherlands

The Rotterdamse Schouwburg (Rotterdam Theatre) was opened on January 10, 1947. There have been some problems in finding suitable productions to fill the large (over one thousand seats) house. In the 1950s, 1960s, and early 1970s two civic companies were lodged in the theatre: the Rotterdamse Toneel and the Nieuw Rotterdamse Toneel, which replaced it. Both companies had checkered careers. There has also been a succession of experimental companies in the city since World War II, many of them quite good, but all with fairly short lives.

Since 1976 the situation has radically altered with the establishment of the RO Theatre founded by Franz Marijnen, who is one of Holland's hottest *regisseurs*. Marijnen is actually Flemish by birth, but all his work has been done either in the Netherlands or in West Germany (principally Hamburg's Deutsches Schauspielhaus). In 1976 Marijnen staged a production of Oskar Panizza's *Love Council* as a sort of test production. It proved so successful that the following fall Marijnen opened a resident company in the Schouwburg.

The first season (1977–1978) opened with Marijnen staging a production of Hugo Claus' *Het Huis van Labdakus* (*The House of Labdakus*), a play much admired in the Netherlands. It was a moderate success, but the second play was a substantial success, a project with Jérôme Savary staging, *1001 Nacht*, (*1001 Nights*). This was followed by another hit, Jean Genet's *The Balcony*.

The next season, Marijnen staged a light and inventive production of Carlo Goldoni's *The Servant of Two Masters* (with Peter Tuinman as Arlecchino), which toured extensively throughout the Netherlands.

The 1979–1980 season opened with a big success, a production of Shakespeare's *King Lear* by the East German *regisseurs* Manfred Karge and Matthias Langhoff, with John Kraaykamp, Sr., as the King. The sets were by Gero Troike, who also is East German. This was followed by a premiere production entitled *Wasteland*, which was staged by Marijnen with choreography by Hans Tuerlings. The subject of this disturbing evening was the effect of an atomic blast. This season also featured two versions of Genet's *The Maids* (one staged by Wolfram Kremer and the other by Marijnen) and the Tom Stoppard/André Previn *Every Good Boy Deserves Favor* done with the Rotterdams Philharmonisch Orkest (conducted by David Zinman or Roelof van Driesten) and staged by Marijnen.

The next season (1980–1981) opened with Marijnen directing one of his specialties, Shakespeare's *A Midsummer Night's Dream*. The season closed with a lively and comic modern dress version of Molière's *Tartuffe*, with the production by Marijnen. After *Tartuffe* closed in Rotterdam, it went on a long tour of the Netherlands and Belgium.

The RO Theatre houses two major theatres within its building: a large theatre with seats for over one thousand, and a small Piccolo with variable seating (usually one hundred). The theatre does four productions a year, with Marijnen staging at least two. The company has nine men and four women in a permanent status; the rest of the troupe are guests. The company also has a permanent dramaturge and a technical staff. The company's budget runs to 2.5 million guilders, which is all subsidy. Box office receipts are returned to the government. The company has no subscriptions, although the theatre in which it is housed does have an extensive program that includes all sorts of theatre performances, including those of the RO Theatre. The company averages about 75 to 80 percent attendance per production.

The company does not strive for huge commercial success (although it has obviously had some), nor is it a star-oriented company. Its feeling is toward ensemble. During the first season the company toured, but in succeeding seasons it did rather less touring. Its main duty, it feels, is toward the city of Rotterdam. So far it has served its home city well.

LEON M. AUFDEMBERGE

Portugal

INTRODUCTION

The Portuguese theatre presents a paradox: the country has a long tradition of doing plays but has yet to produce a major dramatist. The only playwright to achieve some fame outside the country was Gil Vicente, who wrote in the sixteenth century and who in some histories is claimed by Spain, inasmuch as the language of his plays alternates between a very literary Spanish and an early Portuguese. He cannot be called a major playwright, however; the country's only other playwright of note is João Baptista da Almeida-Garrett (the real Father of Portuguese drama), whose play *Frei Luis de Sousa* (1843) is Portugal's national drama.

Portugal, like many countries in Western Europe, has undergone decentralization in recent years which has been much to the country's good. Until fairly recently, Portuguese theatre was the theatre of Lisbon. Now companies, most of which receive some form of government subsidy, dot the whole of the country. The major company outside Lisbon is undoubtedly the Teatro Sperimental do Oporto, which has fostered new playwrights and introduced playgoers in the North to an international repertory.

The best theatre in Portugal is still found in Lisbon. Lisbon's commercial theatres feature a wide variety of plays, much as the theatres of New York, London, or Paris do. The commercial houses present current hits from abroad, classic plays, or works by contemporary Portuguese playwrights. Portugal, similarly to many other Southern European countries, admires acting; the average Lisbon playgoer is less apt to ask who wrote the play than who was in it.

Apart from decentralization, the most important change in the Portuguese theatre has been its loss of censorship. Since the 1920s (and even before that), conditions of censorship in Portugal sapped almost all creative ability, and, until the late 1960s, plays were still being closed by censors, often for frivolous reasons. Even the prestigious Teatro Nacional Dona Maria II was not immune.

Another significant change in the Portuguese theatre is the recent rise in importance of the *encenação* or stage director. As mentioned earlier, until recently Portuguese theatre was a theatre of stars. Portugal now has a number of strong *encenaçãos*, as well as important ones from abroad such as José Tamayo and Michael Benthall. Portuguese productions are also beginning to play abroad at various festivals.

In an effort to encourage playwrights, the government awards small subsidies to young playwrights. All of the theatres described in the following articles have administrators who read a number of plays each season with an eye to production. Perhaps from this will come the great playwright of whom Portugal has long dreamed.

LEON M. AUFDEMBERGE

NATIONAL THEATRE OF DONA MARIA II
(Teatro Nacional Dona Maria II)
Praça don Pedro IV (Rossio)
Lisbon, Portugal

The first notice of a play in Lisbon came as early as 1471 with *Entremés do Anjo* (*The Business of an Angel*). Later in the north of the country, Gil Vicente, still considered Portugal's greatest playwright, began writing plays. It was not until the early nineteenth century, however, that Portugal began to build playhouses in great numbers. From this time the theatre was dominated by either Spanish or Italian influences.

The idea of establishing a national theatre for Portugal came in 1836 when Joachim Larcher, civil governor for the city of Lisbon, and João Baptista da Almeida-Garrett, then Portugal's leading poet and playwright, presented to Queen Dona Maria II a plan for a theatre, largely built to present modern Portuguese plays. The Iberian Peninsula was experiencing a wave of nationalism at the time; and Garrett, who was also the inspector general for Lisbon's theatres, had already founded the prestigious Conservatório (which still exists) as a school for music and theatre. In 1842 the building, Italian neoclassic in design, was started by the Italian Fortunato Lodi; it looked more like a palace than a theatre. The interior decoration was done by António Manuel de Fonesca. The district chosen for the theatre was the Rocio (now Rossio), and the theatre was built on what is still the major square of the city, Praça don Pedro IV.

The Teatro Dona Maria II (as a semiprivate theatre with government subsidies) opened on April 13, 1846. It played a new work with a long title written by a Portuguese playwright with a long name, *Alvaro Goncalves, o magriço, ou os Doze de Inglaterra* by Jacinto Helidora de Faria Aguiar de Loureire e a Rainha. It was performed ten times in the first season and then forgotten. The acting company was far from forgotten, however, for in its first seasons the company included such important actors as Delfina Rosa do Espírito Santo, Crispianiano Pantaleaõ de Cunha Sargedos, Jose Simoẽs Nunes Borges (whose daughter and granddaughter would also act for the company), and, above all, Emília das Neves e Sousa, generally considered Portugal's greatest actress. Das Neves also played extensively outside Portugal, being especially well received in Brazil.

The organization for the company was patterned after that of the troupe playing at the Teatro da Rua dos Condes, currently managed by Émile Roux, a Frenchman. Most of the acting troupe for Garrett's company came from this theatre. The Roux company's repertory contained many contemporary French works, as well as Portuguese writers, such as Garrett, which the new troupe copied. The actors themselves organized into a society much like that of the Comédie Française. This Sociedade Artistic do Teatro Dona Maria II was dissolved and reformed many times during the nineteenth and twentieth centuries. Among other things, it set rules for actors, such as how much each actor was to be paid, which actors would be members of the society (and thus members of a permanent company), and which would be hired by the season.

Until the turn of the century, the company's repertory derived largely from Portugal and France. Victor Hugo was particularly popular. In the first season, the company played Garrett's *Frei Luis de Sousa*, a work that has rarely been out of the repertory and has remained the most popular play, being performed more than any other play in the company's history. In 1848 Garrett's last play, *Sobrinha do Marqués* (*Niece of the Marqués*), had its premiere by the company.

In the 1840s and 1850s the troupe strove to find new plays from Portuguese writers, none of which proved lasting primarily because from the 1850s until the 1870s, censorship posed a great obstacle to Portuguese theatre. The theatre had its first huge success at the box office in 1849, with José da Silva Mendes Leal, Júnior's play, *O Templo de Salomão* (*The Temple of Solomon*). In this play João Rosa (whose two sons would eventually act here as well) and Josepha Soller had acting triumphs. The audience was convinced this was a great play, but, though well received (it was spectacularly mounted), it has not lasted. In 1853 das Neves, who had been absent several seasons, gave a triumphant performance when she played Marguerite Gauthier in Alexandre Dumas *fils' La dame aux camélias* (*Camille*, translated by Antonio Joaquim de Silva Abranches). Other important plays before her retirement included Friedrich von Schiller's *Mary Stuart* (1854, translated by Mendes Leal); Hugh's *Angelo, Tyrant of Padua* (1855) and *Lucretia Borgia* (1863); and Friederich Halm's *The Gladiator of Ravenna* (1871), as well as great numbers of Portuguese plays.

In the 1850s, too, the company hired several new players: Manuela Lopes Rey, Francisco Alves da Silva Taborada, and Teodorico. In the 1860s the Rosa brothers (João júnior and Augusto) appeared. In the 1870s the theatre began to do many well-made plays, both French (Sardou) and Portuguese, and added even more actors, including Eduardo Brazão, José Ferreira da Silva (frequently considered Portugal's greatest actor), Joaquim Pinto, Virginia, Emilía Adélaide, Augusto Posser, Ángela Pinto, Adelina Abraches, Lucinda Simoës, and Rosa Damasceno.

In the late 1880s and into the turn of the century, Portugal was hit by a new wave of nationalism and republicanism. The plays of this period reflect this spirit. Many of the plays have lasted, being among the most often read and revived in Portugal. Among the best known are João da Câmara's *Os gatos* (*The Cats*, 1888), *Don Alfonso VI* (1890), *Alcáber-Kibir* (1891), *Os velhos* (*The Old Ones*, 1893), *O pântano* (*The Swamp*, 1894), and *A Triste Viuvinha* (*The Sad Little Widow*, 1897); Marcelino Mesquita's *Lenor Teles* (*Lenor Teles*, 1889), *Os castros* (*The Castros*, 1893), *O velho tema* (*The Old Theme*, 1894), *A Dor Suprema* (*The Supreme Pain*, 1895), and *O Regente* (*The Regent*, 1897); Alberto Braga's *O Estuário* (*The Estuary*, 1897); and Vasco de Mendoca Albes' *Os Filhos* (*The Children*, 1900). In 1882 the company began to play Shakespeare with *Othello* (Brazão as Othello and João Rosa júnior as Iago), the translation by Jose Antonio de Freitas, followed by *Hamlet* (1887), and *King Lear* (1903). In 1889 the Rosa brothers and Brazão became managers for the troupe, staying until 1903. They had the good fortune to have Mancini as scene designer for most of their productions. In the 1880s a series of guest productions by other great actors played the theatre, including Eleanora Duse, Sarah Bernhardt, and, most frequently, Italia Vitalini.

From the turn of the century, the company began to tour extensively in Portugal. It had already gone to Brazil in 1893 and would return in 1910 and 1939, but from 1900 on the company began to see the need to act as a touring organization as well, with Oporto, Coimbra, and Braga being the cities it would visit most often. New actors came into the company about this time, including Laura Cruz, Paulo Armstrong, and Maria Pia de Almenida. Beginning in 1900, the repertory became more international but not necessarily very adventurous. (Ibsen and Strindberg were played elsewhere if played at all.) Oscar Wilde was especially popular. In addition, the company began to revive many plays from the Portuguese past, especially Gil Vicente and Garrett. More attention was also paid to a balanced season, split between Portuguese and international writers, classics and moderns. This pattern still exists.

In the 1910s and 1920s a new breed of actor was admitted to the company: such an actor was not so much schooled in the grand tradition but was more influenced by the realistic approach to acting which was spreading through Europe at the time. These actors included Ilda Stichini, Palmira Bastos, José Alves de Cunha, and a husband-and-wife team, José Ricardo e Robles Monteiro and Amélia Rey Colaço, who would eventually become the managers of the troupe. Two good original plays of this period were Augusto de Lacerdo's *O Pasterleiro do Madrigal* (*The Baker of the Madrigal*, 1923) and Raul Brandão's *O Gebo e a Sombra* (*The Old Shabby Woman and the Shadow*, 1927).

Monteiro and Rey Colaço were made heads of the troupe in 1929 and would lead it jointly until 1958, when Monteiro died. Rey Colaço would then become sole head until 1978, probably the longest anyone has ever managed a theatre company. During her tenure the plays became much more international and experimental in approach. At the beginning of her career with the company, she acted in Edward Sheldon's *Romance* (1927), and at the end, she did Friedrich Dürrenmatt's *The Visit from the Old Lady* (1960). This was in the face of the omnipresent censor, who at various stages in the joint or single directorship forbade plays by such writers as Eugene O'Neill, Luigi Pirandello, George Bernard Shaw, Federico García Lorca, J. B. Priestley, Jean Giraudoux, and many Portuguese writers, including José Régio.

Monteiro and Rey Colaço encouraged new playwrights. Rey Colaço had already scored an acting triumph with the company in Alfredó Cortês' *Zilda* (1921) and, under the joint directorship, they staged several new works from him, including *Os gladiodores* (*The Gladiators*, 1933) and above all, *Tá-Mar* (*Behold the Sea*, 1936), which has proved to be his best work, a sensitive picture of the daily lives of Portuguese fishermen. The play has since been revived by the company, most recently in 1955 (staged by Rey Colaço); later it was taken to Paris for the international theatre festival. Other new works done under the joint directorship included Carlos Selvagem's *Dulcinea ou a ultima aventura de D. Quixote* (*Dulcinea or the Last Adventure of Don Quixote*, 1944) and José Régio's *Benilde ou a Virge-mae* (*Benilde, or the Virgin Mother* staged by Rey Colaço in 1947). In 1937 in a centenary celebration in honor of Gil Vicente, a number of his works were played.

Before World War II, the company was largely made up of stars, but, from the late 1940s on, the focus shifted to ensemble. In 1939 the theatre finally became the National Theatre of Portugal, leading to the rise of the *encenação* (the director). The major productions of the 1930s and the early 1940s, in many of which Rey Colaço and Monteiro acted, included Molière's *Le bourgeois gentilhomme* (*The Bourgeois Gentleman*, 1930); Marcelino Mesquita's *Lenor Teles* (1931); João de Camar's *D. Alfonso VI* (1933); Antonio Ferreira's *Castro* (1934); Gil Vicente's *O Amadis de Gaula* (1935); Schiller's *Mary Stuart* (1938); Paul Claudel's *The Tidings as Brought to Mary* (1940); Shakespeare's *A Midsummer Night's Dream* (1941); O'Neill's *Mourning Becomes Electra* (1942), in which Rey Colaço was an outstanding Christine; Pirandello's *Six Characters in Search of an Author* (1943); Shakespeare's *Hamlet* (1943); Wilde's *Lady Windermere's Fan* (1944); and Shakespeare's *Othello* (1944).

Beginning in the mid-1940s, the stager of the play became of major significance, possibly because of Erwin Meyenburg, who joined the company as one of its major stagers in the 1940s. The major productions in the 1940s and 1950s included Gerhart Hauptmann's *The Assumption of Hannele* (1944, *encenação* Meyenburg); José Bruno Carreiro's *Os Maias* (*The Mayans* 1945, *encenação* Rey Colaço and Monteiro); an enormously successful revival of Garrett's *Frei Luis de Sousa* (*Friar Luis de Sousa*, 1945, *encenação* Monteiro); Sophocles' *Antigone* (1945, *encenação* Rey Colaço and Meyenburg); García Lorca's *The House of Bernarda Alba* (1946, *encenação* Meyenburg), with Palmira Bastos, Maria Matos, and Maria Barroso; Molière's *The Miser* (1948, *encenação* Meyenburg): Priestley's *Dangerous Corner* (1949, *encenação* Rey Colaço); Gil Vicente's *Farsa de Inez Pereira* (*Farce of Inez Pear Tree*, 1950, *encenação* Pedro Lemos); Shakespeare's *A Midsummer Night's Dream* (1952, *encenação* Meyenburg); the Spanish Alejandro Casona's *Seven Cries of Sea Knots* (1952, *en-*

cenação Rey Colaço and Monteiro); Lope de Vega's *Silly Girl* (1952, *encenação* Meyenburg); Isabel da Nobrega's *O Filho Prodigo* (*The Prodigal Son*, 1953, *encenação* Montiero); Romeu Correia's *Casaco de Fogo* (*Jacket of Fire*, 1953, *encenação* Lemos); Pirandello's *Right You Are—If You Think You Are* (1954, *encenação* Palmira Bastos); and Cortês' *Tá-Mar* (1955, *encenação* Rey Colaço and Monteiro).

After Monteiro's death in 1958, Rey Colaço continued to expand the repertory to include a variety of playwrights, new to the company, and to hire prominent stagers from abroad, including Michael Benthall, Cayetano Luca de Tena, José Tamayo, and Jacques Sereys. In the late 1950s and into the 1960s came major productions of Arthur Miller's *The Crucible* (translation by Antonio Quadros, 1958); Georges Bernanos' *Dialogues of the Carmelites* (1958, *encenação* Lemos), with Mariana Rey Monteiro (daughter of Rey Colaço and Monteiro); and Dürrenmatt's *The Visit from the Old Lady* (1961, *encenação* Luca de Tena). From the 1930s, great names in Portuguese acting worked at the theatre, including Adelina Abraches, Lucila Simoẽs, Palmira Bastos, Maria Lalande, Alves de Cunha, Nascimiento Fernandes, Mariana Rey Monteiro (best remembered in Shaw's *Saint Joan* in 1956), João Villaret, and Amaret.

In 1964 the interior of the theatre burned, and for the following fourteen years the company played in three local houses, the Teatros Aveneida (which also burned), the Capitolio, and the Trinidade. Rey Colaço remained director, but the theatres were more like a semiprivate company with government subsidies. In these years, the company played a varied repertory, including Shakespeare, Harold Pinter (*The Birthday Party*, 1968, *encenação* Artur Ramos), Sławomir Mrożek (*Tango*, 1971, *encenação* Valveda Silva), and Edward Albee (*A Delicate Balance*, 1967, *encenação* Rey Colaço), as well as Arthur Miller, Albert Camus, Eugene Ionesco, Pedro Calderón de la Barca, Schiller, and Nikolai Gogol. Rey Colaço also used many new actors in the various companies she formed in the houses.

The theatre was finally rebuilt and opened on May 11, 1978, with a work generally attributed to Gil Vicente, *Auto da geração humana* (*Work of the Generations of Men*, *encenação* Carlos Cabral). The company included many actors from the old troupe as well as many new actors. The second play staged was *Alfageme de Santarém* by Garrett (*encenação* Francisco Ribeiro). These first two productions were only mildly successful with the public. The rest of the first season, however, was extremely popular, including Pinter's *Old Times*, which opened the experimental theatre (*encenação* the Argentinian Carlos Quevedo); Shakespeare's *The Merry Wives of Windsor* (*encenação* Ribeiro); and Maxim Gorky's *Sons of the Sun* (*encenação* Luis de Lima), the latter being particularly well attended. There were also performances of Racine's *Phédre* by the company of Antonine Bourseiller, two weeks of American music, an evening with Gisela May singing Brecht songs, an exhibition of the theatre designs of the American George Izenhour, and another exhibition devoted to the theatre of the German Weimar Republic. It was a very exciting season.

The theatre currently is run on a troika arrangement, with Lima de Freitas as the general manager, Francisco Ribeiro as the artistic director, and Pedro Lemos as the stage manager. In its first reopened season the company was composed of thirty-two actors and actresses. All are on one-year contracts, but several have been with the company since the 1930s. The major administrators for the company are state employees, whereas the actors and technical staff are theatre employees.

The major theatre contains eight hundred seats and is similar to its predecessor in design, though obviously its sight lines are much improved. It also contains a small experimental house, which seats two hundred but is unusable. The theatre is located on Lisbon's busiest street and street noises are very audible in the small house. Work is now being done to correct this problem.

Plays are chosen by the troika. The administration tries to avoid politics, seeking out plays and productions that will please everyone. It plans five new works a season, each with a limited run. Current plans are for touring in Portugal and outside. The company would eventually like to tour to Brazil. The 1979–1980 season included more Portuguese plays than before, including several by Camoẽs, the great national poet, *O Judeu* (*The Jew*) by Bernardo Santareno, and Alfredó Cortês' *O Lodo* (*The Mud*). (Spanish writers have been popular in Portugal, especially García Lorca.) The theatre is receptive to new scripts by unproduced playwrights: it employs a literary manager to read scripts, and the government awards prize money for new playwrights. The theatre manager reads the prize scripts with an eye for production. In the first season, the theatre received a government subsidy of 32 million escudos, with an additional 5 million coming in at the box office.

The company is trying to find its public. In the first season, the theatre was frequently filled—except on televised soccer nights, when nobody goes anywhere. Special discounts are given to students, union members, and groups of twenty or more. All seat sales are by single admission, as the Portuguese are far too independent to buy by subscription. The company seems obsessed with making the theatre work, even coming promptly to rehearsals, which is almost unheard of in a Southern European country.

One potential problem for the company revolves around its political orientation. Many Portuguese stage artists are to the left in politics, while the government is conservative. All the same, the government seems to favor a broad program of subsidies in the arts. At least for the present, then, the company's situation is encouraging.

LEON M. AUFDEMBERGE
(Translation help by Doretta Fuhs.)

Spain

INTRODUCTION

Spain has only two important theatre cities, Madrid and Barcelona; the rest of the nation is more or less at the mercy of touring companies. Madrid, with over forty legitimate houses, is decidedly the more important, though Barcelona has more experimental theatre. For a long while Barcelona had no native Catalan theatre, for it was forbidden by Franco; plays had to be done in Spanish or not at all. From 1968 to 1975 Barcelona had a national theatre, named the Teatro Nacional Angel Guimera in honor of a famous Catalan playwright. The theatre was founded by José María Loprena. The theatre did much for the cultural life of Barcelona before foundering in the sea of bureaucracy and eventually sinking.

The major sickness in the Spanish theatre during the Franco era was censorship. From 1939 to the death of Francisco Franco in 1975 (and for a while after), a series of strictures was issued specifying what could not be done in the theatre. While these regulations were not imposed by the Catholic Church, the Church did profit from them. Plays were forbidden to criticize either the government or the Church, and no blaspheming or poking of fun at religion was tolerated. Moreover, even a play that was permitted could be closed by the government. In 1971, for example, the Teatro María Guerrero company staged Bertolt Brecht's *The Caucasian Chalk Circle*, in a production translated by Pedro Lain Entralgo and staged by the prominent director José Luis Alonso. The production received excellent notices, and playgoers bought tickets in advance, a rarity in Spain. Then authorities discovered Brecht was a Communist, and the play was forced to close. Other productions that criticized the United States or even the USSR were forbidden. Not surprisingly, now that censorship has ceased, approximately one-half of Madrid's theatres devoted to drama are doing plays of a sexual nature and are often mildly pornographic.

Until recently, most Spanish companies, except state-supported ones, were built around name actors, much like the old actor/manager companies in England and the United States. Spain has a long literary tradition and an even longer one of acting. Spain has produced very few actors who are internationally known, however.

Spain's playwrights need no introduction. Among the twentieth-century playwrights, Federico García Lorca is the best known and most often presented. For a long time after his death, his plays were forbidden to be performed in much of Spain, not by Franco, as is often erroneously written, but by the Lorca family, who were opposed to Franco. Among contemporary playwrights are Antonio Buero Vallejo, Ramón María del Valle Inclán, Alejandro Casona, and Alfonso Sastre.

Franco did very little for the Spanish theatre. In contrast, the present government is beginning to subsidize not only the companies it favors, but also some theatre troupes critical of government policies. The theatre is not well attended, but at least a beginning has been made.

LEON M. AUFDEMBERGE
(With the assistance of Raphael Fernandez
of the Office of Festivals and Theatres
and translation help by Janine Pefley.)

LLIURE THEATRE
(Teatro Lliure)
Leopoldo Alas, 2
Barcelona, Spain

The Catalan-speaking area of Spain is rich in folklore, and the region has produced several notable playwrights. During the Franco era, however, the Catalan language was forbidden in the schools, and its theatre was reduced to nothing. A permanent Spanish-speaking national theatre flourished in Barcelona during the 1960s. Called the Teatro Nacional Angel Guimera, it foundered despite the best of intentions and died because of politics and poor funding.

In May 1976 a new company was founded in Barcelona. It was called La Sociedad Cooperativa Teatro Lliure, with a troupe of ten actors, three directors, a manager, and two technicians. It was installed in the local Cooperativa de Consum La Lleialtat in the Barrio de Bracia. Its prime movers were Fabiá Puigserver (one of its technicians and stagers), Carlota Soldevila (an actress), and Luis Pasqual. All were from Barcelona. The first production came on December 1, 1976, with a text called *Cami de Nit 1854* (*Night's Way 1854*); it was written, staged, and set by Puigserver, with music by Lluis Llach. The aim of the new theatre was to reestablish the Catalan-speaking theatre in Barcelona.

Except for its first work, the first season for the new company was German in orientation. Following the success of *Cami de Nit*, the company tackled the Brecht/Weill work, *The Small Rise and Fall of the City of Mahagonny*, done in collaboration with the Grup Instrumental Catalá and again staged and set by Puigserver. The rest of the season was made up of Arthur Schnitzler's *The Green Cockatoo* (*dirección* Pere Planella) and Georg Büchner's *Leonce and Lena* (*di-*

rección Luis Pasqual). All four were highly successful. Barcelona once more had a literary theatre company in its midst which did plays in Catalan.

The second season for the troupe opened with a surprise success, Shakespeare's rarely done *Titus Andronicus* (1977), with music by Giuseppe Verdi, staged and set by Puigserver, with Fermí Reixach in the title role. This was followed by *Hedda Gabler* (1978, *dirección* Planella) and then a major success with the Christopher Marlowe/Brecht/Lion Feuchtwanger *The Life and Death of Edward II of England* (1978, *dirección* Pasqual), with Josep María Flotats in the title role. Since then the company has done a series of major productions including Chekhov's *The Three Sisters* (1979, *dirección* Pasqual); Jean Genet's *The Balcony* (1980, *dirección* Planella); and a work adapted from the works of Alfred Jarry, *Operació Ubu*, with the adaptation and staging by Alberto Boadella of Els Comediants, another Barcelona company.

The home theatre for the company is located in the Cooperativa de Consum La Lleiltat and seats four hundred, with the seating flexible. In the first seasons, the company presented four plays a season, generally for two-month runs. Today the company presents three works a season for longer runs. (*The Balcony* ran four months in 1980, the longest run so far for a play.) The company is run as a cooperative, with twenty-seven people employed, of whom five are actors and four are actresses, with extras added as needed. The company has its own ateliers to make scenery. One of the distinctions for the company is a subscription program involving over two thousand people. This is an astronomical number, given the Spaniards' abhorrence of buying tickets ahead. The city receives 10 million pesetas from the Ministry of Culture and 2 million from the local city government, sums that constitute about 25 percent of the theatre's total budget. The company has played in Madrid as well as Barcelona.

The company is modeled after the Piccolo Teatro di Milano in its popular repertory and experimental approach without being too outrageous. In many ways, the company's philosophy was set by its first piece which dealt with an incident in the history of Barcelona, the life and death of Josep Barceló, a local hero. The company is very social in aim and high in purpose. Although it is new, it has a wealth of Catalan history and language as a resource.

LEON M. AUFDEMBERGE

MARIA GUERRERO NATIONAL THEATRE
(Teatro Nacional María Guerrero)
Tamayo y Baus, 4
Madrid, Spain

The María Guerrero has had somewhat the same development as the Spanish National Theatre, producing popular works at its beginning as a national theatre and later a much more serious repertory. The María Guerrero was the first to open, beating the Spanish National by a couple of months. The first manager of this theatre was Luis Escobar, one of Spain's major directors, who co-managed the company with another major director, Huberto Peréz de la Ossa, until 1953. Like the Spanish National, the María Guerrero had a good acting company from the beginning, including Renée Devilliers, María Paz Molinero, Carmen Seco, Luis Pena, María Carmen Diaz de Mendoza y Labariti, and, above all, Elvira Noriega. In its first seasons the company did a repertory of modern works with a few classics for variety (the opposite of the Spanish National), including Eduardo Marquina's *El estudiante endiablado* (*The Devilish Student*, 1941); J. B. Priestley's *Time and the Conways* (1942, *dirección* Escobar); Gil Vicente's classic *Don Duardas* (1942, *dirección* de la Ossa); Augustín de Foxá's *Gente que pasa* (*People Who Go By*, 1942, *dirección* Escobar); Friedrich von Schiller's *Mary Stuart* (1942), with Noriega; Jean Giraudoux's *Amphytrion 38* (1943); Thornton Wilder's *Our Town* (1944, *dirección* Escobar); Augustín de Figueroa's *La Señorita del Mirador* (*The Woman of the Gallery*, 1945), with María Victoria Duca; Juan Ignacio Luca de Tena's *El sombrero de tres picos* (*The Three Cornered Hat*, 1945), based on Pedro Antonio de Alarcón's celebrated novel, with Noriega; Joachim Calvo Sotel's *Plaza de Oriente* (*Marketplace of the Orient*, 1947); and José Zorrilla's *Don Juan Tenorio* (1949), with staging by Escobar and surrealistic sets by Salvador Dali, a production that toured widely and is a landmark in Spanish theatre history.

In the 1950s the repertory became more serious, though popular works remained in order to draw customers. In the early part of the decade the best known productions included Julio Alejandro's *Barricada* (*Barricade*, 1950, *dirección* Escobar and de la Ossa); Victor Ruiz Irarte's *El landao de seis caballeros* (*The Landau with Six Horsemen*, 1950, *dirección* Escobar); T. S. Eliot's *The Cocktail Party* (1951, *dirección* Escobar); Curt Goetz's *The Heiress* (1951, *dirección* Escobar and de la Ossa), with Noriega; and Isabel Suárez's *Buenas Noches* (*Good Night*, 1952), which won the Calderón de la Barca Prize for best new work in 1952.

A new company manager, Claudio de la Torre y Millares, came in 1954 and would remain until 1960. He had been a successful writer before becoming a director, and under his leadership there would be more original plays staged (including a couple of his own), the acting company would be enlarged, and several new directors would be added to the staff. His most interesting productions included de Foxá's *Otono del 3006* (*Autumn of 3006*, 1954, *dirección* Alfredo Marquerie); Juan Antonio de Laigleisa's *La rueda* (*The Wheel*, *dirección* de la Torre), which won the Lope de Vega Prize in 1955; Buero Vallejo's *Hoy es fiesta* (*Today Is a Holiday*, 1955, *dirección* de la Torre); Alfonso Sastre's *El cuervo* (*The Crow*, 1956, *dirección* de la Torre); Enrique Jordiel Ponel's *Eloisa está debajo de un Almendra* (*Eloise Is under an Almond Tree*, 1957, *dirección* José Alonso); and Carlo Goldoni's *The Mad Woman of the House* (adaptation by Pérez Galdós, 1958, *dirección* de la Torre).

In 1960 the distinguished critic and writer, Alfredo Marquerie y Mompin, would become manager for two years. Marquerie y Mompin was extremely prolific as a writer, with over twenty books on the theatre and several plays to his credit before his death in 1974. During his tenure Marquerie y Mompin would stage several works, but the major productions were by José Alonso, who directed Chekhov's *The Cherry Orchard* (1960); Lopez Arrand's *Cerca de las estrellas* (*Close to the Stars*, 1961); and Eugene Ionesco's *Rhinocéros* (1961), with José Bódalo. In 1962 Alonso became manager, staying until 1973, when the theatre was reorganized and he became a freelance director again. During these years the company became Spain's major troupe, noted especially for its experimental staging and broad repertory. Alonso liked touring and took his company throughout Spain, especially Valencia, Barcelona and Seville. In 1969 he also made a major trip to South America (assisted by Enríque Llovet and Victor Catena). In seven months the company staged a repertory of five plays for ten countries in fifteen different theatres. Since then the company has made other international tours.

Among the biggest productions were Miguel Unamuno's *La difunta* (*The Dead One*, 1962); Lope de Vega's *La bella mal mariada* (*The Beautiful Unhappily Married Woman*, 1962); Antonio Gala's *Los verdes campos del Edén* (*The Green Fields of Eden*, 1963), which was one of the most notable plays to come out of Spain in the last twenty years and won a Calderón de la Barca Prize; Eugene O'Neill's *Mourning Becomes Electra* (1965), with Nuria Espert; Carlos Archies' *El Señor Adrian, El Primo* (*Señor Adrian, the Dupe*, 1966); Luigi Pirandello's *Right You Are—If You Think You Are* (1967); Valle Inclán's *La rosa de papel* (*The Paper Rose*) and *La cabeza de Bautista* (*The Head of Bautista*), a double bill staged in 1967; Pedro Calderón de la Barca's *La dama duende* (*The Phantom Lady*, 1967); Maxim Gorky's *The Lower Depths* (1968); Miguel Mihura's *Tres sombreros de copa* (*Three Top Hats*, 1969); Brecht's *The Caucasian Chalk Circle* (1971); Benito Peréz Galdó's *Misericordia* (*Misery*, in an adaptation by Alfredo Mañas, 1972); Gaston Baty's *Dulcinea* (1972); and Chekhov's *The Three Sisters* (1973).

After Alonso left in 1973, nothing seemed to go right for the company; several managers kept forming new companies and some of the same actors stayed on. The few notable productions of the period included José María Camps' *El edicto de gracia* (*The Edict of Grace*), which won the Lope de Vega Prize in 1972 (*dirección* José Oscuna), and Francisco Nieva's adaptation of Aristophanes' *The Peace* (1977), in a grotesque but gorgeous production by Michael Conelo with Carlos Lemos (1977).

Finally, in 1978 the Spanish government stepped in, and the company was taken over by a new agency, the Centro Dramatico Nacional. In its first season the company at the María Guerrero presented Rafael Alberti's *Noche de guerra en el Museo del Prado* (*Night of War in the Prado Museum*, *dirección* Richard Salvat); the Peter Weiss adaptation of Kafka's *The Trial* (*dirección* Manuel Gutiérrez); and Zorilla's *¡Abre el Ojo!* (*Open Your Eyes!*, *dirección* Fernando Fernán Goméz), all of which received good reviews and were well attended.

In the 1970s the theatre played host to a number of visiting companies, including the Teatro Nacional de Honduras, the now defunct Teatro Nacional Angel Guimera, and the Teatro Nacional de Juventudes.

LEON M. AUFDEMBERGE

NATIONAL DRAMA CENTER
(Centro Dramatico Nacional)
Tamayo y Baus, 4
Madrid, Spain

In the aftermath of Franco's death, the theatre in Spain encountered a period of turmoil with the Spanish National Theatre closed because of fire and the National Theatre María Guerrero passing through several managers. Today some stability has been achieved. The National Drama Center is now under the supervision of the Ministry of Culture, under the Department of National Theatres and Festivals of Spain, with its home office in the María Guerrero National Theatre.

The National Drama Center has three theatres: the newly reopened Teatro Español, the Teatro María Guerrero, and the Teatro Bellas Artes. The Teatro Español is one of Madrid's oldest; it opened its doors in 1807 and was built on the site of an even older theatre. The house was built by a well-known Spanish architect, Juan de Villanueva, and was originally called the Teatro Principe. It was built to hold 1,000 spectators, and throughout most of the nineteenth century it was the major theatre in Madrid for prose drama. In the early part of the century the theatre was acquired by the Ayuntamiento (the city hall) of Madrid, which controls the theatre. The María Guerrero was built in 1885 by Augustin Ortiz de Villajos. It was built for and was long managed by Spain's great actress María Guerrero, whom at least the Spaniards consider the equal of Sarah Bernhardt. The theatre was extensively remodeled in 1969–1970 by José Luis Manzano Monis. It holds 850 seats and is one of Spain's loveliest theatres. The Teatro Bellas Artes was built within the Bellas Artes in 1961 by Ignacio Basel and Angel de la Morena (with José Tamayo in on the planning). The house is extremely comfortable and has 496 seats.

The work of the two theatres is really the work of the National Drama Center. There is a common list of actors (about sixty at present), who are hired for the season and work from theatre to theatre. (Many actors, however, are likely to stay closely identified with one house). In the 1979 and 1980 season some actors were hired for only one play as Spain has far too many unemployed actors and the Ministry of Culture wished to see as many working as possible.

The ticket prices in the theatre are low; discounts are given to students (there are even student performances), soldiers, and groups of people who buy blocks of tickets. All seats are by single sale as the Spanish temperament does not favor subscriptions. Generally, too, seats are bought at the last minute, and long lines in front of box offices just before curtain time are a common sight in all Madrid theatres. The Spanish theatregoer also views acting as the best facet of a theatre production. Nonetheless, in the last few years directors have become much more important. Each theatre mounts three works a season. The works are selected by the artistic director, with the *comisario* (the "man on the spot") overseeing the business aspects of the company theatre he represents. Plays are done for specific runs and then tour. For the 1979 to 1980 season the National Drama Center received 45 million pesetas in subsidy.

LEON M. AUFDEMBERGE

SPANISH NATIONAL THEATRE
(Teatro Nacional Español)
Principe, 25
Madrid, Spain

Madrid's theatre was devastated by the Spanish Civil War. Many of Spain's major artists disappeared. Federico García Lorca, Spain's greatest playwright, was killed under circumstances that are still being debated, and Margarita Xirgú, its most renowned actress, went to South America and did not return because of her differences with the Franco regime. In an effort to help the theatre in 1940, the Franco regime decided to open three national theatres, one for opera and two for spoken drama. The houses for drama were established to foster an appreciation of the drama of Spain, both classic and modern. Two theatres were to be used as homes for the newly formed National Theatre: the Spanish National Theatre (Teatro Español) for classic drama, and the María Guerrero for modern writers.

In its first years (1940–1942) the Spanish National Theatre was managed by Felipe Lluch, who had been drama critic for *El Debate* and during the Civil War had been the managing director of the Teatro de Arte y Propaganda. He headed the Spanish National Theatre until his death in 1942 and was succeeded by Cayetano Luca de Tena, one of Spain's most noted directors of classical plays, who would be its manager until 1953. Luca de Tena tried to balance the repertory between Spanish and other classics, with an occasional modern work for variety. His productions featured some of Spain's most notable classics actors, including Mercedes Prendes and Guillermo Marin. Luca de Tena staged the first major success for the company in 1941, with Fernando de Rojas' *La Celestina*; he would follow this production with other classics, such as Lope de Vega's *La discreta enamorada* (*The Clever Girl in Love*, 1945); Shakespeare's *A Midsummer Night's Dream* (1945); Lope de Vega's *La mal casada* (*The Mismatched Girl*, 1947); Tirso de Molina's *Don Gil de calzas verdes* (*Don Gil of the Green Stockings*, 1947); Victor Hugo's *María Tudor* (1947), with Prendes; Molière's *Le bourgeois gentilhomme* (*The Bourgeois Gentleman*, 1948), in a translation by José López Rubio; and Hugo's *Ruy Blas* (1952), with Prendes.

While the Spanish National Theatre was intended primarily as a classics house, some modern plays were also staged there, including the premiere of Augustín de Foxá's *Baile en capitania* (*Dance of the Captainry*, 1944, *dirección* Juan Ignacio Luca de Tena), with Prendes; Antonio Buero Vallejo's *Historia de una escalera* (*Story of an Apartment House Staircase*, *dirección* Luca de Tena), which won the coveted Lope de Vega prize as the best play of the year in 1949; José López Rubio's *Celos del aire* (*Jealous of the Air*, 1950, *dirección* Luca de Tena); and the same author's *Veinte y cuarenta* (*Twenty and Forty*, 1951, *dirección* Luca de Tena), with Marin and Susanna Canales. There would also be notable productions of Patrick Hamilton's *Gaslight* (1948, *dirección* Luca de Tena) and Peter Ustinov's *The Love of Four Colonels* (1953, *dirección* Alfredo Marquerie y Mompin, who would later become head).

José Tamayo became the head in 1954 and continued what Luca de Tena had begun. Tamayo is still one of Spain's most able and most lavish theatrical directors and had already done a well-staged production of Seneca's *Thyestes* (among others) in 1945 for the troupe, before he became its general manager. Tamayo would direct many works for the theatre before he left, including Sophocles' *Oedipus* in a translation by José María Pemán, with Francisco Rabal, Prendes, and Marin (1945); Jean Anouilh's *The Lark* (1954), with María Carillo (1954); Edmond Rostand's *Cyrano de Bergerac* (1955); Diego Fabbri's *The Trial of Jesus* (1956), with María Dolores Prandera; Lope de Vega's *La estrella de Sevilla* (*The Star of Seville*, 1957); Luigi Pirandello's *Henry IV* (1957), with Carlos Lemos (1957); a major revival of Jacinto Benavente's *Los interes creados* (*The Bonds of Interest*, 1958); Buero Vallejo's *Un soñador para un pueblo* (*A Handkerchief for a Town*, 1958); and Friedrich Dürrenmatt's *The Visit from the Old Lady* (1959), with Irene López Heredias as Klara. Perhaps the best staging job he did was the premiere of Buero Vallejo's *Las meninas* (*The Ladies-in-Waiting*), based on the life of Velásquez, which featured Carlos Lemos as the painter, with sets by Burgos. In the last two years of his managerial post, Tamayo directed two exceptional productions: Eduardo Marquina's *En Flandres se ha puesto el sol* (*In Flanders the Sun Has Set*, 1961) and a marvelously vital Lope de Vega's *Fuenteovejuna* (1962).

In 1962 Tamayo left to head a number of projects, and Luca de Tena returned for two seasons as manager. In these two seasons, he staged productions of Calderón de la Barca's *No hay burlas con el amor* (*No Trifling with Love*, 1963) and a return production of Shakespeare's *A Midsummer Night's Dream* (1964). Adolfo Marsillach, who had acted with the company, became its head in 1965; his major production was Lope de Vega's *Las siete infantes de Lara* (*The Seven Infants of Lara*, 1965). He was followed by Miguel Narros in 1966, and under him the repertory was more adventurous. (Spain was beginning to loosen up politically at that time.) Notable productions in this era included Augusto Moreto's *El lindo Don Diego* (*Pretty Don Diego*, 1966, *dirección* Luca de Tena); Shakespeare's *King Lear*, in an adaptation by Benavente (1967, *dirección* Narros); Cervantes' *El cerco de Numancia* (*The Siege of Numantia*, 1967, *dirección* Narros); Molière's *Les femmes savantes* (*The Learned Ladies*, 1968, *dirección* Narros); the premiere of Guillén de Castro's *Las mocedades del Cid* (*The Youth-*

fulness of the Cid, 1968, *dirección* Narros); and José Camon Aznar's tragic *Hitler* (1969, *dirección* Modesto Higueiras), a play that would have been forbidden ten years earlier.

In the 1970s the company's repertory became even more daring, under the directorship of Alberto Gonzales Vergel (1970–1975), who also tried to keep seasons balanced between classics and moderns, Spanish and outside. The best productions of the era were staged by the manager, including Lope de Vega's *La estrella de Sevilla* (1970); Shakespeare's *Othello* (1971), with Carlos Bellestros; Seneca's *Medea*, in a translation by Miguel de Unamuno (1972); and Francisco de Quevedo's *El buscón* (*The Searcher*, 1972). Later the company would do Ramón del Valle Inclán's *Tirano banderas* (*Tyrant Flags*, 1974), in an adaptation by Enrique Llovet (staging by Tamayo), and Juan Guerrero Zamora's *La nueva fiercilla domada* (*The New Taming of the Shrew*), based on Shakespeare and staged by Zamora in 1975.

LEON M. AUFDEMBERGE

Switzerland

INTRODUCTION

Each of the four major languages in Switzerland—German, French, Italian, and Romanisch (a pure language)—has its own form of theatre, loosely banded together by the Swiss Theatre Union, formed in 1920, with headquarters in Zurich.

Each year, the Swiss Society of Human Sciences publishes a yearbook in three of the languages—*Szene Schweiz*, *Scène Suisse*, and *Scena Svizzerzia*—which lists all activities in theatres throughout Switzerland. Switzerland has twenty municipally owned theatres, seven of which have their own companies. In addition, a number of commercially sponsored plays tour each year, and plays from either Germany or France are apt to make it over the line.

The main companies in the country are located either in the French- or the German-speaking areas. Both areas have rather traditionally oriented companies with the usual director/stager operation, copied from ancient German models. Aside from this it is difficult to generalize about the Swiss theatre.

The French theatre is largely centered in Geneva, which has a surprising number of fine companies and perhaps the major opera in all Switzerland. Geneva's taste in theatre tends to be rather conservative, although there is a rather high regard for experimental *metteurs-en-scène*. There are also several good French-speaking companies outside Geneva.

The problem in the German-speaking theatres is in determining whether Basel or Zurich is best. These two companies have traditionally jockeyed for position. During World War II, Zurich was the predominant theatre of all German-speaking countries. Since then there has been more of a seesaw. Zurich has the advantage of a longer tradition, a physical theatre with many associations (which has just been renovated), and a *direktor* (manager) who has to think only of plays. (In Basel the *direktor* also runs the opera.) Basel has the advantage of a new theatre, which is one of the best equipped in Europe, and a much more cosmopolitan population with wider tastes. Both have a good deal of civic support.

Most municipally run theatres in Switzerland are governed by boards of directors, a system that is both good and bad. The boards generally see that the theatres are well funded and are on a solid financial footing. Most board members, however, come from the business community, know little about the artistic running of a house, and generally try to meddle. In the last few years, for example, the Züricher Schauspielhaus fired its head because his taste was not to the board's liking.

The German-Swiss theatre has produced two major playwrights since World War II: Friedrich Dürrenmatt and Max Frisch. Before the war, Carl Zuckmayer was Switzerland's leading playwright. His play *Der Hauptmann von Köpenick* (*The Captain from Köpenick*, 1931) is one of the classics of the international theatre. Since the end of the war, his major contribution has been *Des Teufels General* (*The Devil's General*, 1946), perhaps Switzerland's most frequently produced play of the postwar era. Dürrenmatt has been both a dramaturge and a *regisseur*, as well as a playwright with a long list of plays produced in all four German-speaking countries and abroad. He is best known in the United States for his version of *Der Besuch der alten Dame* (literally *The Visit from the Old Lady*), which was done by the Lunts in a somewhat cleaned up version as *The Visit*. Frisch has also been a dramaturge, whose major play *Andorra* (1961) is probably the most direct attack on Germany's anti-Semitism. Both dramatists have been most often connected with the Züricher Schauspielhaus.

LEON M. AUFDEMBERGE

CITY THEATRE OF BASEL
(Basel Stadttheater)
Theaterstrasse 1
CH-4000 Basel, Switzerland

The City Theater of Basel opened on October 4, 1834, with *Die Krone von Cypern* (*The King of Cyprus*) by a forgotten author. This was a guest performance by a visiting troupe, and throughout most of the century the theatre played host to a series of troupes from Switzerland and Germany. This first theatre was replaced by a new one in 1875. In 1890 the idea of a permanent company was formulated. Most of the activity of the late nineteenth century, however, was directed toward opera. It was not really until World War I that, under the influence (but not the person) of Max Reinhardt, plays became a part of Basel's theatre life.

In the 1920s, and especially under Otto Henning, the Basel took on a new vigor. Adolf Appia worked there for a while in the operatic part of the theatre. In 1919 Oskar Waelterlin began a long and distinguished career at the Basel, first as *regisseur* and then, from 1925 to 1932, as its director. Egon Neudegg followed in 1932 and remained until 1949. He was its intendant during the great days of the exit from Germany, but most of the major talent went to Zurich. A few great German artists came to work there in the war years, including Albert

Bassermann, the dancer Harald Kreutzberg, the *regisseur* Leopold Lindtberg, the designer Teo Otto, and the actor and *regisseur* Leonhard Steckel.

After Neudegg left, the directorship became split. Kurt Horwitz took over the Schauspielhaus directorship from 1946 to 1950, giving large space to new French playwrights and to Swiss writers, such as Friedrich Dürrenmatt and Max Frisch. The world premiere of Dürrenmatt's *Romulus der Grosse* (*Romulus the Great*) was staged there in 1949, with Horwitz as director and Ernst Ginsberg as the title character. After Horwitz left, the house seemed to suffer from a lack of leadership, although the opera house continued to prosper. One person helped bring continuity to the company. This was Adolf Zogg, who had been part of the cultural administration of the theatre since the 1950s.

Werner Düggelin's arrival in 1969 as intendant for both plays and operas put an end to the indecisive leadership. He formed a team, with Dürrenmatt as dramaturge and Hans Hollmann as leading *regisseur*, and practically overnight Basel became an important theatre city. Under Düggelin a new theatre was opened in 1975. Even before the theatre opened, Hollmann staged in the foyer of the unfinished theatre one of the truly remarkable productions of the twentieth century, Karl Kraus' *Die letzen Tage des Menschheit* (*The Last Days of Mankind*), done over two nights. The production ran for more than eight hours. The house was limited to 375 spectators. Hollmann staged other works, including *Macbeth* (1972) in an adaptation by Heiner Müller; Odön von Horváth's *Kasimir und Karoline* (1969); *Titus, Titus* (after Shakespeare's *Titus Andronicus*), which was very violent indeed; Molière's *The Doctor in Spite of Himself* (1972); and *Othello* (1977), as well as Wagner's Ring Cycle for the opera house. In 1975 he became head of the theatre.

The next notable premiere of the Düggelin era was Dieter Forte's *Thomas Munzer oder Die Einführung des Buchhaltung* (*Thomas Munzer, or the Introduction of Book-keeping*, 1970, *regie* Kosta Spaic), Horst Seide's production of Chekhov's *The Cherry Orchard*, Joseph Papp's *The Naked Hamlet* (1973), and Düggelin's excellent *Twelfth Night* (1971) and staging of Heinrich Heinkle's *Olaf und Albert* (1973). Unfortunately, Dürrenmatt remained only briefly as dramaturge, but he did stage his own *Der Besuch der alten Dame* (*The Visit from the Old Lady*), before he resigned over a production of a Peter Hacks play. The Düggelin-Hollmann era was a great one. Its current intendant is Horst Statkus, formerly intendant at Heidelberg.

The theatre in which most of the plays are done is one of the most modern in Europe. Its main theatre seats one thousand spectators, and the stage can be used for opera, with a large orchestra pit, a schauspielhaus (with the pit covered over), and an arena theatre. In addition, the company uses two theatres for more experimental works. The company is fairly large (thirty-one men and twenty-one women), and probably more actors will be brought in with a new intendant. There are four permanent *regisseurs* and three guest *regisseurs* each season. The subsidy for the theatre is 20 million Swiss francs per year, with an additional 3 million francs in box office receipts.

The philosophy of the theatre is an aggressive one. All people are considered equal, and all doors are open. This policy has had some repercussions, largely in productions that shocked people (for example, Hollmann's *Othello* in 1977), but subscribers keep coming back each season. Fourteen plays are done each year, and popular plays from other seasons are repeated. A special effort is made to attract students. The City Theatre of Basel also likes to have other companies share its stages, particularly a French one from Geneva, as Basel has a largely French-speaking population.

What is the special character of Basel? First, both Düggelin and Hollmann were equally interested in opera and plays and gave them equal treatment; an intendant usually favors one form over the other. Second, the choice of plays has been wide and varied. Third, the choice of *regisseurs* has included some of the finest directors in Switzerland and Germany.

LEON M. AUFDEMBERGE

ROMAND POPULAR THEATRE
(Théâtre Populaire Romand)
Lepold-Robert 83
La Chaux-de-Fonds 2300, Switzerland

The history of the Romand Popular Theatre can be divided into two parts: during the first part, the company was very broke, toured a lot because it had to, and had its headquarters in a farm at Chézard; during the second, it achieved financial stability and toured simply because it liked to serve its area. There had been an earlier Romand Popular Theatre under the direction of Marcel Tassimot, which toured with Heinrich von Kleist's *The Broken Jug* and Molière's *Les fourberies de Scapin* (*The Cheats of Scapin*) during its one season (1959–1960) before its death. In 1961 a new company was formed, headed by Charles Joris, who is still its director. The company's first performance was Bernard Liègme's *Murs de la Ville* (*Walls of the Town*) in November 1961. Liègme had created this piece for the company, although it was based on improvisations by the company. The first production had its premiere in Locle and was staged by Joris, who also acted in it. (Unless otherwise stated, Joris staged all works mentioned here.) The troupe, severely hampered by lack of funds, lived a communal existence at a farm at Chézard.

In March 1962 the company presented a work by another Swiss author, Henri Deblüe's *Le procès de la truie* (*The Trial of the Sow*), and at the end of the season it received a subsidy from the Pro Helvetia organization. In July of the same year, it played at the open air festival at Estavayer-le-Lac. In September came Charles Prost's work, *Adieu Jérusalem*, which dealt with the war in Algeria and was dimly viewed by the French government. November of the same year saw the troupe performing for the first time in France at the Comédie de l'Est at Strasbourg. By the following year, the company had established itself well enough so that the canton of Neuchâtel gave the young troupe its first official subsidy. Other subsidies would follow in due course.

In the next seasons the company enlarged its touring policy (partly from necessity) and made a name for itself in the variety of plays it produced: Ben Jonson's *The Alchemist* (1963); Sean O'Casey's *The Shadow of a Gunman* (1963); Carlo Goldoni's *The Mistress of the Inn* (1964); Chekhov's *The Three Sisters* (1965); Pierre Marivaux's *Le legs (The Legacy)* and *L'epreuve (The Trial*, 1965); and Molière's *Don Juan* (1965). In April 1964 came *Jeunesse 64*, which was the first collective exercise for the company and would not be the last. In January 1966 the company began to receive regular salaries of 500 francs a month, but this did not ward off financial chaos. Fortunately, a number of institutions bailed the company out, and it survived.

The company presented two works in 1966: Bernard Liègme's *Le soleil et la mort (The Sunshine and Death)*, which was a premiere, and Lope de Vega's *Fuenteovejuna*. Maxim Gorky's *The Petty Bourgeois* had its first performance at the Theatre de La Chaux-de-Fonds in 1967, the same year the company published the first issue of its journal, *Bulletin des Amis du TPR*. The Gorky piece had a long tour in both France and Switzerland. In June 1967 the company presented its first work for schools, *Molière et nous (Molière and Us)*, which includes scenes from *Le bourgeois gentilhomme*, and began to institute classes for actors.

The second phase began when the troupe was installed in January 1968 at La Chaux-de-Fonds and in May began to receive a regular official subsidy. The company has moved frequently and to date has rented over thirty places in the city in which to work or rehearse, though from 1969 to 1974 it did have a Petite Salle, which was a center for its activities. In the late 1960s and into the early 1970s, it began to receive more invitations to play in theatres in both Switzerland and France. Its plays began to be more concerned with social ideas. Its first Brecht play, *Man Is Man* (1968), was a good production but attracted poor audiences. The works done at this time reflect the company's social consciousness: a collective play for adolescents called *La Bataille d'Hernani (The Battle of Hernani*, 1968); Chu Su Chen's *Quinze Rouleaux d'Argent (Fifteen Rolls of Silver*, 1969, *mise-en-scène* Gaston Jung); Angelo Beloco's *Les Histoires de Ruzzante (The Stories of Ruzzante*,1969); and a collective children's play, *Le Roman de Renart (The Novel of Renart)*, which played at Turin, Berlin, and Venice and in 1976 made an extensive tour of Mexico. In 1968 came the first Biennale at La Chaux-de-Fonds, which featured lectures and troupes from the area and which would become a permanent event, emphasizing a different theme or problem on each return.

Since 1970 the troupe has continued to widen its activities. First, it has done collective scripts touching on a variety of problems. Among these are *Le Reporter dans la Ville (The Reporter in the Town*, 1970), which is directed toward young children; *Le Journal, Service public, Enterprise commercial (The Newspaper, Public Service, Commercial Enterprise*, 1970), which addressed itself to adolescents; *Dossier Antonio Salvi* (1971), which concerns the problems of immigration; and two works that deal with Le Corbusier (who comes from the city); *Gare au Corbu* (*The Railroad Station at Corbu*) and *Le Corbusier—Le Bâtisseur* (*Le Corbusier—The Builder*, both 1975). It also has done a number of premieres of modern authors, including Bernard Liègme's clown show, *Augustes* (1972); Peter Terson's *Mooney et ses Caravanes* (*Mooney and His Caravans*, 1973), which was adapted from works of Henkel and Gatti; Franz Xaver Kroetz's *Maria Magdalena* (1974, *mise-en-scène* Jong); and an adaptation from E.T.A. Hoffman, *Princess Brambilla* (1980). There have also been children's plays, with a special hit in *Decouverte* (*Discovery*, 1975).

Perhaps the most popular productions, however, have been reworkings of plays of the past. The company even made a success of Marivaux's *Le Prince travesti* (*The Prince in Disguise*, 1969). In 1971 Joris' production of Chekhov's *Uncle Vanya* used a montage of texts, which accompanied the play; this *envionnement-animation* (audience participation in the play) has become the trademark for the company. An adaptation of Carlo Goldoni's *The Military Lover* (1973, *mise-en-scène* collective) became a springboard for a discussion of woman's place in the modern world.

The production that has become the company's biggest and most prestigious ever is Shakespeare's *King Lear* (1977), with Guy Touraille in the title role. The company rehearsed for six months and continued to work on the production after it opened. In preparation, its actors went through a vigorous program, which included music training, dancing, singing, martial arts, tai-chi chuan, and acrobatics. The work was not strictly Elizabethan; rather, it spoke to a highly modern viewpoint. It toured extensively in Switzerland, France, and West Germany. Since then the company has gone on to a mixture of classic and modern, including John Arden's *Work House Donkey* (1978); Brecht's *The Good Woman of Setzuan* (1979), with Jacqueline Payelle as Shen Te/Shui Ta; and Pierre Corneille's *Sophonisbe*, with Liécane in the title role.

The Romand Popular Theatre has one of the most extensive programs of activities of any theatre in Europe. Its primary function is its production of plays; it generally does two large productions a season, as well as revivals for the road, and sponsors programs (poetry, talks) during the season. Its permanent company, which makes all the decisions, consists of ten actors, five technicians, and six administrators. It sponsors the Biennale, whose theme in 1980 was the formation of the actor. The company publishes its own newspaper, which currently takes the name of the company.

The company is social minded but not necessarily political. The area in which it plays leans toward Socialist ideas. Its plays try to serve a broad public, especially children. Decisions are made by the whole of the assembly (including actors, technicians, and administrators), which meets regularly to discuss matters of play selection and the general running of the company. Hence, although Joris is *directeur*, the company tends to be more a collective than a one-man rule. The company receives its subsidy from three cantons: Neuchâtel, Jura, and Berne

(185,000 francs); four cities: La Chaux-de-Fonds, Le Locle, Bienne, and Delemont (340,000 francs); and a number of foundations and private sources (93,313 francs). It is a comfortably subsidized company, but by no means a wealthy one.

The company has been plagued by its lack of suitable rehearsal space. In 1981 the city bought an old house, Beau Site, as a center for the troupe. About 850,000 francs are needed to renovate it, of which the Swiss government has already contributed 500,000. The troupe is still looking for the remaining 350,000.

LEON M. AUFDEMBERGE
(With thanks to Nicole Simon-Vermot)

ZURICH'S THEATRE
(Zürich Schauspielhaus)
Zeltweg 5
8032 Zurich, Switzerland

Plays have been done in Zurich with some regularity since the Middle Ages, and the city has had a playhouse since the eighteenth century. The playhouse was built by two local builders, Johann Jakob Bodmer and Johann Jakob Breitinger. But the first person to see the need for a theatre with a permanent company was Caroline Birch-Pfeiffer, who was the directoress of the Züricher Akteinentheater, a predecessor of the Schauspielhaus. She was manager from 1837 to 1842, and the theatre likes to consider 1837 as the date of its founding. The company used various playhouses until 1890 when it had a new theatre built for it, the Pfauenkomplex, which remains its home today.

The person who first brought the Schauspielhaus to prominence was Alfred Reucker, director of the theatre from 1901 to 1921. He staged everything from Maxim Gorky's *The Lower Depths* to Brandon Thomas' *Charley's Aunt*. He introduced Zurich to playwrights such as Ibsen, Shaw, and Wedekind. He did well-remembered productions of Gerhart Hauptmann's *Der Biberpelz* (*The Beaver Coat*, 1901), *Die Weber* (*The Weavers*, 1902), and *Rose Bernd* (1904). He invited well-known actors to become part of the company: Johann Terwein, Elisabeth Bergner, Heinrich Cretler, Alexander Moissi, Edwin Althauser, and Paul Hartmann. Then followed a series of minor directors until the leadership of the company was assumed by Ferdinand Reise (1929–1938), who was director when the great exodus from Germany began, which radically changed the complexion of the German theatre.

During the war years, many prominent German names came to Zurich to keep the idea of a free German theatre alive. Kurt Hirschfield came from Darmstadt; Leopold Lindtberg from Berlin; and Leonard Steckel, Therese Giehse, Kurt Horwitz, and Erwin Kaiser from Munich. Karl Paryla was from Vienna. Others who joined the company were the designer Teo Otto (a friend of Brecht), Heinrich Bretler, Leopold Biberti, and Wolfgang Langhoff.

Oskar Wälterlin was director from 1938 to 1961. He staged the German-language premiere of Thornton Wilder's *Our Town* in 1938 and also directed

Wilder's *The Skin of Our Teeth* (1944). Brecht's *Mutter Courage und ihre Kinder* was staged by Leopold Lindtberg in 1941, with sets by Teo Otto and Therese Giehse as Anna Fierling.

Leonard Steckel did the lion's share of great Shakespeare productions, beginning with *Henry IV* (1941), *As You Like It* (1942), *Measure for Measure* (1944), and *The Taming of the Shrew* (1944); the premiere of Brecht's *Der gute Mensch von Sezuan* (*The Good Woman of Setzuan*, 1943) with Maria Becker as Shen Te/Shui Ta; and the German premiere of Brecht's *Das Leben des Galilei* (*The Life of Galileo*, 1943), with himself in the title role.

The Schauspielhaus in Zurich, more than any other force, prepared the way for the furious revival of German theatre after the war. During the years after World War II, three Swiss playwrights emerged, all with some connection to the theatre in Zurich: Carl Zuckmayer, Friedrich Dürrenmatt, and Max Frisch. Carl Zuckmayer, the oldest of the three, spent a large part of World War II in exile in the United States. Perhaps the most frequently performed play in the German language of the postwar era was his *Des Teufels General* (*The Devil's General*), which had its first performance in Zurich in 1946. It was directed by Heinz Hilpert, formerly of the Deutsches Theater in Berlin. Since that date the play has been staged over seventy times in Germany alone and is frequently performed today. Other Zuckmayer plays that had their first performances at the theatre were *Das Leben des Horace A. W. Tabor* (*The Life of Horace A. W. Tabor*, 1964), *Kranichtanz* (*The Dance of the Crane*, 1966), and *Der Rattenfänger* (*The Rat-Catcher*, 1975).

Dürrenmatt's first work *Es steht geschrieben* (*It Is Thus Written*, 1947) was staged by Kurt Horwitz at the Schauspielhaus. Other important dramas followed: *Der Besuch der alten Dame* (*The Visit from the Old Lady*, 1956) with Therese Giehse as the title character, *Die Physiker* (*The Physicists*, 1962), *Herkules and der Stall Augias* (*Hercules and the Augean Stable*, 1963), and *Der Meteor* (*The Meteor*, 1966).

The third of the playwrights, Max Frisch, is probably the most prolific of the three. His first play, *Nun singen wir wieder* (*Now They Sing Again*, 1945), had its premiere at the Schauspielhaus. Frisch also contributed *Die chinesische Mauer* (*The Chinese Wall*, 1946), *Don Juan oder Die Liebe zur Geometrie* (*Don Juan, or The Love of Geometry*, 1952), and his two best known works, *Biedermann und die Brandstifter* (*Biedermann and the Firebugs*, 1958) and *Andorra* (1961). Finally, the theatre presented his work *Biografie* (1968), one of his most antagonistic pieces.

After Wälterlin's death in 1961, a series of directors took over beginning with Kurt Hirschfield. Hirschfield was an admirer of Brecht and had staged the premiere of *Herr Puntila und sein Knecht Matti* (*Mr. Puntila and His Hired Man, Matti*) in Zurich in 1948. The production delighted Brecht. Wälterlin kept the company relatively stable and the repertory international. Leopold Lindtberg stayed as director from 1965 to 1968. Then followed two short directorships: Erwin Parker/Otto Weissert (1968–1969) and Peter Loffler (1970). Loffler's chief distinction was to be head of the theatre when Peter Stein upset Zurich with two productions.

Harry Buckwitz came in 1970, and he once publicly said that his most difficult job was to get people away from their television sets. Buckwitz did several good productions, including Brecht's *The Threepenny Opera* (1973) and *Mother Courage* (1974), Joseph Papp's *Naked Helmet* (1973), Gorky's *Yegor Bulychyov and Others* (1973), and *Richard III* (1977). Since 1978 the head of the theatre has been Gerhard Klingenberg, who was formerly head of the Burgtheater in Vienna. Under his directorship, the Schauspielhaus has been completely renovated.

Zurich has one of the largest companies in Switzerland: thirty-nine men, sixteen women, ten *regisseurs*, and four dramaturges. Because Switzerland recognizes practically every nation in the world, the theatre is in the enviable position of inviting *regisseurs* from other countries to stage plays.

There are generally eleven new productions each year. In addition, the Schauspielhaus invites a number of other theatre companies to share its stage, and it sponsors concerts. The Zürich Schauspielhaus is an exciting house, even though it does not have its brilliance of the war years. Perhaps with a new director and a newly renovated house, people will cease comparing it to the wartime theatre.

LEON M. AUFDEMBERGE

West Germany

INTRODUCTION

Perhaps no other country spends as much money on the theatre per capita as the Federal Republic of Germany. This was true in the nineteenth century and continues to be so today. The quality of theatre is, therefore, very high.

World War II had a devastating effect on German theatre. Not only were approximately 70 percent of all German theatres destroyed, but also many of the most talented theatrical figures emigrated. Among the great actors who left were Therese Giehse, Albert Bassermann, Fritz Kortner, and Ernst Deutsch. Among those who elected to stay were Gustaf Gründgens, Käthe Gold, and Heinrich Georg. Among the *regisseurs*, Max Reinhardt emigrated as did Erwin Piscator, while Gründgens, Heinz Hipert, and Walter Felsenstein remained. All the major playwrights except Gerhart Hauptmann left. No major play was written in Germany from 1933 to 1944.

Today a taboo remains against staging any play written during the Nazi era in any German-speaking theatre. The acting style in this period was heavily bombastic. Part of the work of the German intendants' theatre after the war was to get rid of the bombast, with the work of the (East) Berliner Ensemble leading the way.

By 1946 most of the major theatres were open after having been closed by Hitler in 1944. It was at once clear that things could not operate as they had before, however. In West Germany censorship was dead, though there are still movements, especially by conservative town councils, to revive it. The most amazing occurrence was the rapid recovery of the theatre, both in terms of acting and types of plays performed. The most important change in the postwar era was the enormous power of the *regisseur*.

In all the German-speaking countries (both Germanies, Switzerland, and Austria), the *regisseur* is in command of the theatre company. Most actors have objected to this power and, perhaps in self-defense, many have become *regisseurs* themselves.

Next in importance is the intendant, or general manager, who is in charge of the company. (*Generalintendants* have several companies under their wing: theatre, opera, and ballet.) Most intendants are *regisseurs* as well and stage several works a season; they may also work other houses, particularly if such houses are close by. The intendant works closely with the dramaturge. In most West German houses the intendant and the dramaturge pick the plays and *regisseurs* for one season. Dramaturges translate works, write program notes, cut plays, and do all the preliterary work, before a *regisseur* steps in. A few well-known dramaturges have written plays as well, Bertolt Brecht and Heinar Kipphardt, for example. The intendant also fights with the authorities for subsidies.

The production style in most West German theatres ranges from highly experimental (Bochum) to rather solidly literary and conservative (Munich's Residenz). Companies are generally characterized by the type of *regisseurs* hired. A minor movement away from the *regisseur*-intendant combination has begun, however, and some German houses are now run by administrators. All four of the German-speaking countries complain that there are not enough good ones. Also in woefully short supply are designers and technical people of all kinds. The good designers in West Germany (Wilfred Minks and Günther Schneider-Siemssen) are few in number.

The set-up of the West German house is geared more toward ensemble than toward the star system. A few German actors work in both theatre and films (the Austrian Schells, for example), with guest appearances for part of a season at one company, but most German actors are known solely within Germany. In return for anonymity, German actors receive some security. Most are hired from three to five years, and many theatres have the so-called fifteen-year rule which means that an actor cannot be fired at the end of fifteen years—only retired. Many actors have been with the same companies since the 1920s, and, as they get older, may do only one play a season. Generally, when a new intendant moves into a theatre he brings his own people with him. Thus, many actors are fired and are replaced by those from the intendant's previous company.

Another major lack in West German houses is that of native playwrights. The West German playwright gets 15 percent of the box office income. This is not as generous as it sounds, for most theatre seats are sold by subscription, in which the playwright does not participate. There are masses of foreign imports; a current Broadway or West End success may be done by a number of houses. The other large percentage of repertory comes from classics.

The most popular playwrights in West German houses are Shakespeare and Brecht, followed by Schiller, Molière, and Johann Nestroy. Friedrich Dürrenmatt and Max Frisch, both Swiss, are the contemporary writers most played.

The theatres are marvelously equipped, and the management goes out of its way to see that everyone is comfortable. Most German playgoers buy their seats by subscription and arrive on time. All theatres seem to have bars and serve snacks as well as drinks. At intermission couples walk around the foyers in ritual fashion. The German theatregoer is probably the most pampered person in the world. Most theatre tickets are cheaper than a movie, and theatregoing is quite popular among the young in West Germany.

Approximately 80 percent of all theatre income comes from subsidy. For the privilege of a state-supported theatre, the average West German pays $10 to $15 a year in extra taxes. Many West Germans do not go to the theatre, but support it nonetheless as a matter of civic pride.

There is a great deal of waste in West German theatre. Most productions, especially in the spoken theatre, are scrapped after one year, with the scenery and costumes cannibalized for another production. The West German theatre probably spends too much on production and not enough on original plays. All in all, however, the West German theatre is probably among the best in the world.

LEON M. AUFDEMBERGE

BAVARIAN STATE THEATRE
(Bayerisches Staatschauspiel) (Residenztheater)
Max Josef Platz
8000 Munich, West Germany

Munich may be called the theatre capital of West Germany. Plays have been performed in this Bavarian city since the late Middle Ages, although its first major theatre was not built until 1657, the opera house on the Salvatorplatz. This opera house was rebuilt in 1685 and for almost a century was the major theatre in the city. By the middle of the eighteenth century, the old house was clearly outmoded, so Max III, Joseph, the then *Kurfurst* (Elector), ordered a new house to be built. The architect for the new theatre was François Cuvilliés. The opening production was Ferrandini's opera, *Catone in Utica*, on October 12, 1753, and the first intendant was Baron von Seeau. Part of this theatre is still in existence; a large part, including the ceiling, was destroyed in World War II. In 1943 the wood decoration of the house was removed, divided into two parts, and stored in two barns some distance apart. After the war the house was lovingly restored, and the Altes Residenztheater is now the Cuvilliéstheater and is used for both operas and plays.

The early years of the Residenztheater were largely concerned with the production of opera. Baron von Seeau also included some plays in the repertory which were strictly used for court entertainment. Later theatres in Munich would be for the townspeople. By the early part of the nineteenth century, however, plays began to become extremely important for the court, particularly under the directorship of Baron von Poissl, who staged Goethe's *Faust* in 1830 and productions of Ferdinand Raimund. Theodore Küstner, who was its intendant from 1833 to 1842, included even more contemporary playwrights, especially Franz Grillparzer and Karl Ferdinand Gutskow.

The first intendant in the last part of the nineteenth century was Franz von

Dingelstedt, who brought more modern plays into the repertory and built a strong acting company, including Marie Seebach, Emil Devrient, Heinrich Anschütz, and Theodore Döring. Dingelstedt is best remembered for his productions of Goethe and Schiller, and of Sophocles' *Electra*, which he staged with music by Mendelssohn. For the time he was considered an ideal *regisseur*. Dingelstedt also helped to restore the old Residenztheater, which for some time had been used for other purposes.

Karl von Perfall became director in 1864 and liked both modern plays (Ibsen) and opera (Wagner). He would remain until 1894. He was one of the first directors to have Ibsen done in a German theatre, with productions of *Northern Journey* (1876), *The Pillars of Society* (1878), and *Hedda Gabler* (1891). He also had a first-rate designer, Karl Lautenschlager, who designed many of the great productions, including those of Shakespeare, beginning in 1889 with *King Lear*. Under Perfall's directorship King Ludwig II began his long infatuation with Wagner, which so greatly influenced modern theatre.

Ernst von Possart came to the company in 1864, making his debut as Karl Moor in Schiller's *Die Räuber* (*The Robbers*). Later he would appear as Shylock, Iago, Mefistofele in Goethe's *Faust*, Nathan in Gotthold Lessing's *Nathan der Weise* (*Nathan the Wise*), and Richard III. He became head of the Hoftheater and its *oberregisseur* in 1878, finally becoming general director of both the opera and theatre in 1895. Possart had wide dramatic interests, so his repertory included not only Shakespeare, Goethe, and Schiller, but also new German playwrights such as Gerhart Hauptmann, Hermann Sudermann, and Arthur Schnitzler, as well as many French boulevard successes. In 1887 he toured his company to Holland, Russia, and the United States. (He would return to America in 1911.) Possart trained his actors in a highly declamatory style, which at the time was considered ideal for the classics, but it is questionable how well his actors fared with modern plays. His main designer was Angelo Quaglio, a member of the Quaglio family of designers in Munich from the first opening of the Cuvilliés-designed theatre. In 1882 the Hoftheaters were among the first to use electric lighting.

Between 1910 and 1919, the theatre began to play Georg Büchner; both of his major works were done before the war. The most important actor of this era was Albrecht Steinbruck, who did both classics and modern plays. The Residenz also had a strong acting company in Luise Hohorst, Emil Hofer, Viktor Schwanneke, Gustav Waldau (famous for his Liliom), and his wife, Hertha von Hagen. After World War I, the theatre began to play new German playwrights (Georg Kaiser, Carl Sternheim, and Lion Feuchtwanger), as well as George Bernard Shaw and Ferenc Molnár, particularly under the leadership of Dr. Karl Zeiss during the 1920s. Zeiss was extremely adventurous in repertory—to the point where some thought him pornographic. Elisabeth Bergner came in the 1920s and is especially remembered for her playing of Hugo von Hofmannsthal's *Der Schwierige* in 1924.

During National Socialism, the theatre played many classics, the most notable being the Shakespeare cycle which Hans Schweikart did from 1934 to 1938. Most of the modern plays as staged by the intendant Alexander Galling were "safe." In 1944, after a performance of Ludvig Holberg's *Don Ranudo de Colibrados* (or *Poverty and Pride*), the theatre was destroyed.

On May 18, 1945, the theatre reopened with Lessing's *Nathan der Weise*, with Paul Verhoeven as the intendant. This play would be done over one hundred times in the company's new home, the Theater am Brunnenhof, with performances over four seasons. The repertory included many German playwrights not seen in the Nazi era, as well as new playwrights such as T. S. Eliot and Thornton Wilder, whose *The Skin of Our Teeth* was one of the most often played in the postwar era.

Verhoeven was followed by Alois Johannes Lippl, who was head from 1948 to 1953 and wrote some plays for the company. Lippl extended the repertory even more with modern works and invited prominent *regisseurs* to work at the theatre, especially Jürgen Fehling and Bruno Hübner. New playwrights, such as Tennessee Williams, Jean Giraudoux, and Federico García Lorca, appeared in the repertory. The acting company comprised such well-known actors as Maria Wimmer, Otto Wernicke, and Hans Bauer.

In 1951 a new Residenztheater opened with Raimund's *Der Verschwende* (*The Prodigal*), the architect being Karl Hocheder. (In 1958 the Cuvilliéstheatre was reopened to some of its original brilliance.) Kurt Horwitz, an actor, *regisseur*, and administrator, became intendant in 1953. Horwitz was especially fond of Molière and mounted several productions of his work during this period, but the best known production of the era was Rudolf Noelte's cut version of Eugene O'Neill's *Mourning Becomes Electra* (1957).

Helmut Henrichs was head from 1958 to 1972. He had been a pupil of Heinz Hilpert and, more than anything, tried to get away from the star system into the feeling of an ensemble. He liked both classics and modern plays and himself staged García Lorca's *Blood Wedding* (1962) and Goethe's *Torquato Tasso* (1967). The best known *regisseur* of this period was Hans Lietzau, who probably did his best work in Munich. Lietzau worked steadily with the company from 1965 to 1968 and returned sporadically thereafter. There he staged Sternheim's *Tabula Rasa*; Büchner's *Woyzeck*; Goethe's seldom played *Die Mitschuldigen* (*The Accomplices*, 1966), which later played New York; an extraordinary production of Paul Claudel's *The Satin Slipper* (1967); Jean Genet's *The Screens* (1968); Shakespeare's *As You Like It* (1968); and Heiner Müller's *Philoktet* (1968).

In 1966 the company came to New York in honor of the Goethe year with *Die Mitschuldigen*, *Woyzeck*, and Hauptmann's *Die Ratten* (staged by Henrichs). The critics liked the company but carped a bit about the repertory. Other good productions during Henrichs' tenure were Lessing's *Minna von Barnhelm* (1962, *regie* Meisl), Ionesco's *Exit The King* (1964), the world premiere of Georges Schéhadé's *The Immigrants* (1964, *regie* Meisl), Chekhov's *The Cherry Orchard*

(1970, *regie* Rudolf Noelte), and Shakespeare's *Coriolanus* (1970), freely adapted and staged by Hans Hollmann.

Kurt Meisl had first come to the Residenz as an actor in 1961 and became its intendant in 1972. He continues to strive for ensemble, but seems more interested in actors than his predecessors had been and has picked *regisseurs* who like to talk to actors. Probably the most newsworthy event of his directorship was his snaring of Ingmar Bergman to do an annual production for the house, his first production being August Strindberg's *A Dream Play* in 1977. The productions done in Meisl's era have been solid rather than experimental and include Walter Felsenstein's staging of the Wallenstein plays (1971), the plays that opened the intimate Theatre im Marstall; Franz Xaver Kroetz's *Globales Interesse*; William Gaskell's look at Edward Bond's *Lear* (1972); Bond's *The Sea*, which was probably one of the most discussed works ever done at the Residenz and played over two seasons (production by Luc Bondy); and Schiller's *Don Carlos* (1974, *regie* Schweikart). In 1974 came Kurt Wilhelm's dramatization of Franz von Kobell's *Der Brandner Kaspar und das ewig Leben* (*Brandner Kaspar and Eternal Life*), which has played over 225 performances and will probably be played as long as there is a Munich. After 1974 came Thomas Bernhard's *Der Präsident* (*The President*, 1976, *regie* Michael Degen); Tom Stoppard's *Travesties* (1976, *regie* Lietzau); Peter Shaffer's *Equus* (1977, *regie* Dieter Kirchlechner); Shakespeare's *Richard II* (1978, *regie* Dietrich Haugk); Chekhov's *The Three Sisters* (1978, *regie* Bergman); and Ibsen's *Hedda Gabler* (1979, *regie* Bergman).

The Bavarian Schauspielhaus has always been a state theatre and is subsidized (17 million marks in 1978). It operates three theatres: the Residenz, which seats 1,039; the Cuvilliéstheater, which it shares with the opera (500 seats); and the small Theater im Marstall, which is used for works that require some intimacy. The repertory is a balanced one: two or three classic plays; two or three works by Bavarian authors (Ludwig Thoma being the favorite); two or three plays from the nineteenth century; two contemporary works and a Brecht each season. The permanent *regisseurs* stage one or two productions a season, which the intendant picks with the help of his staff.

Plays run for only one season, although a few are repeated from the end of one season to the beginning of another. There are seventy-five actors in the company, about 60 percent men and 40 percent women; a total of 450 people are employed by the theatre. Actors generally have a three- to five-year contract, and a few have been in the house for a long while (Erwin Faber since the 1920s). The theatre has about 90 percent average attendance spread over the season. While the audience in Munich is conservative, only a few plays at the Residenz have genuinely shocked them, the most recent example being Edward Bond's *Lear*. Most tend to return season after season. The audience generally likes more popular works, such as Nestroy, even with his heavy Viennese dialect.

LEON M. AUFDEMBERGE

BOCHUM PLAYHOUSE
(Bochum Schauspielhaus)
Königsallee 15
4630 Bochum, West Germany

In 1915, when a new theatre was built in Bochum, the Stadtheater Bochum, the city fathers decided the time was ripe to establish a local company. The first production in the new theatre was Friedrich von Schiller's *Don Carlos*, staged by the visiting troupe from Düsseldorf Playhouse, with a special prologue written by its great actress-director, Louise Dumont. In 1919 a permanent company was formed. The opening performance was Franz Grillparzer's *Des Meeres und der Liebe Wellen* (*The Sea and Its Lovely Waves*), staged by the intendant, Saladin Schmitt, who led the company from 1919 to 1949.

Schmitt was one of Germany's leading old-line *regisseurs*, very correct and severely disciplined. He was considered an expert in the staging of Shakespeare, Schiller, Goethe, and Heinrich von Kleist. The Schmitt era in Bochum is a history of one classic production after another. Schmitt brought great actors to Bochum, including Horst Caspar, who played Hamlet at Bochum and elsewhere. Schmitt did cycles of authors, including several Shakespeare cycles. The theatre was destroyed in 1944 by an air raid.

The company reopened on December 12, 1945, in the Parkhausbühne with Grillparzer's *Weh dem, der lügt* (*Thou Shalt Not Lie*). In 1949 Schmitt, after leading his company for thirty years, said farewell with a production of Shakespeare's romantic *Cymbeline*. He was replaced by Hans Schalla, whose first production for Bochum was *Measure for Measure* (1949).

Schalla liked the classics as much as his predecessor had and so chose Shakespeare's *Richard III* (staged by himself) to open a new playhouse (one of Germany's best designed), built by Gerhard Graubner, on September 23, 1953. The repertory of the new theatre was filled with new authors, particularly American and French; the company was especially noted for its productions of Jean Anouilh. Schalla's most outstanding productions, which he staged, were Shakespeare's *As You Like It* (1954), *The Taming of the Shrew* (1957), and *Othello* (1961). Schalla brought Max Fritzsche to Bochum as his lead designer in 1954, and the two worked out what is known as the "*Bochumstil*," which were productions with sets full of abstractions, wide use of space, and good lighting. Fritzsche is best remembered for his designs for George Bernard Shaw's *Saint Joan* (1956), *Othello* (1961), and Tom Stoppard's *Rosencrantz and Guildenstern Are Dead* (1967). At the end of his career Schalla did a lot of staging of Christopher Fry and John Arden. In 1972 Schalla retired from Bochum to be replaced by Peter Zadek, who had already staged some plays there and was certainly one of Germany's most influential *regisseurs*.

Schmitt and Schalla were both traditionalists in the staging of Shakespeare. Zadek was anything but a traditionalist and had been a member of the "*shockstil*" (shocking style) group, which had come out of Bremen. His productions of

Shakespeare shocked many of the traditionalists of the town. For example, in 1973, Hans Mahnke played Shylock as anything but sympathetic, and many members of the audience were uncomfortably reminded of Germany's traditional anti-Semitism. The same year Zadek staged his extremely famous clown show production of *King Lear*, with his favorite actor, Ulrich Wildgruber, as the title character. The production, which used silent movie techniques and elements of shock and farce, was a collective exercise, with the actors working with the *regisseur* to solve the problems of staging. Under Zadek, the company played frequently at the Berlin Festival and in the Capital Festival in Paris. In 1974 Zadek staged a highly acclaimed production of Heinrich Mann's novel *Professor Unrath* (upon which the movie *The Blue Angel* is based), with Hannelore Hoger as Rose Froehlich. *Hamlet* (with Wildgruber again) came in 1977 as did Ibsen's *Hedda Gabler*.

Many of Zadek's best productions were staged outside the theatre where he escaped its confines. Zadek also brought other famous people to work at the house, including Tankred Dorst, one of West Germany's best playwrights. Also a first-rate dramaturge, Dorst has had two of his best works done as premieres at Bochum: *Kleiner Mann, was nun?* (*Little Man, What's Up?*, 1971), which was co-authored with Fallada and Zadek and which eventually was done on German television, and *Eiszeit* (*Ice Age*, 1973). Both works were well staged by Zadek and were controversial. Maria Schell made a guest appearance in 1977 in Fernando Arrabal's *The Tower of Babel*, with the author as *regisseur*. Lee Strasberg came in the same year to do a workshop with actors of the company. Zadek also helped organize Shakespeare weeks at Bochum at which prominent scholars would talk about the English playwright.

In 1977 Zadek left and was replaced by Lew Bogdan, who was only a temporary replacement and followed Zadek's policy of making things happen. In the fall of 1979 Claus Peymann took over and began a new chapter for the company. (See the article on the Stuttgart-Württemberg State Theatre for a description of Peymann's contributions to Stuttgart.)

Bochum has had good fortune in hiring intendants. It also has one of the heaviest production schedules in West Germany, generally doing about twenty-two works a season (with nary a revival), balanced between the classics and modern plays, as well as a healthy children's theatre. Its acting company numbers around eighty (more men than women), and about sixteen *regisseurs* are hired each season, including some of West Germany's best names. There are two houses in the theatre complex: a large house (the Schauspielhaus), which seats 922; and the smaller Kammerspiele, with places for 401. It has a large number of subscribers, some of whom occasionally grumble about the modern style of production but nevertheless keep returning. Since Bochum does not have an opera company, it invites the opera company from nearby Gelsenkirchen to present about twenty musical works a season in its theatre.

Bochum has always been a *regisseur*'s house, with a special affinity for the classics. The style of staging them, however, has varied widely in the last few years. In addition, in the last few years, Bochum has tried to give its playgoers something special in terms of a project each season. In 1978 Pina Bausch, one of West Germany's best choreographers, developed a choreographic/acting piece entitled *Er nimmt sie an der Hand und führt sie in das Schloss die anderen folgen* (*He Takes Her by the Hand and Takes Her into the Castle, the Others Follow*), the title coming from a stage direction in Shakespeare's *Macbeth*. Arrabal has worked as a *regisseur* with the company, and Pip Simmons, one of England's most radical stagers, has been a recent guest.

With the announcement of Peymann's appointment, many members of the permanent company were upset because they feared he would bring a whole new group of actors with him, most from Peymann's previous theatre in Stuttgart. This has proven true. The last two intendants at Bochum have been very much directors, interested in a wide variety of projects. Peymann is of the same mold, with a much more political bent. The future looks promising for the Bochum Playhouse, and it seems likely to keep its reputation as a place where things happen.

LEON M. AUFDEMBERGE

CITY STAGES OF BERLIN
(Staatliche Schauspielbühnen Berlins)
1 Berlin 12, Bismarckstrasse 110
(Schlosspark Theater, Schlosstasse 48)
12 West Berlin, West Germany

At the end of the nineteenth century many "freien theaters" ("free theatres") were built in Germany. These were companies without governmental support, generally set up by reformers, which sought to provide theatre at low cost for a large public. Typical of these was the Schiller Theatre, founded by Dr. Rapheal Löwenfeldt, which opened its doors, on August 30, 1894, in the Neues Wallner-Theater (built in 1864 as a house for light comedies). The opening production was appropriately Friedrich von Schiller's *Die Räuber* (*The Robbers*), staged by Löwenfeldt. From the beginning the theatre was popular with people of the area. On September 3, 1902, a second theatre was added in Chausseestrasse (in the old Friedrich-Wilhelm-Städtisches Theater), opening with Schiller's *Die Braut von Messina* (*The Bride of Messina*). The *regisseur* for the productions was Löwenfeldt, who kept both theatres active.

Löwenfeldt had been an author and a dramaturge before opening his company, and his great aim was to offer low-priced classics. In 1907 a third theatre was opened on Bismarckstrasse (the second dropped out at that time), especially designed for the company by Max Littmann and named the Schiller. Löwenfeldt was director of the company until his death in 1910. Until World War I, the theatre was known as a classics house; after the war, it played a much more modern repertory. The main *regisseur* in the 1920s was its director, Professor Leopold Jessner, who staged a series of remarkable productions of Molière,

Shakespeare, Frank Wedekind, Friedrich Hebbel, Gerhart Hauptmann, and Sophocles. He influenced many German *regisseurs*, including Jürgen Fehling, Gustaf Gründgens, and the young Brecht. Eventually, he emigrated and made his way to Hollywood.

Immediately before World War II, the Schiller had two houses, the Wallner and the Schiller. After Jessner left, the theatre had a series of directors, most of whom stayed for only brief periods. The best known of these was Ernst Legal who had been an actor and *regisseur* under Jessner. In 1938 the Schiller was renovated, reopening with Schiller's *Kabale und Liebe* (*Intrigue and Love*), a production by the new intendant, Heinrich George. George was one of Germany's ace stagers in the 1930s and 1940s, but, unfortunately, he was also a great follower of National Socialism. George did many classics, his forte, as well as a number of Nazi works. Walter Felsenstein and Fehling were the principal *regisseurs*, in addition to himself. The Schiller was destroyed in 1943, and the company disbanded in 1944.

The Allied authorities did not consider George to be a suitable intendant for the company, so when the company reopened in 1945, Boleslaw Barlog became its head. Barlog had been a student of Heinz Hilpert and was well versed in all forms of theatre. His forte was staging realistic plays with a heavy sense of atmosphere. He was a firm believer in type casting. He reformed his company in the Schlosspark Theatre, which was built in 1921 and before the war had played an abundance of light comedies and operettas.

Barlog made the company's reputation. In the early days after the war, the company played for whatever it could. Barlog said the company had a theatre and costumes, but lacked nails. Audiences began to pay in that commodity. Frequently, the company was paid in food or 20 pfennigs. In his ill-equipped theatre, Barlog created miracles. His first success was the old American chestnut by George Abbott and John Cecil Holm, *Three Men on a Horse*, which was played 291 times. At the Schlosspark theatre, Barlog was to stage the German premiere of Eugene O'Neill's *Ah, Wilderness!* (1947); George Bernard Shaw's *Androcles and the Lion* (1947); William Saroyan's *The Time of Your Life* (a German premiere of 1948); Christopher Fry's *The Lady's Not for Burning* (1950); and many works that formed the company's international repertory. He also staged new German works, such as the obligatory (for a postwar German house) Carl Zuckmayer's *Des Teufels General* (*The Devil's General*, 1948); Fritz Hochwälder's *Das Heilige Experiment* (*The Saintly Experiment*, 1949); and Walter Schäfer's *Die Verschwörung* (*The Conspiracy*, 1949). Willi Schmidt was his assistant *regisseur* and staged many of the plays, including the usual Shakespeare, Schiller, Nikolai Gogol, and Johann Nestroy, as well as John Steinbeck's *Of Mice and Men* (1948).

In 1950 these two men were joined by Karl Heinz Stroux as a guest *regisseur*, and the triumvirate made the Schiller one of the best in Germany. (There was as yet only one Germany, and people from the Soviet Zone came to the theatre until the wall went up). In 1949 Felsenstein returned to the Schiller to stage

Goethe's *Torquato Tasso*. On December 6, 1951, a new Schiller Theatre opened with Schiller's *Wilhelm Tell*. In 1959 a small third theatre was opened, the Werkstett, to play experimental works.

In the 1950s came a series of triumphs for the theatre, particularly those of Ernst Barlach's staging. The repertory was extremely varied, with productions coming from all ages and times. Barlog had important actors and certainly distinguished *regisseurs*. The best-received productions included Barlog's staging of Ibsen's *Nora* (*A Doll's House*, 1956), with Käthe Braun and Jürgen Fehling's production of Schiller's *Mary Stuart* (1952), with Elisabeth Flickenschildt and Martin Held. Erwin Piscator came in the mid-1950s to stage both William Faulkner's *Requiem for a Nun* (1955) and his own dramatization of Tolstoy's *War and Peace* (1956). In 1951 Albert Bassermann would say farewell to the stage, playing Attinghausen in Schiller's *Wilhelm Tell* (1951, the year before he died). The repertory also included many Tennessee Williams plays, along with the plays of Jean Giraudoux and Jean Anouilh.

In the 1960s, with three theatres to fill, activities became highly frantic but distinguished. Barlog staged the German premiere of Edward Albee's *Who's Afraid of Virginia Woolf?* (1963), which played an astounding 114 times at the Schlosspark before touring. He also did productions of Peter Nichols' *A Day in the Death of Joe Egg* (1968), Georges Feydeau's *A Flea in Her Ear* (1968), and many others. The two most important premieres under his direction were done in the sixties. The first was the Peter Weiss work with the remarkable title (usually cited simply as *Marat/Sade*) *Die Verfolgung und Ermordung Jean Paul Marats, dargestellt durch die Schauspielgruppe des Hospizes zu Charenton under Anleitung des Herrn de Sade* (*The Persecution and Assassination of Jean Paul Marat as Performed by the Inmates of the Asylum of Charenton under the Direction of the Marquis de Sade*, 1964, *regie* Konrad Swinarski), with Peter Mosbacher and Ernst Schröder debating the revolution in the bathhouse. In 1966 Hansjörg Utzerat staged Gunther Grass' thinly disguised portrait of Brecht during the Berlin Uprisings of 1953, *Der Plebejer proben der Aufstand* (*The Politicians Rehearse the Uprising*). Both have since been much staged, especially the Weiss work. Samuel Beckett came as a *regisseur* for productions of his own works: *Endgame* (1962) and *Krapp's Last Tape* (1969), with Martin Held. He would return to direct *Waiting for Godot* (1974) and others. Three of West Germany's top *regisseurs* would be guests in the 1960s: Fritz Kortner (Max Frisch's *Andorra*, 1962), Hans Schweikart (Harold Pinter's *The Homecoming*, 1966), and Hans Lietzau (Tom Stoppard's *Rosencrantz and Guildenstern Are Dead*, 1967). The Romanian *regisseur*, Liviu Ciulei, staged a remarkable Georg Büchner's *Dantons Tod* (*Danton's Death*) in 1968 with himself in the title role. Hans Hollmann came in 1970 to do a well-thought-out but highly controversial production of Schiller's *Kabale und Liebe* (*Love and Intrigue*).

In 1971 Barlog resigned, to be replaced by Hans Lietzau; both men had wide tastes in drama and both were *regisseurs*/intendants. Lietzau staged many productions, but none had the same sharp quality that marked the Barlog era. Even so, many have been well-received in the last few years, including such works as Bond's *Lear* (1973, *regie* Lietzau); Aristophanes' *The Birds* (1973, *regie* Dieter Dorn), in which the title characters wore artificial phalluses which amused and shocked many playgoers; the world premiere of Harmut Lange's *Die Ermordung des Aias, oder Ein Diskurs über das Holzhacken* (*The Murder of Ajax, or a Discussion of Woodcutting*, 1974, *regie* Lietzau), which Lange tried to close; Chekhov's *Ivanov* (1974, *regie* Lietzau); Simon Gray's *Butley* (1974, *regie* Lietzau), with Martin Senrath; Eugene O'Neill's *Long Day's Journey into Night* (1976, *regie* Willi Schmidt), with Martin Held and Marianne Hoppe as the elder Tyrones; Harold Pinter's *No Man's Land* (1975, *regie* Lietzau), with Held as Hirst; Ibsen's *Hedda Gabler* (1977, *regie* Niels-Peter Rudolph); and Chekhov's *The Cherry Orchard* (1978, *regie* Lietzau). Although Lietzau has had many first-rate *regisseurs*, he never achieved his own high level of brilliance when staging works at the Residenz in Munich. Perhaps the intendant/*regisseur* combination was too much. In 1980 he was replaced by Boy Gobert, formerly of the Burgtheater in Vienna and the Thalia in Hamburg.

The Schiller has three theatres over which to spread its activities: the Schiller itself (1,103 seats), the Schlosspark Theatre (478 seats), and the Werkstatt (with room for a comfortable 60). The acting company is one of the largest in West Germany: eighty men and forty women. There is no "cardinal sin" in playing or staging in one of the small houses. There are seventeen *regisseurs* in each season, most of whom are guests. They stage eight works in the large house, seven in the Schlosspark, and five in the Werkstatt. Plays and *regisseurs* are chosen by the intendant, with the season generally balanced between the classics and moderns, Germans and non-Germans. All are available to subscribers.

The Schiller was once one of the leading theatres in West Berlin, but after Barlog left some of the life went out of the company. It still has some of West Germany's best actors, especially Martin Held, but its productions are not done with the care of the 1960s. It still has one of the greatest subsidies in West Germany (17.8 million marks), but the guiding force of a Barlog is missing. Even Beckett took something of a critical drubbing on his last staging. In the 1970s too many productions seemed at best perfunctory. Perhaps under Gobert's leadership the old luster will return.

LEON M. AUFDEMBERGE

COLOGNE CITY THEATRE
(Bühnen der Stadt Köln)
Schauspiel Köln, Offenbachplatz
5000, Cologne, West Germany

Joseph Von Kurz was given permission in 1767 to construct a permanent wooden theatre in the Heumarkt of Cologne. Another theatre, this time of stone, followed in 1783, initially occupied by the company of Johannes Böhm, whose troupe was probably the best Cologne had seen to that time. This theatre was occupied by a French troupe during the Napoleonic wars. The first important permanent director for the theatre in Cologne was Friedrich Sebold Ringelhart (1820–1832), who was big on modern German plays of the period. In 1829 a new Stadttheater opened with Spohr's *Jessonda*. After Ringelhart's departure, the theatre in the city went into decline and was known as "die schlechteste Theaternehmung" (figuratively, a difficult place where people go to take punishment).

Friedrich Spiegelberger (1840–1846) brought R. J. Bendix, a well-known playwright, as dramaturge to the theatre, which meant a high quality of plays. From 1853 to 1855 the company was managed by Ferdinand Roder, who was keen on opera, particularly Wagner. Adolph Theadore L'Arronge (1858–1863) brought the important actress, Ellen Franz, to the city and presented lots of Offenbach. He also opened the Victoria Theatre as a summer theatre for the company. In 1859 the Stadttheater burned, and another theatre opened in 1862 with Goethe's *Egmont*. The company was managed in 1863–1869 by Moritz Ernst, who emphasized acting.

The Stadttheater burned again in 1869, and the company played the Thalia. The new Stadttheater in der Glockengasse opened on September 1, 1872 (architect Julius Raschdorff), with Gotthold Lessing's *Minna von Barnhelm* and Magda Irschick in the title role. The company was managed at this time by Heinrich Behr (1875–1881), who was considered very efficient in his running of both the opera and theatre wings. Ernst returned and served from 1875 to 1881, being particularly good in the staging of plays. Under his leadership, the theatre was known as a *regisseur*'s theatre.

The era of Julius Hofmann (1881–1904) was good for both operas and plays, with many modern playwrights' work done for the first time in Cologne, particularly Ibsen. Hofmann brought a number of prominent actors to his company, including Otto Beck (who did modern plays) and Ernst Lewinger (who doubled as a *regisseur*); Adele Doré, as well as Max Grube and Carl Dalmonico as *regisseurs*, with Dalmonico influenced by the work of the Meininger troupe. On September 6, 1902, a new theatre for opera opened (architect Karl Moritz) with a prologue by Joseph Lauff, Goethe's *Vorspiel auf dem Theater* (*Prelude on the Stage*), and the third act of Wagner's *Die Meistersinger von Nurnberg* (*The Master Singer of Nuremberg*).

With the coming of Max Martersteig in 1905, Cologne had its first highly important period of both theatre and opera. Martersteig was an actor, *regisseur*, writer, theatre historian, and, above all, a reformer with his great work in imposing a uniform style on the works he staged, with heavy emphasis on psychology. The repertory he staged included the usual Shakespeare, Schiller, and Goethe. He was also a Friedrich Hebbel enthusiast, and he admired modern writers such as Ibsen, Herbert Eulenberg, and Wilhelm Schmidtbonn. Among the innumerable productions he staged at Cologne were Schiller's *Wallenstein* cycle (1905); Ibsen's *The Master Builder* (1906); Goethe's *Iphigenia auf Tauris*

(1906); Shakespeare's *Hamlet* (1906), *Henry IV* (1907), with Fritz Odemar as Falstaff, *Richard II* (1908), with Richard Lindner in the title part, and *Othello* (1908), with Theodor Becker as Othello; Hebbel's *Gyges und sein Ring* (*Gyges and His Ring*, 1908); and Hauptmann's *Florian Geyer* (1909). Martersteig left in 1911 for Leipzig and was replaced for two seasons by Otto Purchian, whose tenure was noted for two premieres: Gerdt von Bassewitz's *Schaharazade* (1911, *regie* the author) and Detmar Sarnwtzki's *Der Eroberer* (*The Conqueror*, 1913, *regie* Hans Werckmeister). Fritz Rémond came in 1913. While his background was opera (he was a noted tenor), he did a number of fine things for the acting company, transforming it into a highly experimental company. He had several noted *regisseurs* (Johannes Tralow, Gustav Hartung, Ernst Hardt, and Theo Modes), and his acting company included Maria Koppenhofer, Elisabeth Lennartz, and Gillis von Rappard. He began rather conservatively with cautious productions: the premiere of Bassewitz's *Die Sunamiten* (*The Sunamites*, 1914, *regie* Rémond); Pedro Calderón's *The Mayor of Zalamea* (1915, *regie* Rémond), with Otto Egerth in the title role; Hebbel's *Herodes und Mariamne* (1916, *regie* Rémond); Schiller's Wallenstein cycle (1917, *regie* George Kiesau); Hebbel's *Die Niebelungen* (1919, *regie* Tralow); and Shakespeare's *King Lear* (1921, *regie* Otto Liebscher), with Eggerth as the King, and *Macbeth* (1923, *regie* Liebscher).

Beginning in 1924, however, the emphasis shifted to experimentation, with many plays or classics treated in an expressionistic manner: O'Neill's *The Hairy Ape* (1924, *regie* Hartung), with Heinrich George as Yank; Paul Kornfeld's *Shakuntula* (1925, *regie* Hartung); the premiere of Knut Hamsun's *Queen Tamara* (1925, *regie* Hartung); the premiere of Fritz von Unruh's *Heinrich aus Andernach* (1925, *regie* Hartung), with Carl Ebert in the title role; Brecht's *Das Leben Eduard II von England* (*The Life of Edward II of England*, 1926, *regie* Hardt); Franz Werfel's *Paulus unter den Juden* (*Paul under the Jews*, 1926, *regie* Modes); Heinrich von Kleist's *Amphytrion* (1927, *regie* Leopold Jessner); and Schiller's Wallenstein cycle (1927, *regie* Modes). Many of these productions were set by T. C. Pilartz, who was Cologne's chief designer.

In 1928 the opera and drama companies split, and the office of *generalintendant* disappeared for a while. Theo Modes took over the acting company. He was considered a lavish *regisseur* who wrote as well as he staged, with his primary love being the classics. The emphasis in this period was the classics, but there were still some modern plays. The most outstanding productions were Shakespeare's *Julius Caesar* (1928, *regie* Modes); Lessing's *Nathan der Weise* (*Nathan the Wise*, 1929, *regie* Modes); Schiller's *Mary Stuart* (1929, *regie* Alfons Godard); both parts of Goethe's *Faust* (1929, *regie* Modes), with sets by Ludwig Sievert; and Karl Maria Finkelburg's *Amnestie* (1930, *regie* Hans Rodenburg).

Under Fritz Holl (1930–1933), the company became the Deutsches Theater am Rhein. The companies of the Düsseldorfer Schauspielhaus combined with the acting company at Cologne, but the union did not last long. Holl preferred the classics, especially Shakespeare. Among his most important productions were Goethe's *Egmont* (1930, *regie* Holl); Shakespeare's *Troilus and Cressida* (1930, *regie* Holl); Hermann Rossman's *Fliegen* (*To Fly*, 1932, *regie* Alfons Godard), with Jochen Poelzig as Frank; and Shakespeare's *The Merchant of Venice* (1932, *regie* Holl).

Under National Socialism, the company became the Bühnen der Hansestadt Köln and was directed by Alexander Spring, who was known chiefly for his friendship with the Wagner family. The acting company during these years was reduced, but it retained one actor who became extremely popular in West Berlin after the war, Ernst Wilhelm Borchert. There was also a mass of guest artists. As was true of most German companies during the period, the repertory consisted almost totally of classics. They were staged mainly by three *regisseurs* (all of whom had strong postwar reputations): Hans Schalla, Paul Riedy, and Alfons Godard. Erich Metzoldt frequently did the sets. The company toured extensively during the war years, particularly in the occupied countries. Among the best productions were Kleist's *Prinz Friedrich von Homburg* (*The Prince of Homburg*, 1933, *regie* Godard) and *Das Käthchen von Heilbronn* (1934, *regie* Richard Dornseiff); Goethe's *Götz von Berlichingen* (1935, *regie* Dornseiff); Shakespeare's *Othello* (1936, *regie* Seigfried Sioli), with Rudolf Wittgen as Othello, and *Much Ado About Nothing* (1937, *regie* Godard); Schiller's Wallenstein cycle (1938, *regie* Riedy); Shakespeare's *Hamlet* (1938, *regie* Godard), with Borchert as the title character; Kleist's *Amphytrion* (1939, *regie* Riedy); Shakespeare's *King Lear* (1940, *regie* Riedy); both parts of Goethe's *Faust* (1941/1942); Goethe's *Clavigo* (1941, *regie* Riedy); Schiller's *Kabale und Liebe* (*Intrigue and Love*, 1942, *regie* Schalla); Aeschylus' *Oresteia* (1943, *regie* Schalla); and Schiller's *Mary Stuart* (1944, *regie* Schalla). All the theatres in the city were destroyed during the war, and many members of the company were killed in the air raids of 1943 and 1944.

The first play staged after World War II was Shakespeare's *A Midsummer Night's Dream*, done in September 1945, with the production by Wilhelm Pilgram and Alois Garg. The first head of the theatre in the postwar era was Karl Pempelfort, who was head of the Schauspiel from 1945 to 1951.

The first theatres the company used after the war were the Kammerspiele and Studio and the Aula of the university. In the first seasons the repertory included many new plays, especially Paul Claudel's *The Satin Slipper* (1946, *regie* Pempelfort), which was the first standing-room-only play of this troublesome period. There were also big productions of Shakespeare's *Hamlet* (1946, *regie* Pempelfort), with Garg as Hamlet, and Strindberg's *A Dream Play* (1947, *regie* Schalla).

Herbert Maisch became *generalintendant* in 1947 and stayed until 1959. This was a highly productive era, with many plays and an extremely broad repertory. Two especially popular actors were Kaspar Brüninghaus and Deltgen. Maisch built his seasons well, with both classics and modern works popular during the period, done by a series of well-chosen *regisseurs*: Eliot's *Murder in the Cathedral* (1947, *regie* Pempelfort); Schiller's *Don Carlos* (1947, *regie* Maisch);

Carl Zuckmayer's *Des Teufels General* (*The Devil's General*, 1948, *regie* Maisch), with Deltgen as Harras; Schiller's *Die Räuber* (*The Robbers*, 1949, *regie* Maisch); O'Neill's *Mourning Becomes Electra* (1949, *regie* Friedrich Siems); Shaw's *Saint Joan* (1950, *regie* Siems), with Edith Teichmann as Joan; Molière's *Tartuffe* (1950, *regie* Maisch), with Deltgen as the hypocrite; Fry's *The Lady's Not for Burning* (1951, *regie* Siems); Williams' *A Streetcar Named Desire* (1952, *regie* Deltgen); Shakespeare's *Richard III* (1953, *regie* Siems), with Brüninghaus in the title role; Miller's *The Crucible* (1954, *regie* Hans Bauer), with Deltgen as John Proctor; Brecht's *Das Leben des Galilei* (*The Life of Galileo*, *regie* Siems), with Brüninghaus as Galileo; Strindberg's *The Ghost Sonata* (1955, *regie* Bauer); Brecht's *Der gute Mensch von Sezuan* (*The Good Woman of Setzuan*, 1956, *regie* Siems); Shakespeare's *Hamlet* (1957, *regie* Siems); the Euripides/Braun *The Trojan Women* (1958, *regie* Siems), with Hermine Körner as Hekuba; Else Lasker-Schuler's *Die Wupper* (1958, *regie* Bauer); and Schiller's Wallenstein plays (1959, *regie* Maisch). One of Maisch's last acts as *generalintendant* was to stage the opening production in a new opera house (architect Wilhelm Riphan), which the acting company used as well. The production was Weber's *Oberon*, first performed on May 8, 1957.

Oscar Fritz Schuh became *generalintendant* in 1959. Not since Martersteig's era had Cologne had a head who knew opera as well as theatre, bringing both companies to real prominence. Schuh turned the Schauspiel into a real *regisseur*'s theatre with a series of distinguished groups working there, including Hans Lietzau, Hans Bauer, Charles Regnier, and himself. Schuh's own staging style tended toward the anti-illusionistic, often with abstract sets and much semichoreographed movement. In the first half of Schuh's directorship, these productions emerged as winners: O'Neill's *Ah, Wilderness!* (1960, *regie* Lietzau); Hauptmann's *Rose Bernd* (1960, *regie* Lietzau); Eliot's *The Elder Statesman* (1960, *regie* Schuh), with Bernhard Minetti as Lord Claverton; Hauptmann's *Fuhrmann Henschel* (1961, *regie* Lietzau), with Brüninghaus in the title role; and Molière's *The Miser* (1962, *regie* Hans Karl Zeiser), with Minetti as Harpagon.

On September 8, 1962, Schuh staged Schiller's *Die Räuber*, with sets by Caspar Neher (Schuh's favorite designer), which opened the new Schauspielhaus (architect Riphan), a companion building next to the opera. A number of large productions followed in the aftermath of the opening: Büchner's *Woyzeck* (the Schuh/Neher combination); Wilder's *The Matchmaker* (*regie* Regnier), with Grete Mosheim as Dolly; and Williams' *The Night of the Iguana* (*regie* Regnier). In the season left to Schuh there would be several big productions, including Max Frisch's *Andorra* (1963, *regie* Lietzau) and Schuh's staging of Shakespeare's *Richard III* (1963), with Helmut Qualtinger as the crafty king.

Schuh left in 1963 to go to the Deutsches Schauspielhaus in Hamburg. Arno Assmann became his replacement. Assmann with his chief producer, Max Peter Amman, tried more experimentation with plays, particularly the classics. (Both seemed to be influenced by Jan Kott). Assmann was not nearly as successful as Schuh had been. The repertory was much more political, with Brecht frequently played. His best productions were balanced between the classics and the moderns, done by a broad series of *regisseurs*, both regulars with the company and guests. There were also guests in the acting company. Among the better productions were Kleist's *Der zerbrochene Krug* (*The Broken Jug*, 1964, *regie* Zeiser), with Brüninghaus as Adam; Brecht's *Mutter Courage und ihre Kinder* (*Mother Courage and Her Children*, 1964, *regie* Peter Palitzsch), with Ursula von Rechnitz as Anna Fierling; O'Casey's *Juno and the Paycock* (1965, *regie* Palitzsch), with sets by Wilfred Minks; Shakespeare's *Richard II* (1966, *regie* Amman), with Peter Lierck in the title role; Brecht's *Der kaukasische Kreide Kreis* (*The Caucasian Chalk Circle*, 1967, *regie* Amman); Harold Pinter's *The Homecoming* (1967, *regie* Deltgen), with Deltgen as Max; and Kleist's *Prinz Friedrich von Homburg* (1968, *regie* Hans Joachim Heyse).

The years 1968 to 1979 are frequently referred to as the Hansgünther Heyme era in Cologne, but this designation is not completely accurate. Actually, Heyme began as head of the Schauspiel under the *generalintendant* Claus Helmut Drese, who served at Cologne from 1968 to 1975. Drese, however, kept a very low profile that caused one critic to dub the Opera and Schauspiel (which are high pitched) the "Denkmal des unbekannte" ("monument to the unknown") intendant. During the period, Heyme made the company a real *regisseur*'s organization, with the classics radically treated, almost to the point of anti-heroism. Among the most daring productions of his tenure were his staging of Sophocles' two Oedipus plays (1968), with Karl-Heinz Pelser in the title roles; Schiller's Wallenstein cycle (1969, *regie* Heyme), with Pelser again as the protagonist (this played Milan); Tankred Dorst's *Toller* (1969, *regie* Heyme); Brecht's *Turandot oder der Kongress des Weissacher* (*Turandot or the Congress of Whitesashers*, 1970, *regie* Heyme), which toured; Chekhov's *Uncle Vanya* (1971, *regie* Valentin Jeker); Brecht's *Mann ist Mann* (*Man Is Man*, 1972, *regie* Ulrich Grieff); Hebbel's *Die Niebelungen* (1973, *regie* Heyme); Alfred Jarry's *Ubu Roi* (1973, *regie* Ciulli); Schiller's *Die Jungfrau von Orleans* (*The Maid of Orleans*, 1974, *regie* Heyme), with Nüsse as Johanna; and Luigi Pirandello's *Six Characters in Search of an Author* (1975, *regie* Ciulli).

The opera and theatre companies split in 1975. The post of *generalintendant* was abolished, and Drese went off to head the opera in Zurich. The management of the theatre was turned over to a *direktorium* (board of directors). The first *direktorium* was to have been Heyme, Ciulli, and the English Geoffrey Reeves, but Reeves dropped out early to be replaced by Angelika Hurwicz, herself dropping out after one season and replaced by Hans Schulze. The *direktorium* continued the radical experiments of their predecessors, but made a more conscious effort to achieve uniformity of style. The most notable productions included Strindberg's *A Dream Play* (1975, *regie* Ciulli); Sophocles' *Women of Trachis* (1976, *regie* Heyme); Goethe's *Faust II* (1977, *regie* Heyme); Ernst Barlach's *Der Arme Vetter* (*The Poor Cousin*, 1977, *regie* Ciulli); Chekhov's *The Cherry Orchard* (1978, *regie* Ciulli); and Shakespeare's *Hamlet* (1979, *regie* Heyme), with Wolfgang Robert as Hamlet.

Heyme dropped out for Stuttgart in 1979. The new *direktorium* consists of Volker Canaris (dramaturge), Jürgen Flimm (*regisseur*), and Ludwig Von Otting (business). This *direktorium* is moving toward more original scripts and projects and a much more socially responsive theatre, though not necessarily totally political. In addition, the company has made more use of theatres around the city. It has also moved toward more experimentation, which has caused some controversy. The following productions were heavily attended: Kleist's *Kätchen von Heilbronn* (1979, *regie* Flimm), with Katharina Thalbach in the title role; Shakespeare's *The Merchant of Venice* (1979, *regie* Palitzsch), with Hermann Lause as Shylock; the premiere of Peter Greinert's *Kiez* (1980, *regie* Walter Bockmayer); Witold Gombrowicz's *Yvonne, Princess of Burgundia* (1980, *regie* Luc Bondy); Samuel Beckett's *Happy Days* (1980, *regie* Bondy), with Christa Berndl as Winnie; Heiner Müller's *Mauser* (1980, *regie* Christof Nel); Brecht's *Baal* (1981, *regie* Flimm), with Hans-Christian Rudolph as Brecht's monstrous title character; Maxim Gorky's *The Lower Depths* (1981, *regie* Jürgen Gosch); and Büchner's *Leonce und Lena* (1981, *regie* Flimm).

The Cologne Schauspiel uses three main houses: its Schauspielhaus (with 920 seats), its Kammerspiele (remodeled in 1964 with 314 seats), and the Schlosserei (Workshop) im Schauspielhaus (with flexible seats). It does about eight new productions in the Schauspielhaus, two in the Kammerspiele, six programs in the Schlosserei, and one in the hall on Oskar-Jäger-Strasse. The company numbers twenty-two women and thirty-nine men, and it has guest actors. Approximately eleven *regisseurs* are used every year and nine dramaturges, with the dramaturges doing many of the special projects. Plays are chosen by the *direktorium*, with the dramaturge's help, and are split between classics and modern. When choosing plays, the acting company is kept very much in mind, and an effort is made to get away from using guests. The company has done some work on television and some touring, both in the area and occasionally in large cities. Its current budget runs to 18.9 million DM, of which 15.8 million DM is subsidy. The attendance runs to 82 percent capacity. It has 2,686 people on subscription, and its own newspaper, *Theaterzeitung*, informs subscribers of events.

The company has attempted to obtain the involvement of more people in its activities. The whole organization is making a special effort to attract young people and Cologne's many foreign workers. The dramaturges and acting company are working on scripts dealing with the history of the city.

The company's most pressing problem centers on its relationship with the opera. Although the two companies are autonomous, they share a common technical staff. As the opera schedule is extremely ambitious, the technical staff often appears to favor the operatic productions. The second problem has been with the Schauspielhaus itself, which, though handsome, is built on a rather narrow lot and has somewhat inadequate backstage space. The problem is aggravated by the fact that the Schauspielhaus is in the middle of the city, leaving literally no room to build.

LEON M. AUFDEMBERGE
(With thanks to Uta Bitterli.)

DÜSSELDORF PLAYHOUSE
(Düsseldorfer Schauspielhaus)
Belichstrasse 1
4000 Düsseldorf, West Germany

In 1805 a national theatre was founded in Düsseldorf, the Bergisches Nationaltheater, by Friedrich Carl Gollnick and Gustav Wohlbrück. By 1813 this theatre had prospered so much that it was able to publish a yearbook, the *Bergisches Theater-Almanach*, which is considered a landmark in the German theatre. Karl Immermann headed the city theatre from 1834 to 1837. He invited great names to the theatre, especially Wilhelm Schadow (the painter); Karl Schnasse (the art historian); Felix Mendelssohn (the great composer); and two playwrights, Friedrich von Vechtritz and Michael Beer. Immermann's whole concept of the theatre was highly romantic, and he had a taste for a wide variety of plays. He produced model productions of many Shakespearean works, including *Macbeth*, *Hamlet*, *King Lear*, *As You Like It*, and *Romeo and Juliet*; Heinrich von Kleist's *Prinz Friedrich von Homburg* (*The Prince of Homburg*); and Schiller's *Wallensteins Tod* (*Wallenstein's Death*). He was one of the first people to stage Spanish plays, including Calderón de la Barca's *Life Is a Dream* and *The Mayor of Zalamea*. In addition, there were also productions of works by Johann Wolfgang von Goethe and Johann Ludwig Tieck. Several of his own works were also produced, although they are not much read anymore. The best of these is probably *Merlin* (1832), inspired by Goethe's *Faust*. Immermann is considered one of the greatest theatrical innovators of his time. The Stadttheater (it became one in 1834) went downhill after his demise.

From time to time efforts were made to rejuvenate the company, particularly by Karl Simon and Eugen and Ida Stägemann (prominent actors). In 1905 the new Düsseldorfer Schauspielhaus was built under the direction of Gustav Lindemann, and opened a great era in the Düsseldorf theatre. The first production for the new house was Friedrich Hebbel's *Judith* on October 14, 1905. The lead role was played by Lindemann's wife, Louise Dumont, who was one of Germany's great Ibsen actresses. The two created a series of excellent productions, most notably of Ibsen, including *Ghosts*, *Emperor and Galilean*, *Hedda Gabler*, *Rosmersholm*, *The Lady from the Sea*, *Peer Gynt*, and *When We Dead Awaken*.

Lindemann also staged great productions of Leonid Andreyev's *The Life of a Man* (1908); Shakespeare's *Henry IV* (1915); Euripides' *The Trojan Women* (1931); and the greatest triumph of his life, both parts of Goethe's *Faust* in 1932, the year he left Düsseldorf. He also did productions of playwrights who were just emerging in Germany such as Frank Wedekind, Hans José Rehfisch, Ernst Barlach, Walter Hasanclever, and Gerhart Hauptmann. Many of those who were trained by Lindemann later made names for themselves in the German theatre, including Wolfgang Langhoff, Richard Weichert, Bertold Vierthel, Herman Greid, Paul Heckels, Willy Kleinau, and Gustaf Gründgens. After the duo left for Berlin, the fortunes of the Schauspielhaus dropped considerably. During World

War II, the house was renovated only to be destroyed in the last days of the war. This marked the end of an era.

During World War II Wolfgang Langhoff went into exile in Zurich, where he spent the war years learning new staging techniques and discovering new playwrights. He was chosen to open the Düsseldorf Playhouse in 1945 at the Theater am Worringerplatz. Langhoff brought with him a knowledge of what had been going on during the war elsewhere, and he introduced his Düsseldorf audiences to new playwrights. He was followed, in 1947, by Gustav Gründgens, one of Germany's great *regisseurs*. It was Gründgens who, more than anyone else, made the Schauspielhaus an international house.

Gründgens was one of the last of the old school of German *regisseurs* who were meticulous in their staging methods. He had worked as an actor under the Dumont-Lindemann team in Düsseldorf before moving on to various German cities. During World War II he was intendant of one of the most prestigious theatres in Berlin and all Germany, the Staatstheater. But it was at Düsseldorf that Gründgens first found the freedom to stage as he chose. He created a fantastic number of productions, acted in a great many, and chose the plays his audiences were to see. Because of his immense personal popularity, great actors began to congregate in Düsseldorf: Werner Krauss (partly forgiven for his sins of the Nazi era), Marianne Hoppe, Käthe Dorsch (famous for her title characters in Frederick Bruckner's *Elizabeth of England* and Friedrich Dürrenmatt's *The Visit from the Old Lady*), and Elisabeth Flickenschildt (who was famous for practically anything she chose to play). Gründgens introduced his audience to plays forbidden in the Nazi era, such as Jean-Paul Sartre's *The Flies* (1947) and Thomas Wolfe's *Mannerhouse* (1953), which is scarcely known in the United States but is a staple in the German theatre. He staged many notable productions, including Chekhov's *The Seagull* (1947); Goethe's *Faust* (1949); T. S. Eliot's *The Family Reunion* (1950) and *The Cocktail Party* (1951), with himself as the analyst and Flickenschildt as Julia; Schiller's *Die Räuber* (*The Robbers*, 1951); Shakespeare's *All's Well That Ends Well* (1954); and Eliot's *The Confidential Clerk* (1954), before saying farewell to the city with Wolfgang Hildesheimer's *Der Drachenthron* (*The Throne of the Dragon*), in 1955. It had been a great era, and Düsseldorf was reluctant to lose him to Hamburg.

Gründgens was followed by a different sort of intendant, one who was also an excellent *regisseur*, Karl Heinz Stroux (1955–1972). Under his leadership a new theatre (actually a complex of two) opened in 1970 (architect Bernhard Pfau) with Georg Büchner's *Dantons Tod* (*Danton's Death*). Stroux liked a wide variety of plays, as had Gründgens, but his taste ran more toward the experimental and the avant-garde. For a while, the theatre was known as the German capital of the theatre of the absurd. Most of Eugene Ionesco's works written in these years had their German premieres in the house. One of his major plays, *Rhinocéros* (1959, *regie* Stroux), had its world premiere here. Elisabeth Bergner came to do Eugene O'Neill's *Long Day's Journey into Night* (1956) and Jean Giraudoux's *The Madwoman of Chaillot* (1964).

Stroux staged classics: Shakespeare's *King Lear* (1956); Schiller's *Wilhelm Tell* (1959); Shakespeare's *Othello* (1967, sets by Teo Otto), with Wolfgang Reichmann as the Moor; Goethe's *Faust I* (1967); Schiller's *Wallenstein* (1968); and Shakespeare's *Richard III* (1960 and 1972). In 1969 the season opened with the Peter Weiss *Trotsky in Exile* (*regie* Harry Buckwitz), but at the final dress rehearsal the student audience so objected to the play that the actors were able to get through only the first half.

Ulrich Brecht succeeded Stroux, staying until 1978. Brecht had a background as a *regisseur* and an actor, but it was clear from the beginning that he was not the intendant his predecessors had been. Careful was the word which one critic applied to his directorship when he left. There were, however, good productions during his tenure, including Odön von Horváth's *Italienische Nacht* (*Italian Night*, 1972, *regie* Luc Bondy); Büchner's *Leonce and Lena* (1973, Bondy again); Molière's *The Miser* (1973, *regie* Brecht), with Hans Korte as Harpagon; Kai Brooks' production of Gotthold Lessing's *Minna von Barnhelm* (1973); Büchner's *Woyzeck* (1974, *regie* Wolfgang Seesman); John Webster's *The Duchess of Malfi* (1974, *regie* Brook); Lessing's *Nathan der Weise* (*Nathan the Wise*, 1975, *regie* Brecht). In 1976 Günther Beelitz became intendant.

Düsseldorf has two theatres in its house, a Grosses Haus, which seats 1,036, and the Kleines Haus, which seats 250 to 300. The theatre itself is located in the center of Düsseldorf (close to Gustaf Gründgenplatz); photos of it are frequently reproduced in histories of architecture. It has a large acting company of fifty men and thirty women. The theatre does ten to eleven works each year in the large house, ten in the smaller house, and a number of plays for children. The annual budget is 23 million marks (about $13 million), of which 17 million marks are in subsidy. It publishes one of the best theatre magazines in Germany, *Scene 10*, which contains news about repertory and casts. There are ten *regisseurs* each season (mostly guests) and four permanent dramaturges. It is a well-run house, rather safe but solid. The public seems to like it, and attendance runs at a healthy 80 percent capacity.

LEON M. AUFDEMBERGE

ESSEN CITY THEATRE
(Theater der Stadt Essen)
Postfach
4300 Essen 1, West Germany

By the 1880s various people in Essen tried to convince the local city fathers of the need to open a theatre, financed by the city. The theatre (architect Heinrich Seeling) finally became a reality on September 16, 1892, opening with Gotthold Lessing's *Minna von Barnhelm*, staged by its first intendant, Albert Berthold. Berthold had been working in the city since 1877 and was one of the prime movers in getting the city to build a theatre, with part of the financing from Alfred Krupp. Berthold staged classics and opera in the theatre during his two years as intendant. All were very conservative productions, with himself staging such works as Schiller's *Don Carlos* (1892), Goethe's *Faust* (1893), and Shakespeare's *Hamlet* (1893).

The next intendant, Louis Ockert (1894–1900), continued the conservative repertory of his predecessor, but did begin a program of touring productions to nearby Münster in 1895. His successor, Hans Gelling (1900–1907), showed a preference for Schiller, guest productions, and actors such as Adalbert Matkowsky. In 1904 the company combined with the Dortmund company, an arrangement that lasted until 1907. Gelling had the usual classics in the repertory as well as modern playwrights such as Ibsen, George Bernard Shaw, Arthur Schnitzler, and Hugo von Hofmannsthal.

George Hartmann stayed from 1907 to 1912 and continued Gelling's classics/modern policy, expanding the number of plays every season to sixty. Johannes Maurach (1912–1918) favored two playwrights, Ibsen and Schiller, and brought many prominent guests to the opera. Then followed two short directorships, Willy Becker (1918–1920) and Paul Trede (1920–1921). Becker promoted popular plays to bring people into the theatre, including his own productions of Hans Müller's *Der Schöpfer* (*The Creator*, 1918) and Gerdt von Bassewitz's perennial *Peterchens Mondfahrt* (*Little Peter's Moon Journey*, 1919). The repertory of Trede's lone season included many classics such as Shakespeare's *The Merchant of Venice* and Schiller's *Kabale und Liebe* (*Intrigue and Love*, both 1920 and *regie* by Hanns Donadt).

Stanislaus Fuchs (1921–1931) was intendant during Germany's inflation crisis and tried everything to make people come to the theatre. He increased the quality by cutting down the number of plays and introduced many modern playwrights in the repertory. In 1926 he opened the Waldtheater the same year as the founding of the Essener Volksbühne, which provided theatre tickets at low prices. On October 18, 1927, a new Schauspielhaus was opened (refashioned from the former Kriegerheim), with Heinrich von Kleist's *Prinz Friedrich von Homburg* (*The Prince of Hamborg*, *regie* Martin Kerb) as the first play. The repertory during these years included many new playwrights, such as Georg Kaiser, Ernst Toller, and Gerhart Hauptmann. Some of the most often played works of the period were Ibsen's *Peer Gynt* (1921, *regie* Fuchs), Goethe's *Faust* (1922, *regie* Fuchs), Hauptmann's *Rose Bernd* (1923, *regie* Alfons Melchinger), Kaiser's *Nebeneinander* (*Side by Side*, *regie* Melchinger), Friedrich Hebbel's *Die Niebelungen* (*The Niebelungen*, *regie* Hans Weitag), Schiller's Wallenstein cycle (1926, *regie* Weitag), Shakespeare's *Hamlet* (1927, *regie* Fuchs), Schiller's *Kabale und Liebe* (*Intrigue and Love*, 1928, *regie* Kerb), Molière's *The School for Wives* and *The Miser* (1928, *regie* Willibald Froon), Schiller's *Wilhelm Tell* (1930, *regie* Friedrich Sebrecht), and Carl Zuckmayer's *Der Hauptmann von Köpenick* (*The Captain from Köpenick*, 1931, *regie* Herbert Waniek). Many of these plays had sets by Carl Wild, who headed the technical department from 1913 to 1927. After his death in 1927, Caspar Neher filled Wild's post for a time. Another prominent member of the company during this period was Kurt

Jooss, leader of the Tanzgruppe. In 1931 Fuchs left primarily because of the company's serious financial problems.

Alfred Noller came as head of the Schauspiel in 1931, becoming intendant in 1933. Noller had two major problems: finances and the Nazis. The first problem was solved with his *Fusionspläne* which combined certain operations with those of other local theatres. In dealing with the second difficulty, Noller turned his back on the previous modern repertory to produce season after season of classics and forge a style that was best adapted to the playing of them. In his first seasons, the big productions included both modern and classic plays: Goethe's *Faust* (1931, *regie* Noller), Ibsen's *Peer Gynt* (1931, *regie* Noller), and Zuckmayer's *Katharina Knie* (1932, *regie* Noller). After National Socialism there would be many more classics, with special attention paid to those staged in the Waldtheater. (National Socialism was big on "folk theatre.") The following productions (all staged by Noller) were especially praised: Shakespeare's *The Taming of the Shrew* (1933), Schiller's *Mary Stuart* (1934), Hebbel's *Die Niebelungen* (1934), Shakespeare's *The Two Gentlemen of Verona* (1935), Goethe's *Iphigenie auf Tauris* (*Iphigenia in Tauris*, 1936), Shakespeare's *Hamlet* (1937), and *A Midsummer Night's Dream* (1938), and Goethe's *Faust* (1940).

Karl Bauer had been intendant at Göttingen before he came to Essen, and he would be one of the few intendants to keep his position after the war, staying from 1940 to 1958. Bauer's repertory, like that of his predecessor, was heavy in classics. While he also promoted many current plays, it was the classics that received the care. A few productions stood out in the early part of Bauer's era, all staged by Erich Fritz Brücklmeier: Sophocles' *Antigone* (1941), Hauptmann's *Iphigenie in Delphi* (1942), Schiller's *Mary Stuart* (1942), and Goethe's *Torquato Tasso* (1943). On March 5, 1943, the Schauspiel was destroyed, and for the rest of the war the company played in various theatres, continuing its heavily classical program with a couple of standouts: Kleist's *Der zerbrochene Krug* (*The Broken Jug*, 1943, *regie* Karl Heinz Stroux) and Goethe's *Faust* (1943, *regie* Brücklmeier). On March 26, 1944, the opera house was also destroyed, but the company continued to perform until June 1944.

The theatre company reopened on August 8, 1945, with a double bill of two Goethe plays, *Die Mitschuldigen* (*The Accomplice*) and *Die Geschwister* (*The Brothers and Sisters*), both staged by Brücklmeier at the Theater in Velbert. During the postwar years the company played in a variety of temporary and makeshift theatres in and around the city, with the Waldtheater its only good house. The repertory at first relied on the classics, with the company doing a long Goethe cycle in 1949. As the company developed, however, more and more modern plays began to enter the repertory. In the first postwar seasons the following productions were considered significant: Molière's *The Imaginary Invalid* (1945, *regie* Bauer), Goethe's *Faust* (1946, *regie* Bauer), Franz Werfel's *Jacobowsky und der Oberst* (*Jacobowsky and the Colonel*, 1947, *regie* Theodore Haerten), Shakespeare's *Hamlet* (1948, *regie* Bauer), Zuckmayer's *Des Teufels General* (*The Devil's General*, 1948, *regie* Haerten), Goethe's *Stella* (1949, *regie* Gustav Rudolph Sellner), Walter Schäfer's *Die Verschwörung* (*The Conspiracy*, 1949, *regie* Sellner), Kleist's *Amphytrion* (1950, *regie* Sellner), and the Calderón/Hugo von Hofmannsthal *Great World Theatre* (1950, *regie* Sellner). On December 29, 1950, the opera house reopened (architect for the rebuilding I. Seidenstrik) with Wagner's *Die Meistersinger*. The acting company used the Ruhrokohlehaus and the Humboldt Aula in 1955 and 1956, respectively. In the years remaining, Bauer expanded the repertory enormously. In his last years as intendant, most of the better works were modern, often by some of West Germany's most notable *regisseurs*. Especially remembered are Federico García Lorca's *Dona Rosita Remains Single* (1951, *regie* Sellner), which opened the night after *Meistersinger*, Schiller's Wallenstein cycle (1951, *regie* Günther Sauer), George Bernanos' *The High Gifted Fear* (1952, *regie* Bauer), Shakespeare's *Troilus and Cressida* (1953, *regie* Sauer), the premiere of Reinhold Schneider's *Innozenz und Franziskus* (1954, *regie* Heinz Dietrich Kenter), William Saroyan's *Sam Ego's House* (1954, *regie* Kenter), John Patrick's *The Teahouse of the August Moon* (1954, *regie* Peter Hamel), Schiller's *Die Verschwörung des Fiesko zu Genua* (*The Conspiracy of Fiesco Against Genoa*, 1955, *regie* Kenter), T. S. Eliot's *The Cocktail Party* (1956, *regie* Bauer), and Eugene O'Neill's *Mourning Becomes Electra* (*regie* Erwin Piscator).

Erich Schumacher had been a dramaturge before becoming an intendant. His early interest in Shakespeare later developed into a real devotion to Bertolt Brecht, the most frequently played writer during Schumacher's tenure. Schumacher made the company much more a *regisseur*'s theatre, pulling in Europe's most famous, including Erwin Piscator, Harry Buckwitz, Peter Palitzsch, Jean-Louis Barrault, Roger Blin, and Kazimierz Dejmek. His most interesting productions were generally twentieth century in origin: Brecht's *Der kaukasische Kreide Kreis* (*The Caucasian Chalk Circle*, 1958, *regie* Kenter), Arthur Miller's *The Crucible* (1958, *regie* Piscator), Schiller's *Die Räuber* (*The Robbers*, 1959, *regie* Piscator), the premiere of Paul Claudel's *Head of Gold* (1959, *regie* Schumacher), Brecht's *Schweyk im zweiten Weltkrieg* (*Schweyk in the Second World War*, 1960, *regie* Buckwitz) with Hans Ernst Jäger in the title role, Jean Anouilh's *Becket, or the Honor of God* (1961, *regie* Piscator), Georg Büchner's *Woyzeck* (1961, *regie* Palitzsch), Claudel's *The Book of Christopher Columbus* (1962, *regie* Barrault), Max Frisch's *Andorra* (1962, *regie* Joachim Fontheim), Paul Fechter's *Der Zauberer Gottes* (*The Magic of God*, 1965, *regie* Freidrich Brandenburg) with Jäger as the protagonist, Armand Gatti's *The Second Existence of Lagers Tatenberg* (1965, *regie* Joachim Fontheim), Brecht's *Die heilige Johanna der Schlachthöfe* (*Saint Joan of the Stockyards*, 1966, *regie* Fontheim), Nikolai Gogol's *The Inspector General* (1966, the first *regie* by Dejmek in West Germany), Fernando Arrabal's *The Great Ceremony* (1966, *regie* Dieter Reible), Jean Genet's *The Screens* (1967, *regie* Blin), Shakespeare's *Richard II* (1968, *regie* Claus Leininger), the premiere of Hans Magnus Enzenberger's *Das Verhör vor Habana* (*The Examination of Havana*, 1970, *regie* Hagen Müller-Stahl), first done at the Ruhrfestspiele in Recklinghausen, the premiere of Weiss' *Die*

Versicherung (*The Assurance*, 1971, *regie* Hans Neuenfels) with sets by Wilfred Minks, the premiere of Rolf Hochhuth's *Die Hebamme* (*The Midwife*, 1971, *regie* Schumacher), Frank Wedekind's *Franziska* (1972, *regie* Alois Michael Heigel), and the premiere of Hochhuth's *Lysistrate* (1974, *regie* Schumacher). In the 1967–1968 season the company went to Poland with two plays.

From 1974 to 1978 Jurgen-Dieter Waidelich was the *generalintendant* and continued the company's established policies, playing at the Ruhrfest in Recklinghausen. Waidelich kept many of the same *regisseurs* of the previous period, emphasized twentieth-century plays, and began to do more plays for children. The most popular productions of this period were decidedly twentieth-century works: Paul Foster's *Elizabeth I* (1975, *regie* Liviu Ciulei), Chekhov's *The Cherry Orchard* (1975, *regie* Liviu Ciulei) with Joanna Maria Gorvin as Madame Ranevskaya, Klaus Budzinski's antiwar revue *Hurra, wir sterben* (*Hurrah, We Die*, 1976, *regie* Dieter Reible), and Gombrowicz's *The Operetta* (1977, *regie* Dejmek).

Ulrich Brecht came in 1978 and brought a much more balanced view to the repertory company. His tenure has been marked by more experimentation, particularly in terms of classics. The following productions have been deemed important: the premiere of Yvonne Keuls' young people's play *Abgespielt* (*Played Out*, 1979, *regie* Edgar Cox/Herman Wintsch), the premiere of Franz Xaver Kroetz's *Der stramme Max* (*The Sturdy Max*, 1979, *regie* Wolf Seesemann), Georg Kaiser's *Gas* (1979, *regie* Carsten Bodinus), Alfred Jarry's *Ubu Roi* (1979, *regie* Dejmek), Kleist's *Prinz Friedrich von Homburg* (*The Prince of Homburg*, 1980, *regie* Brecht), and Schiller's Wallenstein cycle (1981, *regie* Brecht), with Hans Korte as the protagonist.

The company at Essen does sixteen new productions a year as well as revivals of works from the previous season. These productions are split among its various theatres: the Opernhaus (637 seats), the Rathaus-Theater (250 seats), the Humboldt Aula (546 seats), and the Casa Nova (flexible seating from 100 to 300 seats). The repertory includes plays from the present and the past, as well as children's and young people's plays. The Schauspiel has an acting company of twenty-two men and nine women plus guests, with a separate company for the Kinder- und Jugendtheater. Plays are selected by the intendant with his staff, especially the dramaturge David Esrig, current *schauspiel direktor*. The 1980–1981 budget ran to 24.6 million DM, of which 20.6 million DM was subsidy. Attendance runs from 77 percent in the Humboldt Aula to 92 percent in the Rathaus. The company publishes its own newspaper called *Theater Journal* which carries news of upcoming events in opera, ballet, and spoken theatre.

As with many German houses, the dramaturgical staff (five at present) and the technical staff work for both the music and theatre wings of the organization, with Ulrich Brecht staging works for both. It is an exceedingly ambitious organization doing twenty-six productions a year. While the company tries not to offend, it is by no means conservative. One of the recurrent themes in the life of every *generalintendant* since the 1940s has been the desire for a new opera

house. This is the company's chief need as the old one is much too small and
rather antiquated, charming as it may be.

LEON M. AUFDEMBERGE
(With thanks to Vera Noll.)

FRANKFURT'S THEATRE
(Schauspiel Frankfurt)
Theaterplatz
Frankfurt-am-Main, West Germany

Frankfurt-am-Main has a very long theatre history going back to the fifteenth
century when a passion play was presented in the Römerberg (the old section
of Frankfurt largely destroyed in the war). Its theatre history has been the subject
of many books. Suffice to say here that by the end of the eighteenth century
traveling groups visited the city with some regularity. The idea of a permanent
city theatre can probably be traced to the presentation of *Erwin und Elmire* by
J. André in 1777 by the Seyler company, who decided to stay. Seyler had
originally been a member of the Nationaltheater in Hamburg and would present
Shakespeare, Gotthold Lessing, and other playwrights to delighted theatregoers.

In 1782 a Stadtisches Comodienhaus was built by the Grossmanschen troupe
who produced *Hanno Fürst in Norden* by Johann Christian de Bock. This was
followed by doses of Schiller and other German playwrights. In 1792 the Na-
tionaltheatre was inaugurated, and by the middle of the next century, prominent
regisseurs and actors made the city their home. In 1855 a new prose theatre was
built, followed in 1880 by the opera house (architect Lorenz Ritter). (The opera
house was destroyed in World War II, and its ruins are still to be seen.) By the
turn of the century, there was a need for a new prose theatre in the town. Frankfurt
had considerable wealth (members of the Kahn and Rothschild families lived
there), and various permanent troupes played year-round. In 1902 a new theatre
was built (architect H. Seeln), opening with scenes from Goethe's *Faust I* and
Schiller's *Wallenstein*. It, too, was partially destroyed in World War II, but it
was later rebuilt and is now the opera house for the city. The intendant for the
theatre was Paul Jensen, who was fond of German classic plays and pursued a
conservative course, both in terms of actors and repertory, until World War I.

In 1911 a new private theatre company, the Neue Theater, opened its doors
and its program influenced the Schauspielhaus. Arthur Hellmer served as intendant. Until the theatre company disbanded in 1935, it played a wide repertory,
including Henrik Ibsen, August Strindberg, Gerhart Hauptmann, Frank Wedekind, and Arthur Schnitzler, in contrast to the more conservative city-subsidized
theatre. Important actors came to the Neue, including Alexander Moissi, Käthe
Gold, Marianne Hoppe, and the young Helen Weigel.

In 1917 Dr. Karl Zeiss became *generalintendant*, in charge of both opera and
plays. Taking his cue from the Neue, he made the Schauspielhaus much more
in tune with twentieth-century theatre. He infused new life into the classics (he

saw Schiller as pre-expressionistic), and he introduced audiences to Strindberg, George Bernard Shaw, Georg Kaiser, and many others. Important premieres were presented about this time, including Arnold Zweig's *Ritualmord in Ungarn* (*Ritual Murder in Hungary*) in 1914 and *Der Marquis von Arcis* (1917). Zeiss stressed the importance of the dramaturge and invited Richard Weichart (*regisseur*) and Carl Ebert (actor and later *regisseur*) to join the company, as well as K. F. Delavilla (chief designer). Zeiss had a rough time of it in conservative Frankfurt; he was accused of being a pornographer and of making the theatre a place for spreading propaganda. In 1920 he was replaced by Weichart.

Weichart made the theatre much more conservative, but not sufficiently conservative to please the public. He stressed the idea of ensemble, in which acting would be an important element. He did, however, play some works of new German playwrights, as had his predecessor, and he added new ones, such as Bertolt Brecht and Luigi Pirandello. For a short while, Oskar Kokoschka worked here as a designer in the 1920s. Weichart left in 1932, returning after World War II.

During most of the 1930s and the war years, the intendant was Hans Meissner, who followed the safe course of most intendants under National Socialism, playing many classics or innocuous comedies. His chief contribution was in the drama festivals he produced in the Römerberg. Particularly well remembered is his production of *Hamlet*, in the Römerberg in 1938, with Wolfgang Buttner as the title character. Many actors left the company to emigrate because of racial or political reasons or dissatisfaction with Meissner's leadership. In 1944 the theatre was largely destroyed, but by that time nearly all German theatres had closed.

The company opened in the Börsensaal (stock exchange) in September 1945, with *Ingeborg* by Curt Goetz, under the leadership of Toni Impehoven. In this temporary house, Frankfurt theatregoers for the first time saw new playwrights such as Thornton Wilder, Carl Zuckmayer, Jean Anouilh, and Jean Giraudoux. The most important *regisseur* was Fritz Rémond. In 1947 Heinz Hilpert became *generalintendant* for one year followed by Weichart who returned once more to Frankfurt. During Weichart's tenure there would be important productions of Wolfgang Borchert's *Draussen vor der Tür* (*The Man Outside*, 1947); Arthur Miller's *Death of a Salesman* (1950), with Martin Held; and Christopher Fry's *The Lady's Not for Burning* (1951, *regie* Verhoven).

Harry Buckwitz came in 1951, staying until 1968 as intendant of all Frankfurt theatres. This was time of great rebuilding in Frankfurt, especially in the Schauspielhaus. Under Buckwitz the Frankfurt Schauspielhaus became one of the leading theatres in Germany, famous for playing a wide variety of plays in varied styles. Well-known actors such as Lothar Müthel and Oskar Werner came to Frankfurt; Werner is best remembered for his Hamlet of 1953 under Lothar Müthel's direction. The great specialties of the house were modern French playwrights, such as Anouilh and Giraudoux, and, of course, German classics, but the company was equally adept at playing Arthur Miller, Arthur Kopit, and

Chekhov (who had been little played before the war). Buckwitz was an early champion of Brecht in West Germany and played him frequently when Brecht was most critical of the West German government. Buckwitz is remembered in particular for staging Brecht's *Der gute Mensch von Sezuan* (*The Good Woman of Setzuan*, 1952); Miller's *The Crucible* (1955); Brecht's *Der kaukasische Kreide Kreis* (*The Caucasian Chalk Circle*, 1955), with Käthe Reichl as Gruscha and Ernst Jager as a great Azdak. Brecht's *Mutter Courage und ihre Kinder* (*Mother Courage and Her Children*, 1959), with Therese Giehse repeating the title role she had originated in Zurich during the war years; Friedrich Dürrenmatt's *Frank V* (1960); Brecht's *Das Leben des Galilei* (*The Life of Galileo*, 1961); Ibsen's *Peer Gynt* (1962); Brecht's *Die heilige Johanna der Schlachthöfe* (*Saint Joan of the Stockyards*, 1963); and the Peter Weiss play *Vietnam Discourse*, with the remarkable full title of *Diskurs über die Vorgeschichte und den Verlauf des lang Andauernden Befreiungkrieges in Viet Nam als Beispiel für die Notwendigkeit des bewaffneten Kampfes der Unterdrückten gegen ihre Unterdrücker sowie über die Versuche der Vereinigten Staaten von Amerika die Grundlagen der Revolution zu vernichten* (*Discourse on the Background and Course of the Long-lasting War of Liberation in Viet Nam as an Example of the Necessity of Armed Struggle by the Oppressed Against Their Oppressors as Well as Attempts of the United States of America to Destroy the Bases of Revolution*). The Weiss play was a world premiere staged in 1968.

Many important *regisseurs* worked with Buckwitz, including Lothar Müthel and Heinrich Koch. Koch staged the opening production, Goethe's *Faust I*, when a new Schauspielhaus was opened on December 14, 1963. In 1952 the theatre began semiregular touring. Buckwitz gradually reformed the company's playing style. Most of the original company had been trained in the old style of German declamation, and under Buckwitz the style became lighter and freer and certainly more versatile. It was no small undertaking.

Ulrich Wilhelm Erfurth became director in 1968, to remain until 1972. His regime was largely marked by his differences of opinion with the city council. There were a number of remarkable works during his years, including Goethe's *Götz von Berlichingen* (1968, *regie* Reible); Jean-Claude Van Itallie's *America Hurrah!* (1968, *regie* Wolfgang Mehring); Aristophanes' *The Acharnians* (1969, *regie* Ulrich Brecht); Shakespeare's *Richard II* (1969, *regie* Reible); Hugo von Hofmannsthal's *Der Mann von Rabinal* (*The Man from Rabinal*, 1969, *regie* Gunther Amberger); Hauptmann's *Florian Geyer* (1970, *regie* Richard Münch); and Odön von Horváth's *Italienische Nacht* (*Italian Night*, 1970, *regie* Wolf Dietrich). As can be seen from the list, Erfurth liked plays with a social theme; he was followed by a man of similar taste.

In 1972 Peter Palitzsch joined the company as chief *regisseur*. Before coming to Frankfurt he had worked as Brecht's assistant at the Berliner Ensemble, later becoming chief dramaturge and a *regisseur* there. He worked in Stuttgart as intendant before coming to his present job. At the time of his arrival, the role of intendant was abolished, and, in a move toward democratization, a *direktorium* of three people was established: Palitzsch (who is still a member) and two others elected by the company. Paltizsch has made this very much a *regisseur*'s house. However, actors are not ignored, as is shown by the case of Peter Roggisch, certainly one of West Germany's best actors, who followed Palitzsch to Frankfurt. Palitzsch has tried to balance the choice of plays and staging style and has not tried to overspecialize.

Also to Palitzsch's credit, he has not tried to keep all the staging plums to himself. The outstanding productions of the last few years have been split among a variety of *regisseurs*. The theatre is especially proud of the following since 1972: Lessing's *Emilia Galotti* (1973, *regie* Palitzsch); Frank Wedekind's *Frühlings Erwachen* (*Spring's Awakening*, 1973, *regie* Palitzsch); Pedro Calderón's *Life Is a Dream* (1973, *regie* August Fernandes), with Peter Roggisch as King Sigismund; Brecht's *Baal* (1973, *regie* Hans Neuenfels); Ibsen's *A Doll's House* (1973, *regie* Neuenfels); Horst Laubner's *Der Dauerklavierspieler* (*The Monstrous Piano Player*, 1974, *regie* Luc Bondy); Strindberg's *Playing with Fire* (1974, *regie* Löscher); Witold Gombrowicz's *The Operetta* (1975, *regie* Neuenfels); Brecht's *Herr Puntila und sein Knecht Matti* (*Mr. Puntila and His Hired Man, Matti*, 1975, *regie* Palitzsch); a shocking Euripides' *Medea* (1976, *regie* Neuenfels); Ernst Barlach's *Der Armen Vetter* (*The Poor Cousin*, 1976, *regie* Frank P. Steckel); Dario Fo's *Not Paid* (1976, *regie* by the Milanese *regisseur*, Arturo Corso); Shakespeare's *A Midsummer Night's Dream* (1977, sets and staging by Wilfred Minks, West Germany's best designer); Shakespeare's *Othello* (1978, *regie* Palitzsch); Ibsen's *The Master Builder* (1978, *regie* Palitzsch); and Sophocles' *Oedipus* (1979, *regie* Neuenfels).

The Schauspielhaus in Frankfurt is located in the heart of the commercial district, next door to the opera house with which it is in close cooperation. (Technical staffs build sets for both.) Like most German theatres, it has two theatres, the Schauspielhaus which seats 1,387, and the Kammerspiel, which seats 200. Actors and *regisseurs* work the two houses; some of the best work is done in the Kammerspiel. Both houses are well equipped, but the architectural style (designed by architects Apel and Beckett) is a bit cold. They are comfortable houses, however, with a bar and large foyers, where patrons may walk during intermissions.

The Schauspielhaus company numbers about sixty-five (forty men, twenty-five women) and is relatively stable. Like most German-language houses, it plays ten months a year. Frankfurt generally runs later than most German houses, linking its season with that of the opera house, which is tied to the tourist season. The theatre belongs to the city, and the subsidy for the three companies (theatre, opera, and ballet) is 45 million DM ($25 million), of which the Schauspielhaus receives 12 million DM. Eight new productions a year are presented in the Schauspielhaus and five in the Kammerspiel. Although most plays run only one season (thirty performances on an average), popular plays are run over into the next season. If a production proves wildly popular (as did its all-actor production of the Ralph Benatzky operetta *Im Weissl Rossl*, known in English as *White Horse Inn*), extra performances are scheduled.

Of course, subscriptions are available. The public has had an on again-off again relationship with the house since Palitzsch's arrival. For popular attractions the house has been filled, but for several productions audiences have been extremely small.

Under Palitzsch's leadership, the Schauspielhaus was much more democratic. Although the house was called "Palitzsch's house," most decisions were made by the *direktorium*, which helped to spread decisions throughout the company. Palitzsch was largely responsible for staging aspects. *Regisseurs* were chosen by Palitzsch and the *direktorium*, with some voice given to the actors themselves.

In 1980 Palitzsch left the company. Some continuity was assured when Wilfred Minks (a designer-*regisseur*) and Johannes Schaaf were announced as members of the *direktorium* in 1980. As a result, the Schauspielhaus in Frankfurt will probably not lose its place among the top German houses.

LEON M. AUFDEMBERGE

GERMAN PLAYHOUSE
(Deutsches Schauspielhaus)
Kirchenallee 39
2000 Hamburg, West Germany

When the German Playhouse was organized in 1899 as a commercial theatre by a group of middle-class citizens, Hamburg had two prominent theatre companies in operation, the Stadttheater and the Thalia. The Stadttheater was too concerned with opera (it would drop its theatre company in the middle 1920s), while the Thalia did far too many comedies. It was hoped that the new theatre organization would do more classics and do them well, as well as modern serious works—but not too radical—interspersed with light comedies in order to balance the budget.

The company opened its new theatre on September 15, 1900, with Goethe's *Iphigenia auf Tauris* (*regie* Cord Hachmann). Stelle Hohenfels played the title character, and Carl Wagner also appeared in the production. Also in the new company were Franziska Ellmenreich, one of Germany's great classical actresses, Robert Nhil, Ludwig Max, and Ernst Koehne.

The first intendant for the theatre was Alfred Freiherr von Berger, who had worked at the Burg in Vienna before coming to Hamburg. His whole tenure was marked by an earnest endeavor to give customers what they wanted—big, heavily produced classics and comedies. What they did not want Berger gave them as well, modern playwrights. Berger presented ten Ibsen plays and championed Friedrich Hebbel. During most of the seasons, Berger presented cycles of playwrights, and most of the major works done in the period were originally part of longer lists by the same playwright. Among his major efforts could be listed the following (productions without *regisseurs* belong to Berger): Hermann Suder-mann's *Johannisfeuer* (1900, *regie* Hachmann); Friedrich von Schiller's Wal-lenstein cycle (1901) and *Mary Stuart* (1901, *regie* Ernst Koehne), with Ellmenreich in *Mary Stuart*; Shakespeare's *King Lear* (1902), with Rudolf Schildkraut as Lear; Friedrich Hebbel's *Herodes und Mariamne* (1903) and *Gyges und sein Ring* (*Gyges and His Ring*, 1903); Shakespeare's *The Merchant of Venice* (1904), with Schildkraut as Shylock; Schiller's *Die Braut von Messina* (*The Bride of Messina*, 1904); Hebbel's *Die Niebelungen* (1905); Schiller's *Don Carlos* (1905); Shakespeare's *Julius Caesar* (1906); Goethe's *Faust* (1907), with Nhil as Mephistopheles; Shakespeare's *Hamlet* (1908); and Ibsen's *A Doll's House* (1909). The big hit, however, was Wilhelm Meyer-Forster's *Alt-Heidel-berg* (*Old Heidelberg*, 1902, *regie* Carl Heine), which Americans know as the basis for the Sigmund Romberg operetta *The Student Prince*. The play was in the repertory until the 1930s and is the most often-produced work in the history of the theatre, having been given 145 times during the Berger regime alone.

Berger left in 1909, and the theatre was run for a short while by Ernst Koehne, with Carl Hagemann serving as intendant from 1910 to 1913. He did the usual classics and many more modern playwrights (such as August Strindberg, Frank Wedekind, and Arthur Schnitzler), which caused some controversy. Two actors who were prominent during his tenure were Max Montor and Alex Otto, both of whom were long associated with the theatre. Among the most prominent works performed under his directorship were Oscar Wilde's *A Woman of No Importance* (1910); Schnitzler's *Anatol* and Hebbel's *Gyges und sein Ring* (both 1911); and Goethe's *Torquato Tasso* and Hebbel's *Die Niebelungen* (both 1913), all of which were staged by Hagemann.

Max Grube (1913–1918) had been an actor with the Hoftheater in Meiningen, where he learned the realistic style of the troupe. The great works done during his period were largely classic plays, though plenty of comedies and sentimental and patriotic works were done during the war years. The best of Grube's pro-ductions had two things in common—large casts staged by Grube himself (un-credited productions are by Grube): Shakespeare's *Love's Labour's Lost* (1913); Shaw's *Pygmalion* (1914, *regie* Walter O. Stahl); Schiller's *Die Braut von Messina* (1914); Schiller's *Don Carlos* (1915), with Nhil as Philip; Ferdinand Raimund's *Die Verschwender* (*The Prodigal*, 1917, *regie* Stahl); Goethe's *Faust* (1917), with Montor as Faust; and Shakespeare's *King Lear* (1917), with Otto as Lear.

Paul Eger was intendant from 1918 to 1925. This was a period of runaway inflation in Germany, with Eger struggling to keep the theatre financially solvent. He would use operetta seasons during the summer to help pay for the winter seasons. The theatre was closed for a time, after the Armistice and during the political unrest of 1919 and the general strike of 1920. His important productions were plays from many periods: Goethe's *Iphigenia auf Tauris* (1918, *regie* Eger); Wedekind's *Frühlings Erwachen* (*Spring's Awakening*, 1919, *regie* Eger); Ger-hart Hauptmann's *Die Weber* (*The Weavers*, 1919, *regie* Alex Otto); Shakespeare's *Macbeth* (1920, *regie* Eger); Hauptmann's *Der Biberpelz* (*The Beaver Coat*, 1920, *regie* Otto); Schiller's *Wilhelm Tell* (1920, *regie* Otto); Ibsen's *Peer Gynt* (1921, *regie* Svend Gatte); Shakespeare's *Hamlet* (1921, *regie* Albert Heine), with Reinhold Lütjohann in the title role; Hauptmann's *Fuhrmann Henschel* (1922, *regie* Otto); Hebbel's *Gyges und sein Ring* (1922, *regie* Hermann Wlach); Goethe's *Faust* (1924, *regie* Werther); the premiere of Hauptmann's *Veland* (1925, *regie* by the author), with Otto Werther as Veland; Luigi Pirandello's *Six Characters in Search of an Author* (1925, *regie* Arnold Marlé); and Shakespeare's *The Merchant of Venice* (1925, *regie* Werther).

Erich Ziegel managed the company for only a short time (1926–1928), but he accomplished some important things. His repertory was extremely modern, with two playwrights appearing for the first time in the repertory, Bertolt Brecht and Hans Henny Jahnn. He had serious financial problems, but scraped up enough capital to partly renovate the theatre in 1926. Most of the biggest audience-pleasers during the short Ziegel tenure were classics: Schiller's *Die Verschwörung des Fiesko zu Genua* (*The Conspiracy of Fiesco Against Genoa*, 1926, *regie* Ziegel), with Gustav von Wangenheim as Fiesko; the Brecht/Marlowe *Das Leben Eduard II von England* (*The Life of Edward II of England*, 1926, *regie* Ziegel), with Hans Otto in the title role; Hans Henny Jahnn's *Medea* (1927, *regie* Hanns Lotz); Heinrich von Kleist's *Das Käthchen von Heilbronn* (1927, *regie* Otto Werther); Schiller's *Die Jungfrau von Orleans* (*The Maid of Orleans*, 1927, *regie* Lotz), with Maria Eis as Johanna; Hebbel's *Die Niebelungen* (1928, *regie* Lotz); and Hugo von Hofmannsthal's *Der Turm* (*The Tower*, 1928, *regie* Otto Werther).

Because of financial conditions Hermann Röbbeling took over both the Deutsches Schauspielhaus and the Thalia from 1928–1932. He tried a little of everything to balance the books, from guest actors to guest productions—anything that would attract attention and draw spectators. One effort early in this period became the recipient of one of the first stinkbombs to go off in a theatre, set off at a production of Ferdinand Bruckner's *Die Verbrecher* (*The Criminals*, *regie* Arnold Marlé), in December 1928, probably because Bruckner was Jewish. Many of Röbbeling's major productions included plays that would be forbidden during the Nazi era: Schiller's *Die Räuber* (1929, *regie* Röbbeling); Gustav Freytag's *Die Journalisten* (1929, Otto Werther); Bruckner's *Elisabeth von England* (1930, *regie* Marlé), with Eis as the titled queen; Franz Grillparzer's *Medea* (1930, *regie* Gerhard Bünte); Goethe's *Iphigenia auf Tauris* (1931, *regie* Georg von Terramare); Carl Zuckmayer's *Der Hauptmann von Köpenick* (*The Captain from Köpenick*, 1931, *regie* Röbbeling), with Bruno Harprecht as Voigt; and Goethe's *Torquato Tasso* (1932, *regie* Terramare). In 1932 Röbbeling was made head of the Burg in Vienna, a job he lost after the Anschluss.

The years of Karl Wüstenhagen (1932–1945) coincided with National Socialism. Wüstenhagen kept mainly to the classics and maintained a fairly stable acting company. Some of his best actors, however, were lost to Berlin. Certain changes were instituted during these years. The first was a change in company name to Staatliches Schauspielhaus in Hamburg; the second was the founding of a theatre school, which existed from 1935 to 1950; and the third was the use of a second house for plays, the Kleines Haus in the Volkstheater in Altona. The most widely heralded productions during this period were three by Jürgen Fehling, early in the period. They were lavishly set by Cesar Klein, who was the major designer in the theatre during this era and in the postwar years as well.

The three Fehling productions were Schiller's *Don Carlos* (1935), with Wüstenhagen as Phillip; Gotthold Lessing's *Minna von Barnhelm* (1935), with Ehmi Bessel in the title role; and Hebbel's *Kriemhilds Rache* (*Kriemhild's Revenge*, 1936), with sets by Karl Gröning and Werner Hinz as Gunther. Other major productions of the era were by some of the major *regisseurs* in Germany: Hauptmann's *Florian Geyer* (1932, *regie* Günter Haenel); Hebbel's *Die Niebelungen* (1933, *regie* Heinz Dietrich Kenter); *Wilhelm Tell* by Schiller (the most often played playwright during the period), staged by Haenel in 1933; Shakespeare's *King Lear* (1934, *regie* Adolf Rott), with Wüstenhagen as Lear; Schiller's Wallenstein cycle (1936, *regie* Hans Schweikart); Goethe's *Iphigenia auf Tauris* (1937, *regie* Bünte); Schiller's *Mary Stuart* (1940, *regie* Wüstenhagen), with Maria Wimmer as Elisabeth; both parts of *Faust* (1940, *regie* Wüstenhagen), with Robert Meyn as Mephisto; Ludwig Thomas' *Moral* (1943, *regie* Heinz Stieda); Shakespeare's *Macbeth* (1943, *regie* Robert Michal), with Wüstenhagen and Wimmer as the royal couple; and Ibsen's *The Pillars of Society* (1944, *regie* Bünte).

Theoretically, all German theatres were closed in October 1944, but the company played through April 1945. Although the Schauspielhaus was hit several times by bombs during air raids in 1940, 1941, and 1943, it survived the war.

The first play staged in Hamburg after the war was Hofmannsthal's *Jedermann* (*regie* Bünte), done in St. John's Church in Hamburg-Harvestehude on August 8, 1945, with Hinz as Jedermann. The company was composed of actors from both the Thalia and the Schauspielhaus (it took its old name back after the war), and other houses. The first postwar leader for the Schauspielhaus was Rudolf Külüs. During the opening seasons, the company played in various theatres around the city because the British forces had requisitioned the theatre as a garrison theatre (until 1949). The company was occasionally allowed to play there, however. During his sole season as head, Külüs was heavy on old favorites, including Lessing's *Nathan der Weise* (1945, *regie* Helmut Gmelin), with Walter Süssenguth as Nathan; Shakespeare's *The Taming of the Shrew* (1945, *regie* Helmut Käutner); Ferenc Molnár's *Liliom* (1946, *regie* Otto Kurth), with Gisela von Collande as Julie.

Arthur Hellmer had been the founder and head of the Neue Theatre in Frankfurt, which had been one of Germany's most experimental houses. During the Nazi era, he emigrated first to Austria and then to England. The company's repertory during his two seasons (1946–1948) included a variety of classics, as well as many modern playwrights, such as Bertolt Brecht, Ernst Barlach, Eugene O'Neill, Jean Giraudoux, and Carl Zuckmayer. During these seasons the company played in the Gewerkschaftshaus am Besenbinderhof, the Altonaer Kassenhalle, the Altonaer Haus der Jugend, the Schauspielhaus, and a variety of others. Among Hellmer's major productions were Shakespeare's *The Tempest* (1946, *regie* Heinrich Koch), with Hinz as Prospero; Giraudoux's *Ondine* (1946, *regie* Koch); O'Neill's *Mourning Becomes Electra* (1947, *regie* Alfred Noller); the German premiere of Zuckmayer's *Des Teufels General* (*The Devil's General*, 1947, *regie* Friedrich Brandenburg), with Meyn as Harras; Shakespeare's *Much Ado About Nothing* (1948, *regie* Paul Mundorf); and Shaw's *Caesar and Cleopatra* (1948, *regie* Hans Schalla).

Albert Lippert arrived in 1948 as head of the theatre, and the following year the company began to play in its theatre full time. Lippert was an actor and *regisseur* who used a series of distinguished actors and *regisseurs* to bring the company to its fullest height. The *regisseurs* included Hermine Körner, Werner Krauss, Karl Heinz Stroux, and Erwin Piscator. The repertory of this period was a compendium of world classics and important new plays. Lippert neglected almost no era of the theatre, often emphasizing guest artists. Among the star-studded productions were Brecht's *Herr Puntila und sein Knecht Matti* (*Mr. Puntila and His Hired Man, Matti,* 1948, *regie* Lippert), with Willy Kleinau as Puntila; Giraudoux's *The Madwoman of Chaillot* (1949, *regie* Stroux), with Körner in the title role; Goethe's *Faust* (1949, *regie* Lippert); Goethe's *Iphigenia auf Tauris* (1950, *regie* Lothar Müthel), with Horst Caspar as Orest; Federico García Lorca's *Blood Wedding* (1950, *regie* Stroux), with Körner as the mother; Aeschylus' *The Oresteia* (1950, *regie* Gustav Rudolf Sellner); Shakespeare's *King Lear* (1951, *regie* Ulrich Erfuth), with Krauss as Lear; Gerhart Hauptmann's *Vor Sonnenuntergang* (*Before Sunset,* 1951, *regie* Bünte), with Krauss as Clausen; Schiller's *Mary Stuart* (1951, *regie* Körner), with Maria Becker as Elisabeth; Zuckmayer's *Der Hauptmann von Köpenick* (*The Captain from Köpenick,* 1951, *regie* Robert Meyn), with Krauss as Voigt; Grillparzer's *Ein Bruderzwist in Habsburg* (*Fraternal Strife in Habsburg,* 1952, *regie* Lippert), with Krauss as Rudolph; Ibsen's *Peer Gynt* (1952, *regie* Koch), with Will Quadflieg in the title role; Pedro Calderón's *Life Is a Dream* (1953, *regie* Koch), with Quadflieg in the title role; Kleist's *Penthislea* (1954, *regie* Koch), with Wimmer in the title role; Tennessee Williams' *El Camino Real* (1954, *regie* Lippert), with Lil Dagover as Marguerite Gautier; and Hauptmann's *Die Ratten* (*The Rats,* 1955, *regie* Stroux), with Käthe Dorsch as Frau John.

So many books have been written on the career of Gustaf Gründgens that a summary of his era (1955–1963) is difficult. Gründgens had been intendant at the Düsseldorf Playhouse before coming to Hamburg; many of the actors and *regisseurs,* as well as the repertory, were transferred from Düsseldorf to Hamburg. Here, however, Gründgens had less hassle with finances and was allowed a larger ensemble and a clearer field. In terms of repertory, he balanced classics and modern, staging several important premieres, including plays by Brecht, Jahnn, Lawrence Durrell, and Zuckmayer. His acting company included some of Germany's most prestigious actors, notably Elisabeth Flickenschildt, Johanna

Maria Gorvin, and Maximilian Schell. He demanded the best *regisseurs* working in Germany: Ulrich Erfurth, Peter Gorski (Gründgens' adopted son), Heinz Hilpert, Leopold Lindtberg, Rudolf Noelte, Max Ophüls, Oscar Fritz Schuh, and so on. In the earlier part of Gründgens' tenure there was a series of much-reviewed productions (those without *regisseurs* are Gründgens'): Schiller's *Wallensteins Tod (Wallenstein's Death*, 1955, *regie* Erfurth), with Gründgens as Wallenstein; the premiere of Zuckmayer's *Das kalte Licht (The Cold Light*, 1955); T. S. Eliot's *The Confidential Clerk* (1955); Thomas Wolfe's *Mannerhouse* (1956), with Gründgens as General Ramsay; the premiere of Jahnn's *Thomas Chatterton* (1956); the premiere of Curt Goetz's *Nichts Neues aus Hollywood (Nothing New Out of Hollywood*, 1956), with Gründgens as Cliff Clifford; Ibsen's *The Wild Duck* (1956, *regie* Noelte), with Hinz as Hjalmar; Friedrich Dürrenmatt's *Der Besuch der alten Dame (The Visit from the Old Lady*, 1956, *regie* Erfurth), with Flickenschildt as Claire; and Shakespeare's *Henry IV* (1956, *regie* Lindtberg).

Then on April 21, 1957, came Gründgens' most famous production, Part One of Goethe's *Faust*. Quadflieg starred as Faust, Ella Büchi as Gretchen, Flickenschildt as Marthe Schwerdtlein, and Gründgens as Mephistopheles, with sets by Teo Otto. This production was the culmination of all Gründgens had learned in his theatrical life. It was a highly theatrical production, full of energy, light, movement, and vitality—very much an atomic age Faust. Eventually, part two followed in 1958, with both parts recorded and part one filmed in 1961. Every time the work came up in the repertory in Hamburg, crowds stretched around the block to buy seats. The work played tours in West Germany and eventually was taken to the USSR in 1959 and New York in 1961.

Although *Faust* was Gründgens' last great production, there were many very good ones left (again unattributed productions belong to Gründgens): John Osborne's *The Entertainer* (1957, *regie* Hilpert), with Gründgens as Archie; Georg Büchner's *Dantons Tod (Danton's Death*, 1958); Eugene O'Neill's *A Touch of the Poet* (1958, *regie* Erfurth), with Hinz as Con; Christian Grabbe's *Don Juan and Faust* (1959), with Quadflieg as Don Juan; the premiere of Brecht's *Die heilige Johanna der Schlachthöfe (Saint Joan of the Stockyards*, 1959), with Hanna Hiob (Brecht's daughter) in the title role and sets by Caspar Neher; Schiller's *Mary Stuart* (1959), with Flickenschildt as Elisabeth; the premiere of Lawrence Durrell's *Sappho* (1959), with Flickenschildt in the title role; Shaw's *Caesar and Cleopatra* (1959, *regie* Gründgens and Karl Vibach), with Gründgens and Ingrid Andree as the title characters; Hebbel's *Gyges und sein Ring* (1960), with Gründgens as Kandaules; Shakespeare's *The Tempest* (1960, *regie* Sellner), with Gründgens as Prospero; Strindberg's *Miss Julie* (1960), with Gorvin in the title role; the premiere of Dieter Waldmann's *Von Bergamo bis Morgen früh (From Bergamo to Early Morning*, 1960), with Heinz Reincke as Harlequin; the premiere of Durrell's *Actis* (1961); Giraudoux's *Amphytrion 38* (1961, *regie* Gorsky); Tirso de Molina's *Don Gil of the Green Hose* (1961), with Gorvin as Donna Juana; the premiere of Siegfried Lenz's *Zeit der Schuldlosen (Time of*

Innocence, 1961, *regie* Gorski); Schiller's *Don Carlos* (1962), with Gründgens as Philip (his last role); Strindberg's *The Dance of Death* (1963), with Hinz and Gorvin as the battling couple; and Shakespeare's *Hamlet*, with Maximilian Schell in the title role, which was Gründgens' last production (1963). He became a suicide in the same year.

Although Gründgens' shadow lay heavily over the man who followed him, Oscar Fritz Schuh, all things considered, Schuh did very well in his years (1963–1968). He emphasized more experimentation, with a freer look in the staging of classics. Gründgens was literary, and the emphasis of his productions (and the Schauspielhaus) was on solidity and form. Schuh was anti-illusionistic and mythic. He persuaded a number of new *regisseurs* to come to Hamburg, including Werner Düggelin, Fritz Kortner, and Hans Lietzau. The most often performed playwrights during this period included Edward Albee, O'Neill, and Shakespeare. Schuh heavily favored twentieth-century plays, as is clear from the following list: Strindberg's *A Dream Play* (1963, *regie* Schuh), with Gorvin as Indra's daughter; Albee's *Who's Afraid of Virginia Woolf?*; Molière's *The Imaginary Invalid* (1964, *regie* Kortner), with Curt Bois as the title character; Shakespeare's *A Midsummer Night's Dream* (1965, *regie* Schuh); O'Neill's *Mourning Becomes Electra* (1965, *regie* Gerhard Klingenberg); Hebbel's *Judith* (1966, *regie* Lindtberg), with Rolf Boysen in the title role; Strindberg's *The Father* (1967, *regie* Kortner), with Hinz and Wimmer as the unhappily married couple; Goethe's *Egmont* (1967, *regie* Schuh), with Walter Reyer; Harold Pinter's *The Homecoming* (1967, *regie* Dieter Giesing), with Bernhard Minetti as Max; and Wedekind's *Die Liebestrank* (*The Love Potion*, 1968, *regie* Harry Meyen). In this era the company began to work in television.

Schuh was followed by four different intendants. The first was Egon Monk, who had worked at the Berliner Ensemble in East Berlin and West German television, and promised a rousing repertory, as well as a series of new actors. He staged the premiere of his own (with Claus Hubalek) *Uber den Gehorsam* (*Over Respectable People*) and Schiller's *Die Räuber*, both in September 1968; in the middle of October he left. Gerhard Hirsch became intendant, serving from October 16, 1968, to October 31, 1969. He pulled off a number of really fine things during this short time: Max Frisch's *Biografie* (1968, *regie* Koch), with Gorvin as Antoinette; Büchner's *Woyzeck* (1969, *regie* Niels-Peter Rudolph); Brecht's *Herr Puntila und sein Knecht Matti* (*Mr. Puntila and His Hired Man, Matti*, 1969, *regie* Schweikart); and Molière's *Tartuffe* (1969, *regie* Karl Paryla).

Hans Lietzau followed from November 1969 to December 1971. He sought a balance between classics and modern; the following works were heavily attended: Goethe's *Clavigo* (1969, *regie* Fritz Kortner), with Thomas Holtzmann as Clavigo; Arthur Kopit's *Indians* (1970, *regie* Lietzau), with Rolf Boysen as Buffalo Bill; Shakespeare's *Richard II* (*regie* Lietzau); Chekhov's *The Cherry Orchard* (1970, *regie* Lietzau), with Gorvin as Madame Ranyevskaya; and the premiere of Thomas Bernhard's *Ein Fest für Boris* (*A Feast for Boris*, 1970, *regie* Claus Peymann). Rolf Liebermann then took over (December 1970 to

December 1971). He liked to experiment; thus, on April 8, 1971, he opened a second house, the Malersaal, for smaller productions, with the opening work Edward Bond's *The Pope's Wedding* (*regie* Peter von Wiese). There were two big Feydeau successes in his year and three well-staged productions (all in 1971): Christopher Hampton's *The Philanthropist* (*regie* Dieter Dorn), Peter Weiss' *Hölderlin* (*regie* Peymann), and Molière's *The Miser* (set and production by Minks). The following year, Liebermann took over the reins and revitalization of the Paris Opera.

The tenure of Ivan Nagel (1972–1979) can be summed up quite simply: he took chances, and even his severest critics have to admit the whole era was not dull. Nagel, a former theatre critic, transformed the company into a real *regisseur*'s house in which people were given considerable freedom to experiment. A regular series of premieres was also held. The freedom resulted in some controversy, particularly in the handling (some critics said "mangling") of classics, notably in Peter Zadek's King-Kongish *Othello* (1976), with Wildruber as the Moor. It was a highly charged era, full of brilliance in many productions: the premiere of Franz Xaver Kroetz's *Stallerhof* (*Staller Farm*, 1972, *regie* Ulrich Heising), with Eva Mattes as Beppe; Maxim Gorky's *The Barbarians* (1972, *regie* Dieter Giesing); Strindberg's *The Pelican* (1973, *regie* Claus Peymann), with Gorvin as the mother; the premiere of Tankred Dorst's *Eiszeit* (*Ice Age*, 1973, *regie* Dieter Hackmann); Schiller's *Die Jungfrau von Orleans* (1973, production and sets by Wilfred Minks), with Mattes as Johanna; Peter Shaffer's *Equus* (1974, *regie* Schweikart), with Quadflieg as Dysart; Molière's *The Misanthrope* (1975, *regie* Noelte), with Quadflieg as Alceste; Zadek's farcical view of Ibsen's *The Wild Duck* (1975); O'Neill's *Long Day's Journey into Night* (1975, *regie* Noelte), with Quadflieg and Wimmer as the elder Tyrones; Hauptmann's *Der Biberpelz* (*The Beaver Coat*, 1977, *regie* Jérôme Savary); Brecht's *Der gute Mensch von Sezuan* (*The Good Woman of Setzuan*, 1977, *regie* Giorgio Strehler); Ibsen's *Ghosts* (1977, *regie* Luc Bondy); Shakespeare's *The Winter's Tale* (1978, *regie* Zadek), with Wildgruber as Leontes; Kleist's *Prinz Friedrich von Homburg* (*The Prince of Homburg*, 1978, *regie* the Karge/Langhoff team); and S. Ansky's *The Dybbuk* (1979, *regie* Arie Zinger). Nagel took his company to various places in the city to perform, regularly to various theatre festivals, and most repeatedly to Berlin.

Nagel left in 1979 to pursue the world of festivals, and for one season, the company was taken over by Rolf Mares and Gunter König. Although this was a pick-up season in terms of *regisseurs*, it was a good one with an outstanding production of George Bernard Shaw's *A Doctor's Dilemma* (1979, *regie* Noelte). In the fall of 1980 Niels-Peter Rudolph, an actor/*regisseur* combination, took over the company as intendant, giving the theatre a more socially conscious complexion. As the theatre is part of a complete renovation in the area, the old Malersaal was closed and a new one opened on October 1, 1981, with Euripides' *Medea* (*regie* Barbara Bilabel). Rudolph has maintained the company's balanced repertory and has done much experimentation in classics. His major works have come from many eras: Jakob Lenz's *Der Hofmeister* (*The Tutor*, 1980, *regie* Christof Nel); Beckett's *Endgame* (1981, *regie* Peter Loscher); Shakespeare's *Pericles* (1981, *regie* Augusto Fernandes), with Karl Heinz Stroux as Gower; and Schiller's *Die Verschwörung des Fiesko zu Genua* (1981, *regie* Rudolph), with Wildgruber as Fiesko.

The German Playhouse normally does ten new productions in its Grosse Haus, which seats 1,165, and six in the Malersaal (Deutsches Schauspielhaus in der Kampnagel-Fabrik). The intendant together with his staff selects the plays and splits them between old and new, with all works having some social idea. Those done in the Malersaal are generally modern. There are thirty-six actors and seventeen actresses in the acting company, in addition to guests; the organization also employs five dramaturges, eight *regisseurs* (two of whom are guests), and the usual technical staff.

During Nagel's time, a number of productions upset people; as a result, the company is striving for a more balanced approach without becoming dull and still tries to be as experimental as possible. There are around two thousand people on subscription, which is not enormous, but the Hamburger Volksbühne and Kulturring der Jugend bring in more people. The theatre generally runs to 70 percent capacity, with its annual budget totaling 20 million DM, of which 17 million is subsidy. It publishes its own paper, *Schauspiel*, to let spectators know about forthcoming productions; the local tourists' bureau publishes several more general information sheets.

The special excellence of the German Playhouse has been apparent throughout its history. Beginning as primarily a classics house, it has progressed through a series of changes to become a theatre that mixes the best of modern works with highly charged productions from the past.

LEON M. AUFDEMBERGE
(With thanks to the Publicity
Department of the theatre plus
Christel Benner of the Universität Hamburg.)

GERMAN THEATRE IN GÖTTINGEN
(Deutsches Theater in Göttingen)
Theaterplatz 11
3400 Göttingen, West Germany

Like its sister city of Oxford, Göttingen has a long tradition of student-acted plays and an equally long tradition of faculty mistrust. It also has a long history of traveling troupes, who began to visit the city sporadically in the seventeenth century and by the next century were making regular visits. At the beginning of the nineteenth century Göttingen had an improvised theatre, the Zeughaus, with many prominent troupes playing there, including the companies of Abt and Grossman, and Konrad Ekhof. The first Stadttheater came in 1834, with places for eight hundred spectators. In the 1850s a number of famous players performed in it, including Karl Devrient and Marie Seebach, followed later by Carl Sonntag and Franziska Ellmenreich. On January 10, 1887, the Stadttheater burned, and for three years Göttingen had an interim theatre.

On September 30, 1980, a new Stadttheater opened (architect Nierenheim assisted by Baumeister Schnitger) with Friedrich von Schiller's *Wilhelm Tell*. It was staged by the director, Norbert Berstel. Berstel patterned the running of his company (which included opera and ballet, as well as drama) after Otto Brahm's Lessing Theater in Berlin. As money was scarce, he emphasized repertory and ensemble. Nonetheless, he did bring a number of famous actors as guests to the theatre, including Ellmenreich, Josef Kainz, Clara Ziegler, Anna Haverland, and Sarah Bernhardt. In terms of repertory, he favored a balance between classics and modern, especially Gerhart Hauptmann, Hermann Sudermann, and Max Halbe. In terms of classics he liked *Sturm und Drang* and Greek tragedy. The biggest productions of his tenure included his own productions of Sophocles' two Oedipus plays (1898) and Goethe's *Faust II* (1901).

Willy Martini, head from 1906 to 1917, also favored a balance of classics and modern, with his favorite modern contemporary writers being George Bernard Shaw, Leo Tolstoy, and Gerhart Hauptmann. He also engaged guest actors, bringing Friedrich Kayssler and Albert Bassermann to Göttingen. Among his permanent acting company were Harry Liedtke, one of Germany's first movie actors, and Käthe Haack. Martini's own personal favorite among the productions he staged was Oscar Wilde's *An Ideal Husband* (1916). During World War I the theatre was closed for a while. From 1917 to 1919 the theatre was managed by Philip Werner, which was good for opera but not for plays.

Otto Werner, who was director from 1919 to 1929, was especially good in staging classics, Shakespeare, Goethe, Ibsen, and the new expressionistic playwrights. Again there were guests, including Werner Krauss, Paul Wegener, and Hermine Körner. The most important work in this period was the beginning of the important Händel Festival, frequently conducted by Robert Hager. Paul Stiegler (1929–1936) continued the festivals, but he was extremely conservative in his choice of plays: his sole emphasis was on classics. His most popular works were from the past: Shakespeare's *Julius Caesar* (1930) and *Twelfth Night* (1932, both staged by Stiegler); Schiller's *Die Räuber* (*The Robbers*, 1934, *regie* Hans-Wilhelm Kleffner); and Alexander Scribe's *A Glass of Water* (1935, *regie* Rudolf Morsbach). Stiegler was the first head to call himself an intendant.

Karl Bauer (1936–1940) put together a very conservative repertory. He had two excellent *regisseurs* in his company, Heinrich Koch and Walter Jockish, with Bauer himself very strong in staging Shakespeare. These years were heavy in classics, which began to be reviewed in the Berlin papers: Shakespeare's *Hamlet* (1936, *regie* Bauer), with Eduard Benoni in the title role; *Romeo and Juliet* (1937, *regie* Bauer); Shaw's *Pygmalion* (1937, *regie* Bauer); Shakespeare's *Macbeth* (1939, *regie* Koch) and *The Tempest* (1939, *regie* Bauer).

Gustav Rudolf Sellner became the first truly renowned head of the theatre in 1940, remaining until 1943. Although the company's repertory was severely limited, Sellner managed to make the acting company important largely through his own staging style. He brought important guests to the company, including Heinrich George. His best productions were a string of classics, highly literate, highly disciplined, and all staged by himself: Pedro Calderón's *Mayor of Zalamea* (1940), with George as Pedro Crespo; Sophocles' *Electra* (1940); Schiller's *Don Carlos* (1941) and the Wallenstein cycle (1941); Shakespeare's *The Merchant of Venice* (1942); and Heinrich von Kleist's *Amphytrion* (1943). Sellner was also to change the name of the company to the Theater der Stadt Göttingen. From 1943 to 1944 the theatre was managed by Hans K. Friedrich, whose main accomplishment was a classic theatre festival in 1944, which included Sophocles' *Antigone* (*regie* Heinrich Buchmann) and Friedrich Hebbel's *Gyges und sein Ring* (*Gyges and His Ring*, *regie* Friedrich). In September 1944 the theatre closed; and it was one of the most important theatre buildings in Germany to survive the war.

The theatre reopened on August 4, 1946, with *God Save the Queen* (Göttingen was in the British Zone), followed by Mozart's *The Marriage of Figaro*. The first intendant after the war was Fritz Lehmann, who brought a new and exciting repertory to his theatre, even though his field was opera. He produced a mixture of classics and modern: T. S. Eliot's *Murder in the Cathedral* (1947, *regie* Heinz Dietrich Kenter); Carl Zuckmayer's *Des Teufels General* (*The Devil's General*, 1948, *regie* Kurt Hübner), with Oskar Dimroth as Harras; Goethe's *Faust I* (1948, *regie* Kenter); the premiere of Albert Haushofer's *Chinesische Legend* (1948, *regie* Kenter); Friedrich Dürrenmatt's *Romulus der Grosse* (*Romulus the Great*, 1949, *regie* Karlheinz Striebing); Goethe's *Torquato Tasso* (1949, *regie* Peter Stanchina); Jean Anouilh's *Medea* (1950, *regie* Hermann Kühn); and H. Kaminski's *Das Spiel von König Aphelius* (*The Play of King Aphelius*, 1950, *regie* Lehmann).

From 1950 to 1966 Heinz Hilpert was the intendant, and with him Göttingen came to have an exceedingly important theatre. Hilpert was a disciple of Max Reinhardt and had worked with him at the Deutsches Theater in Berlin before Reinhardt's exit to America. During the war Hilpert had been head of the Deutsches Theater as well as the Theater in der Josephstadt in Vienna. After the war he had worked in Switzerland and then in Frankfurt and Stuttgart. When asked to come to Göttingen, he brought some actors with him. Hilpert's first major decision was to drop the opera and ballet companies. The second was to change the name of the company to the Deutsches Theater in Göttingen, reorganizing the company as a limited corporation (the GmbH organization). His acting company was extremely good and he brought, either as full-time actors or guests, such actors as Mila Kopp, Hilde Krahl, Erich Ponto, Angela Salloker, Helene Thimig-Reinhardt, Else Bassermann, and Grete Wurm. He also had a series of excellent *regisseurs* who worked with him. The most important was Eberhard Müller-Elmau, who is still with the company.

Hilpert brought a wide variety of plays, split between classics and modern works. He staged several significant premieres, including two by Carl Zuck-mayer, *Der Gesang im Feuerofen* (*The Song in the Oven*, 1950) about the French Resistance, and *Ulla Winblad* (1953). He also acted.

Season after season, Hilpert provided absolutely top-line plays done in solid productions with major actors in the leading roles: Kleist's *Der zerbrochene Krug* (*The Broken Jug*, 1951), with Hilpert staging and playing Adam; Haupt-mann's *Hanneles Himmelfahrt* (*The Assumption of Hannele*, 1952, *regie* Hilpert); Goethe's *Faust I* (1953, *regie* Müller-Elmau); Shakespeare's *King Lear* (1955, *regie* Hilpert), with Gerhard Giesler in the title role; García Lorca's *Doña Rosita Remains Single* (1955, *regie* Fritz Schindel), with Salloker, Kopp, and Basser-mann in the lead female roles; Christopher Fry's *The Dark Is Light Enough* (1955); Hauptmann's *Michael Kramer* (1956), with Hilpert staging and playing the title role; Walter Hasanclever's *Skandal in Assyrien oder Konflikt in Assyrien* (*Scandal in Assyria or Conflict in Assyria*, 1957, *regie* Hilpert); Tennessee Williams' *Cat on a Hot Tin Roof* (1958, *regie* Hilpert), with Hilpert as Big Daddy; Shakespeare's *Hamlet* (1959, *regie* Hilpert), with Karl Walter Dreis in the title role; Shaw's *Saint Joan* (1960); Shakespeare's *Troilus and Cressida* (1961, *regie* Hilpert); Jerome Kilty's *Dear Liar* (1962, *regie* Müller-Elmau), with Hilpert as Shaw and Salloker as Mrs. Patrick Campbell; Zuckmayer's *Die Uhr schlagt eins* (*The Clock Strikes Once*, 1962, *regie* Hilpert); and a string of Shakespearean plays, all staged by Hilpert.

Hilpert's replacement was Günther Fleckenstein, who is still intendant. Like Hilpert, he has been an actor, is highly literary, works for ensemble, and puts together exceedingly ambitious seasons of plays. Fleckenstein has had more cycles of playwrights, however, in the last few years Göttingen has seen a number of plays by Aristophanes, Brecht (there is usually one every season), Rolf Hoch-huth, Shakespeare, Chekhov, O'Neill, and, above all, the East German, Peter Hacks. While Hilpert liked his guest artists, Fleckenstein has relied on his ensemble alone. Both men have seen Göttingen as a place where young *regisseurs* might be given a fair hearing, though Fleckenstein probably has the better track record.

A comparison of the two intendants' most significant productions reveals more modern works in the Fleckenstein years: Sophocles' *Antigone* (1966, *regie* Fleck-enstein); the premiere of Hacks' *Amphytrion* (1967, *regie* Eberhard Pieper); Shakespeare's *A Midsummer Night's Dream* (1968, *regie* Roberto Ciulli-Chen-trens); the premiere of Wolfgang Diechsel's *Agent Bernd Etzel* (1968, *regie* Fleckenstein); Hacks' *Margarete in Aix* (1969, *regie* Fleckenstein); Hacks' *Polly, oder Die Schlacht am Blue Water Creek* (*Polly, or the Battle on Blue Water Creek*, 1970, *regie* Fleckenstein); Dieter Forte's *Martin Luther und Thomas Münzer oder Die Einführung der Buchhaltung* (*Martin Luther and Thomas Mün-zer or the Introduction of Bookkeeping*); the premiere of Hochhuth's *Die He-bamme* (*The Midwife*, 1972, *regie* Fleckenstein); Machiavelli's *Clizia* (1972, *regie* Ciulli-Chentrens); Brecht's *Das Leben des Galilei* (*The Life of Galileo*, 1973, *regie* Müller-Elmau); Sophocles' *Oedipus Tyrannos* (1973, *regie* Fleckenstein); Schiller's *Die Räuber* (*The Robbers*, 1974, *regie* Peter Eschberg); Georg Büchner's *Dantons Tod* (*Danton's Death*, 1975, *regie* Hans Schalla); Albert Camus' *Caligula* (1975, *regie* Fleckenstein); Hochhuth's *Tod eines Jäger* (*Death of a Hunter*, 1977, *regie* Fleckenstein); Ivan Turgenev's *A Month in the Country* (1978, *regie* Adam Hanuskiewicz); Shakespeare's *Antony and Cleopatra* (1979, *regie* Jan Kulcyzynski); Hochhuth's *Die Juristen* (1980, *regie* Fleckenstein); Chekhov's *Platonov* (1980, *regie* Hanuskiewicz); and Hacks' *Senecas Tod* (*Seneca's Death*, 1981, *regie* Hannes Fischer).

As a university city, Göttingen has produced a theatre of high literary standards. Consequently, a typical season will include authors such as Shakespeare, Goethe, Schnitzler, Aristophanes, Hauptmann, Pagnol, Kohout, and Hochhuth. The company does twelve to fourteen new productions a year, as well as revivals from the previous season. In addition, a children's play and a young people's play are presented. The company also does special attractions during the season such as informal talks, lectures, discussions, and poetry readings. The acting ensemble numbers twenty-six men and fifteen women, three dramaturges, and a large technical staff. The company employs around eight guest *regisseurs* a year. Three or four more are permanent; one of these is the intendant and stages at least two works a year. Plays and *regisseurs* are selected by the intendant, assisted by his dramaturge staff, currently headed by Norbert Baensch.

The company thinks of itself as primarily an ensemble theatre, rather than a *regisseur*'s theatre. Considerable experimentation is done in staging, however. Productions are rehearsed six to eight weeks, and actors work about five days a week. Fleckenstein tries not to overwork them. A work is done only one season. The exception is the popular work or a work done only at the end of the season which may be carried over until the next season, with two seasons being the maximum. The theatre holds around 550 people and runs to 80 percent capacity during a season. The annual budget is 7.4 million DM, of which 6.2 million DM is subsidy. The company publishes its own newspaper, *DT, aus dem Deutschen Theater*.

Fleckenstein is now revamping the theatre in order to provide more rehearsal space and better technical facilities.

LEON M. AUFDEMBERGE
(With thanks to Günther Fleckenstein
and Norbert Baensch.)

MANNHEIM NATIONAL THEATRE
(Mannheim Nationaltheater)
Am Goetheplatz
6800, Mannheim, West Germany

In 1720 Karl Philipp von der Pfalz established a Residenz in Mannheim and in 1742 opened an Opernhaus in the castle. This baroque Schlosstheater was designed by Alessandro Galli di Bibiena and was inaugurated in January 1742 with Carlo Grua's opera, *Meride*, in honor of the marriage of Karl Philipp's son Karl Theodore. Mostly opera was done at the theatre. A French theatre troupe occupied it in 1770, largely because Karl Theodore was a friend of Voltaire and much admired French culture. In the mid-1770s the theatre was occupied by the Marchandsche Gesellschaft.

Soon after, Karl Theodore decided to build a new theatre. Its architect was Lorenzo Quaglio, and it was to be the envy of all other rulers in Germany. This new national theatre was opened on January 1, 1777, by the Marchandsche Troupe. The first performance by a permanent company came on October 7, 1779, with an adaptation of Carlo Goldoni's *Un curioso accidente* done in German as *Geschwind ehe es jemand erfahlt* (*Quick Before Someone Hears It*). The first intendant for the permanent company was Wolfgang Herbert von Dalberg, who ran the theatre until 1802.

In many ways the company's opening years were the golden years of the Mannheim theatre, for this acting company included some of the most important actors of the time: Heinrich Beck, Johann David Beil, Johann Michael Boeck, and especially August Wilhelm Iffland, who also wrote plays for the company. The most important premieres Mannheim has witnessed came early in Dalberg's era: Friedrich von Schiller's *Die Räuber* (*The Robbers*, 1782), with Iffland as Franz Moor, and *Die Verschwörung des Fiesko zu Genua* (*The Conspiracy of Fiesco Against Genoa*, 1784), with Boeck as Fiesco, as well as early productions of several of Schiller's other plays. Schiller was resident poet for the theatre from 1783 to 1784 but disliked the city. In addition to Schiller's works (which after a few performances were generally dropped from the repertory), the company did Shakespeare, Goldoni, Goethe, Gotthold Lessing, August von Kotzebue, and Iffland. Unfortunately, the deaths of Boeck (1793) and Beil (1794) and Iffland's departure for Berlin, together with bad finances, made the last years of Dalberg's era rather unhappy (there was also a war on). The one bright spot was the noted actor Ferdinand Esslair who worked briefly for the company at the beginning of the nineteenth century. After Dalberg, the theatre passed to his son-in-law, Freiherr von Venningen (1803–1816), who tried to do what he had done. There followed a series of intendants who are not mentioned in German theatrical dictionaries.

From 1839 to 1890 control of the theatre passed to the city (the Bürgerlichen Periode), with the company run by an *oberregisseur* (main stage manager). The best known of the early ones was Philipp Jacob Düringer, who served as *oberregisseur* from 1848 to 1853. Düringer staged many works, including Schiller; some were especially for his wife, Caroline. The next in terms of fame was August Wolff (1858–1867 and 1873–1876), who was a disciple of Franz Dingelstedt. Wolff's *regie* style was much like that of Weimar at the time. Wolff did long cycles of Shakespearean works, including one of the comedies (1868–1869), and all the histories from *Richard II* to *Richard III* (1871–1872), Schiller/ Wallenstein plays (1868), and Sophocles' Theban cycle (1872). Wolff also had the help of two fine actors, Hermann Jacobi and Albrecht Herzfeld, both of whom were excellent in classic roles. Julius Werther took over (1868–1873), was replaced by Wolff, and later returned (1877–1884). Werther was best at staging classics, including the first Mannheim production of the second part of Goethe's *Faust* (1882).

Three famous *regisseurs* were also *oberregisseurs* in the latter half of the nineteenth century. The first was Otto Devrient (1876–1877) who was an early champion of Ibsen and brought the first Ibsen play to Mannheim, *The Vikings from Helgoland* (1877). Jocza Savits (1884–1885) was later famous in Munich for staging Shakespeare, which he also did at the national theatre. Max Martersteig was head only five years (1885–1890) but these were the best five years in the history of the theatre in Mannheim during the nineteenth century. Martersteig was an actor/*regisseur*/theatre historian, and his style of staging was highly disciplined. His greatest love was Grabbe; he also liked Henrik Ibsen and Hermann Sudermann, and the usual classics, frequently with August Bassermann in the lead role. Among Martersteig's major productions in the city were Goethe's *Torquato Tasso* (1885); Shakespeare's *Coriolanus* (1885); a cycle of King plays, including many from Shakespeare (1886–1887); a cycle of Shakespearean comedies (1887–1888); Goethe's *Götz von Berlichingen* (1887); and three Ibsen works, all with Bassermann as the protagonist: *Brand* (1887), *The Pillars of Society* (1888), and *An Enemy of the People* (1888). One might add that from Düringer on, all the *regisseur* heads of the theatre, including Martersteig, staged Wagner. Eventually, Martersteig tired of quarreling with the local committee who hired him, and in 1890 he left.

After 1890 the theatre again had intendants, with the first Freiherr Carl von Stengel (1890–1892), who was followed by Aloys Prasch (1892–1895). It was under Prasch that the theatre again became a Hoftheater (1893). Both Stengel and Prasch were noted for their basic conservatism. August Bassermann (1895–1904) had three excellent actresses in his company, Lucie Lissl, Toni Wittels, and Helen Burger, and one actor, Hans Godeck. In the repertory were many classics (much admired) and some of the new psychological playwrights (not all admired). Then followed the brief tenure of Julius Hoffman (1904–1906), which was marked by a number of classic productions.

Carl Hagemann (1906–1910 and 1915–1920) saw the theatre through the days of World War I and its return to city control. Hagemann favored a very modern repertory. He was very fortunate in having two of Germany's leading designers at work in the theatre, Adolf Linnebach and Ludwig Sievert. Hagemann brought young *regisseurs* to Mannheim, particularly in his second period. In his first period Hagemann presented Shakespeare's *Hamlet* (1907); Friedrich Hebbel's *Gyges und sein Ring* (*Gyges and His Ring*, 1908); Goethe's *Faust* (1909); the Schiller Wallenstein cycle (1909); and Ibsen's *Crown Pretenders* (1910). In the second period, Hagemann shared the important productions with other *regisseurs*: Hebbel's *Judith* (1917, *regie* Richard Weichart); the premiere of Walter Hasanclever's *Sohn* (*Son*, 1918, *regie* Wiechert); and Georg Büchner's *Leonce and Lena* (1918, *regie* Hagemann)—all three with sets by Sievert.

After Hagemann's departure there was a series of short-lived intendants, which, with the runaway inflation and general postwar unrest, made conditions in the company very unsettled. The first of these intendants was Saladin Schmitt (1920–1921), who was later famous in Bochum for his staging of Shakespeare. In Mannheim he was noted for some classics, such as his opening, *As You Like It* (*regie* Schmitt). The work of two other *regisseurs* was more experimental: Hanns Lotz, who staged *Julius Caesar* (1920) in the local Nibelungensaal, and Wilhelm Kolmar, whose production of Emil Gött's *Schwarzkünstler* (*Black Artist*, 1921) aroused comment. Adolf Kraetzer (1921–1923) had serious problems with inflation, but he employed two excellent *regisseurs* in his second season, Artur Holz and Eugene Felber, both experimental. August Zoepffel took over for one season as temporary intendant (1923–1924).

Francesco Sioli came in 1924 and brought a good deal of solidity to the company. Under Sioli the repertory contained a mixture of classics and modern, mostly expressionistic, playwrights, including Arnolt Bronnen, Georg Kaiser, Frederich Wolf, Bertolt Brecht, and Carl Zuckmayer. Sioli also brought new actors and *regisseurs*, and made a rather lively theatre. Among the offbeat plays the company was doing in these years were Max Zweig's *Ragen* (*To Tower*, 1924, *regie* Sioli); Shakespeare's *Pericles* (1924, *regie* Sioli); the premiere of Arnold Bronnen's *Rheinische Rebellen* (*Rhein Rebels*, 1925, *regie* Sioli); the premiere of Carl Sternheim's *Schule von Uznach* (*School of Uznach*, 1926, *regie* Heinz Dietrich Kenter); Fritz von Unruh's *Bonaparte* (1927, *regie* Kenter); Christian Grabbe's *Don Juan und Faust* (1928, *regie* Kenter); Shakespeare's *Hamlet* (1928, *regie* Sioli), with Birgel in the title role; Brecht's *Trommeln in der Nacht* (*Drums in the Night*, 1928, *regie* Kenter); Shakespeare's *The Merchant of Venice* (1929, *regie* Gerhard Storz), with Karl Marx as Shylock; and Schiller's *Die Räuber* (*The Robbers*, 1930, *regie* Kenter). In the 1929–1930 season there was a big festival which pulled in a number of guests, including Albert Bassermann, nephew of the old intendant.

Herbert Maisch (1930–1933) liked new repertory and did some experimentation, but for the most part he was conservative in his choice of plays and styles of staging. He liked guest artists, both actors and *regisseurs*,with his most important work in the classics: Goethe's *Urgötz* (1930, *regie* Richard Dornseiff); Zuckmayer's *Der Hauptmann von Köpenick* (*The Captain from Köpenick*, 1931, *regie* Maisch), with Ernst Langheinz as Voigt; Schiller's Wallenstein cycle in one evening, fourteen-and-one-half hours, (1932, *regie* Maisch); and Shakespeare's *King Lear* (1933, *regie* Dornseiff), with Karl Zistig.

Friedrich Brandenburg followed (1933–1945). Brandenburg seems to have alternated between subservience and hostility to the Nazis and had some problems with the Nazi regime. Walter Erich Schäfer, who was his dramaturge from 1934 to 1938, was later famous as *generalintendant* in Stuttgart. On the whole, the repertory was conservative, with not too many light comedies or too much Nazi propaganda. In 1937 the company began to use the Rokokotheater in Schwetzinger. Its best productions were classics (uncredited productions are Brandenburg's): Schiller's *Kabale und Liebe* (*Intrigue and Love*, 1933); Shakespeare's *Henry IV* (1934); Schiller's *Don Carlos* (1935); Shakespeare's *Hamlet* (1936), with Birgel as Hamlet; Schiller's Wallenstein cycle (1937); Heinrich von Kleist's *Prince Friedrich von Homburg* (*The Prince of Homburg*, 1939); Lope de Vega's *Since When Our Wine?* (1940, *regie* Hellmuth Ebbs); Shakespeare's *Measure for Measure* (1942); Grabbe's *Don Juan und Faust* (1943, *regie* Willi Rohde); and Schiller's *Die Verschwörung des Fiesko zu Genua* (1944). In 1943 the national theatre was destroyed by bombs, and the company played on elsewhere.

In the immediate postwar years there were many new plays and frequent changes of intendants. The first play done in Mannheim after the war was Hugo von Hofmannsthal's *Jedermann* (*Everyman*) on October 1, 1945 (*regie* Roland Ricklinger), with Viktor Stefan Gortz in the title role. The main theatre used after the war was the national theatre in Lichtspielhaus (Schauburg in der Breitenstrasse), and the first intendant after the war was Carl Onno Eisenbart, who stayed only one season (1945–1946). The big success that season was Curt Götz's *Dr. Med. Hiob Prätorius* (1945, *regie* Ricklinger). Erich Kronen (1946–1947) presented many new plays, with his most immediate successes in classics: Schiller's *Don Carlos* (1946, *regie* Ricklinger) and Lessing's *Nathan der Weise* (*Nathan the Wise*, 1946, *regie* Willi Hanke). Richard Dornseiff stayed two seasons (1947–1949) and added several new people to the acting company. He especially liked three playwrights—Jean-Paul Sartre, Oscar Wilde, and Frank Wedekind, although the biggest productions came from none of these: Shakespeare's *A Midsummer Night's Dream* (1947, *regie* Dornseiff); Jean Giraudoux's *The War of Troy Will Not Take Place* (1948, *regie* Vasa Hochmann); Carl Zuckmayer's *Des Teufels General* (*The Devil's General*, 1948, *regie* Dornseiff), with Birgel as Harras; and Schiller's *Wilhelm Tell* (1949, *regie* Dornseiff). Richard Payer (1949–1950) was another one-season man, who did a lot of twentieth-century repertory, such as Georg Kaiser's *Das Opfer des Agnete* (*The Offering of Agnete*, 1950, *regie* Dornseiff). Then followed *Vorsitzender des Vorstandkollegiums*, led by Florian Waldeck (1950–1951), which continued the policy of new plays, including Arthur Miller's *Death of a Salesman* (1950, *regie* Riedy), with Langheinz as Willy.

Hans Schüler was intendant for many years (1951–1963). These years were marked by the production of many plays and new playwrights. Schüler had been at Leipzig during the war years, and he tried to meet the public in Mannheim as he had done in Leipzig. He was primarily interested in opera in his years at Mannheim and turned over the running of Schauspiel to various people. In 1952 he opened a second house for plays, the Haus am Friedrichplatz. In the early part of the Schüler tenure, the productions were rather academic in style without being pedantic. Later, from the mid-1950s on, particularly in the work of Erwin Piscator and Heinz Joachim Klein, the productions became much freer in style. Among Schüler's early productions were Schiller's Wallenstein plays (1951, *regie* Riedy); Shakespeare's *As You Like It* (1951, *regie* Heinrich Sauer); Shakespeare's *Hamlet* (1952, *regie* Riedy); T. S. Eliot's *The Cocktail Party* (1952, *regie* Sauer); Brecht's *Mutter Courage und ihre Kinder* (*Mother Courage and Her Children*, 1953, *regie* Riedy); Kleist's *Prinz Friedrich von Homburg* (1953, *regie* Riedy); the German premiere of Sidney Kingsley's *Darkness at Noon* (1954, *regie* Riedy, who left soon after); Miller's *The Crucible* (1954, *regie* Piscator); Schiller's *Kabale und Liebe* (1955, *regie* Heinz Hilpert); Brecht's *Der kaukasische Kreide Kreis* (*The Caucasian Chalk Circle*, 1956); and Eugene O'Neill's *Mourning Becomes Electra* (1956, *regie* Klein).

A new complex of theatre buildings was built in the 1950s: Das Grosses Haus and Das Kleine Haus, opening on January 13, 1957. The first opened with Weber's *Der Freischütz* (*regie* Schüler), and the second with Schiller's *Die Räuber* (*regie* Piscator), with sets by Paul Walter and Ernst Ronnecker as Karl Moor. With the new theatre, Schüler began using guest artists in the acting company and larger scale productions.

Among the successes of the second part of the Schüler tenure were Shakespeare's *Henry IV* and *King Lear* (both 1957, *regie* Klein), with Werner Krauss as King Lear; Schiller's *Wilhelm Tell* (1958, *regie* Piscator); Schiller's Wallenstein cycle (1959, *regie* Maisch in a return visit); Max Frisch's *Biedermann und die Brandstifter* (*Biedermann and the Firebugs*, 1959, *regie* Piscator); Ferdinand Raimund's *Der Bauer als Millionär* (*The Peasant as Millionaire*, 1960, *regie* Bruno Hübner); the premiere of Tankred Dorst's *Gesellschaft in Herbst* (*Society in Autumn*, 1960, *regie* Klein); and both parts of Goethe's *Faust* in a conservative but very satisfying production (1961–1962, *regie* Klein), with Ernst Ginsberg as Mephisto.

Ernst Dietz (1963–1972) was an actor and *regisseur* who had worked in both the musical and spoken theatre before coming to Mannheim. He added a Studiobühne in the Kunsthalle as a second house for more experimental plays. He presented a mixture of classic and modern works: Schiller's *Don Carlos* (1963, *regie* Dietz); Shakespeare's *Twelfth Night* (1964, *regie* Dietz); Büchner's *Dantons Tod* (*Danton's Death*, 1964, *regie* Werner Kraut); Shakespeare's *Hamlet* (1965, *regie* Kraut), with Klaus Nagelen in the title role; Brecht's *Die heilige Johanna der Schlachthöfe* (*Saint Joan of the Stockyards*, 1966, *regie* Ulrich Brecht); Zuckmayer's *Der Hauptmann von Köpenick* (*The Captain from Köpenick*, 1967, *regie* Ilo van Janko), with Joseph Offenbach as Voigt; the brothers Capek's *Insect Comedy* (1969, *regie* Vaclav Hudecek); Shakespeare's *Romeo and Juliet* (1969, *regie* Janko); Schiller's *Mary Stuart* (1970, *regie* Dietz); Shakespeare's *Othello* (1971, *regie* Janko); yet another Schiller's *Die Räuber* (1971, *regie* Hans Neuenfels); and Rainer Maria Fassbinder's *Bremen Freiheit* (*Bremen Freedom*, 1972, *regie* Rolf Müller).

Michael Hampe (1972–1975) had been a dramaturge and worked with Leopold Lindtberg before coming to the company. His era reflected his youth, as he moved to more democracy in the company, more political plays, and more experimentation in production. He especially relied on two *regisseurs*, Hagen Müller-Stahl and Jürgen Flimm. (Walter Felsenstein came to the opera as well.) But it did not work. Some works, however, were brilliant: Wedekind's *Marquis von Keith* (1972, *regie* Müller-Stahl); Büchner's *Leonce und Lena* (1973, *regie* Flimm); Maxim Gorky's *Enemies* (1973, *regie* Müller-Stahl); and Jean Genet's *The Balcony* (1974, *regie* Keith Hack).

The current *generalintendant* for the company is Arnold Petersen (1975 on), who has kept the company vital. He has used both Das Kleine Haus and a Studiobühne in Werkhaus for plays, also doing one play in Das Grosse Haus. He has made the company more adaptable to a variety of *regisseurs'* styles, particularly those of Claus Leininger and Jürgen Bosse. The company has added an annual Schiller Tage, where companies from everywhere bring Schiller dramas to Mannheim (begun in 1978); and an annual theater festival (since 1980), which brings companies in from everywhere to do experimental plays. Since this revitalization, the company has been going to other places as well, most notably the Berlin Theatertreffen. The repertory in the last few years has been very wide, with many contemporary plays and a steady concentration of plays of the 1920s. Some of the high points of the last few years have been Wolf's *Cynakli* (1975, *regie* Bosse); Hebbel's *Maria Magdalena* (1976, *regie* Bosse); Brecht's *Der kaukasische Kreide Kreis* (*The Caucasian Chalk Circle*, 1976, *regie* Leininger); Odön von Horváth's *Der Bergbahn* (*The Mountain Track*, 1977, *regie* Bosse), which played Berlin; the premiere of Volker Braun's *Guevara* (1977, *regie* Bosse), with Peter Rühring in the title role; Shakespeare's *Richard III* (1979, *regie* Bosse), with Rühring again in the title role; Goethe's *Clavigo* (1979, *regie* Benjamin Korn); Martin Sherman's *Bent* (1980, *regie* Bosse); Schiller's *Die Jungfrau von Orleans* (*The Maid of Orleans*, 1980, *regie* Volker Geissler); Horváth's *Geschichten aus dem Wiener Wald* (*Tales of the Vienna Woods*, 1981, *regie* Bosse); Wedekind's *Lulu* (1981, *regie* Bosse), with Helga Grimme in the title role; and Ibsen's *The Wild Duck* (1981, *regie* Heinz Kreidl). The company's greatest success in its history, in terms of a single production, may have been Bosse's production of Arnold Bronnen's *Vatermord* (*Patricide*, 1979), which played the Berliner Theatertreffen.

The Mannheim National Theatre operates primarily two theatres for plays: Das Kleine Haus, which has flexible seating (from 600 to 700 places), and the Studiobühne in Werkhaus (110 to 130 places), with the musical part of the organization using Das Grosse Haus (1,200 to 1,300 places). The Schauspiel uses it for at least one play a season. The company has ten actresses and twenty-seven actors, as well as guests and players who work only part of the season, five dramaturges, and seven *regisseurs*. The company does ten new plays a season, as well as revivals of works from the previous season. It publishes its own paper, *Nationaltheater*. Its annual budget runs to 41.6 million DM, of which 34.3 million is subsidy, which, of course, includes funds for the musical part of the organization. The whole operation has been running to around 85 percent capacity during recent seasons. There is also a Kinder- und Jugendtheater am Nationaltheater Mannheim ''Schnawwl,'' which is a separate organization that does plays for children and young people, under the jurisdiction of the main organization. The large technical staff works for all three organizations.

The theatre plays seven days a week, but no actor works that many days. The company has toured and worked on television. In 1982 it traveled to the People's Republic of China, a "reciprocal tour," as the People's Art Theatre of Peking has played at Mannheim.

LEON M. AUFDEMBERGE
(With thanks to Germana Kampa)

MUNICH'S INTIMATE THEATRE
(Münchner Kammerspiele)
Naxunukuabstrasse 22
8000 Munich, West Germany

The first name of Munich's Intimate Theatre was Zum grosse Wurstel (or Grand Guignol). Its first production was a bill of one acts, Friedrich Freska's *Die Dame im Kamin* (*The Woman in the Chimney*); Heinrich Mann's *Varieté*; and A. L. Brody's *Der alte Fürst* (*The Old Count*), staged by its first director, Eugen Robert on January 10, 1911. The early company members were Erwin Kalser, Ida Roland, and Gustl Weggert. The first theatre for the company was the Münchener Lustspielhaus.

From the beginning the repertory was decidedly modern, including Anton Chekhov, August Strindberg, George Bernard Shaw, Arthur Schnitzler, and Frank Wedekind. Its emphasis on the very modern led to trouble with the censor; for example, there was a big fight over Carl Strenheim's *Die Hose* (*Underpants*, 1911, *regie* Robert). In 1912 the name of the company was changed to the Münchner Kammerspiele. Among the many works Robert staged for the company in his brief tenure were Chekhov's *The Seagull* (1911); Strindberg's *The Father* (1911); the premiere of Wedekind's *Oaha* (1911); Leonid Andreyev's *The Life of Men* (1912); and the premiere of Wedekind's *Franziska* (1912).

Robert quarreled with his board of directors, quit in 1913, and was replaced by Erich Ziegel (1913–1916). Among the actors who joined the company during the Ziegel years were Marjam Horwitz, Walter Lantzsch, and Paul Marx, and such guest actors as Irene Treisch and Albert Streinrück. The first dramaturge for the company was Hugo Ball, later one of the leaders of the Dada movement in Zurich. The company's repertory became even more advanced, with a cycle of Strindberg plays and many by Wedekind. One of the people to join the theatre at this time as chief dramaturge and managing director was Otto Falckenberg, the great man of the Kammerspiele. The better productions of the Ziegel period included many of Strindberg's plays: *The Bridal Crown* (1914, *regie* Ziegel), with Triesch as the protagonist; *The Dance of Death* (1915), with Streinrück staging the work and playing Edgar; the premiere of *The Ghost Sonata* (1915, *regie* Falckenberg); and *To Damascus* (1916, part one *regie* Arnold Marlé and parts two and three Falckenberg).

Ziegel left in 1916 and was replaced for one year by the noted theatre critic Hermann Sinsheimer, whose season had little financial success. The important productions of this year included Sophocles' *Antigone* (1916, *regie* Sinsheimer); and the premiere of Georg Kaiser's *Von morgen bis mitternachts* (*From Morning to Midnight*, 1917, *regie* Falckenberg). In September 1917 Falckenberg became the head and remained in charge until 1944. His tenure is considered a great one. Some great actors worked with him, including Maria Koppenhöfer, Erwin Faber, Arnold Marlé, Kurt Horwitz, and Sibylle Binder. But it was the repertory and productions that made the company justly famous. Playwrights were introduced to Munich, especially writers from the new expressionistic group such as Georg Kaiser, Sternheim, Essig, Walter Hasanclever, and Brecht. In addition, the company began to play the classics with some regularity in 1917. There were problems with some works, especially the premiere of Wedekind's *Schloss Wetterstein* (*Wetterstein Castle*, 1919, *regie* Erwin Kalser), which brought Falckenberg into conflict with both the clergy and the police. The big hits of the years 1917 to 1926 included the following, many of which were set by Otto Reigbert (uncredited productions are by Falckenberg): Shakespeare's *The Winter's Tale* (1917); the premiere of Kaiser's *Die Koralle* (*The Coral*, 1917); a very balletic production of Tirso de Molina's *Don Gil of the Green Stockings* (1920); Shakespeare's *A Midsummer Night's Dream* (1920) and *As You Like It* (1920), with Bergner as Rosalinde; Schiller's *Die Verschwörung des Fiesko zu Genua* (*The Conspiracy of Fiesco Against Genoa*, 1921); Arnolt Bronnen's *Vatermord* (*Patricide*, 1922); Ernst Barlach's *Der tote Tag* (*The Dead Day*, 1924); the premiere of the Brecht/Marlowe *Das Leben Eduard II von England* (*The Life of Edward II of England*, 1924, *regie* Brecht), with sets by Caspar Neher; Shakespeare's *Troilus and Cressida* (1925); Büchner's *Woyzeck* (1925, *regie* Schweikart), with Helene Weigel as Marie; Shakespeare's *A Midsummer Night's Dream* (1925); and Paul Raynal's *Das Grabmal des unbekannten Soldaten* (*The Monument to the Unknown Soldier*, 1926).

Because of bankruptcy, Falckenberg moved his company to another theatre in 1926. This was the Schauspielhaus which had been built in 1901 (architect Richard Riemerschmid) and whose architectural style was German art nouveau. The years 1926–1933 had their good and bad points. The good was seen in the repertory, which included many of the playwrights mentioned above, as well as new ones such as Ferdinand Bruckner, Frederich Wolf, and boulevard works for which the Schauspielhaus was noted. Another strength was the acting company, many members having come from the Schauspielhaus company. Among them were Therese Giehse, Käthe Gold, Berta Drews, Ehmi Bessel, Ewald Balser, Marianne Hoppe, O. E. Hasse, and Heinz Rühmann. In this period Falckenberg began to use a great variety of *regisseurs* besides himself, such as Berthold Viertel, Richard Révy, and Hans Schweikart. Even Max Reinhardt came in 1931 to stage two works, Goethe's *Iphigenia auf Tauris* (*Iphigenia in Tauris*) and *Stella*; Helen Thimig (Frau Reinhardt) was the lead actress in both productions. Falckenberg had a small studio in this period for experimental plays.

The productions that made theatrical history in the era were from all periods. Falckenberg staged the classic works. A partial list of these would include the following (uncredited productions are again by Falckenberg): Büchner's *Dantons Tod* (*Danton's Death*, 1926), which was the first play in the Schauspielhaus; the premiere of Bruno Frank's *Zwölftausen* (*Twelve Thousand*, 1927); the premiere of Bruckner's *Krankheit der Jugend* (*Youth Sickness*, 1927, *regie* Julius Gellner); Luigi Pirandello's *Henry IV* (1927, *regie* Robert Forster-Larinaga), with Moissi in the title role; Ibsen's *Peer Gynt* (1927, *regie* Révy); Gerhart Hauptmann's *Der Biberpelz* (*The Beaver Coat*, 1928, *regie* Révy), with Giehse as Frau Wolff; Wedekind's *Lulu* (1928), with Margharete Koeppke as Lulu; the premiere of Peter Martin Lampel's *Revolte in Erziehungshaus* (*Revolt in the House of Correction*, 1929, *regie* Gellner); Max Mell's *Nachfolge—Christi Spiel* (*Imitation of Christ Play*, 1929, *regie* Gellner); the Brecht/Weill *Die Dreigroschenoper* (*The Threepenny Opera*, 1929, *regie* Schweikart), with sets by Neher and Horwitz as Mackie; Wolf's *Cyankali* (1930); Shaw's *Caesar and Cleopatra* (1930, *regie* Révy), with Krauss as Caesar; Shakespeare's *Hamlet* (1930), with Balser as Hamlet; Döblin's *Die Ehe* (*The Married State*, 1930); Ibsen's *A Doll's House* (1931), with Bessel as Nora; the premiere of Richard Billinger's *Rauhnacht* (*Raw Night*, 1931); Bruckner's *Elisabeth von England* (1932, *regie* Gellner), with Körner as Elisabeth; Ibsen's *The Wild Duck* (1932), with Gold as Hedwing; and Hauptmann's *Die Ratten* (*The Rats*, 1932).

The negative side of the years 1926–1933 had to do with the theatre's conflict with two groups: the police and the Nazis. The police closed several of the productions listed above, namely Bruckner's *Die Verbrecher*, *Cyankali*, and *Die Ehe*. The Nazis disrupted productions and put pressure on the local authorities to close plays, particularly those done in the studio.

The era of National Socialism meant drastic changes to the company in terms of actors, repertory, and especially style of playing and staging. Many of Falckenberg's old actors left Germany; Horwitz and Giehse went to Switzerland but returned after the war. Most of the new plays done during 1933–1944 are lost in oblivion. Apparently, Falckenberg did very few of the sentimental dramas the Nazis were pushing. Instead, Falckenberg staged a great number of classics. As seen by the photos, the plays were heavier and contained much pictorial scenery. Nonetheless, there were some fine sets by Eduard Sturm. There were some new actors, namely, Friedrich Domin, Maria Nicklisch, Elisabeth Flickenschildt, Kurt Meisel, Heidemarie Hatheyer, and, above all, Horst Caspar, who did a series of great classic heroes. The new *regisseurs* included Domin, Karl Heinz Martin, and Heinz Dietrich Kenter. In 1939 the city took control of the theatre, and in the following year the Schauspielhaus was remodeled.

German theatres of the time would like to be remembered for their productions of the classics. Not all the classic productions seemed to be to the Nazis' liking, however. The works most often produced during the era include the following (uncredited productions are by Falckenberg): Shakespeare's *As You Like It* (1933), with Gold as Rosalind, and *Cymbeline* (1934); Lessing's *Minna von Barnhelm* (1934, *regie* Domin), with Käthe Dorsch in the title role; Schiller's *Die Räuber* (*The Robbers*, 1934); Schiller's *Don Carlos* (1936); Shakespeare's *Troilus and*

Cressida (1936); Kleist's *Prinz Friedrich von Homburg* (1938), with Caspar in the title role; Tirso de Molina's *Don Gil of the Green Hose* (1939); Goethe's *Torquato Tasso* (1939), with Caspar as Tasso; Shakespeare's *Hamlet* (1939), with Caspar as Hamlet; Christian Grabbe's *Hannibal* (1940, *regie* Martin); Shakespeare's *A Midsummer Night's Dream* (1940); Schiller's *Mary Stuart* (1940), with Mila Kipp in the title role; Friedrich Hebbel's *Gyges und Sein Ring* (*Gyges and his Ring*, 1941), with Caspar as Gyges; Shakespeare's *Othello* (1942), with Domin as Othello; Grabbe's *Kaiser Heinrich VI* (1942, *regie* Kenter); and Goethe's *Urfaust* (1944). The Nazis hated the theatre itself (Jugendstil—German art nouveau— was a decadent style), and there were plans to tear it down. In July 1944 the theatre was partly destroyed in the bombing raids, and at the end of the war the theatre was turned into a factory.

Falckenberg was forcibly removed from his theatre in 1945 and denounced as a Nazi. In 1947, shortly before his death, he was rehabilitated. The first intendant after the war was Erich Engel, who had worked with Brecht in the 1920s and at the Deutsches Theater in Berlin during the Nazi era. The first production after the war in the rebuilt theatre was Shakespeare's *Macbeth* (*regie* Domin), opening on October 12, 1945, with Domin and Nicklisch as the Scottish rulers. Many critics thought the play mirrored current events. With finances low, the theatre was combined with the Volkstheater until 1949. New actors came, including Maria Koppenhöfer, Hans Christian Blech, and Bruno Hübner. Even though theatre conditions were bleak after the war, Engel managed to present a full season in his first year.

The repertory for the Engel years (1945–1947) included many plays forbidden during the Nazi era, especially Thornton Wilder's *Our Town* (1945, *regie* Engel); Jean Giraudoux's *The War of Troy Will Not Take Place* (1946, *regie* Martin Hellberg); Odön von Horváth's *Der jüngste Tag* (*Doomsday*, 1947, *regie* Harry Buckwitz); and Jean Anouilh's *Eurydice* (1947, *regie* Engel). In 1947, the company was playing in three theatres: the Schauspielhaus, the Volkstheater in Bayerischen Hof, and the Postssal Pasing. In his second season Engel hired a new scene designer, Wolfgang Znamanacek, who would remain with the theatre until 1953.

Hans Schweikart's years as intendant—1947–1963—were both very long and very good. Schweikart had been an actor and *regisseur* at various theatres in Germany, including the Kammerspiele; his work there had been satisfactory but not outstanding. At the Kammerspiele, however, he became one of the most important *regisseurs* in West Germany. The repertory of the company during the whole Schweikart era was well chosen and well balanced between classics and modern works. The acting company had a solid core of the finest actors in Germany, including Maria Wimmer, Peter Lühr, Maria Nicklisch, and Paul Verhoeven (also a *regisseur*), as well as guests who came either for a long while, such as Giehse and Erich Ponto, Paul Dahlke, Martin Held, Leonhard Steckel, and Fritz Kortner (the last two staged plays as well), or for only one play. During his tenure the theatre changed from primarily an actors' theatre to an actors/

regisseurs' house. Many important *regisseurs* came to work at the Kammerspiele, ranging from Bertolt Brecht to Erwin Piscator (political plays) to Schweikart himself and Fritz Kortner (many plays). Schweikart also hired noted designers during the period, including Znamanacek, Caspar, Teo Otto, Jorg Zimmermann, and Jürgen Rose.

One thing was certain, the Schweikart seasons were very much alike in terms of repertory and class. In his first seasons, it was perhaps the actors and the repertory which made the news as in the following (uncredited productions belong to Schweikart): Paul Claudel's *The Satin Slipper* (1947, *regie* Domin); Zuckmayer's *Des Teufels General* (*The Devil's General*, 1948, *regie* Buckwitz), with Dahlke as Harras; Giraudoux's *The Madwoman of Chaillot* (1948), with Koppenhöfer in the title role; Brecht's *Herr Puntila and sein Knecht Matti* (*Mr. Puntila and His Hired Man, Matti*, 1949); Goethe's *Faust II* (1949), with Paul Hoffmann as Mephisto; the Brecht/Weill *Die Dreigroschenoper* (*The Threepenny Opera*, 1949, *regie* Buckwitz); Hauptmann's *Der Biberpelz* (*The Beaver Coat*, 1949, *regie* Lühr), with Giehse in her old part; Strindberg's *The Father* (1949, *regie* Kortner), with Kortner and Wimmer as the battling couple; Miller's *Death of a Salesman* (1950), with Ponto as Willy; Brecht's *Mutter Courage und ihre Kinder* (*Mother Courage and Her Children*, 1950, *regie* Brecht), with Giehse in the title role she had created in Zurich in 1941 (sets by Otto); Albert Camus' *State of Siege* (1950); Tennessee Williams' *A Streetcar Named Desire* (1951, *regie* Paul Verhoeven), with Nicklisch as Blanche; Büchner's *Dantons Tod* (*Danton's Death*, 1951), with Caspar as Danton (he died the next year); Lessing's *Minna von Barnhelm* (1951, *regie* Kortner); and Sidney Kingsley's *Detective Story* (1952).

Schweikart's premiere production of Friedrich Dürrenmatt's *Die Ehe des Herrn Mississippi* (*The Marriage of Mr. Mississippi*) in 1952 marks the starting point for a change in the company's policy: after that year the company had premieres by well-known playwrights. The company continued to do the same balanced repertory. Kortner and Schweikart were in charge of the major productions as can be seen in the following listing (uncredited productions again belong to Schweikart): Hebbel's *Herodes und Miriamne* (1952, *regie* Kortner), with Kortner as Herodes and Wimmer as Mariamne; Hauptmann's *Die Ratten* (*The Rats*, 1952), with Giehse as Frau John; Williams' *The Rose Tattoo* (1953, *regie* Kortner), with Wimmer as Serafina; the premiere of Dürrenmatt's *Ein Engel kommt nach Babylon* (*An Angel Comes to Babylon*, 1953); Shakespeare's *Hamlet* (1954, *regie* Leopold Lindtberg); Miller's *The Crucible* (1954), with Blech as Proctor; Samuel Beckett's *Waiting for Godot* (1954, *regie* Kortner); the premiere of Peter Hacks' *Eröffnung des indischen Zeitalters* (*Opening of the Indian Age*, 1955); Dürrenmatt's *Der Besuch der alten Dame* (*The Visit from the Old Lady*, 1956), with Giehse as Claire; Jean-Paul Sartre's *The Devil and the Good Lord* (1956, *regie* Hans Schalla); Shakespeare's *Twelfth Night* (1957, *regie* Kortner), and the premiere of Erich Kästner's *Die Schule der Diktatoren* (*The School for Dictators*, 1957).

On December 7, 1957, Schweikart opened a Werkraumtheater which increased the number of productions each year and made possible more experimental work both in terms of plays chosen (more absurdist plays, for example) and new approaches to staging works. At this time greater freedom in staging was being seen all over West Germany. Certainly, the Kammerspiele was one of the leaders in the movement, particularly in the experimental approach to classics. Among the productions of this period were Wolfgang Borchert's *Draussen vor der Tur* (usually translated as *The Man Outside*, 1957, *regie* August Everding), which opened the Werkraumtheater; Eugene Ionesco's *The Chairs* (1958), with Tilla Durieux and Lühr as the old couple; John Osborne's *Look Back in Anger* (1958, *regie* Everding); Brecht's *Das Leben des Galilei* (*The Life of Galileo*, 1959), with Domin as Galileo; Schiller's *Don Carlos* (1959, *regie* Erwin Piscator); Sternheim's *1913* (1960, *regie* Piscator); Shakespeare's *Timon of Athens* (1961, *regie* Kortner), with Romuald Pekny as Timon; and Gorky's *Wassa Schelesnowa* (1951, *regie* Horwitz), with Giehse in the title role.

On November 1, 1961, Schweikart staged a bill of one acts, which opened the Neues Werkraumtheater. The whole evening was entitled *Selbstgespräche*: Chekhov's *On the Harmfulness of Tobacco*; Aldo Nicolai's *Salt and Tobacco*; Carlo Terron's *The Black Widow*; and Beckett's *Krapp's Last Tape*. In his last seasons Schweikart staged the following major productions: Max Frisch's *Andorra* (1962, *regie* Schweikart); the premiere of Brecht's *Fluchtlingsgespräche* (*Fugitive Conversation*, 1962, *regie* Piscator); Chekhov's *The Cherry Orchard* (1962, *regie* Lühr), with Nicklisch as Madame Ranyevskaya; Shakespeare's *Othello* (1962, *regie* Kortner), with Rolf Boysen as Othello and Pekny as Iago; Dürrenmatt's *Die Physiker* (*The Physicists*, 1962, *regie* Schweikart); and Shakespeare's *Richard III* (1963, *regie* Kortner), with Pekny as Richard.

Although Schweikart stepped down as intendant in 1963, he continued to work as an actor and a *regisseur* for the company with the new head, August Everding (1963–1973), who had been an important *regisseur* with the company. His repertory policy remained substantially the same as Schweikart's. There were also many premieres, new *regisseurs*, and new actors—even some controversies in the era, which might be an indication of its liveliness. One of Everding's major innovations was his *Woche der Werkraumtheater*, which brought experimental guest productions from both West Germany and abroad to Munich. The 1972 season, the year of the Olympics, was an exceptional one.

A string of major productions was staged during Everding's years. Unfortunately, however, one major *regisseur* died in 1970, Fritz Kortner, who is remembered for his many productions with the theatre as well as his acting. Some of the major productions were as follows (uncredited productions belong to Everding): Büchner's *Leonce und Lena* (1963, *regie* Kortner); Albee's *Who's Afraid of Virginia Woolf?* (1963), with Lühr and Nicklisch as George and Martha; Roger Vitrac's *Victor or the Children of Force* (1963, *regie* Jean Anouilh and Roland Piétri); the premiere of Heinar Kipphardt's *In der Sache J. Robert Oppenheimer* (*In the Case of J. Robert Oppenheimer*, 1964, *regie* Paul Verhoeven);

Brecht's *Herr Puntila und sein Knecht Matti* (1964), with Martin Held as Puntila; Schiller's *Kabale und Liebe* (1965, *regie* Kortner); the premiere of Kipphardt's *Joel Brand* (1965); the premiere of Peter Weiss' *Die Ermittlung* (*The Investigation*, 1965, *regie* Verhoeven); Horváth's *Geschichten aus dem Wiener Wald* (*Tales of the Vienna Woods*, 1966, *regie* Otto Schenk), with Helmet Lohner as Alfred; Edward Bond's *Saved* (1967, *regie* Peter Stein), done in Bavarian dialect; Strindberg's *Miss Julie* (1967, *regie* Kortner), with Ingrid Andree as Julie; Frisch's *Biografie: Ein Spiel* (*Biography: A Play*, 1968); Brecht's *Im Dickicht der Stadte* (*In the Jungle of the Cities*, 1968, *regie* Stein); Miller's *The Prize* (1968, *regie* Schweikart); a huge controversy with Weiss' *Vietnam Diskurs* (*Vietnam Discourse*, 1968, *regie* Stein and Wolfgang Schwiedrzik), which ended with a collection for the North Vietnamese (it was quickly closed); Georges Feydeau's *The Girl from Maxim's* (1970, *regie* Dieter Giesing), with Andree as La Mome Crevetee; Frank Wedekind's *Der Marquis von Keith* (1970, *regie* Giesing), with Ulrich Haupt and sets by Jürgen Rose; the Brecht/Marlowe *Das Leben Eduard II von England* (1970, *regie* Hans Hollmann), with Pekny as Eduard; Wolfgang Bauer's *Change* (1970); Nikolai Erdman's *The Suicide* (1971), with Stefan Wigger as the title character; a dramatization of Wagner's *Der Ring des Niebelungen* (1971, *regie* Heising); Albee's *All Over* (1972), with Grete Mosheim as the wife; the premiere of Rolf Hochhuth's *Die Hebamme* (*The Midwife*, 1972); Chekhov's *Uncle Vanya* (1972, *regie* Erwin Axer), with Cornelia Froboess as Sonia; Arnold Wesker's *The Old Ones* (1973, *regie* the author); Ionesco's *Macbett* (1973, *regie* Liviu Ciulei), with Heinz Baumann in the title role; and Lessing's *Nathan der Weise* (*Nathan the Wise*, 1973, *regie* Schweikart). Lessing's work was Schweikart's last production with the company; he died in 1975, remembered, as was Kortner, for both his acting and staging.

On May 1, 1973, Hans-Reinhard Müller was named intendant, in the tradition of *regisseur*/intendants who have headed the house. With Müller the theatre has definitely become a *regisseur*'s house; at the same time the theatre continues to have one of the strongest acting ensembles in West Germany. The Müller era started out largely with pick-up *regisseurs*. They had several fine productions: Neil Simon's *The Sunshine Boys* (1974, *regie* Boleslaw Barlog), with Ruhmann and Verhoeven; Brecht's *Die heilige Johanna der Schlachthöfe* (*Saint Joan of the Stockyards*, 1974, *regie* Benno Besson), with Ursula Karusseti as Johanna Dark; Ramón María del Valle Inclan's *Word of God* (1974, *regie* Johannes Schaaf); and Hauptmann's *Einsame Menschen* (*Lonely People*, 1975, *regie* Peter Palitzsch).

Then, in the fall of 1975, Ernst Wendt came as chief dramaturge and Dieter Dorn as managing director. Together they radically changed the theatre. Staging became much more experimental and more concept-oriented. The highly literary Wendt and Dorn have been particularly strong in the classics. They have presented Schiller's *Kabale und Liebe* (*Intrigue and Love*, 1978, *regie* Wendt); Shakespeare's *A Midsummer Night's Dream* (1978, *regie* Dorn); Schiller's *Mary Stuart* (1979, *regie* Wendt), with Froboess in the title role; Heinrich von Kleist's

Das Käthchen von Heilbronn (1979, *regie* Wendt); Shakespeare's *Twelfth Night* (1980, *regie* Dorn), with Thomas Holtzmann as Malvolio; Shakespeare's *Hamlet* (1980, *regie* Wendt), with Lambert Hamel as Hamlet; Hebbel's *Maria Magdalena* (1981, *regie* Hans Lietzau); and Goethe's *Torquato Tasso* (1981, *regie* Wendt).

The theatre has always prided itself on its modern works, which form the core of its repertory. On paper, the repertory has been much the same since the Schweikart era, but in the Müller era varied approaches were taken; it is, therefore, difficult to generalize as to what sort of production works best at the theatre. The modern plays done in the last seasons include Shaw's *The Doctor's Dilemma* (1975, *regie* Rudolf Nolte); Ibsen's *Ghosts* (1975, *regie* Müller), with Inge Birkmann as Mrs. Alving; Harmut Lange's *Die Gräf von Rathenow* (1976, *regie* Bernd Fischerauer); Genet's *The Balcony* (1976, *regie* Wendt), with Agnes Fink as Irma; García Lorca's *Dona Rosita Remains Single* (1977, *regie* Wendt); Wedekind's *Lulu* (1977, *regie* Dorn), with Froboess as Lulu; the premiere of Heiner Müller's *Germania Tod in Berlin* (*Germania Dead in Berlin*, 1978, *regie* Wendt); D. L. Coburn's *The Gin Game* (1978, *regie* Müller), with Nicklisch and Lühr as the unhappy old couple; Strindberg's *The Dance of Death* (1978, *regie* Harald Clemen), with Pekny as Edgar; Ibsen's *The Wild Duck* (1979, *regie* Müller); Luigi Pirandello's *The Giants of the Mountain* (1980, *regie* Wendt); Hans Henny Jahnn's *Medea* (1981, *regie* Wendt); and Chekhov's *Platonov* (1981, *regie* Thomas Langhoff).

George Tabori, one of the company's prominent *regisseurs*, has done a series of programs. Tabori's projects have been staged in either the Werkraum or the Stadtteil Zirkus-Atlas. He has staged a special project (based on Kafka) called *Der Verwandlung* (*The Conversion*, 1977), another based on Shakespeare's *The Merchant of Venice* and called *Shylock 44* (1978), his own play *My Mother's Courage* (1979), and the Tabori/Enzenberger *Der Untergang der Titanic* (*The Sinking of the Titanic*, 1980).

The company uses two houses: its Schauspielhaus (renovated most recently in 1970 to bring it back to its Jugendstil, or art nouveau style, with 730 seats) and the Werkraumtheater (299 seats). Both houses may seat fewer for certain productions. The company also controls the Theater der Jugend (Young People's Theatre) which since 1977 has been in the Schauburg am Elisabethplatz (520 seats).

In an average season, the company mounts eight major productions in the Schauspielhaus and three in the Werkraumtheater. In addition, it may carry over popular productions from previous seasons. The acting company has sixteen women and thirty-three men, as well as guests who work part of the season or one play. Six dramaturges and eight *regisseurs* also work for the theatre; the dramaturges are permanent, and the *regisseurs* are about one-half guests and one-half permanent. *Regisseurs* are generally allowed to pick their own designer. The productions in the Werkraum are frequently popular with the young of Munich. A really well-done work, such as the 1973 production of Ulrich Plenzdorf's *Die neue Leiden des jungen W.* (*The New Sorrows of Young W.*, *regie* Calus Emmerich), can have a very long run.

The organization controls the Otto-Falckenberg-Schule, which is the theatre school for the Landeshaupstadt München. Its head is Hans-Reinhard Müller. The school is an intensive three-year program that trains primarily actors. Many members of the company also work for the school, and third-year students may act in plays for the Kammerspiele.

The company selects plays that will sharpen the consciousness of the spectator. It definitely rejects the museum approach; even classics must have some relevance to contemporary life. This contemporary philosophy occasionally gets the theatre in trouble. In 1956, for example, the local cardinal preached against Sartre's *The Devil and the Good Lord* (which meant good attendance); more recently (in 1976), some locals objected to Genet's *The Balcony*, and Wendt and the acting company were hauled in. The net result was fifty sold-out houses. Munich tends to be rather conservative and strongly Catholic, and there have been some walk-outs in recent seasons. Actors do not mind it too much but wish spectators would leave quietly. Nevertheless, spectators remain loyal and subscribers currently number around four thousand. The current budget for the company runs to 23.3 million DM, of which 20.5 million is subsidy (paid by the city). There are also guest performances.

The company would like to increase touring but is deterred by the cost; it has gone to Russia (1977 with *Minna von Barnhelm*), Bucharest, and Finland. It would also like to do more work on television which has the lure of fame and money.

LEON M. AUFDEMBERGE
(With thanks to Wolfgang Zimmermann.)

STATE THEATRE OF DARMSTADT
(Staatstheater Darmstadt)
Auf dem Marienplatz
61000 Darmstadt, West Germany

In 1810 George Moeller was commissioned to begin a theatre (actually a neoclassic temple with a fly gallery) for Darmstadt, and in 1819 the theatre opened with Spontini's *Ferdinando Cortez*. This building still exists in the center of town, partly in ruins, and there are plans to restore it as a concert house. In 1879 the theatre burned and was immediately restored.

After World War I the balance between operas and plays improved. In 1918 the theatre was named the Hessisches Landestheater, and in the 1920s it was known as one of the most advanced in Germany. The company began to play a variety of new playwrights (its productions of expressionist plays were well known). Several important premieres were done here: Fritz von Unruh's *Louis Ferdinand, Prinz von Preussen* (1922), Brecht's *Mann ist Mann* (1926), and

Georg Kaiser's *Mississippi* (1930). In the postwar era it had several good intendants, all of whom were *regisseurs* as well: Gustav Hartung (1920–1924 and 1930–1933), Ernst Legal (1924–1927), and Carl Ebert (1927–1931). Hartung showed a preference for new German drama; Legal was famous as both an actor and a *regisseur*; and Ebert staged operas and plays, his best known productions of plays at Darmstadt being Shakespeare's *The Winter's Tale* (1927), Goethe's *Egmont* (1927), Shakespeare's *Hamlet* (1930) and *A Midsummer Night's Dream* (1930). The young Rudolph Bing was his assistant at Darmstadt and according to his autobiography, *1001 Nights of Opera*, learned how to run a company from Ebert. A number of good actors worked in the 1920s, including Käthe Gold, Hans Liebelt, Karl Paryla, and Kurt Hirschfeld.

The company's experimentation ceased during the Nazi era. Most productions were of classic plays, the best known being Hans Schalla's *Don Carlos* by Schiller in 1937. In 1944 Moeller's theatre was bombed and leveled in forty minutes, but by that time most German theatres had already closed.

In 1945 the theatre reopened in three houses: the Theater im Schloss, the Orangeriehaus, and the Stadthalle. The first intendant was Wilhelm Heinrich, who served from 1945 to 1946. The most important production of this year was Jean Anouilh's *Antigone*. The next intendant was Walter Jackesih (1946–1948), and Karl-Heinz Stroux was named head of the Schauspielhaus for a while. Stroux is still one of Germany's leading *regisseurs*. In the brief time he was at Darmstadt, he did one of the first German productions of Wilder's *The Skin of Our Teeth*. In 1948 Dr. Siegmund Skraup became intendant, staying until 1951, and it was he who began to expand the repertory to include more modern playwrights. His most important productions were Bertolt Brecht's *Mutter Courage und ihre Kinder* (*Mother Courage and Her Children*), Arthur Miller's *All My Sons*, and Goethe's *Götz von Berlichingen mit der eisernen Hand* (*Götz von Berlichingen with the Iron Hand*).

In 1951 came Gustav Sellner, who would radically change the theatre. Even though the playhouses Sellner worked in were far from ideal, he made the company a leader in Germany, largely because of the strength of his own productions. Sellner's staging style was highly theatrical; he liked plays that were mythic and in which he could exhibit his favorite devices: lots of movement, masks, dance, music, and stark sets. The Darmstadt company became one of the principal houses for theatre of the absurd in Germany in the Sellner era. His best known productions include Shakespeare's *King Lear* (1951), Ernst Barlach's *Der Graf von Ratzeburg* (*The Count of Ratzeburg*, 1951), Christopher Fry's *Venus Observed* (1951), Sophocles' *Oedipus Tyrannos* (1952), Federico García Lorca's *Blood Wedding* (1953), Sophocles' *Electra* (1953), the German premiere of Tennessee Williams' *Camino Real* (1954), Georg Büchner's *Dantons Tod* (*Danton's Death*, 1954), Eugene Ionesco's *Victims of Duty* (1958), the Sophocles/Ezra Pound *Women of Trachio* (1959), and Shakespeare's *The Tempest* (1959). The production of *Oedipus Tyrannos* established the company as one of the most experimental in Germany. Sellner attracted other great *regisseurs* to Darmstadt, including Erwin Piscator, who adapted Tolstoy's *War and Peace* for the stage in 1955.

Since Sellner there have been three intendants: Gerhard Hering (1961–1970), Gunther Beelitz (1970–1976), and Kurt Horres (1976 to the present). Hering favored the classics, and his tenure began with a number of classic productions, including his own: a Lessing cycle consisting of *Emilia Galotti* (1961), *Minna von Barnhelm* (1962), *Miss Sara Sampsoro* (1965), and *Nathan the Wise* (1969). He also staged one of the first German productions of Jean Genet's *The Blacks* (1964) and *The Balcony* (1967).

In 1970 a new opera theatre was opened with Beethoven's *Fidelio*, and that same year Günther Beelitz became general intendant. Beelitz was probably more at home with the Schauspielhaus than with the opera part. He invited some good *regisseurs* in his time, though not of the same quality as Sellner's, and he favored a well-balanced season, split between classics and moderns. Among his best remembered productions were Odön von Horváth's *Zur schönen Aussicht* (*For a Good View*, 1971), Büchner's *Woyzeck* (1972), Alfred de Musset's *Lorenzaccio* (1973), Goethe's *Stella* (1975), and Büchner's *Leonce und Lena* (1975).

Beelitz left in 1976 to become head of the Düsseldorf Schauspielhaus where he would have no responsibilities for opera. His replacement was Dr. Kurt Horres, a well-known opera *regisseur*. He has left the running of the Schauspielhaus to Lothar Trautman, who has become its principal *regisseur*. In the last few years there have been some noteworthy productions, including Büchner's *Dantons Tod* (1976, *regie* Trautman); Brecht's *Herr Puntila und sein Knecht Matti* (*Mr. Puntila and His Hired Man, Matti*, 1978, *regie* Roland Gall); and Schiller's *Die Räuber* (*The Robbers*, 1979, *regie* Trautman).

Generally, five plays are done each season in the Kleines Haus and four in the smaller Werkstadt; most of the staging is done by guest *regisseurs*. The intendant and the director of the Schauspielhaus choose the season, which is set a year ahead. Plays are balanced between modern and classics; Büchner is probably the most often repeated German playwright, and Shakespeare the most popular foreign playwright. The theatre tries to do at least one world premiere a season. If a play proves very popular, it may be revived. The Schauspiel works in conjunction with the opera; it shares technical staff, and even subscribers may belong to the opera and either of the playhouses. Suburban people seem to prefer operettas or light plays. In the opera, the classics are most popular, but the opera company likes to mount at least one new work a season (for example, Benjamin Britten's *Death in Venice*). The theatre tours small towns in the area and works in close conjunction with the theatres at Kassel and Wiesbaden, sharing a ballet company with the Wiesbaden theatre.

The acting company consists of eleven women and twenty-two men, and other actors are hired if necessary. The theatre also employs four dramaturges (three for plays, one for opera) and a huge technical staff. The budget for the theatre is large—24 million DM, of which 3 million comes from the box office and the rest from subsidies (52 percent from the state of Hesse and the remainder from the city of Darmstadt). The company is conservative, staging high-level, but not very experimental, evenings in the theatre.

The two main theatres are far too large for the town. Hence, even with a large number of subscribers (twenty-four thousand), there are frequently too many empty seats. For this reason the company is rather conservative in its choice of musical and operatic works. Under Beelitz there were many great performances by outside theatres; these have dwindled. In the future, the director of the Schauspielhaus would like more experimentation and more touring. The theatre is loved by the people of the town, and its record of good productions is a source of some civic pride.

LEON M. AUFDEMBERGE
(With thanks to the theatre staff.)

STUTTGART-WÜRTTEMBERG STATE THEATRE
(Stuttgart-Württembergische Staatstheater)
Oberer Schlossgarten 6
7000 Stuttgart, West Germany

Stuttgart's first permanent theatre, the Neuen Lusthause, was erected in the late sixteenth century. Traveling companies played there, and by the end of the seventeenth century, opera played regularly in the city. During the eighteenth century, practically every important touring company scheduled engagements in the city. In 1750 the Lusthause was remodeled, opening on August 30 of that year with K. H. Graun's opera *Artaserse*. It is to this date that Stuttgart's company generally traces its beginning. A theatre for plays, the Kleines Theater an der Plaine (architect K.F.H. Fischer), was established in 1780. The first important director for all theatres in Stuttgart was Christian Friedrich Schubart (1787–1791). The Lusthause, renamed the Hoftheater, was remodeled in 1812, with more rings added.

Under Wilhelm I (1817–1846), the court began to broaden its taste to include more plays, especially German drama. During much of his reign, the Hoftheater intendant was Graf Karl von Leutrum-Ertigen. From 1829 to 1841, he brought a succession of fine actors to the company, including Feodor Löwe (also a *regisseur*), Ludwig Wallback, Karl Seydelmann, Theodor Doring, Eduard Gnauth, Heinrich Moritz, Therese Peche, and August Lewald as a *regisseur*. The theatre gained renown with such productions as Esslair's playing of Shakespeare's *King Lear* (1830); the first Stuttgart production of Goethe's *Faust* (1832), with Seydelmann as Mephisto; and the first Stuttgart Wallenstein cycle of Schiller (1839, *regie* Löwe). From 1841 to 1845, the intendant was Graf von Taubenheim, who continued Leutrum-Ertigen's policies.

The Hoftheater was rebuilt in 1846, the same year Freiherr Ferdinand von Gall became head, bringing with him one of Stuttgart's greatest actors of all time, Karl Grunert. Von Gall brought excitement to repertory and acting. Grunert played all his great parts in Stuttgart, including Macbeth, Hamlet, King Lear, Othello, and Karl Moor in Friedrich von Schiller's *Die Räuber* (*The Robbers*). He frequently appeared with Amelie Stubenrach, who is especially remembered for her Schiller roles. Franz Dingelstedt was dramaturge for the company from 1846 to 1851 and also staged plays. Other actors who played during von Gall's tenure included Adolf Wertzel, Elenore Wahlmann, and Antoine Wilhelmini.

In 1869 von Gall was followed by Hofkammerpräsident von Gunzert and then by Fodor Wehls (1869–1884), whose repertory included Goethe, Schiller, and Shakespeare, as well as Christian Grabbe and Franz Grillparzer. In 1883 the Hoftheater was again rebuilt and was one of the first German theatres to use electric lighting. Ibsen first came to Stuttgart in 1879 with *The Pillars of Society*.

With Julius Werther as head (1884–1890), the theatre became modern—many thought too modern. Werther was noted for his advanced repertory, especially Ibsen, and for his acting company, which included August Junkermann (adept at comedy), Karl Salomon, Kathi Frank (great in Schiller), Charlotte Wolter, and Friedrich Haase, as well as Louise Dumont, one of Germany's first Ibsen actresses. Werther favored Schiller and Grillparzer in his repertory, but it was his Shakespearean productions that were the most admired, including *The Winter's Tale*, *Richard II* (both 1885), and *Henry V* (1887). His splashiest production was the Schiller Wallenstein cycle (1889), with guest Friedrich Mitterwurzer as Wallenstein and Dumont as Thekla.

There followed a brief period when the company foundered with no head (1890–1892); in 1892 it was taken over by Baron Joachim Elder Herr zu Putliss who carried the theatre through World War I. The company was considerably enlarged during this period and included such names as Dumont, Alfred Gersach, Egmont Richter, August Ellmenreich, Gertrud Eysoldt, Emmy Remolt-Jessen, Alexandrine Rossi, and Raoul Aslan, as well as many guest artists. Putliss was the first intendant to see the importance of *regisseurs*. In his early years, however, it was the lead actor who got the publicity. Thus, the journals of the time herald such performances as Shakespeare's *The Merchant of Venice* (1892), with Dumont as Portia; Grillparzer's *Die Judin von Toledo* (*The Jewess of Toledo*, 1894), with Eysoldt as Rachel; and Ibsen's *Rosmersholm* (1896), with Dumont as Rebekka West.

On January 19, 1902, the Hoftheater burned, and an interim theatre opened on October 12, 1902 with Richard Wagner's *Tannhäuser*. The new theatre was larger than the old one, and productions became more ambitious. Around 1905 programs began to mention the *regisseur*. Among the better productions of this period were Schiller's *Die Braut von Messina* (*The Bride of Messina*, 1904), with Alexandrine Rossi as Isabella; Gerhart Hauptmann's *Olga* (1905), with Irene Treisch in the title role; and the premiere of Julius Babb's *Das Blut* (*The Blood*, 1908, *regie* Viktor Stephany). In the 1911–1912 season Stuttgart presented an important Ibsen cycle.

On September 14, 1912, a new opera house opened, the Grosses Haus. The program included Goethe's prologue "Vorspiel auf der Theater," an orchestral concert, Act II of Wagner's *Meistersinger*, and Schiller's Demetrius fragment (*regie* Hans Merry). The Kleines Haus opened the next day with Gustav Freytag's *Die Journalisten* and Act III of Mozart's *The Marriage of Figaro*. With the opening of the new theatre there was considerable interchange with other theatres in Germany. The 1912–1918 period was extremely brilliant, including the premiere of Richard Strauss' *Ariadne auf Naxos* (first version), coupled with Molière's *Le bourgeois gentilhomme* (*regie* Max Reinhardt), with Jeritza as Ariadne; George Bernard Shaw's *Caesar and Cleopatra* (1913, *regie* Stephany); Schiller's *Don Carlos* (1913, *regie* Merry), with Aslan again in the title role; Shaw's *Pygmalion* (1914, *regie* Stephany), with Richter as Henry Higgins; Shakespeare's *Henry IV* (1914, *regie* Wilhelm von Scholz); Hauptmann's *Florian Geyer* (1914, *regie* Walter Bloem), with Kurt Junker in the title role; Friedrich Hölderlin's *Der Tod des Empedokles* (*The Death of Empedokles*, 1916, *regie* von Scholz); Shakespeare's *Othello* (1916, *regie* Richter), with Albert Bassermann (a guest) in the title role; Schiller's Wallenstein cycle (1917, *regie* Stephany), with Richter as Wallenstein; Friedrich Hebbel's *Herodes und Mariamne* (1918, *regie* Stephany); and Shakespeare's *Troilus and Cressida* (1918, *regie* von Scholz).

On November 13, 1918, after a production of Schiller's *Don Carlos*, the company went from the Königliche Hoftheater to the Württembergischen Landestheater, becoming a state theatre after World War II. In the aftermath of these changes Putliss lost his post, and the company was run for two seasons by Viktor Stephany.

In 1920 the company was taken over by Albert Kehm, who remained in the post until the Nazis took over Germany. This was a brilliant era despite financial problems, not only because of the new repertory, but also because of the great productions that came out of Stuttgart. The repertory contained the usual classics, but there were also new playwrights such as Friedrich Wolf, Bertolt Brecht, Hans Werfel, and Ernst Barlach, as well as some premieres. The company included such well-known actors as Oskar Hofmeister, Christian Friedrich Kayssler, Mila Kopp, Fritz Wisten, and Emmy Sonnemann (later Frau Göring); and two noted designers, Oskar Schlemmer from the Bauhaus and Felix Cziossek, both of whom tended to the abstract and geometric.

During the last part of the Putliss era, critics from all over Germany had occasionally reviewed productions at Stuttgart; during the Kehm years works were frequently reviewed, especially the premieres. Kehm was a famed *regisseur* himself, and he had the advantage of three talented *Schauspieldirektors*: Fritz Holl (1920–1924), Wolfgang Hoffmann-Harnisch (1924–1927), and Friedrich Brandenburg (1927–1933). The more important works of the Kehm period include the premiere of Wilhelm von Scholz's *Der Wettlauf mit dem Schatten* (*The Race with the Shadow*, 1920, *regie* the author); Werfel's *Der Spiegelmensch* (*The Mirror Person*, 1921, *regie* Holl); Ibsen's *Peer Gynt* (1920, *regie* Holl); Aeschylus' *The Oresteia* (1920, *regie* Holl); August Strindberg's *A Dream Play* (1923, *regie* Holl); Shakespeare's *Othello* (1923, *regie* Brandenburg), with Wisten as Iago; Georg Büchner's *Dantons Tod* (*Danton's Death*, 1924, *regie* Hoffmann-Harnisch); Shakespeare's *Henry IV* (1924, *regie* Hoffmann-Harnisch); the premiere of Barlach's *Die Sündflut* (*The Flood*, 1924, *regie* Hoffmann-Harnisch); Strindberg's *Gustav III* (1924, *regie* Hoffmann-Harnisch), with Wisten as Gustav; Goethe's *Niedhardt von Gniesenau* (1925, *regie* Hoffmann-Harnisch); Schiller's *Die Räuber* (*The Robbers*, 1925, *regie* Kehm); the premiere of Barlach's *Der Blaue Boll* (*The Blue Boll*, 1926, *regie* Brandenburg); Schiller's Wallenstein plays (1926, *regie* Hoffmann-Harnisch); Alfred Neumann's *Der Patriot* (1927, *regie* Brandenburg); Shakespeare's *Richard III* (1927, *regie* Brandenburg), with Wisten as Richard; Brecht's *Mann ist Mann* (*Man Is Man*, 1938, *regie* Brandenburg); Sophocles' *Oedipus Tyrannos* (1929, *regie* Brandenburg), with Wisten as Oedipus; Carl Zuckmayer's *Katherine Knie* (1929, *regie* Brandenburg); Shakespeare's *Coriolanus* (1930, *regie* Brandenburg); the premiere of Ossip Symow's *Schatten über Harlem* (*Shadow over Harlem*, 1931, *regie* Brandenburg); Shakespeare's *The Merchant of Venice* (1931, *regie* Brandenburg), with Wisten as Shylock; and Shakespeare's *A Midsummer Night's Dream* (1932, *regie* Brandenburg). Kehm was considered extremely leftist, and in his last seasons the Nazis frequently interrupted his productions with whistling and booing.

In 1933 Kehm was removed from his post and replaced by Otto Krauss. All the important people of the Kehm era were lost to Berlin, exile, or hiding. The years of National Socialism were the years for classics, particularly German classics, with heavy realistic scenery and lots of stage pictures. The big productions of the Krauss years included the following (uncredited productions belong to Krauss): Schiller's *Wilhelm Tell* (1933), *Die Räuber* (1933, *regie* Karl Hans Bohm), and *Don Carlos* (1934); Heinrich von Kleist's *Penthislea* (1935, *regie* Bohm); and both parts of Goethe's *Faust* (1936).

Gustav Deharde took over from 1937 to 1944. Deharde had a better range of *regisseurs* than had Krauss, including himself, Paul Riedy, Helmut Henrichs, and Karl Heinrich Ruppel. All of them would be in Stuttgart after 1945, except Deharde, who died soon after the war. Works done in the Deharde period include Schiller's *Don Carlos* (1937, *regie* Deharde); Shakespeare's *Hamlet* (1937, *regie* Dornseiff), with Rudolf Fernau as Hamlet (perhaps the most played work during the era of National Socialism); Schiller's *Die Räuber* (1938, *regie* Deharde); Shakespeare's *Richard III* (1939, *regie* Dornseiff), with Walter Richter in the title role; Gotthold Lessing's *Emilia Galotti* (1940, *regie* Dornseiff); Schiller's Wallenstein cycle (1940, *regie* Dornseiff); Hölderlin's *Der Tod des Empedokles* (*The Death of Empedokles*, 1942, *regie* Riedy); Shakespeare's *Measure for Measure* (1943, *regie* Riedy); Sophocles' *Antigone* (1944, *regie* Henrichs); and Hebbel's *Gyges und sein Ring* (*Gyges and his Ring*, 1944, *regie* Henrichs). In the fall of 1944, all theatres closed in Germany, and a short while later the Kleines Haus was destroyed by bombs.

As early as April 1945, plans were made to reopen the theatre in Stuttgart, with Max Roth made temporary intendant on May 1. Then, on June 21, Albert Kehm was made intendant for the theatre. The first play, Hugo von Hofmannsthal's *Jedermann* (*regie* Henrichs), was presented on August 4, 1945. It was followed by a full and very ambitious season. The main houses used for plays were the Grosses Haus and the Mörike Oberschule. Kehm remained only one year, but he presented many plays which had been forbidden in the Nazi era: Lessing's *Nathan der Weise* (*Nathan the Wise*, 1945, *regie* Henrichs); Romain Rolland's *Play of Love and Death* (1946, *regie* Henrichs); and Anouilh's *Antigone* (1946), with Christine Kayssler.

In May 1946 Bertil Wetzelberger (an opera man) was made *generalintendant*, and Ruppel became the *Schauspieldirektor*. The company's repertory from 1946 to 1949 was formed from classics and the new plays. Among the actors in the company were Hermine Körner (also a *regisseur*), Mila Kopp, Erich Ponto, Gisela Uhlen, Paul Hoffmann (also a *regisseur*), with Riedy, Henrichs, and Still remaining as *regisseurs*. On December 22, 1946, a Kammerspiele was opened in the Grosses Haus with Thornton Wilder's *The Skin of Our Teeth* (*regie* Riedy), with Uhlen as Sabina. Among the important works of the Wetzelberger tenure were Eugene O'Neill's *Mourning Becomes Electra* (1946, *regie* Henrichs); Ibsen's *Ghosts* (1946, *regie* Henrichs), with Körner as Mrs. Alving; Federico García Lorca's *Blood Wedding* (1947), with Körner staging and playing the mother; Albert Camus' *Caligula* (1947, *regie* Henrichs), with Hoffmann as Caligula; Carl Zuckmayer's inevitable *Des Teufels General* (*The Devil's General*, 1948, *regie* Riedy), with Hoffmann as Harras; Frederich Bruckner's *Heroische Komödie* (1948, *regie* Hoffmann), with Körner as Madame de Staël; Jean-Paul Sartre's *Dirty Hands* (1949, *regie* Henrichs); and Brecht's *Herr Puntila und sein Knecht Matti* (*Mr. Puntila and His Hired Man, Matti*, 1949, *regie* Riedy).

Walter Erich Schäfer had been a dramaturge at Stuttgart from 1929 to 1933, and he had also been a likable playwright during National Socialism (patriotic but not fascist). At the end of 1949, he was made *generalintendant*, staying until 1972 and seeing changes in the theatre. Schäfer insisted on high literary merit; other than that requirement, he gave considerable autonomy to the people who ran the branches of the organization. Even though he particularly disliked the plays of T. S. Eliot, he allowed them to be done. The main theatres used for plays were the Kammerspiele and the old Schauspielhaus, with the Grosses Haus used occasionally. There were five *Schauspieldirektors* during the Schäfer years, all of whom were very different in policy and their approach to repertory.

The first was Paul Hoffmann (1950–1958), who had as his *Oberspielleiter* Erich Fritz Brücklmeier. Hoffmann was both an actor and a *regisseur*, somewhat in the classic manner of the old German school. The plays he did were a mixture of classics (all five directors would present classics), with a rather conservative choice of new plays. Hoffmann used many guest artists and toured extensively. The important works of the first part of Schäfer's tenure were as follows (uncredited productions are Hoffmann's): Shakespeare's *Hamlet* (1950, *regie* Brücklmeier), with Hoffmann as Hamlet; Schiller's *Don Carlos* (1950); Shakespeare's *Troilus and Cressida* (1951, *regie* Brücklmeier), with Ponto as Thersites; Miller's *Death of a Salesman* (1951), with Ponto as Willy; Eliot's *The Cocktail Party* (1951); Shaw's *Saint Joan* (1952), with Edith Heerdgen as Joan; Shakespeare's *Othello* (1952), with Hans Mahnke as the Moor; Ludwig Thomas' *Moral* (1953, *regie* Henrichs); Shakespeare's *Henry IV* (1954); Lessing's *Nathan der Weise* (*Nathan the Wise*, 1954), with Ponto as Nathan; John Patrick's *The Teahouse of the August Moon* (1954, *regie* Brücklmeier); the Dumas/Sartre *Kean* (1954, *regie* Werner Kraut), with Hoffmann in the title role; Schiller's *Mary Stuart* (1955), which was the high point of Hoffmann's era, with Elisabeth Flickenschildt as Elisabeth and Gisela von Collande as Maria (it toured); N. Richard Nash's *The Rainmaker* (1955, *regie* Brücklmeier), with Ponto as Curry; Hauptmann's *Der Biberpelz* (*The Beaver Coat*, 1956, *regie* Peter Haenel), with Kopp as Frau Wolff; Goethe's *Götz von Belichingen* (1957, *regie* Dietrich Haugk); Shakespeare's *The Merchant of Venice* (1957, *regie* Kraut), with Ponto as Shylock (his last role before his death); Shakespeare's *Macbeth* (1957, *regie* Günther Rennert), with Flickenschildt and Walter Richter as the royal couple; and Brecht's *Mutter Courage und ihre Kinder* (*Mother Courage and Her Children*, 1958, *regie* Brücklmeier).

Dietrich Haugk (1958–1960) was more socially aware and considerably more experimental in both staging and repertory. His *regisseur*, Peter Palitzsch, was a Brecht disciple. Haugk continued to use guest artists, but the most important works of his tenure were modern plays, including the premiere of Brecht's *Der Aufhaltname des Arturo Ui* (*The Resistible Rise of Arturo Ui*, 1958, *regie* Palitzsch, with Manfred Wekwerth), with Wolfgang Keiling as Ui; O'Neill's *A Touch of the Poet* (1958, *regie* Günther Haenel), with Hoffmann as Con; Brecht's *Das Leben Eduard II von England* (*The Life of Edward II of England*, 1959, *regie* Palitzsch), with Käthe Reichel in the title role; Chekhov's *Platonov* (1959, *regie* Haenel), with Adolf Wohlbrück in the role of Platonov; Archibald MacLeish's *J. B.* (1959, *regie* Rennert); and Molière's *Tartuffe* (1960, *regie* Brücklmeier).

It was during the tenure of Günther Lüders (1960–1963) that a new Kleines Haus opened on October 6, 1962, with Strauss' *Ariadne auf Naxos* (with Leonie Rysanek) and Molière's *Le bourgeois gentilhomme* (*regie* Rennert). The repertory during this period was diversified and maintained a nice balance. Among the most important productions were Zuckmayer's *Der Hauptmann von Köpenick* (*The Captain from Köpenick*, 1960, *regie* Günther Haenel), with Lüders as Voigt; Brecht's *Die heilige Johanna der Schlachthöfe* (*Saint Joan of the Stockyards*, 1960, *regie* Benno Besson), with Käthe Reichl as Johanna Dark; O'Neill's *Long Day's Journey into Night* (1961, *regie* Gustav von Manker), with Heerdgen and Hoffmann as the elder Tyrones; Ibsen's *An Enemy of the People* (1961, *regie* Haenel), with Lüders as Stockmann; Georges Schéhadé's *The Journey* (1961, *regie* Rennert); Büchner's *Dantons Tod* (*Danton's Death*, 1962, *regie* Palitzsch); and Schiller's *Die Räuber* (1963, *regie* Hanskarl Zeiser). This was a good era for design, particularly the work of Leni Bauer-Ecsy, which was remarkable for its atmospheric feeling.

Karl Vibach (1963–1966) was perhaps the most energetic of the five directors. He tried a much more popular approach to repertory, including several American musicals. Both Vibach and Lüders had worked with Gründgens and had learned a good deal about balancing a season. Of the many premieres of the period, those of Martin Walser were the most important. The most significant productions included the premiere of Walser's *Überlebensgross Herr Krott—Requiem fur einen unsterblichen* (*Larger Than Life Herr Krott—Requiem for the Undying*, 1963, *regie* Palitzsch), with Hans Mahnke as Krott; Anouilh's *Poor Bitos* (1964, *regie* Heinrich Schnitzler); Carl Sternheim's *Der Snob* (1964, *regie* Rudolf Noelte); the premiere of Walser's *Der Schwarze Schwan* (*The Black Swan*, 1964, *regie* Palitzsch); Chekhov's *The Three Sisters* (1965, *regie* Noelte); Schiller's *Mary Stuart* (1965, *regie* Gustav von Manker); and Schiller's *Wilhelm Tell* (1966, *regie* Vibach), with Peter Roggisch as Gessler.

Peter Palitzsch became *Schauspieldirektor* in 1966 and remained in that position until 1972. He had worked at the Berliner Ensemble in East Germany before coming over to West Germany, and he tried some of the Brechtian approaches to staging and running the company (for example, his rehearsal methods, with much discussion, and his semi-Marxist staging of the classics). His choice of repertory was very socially minded, particularly his premieres, but it was far from doctrinaire and was well balanced. He also built his seasons around common themes, such as "revolution." Palitzsch emphasized the *regisseur*; at the same time he had the best ensemble of any company in West Germany, including Roggisch, Hans-Christian Blech, and Elisabeth Trisenaar.

The most significant productions of this successful period included the following (uncredited productions are Palitzsch's): Kleist's *Prinz Friedrich von Homburg* (*The Prince of Homburg*, 1966, *regie* Heinz Schirk); Arden's *Live Like Pigs* (1966); the Molière/Tankred Dorst *The Miser* (1967, *regie* Peter Zadek), with Lüders as Harpagon; Horváth's *Italienische Nacht* (*Italian Night*, 1967, *regie* Hans Hollmann); Chekhov's *The Cherry Orchard* (1968, *regie* Peter Zadek); Shakespeare's (more or less) *Der Dritte Richard* (*The Third Richard*, 1968, *regie* Palitzsch), with Blech as Richard III; the premiere of Tankred Dorst's *Toller* (1968, *regie* Palitzsch), with Roggisch in the title role; Shakespeare's *Henry IV* (1969, *regie* Palitzsch); Roger Vitrac's *Victor or the Children of Might* (1969, *regie* Hans Neuenfels); Sean O'Casey's *The Silver Tassie* (1970, *regie* Zadek); Brecht's *Mutter Courage und ihre Kinder* (*Mother Courage and Her Children*, 1970); Kleist's *Penthislea* (1970, *regie* Klaus Michael Grüber); the premiere of Peter Weiss' *Hölderlin* (1971), with Roggisch in the title role; Sternheim's *Burger Schippel* (1971, *regie* Niels-Peter Rudolph); Ibsen's *A Doll's House* (1972, *regie* Neuenfels), with Elisabeth Trisenaar as Nora; and Shakespeare's *Hamlet* (1972), with Roggisch as Hamlet. This was also a good era for design, with Wilfried Minks doing the sets for *Die Rosenkriege*, *Marija*, *Toller*, and *The Cherry Orchard*.

The year 1972 was a great turning point in many German houses. At that time Schäfer went into retirement and Palitzsch left for Frankfurt, taking a lot of the good actors with him, especially Roggisch and Trisenaar. Schäfer's replacement was Hans Peter Doll, who is still *generalintendant* today and, like Schäfer, was a dramaturge before becoming a *generalintendant*. Before coming to Stuttgart, he had been at Braunschweig. All three of his *Schauspieldirektors* have used different methodologies. The first of these was Alfred Kirchner (1972–1974), who had been a tested *regisseur*, particularly at Bremen, before coming to Stuttgart. Kirchner had no particular program in mind, and his *regisseurs* were strictly a pick-up group. Nevertheless, his two seasons were very successful, especially Shakespeare's *Romeo and Juliet* and David Storey's *The Changing Room* (both 1972, both *regie* Kirchner); Hauptmann's *Michael Kramer* (1973, *regie* Friedrich Beyer); Dorst's *Eiszeit* (*Ice Age*, 1973, *regie* Fritz Zecha), with Hans Mahnke as Kristian; and Witold Gombrowicz's *The Marriage* (*regie* Beyer).

Claus Peymann had been a *regisseur* at many theatres before taking over the job of *Schauspieldirektor* (1974–1979). His was an extremely literary, experimental age with many brilliant productions. Peymann brought a first-rate team to Stuttgart, including his head dramaturge Hermann Beil. Peymann and Palitzsch were contrasts in many ways. With Palitzsch, the company had many excellent actors; Peymann had only a few, such as Bernhard Minetti or Kirsten Dene, but worked hard for ensemble. Palitzsch welcomed political statements in plays; Peymann believed politics and the theatre did not mix (practically, this meant only early Brecht was done), though Peymann did stage political works at the end. Attendance in the Schauspiel ran to over 90 percent capacity under Peymann, who particularly appealed to the young. In a 1976 *Theatre Heute* poll of twenty-seven critics as to the most important company in the German-speaking world, sixteen named Stuttgart. In a 1979 poll of twenty-nine critics, twenty-two chose Stuttgart.

The list of the most important plays during the Peymann period is a lengthy one (uncredited productions are Peymann's): the premiere of Gerlind Reinshagen's *Himmel und Erde* (*Heaven and Earth*, 1974); Schiller's *Die Räuber* (*The Robbers*, 1975); Horváth's *Geschichten aus dem Wiener Wald* (*Tales of the Vienna Woods*, 1975, *regie* Horst Zankl); Kleist's *Das Käthchen von Heilbronn* (1975), played in a circus motif; Brecht's *Trommeln in der Nacht* (*Drums in the Night*, 1975, *regie* Christof Nel); Camus' *The Just* (1976), which turned out to be very important; the premiere of Thomas Bernhard's *Minetti* (1976), with Minetti playing himself; both parts of Goethe's *Faust* (1977), with sets by Achim Freyer; Shakespeare's *A Midsummer Night's Dream* (1977, *regie* Kirchner); Goethe's *Iphigenia auf Tauris* (*Iphigenia in Tauris*, 1977), with Dene as Iphigenia; Molière's *Tartuffe* (1978, *regie* Valentin Jeker); the premiere of Bernhard's *Immanuel Kant* (1978); the premiere of Thomas Brasch's *Rotter* (1978, *regie* Christof Nel); Chekhov's *The Three Sisters* (1978); Shakespeare's *Measure for Measure* (1979, *regie* B. K. Tragelehn); and the premiere of Bernhard's *Vor Dem Ruhestand* (*Before the Retirement*, 1979), which was Peymann's last production.

Despite Peymann's claim that politics and theatre do not mix, he did many plays that dealt with Germany's contemporary social conditions. During the political murders of 1977, he staged Camus' *The Just*; in addition, he devised programs and special evenings that addressed the problems of modern Germany. Indeed, politics led to Peymann's resignation. Peymann had objected strenuously to a very prominent local official who had been an ardent Nazi, but whose memory about his activities during the period had become conveniently blank. Eventually, the local council demanded an accounting of what Peymann himself had done during the war, and the police asked for a theatre boycott. The Stuttgarter *oberbürgermeister* Manfred Rommel, son of the famous general, tried to steer a middle course, saying that Peymann could not be held accountable for political happenings in Germany, past or present. Rommel admired Peymann's work tremendously, but eventually all the problems were blown out of proportion, and by 1980, Peymann had left for Bochum, taking a large part of the acting company and his staff with him.

The job of running the Schauspiel was offered to several people, but because of its explosiveness, no one seemed interested. Then Hansgünther Heyme, who was at Cologne, accepted. He formed a new team, most of whom were from Cologne, and hired a mass of new actors. Heyme has had many problems at Stuttgart, not all of which have been of his own making. The main problem seems to lie with the press. Peymann was very popular in Stuttgart, not only with his audiences, but also with the press. As a result, Heyme never seems to satisfy the local press, although he does receive good reviews in the national magazines.

There have been many good evenings in the Stuttgart theatre in the last seasons, mostly staged by Heyme or his *oberspielleiter*, Günter Krämer, including Schiller's *Don Carlos* (1979, *regie* Heyme), with Hans Schulze as Philip; Arthur Schnitzler's *Komödie der Verführung* (*Comedy of Seduction*, 1980, *regie* Heyme); Strindberg's *The Dance of Death* (1980, *regie* Krämer), with Gisela Stein as Alice and Fritz Lichterhahn as Edgar; the premiere of Tankred Dorst's *Die Villa* (1980, *regie* Krämer); Lessing's *Minna von Barnhelm* (1980, *regie* Heyme); and Goethe's *Stella* (1981, *regie* Berndt Renne), with Sabine Wegner as Stella.

Stuttgart has two theatres, the Kleines Haus (which seats 700 to 851) and the Kammertheater (which seats 220 but can be flexible). Occasionally the company plays in the foyer of the theatre. The acting company numbers twenty-eight men and fourteen women plus guests; there are five dramaturges and a large technical staff, which works for the acting company, the ballet, and the opera. Around twelve *regisseurs* are hired every season, three of whom are resident. The acting company does about six new productions each season, split between the two houses, as well as revivals of works from the previous season. While both classic and modern plays are staged, many more modern works are done. The budget for the whole operation (opera, spoken drama, and ballet) runs to 70.5 million DM, of which 58.6 million is subsidy, one-half of which comes from the city and one-half from the state. Current attendance runs to 78 percent capacity in the Kleines Haus and 73 percent capacity in the Kammertheater, which represent decreases from the Peymann era.

The theatre has a small company within it that does more avant-garde works through the large subscription program. One of the company's major problems is to regain subscribers (currently there are around six thousand).

LEON M. AUFDEMBERGE
(With thanks to Verena Knorr, Hermann Beil, and Peter Kleinschmidt; translation help by Ingrid Dubberke and Paul E. Hofman.)

THALIA THEATER
Raibosen–67
2000 Hamburg, West Germany

Hamburg has two subsidized theatres—the Thalia and the German Playhouse— and, like those in Munich, they are a study in contrasts. Their polite but strong rivalry keeps both on their theatrical toes. Both theatres play a wide and varied repertory and insist upon a balanced season, but their histories and operating procedures are quite different.

The Thalia was founded in 1843 on Pferdmarkt (now Gerhardt Hauptmann Platz) by Chéri Maurice, an established theatre figure who was to direct the theatre for fifty years. On opening night, November 9, 1843, three plays were presented, the major production being A. B. Herrmann's *Der Freundschaftdienst* (*The Service of Friendship*). Most of the repertory throughout Maurice's directorship consisted of extremely popular pieces: Johann Nestroy, Ferdinand Raimund, and the like, and endless amounts of parody and French vaudeville. Many of the plays performed are now fairly forgotten, but the theatre did attract a first-rate acting company from the very beginning. The chief distinction of Maurice's directorship, apart from its longevity, was his ability to hold together an acting company.

By the 1870s, however, some classics were introduced, and Goethe and Schiller began to be part of the repertory. Ibsen was first played in 1878 with *The Pillars of Society*, and the play which the Germans call *Nora* (better known as *A Doll's House*) followed in 1880. Maurice died in 1893, the same year he celebrated his fiftieth anniversary as leader of the Thalia.

Maurice was followed by a series of directors, including Bernhard Pollini and a double directorship of Bittong and Max Bachur, under whom modern serious plays began to be done more frequently. The bulk of the repertory continued to be light comedy, however. In 1900 the Hamburg German Playhouse (Deutsches Schauspielhaus) opened, enlisting the aid of part of the Thalia's acting company. This loss was more than made up by Leopold Jessner, who first came to the Thalia as a *regisseur* in 1904 and was its mainstay until 1915. Jessner's repertory at the Thalia reflects the drama of the times, but his best remembered productions are Beaumarchais' *The Marriage of Figaro* (1907) and Molière's *Tartuffe* (1911). In 1912 a new Thalia Theatre was opened with scenes from various plays, in which the intendant, Max Bachur, chose to show off the whole company: Otto Ernst's *Der Einzug* (*The Entrance*); Goethe's *Die Laune des Verliebten* (*The*

Humor of Falling in Love); Paul Heyse's *Under Brüdern* (*Under Brothers*); and Frank Wedekind's *Der Kammersänger* (*The Court Singer*). The architects for the new house were Lundt and Kallmorgen, and the theatre held thirteen hundred seats. It was to be the company's pride until it was destroyed in World War II. With the opening of the new theatre, the Thalia began a program of inviting other theatre companies to share its stage.

In 1915 Herman Röbbeling became the intendant. Under his directorship, the Thalia would finally emerge as one of the leading houses in Germany. He introduced Thalia audiences to playwrights such as Herbert Eulenberg, August Strindberg (who became a Röbbeling staging specialty), George Bernard Shaw, and Lion Feuchtwanger. Actors such as Alexander Moissi, Wilhelm Bednow, Julius Kobler, and Berthe Gast were part of the company. In 1918 the theatre celebrated its seventy-fifth anniversary with Roderick Bendix's *Der Kaufmann* (*The Merchant*) in a production by Hans Andersen.

The 1920s were a difficult time economically for all German theatres, and the Thalia suffered along with the rest. Röbbeling was able to help keep the theatre afloat by enlarging the repertory (more Shaw, Luigi Pirandello, Somerset Maugham, and the new Germans, such as Bertolt Brecht) and by adding new actors to the company, such as Paul Barnay, Hans Wengraf, Maria Eis, Heinz Stieda, Heinz Salier, Marianne Wentzel, and Willy Maertens, who would eventually become intendant of the company. There were also many comedies to help balance the season and budget. In 1928 Röbbeling became director of both the Thalia and the German Playhouse in an economy move, but this post lasted only a short while.

In the 1930s the Thalia began to bring in more guest artists to enlarge its audience. Fritz Massary came in 1930 to play in the *First Mrs. Selby*; John Ervine and Fritz Kortner appeared in 1931 in Gerhart Hauptmann's *Professor Bernhardi*, and Elisabeth Bergner portrayed Alkmena in Jean Giraudoux's *Amphytrion 38*. In 1932 Röbbeling left, to be replaced by Erich Ziegel, who stayed only two years. The directors under National Socialism were Paul Mundorf and Ernst Leudesdorff (1934–1942) and Robert Meyn (1942–1945). With regard to repertory, Shaw continued to be popular at the Thalia up to the eve of the war, but many more classics were done during the war, especially Goethe, Schiller, and Lessing, as well as comic writers such as Carlo Goldoni and Molière. There were also many new modern comedies that are best forgotten. In 1943 the theatre celebrated its one-hundredth anniversary with Gustav Freytag's *Die Journalisten*, in a production by the intendant Meyn. During part of the war years the opera company used the theatre because its own house had been destroyed. In 1944 the theatre closed along with the rest of the German houses, and in the following year most of the theatre was destroyed by Allied bombs.

The theatre company reformed in 1945 and played in a variety of improvised theatres, including St. John's Church and the Altonaer Sparkasse, but its main house was to be the Haus Schlankreye. The first intendant after the war was Willy Maertens, who had been an actor at the Thalia. In the years following the war, there were many new playwrights to be absorbed. In 1946 a partially restored Thalia (seating six hundred) would open with *As You Like It*. Molière and Ferenc Molnár were very popular during the early postwar years, as were Noel Coward and Tennessee Williams. Maertens staged such works as Shaw's *The Doctor's Dilemma* (1948), Hauptmann's *Die Ratten* (*The Rats*, 1949), Oscar Wilde's *An Ideal Husband* (1949), Tennessee Williams' *A Streetcar Named Desire* (1950), Christopher Fry's *The Lady's Not for Burning* (1950), Molière's *Tartuffe* (1952), and Wilde's *Lady Windermere's Fan* (1953). Hans Lietzau came in to stage Ibsen's *Hedda Gabler* (1949) and one of the first German productions of Arthur Miller's *Death of a Salesman* (1950), with Maertens as Willy. In 1952 Leo Mittler staged one of the most memorable productions in the Thalia's history, Williams' *The Rose Tattoo*, with Inge Meysel as Serafina. There were also light comedies, including Mary Chase's play about the rabbit, *Mein Freund Harvey* (*Harvey*).

In December 1960 the Thalia opened a new house with Shaw's *Saint Joan*, and before Maertens left in 1964 there would be outstanding productions of Goethe's *Die Mitschuldigen* (*The Accomplices*), Molière's *Sganarelle* (1961, *regie* Heinz Dietrich Kenters), and Shakespeare's *The Comedy of Errors* (1963, *regie* Hans Rothe).

Dr. Kurt Roeck took over in 1964 and continued his predecessors' policies of balanced seasons. He hired new *regisseurs* and increased the number of subscribers. His particularly outstanding productions were Jean Anouilh's *The Lark* (1964, *regie* Roland Pietri); Miller's *After the Fall* (1965, *regie* Heinrich Käutner), with Viktor de Kawa and Ingrid Andree; Ibsen's *Peer Gynt* (1966, *regie* Otto Wilhelm), with Ulrich Haupt; Arthur Schnitzler's *Der Einsame Weg* (*The Lonely Way*, 1966, *regie* by the playwright's son Heinrich); Michael Stewart/Jerry Herman's *Hello, Dolly!* (1966, *regie* Jean-Pierre Ponnelle); Arnold Wesker's *The Kitchen* (1967, *regie* Axel von Ambesser); Peter Ustinov's *The Unknown Soldier and His Wife* (1967, *regie* Boy Gobert); and Ferdinand Bruckner's *Elisabeth von England* (*Elizabeth of England*, 1967, *regie* Hans Balzer), with Heidimarie Hatheyer in the title role.

Roeck was followed by Boy Gobert, who trained as both an actor and *regisseur* in Hamburg. From 1960 to 1969 he worked as an actor at the Burgtheater in Vienna. Gobert brought the house forward and is genuinely respected in Hamburg. Because of his acting career his focus as intendant was on ensemble, although good *regisseurs* still worked regularly at the Thalia. Gobert continued the policy of balanced seasons, with classics and modern authors, but there were some experiments with productions, particularly in the work of Hans Neuenfels and Hans Hollmann. During his tenure the Thalia opened a small experimental house, the "tik," in the local art museum.

Gobert left a long list of distinguished productions: Molnar's *Liliom* (1964, *regie* Hans Deppe), with Harald Jahnke; Nikolai Gogol's *The Inspector General* (1969, *regie* Gobert); Williams' *The Seven Descents of Myrtle* (1969, *regie* Detlef Sierck); Shakespeare's *Troilus and Cressida* (1970, *regie* Hollmann); George

Farquhar's *The Beaux' Stratagem* (1971, *regie* William Gaskill); Frank Wedekind's *Lulu* (1971, *regie* Dieter Giesing); Shaw's *Heartbreak House* (1971, *regie* Gobert); Harold Pinter's *Old Times* (1972, *regie* Hans Schweikart); Shakespeare's *Richard III* (1973, *regie* Hollmann), with Gobert as the crafty king and Elizabeth Flickenschildt as the mad Queen Margaret; Cole Porter's *Kiss Me, Kate* (1973, *regie* Helmut Braun); Odön von Horváth's *Geschichten aus dem Wiener Wald* (*Tales of the Vienna Woods*, 1973, *regie* Flimm); Pinter's *No Man's Land*, 1974, *regie* Gobert); Schiller's *Mary Stuart* (1975, *regie* Gobert), which later toured Russia; Edmond Rostand's *Cyrano de Bergerac* (1975, *regie* Flimm), with Gobert as the title character; Wilde's *Lady Windermere's Fan* (1976, *regie* Gobert); an antifascist production by Hans Hollmann of Shakespeare's *Coriolan* [*sic*], with Gobert in the title role and Flickenschildt as Volumnia (1977); Trevor Griffith's *The Comedians* (1977, *regie* Peter Zadek, who normally works at the German Playhouse), with Gobert as Chancellor; Molière's *Don Juan* (1977, *regie* Peter Striebeck); the Bob Fosse/Fred Ebb/John Kander musical *Chicago* (1977, *regie* Baumann); and Shakespeare's *Hamlet* (1978, *regie* Hans Neuenfels).

The Thalia started as a popular house, and it still has that reputation. But in its defense, it has one of the largest numbers of subscribers in all West Germany (twenty-four thousand), and its attendance runs a high 90 percent capacity. Year after year, almost from the very beginning, the theatre has tried to give the public what it wants. The Thalia does nine or ten productions in its main house, which seats one thousand, every year and five to six in the "tik" (seating four hundred). Actors and *regisseurs* work back and forth between the two theatres, and occasionally a production from one theatre is transferred to the other. It tries to balance its plays between classics and moderns; it has a special affinity for British works, with Pinter as a house specialty. In addition, the house has done six works by the East German writer Peter Hacks.

Its acting company numbers about seventy-five, of whom forty-five are men and thirty are women. A few actors come as guests but are required to stay a reasonable amount of time. It has two resident *regisseurs*; the rest of the productions are by guests. A large technical staff works five-day weeks, but as the theatre plays seven days a week, weekends are not assured days off. The Thalia plays up to nine performances a week, with eight the general rule.

In recent years, by hiring some of West Germany's best freelance *regisseurs*, the Thalia's staging standard has been quite high. Most *regisseurs* there tend to be conservative rather than experimental.

Most actors like the company because the *regisseurs* talk with them and do not make them feel like puppets. Some Thalia plays have recently been done on television, which means both fame and extra revenue. The budget for the theatre is a comfortable 15.6 DM, of which 11.2 million is subsidy. In 1974, Ulrich Hartmann, a Social Democratic senator, proposed cutting the budget of both Hamburg theatres 20 percent, but it was promptly vetoed. When the curtain rose at the next performance in the Thalia, the audience applauded in a show of appreciation.

Despite the outward appearances of St. Pauli and the Reeperbahn, Hamburg is a fairly conservative city and the Thalia is a basically conservative house. It had one major uproar in recnt years when, in a production of Dieter Forte's *Martin Luther und Thomas Münzer oder die Einführung der Buchhaltung* (*Martin Luther and Thomas Münzer or the Introduction of Bookkeeping*), an actor was crucified nude on the stage and a large sector of the audience objected.

The Thalia would like to tour more, finances permitting. Its most recent major tour was to Russia, with Schiller's *Mary Stuart*, which was two years in the planning. It would also like to do more musicals and have more *regisseurs* from outside Germany. William Gaskill, of Britain's National Theatre, has been there, and in the 1978–1979 season, George A. Towstonogow, director of the Maxim Gorky theatre of Leningrad, staged a dramatization of Dostoyevsky's *The Idiot*.

Taking many of his staff with him, Gobert resigned in 1980 to take over the Schiller Theatre in West Berlin. Peter Striebeck, who had worked at the Thalia as a *regisseur*, took over as intendant.

LEON M. AUFDEMBERGE
(With assistance from Dr. Gerhard Blasche
of the Thalia.)

THEATRE OF THE FREE CITY OF BREMEN
(Theater der Freen Hansestadt Bremen)
Brieffach 101046
2800 Bremen, West Germany

Bremen's first permanent theatre, the Schauspielhaus auf der Junkern Bastion, opened in 1792, with a performance of *Bürger-Gluck* (*Citizen Fortune*) by Joseph Marius von Babo. Both opera and spoken drama were performed there by resident and traveling troupes, with August Wilhelm Iffland and August von Kotzebue being the most often performed of contemporary German dramatists. The Schauspielhaus was the center of Bremen's cultural life until October 16, 1843, when a new theatre, the Theater auf dem Wall am Bischofstor (architect Heinrich Seeman), opened with J. L. von Deinhardstein's *Hans Sachs*. The first head of the theatre was K. A. Ritter. This theatre became the home of both opera and theatre performances until its destruction in World War II. The company was celebrated for its performances of Shakespeare, the German writers Karl Gutzkow and Heinrich Laube, and the Austrian Franz Grillparzer. Wagner was enormously popular from the 1870s on. The theatre's chief claim to fame in the last part of the nineteenth century was Heinrich Bulthaupt, who worked there as a dramaturge in the 1870s and contributed several plays. His chief contributions were his observations on various playwrights, particularly Shakespeare and Lessing.

Under the directorship of Friedrich Erdmann-Jesnitzer (1896 to his death in 1906) and his fellow *regisseur* Gustav Burchard, the company's repertory advanced new staging ideas for both classic and modern works. Both *regisseurs* favored large-scale productions, but there were also small-scale productions of plays by Henrik Ibsen, Frank Wedekind, and Arno Holz, as well as a remarkable number of premieres with guest appearances by some of Germany's most important actors. Among the works done during Bremen's first important theatre era were Edmond Rostand's *Cyrano de Bergerac* (1900, *regie* Erdmann-Jesnitzer), with Carl Eckelmann in the title role; Aeschylus' *Oresteia* (1901, *regie* Erdmann-Jesnitzer); Bjørnstjerne Bjørnson's *Beyond Human Power* (1902, *regie* Erdmann-Jesnitzer); Max Dreyer's *Der Probenkandidat* (*The Candidate for the Experiment*, 1902, *regie* Burchard); both parts of Goethe's *Faust* (part one, Burchard; part two, Erdmann-Jesnitzer), with Friedrich Holthaus as Mephisto; and Schiller's *Demetrius* fragment (1907, *regie* Burchard), with Franiskz Ellmenreich as Marfa.

After Erdmann-Jesnitzer's death, the company was managed for awhile by his wife. Although Burchard tried to keep the company in line, he did not succeed. Fortunately for Bremen, a new theatre company, the Bremer Schauspielhaus, made its appearance in the city in 1910. Despite financial problems, it became one of the most advanced companies in Germany. The founders of the theatre company were Eduard Inchon and Johannes Wiegand. Wiegand served as director of the company during most of its existence. The first Schauspielhaus was in the Neustadt district of Bremen (architects J. W. Ostwald and Walter Goring). A new theatre was inaugurated on August 15, 1913 (architects August Abbenheusen and Otto Blendermann), opening with a production of Oscar Wilde's *A Woman of No Importance* (*regie* Wiegand). The second production, a modern-dress version of *Hamlet* staged by the young Gustav Hartung, was more startling.

In its early years the Schauspielhaus employed guest actors, but the most important work was done by the resident company alone. The repertory of the troupe was that of the most advanced German houses, including the expressionist playwrights of the postwar era and foreign writers, such as George Bernard Shaw and later Eugene O'Neill, as well as productions of classics done in experimental ways. The permanent company had strong performances by actors such as Paul Werth, Rosa Conradi, Justus Ott, Otto Mathes, Willy Kleinau, and a local favorite, Dora Maria Herwelly. During the first years of its existence, there were a number of outstanding productions, which included Frank Wedekind's *Frühlings Erwachen* (*Spring's Awakening*, 1918, *regie* Weigand); Sophocles' *Oedipus Tyrannos* (1912, *regie* Inchon); Ferdinand Bruckner's *Elisabeth von England* (1930, *regie* Wilhelm Chmelnitzky), with Herwelly in the title role; Shakespeare's *Twelfth Night* (1931, *regie* Deglef Sierck); Karl Lerb's *U. B. 116* (1931, *regie* Chmelnitzky); Wedekind's *Lulu* (1932, *regie* Chmelnitzky); and Gerhart Hauptmann's *Hamlet in Wittenburg* (1932, *regie* Inchon).

After the Nazis came to power, the company concentrated on the classics, most of which were staged by Hans Tannert whose style was heavily pictorial and very literary, and involved huge casts. Some of the major productions Tanner staged included Ibsen's *Peer Gynt* (1938); Schiller's *Don Carlos* (1938); and Shakespeare's *Othello* (1942), with Willy Kleinau in the title role. Wiegand died in 1940 and the directorship passed to Inchon, who died in 1943. In the same year the acting companies of the Schauspielhaus and the Stadttheater were combined under the name of the Theater der Hansestadt, Bremen.

Little has been written about the Bremer Stadttheater, nor are there many reviews of the theatre's productions in contemporary German publications. Both Hubert Reusch (1908–1910) and Julius Otto (1910–1925) were noted for their conservative style and choice of plays. The best known *regisseur* to work at the Stadttheater during the Otto era was Alwin Kronacher, who worked in Bremen during World War I and whose interest was in staging German naturalistic drama, including two plays by Hauptmann, *Die Ratten* (*The Rats*, 1916) and *Fuhrmann Henschel* (1918). Bremen adored Willy Becker whose tenure (1925–1938) was marked by his choice of excellent classic and modern plays. The most highly praised productions were Goethe's *Faust* (1927, *regie* Adolph Rampelman); Schiller's *Mary Stuart* (1932, *regie* Walter Falk); and Becker's own production of Shakespeare's *Hamlet* (1937). Curt Gerdes' (1938–1944) best productions came at the end of his directorship, with Goethe's *Torquato Tasso* (1943, *regie* Gerdes), with Kleinau in the title role, and Shakespeare's *Twelfth Night* (1944, *regie* Richard Dornseiff). Neither Gerdes nor either of the local theatres, however, survived the war.

The first theatre to open after the war was the Bremer Künstlertheater, which opened in the old Concordia Gastatte on September 19, 1945, under the directorship of Willy Kleinau. This company was led by Kleinau (1945–1946), Erich Keddy (1946–1947), and Gillis von Rappard (1947–1949). The repertory was forward-looking and included many plays forbidden in the Nazi era as well as new plays. Some of its major hits included Gotthold Lessing's *Nathan der Weise* (*Nathan the Wise*, 1945, *regie* Dornseiff); Molière's *The Miser* (1947, *regie* von Rappard); O'Neill's *Mourning Becomes Electra* (1948, *regie* von Rappard); Carl Zuckmayer's *Des Teufels General* (*The Devil's General*, 1948, *regie* von Rappard), with Wolfgang Engels as Harras; and Ibsen's *Ghosts* (1948, *regie* von Rappard), with Herwelly as Mrs. Alving.

The Bremer Kammerspiele opened on February 21, 1946, under the directorship of Walter Koch and Heinz Suhr, both of whom had worked in Bremen during the war. Koch and Suhr were heads from 1946 to 1947, followed by Erich-Fritz Brücklmeier (1947–1948) and Ernst Karchow (1948–1949). The Kammerspiele repertory was much like that of the Künstlertheatre, including classics (German and international) and modern works. Its most important productions included Marcel Pagnol's *To the Golden Anchor* (1945, *regie* Oskar Schättinger); Goethe's *Torquato Tasso* (1947, *regie* Brücklmeier); Thornton Wilder's *Our Town* (1948, *regie* Friedrich Mellinger); and Lope de Vega's *Di quando acá nos vino?* (*When He Came to Us*, 1948, *regie* Karchow), translated into German as *Was kamm denn da ins Haus?*

Both companies were assimilated into the Theater der Freien Hansestadt Bremen in 1949, which was a city-subsidized theatre. However, Bremen does have one private theatre company, the Niederdeutsches Theater, which is still in existence and does dialect plays. It opened in October 1945 under the directorship of Ernst Waldau and Walter Ernst, with Ernst still serving as head today. In November 1947 it opened a new theatre (designed by Waldau) with a production of Fritz Stavenhagen's *De ruge Hoff.*

The first production of a play for the Theater der Freien Hansestadt Bremen took place on August 25, 1949, with Goethe's *Stella*, staged by Willi Hanke, who was *generalintendant* from 1949 until his death in 1954. This play was staged in the Behelfstheater (better known as the "Glocke"). The following year, on August 28, 1950, the company played for the first time in its new theatre, the Theater am Goetheplatz, which had been fashioned from the ruins of the old Schauspielhaus (architect for the rebuilding Hans Storm). Hanke pursued a vigorous program, often with well-known guest artists. Hanke's opening production at the Theatre am Goetheplatz was Goethe's *Egmont* (*regie* Hanke), with Paul Hartmann. Other productions included Tennessee Williams' *A Streetcar Named Desire* (1951, *regie* Hannes Razum); Goethe's *Faust* (1951, *regie* Walter Thomas); Sophocles' *Oedipus Tyrannos* (1952, *regie* Günther Stark), with Wolfgang Engels in the title role; Schiller's *Mary Stuart* (1953, *regie* Stark), with Gisela von Collande as Maria; and Carl Zuckmayer's *Der Hauptmann von Köpenick* (*The Captain from Köpenick*, 1954, *regie* Robert Meyn), with Werner Krauss as Voigt.

Albert Lippert took over in 1955, bringing with him his knowledge from his years at the German Playhouse in Hamburg. Since Lippert was most interested in poetic drama, many of his productions were heavy in atmosphere. With Lippert came one of Germany's leading designers, Günther Schneider-Siemssen. Lippert's major productions included Arthur Miller's *The Crucible* (1955, *regie* Razum); Heinrich von Kleist's *Prinz Friedrich von Homburg* (*The Prince of Homburg*, 1955, *regie* Lippert); Shakespeare's *King Lear* (1956, *regie* Razum), with Albert Hoerrmann as Lear; Schiller's Wallenstein cycle (1957, *regie* Lippert); Federico García Lorca's *Blood Wedding* (1958, *regie* F. P. Buch); Schiller's *Don Carlos* (1959, *regie* Buch), with Lippert as Philip II; Williams' *The Glass Menagerie* (1961, *regie* Jockish); and Georges Bernanos' *Dialogues of the Carmelites* (1962, *regie* Lippert).

Kurt Hübner became *generalintendant* in 1962. He helped make Bremen the most important theatre city outside of Berlin for real experimentation in either Germany. Hübner had been an actor, dramaturge, and *regisseur* at Hanover; he had also worked at other theatres before coming to Bremen. His idea was simple in the statement but complicated in the execution: find the best young *regisseurs* in West Germany who were experimenting with productions, turn them loose in Bremen, and then find an acting company (mostly young) pliable enough to play what the *regisseur* wanted. Among the *regisseurs* who came to Bremen were Hübner himself, Hans Neuenfels, Alfred Kirchner, Peter Palitzsch (perhaps the only "solid" *regisseur* in this list), Kai Braak, Charles Lang, Klaus Michael Grüber, Harmut Gehrke, Rainer Maria Fassbinder (who also wrote for the company), Wilfred Minks (also Hübner's major designer), Johannes Schaaf, Peter Stein, and Germany's leading *wunderkind* of the era, Peter Zadek. The acting company included Marget Carstensen, Edith Clever, Bruno Ganz, Hans Peter Hallachs, Jutte Lampe, Hilde Mikulicz, and Bernhard Minetti. Among the designers of the era were Jürgen Rose, Eduardo Arroyo, Lucian Damiani, and Wilfred Minks, currently West Germany's leading designer.

From these people Hübner forged the "Bremer Stil" or "Shock (*sic*) Stil," which was composed of elements from Antonin Artaud, Vladimir Meyerhold, Bertolt Brecht, Sergei Eisenstein, Erwin Piscator, and whatever was current at the time. The theatrical activities of the years 1962–1973 were very important— so important that one critic, Siegfried Melchinger, once equated the best in German theatre at the time with Bremen (*Theater Heute*, March 1967, pages 28–33). Basically, the "Bremer Stil" meant that all major productions were more-or-less concept productions.

In Peter Zadek's production of Shakespeare's *Henry V*, called *Henry Held* (*Henry Hero*), the concept was not to present a heroic play but rather to attack jingoism. Zadek set his 1966 production of Schiller's *Die Räuber* (*The Robbers*) against big Pop Art posters in the style of Robert Rauschenberg. Both had sets by Minks. In order to provide for more experimentation, Hübner opened the Concordia in 1971, with Witold Gombrowicz's *Yvonne, Princess of Burgundia* (*regie* and sets by Minks). The Concordia had been an old movie-house in which a number of *regisseurs* directed productions that were heavy on environment. It might be added that the company played a number of engagements outside Bremen, including the theatre festivals at Paris, Berlin, and London, and did many plays on television and radio.

A list of the major works performed during the period must be highly selective as practically every issue of *Theater Heute*, West Germany's major theatre magazine, included a review of something the Bremen theatre was doing. The company's most celebrated productions included John Osborne's *Luther* (1962, *regie* Zadek); Brendan Behan's *The Hostage* (1962, *regie* Zadek); Shakespeare's *A Midsummer Night's Dream* (1963, *regie* Zadek); Meredith Wilson's *The Music Man* (1963, *regie* Zadek); Brecht's *Der Kaukasische Kreide Kreis* (*The Caucasian Chalk Circle*, 1964, *regie* Palitzsch); Brecht's *Der Aufhaltsame des Arturo Ui* (*The Resistible Rise of Arturo Ui*, 1964, *regie* Palitzsch); Brendan Behan's *The Quare Fellow* (1964, *regie* Zadek); Shakespeare's *Romeo and Juliet* (1964, *regie* Hübner); Shakespeare's *Hamlet* (1965, *regie* Hübner); Frank Wedekind's *Frühlings Erwachen* (*Spring's Awakening*, 1965, *regie* Zadek); Shakespeare's *Macbeth* (1966, *regie* Hübner); John Osborne's *A Patriot for Me* (1966, *regie* Zadek); the Sophocles/Friedrich Hölderlin *Antigone* (1966, *regie* Hübner); the premiere of Martin Speer's *Jagdzenen aus Niederbayern* (*Hunting Scenes from Lower Bavaria*, 1966, *regie* Rolf Becker); Schiller's *Kabale und Liebe* (*Intrigue and Love*, 1967, *regie* Stein); Shakespeare's *The Comedy of Errors* (1968, *regie* Zadek); Ibsen's *Peer Gynt* (1968, *regie* Hübner); Schiller's *Don Carlos* (1969, *regie* Hübner); Goethe's *Torquato Tasso* (1969, *regie* Stein); Shakespeare's *The Tempest* (1969, *regie* Grüber); Gotthold Lessing's *Nathan der Weise* (*Nathan the Wise*, 1970, *regie* Hübner); the Speer/Shakespeare *Der Kunst der Zähmung*

(*The Art of Taming*, 1971, *regie* Hübner); Schiller's *Mary Stuart* (1972, *regie* Minks); Shakespeare's *Twelfth Night* (1972, *regie* Alfred Kirchner); Samuel Beckett's *Krapp's Last Tape* (1973, *regie* Grüber); and Shakespeare's *Troilus and Cressida* (1973, *regie* Hübner—his last at Bremen).

Hübner's tenure was not free of controversy, on stage or off, as he quarreled with many people including the city fathers. In 1973, he left Bremen for Berlin where he is now head of the Freie Volksbühne.

On coming to Bremen, Peter Stoltzenberg (Hübner's follower) had promised the local authorities a more sensible approach to productions by avoiding experimentation. Experimental productions did come at the end of his tenure (1973–1978), with the work of George Tabori. Hübner had success with both classics and modern works. Most of the best works of the Stoltzenberg era were modern: Maxim Gorky's *Enemies* (1973, *regie* Matthes Masuth); Beckett's *Waiting for Godot* (1973, *regie* Samy Molcho); Georg Büchner's *Woyzeck* (1974, *regie* Christof Nel); Charles Mère's *The Marquis de Sade* (1976, *regie* Bernd-Maria Krieger); Hauptmann's *Die Ratten* (*The Rats*, 1976, *regie* Dieter Rieble); Odön von Horváth's *Kasimir und Karoline* (1977, *regie* Rieble); and Shakespeare's *Hamlet* (1978, *regie* Tabori), with large doses of nudity and much of it played in a bed.

Stoltzenberg left in 1978 and was replaced by Arno Wüstenhofer. The years 1978–1980 constituted an astonishing period, almost the equal of the Hübner era. With Wüstenhofer came Frank-Patrick Steckel, as director of theatre activities, and Klaus Völker, as dramaturge. The byword for the Wüstenhofer period was "experimentation." The first production, Hans Henny Jahnn's *Die Kronüng Richards III* (*The Coronation of Richard III*, *regie* Steckel), was done in the local stockyards with the audience walking around during the performance. A list of important productions from this period would include Schiller's *Mary Stuart* (1978, *regie* Nicolas Brieger), with Barbara Petrich in the title role and sets by Johannes Schutz; August Strindberg's *To Damascus* (1979, *regie* Steckel); Chekhov's *The Three Sisters* (1979, *regie* Brieger); Goethe's *Stella* (1979, *regie* Peter Mussbach); Plato's *Symposium* (1979, *regie* Wolf Redl), with Norbert Schwientek as Socrates; Shakespeare's *Richard II* (1980, *regie* Stekel), with Peter Roggisch as the king; *Hamlet* (1980, *regie* Jürgen Gosch), with Wolf Redl in the title role; Ulrika Minhof's *Bambule* (1981, *regie* Nikola Weisse and Gustav Gisiger); Molière's *Tartuffe* (1981, *regie* Ernst Wendt); and Tankred Dorst's *Die Villa* (1981, *regie* Steckel).

The Hübner and Steckel-Wüstenhofer eras are well documented in the local papers (and throughout West Germany). The people of Bremen were pleased to see Bremen's name in publicity about the company. In the spring of 1981, the local fathers had to cut 5 million DM from the theatre's operating budget, which meant Steckel was forced to leave and theatre operations had to be curtailed. A series of protest meetings was scheduled by the public and the acting company, culminating in a giant mass meeting on October 31, 1981. "Gegen den Bremen Theatertod" brought many theatrical celebrities from the Hübner era back to

Bremen, including Hübner himself, Zadek, Ganz, and Stein. The net result was a sadly abbreviated season for the theatre, opera, and ballet.

The company normally does twelve new productions a year and it may carry over productions from the previous season. The acting company includes thirteen men and ten women, in addition to guests. Within the company is a small ensemble called the Grüppe Zauberflöte (Magic Flute) which employs three dramaturges and six *regisseurs*, one of whom, Jürgen Gosch, is from East Germany. The company plays in three main houses: the Theater am Goetheplatz (989 seats), which is normally used for opera and ballet; the Kammerspiele in der Böttcherstrasse (196 seats), which is the same Kammerspiele of the postwar era; and the big room stage, the Concordia (200 places with flexible seating), which is used for modern and experimental theatre. The whole operation has been receiving a 27 million DM subsidy, and the theatre usually has 83 percent capacity.

The people of Bremen, believing that theatre can change people, reject any sort of museum feeling in the theatre—hence, the liveliness of both the productions and the acting. The company is much admired throughout German-speaking Europe.

LEON M. AUFDEMBERGE

THEATRE ON THE HALLESCHEN CANAL
Schaubühne am Halleschen Ufer
Hallesches Ufer 32
1000 West Berlin 61, West Germany

In the few short years since its founding, the Theatre on the Halleschen Canal has grown from a small collective to the most adventurous in West Germany. Its *regisseurs* are among the most prestigious in West Germany, and its productions are reviewed by all major critics in the West, and occasionally in the East, as the philosophy of the company is West German Marxism.

The company was actually founded in 1962, when a group of students rented a building on one of the canals in West Berlin (Halleschen Ufer) and formed a collective to produce plays, away from the commercial aspects of the West Berlin theatre. The plays they produced came from a variety of sources: Arnold Wesker, Sternheim, Carlo Goldoni, Shakespeare, Samuel Beckett, and many others. The group was Marxist but not rigidly so. From the beginning the company was popular with the public because of its low prices and the quality of its productions, even though the acting was frequently judged mediocre.

In the early 1960s, Peter Stein, then one of Germany's young and very experimental *regisseurs*, eyed the company as a possible place to settle. He had worked with Kurt Hübner at Bremen, later staging several works at Zurich (extremely upsetting to the Swiss), and a production of Peter Weiss' *Vietnam Diskurs* (*Vietnam Discourse*) at Munich's Intimate Theatre, which had ended with a collection for the Vietcong. In 1968 Stein staged a repeat production at the Schaubühne and in 1970 went on to do two more, Edward Bond's *Early Morning* and Thomas Middleton's *The Changeling*. He brought some actors with him who had worked at Bremen (Edith Clever, Werner Rehm, and Jutta Günther Lempe, who would eventually settle in Berlin). In 1970 it was decided that Stein and his actors would stay; Jürgen Schitthelm and Klaus Weiffenbach, remaining from the old Schaubühne, would act as managers. In October of that year Stein staged his first production for the newly formed all-professional troupe, Brecht's *Die Mutter* (*The Mother*), with Therese Giehse (of Zurich, Munich, and the Berliner Ensemble) as the title character. It was greeted with cheers and firmly launched the company.

From the beginning of Stein's involvement as principal *regisseur*, certain decisions were made. The company acted as a collective with all major decisions made by all members of the company. Actors never read "cold" for a part. There would be no intendant; rather a board of governors, who would be part of the collective, would overlook the business end of the company, and actors would suggest both choice of play and preparation of a work. Differences of opinion—and there were many—would be openly aired, and salaries were to be paid according to need. The ensemble was to attend workshops on Marxism; 70 percent of the budget came from a West German subsidy, and the rest from box office receipts. Everyone had a voice in the expenditure of funds.

Dieter Sturm, who arrived with Stein, served as principal dramaturge for the company. He and Stein, concerned about the quality of the company's work, frequently spent up to fourteen hours a day with the company. Actors were required to attend all rehearsals of *Die Mutter* and were asked to make comments after the rehearsal of a scene. The second play was anything but Marxist: Peter Handke's *Der Ritt über der Bodensee* (*The Ride across Lake Constance*), directed by Claus Peymann and first performed in January 1971. Because of the nature of the plays, both Bonn and Berlin made movements to stop the payment of the subsidy of the company. Fortunately, the publicity the company was receiving in the West German press put a quick stop to this attempt.

In May 1971 the troupe had its first enormous success. Some critics said it was the most important play production in West Germany since the end of World War II. Stein's staging of Ibsen's *Peer Gynt* was hailed by the *Theater Heute* as the major event of 1971. The work was staged in seven sections and over two evenings, with six actors playing seven stages in Peer's life. (One of the young Peers came back later as an older Peer.) The company studied a number of aspects of nineteenth-century life (including pornography) and aspects of Ibsen's career. The play was staged in an enormous exhibition hall, with room for seven hundred spectators on two sides. The play was interpreted as a contemporary comment on Peer's aspirations in a bourgeois society. Eventually, it was televised; it also played a not-too-happy engagement in Zurich. In 1972 Stein produced Vsevolod Vishnevsky's *The Optimistic Tragedy*, an old favorite at the nearby Berliner Ensemble, and Heinrich von Kleist's *Prinz Friedrich von Homburg* (*The Prince of Homburg*), which was played as a dream. Botho Strauss, one of West Germany's leading dramatists, served as dramaturge for the production. In the same year, Klaus Michael Grüber did the staging for Odön von Horváth's *Geschichten aus dem Wiener Wald* (*Tales of the Vienna Woods*), and in 1974, he and Stein did a joint production of *The Bacchae*, with the set by Gilles Aillaud and Eduardo Arroyo, consisting of 100,000 watts of neon tubing. The text was part Euripides, part Wittgenstein, part mumbling, and part Hübner, with Edith Clever scoring a solid success as Agave and Bruno Ganz as Pentheus. There were also horses, meat-eating dogs, and gobs of blood and violence.

In 1974 Stein staged and later filmed a poetic and atmospheric *Summer Guests* by Maxim Gorky, which he adapted to stress the parallels between the bourgeois society of Gorky's day and present-day West German society. In the same year he staged a two-part work which he adapted called *Shakespeare's Memory*, also done later on West German television. It was performed in the enormous cavern of the film studios of the CCC in Spandau, the evening consisting of a series of lectures, scenes, readings, and music of the period, depicting Shakespeare and his world.

Stein used the same studio for his production of Shakespeare's *As You Like It* (1977), which began with the audience standing in a modified Elizabethan theatre and with all the court scenes being played one after another. From there, the spectators went through a long maze filled with greenery and were then ushered into the forest of Arden, complete with passageways, gangplanks, houses, Robinson Crusoe (or something like him), a stuffed stag, and so on, and seats for the audience. The whole of the forest of Arden was enormous; yet the actors were clearly heard, especially the Jacques who tired of the German in "All the world's a stage" speech and recited it in English to great audience applause. The first scenes at court were played in Elizabethan dress, as was the final wedding scene; the rest were in modern dress. Stein had no curtain call, yet the audience stood applauding for fifteen minutes after the wedding float, which carried the actors off, had disappeared.

In December 1977 the company presented an elaborate adaptation of Friedrich Hölderlin's *Hyperion, oder die Ermit in Griecheland* (*Hyperion, or the Investigation of Greece*), entitled *Winterreise* (*Winter Journey*), with the staging entrusted to Grüber in the Olympic Stadium. Most West German critics in their annual poll in *Theatre Heute* thought it the theatrical event of the 1977–1978 season. In the 1978–1979 season Lucy Bondy did a stylish representation of Alfred de Musset's *No Trifling with Love*. In the 1979–1980 season Stein staged the world premiere of Strauss' *Gross und Klein* (*Big and Little*), with Edith Clever, followed by the American Bob Wilson's *Death and Destruction and Detroit*, staging by the author. A majority of critics in *Theater Heute* voted both plays to be the best new plays of the season, German and foreign, respectively. In 1980 Stein staged Aeschylus' *The Oresteia*.

The company has been together since 1970, and, as is inevitable, there have been some splits. Peymann went to Stuttgart and then to Bochum, and Giskes went to Hamburg, but many members of the original Stein company remain.

There are now twenty-two actors and eight actresses in the permanent company. The troupe generally mounts four plays a season (it must do this number to receive a subsidy), and attendance is an extremely high 97 percent capacity. The theatre in which the company does most of its work is very small, seating only 539, and the West German government is considering building a new theatre for the company. The company likes to tour, but obviously many of its best productions cannot fit ordinary theatres.

The company has resisted the temptation to become just an ordinary mill to grind out productions or do a play for the fun of it. Its subsidy is high, but it does not take it for granted. The company itself is extremely cooperative, even with visiting American scholars. Conditions in the company are perhaps the most ideal in West Germany, and each production is approached with enormous care.

LEON M. AUFDEMBERGE

THEATRE ON THE LEHNINER PLATZ
(Schaübuhne am Lehniner Platz)
Kurfürstendamm 153
1000 West Berlin 31, West Germany

The Theatre on the Lehniner Platz was founded by Leni Langenscheidt, Waltraud Mau, Jürgen Schitthelm, and Klaus Weiffensbach as the Schaubühne am Halleschen Ufer in 1962. (The Hallesches Ufer is one of the many canals in Berlin.) The building they used (architect Jacobs) was not intended as a theatre and had been built in 1960 as a Social Democratic office, but the founders created a 539-seat theatre and opened with Arno Suassuna's *Auto da compadelida*, which the Germans call *Das Testament des Hundes* (*regie* Konrad Swinarski), on September 21, 1962. The company's repertory and its methodology were greatly influenced by the work of the Berliner Ensemble and the Piccolo Teatro of Milan; they were social as well as popular, with both revolutionary plays and absurdist works.

Most of the company's early productions were modern and relied heavily on the work of several *regisseurs*, Konrad Swinarski, and Hagen Müller-Stahl, with Harmut Lange as a dramaturge/*regisseur*. Critics admired the organization's vigor and its freedom of production; from the first the theatre was a *regisseur's* company. It might be added that the Schaubühne began touring early in its career. In the first years of its life, the Schaubühne presented the following, which were much admired: Arnold Wesker's *Roots* (1963, *regie* Müller-Stahl); Alesander Siskowo-Kobylin's *Tarellkin's Death* (1964, *regie* Swinarski); Odön von Horváth's *Kasimir und Karoline* (1964, *regie* Müller-Stahl); the Sophocles/Friedrich Hölderlin/Bertolt Brecht *Antigone* (1965, *regie* Claus Peymann); Marieluise Fleisser's *Der starke Stamm* (*The Strong Stock*, 1966, *regie* Müller-Stahl); Peter Hacks' *Die Schlacht bei Lobositz* (*The Battle near Lobositz*, 1966, *regie* Wolfgang Schwiedrzik and Harmut Lange); the premiere of Lange's *Die Erlösung des Gelehrten Chien Wan-hsüan* (*The Redemption of the Learned Chien Wan-*

hsüan, 1967, *regie* Schwiedrzik); Brecht's *Im Dickicht der Städte* (*In the Jungle of the Cities*, 1968, *regie* Müller-Stahl); and Nikolai Erdman's *The Suicide* (1969, *regie* Müller-Stahl).

In 1968 Peter Stein staged a production of Peter Weiss' *Vietnam Diskurs* (*Vietnam Discourse*) at Munich's Intimate Theatre, a production so radical it was soon closed. The same year Stein was asked to repeat the production at the Schaubühne, with the same result: a few performances and then it was shut down. Stein had gone on to stage Schiller's *Kabale und Liebe* (*Intrigue and Love*, 1968) and Goethe's *Torquato Tasso* (1969) at Bremen, followed by two highly radical productions in Zurich, Edward Bond's *Early Morning* (1970) and Thomas Middleton and Matthew Rowley's *The Changeling* (1970).

In 1970 Stein was asked to reorganize the company along more radical lines. Working with Dieter Sturm (a dramaturge who had been with the company at the beginning and had left), Claus Peymann, and others, he drew up a working plan for the collective running of the theatre, which was put into effect. A group of young actors with whom Stein had worked at Bremen (Edith Clever, Jutta Lampe, Werner Rehm, and Bruno Ganz) would form the nucleus of the company. The model for the collectivization would be the Berliner Ensemble, and the idea for the *regisseurs'* work came largely from Hübner in Bremen. Plays would be attacked from a variety of angles, with actors participating in all lines. The play's social ideas as in the staging of Ibsen's *Peer Gynt*, would be discussed at length, and the company would study Victorian pornography. The result was a highly experimental, very political theatre, though not radical in either department. Much of the company's success lay not only in its *regisseurs*, but also its dramaturges, namely, Botho Strauss (now one of West Germany's leading playwrights) and Sturm. The first play Stein staged for the organization was the Bertolt Brecht/Maxim Gorky *Die Mutter* (*The Mother*, October 8, 1970), with Therese Giehse (as guest) as Pelageja Wlassowa. The new approach to theatre was the focus of discussion in the West German Berlin papers the next day.

After *Die Mutter*, Stein staged the next three works: Peter Handke's *Der Ritt über den Bodensee* (*The Ride across Lake Constance*), H. M. Enzenberger's *Das Verhor von Habana* (*The Examination of Havana*), and Gerhard Kelling's *Die Auseinandersetzung* (*The Explanation*, all 1971). Then in May 1971 Stein unveiled his two-part production of Ibsen's *Peer Gynt*, which *Theater Heute* selected as the best production of 1971. The production literally made the company one of the most famous in Europe. With Lampe as Solvej and Clever as Asse, there were five Peers to play the title role in seven progressions: Michael König (1), Ganz (2 and 7), Wolf Redl (3 and 5), Dieter Laser (4), and Rehm (6). The sets were by Karl-Ernst Hermann and the dramaturgy by Strauss.

After *Peer Gynt* the company staged a string of highly experimental productions (uncredited productions throughout are Stein's): Hugo von Hofmannsthal's *Das gerettete Venedig* (*Venice Preserved*, 1971, *regie* Jan Kauenhowen and Frank-Patrick Steckel); Vsevolod Vishnevsky's *The Optimistic Tragedy* (1972); Horváth's *Geschichten aus dem Wiener Wald* (*Tales of the Vienna Woods*, 1972, *regie* Klaus Michael Grüber); Heinrich von Kleist's *Prinz Friedrich von Homburg* (*The Prince of Homburg*, 1972), with Ganz in the title role; Marieluise Fleisser's *Fegefeuer in Ingolstadt* (*Purgatory in Ingolstadt*, 1972); Botho Strauss' *Die Hypochonder* (*The Hypochondriac*, 1973, *regie* and sets by Wilfried Minks); and the Strauss adaptation of Eugene Labiche's *Pots of Money*, called *Das Sparschwein* (*The Piggy Bank*, 1973).

In 1973 came two evenings (side by side) called *Antikenprojekt*: the first under Stein's direction was called *Übungen für Schauspieler* (*Exercises for Actors*), and the second was based on Euripides' *The Bacchae* (*dramaturgie* Dieter Sturm, *regie* Grüber), with Ganz as Pentheus and Clever as Agave. These productions signaled an increasingly collective approach to projects that had been building since Stein came to the company. The mid-1970s saw the company's continued operation, doing both set scripts and projects, classic and modern, played in the home theatre, in the Berlin's Messehalle, or the CCC Studios. Among these works were Peter Handke's *Die Unvernünftigen sterben aus* (*The Fools Are Dying Out*, 1973); Heiner Müller's *Der Lohndrucker* (*The Undercutter*, 1973, *regie* Steckel); Gorky's *Summer Guests* (1974); a project (*dramaturgie* Sturm) based on the works of Friedrich Hölderlin called *Empedokles. Hölderlin lesen* (*Empedokles. Hölderlin Lecturing*, 1975, *regie* Grüber), with Ganz as the protagonist; Brecht's *Der Untergant des Egoisten Fatzer* (*The Sinking of the Egotistical Fatzer*, 1976, *regie* Steckel); a project called *Shakespeare's Memory* (1976, devised and staged by Stein) and done in the CCC Studio; Alfred de Musset's *No Trifling with Love* (1977, *regie* Bondy); an adaptation from Courteline called *Die ganz begreifliche Angst von Schlagen* (*The Comprehensible Fear of Being Hit*, 1977, *regie* collective); and Shakespeare's *As You Like It* (1977), with Lampe as Rosalind, done in the CCC Studios.

The production of *Winterreise* (*Winter Journey*) came in December 1977 (*regie* Grüber), a production that could be called the ultimate in the Schaubühne history. The work was staged by Grüber in the Olympia-Stadion, before a mock-up of the old Anhalter-Bahnhof, which had been destroyed in the war (designed by the Italian Antonio Recalcati). The work was based on the writings of Hölderlin, adapted by Grüber (*dramaturgie* Bernard Putrat and Ellen Hammer), and concerned the metaphysical journey of Hyperion (Willem Menne), with Hölderlin's words (particularly from *Hyperion*) flashed on the scoreboard. The work also recalled Schubert's great cycle of the same name. Although many playgoers were puzzled, most were moved as the production progressed through time, and both metaphysical and actual space. (There was an actual track meet during the production.) While the work was done for a very short run (eight performances), fortunately it was filmed.

Since *Winterreise*, the company has retained its experimental policy and has moved in several different directions. First, it has produced more social plays, including some in Turkish, with which Stein hoped to pull in the local Turkish population. Second, it has invited several very radical *regisseurs* to bring in productions or stage them with the company (Robert Wilson and Meredith

Monk). Third, it has arranged many small-cast shows to balance the big works. Among these productions have been Botho Strauss' *Trilogie des Wiedersehens* (*Three Acts of Recognition*, 1978); the premiere of Strauss' *Gross und Klein* (*Big and Little*, 1978), with Clever as Lottie; Ernst Jandl's *Aus der Fremde* (*Out of Foreign Countries*, *regie* Ellen Hammer); a highly political production of Aeschylus' *The Oresteia* (1980), with Clever as Clytemnestra; Georg Büchner's *Woyzeck* (1981, *regie* König); Nigel Williams' *Class Enemy* (1981); and Franz Xaver Kroetz's *Nicht Fisch, Nicht Fleisch* (*Not Fish, Not Meat*, 1981).

One of the company's chief needs from the beginning was for an adequate theatre. The one on the Hallesches Ufer was too small in terms of audience space and technical facilities. On September 21, 1981, the company inaugurated a new theatre (of this more later), with an all-day production of *The Oresteia*. Since then the company has gone on to experiment with what the new theatre can do in a double bill of Pierre Marivaux's *The Dispute* (1981, *regie* Stein) and *The Sincere Ones* (1981, *regie* Prader); Ernst Barlach's *Der blaue Boll* (*The Blue Boll*, 1981, *regie* Steckel); and a Meredith Monk project. With the move, the company became the Theatre on the Lehniner Platz.

All company decisions are collective, including salaries, casting, and choice of plays. Despite this approach, the organization is known almost universally as Peter Stein's company, with Stein keeping a very open door policy. The company does four to seven plays a season and must do four to keep its subsidy. The permanent acting company totals nineteen men and ten women with guests. (Part of the company is Turkish). In addition, there are three dramaturges and, for the 1981–1982 season, seven *regisseurs*, including Bondy, Grüber, Steckel and Stein. Its current budget is 15 million DM, of which 12.7 million is subsidy. The subsidy is a source of some jealousy among West German intendants as West Germany pays for the life of West Berlin (which includes theatre).

The company has done considerable work on television, several plays have been filmed, and touring has been extensive, even in East Germany. Attendance runs to around 95 percent capacity.

The theatre in which the company plays is one of the high spots of Berlin architecture. Originally built in 1928 by Erich Mendelssohn, the Mendelssohn Complex was very art deco in style with a little Bauhaus. In 1978 the West Berlin Senate voted to equip the renovated theatre (architect Jürgen Sawadg) at the cost of around 30 million DM. The acting space is actually one large room, with a plaster dome at one end, and can be used as one huge theatre or three theatres, with hydraulic jacks under the floor to raise any portion for variable seating of up to 1,500 spectators.

There have been some problems of late, namely, some productions have not been of the customary high quality, with the 1979 production of Schiller's *Die Räuber* (*The Robbers*, *regie* Schafer) so disastrous that West Berlin critics asked themselves some fundamental questions about the future of the theatre. In the last seasons it has lost some actors to other companies or to the more lucrative West German film industry. Still, the Schaubühne remains one of the most experimental and vital theatres in the world.

LEON M. AUFDEMBERGE

Suggestions for Additional Reading

Compiled by Joel A. Adedeji, Leon M. Aufdemberge, Edward J. Czerwinski, Kathy Foley, Mei-shu Hwang, Ho Soon Kim, Colby H. Kullman, Michael Mullin, Robert Page, Lance Reppert, Farley Richmond, Andrew T. Tsubaki, Surapone Virulrak, Carla Waal, and George Woodyard.

GENERAL REFERENCE WORKS

Anderson, Michael, et al. *Crowell's Handbook of Contemporary Drama*. New York: Thomas Y. Crowell Company, 1971.

Bentley, Eric. *In Search of Theatre*. New York: Alfred A. Knopf, 1953.

Esslin, Martin, introd. *The Encyclopedia of World Theatre*. New York: Charles Scribner's Sons, 1977.

Garzanti, Aldo, ed. *Enciclopedia Garzanti dello Spettacolo*. Milan, Italy: Redazioni Garzanti, 1977.

Gassner, John, and Quinn, Edward, eds. *The Reader's Encyclopedia of World Drama*. New York: Thomas Y. Crowell Company, 1969.

Handel, Beatrice, ed. *The National Directory for the Performing Arts and Civic Centers*. 3d ed. New York: John Wiley and Sons, 1978.

Hartnoll, Phyllis, ed. *The Oxford Companion to the Theatre*. 3d ed. London: Oxford University Press, 1967.

Kindermann, Heinz, et al. *Theatergeschicte Europas*. 10 vols. Salzburg: Otto Müller, 1974.

McGraw-Hill Encyclopedia of World Drama: An International Reference Work. 4 vols. New York: McGraw-Hill, 1972.

Matlaw, Myron. *Modern World Drama: An Encyclopedia*. New York: E. P. Dutton and Company, 1972.

Melchinger, Siegfried, and Rischeiter, Henning. *Welttheater*. Braunschweig: Georg Westermann Verlag, 1962.

Mokul'skij, S. S., et al., eds. *Teatral'naja Enciklopedija*. 5 vols. Moscow: Gosudarstvennoe Naučnoe-techincesko Izdatel'stvo, 1961–1967.

Pride, Leo B., ed. *International Theatre Dictionary: A World Directory of the Theatre and Performing Arts.* New York: Simon and Schuster, 1973.

AFRICA

Asein, Samuel O. "African Drama in the African University." *Bulletin of Black Theatre* (Spring/Summer 1974):7–8.

Banham, Martin, and Clive Wake. *African Theatre Today.* London: Pittman Publishing, 1976.

Cary, Robert. *The Story of Reps: The History of Salisbury Repertory Players, 1931–1975.* Salisbury, Rhodesia: Galaxie Press, 1975.

Clark, Ebun. *Hurbert Ogunde, The Making of Nigerian Theatre.* Oxford: Oxford University Press, 1979.

Cornevin, Robert. *Le théâtre en Afrique et à Madagascar.* Paris: Le Livre Africain, 1970.

DeGraft, J. C. "Roots in African Drama and Theatre." In *African Literature Today: 8 Drama in Africa.* Ed. Eldred Durosimi Jones. London: Heinemann, 1976, pp. 1–25.

East, N. B. "African Theatre: A Checklist of Critical Materials." *Afro-Asian Theatre Bulletin* 4, no. 2 (Spring 1969):N3–N17.

Ekom, Ernest. "The Development of Theatre in Nigeria, 1960–1967." *Journal of the New African Literature and the Arts* (Summer and Fall 1971):36–49.

Enekwe, Ossie Onuora. "Theatre in Nigeria: The Modern vs. the Traditional." *Yale/Theatre* 8, no. 1 (Fall 1976):62–67.

Etherton, Michael. "Trends in African Theatre." In *African Literature Today: 10 Retrospect and Prospect.* Ed. Eldred Durosimi Jones. London: Heinemann, 1979, pp. 57–85.

Graham-White, Anthony. *The Drama of Black Africa.* London: Samuel French, 1974.

———. "West African Drama: Folk, Popular, and Literary." Ph.D. Diss., Stanford University, 1969.

Horn, Andrew. "Individualism and Community in the Theatre of Serumaga." In *African Literature Today: 12 New Writing, New Approaches.* Ed. Eldred Durosimi Jones. London: Heinemann, 1982, pp. 22–48.

Irele, Abiola, ed. *Theatre in Africa.* Ibadan, Nigeria: Ibadan University Press, 1978.

July, Robert W. *A History of the African People.* New York: Charles Scribner's Sons, 1970.

Kennedy, J. Scott. *In Search of African Theatre.* New York: Charles Scribner's Sons, 1973.

Mbughini, L. A. "Old and New Drama from East Africa." In *African Literature Today: 8 Drama in Africa.* Ed. Eldred Durosimi Jones. London: Heinemann, 1976, pp. 85–98.

Nketia, J. H. Kwabena. *Ghana—Music, Dance and Drama.* Legon: University of Ghana, 1965.

Obafemi, Olu. "Revolutionary Aesthetics in Recent Nigerian Theatre." In *African Literature Today: 12 New Writing, New Approaches.* Ed. Eldred Durosimi Jones. London: Heinemann, 1982, pp. 118–136.

Vandenbroucke, Russell. "Introduction: African Theatre?" *Yale/Theatre* 8, no. 1 (Fall 1976):6–10.

ASIA

Arlington, L. C. *The Chinese Drama*. New York: Benjamin Blom, 1966.

Arnott, Peter D. *The Theatres of Japan*. New York: St. Martin's Press, 1969.

Baumer, Rachel Van M., and Brandon, James R., eds. *Sanskrit Drama in Performance*. Honolulu: University Press of Hawaii, 1981.

Bhavnani, Enakshi. *The Dance in India*. Bombay: Taraporevala's, 1965.

Bowers, Faubion. *Theatre in the East*. New York: Grove Press, 1960.

Brandon, James R. *Asian Theatre: A Study Guide and Annotated Bibliography*. A University College Theatre Association Publication, American Theatre Association, 1980.

————. *Brandon's Guide to Theatre in Asia*. Honolulu: University Press of Hawaii, 1976.

————, trans. *Kabuki: Five Classical Plays*. Cambridge: Harvard University Press, 1975.

————. *Theatre in Southeast Asia*. Cambridge: Harvard University Press, 1967.

————. *On Thrones of Gold: Three Javanese Shadow Plays*. Cambridge: Harvard University Press, 1970.

————, ed. *Traditional Asian Plays*. New York: Hill and Wang, 1972.

————, with Malm, William, and Shively, Donald. *Studies in Kabuki: Its Acting, Music, and Historical Content*. Honolulu: University Press of Hawaii, 1978.

Ernst, Earle. *The Kabuki Theatre*. Honolulu: University Press of Hawaii, 1974.

Foley, Mary Kathleen. "Sudanese Wayang Golek." Ph.D. Diss., University of Hawaii, 1979.

Fu-sheng, Li. *History of Chinese Drama*. Taipei: Cheng-Chung shu-chü, 1970.

Gargi, Balwant. *Folk Theatre of India*. Seattle: University of Washington Press, 1966.

————. *Theatre in India*. New York: Theatre Arts, 1962.

Gunji, Masakatsu. *Kabuki*. Palo Alto, Calif.: Kodansha International, 1969.

Guritno, Pandam. "Wayang Purwa." *Indonesian Quarterly* 2, no. 1 (1973):75–89.

Hadisoeseno, Harsono. "Wayang and Education." *Education and Culture* 8 (1955):2–19.

Halford, Aubrey S., and Halford, Giovanna M. *The Kabuki Handbook*. Tokyo: Tuttle, 1952.

Hatley, Barbara. "Ludruk and Ketoprak: Popular Theatre and Society in Java." *Review of Indonesian and Malayan Affairs* 7, no. 1 (1973):38–58.

————. "Wayang and Ludruk: Polarities in Java." *The Drama Review* 15, no. 3 (1971):88–101.

Hood, Mantle. "The Enduring Tradition: Music and Theatre in Java and Bali." In *Indonesia*. Ed. Ruth T. McVey. New Haven: Human Relations Area Files Press, 1963, pp. 438–471.

Hooykaas, Chiritiaan. *Kama and Kala: Materials for the Study of Shadow Theatre in Bali*. Amsterdam: North-Holland Publishing Company, 1973.

Inoura, Yoshinobu, and Kawatake, Toshio. *The Traditional Theater of Japan*. Tokyo: Japan Foundation, 1971.

Irwin, Vera, ed. *Four Classical Asian Plays*. Baltimore: Penguin Books, 1972.

Keene, Donald. *Bunraku: The Art of the Japanese Puppet Theatre*. Palo Alto, Calif.: Kodansha International, 1965.

————. *Four Major Plays of Chikamatsu*. New York: Columbia University Press, 1961.

————. *Nō: The Classical Theatre of Japan*. Palo Alto, Calif.: Kodansha International, 1966.

————, ed. *20 Plays of the Nō Theatre*. New York: Columbia University Press, 1970.

Kenny, Don. *A Guide to Kyōgen*. Tokyo: Hinoki Shoten, 1968.

————. *On Stage in Japan*. Tokyo: Shufunotomo Company, 1974.

Korean Center or the ITI. *The Korean Theatre Past and Present*. Seoul: Korean National Commission for UNESCO, 1981.

Kunst, Jaap. *Music in Java: Its History, Its Theory, and Its Technique*. Trans. Emile von Loo. The Hague: Martinus Nijhoff, 1949.

Leiter, Samuel L., trans. *The Art of Kabuki: Famous Plays in Performance*. Los Angeles: University of California Press, 1979.

————. *Kabuki Encyclopedia: An English Language Adaptation of Kabuki Jiten*. Westport, Conn.: Greenwood Press, 1979.

Long, Roger. *Javanese Shadow Theatre: Movement and Characterization in Ngayogyakarta Wayang Kulit*. Ann Arbor, Mich.: UMI Research Press, 1983.

McKinnon, Richard N. *Selected Plays of Kyōgen*. Tokyo: Uniprint, 1968.

Malm, William P. *Japanese Music and Musical Instruments*. Rutland, Vt.: Tuttle, 1959.

————. *Music Cultures of the Pacific, the Near East, and Asia*. Englewood Cliffs, N.J.: Prentice-Hall, 1967.

Mellema, R. L. *Wayang Puppets*. Amsterdam: Koninklijk Instituut voor de Tropen, 1954.

Nippon Gakujitsu Shinkōkai. *The Noh Drama, Ten Plays from the Japanese*. Rutland, Vt.: Tuttle, 1960.

O'Neill, P. G. *Early Nō Drama, Its Background, Character and Development, 1300–1450*. London: Lund Humphries, 1958.

————. *A Guide to Nō*. Tokyo: Hinoki Shoten, 1960.

Peacock, James. *Rites of Modernization: Symbolic and Social Aspects of Indonesian Proletarian Drama*. Chicago: University of Chicago Press, 1968.

Pronko, Leonard C. *Theatre East and West: Prospectives Toward a Total Theatre*. Los Angeles: University of California Press, 1967.

Rangacharya, Adya. *The Indian Theatre*. New Delhi: National Book Trust, 1971.

Rao, P.S.R. Appa. *A Monograph on Bharata's Naatya Saastra: Indian Dramatology*. Hyderabad: Naatya Maalaa Publishers, 1967.

Sakanishi, Shio, trans. *Japanese Folk Plays*. Rutland, Vt.: Tuttle, 1960.

Scott, A. C. *The Classical Theatre of China*. London: George Allen and Unwin, 1957.

————. *The Theatre in Asia*. New York: Macmillan Publishing Company, 1972.

————, trans. *Traditional Chinese Plays, Vol. 1*. Madison: University of Wisconsin Press, 1967.

————, trans. *Traditional Chinese Plays, Vol. 2*. Madison: University of Wisconsin Press, 1969.

————, trans. *Traditional Chinese Plays, Vol. 3*. Madison: University of Wisconsin Press, 1975.

Shaver, Ruth M. *Kabuki Costume*. Rutland, Vt.: Tuttle, 1966.

Shibano, Dorothy Toshiko. *Kyōgen, the Comic as Drama*. Ph.D. Diss., University of Washington, 1973.

Soedarsono. *Dances in Indonesia*. Jakarta: Gunung Agung, 1974.

Takaya, Ted T., trans. *Modern Japanese Drama, an Anthology*. New York: Columbia University Press, 1979.

Tōgi, Masatarō. *Gagaku: Court Music and Dance*. New York: Walker/Weatherhill, 1970.

Traditional Performing Arts of Korea. Seoul: Korean National Commission for UNESCO, 1975.

Ueda, Makoto. *Literary and Art Theories in Japan.* Cleveland: The Press of Western Reserve University, 1967.

Van Buitenen, J.A.B., trans. *Two Plays of Ancient India.* New York: Columbia University Press, 1968.

Vatsyayan, Kapila. *Traditional Indian Theatre: Multiple Streams.* New Delhi: National Book Trust, 1980.

Virulrak, Surapone. *Likay: A Popular Theatre in Thailand.* Ph.D Diss., University of Hawaii, 1980.

Zoetmulder, P. J. "The Wayang as a Philosophical Theme." *Indonesia* 12 (1971):85–96.

AUSTRALIA

Brodsky, Isadore. *Sydney Takes the Stage.* Sydney: Old Sydney Free Press, 1963.

Carroll, Brian. *Australian Stage Album.* Melbourne: Macmillan, 1975.

Encore Australia. (Theatre journal published in New South Wales.)

Fitzpatrick, Peter. *After "The Doll."* Melbourne: Edward Arnold, 1979.

Harcourt, Peter. *A Dramatic Appearance: New Zealand Theatre 1920–1970.* Wellington, New Zealand: Methuen, 1978.

Holloway, Peter. *Contemporary Australian Drama.* Sydney: Currency, 1981.

Irvin, Eric. *Theatre Comes to Australia.* St. Lucia, Queensland: University of Queensland Press, 1971.

Kingston, Claude. *It Don't Seem a Day Too Much.* Kent Town, Australia: Rigby, 1971.

Kramer, Leonie, ed. *The Oxford History of Australian Literature.* Melbourne and New York: Oxford University Press, 1981.

McGuire, Paul. *The Australian Theatre.* London and Melbourne: Oxford University Press, 1948.

Porter, Hal. *Stars of Australian Stage and Screen.* Rigby: Angus and Robertson, 1965.

Rees, Leslie. *A History of Australian Drama.* 2 vols. Sydney: Angus and Robertson, 1978.

Theatre Australia. (Australia's monthly magazine of the performing arts.)

"Theatre in Australia." *Theatre Quarterly* 7, no. 26 (Summer 1977):49–110.

West, John. *Theatre in Australia.* Melbourne, Australia: Cassell, 1978.

Williams, Margaret A., ed. "Drama." In *Australian Writers and Their Work.* Ed. Grahame Johnston. Melbourne and New York: Oxford University Press, 1977.

CANADA

Ball, J., ed. "Theatre in Canada: A Bibliography." *Canadian Literature* 14 (Autumn 1963): 85–100.

Canadian Literature. (A quarterly journal containing criticism and reviews published at the University of British Columbia, Vancouver.)

Canadian Theatre Review. (A theatre magazine published at York University, Downsview, Ontario.)

Grant, Judith Skelton, ed. *Robertson Davies, The Well-Tempered Critic: One Man's View of Theatre and Letters in Canada.* Toronto: McClelland and Stewart, 1981.

Journal of Canadian Studies. (A journal published at Trent University, Petersborough, Ontario.)

Park, Julian, ed. *The Culture of Contemporary Canada.* Ithaca, N.Y.: Cornell University Press, 1957.

Parker, Brian. "Is There a Canadian Drama?" in *The Canadian Imagination.* Ed. David Staines. Cambridge, Mass.: Harvard University Press, 1977.

Performing Arts in Canada. (A magazine published in Ontario, Canada.)

Phelps, Arthur L. "Canadian Drama." *University of Toronto Quarterly* 9 (October 1939): 82–94.

Ripley, John. "Drama and Theatre." In *Literary History of Canada: Canadian Literature in English.* Ed. Carl F. Kinck. Vol. 3. Toronto and Buffalo: University of Toronto Press, 1976.

Story, Norah. *The Oxford Companion to Canadian History and Literature.* Toronto and New York: Oxford University Press, 1967.

Walsh, Paul, ed. *Canadian Theatre Checklist: 1982–83.* Downsview, Ontario: Canadian Theatre Review Publications, 1982.

EASTERN EUROPE

Anderson, Michael, et al., eds. *Crowell's Handbook of Contemporary Drama.* New York: Thomas Y. Crowell Company, 1971.

Burzyński, Tadeusz, and Osiński, Zbigniew. *Grotowski's Laboratory.* Warsaw: Interpress Publishers, 1979.

Czerwinski, E. J., ed. *Slavic and Eastern European Arts Journal.* Special issues devoted to Slavic and Eastern European theatre and drama (Spring 1983 and Fall 1983). Stony Brook, N.Y.: Slavic Cultural Center Press, 1983.

Dabrowski, Stanslaw, et al., eds. *Slownik biograficzny teatru polskiego, 1765–1965.* Warsaw: Państwowe Wydawnictwo Naukowe, 1973.

Esslin, Martin, introd. *The Encyclopedia of World Theatre.* New York: Charles Scribner's Sons, 1977.

Goetz-Stankiewicz, Marketa. *The Silenced Theatre: Czech Playwrights Without a Stage.* Toronto: University of Toronto Press, 1979.

Grodzicki, August. *Polish Theatre Directors.* Warsaw: Interpress Publishers, 1979.

Hausbrandt, Andrzej. *Tomaszewski's Mime Theatre.* Warsaw: Interpress Publishers, 1975.

Marshall, Herbert. *The Pictorial History of the Russian Theatre..* Introd. Harold Clurman. New York: Crown Publishers, 1977.

Mokul'skij, S. S., et al., eds. *Teatral'naja Enciklopedija.* 5 vols. Moscow: Gosudarst-vennoe Naučnoe-technicesko Izdatel'stvo'stvo, 1961–1967.

Raszewski, Zbigniew. *Krótka historia teatru polskiego.* Warsaw: Państwowy Instytut Wydawniczy, 1978.

Segel, Harold B. *Twentieth-Century Russian Drama.* New York: Columbia University Press, 1979.

Semil, Malgorzata, and Wysiński, Elźbieta. *Slownik wspólczesnego teatru.* Warsaw: Wydawnictwa Artystyczne i Filmowe, 1980.

Trensky, Paul I. *Czech Drama Since World War II.* White Plains, N.Y.: M. E. Sharpe, 1978 (Columbia Slavic Studies).

LATIN AMERICA

Adler, Heidrun. *Politisches Theater in Latein-Amerika: Von der Mythologie über die Mission zur Kollektiven Identität.* Berlin: Dietrich Reimer Verlag, 1982.

Boal, Augusto. *Técnicas latinoamericanas del teatro popular: Una revolución copernicana al revés.* Buenos Aires: Ediciones Corregidor Sarci y E., 1975.

Bravo Elizondo, Pedro. *Teatro hispanoamericano de crítica social.* Madrid: Playor, 1975.

Castillo, Susana. *El desarraigo en el teatro venezolano.* Caracas: Editorial Ateneo de Caracas, 1980.

Dauster, Frank. *Ensayos sobre el teatro hispanoamericano.* Mexico: Sepsetentas, 1975.

———. *Historia del teatro hispanoamericano, Siglos XIX y XX.* Mexico D.F.: Ediciones de Andrea, 1973.

Jones, Willis Knapp. *Behind Spanish American Footlights.* Austin: University of Texas Press, 1966.

Luzuriaga, Gerardo. *Popular Theatre for Social Change in Latin America.* Los Angeles: UCLA Latin American Center Publications, 1978.

Lyday, Leon F., and Woodyard, George W. *A Bibliography of Latin American Theatre Criticism, 1940–1974.* Austin: Institute of Latin American Studies, 1976.

———. *Dramatists in Revolt: The New Latin American Theatre.* Austin: University of Texas Press, 1976.

Ordaz, Luis, and Neglia, Erminio G. *Repertorio selecto del teatro hispanoamericano contemporáneo.* Caracas: Editorial Giannelli, 1975.

Rela, Walter. *Teatro brasileño.* Montevideo: Instituto de Cultura Uruguayo-Brasileño, 1980.

———. *Teatro uruguayo, 1807–1979.* Montevideo: Ediciones de Alianza, 1980.

Rojo, Grínor. *Orígenes del teatro hispanoamericano contemporáneo.* Valparaíso: Ediciones Universitarias de Valparaíso, 1972.

Tirri, Nestor. *Realismo y teatro argentino.* Buenos Aires: Ediciones la Bastilla, 1973.

Unger, Roni. *Poesía en Voz Alta in the Theater of México.* Columbia, Missouri: University of Missouri Press, 1981.

Watson Espener, Maida, and Reyes, Carlos José. *Materiales para una historia del teatro en Colombia.* Bogotá: Instituto Colombiano de Cultura, 1978.

MIDDLE EAST

Arberry, A. J. *Classical Persian Literature.* London: Allen and Unwin, 1958.

Browne, E. G. *A Literary History of Persia.* 4 vols. Cambridge, England: University Press, 1953.

Chelkowski, Peter J., ed. *Ta'ziyeh: Ritual Drama in Iran.* New York: New York University Press and Soroush Press, 1979.

Gershoni, Gershon K. *The Hebrew Theatre.* Jerusalem: Israel Digest, 1963.

Kohansky, Mendel. *The Hebrew Theatre: Its First Fifty Years.* New York: KTAV Publishing House, 1969.

Levy, Emanuel. *The Habima—Israel's National Theatre, 1917–1977: A Study of Cultural Nationalism.* New York: Columbia University Press, 1979.

Levy, Reuben. *An Introduction to Persian Literature.* New York: Columbia University Press, 1979.

Shakow, Zara. *The Theatre in Israel*. New York: Herzl Press, 1963.

Theatron 75/76. Tel-Aviv, Israel: Israeli Centre of the ITI, 1976.

SCANDINAVIA

Aarseth, Asbjørn. *Den Nationale Scene: 1901–31*. Oslo: Gyldendal, 1969.

Andersson, Elis. *Tjugofem säsonger: Pjäser och föreställninger på Lorensbergsteatern och Göteborgs Stadsteater 1926–1951*. Göteborg: Erik Hoglunds Bokförlag, 1957.

Anker, Øyvind. *Scenekunsten i Norge fra fortid til nutid*. Oslo: Dansk-Norsk Fond, 1968.

Barba, Eugenio. *The Floating Islands*. Ed. Ferdinando Taviani. Holstebro: Odin Teatret, 1979.

Bergman, Gösta M. *Den moderna teaterns genombrott: 1890–1925*. Stockholm: Bonniers, 1966.

————, ed. *Svensk teater: Strukturförändringar och organisation 1900–1970*. Stockholm: Almqvist and Wiksell, 1970.

————, and Brunius, Niklas, eds. *Dramaten 175 år*. Stockholm: P. A. Norstedt and Söners, 1963.

Brunius, Niklas, Eriksson, Gören O., and Rembe, Rolf. *Swedish Theatre*. Stockholm: Swedish Institute, n.d.

Carrol, Dennis, and Carrol, Elsa. "KOM-teatteri." *ETJ* 30 (1978):376–386.

Dalgard, Olav. *Det Norske Teatret: 1913–1953*. Oslo: Noregs boklag, 1953.

Einarsson, Sveinn. *Theatre in Iceland: 1971–1975*. Reykjavík: Actors Union, et al., 1976.

Ek, Sverker, ed. *Teater i Göteborg: 1910–1975*. 3 vols. Stockholm: Almqvist and Wiskell International, 1978.

Engel, P. G., ed. *Swedish Theatre Today*. Stockholm: Svensk Teaterunion, 1977.

————, and Janzon, Leif. *Sju decennier: Svensk teater under 1900-talet*. Lund: Forum, 1974.

Englund, Claes, and Sanders, Anki, eds. *Teaterårsboken 82*. [Solna]: Svenska Riksteatern/entré, 1982.

Entré. (Theatre journal published in Solna, Sweden.)

Heikkilä, Ritva, ed. *Suomen Kansallisteatteri*. Porvoo: Werner Söderström, 1972.

Henriques, Alf, et al. *Teatret paa Kongens Nytorv: 1748–1948*. Copenhagen: Berlingske forlag, 1948.

Jørgensen, Aage, ed. *Gruppeteater i Norden*. Copenhagen: Samlaren, 1981.

Koskimies, Rafael. *Suomen Kansallisteatteri, II: 1917–1950*. Helsinki: Otava, 1972.

Larsen, Erling. *Endvidere medvirkede—en slags scrapbog*. Copenhagen: n.p., 1982.

Lüchou, Marianne. *Svenska Teatern i Helsingfors*. Helsinki: Svenska Teatern, 1977.

Marker, Frederick J., and Marker, Lise-Lone. *The Scandinavian Theatre: A Short History*. Oxford: Basil Blackwell, 1975.

Martin, Timo, Niemi, Pertti, and Tainio, Ilona. *Suomen teatterit ja teatterintekiiät*. Helsinki: Tammi, 1974.

Neiiendam, Robert. *Det kongelige Teaters Historie: 1874–1922*. 5 vols. Copenhagen: Pio, 1921–1930.

Nygaard, Knut, and Eide, Eiliv. *Den National Scene: 1931–1976*. Oslo: Gyldendal, 1977.

Olsson, Tom J. A. *O'Neill och Dramaten*. Stockholm: Akademilitteratur, 1977.

Ornitofilene; Kaspariana; Ferai. Holstebro: Odin Teatret, n.d.

Rønneberg, Anton. *Nationaltheatret: 1949–1974*. Oslo: Gyldendal, 1974.

————. *Nationaltheatret gjennom femti år*. Oslo: Gyldendal, 1949.

Savutie, Maija. *Finnish Theatre*. Helsinki: Otava, 1980.

Schultén, Marius af. *Benois teaterhus*. Helsinki: Mercators, [1966].

Sejr, Emanuel, with Sven Gundel. *Aarhus Theater gennem 50 aar*. Aarhus: Universitetsforlaget, 1950.

Sjöberg, Alf. *Teater som besvärjelse: Artiklar från fem decennier*. Eds. Sverker R. Ek, et al. Stockholm: P. A. Norstedt and Söners, 1982.

Sjögren, Henrik. *Stage and Society in Sweden*. Stockholm: Swedish Institute, 1977.

Sletback, Nils, ed. *Det Norske Teatret, femti år: 1913–1963*. Oslo: Det norske samlaget, 1963.

Tampereen Työväen Teatteri. Tampere: n.p., 1976.

TDR (The Drama Review) 26, no. 3 (1982):T95.

Theatre in Denmark. No. 14 (1978–1979). Copenhagen: Danish Centre of ITI, [1979].

Theatre in the Five Scandinavian Countries. Stockholm: Nordiska Teaterunionen, 1971.

Theatre in Norway 1979. Oslo: Norsk Teaterunion and ITI, 1979.

Torsslow, Stig. *Dramatenaktörernas republik*. Stockholm: Kungl. Dramatiska teatern, 1975.

20 år med Stockholms Stadsteater: 1960–1980. Stockholm: [Stockholms Stadsteater], 1981.

20th Century Drama in Scandinavia. Helsinki: University of Helsinki, 1979.

Veltheim, Katri, and Tainio, Ilona, eds. *Finnish Theatre Today*. Helsinki: Finnish Centre of ITI, 1971.

Waal, Carla. *Johanne Dybwad: Norwegian Actress*. Oslo: Universitetsforlaget, 1967.

Weckström, Tor. *Chiewitz teaterhus*. Helsinki: Mercators, [1966].

Wiers-Jenssen, H. *Nationaltheatret gjennem 25 aar: 1899–1924*. Christiania: Gyldendalske Bokhandel, 1924.

————, and Nordahl-Olsen, Joh. *Den Nationale Scene: De første 25 aar*. Bergen: Gyldendal, 1926.

UNITED STATES OF AMERICA

Beeson, William, ed. *Thresholds: The Story of Nina Vance's Alley Theatre*. Houston: Wall and Company, 1968.

Berkowitz, Gerald M. *New Broadways: Theatre Across America, 1950–1980*. Totowa, N.J.: Rowman and Littlefield, 1982.

Bharucha, Rustom. "Anatomy of the Regional Theater," *Theatre* (Summer 1979):10–20.

Blum, Daniel, and Willis, John. *A Pictorial History of the American Theatre, 1860–1980*. New York: Crown Publishers, 1981.

Bogard, Travis, Moody, Richard, and Meserve, Walter J. *American Drama*. Vol. 8 of *The Revels of the Drama in English*. London: Methuen and Company, 1977.

Conolly, L. W., ed. *Theatrical Touring and Founding in North America*. Westport, Conn.: Greenwood Press, 1982.

Finnegan, Michael, ed. *Theatre Directory, 1979–1980*. New York: Theatre Communications Group, 1979.

Gard, Robert E., Blach, Marston, and Temkin, Pauline. *Theatre in America: Appraisal and Challenge*. New York: Theatre Arts Books, 1968.

Gassner, John. *Directions in Modern Theatre and Drama*. New York: Holt, Rinehart and Winston, 1966.

Gohdes, Clarence. *Literature and Theatre of the States and Regions of the U.S.A.: An Historical Bibliography*. Durham, N.C.: Duke University Press, 1967.

Gottfried, Martin. *A Theater Divided: The Postwar American Stage*. Boston and New York: Little, Brown, 1968.

Guthrie, Tyrone. *A New Theatre*. New York: McGraw-Hill, 1964.

Hewitt, Bernard. *Theatre U.S.A., 1668–1957*. New York: McGraw-Hill, 1959.

Hill, Errol, ed. *The Presenters/The Participants*. Vol. 2 of *The Theatre of Black Americans*. Englewood Cliffs, N.J.: Prentice-Hall, 1979.

———. *Roots and Rituals/The Image Makers*. Vol. 1 of *The Theatre of Black Americans*. Englewood Cliffs, N.J.: Prentice-Hall, 1979.

Jones, Margo. *Theatre-in-the-Round*. New York: Rinehart and Company, 1951.

Kazan, Elia. "Look, There's the American Theatre!" *Tulane Drama Review* 9, no. 2 (1964):61–83.

Larson, Carl F. W. *American Regional Theatre History to 1900: A Bibliography*. Metuchen, N.J.: Scarecrow Press, 1979.

Little, Stuart W. *Enter Joseph Papp: In Search of a New American Theater*. New York: Coward, McCann and Geoghegan, 1974.

Loney, Glen. *20th Century Theatre*. 2 vols. New York: Facts on File Publications, 1983.

Lowry, W. McNeil, ed. *The Performing Arts and American Society*. Englewood Cliffs, N.J.: Prentice-Hall, 1978.

Morison, Bradley G., and Fliehr, Kay. *In Search of an Audience: How an Audience Was Found for the Tyrone Guthrie Theatre*. New York: Pitman, 1968.

Morris, Lloyd R. *Curtain Time: The Story of the American Theatre*. New York: Random House, 1953.

Novick, Julius. *Beyond Broadway: The Quest for Permanent Theatres*. New York: Hill and Wang, 1968.

Quinn, Arthur Hobson. *A History of the American Drama from the Beginning to the Civil War*. New York: Appleton-Century-Crofts, 1923 and 1943.

———. *A History of the American Drama from the Civil War to the Present Day*. 2 vols. New York: Appleton-Century-Crofts, 1927, 1937, and 1943.

Rockefeller Brothers Fund. *The Performing Arts: Problems and Prospects*. New York: McGraw-Hill, 1965.

Ross, Laura, ed. *Theatre Profiles 5*. New York: Theatre Communications Group, 1982.

Schechner, Richard. "Ford, Rockefeller, and Theatre." *Tulane Drama Review* 10, no. 1 (1965):23–49.

———. "The Regional Theatre: Four Views." *The Drama Review* 8, no. 1 (1968):21–28.

Skal, David J., ed. *Theatre Profiles 4*. New York: Theatre Communications Group, 1979.

Stratman, Carl J. *Bibliography of the American Theatre Excluding New York City*. Chicago: Loyola University Press, 1965.

Taubman, Howard. *The Making of the American Theatre*. New York: Coward-McCann, 1965.

Toffler, Alvin. *The Culture Comsumers: A Study of Art and Affluence in America*. New York: St. Martin's Press, 1964.

Wilson, Garff B. *Three Hundred Years of American Drama and Theatre: From YE BARE*

AND YE CUBB to a CHORUS LINE. Englewood Cliffs, N.J.: Prentice-Hall, 1982.

Young, William C. *Famous Actors and Actresses of the American Stage*. Vols. 3 and 4 of *Documents of American Theater History*. New York: R. R. Bowker Company, 1975.

——. *Famous American Playhouses, 1716–1899*. Vol. 1 of *Documents of American Theater History*. Chicago: American Library Association, 1973.

——. *Famous American Playhouses, 1900–1971*. Vol. 2 of *Documents of American Theater History*. Chicago: American Library Association, 1973.

Zeigler, Joseph Wesley. *Regional Theatre: The Revolutionary Stage*. New York: Da Capo Press, 1977.

WESTERN EUROPE
(excluding Scandinavia)

Addenbrooke, Richard. *The Royal Shakespeare Company: The Peter Hall Years*. London: William Kimber, 1974.

Alberti, Armelo. *Il Teatro dei Pupi*. Milan: Mursia Editore, 1977.

Arpe, Verner. *Knaurs Schauspielführer*. Munich: Draemer Knaur, 1976.

Auburn, Charles V. *Histoire de Théâtre Espagnol*. Paris: Presses Universitaires de France, 1970.

Baecque, Andre de. *Les Maisons de la Culture*. Paris: Seghers, 1967.

——. *Le Théâtre d'aujourd'hui*. Paris: Seghers, 1964.

Barker, Kathleen. *Bristol at Play: Five Centuries of Entertainment*. Bradford-on-Avon, Great Britain: Moonraker Press, 1976.

Barrault, Jean-Louis. *Memories for Tomorrow*. Trans. John Griffin. London: Thames and Hudson, 1974.

——. *The Theatre of Jean-Louis Barrault*. Trans. Joseph Chiari. New York: Hill and Wang, 1961.

Battisteria, Rambelli. *Teatro a Genova*. Genoa: Liguria, 1976.

Bauer, Anton. *Das Theatre in der Josefstadt zu Wien*. Vienna: Manutiuspresse, 1957.

Beauman, Sally. *The Royal Shakespeare Company: A History of Ten Decades*. Oxford: Oxford University Press, 1982.

Beigbeder, Marc. *Le Théâtre en France depuis la Libération*. Paris: Bordas, 1959.

Beprins, P. *Het nederlandstalig toneel in België*. Brussels: Instituut voor Journalisten, 1975.

Bergold, Werner. *50 Jahre Schauspielhaus, 25 Jahre Kammerspiel im Schauspielhaus*. Munich: Suddeutsch Verlag, 1951.

Berlau, Ruth, et al. *Theaterarbeit*. 2d ed. East Berlin: Henselverlag, Kunst und Gesell-schaft, 1967.

Braulich, Heinrich. *Die Volksbühne, Theater und Politik in der Deutschen Volksbühnen-bervegung*. East Berlin: Henschelverlag, Kunst and Gesellschaft, 1976.

Braun, Hans. *The Theatre in Germany*. Munich: F. Bruckmann KG, 1956.

Brown, Frederick. *Theater and Revolution: The Culture of the French Stage*. New York: Viking Press, 1980.

Browne, Terry. *Playwright's Theatre: The English Stage Company at the Royal Court*. London: Pitman Publishing, 1975.

Die Bühne. (Theatre journal published monthly since 1958.)

Carlson, Marvin. *The French Stage in the Nineteenth Century*. Metuchen, N.J.: Scarecrow Press, 1972.

Cézan, Claude. *Le Grenier de Toulouse*. Toulouse: Privat, 1952.

Chapelle, Monique. *Gérard Philipe, notre eternelle jeunesse*. Paris: Robert Laffont, 1966.

Chroniko. (Yearbook listing the theatre activities throughout Greece.)

Clarke, Brenna Katz. *The Emergence of the Irish Peasant Play at the Abbey Theatre*. Ann Arbor, Mich.: UMI Research Press, 1983.

Clausen, Rosemarie. *Theater: Gustaf Gründgens Inszeniert*. Hamburg: Wegner, 1960.

Copfermann, Emile. *La mise en crise théâtrale*. Paris: François Maspero, 1972.

———. *Le Théâtre Populaire, Porquoi?* Paris: François Maspero, 1965.

———. *Planchon*. Lausanne: L'Age d'Homme, S. A., 1969.

———. *Théâtres de Roger Planchon*. Paris: Union Génèrale de Editions, 1977.

Cruet, Francisco. *Historia del Teatro Catala*. Barcelona: Editorial Aedos, 1967.

Cruz, D. I. *Introduçao ao Teatro Português de Século XX*. Lisbon, 1969.

Daiber, Hans. *Deutsches Theater seit 1945*. Stuttgart: Philip Reclam, 1976.

Davies, Cecil W. *Theatre for the People*. Austin: University of Texas Press, 1977.

Day, M. C., and Trewin, J. C. *The Shakespeare Memorial Theatre*. London: Dent, 1932.

Dejean, Jean-luc. *Le Théâtre Française d'aujourd'hui*. Paris: Fernand Nathan, 1971.

Deutsches Bühnen-Jahrbuch (Yearbook listing the theatre activities throughout Germany.)

Devrient, Eduard. *Geschichte der Deutschen Schauspielkunst*. Munich: Langen Müller, 1967.

Drews, Wolfgang. *Theater*. Vienna: K. Desch, 1961.

———, et al. *German Theatre Today*. Velber bei Hanover: Friedrich, 1967.

Dusanne. *La Comédie Française*. Paris: Hachette, 1960.

Duvignaud, Jean, et al. *Itinérarie de Roger Planchon, 1953–1964*. Paris: L'Arche, 1970.

El Espectado y la Critica. (Yearbook listing the theatre activities throughout Spain.)

Ellis, Ruth. *The Shakespeare Memorial Theatre*. London: Winchester, 1948.

Elsom, John. *Post-War British Theatre*. London: Routledge and Kegan Paul, 1976.

———. *Theatre Outside London*. London: Macmillan, 1971.

Fabrego, Xavier. *Teatro o la Vida*. Madrid: Col. Punto de la Referencia, 1976.

Falckenberg, Hans-Geert. *Heinz Hilpert*. Göttingen: Vandenboeck and Ruprecht, 1968.

Findlater, Richard, ed. *25 Years of the English State Company at the Royal Court*. Derbyshire, England: Amber Lane Press, Ltd., 1981.

Franco. Fiorenza. *Eduardo de Filipo*. Rome: Gremese Editore, 1978.

Funke, Chrisoph, et al. *Theater Bilanz, 1945–1969*. East Berlin: Henschelverlag, Kunst und Gesellschaft, 1971.

Gaipa, Ettore. *Giorgio Strehler*. Bologna: Cappelli, 1959.

Gilhiff, Gerd Aage. *The Royal Dutch Theatre in the Hague*. The Hague: Nijhoff, 1936.

Gómez de la Serera, Gaspar. *Gracias y Disgracias del Teatro Real*. Madrid: Ministeria Educacion y Cincio, 1975.

Gontard, Denis. *La Décentralisation Théâtrale*. Paris: Société d'Édition d'Énseignement Supérieur, 1973.

Greeven, Erich August. *110 Jahre Thalia-Theater Hamburg: 1843–1953*. Hamburg: Kayser, 1953.

Guazzotti, Giorgio. *Rapporto sul Teatro Italino*. Milan: Silva, 1966.

Haeusserman, Ernst. *Das Wiener Burgtheater*. Vienna: Fritz Molden, 1975.

Hayman, Ronald. *British Theatre Since 1955: A Reassessment*. Oxford: Oxford University Press, 1979.

————. *The German Theatre*. London: Oswald Wolff, 1975.

Hensel, Georg. *Ein Jahrzehnt Sellner in Darmstadt*. Darmstadt: Reba Verlag GmbH, 1962.

Heym, Heinrich. *Frankfurt und Sein Theater*. Frankfurt: W. Kramer, 1963.

Hinchliffe, Arnold P. *British Theatre 1950–1970*. Totowa, N.J.: Rowman and Littlefield, 1974.

Holden, Michael. *The Stage Guide: Technical Information on British Theatres Published by the Stage Newspaper*. London: Carson and Comerford, 1971.

Holt, Marion. *The Contemporary Spanish Theatre: 1949–1972*. Boston: Twayne Publishers, 1975.

Hunt, Hugh. *The Abbey: Ireland's National Theatre, 1904–1978*. New York: Columbia University Press, 1979.

Hürlimann, Martin. *Das Atlantis Buch des Theaters*. Zurich: Atlantis Verlag, 1966.

————, and Jocker, Emil. *Theater in Zürich: 125 Jahre Stadttheater*. Zurich: Atlantis Verlag, 1959.

Hutchinson, David. *The Modern Scottish Theatre*. Glasgow: Molendinar Press, 1977.

Il Dramma. (Monthly periodical listing theatre activities throughout Italy.)

Isasi Angulo, Armando Carlos. *Diálogos del Teatro español de la postguerra*. Madrid: Ayuso, 1974.

Kaiser, Hermann. *Im Scheinwerfer Darmstadter Theaterinnerungen 1897–1933*. Darmstadt: J. Von Liebig, 1969.

————. *Modernes Theater in Darmstadt, 1910–1933*. Darmstadt: E. Rathe, 1958.

Kemp. T. C., and Trewin, J. C. *The Stratford Festival*. London: Cornish, 1953.

Kipphardt, Heiner, et al. *Deutsches Theater*. East Berlin: Henselverlag, 1957.

Kopp, Paul, et al. *50 Jahre Schweizer Bühnenverband Union des Théâtres Suisses 1920–1970*. Zurich: Herausgegben von Schweizerischen, 1970.

Kraus, Gottfried. *The Salzburg Marionette Theatre*. Trans. Jane Tyson. Salzburg: Residenz Verlag, 1966.

Kunz-Aubert, Ulysses. *Le Théâtre á Genève*. Geneva: Peril Gentil, 1963.

Lang, Jack. *L'État et le Théâtre*. Paris: Librarie générale de droit et de jurisprudence, 1968.

Lange, Friedrich. *Die Welttournee des Burgtheaters*. Vienna: A. F. Koska, 1969.

Larraz, Emmanuel. *Teatro Español Contemperáneo*. Paris: Masson et Cie, 1973.

Leclerc, Guy. *Le T.N.P. de Jean Vilar*. Paris: Union Générale d'Editions, 1971.

Lee, Vera. *Quest for a Public*. Cambridge: P. Schenkerman Publishing Company, 1970.

Lilar, Suzanne. *The Belgian Theatre since 1890*. New York: Belgian Government Information Service, 1950

————. *Sojsante ans de Théâtre Belge*. Brussels: La Renaissance de line, 1952.

London Theatre Record. (Fortnightly periodical listing the theatre activities for London.)

Loup, Kurt. *Das Festliche Haus*. Cologne: Kipenheuer and Witsch, 1955.

Ludwig, Pit. *Licht Bilder 1951–1976: 25 Jahre Theater in Darmstadt*. Darmstadt: Eduard Roether Verlag, 1976.

Luft, Friedrich. *25 Jahre Theater in Berlin*. Berlin: Heinz Spitzing, 1972.

McGarth, John. *A Good Night Out. Popular Theatre: Audience, Class and Form*. London: Eyre Methuen, 1981.

Madral, Philippe. *Le Théâtre hors le murs*. Paris: Ed. de Seuil, 1969.

Mander, Raymond, and Mitchenson, Joe. *The Theatres of London*. London: New England Library, 1975.

Manguao, Luis Molero. *Teatro Español Contemperaneo*. Madrid: Editoria Nacional, 1974.

Manzella, Domenico. *I Teatro di Milano*. Milan: V. Mursia and Company, 1971.

Matos-Sequeiros, Gustavo. *Historia do Teatro Nacional María II*. 2 vols. Lisbon: Publição Comemorativa do Centénario, 1946.

Matthews, Bache. *A History of the Birmingham Repertory Theatre*. London: Chatto and Windus, 1924.

Mayerhöfer, Joseph. *50 Jahre Akademietheater, 1922–1972*. Vienna: Österreichische nationalbibliothek, 1972.

Mignon, Paul. *Jean Dasté*. Paris: Presses Littéraires de France, 1953.

Mohr, Albert Richard. *Das Frankfurter Schauspielhaus 1929–1944*. Frankfurt: Im Verlag von Waldermar Kramer, 1974.

Mohring, Paul. *Von Ackermann biz Ziegel: Theater in Hamburg*. Hamburg: Christians, 1970.

Morckhoven, Paul. *The Contemporary Theatre in Belgium*. Brussels: Belgian Information Documentation Institute, 1970.

Mortero, Gian Renzo. *Il Teatro Populare in Francia*. Rocca San Cascino: Cappelli, n.d.

Mullin, Michael. *Theatre at Stratford-upon-Avon*. Westport, Conn.: Greenwood Press, 1980.

Munzo, Matilde. *Historia del teatro dramatico en España*. Madrid: Editorial Tesorio, 1948.

Nederlands Theater Jaarboek. (Yearbook listing the theatre activities for the Netherlands.)

Nicoll, Allardyce. *English Drama: A Modern Viewpoint*. London: George G. Harrap and Company, 1968.

O'Connor, Gary V. *French Theatre Today*. Bath: Pitman Press, 1975.

Offord, John, ed. *The British Theatre Directory—1979*. New York: Drama Book Specialists, 1979.

O hAodha, Micheál. *Theatre in Ireland*. Oxford: 1974; rpt. Totowa, N.J.: Rowman and Littlefield, 1974.

Olmedilla, A. Martinez. *Arriba el Telon*. Madrid: Aguilar, 1961.

Palmer, Peter. *Schweizer Bühnenwerke Des 20 Jahrhunderts*. Zurich: Züricher Forum, 1972.

Pandolfi, Vito. *Teatro Italiano Contemperaneo*. Milan: A. Schwartz, 1959.

Patterson, Michael. *German Theatre Today*. London: Pitman, 1976.

Petzet, Wolfgang. *Der Münchner Kammerspiel, 1911–1972*. Munich: Kurt Desch, 1973.

Plays and Players. (Monthly publication listing the theatre activities for Great Britain.)

Quardi, Franco. *L'Avanguardia Teatre in Italia*. 2 vols. Turin: Guilio Einaudi, 1977.

Rebello, Luiz Francisco. *Teatro Portuges Contemperaneo*. Madrid: Aguilar, 1961.

Reichl, Kurt. *Stadttheater Basel 1834-1934-1959*. Basel: Pharos Verlag, 1959.

Reiss, Curt. *Gustaf Gründgens*. Hamburg: Hoffman und Kampe, 1965.

Rihle, Gunther. *Theater in Unsere Zeit*. Frankfurt: Suhrkamp, 1976.

Rodríguez Méndez, José María. *Commentarios Imperinente sobre el Teatro Español*. Barcelona: Ediciones Peninsula, 1972.

Rothe, Hans. *Max Reinhardt: 25 Jahre Deutsches Theater*. Munich: R. Piper and Company, 1930.

Roy, Claude. *Jean Vilar*. Paris: Seghers, 1968.

Rüllicke-Weiler, Käthe. *Die Dramaturgie Brecht*. East Berlin: Henselverlag, 1968.

Sarrazin, Maurice. *Comédiens dans une Troupe*. Toulouse: Grenier de Toulouse, 1970.

Sastre, Alfonso. *Drama y Sociedad*. Madrid: Taurus, 1956.

Schreyvogel, Friedrich. *Das Burgtheater*. Vienna: F. Speidel-Verlag, 1956.

Schwab-Felisch, Hans. *Das Düsseldorfer Schauspielhaus*. Düsseldorf: Econ Verlag, 1970.

Serrière, Marie-Thérèse. *Le T.N.P. et nous*. Paris: Libraries Jose-Corti, 1959.

Shaw, Leroy Robert. *The German Theatre Today*. Austin: University of Texas Press, 1963.

Sideres, Giannes. *The Modern Greek Theatre: A Concise History*. Trans. Lucille Vassariaki. Athens: Hellenic Center of the International Theatre Institute, 1957.

Siderif, Yannis. *Le Théâtre Neo-Grec*. Athens: Difros, 1957.

Stegnano, Luciana Picchio. *Richerche sur Teatro Portuguese*. Rome: Visagalli Pasetti, 1969.

———. *Storia del Teatro Portuguese*. Rome: Ediziona del l'Ateneo, 1964.

Surer, Paul. *Cinquante ans de théâtre*. Paris: Société d'Edition d'Enseignement Supérieur, 1969.

Szene Schweiz, Scène Suisse, Scena Svizzerzia. (Annual publication listing the theatre activities for all of Switzerland.)

Taylor, Allison. *The Story of the English Stage*. Oxford: Pergamon Press, 1967.

Teaterjaarbock voor het Nederlandstalig Landstoneel van België. (Annual publication listing the theatre activities for the Netherlands.)

Teatraal. (Monthly publication listing the theatre activities for the Netherlands.)

Teatro Italiano. (Yearbook listing the theatre activities for Italy.)

Temkine, Raymonde. *L'enterprise théâtre*. Paris: Editions Cujas, 1967.

Theater der Zeit. (Monthly publication listing the theatre activities for East Germany.)

Theater Heute. (Publication presenting a yearly compilation of theatre activities in West Germany, Austria, and German-speaking Switzerland.)

Touzoul, Melly, and Touzoul, Tephany. *Jean Vilar, mot pour mot*. Paris: Editions Stock, 1972.

Travail théâtral. (Publication issued three times a year listing international theatre activities.)

Trewin, J. C. *The Birmingham Repertory Theatre: 1913–1963*. London: Barrie and Rockliff, 1963.

Trilse, Christoph, et al. *Theater Lexicon*. East Berlin: Henschelverlag, Kunst and Gesellschaft, 1977.

Van Tieghen, Philipe. *Les grands acteurs contemporaines*. Paris: Presses Universitaires de France, 1963.

Vasla, M. *Le Théâtre grec modern de 1453 to 1900*. Berlin: Akademie Verlag, 1960.

Wächter, Hans Christof. *Theater im Exil*. Munich: Carl Hansen Verlag, 1973.

Wagner, Hans. *200 Jahre Münchner Theaterchronick, 1750–1950*. Munich: Lerche, 1965.

Wahnrau, Gerhard. *Berlin Stadt der Theater*. 2 vols. East Berlin: Henschelverlag, Kunst and Gesellschaft, 1957.

Weddigen, Otto. *Geschichte der Theater Deutschlands*. Berlin: Ernst Frensdorff, n.d.

Weintraub, Stanley, ed. *British Dramatists Since World War II*. 2 vols. Detroit, Mich.: Gale Research Company, 1982.

Wol, Joseph. *Theater und Film im Dritten Reich*. Gütersloh: Sigbert John Verlag, 1964.

Zivier, Georg. *Schiller Theater*. West Berlin: Stapp Verlag, 1963.

Zoff, Otto. *The German Theatre Today*. Milwaukee: Marquette University Press, 1960.

Index

About the Contributors

JOEL A. ADEDEJI is professor of theatre arts and chairman, Theatre Arts Department, University of Ibadan, Nigeria. He holds a Ph.D. in drama from the University of Ibadan, Nigeria. A UNESCO consultant on the promotion and presentation of the performing arts in Africa, Dr. Adedeji is an elected fellow of the Royal Society of Arts (Great Britain) and a licentiate of the Royal Academy of Music (Great Britain). Author of several articles in journals and books on African drama and theatre, he has also directed many plays for the African stage. He is currently working on a book, *Traditions of African Theatre*.

MARIANNE ARIYANTO received an M.A. in dance at the University of California at Los Angeles in 1970. After studying Balinese dance at the Center for World Music in the summers of 1972, 1974, and 1975, she studied dance in Bali on a Fulbright Scholarship during 1977 and 1978. She is currently assistant professor of dance and artistic director of the Nebraska Dance Ensemble at the University of Nebraska-Lincoln. She has also taught at the University of Wisconsin-Stevens Point and the College of St. Teresa in Winona, Minnesota.

LEON M. AUFDEMBERGE, a B.A. from Baker University and a Ph.D. from Northwestern University, teaches at Kendall College and Harpers College, both in Chicago, Illinois.

STEFÁN BALDURSSON was formerly theatre secretary of the National Theatre of Iceland, where he was active as a director of classics, modern drama, and world premieres of Icelandic plays. He is presently a director and co-artistic director of the Reykjavík Theatre Company. He was educated in Reykjavík College and Stockholm University, where he studied theatre and film.

DANIEL BARRETT is adjunct assistant professor of English at Iowa State University. His articles on nineteenth-century drama and theatre have appeared in various journals, and he is a contributor to *Women in the American Theatre*.

BEVERLY ANN BENSON is adjunct professor of English at Florida Institute of Technology and previously taught at the University of Kansas and at Iowa State University. Her research interests include analyzing the writing skills of native and nonnative speakers of English, as well as designing appropriate classroom methods to meet the individualized needs of basic writers. Her teaching experience includes courses in drama, linguistics, and composition, as well as English as a second language.

ELEANA BERLOGEA is one of Romania's finest theatre critics. She has written several books on world theatre, most notably a study resulting from research in various theatres in the United States. Professor Berlogea is associated with the Institute of Theatre and Film in Bucharest.

JO BRANTLEY BERRYMAN has earned a Ph.D. from the University of Southern California and is now a member of the humanities faculty at the California Institute of the Arts. Director of the Poetry Series *CalArts* since 1977, she is also author of *Circe's Craft: Ezra Pound's HUGH SELWYN MAUBERLY* (1983). Her articles and reviews have appeared in *Paideuma, The South Atlantic Quarterly, Southern Humanities Review*, and the *Encyclopedia of Twentieth Century Literature*, among others.

JAMES BEYER holds a doctorate in American literature from the University of Kansas. In 1982–1983 he served as foreign expert at the University of Zhengzhou, the People's Republic of China. He is now an instructor at Iowa State University.

KATHLEEN COLLINS BEYER has taught at Maharani's College, Jaipur, India; at the University of Kansas; at the University of Zhengzhou, the People's Republic of China; and at Iowa State University. Her doctoral research focused on E. M. Forster's *The Hill of Devi*.

SEBASTIAN BLACK is senior lecturer in English at the University of Auckland. He has written extensively on the New Zealand theatre, notably in the *New Zealand Listener, The Walk*, and *Act*.

JILL N. BRANTLEY is professor of English and sociology at Northern Virginia Community College. She formerly taught at the University of Kansas, where she received her Ph.D. in American Studies after earning her B.A. in English at Pomona College. She has done postdoctoral work at George Washington University and Georgetown University and was a National Endowment for the Humanities Summer Seminar Fellow at Princeton University. Her major research interest is the relation between society and literature. She is associate editor of *From Three Sides: A Reader for Writers*.

KAZIMIERZ BRAUN, director of the Contemporary Theatre in Wroclaw, is one of Poland's finest young directors and critics. He has written six books, including a definitive work in Polish on world theatre. Dr. Braun has toured with his company throughout Eastern and Western Europe and directed the American premiere of Tadeusz Różewicz's *White Marriage* at the Slavic Cultural Center in 1975.

JOHN BROCKINGTON is head of the Department of Theatre at the University of British Columbia.

OTTO BÜHRING is leader of the Press Department of the Folk Theatre in Copenhagen. Previously employed by the municipal library system in Greater Copenhagen and as a journalist, he has written numerous articles on literature, theatre, and ballet. He received his education from the universities of Oslo and Copenhagen and has an M.A. in history and Scandinavian languages and literature.

DEENA BURTON studied Indonesian dance at the Center for World Music before taking up residence in Java where she trained in Javanese and Cirebonese dance over three years. She has performed these genres in both Indonesia and America. She is currently completing an M.A. in arts administration at Columbia University and is administrative director of the Bali-Java Dance Theatre.

FERNANDO GONZÁLEZ CAJIAO holds an M.A. (1962) in theatre from Baylor University. He is an actor, director, scholar, and author of eight plays. He is an official translator of English and French, as well as professor of theatre and languages.

PETER J. CHELKOWSKI is currently professor of Persian and Iranian Studies, director of the Hagop Kevorkian Center for Near Eastern Studies, and chairman of the Department of Near Eastern Languages and Literatures at New York University. He is editor of *Ta'ziyeh: Ritual Drama in Iran*, which was published by New York University Press in 1979. He has earned degrees in Oriental philosophy from Jagiello University in Cracow, Poland, and in Persian literature from Tehran University; he has also done postgraduate work in the history of the Islamic Near East at the School of Oriental and African Studies at the University of London.

PEGGY ANN CHOY has an M.A. in Southeast Asian studies from the University of Michigan and a B.A. in anthropology. She spent four and one-half years in Central Java studying dance, and has performed and taught Javanese dance in Hawaii and Michigan. She has made presentations through the artists-in-the-schools program in Hawaii.

EBUN CLARK teaches in the Department of English at the University of Lagos in Nigeria and is author of *Hurbert Ogunde, The Making of Nigerian Theatre* (Oxford University Press, 1979).

EDWARD J. CZERWINSKI is professor of Slavic and Comparative Literature at SUNY, Stony Brook. He is also executive director of the Slavic Cultural Center, located in Port Jefferson, New York. Recipient of the Chancellor's Award for Teaching and the Distinguished Teaching Award from the New York State Teachers of Foreign Languages, he has also written over a hundred articles and studies dealing with Slavic literature and drama. He has translated seven books from Polish, Serbo-Croatian, and Russian; he has just finished the second issue of *Slavic and Eastern European Arts*, which is devoted to *Pieces of Poland: Four Polish Dramatists*; and he is on the Editorial Board of *World Literature Today, Comparative Drama, Twentieth Century Literature*, and *Gradiva*.

ALBERTO DALLAL, as a critic of theatre and dance, has collaborated with virtually all the cultural reviews of Mexico and many abroad. He has held important publishing positions and is currently professor of criticism, research, and journalism at the National Autonomous University of Mexico. He is the author of two books of plays, three novels, and several books of critical essays.

MARY R. DAVIDSON is a lecturer and administrative assistant in the Department of English at the University of Kansas where she received her Ph.D. in 1981. She has published two essays on Tom Stoppard, one in *Modern Drama* and one in a collection of essays called *Alogical Modern Drama*. She has reviewed theatre for newspapers and for a public radio program, in addition to teaching courses on Shakespeare, the London theatre, and the theatre experience.

CARLOS ESPINOZA DOMÍNGUEZ has worked with the Grupo Teatro de Estudio in Havana. He holds an M.A. in theatre arts and is a faculty member of the Institute of Dramatic

Arts. A regular contributor to *Conjunto*, *Tablas*, and other Cuban journals and newspapers, he has prepared and written the prologues for various anthologies of Cuban theatre.

KATHY FOLEY is assistant professor of theatre arts at the University of California, Santa Cruz. She has as Ph.D. in Asian theatre from the University of Hawaii and has written extensively on Sudanese puppet theatre and South Pacific theatrical performance. She spent one and one-half years in West Java learning traditional puppetry of the Sudanese and has performed extensively in California and Hawaii through the artists-in-the-schools program and for university audiences.

LEONARDO AZPARREN GIMÉNEZ is a professor of theatre at the Universidad Central de Venezuela, where he graduated in philosophy in 1966. He has served as a diplomat in Hungary and Libya and is currently an advisor in the Ministry of Foreign Relations. His publications include *El teatro venezolano* (Inciba; 1966) and *El teatro venezolano y otros teatros* (Monte Avila, 1979).

SVEIN GLADSØ teaches music and drama at a teacher's college in Trondheim, Norway. He has been active with amateur and university theatre as performer, director, and playwright.

DAVID G. GOODMAN is assistant professor of Japanese language and literature at the University of Illinois. From 1969 to 1973 he was editor-in-chief of *Concerned Theatre Japan*. He is also the author of three books in Japanese, including a study of the plays of Satoh Makoto.

THORSTEIN GUNNARSSON studied architecture at the Danish Royal Academy of Fine Arts, archaeology at École Française d'Athénes, and acting at the Reykjavík Theatre Company School of Drama. He has continued at the Reykjavík Theatre Company as actor, director, and playwright. One of the designers of the new theatre building, Gunnarsson is also co-artistic director of the Reykjavík Theatre Company.

BARTHOLD HALLE has been managing director of the Oslo New Theatre since 1967. Prior to 1955 he was on the staffs of the Studio Theatre, Rogaland Theatre, and Folk Theatre. From 1952 to 1962 he worked as a freelance director for theatre, television, film, and radio in Norway.

BILLY J. HARBIN is professor of speech communication and theatre at Louisiana State University (LSU) at Baton Rouge. He has published essays on the early American theatre in the *Theatre Journal*, *Theatre Survey*, and *Theatre Notebook* (London). In October 1981 Professor Harbin and his colleague Gresdna A. Doty co-directed a conference held at LSU celebrating the twenty-fifth anniversary of the English Stage Company at the Royal Court Theatre.

OLGA HARMONY is professor of drama at the National Preparatory School of the National Autonomous University of Mexico. She is also a critic and playwright.

ANNE-CHARLOTTE HANES HARVEY is a lecturer in the Drama Department at San Diego State University. She has also taught at the University of Minnesota, Scripps College, Claremont Men's College, and Harvey Mudd College. Her experience with the theatrical arts includes performing on Swedish stage, radio, and television, as well as acting, costume designing, choreography, translating, and directing in Minnesota and California. She specializes in Scandinavian-American folk music and ethnic theatre.

PATRICIA HASELTINE is associate professor of English and Folklore in the Graduate School of Western Languages and Literature at Tamkang University in the Republic of China. A graduate of the Folklore Department at Indiana University, she has been in Taiwan doing research in Chinese folk drama and narrative since 1975. She has published articles in this field for the *Tamkang Review*, a quarterly of comparative studies between Chinese and foreign literature.

JØRGEN HEINER is a director and literary advisor at the Aarhus Theatre. He has directed operas, stage plays, and radio and television productions, and has frequently written about playwrights, composers, and American musical comedy. Having studied in England, Sweden, and Denmark, Heiner now teaches at the acting school in Aarhus and the Theatre Institute of the University of Copenhagen. He has written books on nineteenth-century directing in Denmark and the director-choreographer August Bournonville.

BARBARA HELIODORA studied in the United States at the undergraduate level and has a doctorate from Brazil. She is the most prominent Shakespearean scholar in Brazil and holds joint teaching appointments in Rio de Janeiro and São Paulo. A director and producer, she has translated works into Portuguese and promotes theatre through various groups.

JACK HIBBERD is an Australian playwright who has written such plays as *Brain Rot: An Evening of Pathology and Violence, Love and Friendship*; *White with Wire Wheels*; *Who?*; *Dimboola*; *One of Nature's Gentlemen*; *A Toast to Melba*; and *Glycerine Tears*.

JAN HOSTETLER received an M.A. in dance from Mills College and trained in Javanese dance at Pamulangan Beksa Ngayugyakarta in Indonesia. She did research in Java from 1976 to 1981 and has performed Javanese dance in Indonesia and the United States. She is currently a Ph.D. candidate in anthropology at Cornell University.

MEI-SHU HWANG, professor of English and theatre and drama at Tamkang University, editor of the *Tamkang Review*, a quarterly of comparative studies between Chinese and foreign literature, also serves on the board of the National Committee of Dramatic Production and Appreciation of Taiwan. His publications, in both English and Chinese, include plays, articles on Chinese and Western literature, drama, theatre, and film, and translations of scripts from English into Chinese and vice versa. Recent collections of his articles in Chinese are *On and Off the Stage* (1980), *Without the Ivory Tower* (1981), and *On Dramatic Literature and Theatrical Arts* (1981).

ÁRNI IBSEN, dramaturge and theatre secretary of the National Theatre of Iceland, has studied drama and English literature at Exeter University in Devon, England. A translator of works by Samuel Beckett, e. e. cummings, and others, he has also written a dramatization of Charles Dickens' *Oliver Twist*, produced by the National Theatre of Iceland in 1981. He is a director and actor as well as a college teacher and a published poet.

KAY IKRANAGARA has a graduate degree in linguistics from the University of Hawaii and has specialized in the Jakarta dialect. She is a longtime resident of Indonesia and is married to one of the major playwrights of modern Indonesian drama.

STIG JARL JENSEN is on the staff of the Documentation Center for Alternate Theatre at the Institute for Theatre Research of the University of Copenhagen. His previous experience includes serving as press manager at the Danish Theatre and working for the Ministry of Cultural Affairs. He has written and produced articles and radio programs on such subjects as Brecht, street theatre, and children's theatre.

STEFAN JOHANSSON, trained in literature, film, and theatre, is a member of the Theatre 9 company in Stockholm. Author of a dissertation on Swedish group theatre during the 1960s, he has worked with the Stockholm Student Theatre, the Marionette Theatre, and the Pistol Theatre. A theatre and film critic at the Swedish Broadcasting Corporation since 1969, Johansson is also a playwright, an actor, and a director.

JUKKA KAJAVA is a theatre critic for the *Helsingin Sanomat* of Helsinki, Finland.

KETU H. KATRAK, an assistant professor of English at Howard University in Washington, D.C., has just completed the *Wole Soyinka Bibliography* for Greenwood Press, Westport, Conn.

VERONICA KELLY received her doctorate from the Graduate School for the Study of Drama, University of Toronto, in 1976. She is currently a lecturer in drama in the English Department, University of Queensland, with a special interest in nineteenth- and twentieth-century Australian drama.

JAMES SCOTT KENNEDY, JR., writer, actor, and director, is a student at Stanford University. He has performed throughout the world in such plays as *Four Lost Boys*, *What's in a Name*, and *King*.

JANIE SYKES KENNEDY is an actress, journalist, educator, and playwright who has performed throughout the world. She holds a B.A. from Howard University, an M.A. from the University of Ghana, and an M.S. from the Columbia University Graduate School of Journalism. Among her credits are *The Rivers of the Black Man* and *No More Shuckin' and Jivin'*.

J. SCOTT KENNEDY, professor of theatre arts at CUNY (Brooklyn College) and author of *In Search of African Theatre* (Scribner's), is a director, educator, playwright, actor, and composer. Known throughout the world, he includes among his many theatrical credits *The King Is Dead*, *Ham's Children*, and *Harlem Celebration*. He has earned the B.A., M.A., and Ph.D. degrees from New York University and has studied at the universities of London, Paris, and Heidelberg.

HO SOON KIM is a professor of drama at Ewha Womans University in Seoul, Korea. She holds an M.F.A. from the Goodman School of Drama of the Art Institute of Chicago and a Ph.D. in theatre from the University of Kansas.

BIRGITTA DAHLGREN KNUTTGEN has taught Swedish language and literature at Harvard University since 1976. She holds a B.A. in comparative literature and an M.A. in German literature, and is now a Ph.D. candidate in Scandinavian and Germanic literature at Harvard University. Her studies in acting and theatre arts in Göteborg, Sweden; New York; and Copenhagen have been complemented by acting assignments in stage, television, and film in Sweden and the United States.

YASUHARU KOBAYASHI specializes in medieval Japanese literature and is professor in the Faculty of Education at Waseda University. Since 1973 he has contributed "Nō, Kyōgen,

Kankei Kenkyu Bunken Mokuroku'' (*An Annual Bibliography on Nō and Kyōgen Theatre*) to *Kanshō*.

MOJCA KRANJC is keeper of the archives and publicity director of the Drama Slovensko Narodno Gedalisce v Ljubjana in Yugoslavia.

COLBY H. KULLMAN, an assistant professor of English at the University of Mississippi, holds a B.A. from DePauw University, an M.A. from the University of Chicago, and a Ph.D. from the University of Kansas. His articles on theatre history, dramatic literature, eighteenth-century literature, interdisciplinary studies, and rhetorical theory have appeared in such journals as the *Ball State University Forum, Journal of English Teaching Techniques, Kansas English, The Mississippi Folklore Register, Studies in Contemporary Satire, Studies in the Humanities, Studies on Voltaire and the Eighteenth Century*, and the *Theatre Journal*.

ERLING LARSEN has been in charge of the administration and management of the Café Teater in Copenhagen since 1976. He previously worked as an actor, technician, and press officer for the company. Specializing in French theatre of the seventeenth century and post-World War II era, he holds a degree from the University of Copenhagen. As a freelance reporter, he covers cultural events and youth activities.

BENJAMIN LETHOLOA LESHOAI holds a Ph.D. and is professor of literature at the University of Bophuthatswana, Mafikeng. Formerly, he was reader at the University of Botswana and Swaziland, University College, Botswana. Among his research interests is the black South African theatre.

EMANUEL LEVY received his B.A. and M.A. from Tel-Aviv University, and his Ph.D. from Columbia University, New York. His book, *The Habima—Israel's National Theater, 1917–1977: A Study of Cultural Nationalism* (Columbia University Press, 1979), was the winner of the 1980 National Jewish Book Award. His other published book is entitled *And the Winner Is: The Politics of the Oscar Award* (1983). Dr. Levy specializes in comparative and political sociology, popular culture and mass communications, and the sociology of theatre and film. Currently at Yeshiva University, Dr. Levy has taught at the City University of New York.

CHRISTIAN LUDVIGSEN has been chairman of the Drama Department, Aarhus University, Denmark, since its founding in 1973. He has written *Moderne teaterproblemer* (1964) and served as co-editor of several issues of *Teatrets Teori og Teknik*. He has translated such playwrights as Samuel Beckett, Eugene Ionesco, and Arthur Adamov, written theatre criticism for magazines and newspapers, and edited dramatic anthologies as well as a book of theatre history. Ludvigsen has been associated with the Fiol Theatre in Copenhagen as dramaturge-animator and with the Odin Theatre as literary advisor.

GERARDO LUZURIAGA, born in Ecuador, holds the Ph.D. in Spanish from the University of Iowa, where he wrote his dissertation on the theatre of Demetrio Aguilera Malta. A scholar and literary critic, he has for many years been professor of Spanish at the University of California at Los Angeles.

JOHN MCCALLUM lectures in drama at the University of New England in Armidale, Australia. He is a recognized authority on contemporary Australian drama, and is also a playwright and critic for the magazine *Theatre Australia* and the Australian Broadcasting Commission.

DONALD F. MCKENZIE, a New Zealander by birth, is professor of English at Victoria University, Wellington. He was formerly a fellow of Corpus Christi College, Cambridge, where he was also Sandars Reader in Bibliography. He is president of the Bibliographical Society, London, and was recently elected a corresponding fellow of the British Academy. His major current project is an edition of William Congreve's complete works for the Clarendon Press, Oxford.

MARYKAY MAHONEY has earned a B.A. from the College of St. Rose, an M.A. from Boston College, and a Ph.D. from the University of Kansas. She is presently teaching part-time at the University of Massachusetts at Boston and at Boston College.

ALINA MAKAREWICZ has visited the United States and has translated works from English. She is a former Polish actress.

ANDRZEJ MAKAREWICZ has won numerous awards for his plays. Fluent in English, Makarewicz has translated several plays from the English language. In 1973 he directed his own work, *Face to Face*, for the Slavic Cultural Center at the Provincetown Playhouse.

LISE-LONE MARKER is professor of theatrical history at the University of Toronto. A Ph.D. from Yale University, she is co-author of *The Scandinavian Theatre: A Short History* and author of *David Belasco: Naturalism in the American Theatre*.

TAMOTSU MATSUDA specializes in Nō theatre research. He is a lecturer at Nimatsu Gakusha University and Kokusai Shōka University in Japan.

RUTH MIKKELSON is associate director of the Office of Residential Programs at the University of Kansas. She was formerly a teacher of English in Rocky River, Ohio; in Madison, Wisconsin; and at the University of Kansas in Lawrence. Her publications include five editions of the *Staff Resource Book* and *Contemporary Literature/Contemporary Problems*.

ALEKO MINCHEY is a theatre director and current head of the International Theatre Institute in Sofia, Bulgaria. He is also director of the Bulgarian Actors' Union, whose managing director is the actor Ljubomir Kabakchiev.

KRASIMIRA MINKOVA is a dramaturge with the Adriana Budevska Dramatic Theatre in Burgas, Bulgaria. She is also a critic.

KENKICHI MIYATA is professor in the School of Education at Waseda University in Tokyo as well as at Wako University, also in Tokyo. He was a graduate student at the University of Washington, Seattle, and still participates actively in the affairs of the Asian Theatre Program of the American Theatre Association.

CARLOS MORALES is currently editor of the *Seminario Universidad*, vice-president of the College of Journalism, and assistant director of the School of Communications Science of the University of Costa Rica. He spent ten years as theatre critic for *La Nación*, *La República*, and *Universidad*.

MICHAEL MULLIN, associate professor of English at the University of Illinois-Urbana, holds an M.Phil. and a Ph.D. in English from Yale University. In 1975 he held an observership with the Royal Shakespeare Company. He has published *Macbeth Onstage*

(1976) and *Theatre at Stratford-upon-Avon, 1879–1978* (2 vols., 1980), as well as more than a dozen articles about Shakespeare's plays on stage, film, and television.

TRINE NAESS is an instructor in dramatic theory at the Norwegian Theatre School, a lecturer at the University of Oslo, archivist of the theatre collection at the University Library in Oslo, and curator of the Theatre Museum in Oslo. After earning a *Magister* degree in theatre from the University of Oslo, she served as research fellow at the University of Trondheim. Naess is author of a book on Norwegian scene designer Arne Walentin entitled *Arne Walentin: Teatermålar og scenograf* (1978).

CAROLYN ELY NEURINGER is a lecturer in English at the University of Kansas and has traveled extensively throughout the British Isles with numerous periods of residence in London.

CHARLES NEURINGER is professor of psychology at the University of Kansas.

JOSEPH J. NEUSCHATZ, born in Romania, is an anesthesiologist at Mather and St. Charles Hospitals on Long Island. Dr. Neuschatz has written several feature stories for leading newspapers and is working on his first book.

IRMELI NIEMI is professor of comparative literature and drama at the University of Turku in Finland. She was president of the Finnish Central Union of Theatre Associations in the 1970s. She is a theatre critic and the author of books on modern European drama and theatre theories, ranging from Stanislavsky to Brook.

COLLIN O'BRIEN teaches in the Department of English at the Nedlands, the University of Western Australia.

ROBERT PAGE is a lecturer in drama at the University of Newcastle. He is a specialist in medieval theatre with teaching interests in Elizabethan, nineteenth- and twentieth-century drama, and Australian drama and theatre. His publications include *The Mystery Plays*, which he translated, edited, and adapted, and various major articles for journals published in Australia, the United Kingdom, and Poland. He both founded and continues to edit the national monthly *Theatre Australia*, and is active as a critic and arts journalist. He has scripted and presented several major documentaries on ABC national television, including *Bertolt Brecht in Australia* and the *Chester Mystery Plays*. He has directed a number of successful productions including the multiaward-winning *Waiting for Godot* and *The Mystery Plays* in Newcastle Cathedral.

GIANNA SOMMI PANOFSKY is former Italian coach of the Lyric Opera of Chicago and former lecturer of Italian at Northwestern University. At present she is co-authoring a history of the Italian workers' movement in Chicago under the sponsorship of the Illinois Labor History Society.

ANTONIO PECCI currently works for the *Seminario Sendero* in Asunción, Paraguay. As a man of theatre, he has been instrumental in establishing theatre groups in the capital in recent years, and recently published an anthology of eight plays titled *Teatro breve del Paraguay* (Asunción, 1981).

JUAN ANDRÉS PIÑA is professor of Spanish literature, a journalist, and master of Spanish American literature in the Catholic University of Chile. He is theatre and literary critic for the journals *Hoy* and *Apsi* in Chile, and presently works as theatre critic and does cultural reporting for the journal *Mensaje* in Santiago, Chile.

JAIME POTENZE is director of the National Arts Fund and reviews plays for *La Nación*, *Criterio*, and *Redacción*. Until 1980 he was theatre and cinema critic for *La Prensa*. He is a practicing lawyer and an expert in copyright laws.

VICTORIA S. POULAKIS is professor of English at Northern Virginia Community College. She formerly taught at the University of Minnesota, where she received her Ph.D. in English and American Literature, and at Temple University. She has received two National Endowment for the Humanities Summer Seminar Grants, the most recent to participate in a seminar on "Shakespeare in Performance" at the University of Iowa.

WALTER RELA is the author of several books on Brazilian theatre and has written reviews for various periodicals on Brazilian and Latin American theatre. He is currently director of the Departamento de Investigaciones y Estudios Superiores de Letras Americanas at the Uruguayan Instituto de Filosofía, Ciencias y Letras. He has presented papers at several North American and Latin American conferences on Latin American theatre.

TOM REMLOV has studied world literature at the University of Oslo and directing at the Drama Centre in London. He has edited *The Experimental High School, Oslo* (1968) and translated several British, American, and Australian plays. Previously a lecturer, actor, and administrator in London, Remlov has also served on the editorial staff of the Oslo New Theatre and the Norwegian theatre. He is presently dramaturge at the Rogaland Theatre, Stavanger, Norway.

FARLEY RICHMOND is professor of theatre at Michigan State University. His publication record is focused on the classical, rural, and modern Indian theatre. Besides teaching a wide range of graduate and undergraduate courses in one of the oldest programs of Asian theatre in the country, he has regularly directed Indian plays with college student actors. He collected material on the modern theatre movement in India during the summer of 1980.

CARMEN J. RODRÍGUEZ is a graduate of the Department of Drama of the University of Puerto Rico and is studying for the M.A. degree in the School of Theatre at Florida State University.

IVAN SANDERS, born in Hungary, is professor of English at Suffolk County Community College in Selden, New York. He has translated numerous plays, poems, and short stories from Hungarian.

ANNE SELBY joined the staff of the Stratford Shakespearean Festival Foundation of Canada in 1969 as assistant to the publicity director. Since 1975, she has served as director of publications at Stratford. Her career has also included other work in journalism and public relations.

RICHARD SHAW is professor of English at the Minneapolis College of Art and Design. He is author of three children's plays which have been performed in Minneapolis, Albany, Omaha, Seattle, and other cities. His adaptation of *Sleeping Beauty* was recently performed at the Kennedy Center in Washington, D.C., at the Saratoga Performing Arts Center, and in Lyon, France, at the Association Internationale de Théâtre pour l'Enfance et pour la Jeunesse World Congress. He has received a National Education Association Creative

Writing Fellowship and a National Education for the Humanities institute grant to the Folger Shakespeare Library and Theater.

JOAN SARGENT SHERWOOD is assistant vice-chancellor for student services at the University of Missouri-Kansas City and teaches the "College Student" on an ad hoc basis for the Department of Educational Administration in the School of Education. She received her B.S. in philosophy at Kansas State University, her M.A. in English at Wichita State University, and her Ph.D. in educational policy and administration at the University of Kansas. She has taught freshman and sophomore composition and literature at Wichita State University and the University of Kansas.

KIRSIKKA SIIKALA attended the Theatre Academy of Finland and Helsinki University and is presently theatre critic of *Helsingin Sanomat* newspaper.

M. NOEL SIPPLE is professor in the Humanities Department of the Northern Virginia Community College.

HENRIK SJÖRGEN is the director of information for the Swedish Institute for Concerts. Educated at the University of Lund, he has been a drama critic and editor. Sjögren is author of *Ingmar Bergman på teatern* (1968), *Regi: Ingmar Bergman* (1969), and *Stage and Society in Sweden* (1979).

THOMAS STADTMILLER works for a government agency in New York and is a specialist in Bulgarian affairs.

GERD STAHL is the dramaturge of the National Theatre in Oslo, Norway.

RAYMOND STANLEY served as correspondent to *Variety* from 1959 to 1977 and is currently Australian correspondent to *Screen International* (London) and *The Stage and Television Today* (London).

BIRGITTA STEENE, formerly on the faculty of Temple University, is a professor in the Scandinavian Department of the University of Washington, Seattle. She is the author of *Ingmar Bergman* and *August Strindberg: The Greatest Fire*.

R. ANDERSON SUTTON is a Ph.D. candidate in ethnomusicology at the University of Michigan. He has taught and performed Javanese gamelan there and at the University of Hawaii, where he completed an M.A. He spent two and one-half years in Java researching traditional performing arts and has published on Javanese and Okinawan performing arts in various scholarly journals. He teaches music at the University of Wisconsin-Madison.

ARNLJOT STRØMME SVENDSEN is a professor and vice-president of the Norwegian School of Economics and chairman of the Board of the National Stage in Bergen. Svendsen has written sociological studies on theatre and music in today's society and a book on dramatist Hans Wiers-Jenssen. He is chairman of the Association of Norwegian Theatres, an organization that represents the management and boards of directors of all theatres in Norway.

ALLEN W.W. TAMAKLOE is senior lecturer in drama and theatre arts at the University of Zambia and director of the Chikwakwa Theatre. A graduate of Brooklyn College, City University of New York, with a Master of Fine Arts degree in speech and theatre, he has also attended the College of Science and Technology at Kumasi, Ghana, and the University of Ghana at Legon. He has directed and acted in many plays, lectured in universities in Ghana and the United States, written several plays (including *Jogolo*), and published articles on African drama and theatre practice.

ANDREW T. TSUBAKI is professor of speech and drama and of East Asian Languages and Cultures, director of the International Theatre Studies Center, and chairperson of the East Asian Languages and Cultures Department at the University of Kansas, and area editor (Japan) for the *Asian Theatre Journal*. He has also completed terms as chairman of the Asian Theatre Program, American Theatre Association, and the University and College Division of the Association of Kansas Theatre. He has been active in the area of Japanese theatre and drama, staging both modern and classic works and publishing several articles dealing with Japanese theatre. Recently, he added Indian Chhau folk dance drama to his specialization.

KATRI VELTHEIM is drama critic for the daily newspaper *Uusi Suomi* in Helsinki.

SURAPONE VIRULRAK is dean of the Faculty of Communication Arts at Chulalongkorn University in Bangkok, Thailand, and serves as Thailand's traditional media expert for the Association of Southeast Asian Nations Cultural Committee and as deputy chairman of the National Cultural Committee of the Ministry of Education. He holds a B.A. from Chulalongkorn University, two M.A.'s from the University of Washington, and a Ph.D. from the University of Hawaii. Professor Virulrak publishes books and articles on Thai theatre and film; among them are *Likay, A Popular Theatre in Thailand* and *Acting and Directing on TV*.

CARLA WAAL is professor of speech and dramatic art at the University of Missouri-Columbia. After earning her M.A. from the University of Virginia and her Ph.D. from Indiana University, she taught at the University of Georgia. Her research on Scandinavian theatre has been assisted by a Fulbright Grant (Norway), a George C. Marshall Fund Grant (Denmark), and a Swedish Institute Scholarship (Sweden). She has published a book on *Johanne Dybwad: Norwegian Actress* (Oslo, 1967); articles on Kurt Hamsun, Henrik Ibsen, and Scandinavian theatre; and translations of the fiction of Bjørg Vik. In addition, she has performed in community and university theatre and on Norwegian television, and has directed plays at the universities of Georgia and Missouri.

LAURA H. WEAVER is assistant professor of English at the University of Evansville, Indiana. Since receiving a Ph.D. in English at the University of Kansas, she has continued to do research in twentieth-century drama. Her essay, "Rugby and the Arts: The Divided Self in David Storey's Novels and Plays," has been published in *Fearful Symmetry: Doubles and Doubling in Literature and Film* (University Presses of Florida, 1981); and "The City as Escape into Freedom: The Failure of a Dream in David Storey's Works" in the *West Virginia University Philological Papers*.

GEORGE WOODYARD is professor of Spanish and works in the central administration at the University of Kansas. He is a specialist in the theatre of Latin America and has been editor of the *Latin American Theatre Review* since its inception at Kansas in 1967. He is the author and editor of several articles, texts, and anthologies on Latin American theatre.

WILLIAM C. YOUNG authored *American Theatrical Arts* (American Library Association, 1971) and the *Documents of American Theater History* series: the two-volume *Famous American Playhouses* (American Library Association, 1973) and the two-volume *Famous*